KARL MARX IN AMERICA

KARL MARX IN AMERICA

ANDREW HARTMAN

THE UNIVERSITY OF CHICAGO PRESS

Chicago and London

The University of Chicago Press, Chicago 60637
The University of Chicago Press, Ltd., London
© 2025 by Andrew Hartman
Published 2025
Printed in the United States of America

34 33 32 31 30 29 28 27 26 25   1 2 3 4 5

ISBN-13: 978-0-226-53748-1 (cloth)
ISBN-13: 978-0-226-53751-1 (e-book)
DOI: https://doi.org/10.7208/chicago/9780226537511.001.0001

Library of Congress Cataloging-in-Publication Data

Names: Hartman, Andrew, author.
Title: Karl Marx in America / Andrew Hartman.
Description: Chicago : The University of Chicago Press, [2025] |
    Includes bibliographical references and index.
Identifiers: LCCN 2024046635 | ISBN 9780226537481 (cloth) |
    ISBN 9780226537511 (ebook)
Subjects: LCSH: Marx, Karl, 1818–1883—Influence. | Communism—
    United States—History. | Socialism—United States—History. |
    United States—Economic conditions.
Classification: LCC HX39.5.A53 .H38 2025 | DDC 335.40973—dc23/
    eng/20241127
LC record available at https://lccn.loc.gov/2024046635

♾ This paper meets the requirements of ANSI/NISO Z39.48-1992
(Permanence of Paper).

I dedicate this book to my mom and Erica.

CONTENTS

INTRODUCTION

KARL MARX, GHOST IN THE AMERICAN MACHINE

Experience has shown that no book on Marx can expect to be
received with anywhere near the same detachment as a book on the
Ammassalik Eskimo or a treatise on the internal constitution of the
stars. Marx's ideas are so much a part of what people fear or welcome
today, his doctrines so intimately connected with the living faith and
hate of different classes and so often invoked by groups with conflicting political allegiances that the very sight of his name arouses a mindset on the part of the reader of which he is largely unconscious.

SIDNEY HOOK

In the early years of radio, the British Broadcasting Corporation aired
a series about famous exiles who had lived in London. One episode
included an interview with an elderly man long retired from a job in
the British Museum's reading room. Did he remember a patron by the
name of Karl Marx, who toiled at the museum for many years on what
would become his magnum opus, *Das Kapital*? At first, the pensioner
drew a blank. But after several clues—Marx sat in the same seat every day; he had a thick graying beard and painful boils on his backside;
he endlessly requested materials about political economy—the man's
memory came alive. "Oh Mr. Marx, yes, to be sure. Gave us a lot of
work 'e did, with all 'is calls for books and papers. And then one day 'e

just stopped coming. And you know what's a funny thing, sir? *Nobody's ever 'eard of 'im since!*"[1]

Marx himself half expected that the first volume of *Das Kapital*, or *Capital*, would tumble into oblivion. As he was preparing to send it to press in 1867, he suggested that his best friend and longtime collaborator Friedrich Engels read *The Unknown Masterpiece* by Honoré de Balzac. This was sardonic. *The Unknown Masterpiece* is a story about a painter who spends decades laboring on a single, perfectly accurate representation of reality. After a fellow artist scorns it as unintelligible, the painter hastily burns it and, with little reason left to live, dies soon after.[2]

Yet Marx's masterpiece was not doomed to oblivion. *Capital* unfolded the workings of capitalism in such profound fashion that people across the planet have been reading it ever since.

To read Marx is to wrestle with the world made by capitalism. That world includes America—*especially* America. Citizens and scholars of the United States have long taken for granted the formative influence of the nation's founding philosophers, such as Thomas Jefferson and James Madison. Historians have also highlighted the imprint made on the United States by Enlightenment thinkers like Adam Smith, John Locke, and Tom Paine. But Marx is rarely considered alongside such luminaries. Yet he pointed to our modern world in ways none of the others did, because capitalism is arguably the single most important feature of modern American life. And because Marx is probably the single most important critic of capitalism, his stamp might be just as telling.[3]

This book investigates the meaning of Karl Marx in America. It begins by asking why Marx looked to the United States as a rich source of material about capitalism. It then dives deeply into the many implications of Americans grappling with Karl Marx from the late nineteenth century to the present, from the first Gilded Age to our current one. Why have an underappreciated number of Americans turned to Marx as a sage in turbulent times? And why have so many Americans who fundamentally disagreed with Marx nonetheless read him to make sense of their worlds?

FIGURE 0.1: Karl Marx, 1875.

On the surface, such a book is absurd. Most Americans have never truly welcomed Marx's ideas with open minds. As the grandfather of communism, Marx has long been demonized as the antithesis of all that is good about America. Capitalism? Marx considered it an economic system premised on exploitation. Religion? A drug to control the masses. Democracy? A sham that provides cover for the ruling class.

And yet.

Despite the time-honored tradition of vilifying Marx, plenty of people living in the United States have expressed dismay at the world created by capitalism. Some of these people have found an ally in Marx, and for good reason. In 1844, while living in the bustling city of Paris, the promising young philosopher observed an awful paradox. "The worker becomes all the poorer the more wealth he produces, the more his production increases in power and size. The *devaluation* of the world of men is in direct proportion to the *increasing value* of the world of things." Wonder and horror are inextricable aspects of capitalism. Nobody is as renowned as Marx for calling attention to this contradiction, the source of alienation for millions.[4]

Marx was hardly alone in recognizing this paradox. In 1846, Ralph Waldo Emerson, writing from a New England that was also undergoing rapid capitalist transformation, expressed similar sentiments.

'Tis the day of the chattel
Web to weave, and corn to grind;
Things are in the saddle,
And ride mankind.

Emerson's friend Henry David Thoreau also agonized over the new arrangements. Using the rapidly expanding railroads as a metaphor for the onslaught of industrial capitalism, Thoreau wrote that "though a crowd rushes to the depot, and the conductor shouts 'All aboard!' when the smoke is blown away and the vapor condensed, it will be perceived that a few are riding, but the rest are run over."[5]

Emerson and Thoreau imagined transcending the messy material world of capitalism. Their writings conveyed a wide-openness that doubled as an alternative to the crowded, smoke-choked cities of industrial capitalism. Their moral vision soothed a growing anxiety about capitalism's foreclosure of independence. As the bards of American naturalism, Emerson and Thoreau remembered a world where a person might confront the vast North American wilderness with little more than their wits and hands. It's no surprise Thoreau built a small cabin on Walden Pond. It's also no surprise that the historian Jill Lepore writes, "Instead of Marx, Americans had Thoreau." Disgust with capitalism has rarely been reason enough for Americans to turn to the ravings of a strange German communist. Especially in a land where homegrown prophets dwelled.[6]

And yet.

Perhaps Marx indeed had something unique to offer Americans. Perhaps Marx answered questions ignored by American political traditions. Perhaps the writer John Cassidy was right when he proclaimed in 1997 that Marx "will be worth reading as long as capitalism endures."[7]

Ever since the late nineteenth century, a subset of Americans have looked to Marx for wisdom. During the Gilded Age, socialists read Marx as an antidote to the unchecked power of the mighty corporations. During the Great Depression, communists turned to Marx as a prophet for transcending the destructive capitalist economy. During the 1960s, young rebels discovered Marx as inspiration for their resistance to the imperialist war machine savaging Southeast Asia. Each of these eras was unique, yet in each, a booming market for Marx emerged because readers believed he provided something missing from American political discourse.

At the time of this writing, in 2024, six years removed from the philosopher's two hundredth birthday, we are living through the fourth Marx boom. Americans are thinking about Marx to a degree not matched since the 1960s, or perhaps even the 1930s.

In 2002, *The Economist* magazine, not one to endorse communist revolution, labeled Marx "prescient." From Manchester to Moscow, from Kansas City to Kinshasa, capitalism "has pitilessly torn asunder the motley feudal ties that bound man to his 'natural superiors,' and has left remaining no other nexus between man and man than naked self-interest, than callous 'cash payment.'" Marx's famous aphorism, "all that is solid melts into air," captured in one pithy sentence capitalism's propensity to destroy.[8]

As the late twentieth-century collapse of communism further enabled capitalism's relentless expansion, events closer to home also propelled a rediscovery of Marx in America. In the fall of 2011, thousands of activists set up camp in the heart of the Manhattan financial district, a vivid demonstration of their discontent with the extensive suffering triggered by the financial meltdown of 2008. Occupy Wall Street advanced a captivating Marx-adjacent narrative to explain a crisis of capitalism. Occupy activists referred to themselves and their fellows as the "99 percent," those who, like Marx's proletariat, had nothing to lose but their chains. The movement targeted the "one percent," those who, as with Marx's bourgeoisie, sucked up, "vampire-like," the productive wealth of society.[9]

Occupy's tangible political achievements are negligible, but a political culture revolving around Marx's ideas arose in its wake. Popular magazines and podcasts dedicated to Marxist politics proliferated. Books by and about Marx enjoyed brisk sales. Marxist reading groups sprouted up. Avowed socialist Bernie Sanders, champion of working-class solidarity, came close to winning the Democratic Party nomination for president in 2016, and again in 2020.[10]

This current Marx boom has stimulated much commentary. Some interpret interest in Marx as an alien event. Others correctly note that Marx never really went away. Yet even these more astute observers avoid wrestling with the historical meaning of that claim. The long and complex history of Americans engaging with Marx offers a corrective, showing that, although Marx's ideas have not been assimilated into American political traditions, neither have they been purged, despite the best efforts of countless anticommunists.[11]

Marx has remained relevant in the United States across more than 150 years because he suggested an alternative perspective on freedom. In a nation long obsessed with the concept, why were so many Americans relatively unfree? In a nation founded on the principles of life, liberty, and the pursuit of happiness, why were so many American lives forsaken? By giving words to a deeply felt sense of exploitation, Marx has long offered compelling answers to these perplexing questions. Labor has changed forms several times since Marx's time. Marx wrote at the inception of an industrial revolution powered by the steam engine. Since then, capitalist modes of production have been revolutionized many times over. Yet the basics Marx described persist. As the source of value in a capitalist economy, labor must be disciplined to maximize profit. Workers in a capitalist society cannot be completely free.[12]

Marx diagnosed capitalism's compulsion to exploit, as well as its compulsion to rule. Capitalism not only extracts labor value from workers; it also strips workers of their autonomy. For Marx, freedom required that people have independence over their work, over their time, over their bodies. Since most people in a capitalist society lack such self-rule and must sell their labor to survive, capitalism is incompatible with freedom. Marx gained purchase in American life because he offered a powerful theory of freedom—one that doubled as a map of an alternative American future.

THE VARIETIES OF KARL MARX IN AMERICA

This book is about how Marx's ideas came into contact with people working out political problems in America. Out of what the historians Christopher Phelps and Robin Vandome call "the Marx-America dialectic," three distinct versions of Marx emerged: the Marx who famously centered labor as the driving force of value in a capitalist society; the Marx whose ideas mixed with other American political traditions to form hybrid political tendencies; and the Marx whose repulsive theories helped liberals and conservatives work out their own ideas about America. These patterns of interpreting Marx sometimes consolidated into groupings or even party alignments. But the borders between them were often malleable. Plenty of Americans moved easily from one variety to the next. Nevertheless, these three orientations toward Marx are worth considering as discrete formations that have shaped the long history of Marx in America.[13]

The first way Americans positioned themselves in relation to Marx is striking for its devotion to his classic theory about labor. Numerous intellectuals, activists, scholars, and politicians were inspired by Marx's notion that capitalism is fueled by the exploitation of workers, including such eminent figures as Eugene Debs, Elizabeth Gurley Flynn, A. Philip Randolph, and Bernie Sanders. In the long, difficult, often-losing struggle to win working-class power in the United States, these Americans fashioned a labor-centric Marx into a political weapon. They looked to Marx as a revolutionary muse because he identified the working class as the agent of liberation in capitalist America.

The creators of a hybrid Marx, the second variety of Karl Marx in America, interpreted the bearded communist in assorted, often unique ways. By adapting Marx to a variety of American situations, by cross-fertilizing Marxism with traditions like Christianity, republicanism, populism, pragmatism, black nationalism, indigeneity, Keynesianism, feminism, and more, these architects demonstrated the elasticity of his ideas *and* the diversity of American history. Hybrid versions of Marx have thus been repeatedly constructed and reconstructed.

The third variety of Karl Marx, the array of unfavorable interpretations, speaks to the exceptional degree to which anticommunism has shaped the United States. In the late nineteenth century, reactionaries began blaming Marx for disturbing events, from the Paris Commune of 1871 to the Great Railroad Strike of 1877 to the Haymarket Affair of 1886. A few decades later, in the aftermath of the First World War and the Russian Revolution, the federal government rounded up, arrested, and deported over one thousand Marxists. In the decade following the Second World War, a red scare of unprecedented scope swept the nation as fearmongers like Senator Joseph McCarthy sounded the alarm that communists were seeking to remake America into a Marxist hellhole. And now, in the twenty-first century, right-wing personalities blame mildly progressive reforms they find distasteful on a "cultural Marxism" imported by Jews intent upon destroying America.

Anticommunist vigilantes have rarely cared about what Marx actually wrote. But a host of conservative intellectuals, sometimes but not always working with fire-breathing reactionaries, have read Marx seriously. Their goal has not been to prove Marx wrong. For them, that's a given. Rather, conservatives have written about Marx to show that American liberalism is dangerous precisely for its proximity to Marxism. Liberal intellectuals, meanwhile, have analyzed Marx to both renounce him and to give meaning to the tradition they have been busy inventing. In staving off fascism and communism, liberalism has proven Marx wrong and America right. In short, the reception of Marx in the United States is a history of left, center, and right, sometimes all at once. Marx has served as a sounding board for Americans from every imaginable political background.

People have long assumed the United States is the quintessential anti-Marxist nation. This book contends that Marx truly matters to American history. Marx the man, the myth, the legend has helped a wide range of people formulate a more precise sense of the stakes of the American project. Americans have long articulated their various notions of freedom in conversation with Marx. For some, the bearded communist philosopher expanded upon and enhanced visions of freedom. For others, he served as a warning about the threats to freedom. On the whole, Marx has been a ghost in the American machine.

But what was America to Marx?

EARLY BIOGRAPHY

Marx scholars have mostly ignored the role the United States played in shaping Marx's mind. This is understandable given the palpable influence of more proximate factors.[14]

Marx was born in 1818 in Trier, a radical city in the Rhineland, now southwestern Germany. His father, Heinrich, hailed from a long line of

rabbis but converted to Christianity when Prussia took control of the
Rhineland in 1815. Marx admired his father but disobeyed his wish that
he commit to a respectable profession such as the law. As a university
student in Bonn and Berlin, Marx cultivated a passion for less pragmatic subjects, specifically poetry and philosophy.

In Berlin, Marx discovered the first great intellectual influence of
his life, Georg Wilhelm Friedrich Hegel, whose philosophy aroused a
generation of young radicals. Hegel taught Marx that abstract thought
had practical value, that he did not need to choose between his fascination with ancient Greek philosophy and his growing desire to intervene
in the world of politics. Heeding this lesson, Marx wrote a dissertation
on an abstract topic, *The Difference Between the Democritean and Epicurean
Philosophy of Nature*, before moving to Cologne in 1842 and dedicating
himself to a somewhat more practical career as a journalist for the radical newspaper *Rheinische Zeitung*.

Marx soon grew critical of the political implications of Hegel's
work. But he forever remained Hegelian in his approach to understanding the world, what is known as dialectics. Marx forever unfolded
the relationship between form and content, ideas and matter, philosophy and politics. His father, who died in 1838, might never have been
satisfied with Marx's career choices, but Marx spent his life trying to
make a practical difference with his gift for abstract thinking.

Marx's first and only romantic love was Jenny von Westphalen, a
noble girl from Trier whom he married in 1843. Jenny was all things to
Marx: romantic companion, mother to their children, first reader of
everything he wrote. After censors shut down the *Rheinische Zeitung* in
1843, the newlyweds moved to Paris. Stimulated by his love for Jenny,
and by the many cultural excitements on offer, especially the Parisian
salons where intoxicating ideas were vigorously debated, Marx was
ripe for another intellectual awakening.

Just as his time in Berlin among Hegel's disciples cemented one
crucial aspect of Marx's thought, living in Paris among the devotees
of French utopian socialists such as Count Saint-Simon and Charles
Fourier made manifest another. Being compelled to imagine a radically

better future forced Marx to reflect on the limitations of present arrangements. Marx grew critical of utopian socialism, but his name will
forever be associated with a blueprint for a better, dare we say utopian,
world. In his dazzling *Paris Manuscripts*, Marx advanced the idea that
life in capitalism is a deeply alienating existence; for him, Jenny was his
only respite in a world of estrangement.

While in Paris, Marx met his lifelong comrade Friedrich Engels,
author of the groundbreaking 1845 book *The Condition of the Working
Class in England*. Marx thus began focusing his acute mind on the English factories at the epicenter of an industrial revolution transforming
the world. After Marx landed in London in 1849, chased into exile by
Prussian counterrevolutionaries, Engels grew even more important
to him. Charged with managing his father's textile factory in greater
Manchester, Engels was able to financially support the impoverished
Marx family, while also providing Marx with an insider perspective on
the factory system.

Life in exile was arduous. Yet Marx took advantage of London's
offerings, especially the British Museum's reading room. In countless
hours there, Marx pored over volumes of economic data. He sought to
truly understand the inner workings of capitalism. He also wanted to
debunk Adam Smith and David Ricardo, the two most prominent representatives of the formidable intellectual tradition known as British
political economy. Whereas Smith and Ricardo pinpointed capitalism's
tendency to divide labor as an efficient means for increasing the wealth
of society, Marx focused instead on how this trend was a method for
further exploiting the working class to maximize profits.

Just as encounters with Hegel in Berlin and utopian socialists
in Paris shaped his mind, so too did this confrontation in London.
Marx forever followed Smith and Ricardo by analyzing capitalism as a
macrosystem that took hold of nations. Yet he also forever unmasked
British political economy as an attempt to naturalize capitalist social
relations by ignoring the inherent class antagonism. In this, credit
should be given to Engels for setting Marx on his fated course.

Scholars have exhaustively mapped out these aspects of Marx's intellectual formation. An accurate topography of Marx's mind has been made known to the world. But this is a map that does not include America.

Until now.

The United States of America also helped shape the revolutionary imagination of Marx. For the man who would change the world, America personified the working-class hero of the future. Marx did not have a personal, physical history in the United States. However, he had an intellectual one, and it still burns.

To that history, we now turn.

1

AMERICAN REVOLUTIONARY

The US Civil War

In the United States of America, every independent workers' movement was paralysed as long as slavery disfigured a part of the republic. Labour in a white skin cannot emancipate itself where it is branded in a black skin.

KARL MARX

Karl Marx had thoughts about the United States. It was, after all, the nation most committed to the economic and social systems formed by capitalism. Indeed, it would have been strange if he had ignored the exhilarating developments across the Atlantic. And yet, the idea that the bearded German troublemaker who championed a "dictatorship of the proletariat" had something significant to say about one of the birthplaces of modern democracy has long provoked confusion. Marx's ideas, after all, gave rise to the communist revolutions that the American state devoted itself to crushing. Even long after the Cold War, the coupling of Marx and America bewilders. But the fact remains that thinking about America helped shape Marx's world-shattering theory of capitalism.

Most proximately, the crucible of the American Civil War raised essential questions that Marx spent the better part of his life seeking to

answer. Who might be free? What does freedom look like? Can someone compelled to labor for another truly be free?

Marx had been pondering these questions well before the Civil War,
of course. Revolutionary stirrings in Europe moved him, along with
Friedrich Engels, to write *The Communist Manifesto*. In it Marx famously
declared that capitalism had divided everyone into two contending
classes, those who owned and those who worked for them. But after
the forces of reaction wiped away working-class revolutionary momentum from the Continent, a humbled Marx looked to the United States
for inspiration.

The Civil War, which Marx interpreted as on par with the American
and French Revolutions, provided him with some of the raw materials he needed to complete the painstaking analysis in *Capital*. This is
ironic, not only because America was subsequently shaped by a profound anticommunism but because Marx often expressed skepticism
that American democracy was capable of liberating humans from the
chains of capitalism. But upon closer inspection, the connections start
to make sense.

THE BIRTH OF THE MARX-AMERICA DIALECTIC

Marx had an abiding interest in North America, dating to his youth
when he genuinely considered emigrating to a faraway land called
Texas. Marx's impression of the United States was first shaped by his
reading of the popular travelogues that circulated in Europe, especially Thomas Hamilton's *Men and Manners in America* (1833), Gustave
de Beaumont's *Marie, or Slavery in the United States* (1835), and Alexis de
Tocqueville's *Democracy in America* (1835 and 1840). From these, Marx
came to appreciate both the potential of popular democracy in a capitalist society and its pitfalls.[1]

More than most nineteenth-century European philosophers, Marx
was a fierce proponent of democracy. He believed the laboring masses
who made up the vast majority should have the power to dictate social
arrangements. But Marx concluded that even the American political

system, arguably one of the most democratic in the world at the time, did not unlock full-fledged human freedom. Americans had to some degree achieved political emancipation, but not human emancipation, and the two were far from the same thing. Identifying the limits of American democracy, which he largely chalked up to constraints imposed by capitalism, contributed to Marx's emerging communism. For him, true democracy could only be accomplished in a socialist setting. The events of 1776, like those of 1789, had been an essential step toward democracy and freedom. But it had not gone far enough.[2]

Marx first fleshed out the distinction between political and human emancipation in his long 1844 essay *On the Jewish Question*, a critical response to Bruno Bauer, his fellow Young Hegelian. Marx and Bauer started from a similar place. As successors to the radical Enlightenment, they saw organized religion as "set up to terrify and enslave mankind," as Thomas Paine worded it. Bauer further contended German Jews were wrong to petition for political emancipation since, until the Prussian state was liberated from religion writ large, such freedom could only ever be partial. Bauer insisted, as Marx paraphrased, "that the Jew should renounce Judaism, and that mankind in general should renounce religion, in order to achieve *civic* emancipation." Freedom from religion would unshackle *all* Germans.[3]

Marx criticized Bauer for misunderstanding the role of religion in relation to political freedom, and more than that, for prioritizing political liberty as if it were enough. For Marx, religion was a manifestation of alienation to which political emancipation offered no solution. The United States presented a unique case study to test Marx's theory since there religion had no rightful claim to the state, *and*, Marx wrote, it was "pre-eminently the country of religiosity, as Beaumont, Tocqueville, and the Englishman Hamilton unanimously assure us." For Marx, the flowering of religion in the United States was a clear sign that humans remained unfree even when emancipated politically. The state had been liberated from religion, but people remained enthralled by superstition. "Therefore," Marx wrote, "*political emancipation* itself is not *human* emancipation."[4]

Marx's disagreement with Bauer stemmed from his divergent understanding of the liberal order ushered in by the American Revolution. Where Bauer supposed religion interfered with "the rights of man" inscribed by that revolution, Marx emphasized that the "right of conscience" was among those hallowed rights. More to the point, so was the right to *property*. The American Revolution divided the political realm, where citizens were in theory equal before a secular state, from the civil realm, where people were free to be their own religious and economic agents even if impinging upon the freedom of others. Nowhere, Marx later wrote, "does *social* inequality obtrude itself more harshly than in the eastern states of North America, because nowhere is it less disguised by political inequality."[5]

The nature of the split between the political and social realms, Marx argued, made "every man see in other men not the realization of his own freedom, but the *barrier* to it." Political emancipation, paradoxically, increased human alienation by empowering the private individual as "the *essential* and *true* man." The sphere of solidarity, or politics, only existed to safeguard the sphere of selfishness, or civil society. "Hence," Marx wrote, "man was not freed from religion, he received religious freedom. He was not freed from property, he received freedom to own property. He was not freed from the egoism of business, he received freedom to engage in business."[6]

Marx's commentary on Bauer was in the end a critique of democracy of the American sort. Political democracy in the United States had emboldened the "egoism of business." Marx wanted more. "Emancipation from *huckstering* and *money*," he wrote, "would be the self-emancipation of our time." Marx saw in capitalistic behavior a kind of religion that was particularly palpable in the United States, home to many of the most devout Christians in the world, and also to some of the more fervent hucksters.

Humans could not form bonds of mutuality when they saw each other as a means to make money. Indeed, Marx argued that money, "the universal self-established *value* of all things," when released from political control, as in the United States, became the "estranged essence of man's work and man's existence, and this alien essence dominates him, and he worships it." The only way to conquer this debilitating form of alienation was for people to free themselves from political *and* economic constraints. The young Marx had pinpointed one of the lasting problems of modern existence, but he did not yet offer much of a solution. How might people achieve political *and* economic freedom? The search for answers became Marx's life project.[7]

Marx's misgivings about political emancipation helped push him to communism. But he continued to appreciate the potential of American democracy. Yes, political liberty was a limited form of freedom. Yes, most American workers were no better off than their European counterparts, forced to labor in harsh conditions, even in the Northern states where chattel slavery had been abolished. Yes, these "masterless slaves," as Hamilton called them, were held captive by a "vassalage of the stomach," confronted by a choice to "submit or starve." Nevertheless, America also demonstrated that political democracy was in fact one possible avenue toward the full emancipation represented by socialism.[8]

Marx's optimism about American democracy was based in part on the influence of the conservative Thomas Cooper, an erstwhile English Jacobin who morphed into an outspoken Southern apologist after relocating to South Carolina. Marx read Cooper's 1826 book *Lectures on the Elements of Political Economy*, which argued universal suffrage would logically result in the elite having their property and wealth expropriated by the impoverished masses. Marx agreed. But he and Cooper disagreed on whether that would be good. For Cooper, such leveling would destabilize all social norms and thus precede society's collapse. For Marx, redistribution was part of a larger historical movement toward human emancipation.[9]

Marx grew somewhat sanguine about socialism in America, due in part to Cooper's analysis. Hamilton's description of the American Workingmen's Party also impressed Marx. With branches established in Philadelphia in 1828 and New York City in 1829, the world's first labor party advanced a socialism that Marx came to embrace. Most European socialists at the time, particularly French ones, believed benevolent, technocratic leaders could devise a classless, conflict-free society. Marx saw that as naive utopianism. In contrast, the "Workies" held that democratic struggle was the most effective way to defeat their enemies. Like Cooper, they believed universal suffrage would unlock wealth redistribution. Thomas Skidmore, who helped found the Workingmen's Party, theorized elites would only feel the full redistributive force of suffrage if it was extended to everyone. Then, electoral democracy might unlock forces that would doom economic aristocracy. This radical Workie attitude inspired Marx to write in 1845 that Americans "have had their own socialist democratic school since 1829." The prototype for Marxist socialism existed in the United States.[10]

Marx's optimism about American democracy did not stifle his cynicism about political emancipation. The twentieth-century American socialist Michael Harrington wrote that Marx "could never decide whether the exceptional characteristics of American society boded good or evil for the socialist movement." American democracy was one big contradiction. While the history of the Workies convinced Marx that universal suffrage was a harbinger of socialism, his growing knowledge of other American developments kept such hopes in check. Thanks to Tocqueville he knew that as long as western lands were cheap and plentiful, Americans were unlikely to foment revolution. Rather than struggle for power in a burgeoning industrial economy, as the Workies had done, many working-class Americans regarded westward expansion as their ticket to freedom. Marx fretted to one his German comrades who was on the verge of moving to the United States that "once you are over there, who can say that you won't lose yourself in the FAR WEST!" The allure of the West persuaded Marx that American "bourgeois society is still far too immature for the class struggle to be made perceptible and comprehensible."[11]

In addition to having a firm grasp on the consequences westward expansion had on class consciousness, Marx was attuned to the disfiguring effect Southern slavery had on American democracy. In the process of analyzing the interrelation of these two sectional problems, he innovated a powerful theory of American democracy. Marx posited that easy access to land in the West, much like universal suffrage, might hasten the onset of socialism. This was because he believed that expansion would accelerate industrial development, a precursor, in his view, to working-class power. But Marx also thought westward expansion was antisocialist in its own right because homesteading tended to weaken the bonds of solidarity. As evidence, he noted that many westward migrants opposed the abolition of slavery because free black people would compete with them for land and jobs. For Marx, such a zero-sum mindset was the death knell of working-class democracy.

Marx was antislavery from early on. He disagreed with all impositions on free labor, especially literal shackles. Marx's abolitionist zeal was a moral position, consistent with his hatred of most forms of hierarchy. It was also strategic. He believed workers everywhere were limited in their freedom so long as workers anywhere were in bondage. Or in his concise wording: "Freedom and slavery constitute an antagonism." Slavery hung like an albatross on the neck of the working class. Not coincidentally, it also severely handicapped American democracy.[12]

Marx placed slavery at the far end of a fluid spectrum of labor exploitation. Slavery was not a fixed condition premised on race but rather a *relation* within a larger hierarchical matrix calculated to coerce people to work. As Marx wrote in 1849: "What is a Negro slave? A man of the black race. The one explanation is as good as the other. A Negro is a Negro. He only becomes a *slave* in certain relations. A cotton-spinning jenny is a machine for spinning cotton. It becomes *capital* only in certain relations. Torn from these relations it is no more capital than gold in itself is money or sugar the price of sugar."[13]

If slavery were abolished, enslaved black people would no longer be forced to work for others. Likewise, if capitalism were abolished, workers would no longer be forced to sell their labor to survive. In big-picture terms, Marx was more attentive to imagining an end to capitalism, yet he doubted that was attainable without first abolishing slavery. Marx kept one eye on the United States, even as mounting political drama in Europe began capturing his attention by the late 1840s. As impending European revolutions stirred Marx to articulate his metavision in *The Communist Manifesto*, it's doubtful he would have arrived at his conceptual framework without first having thought about the United States.

1848!

In 1848, against the backdrop of mounting revolutionary tendencies, Marx and Engels were tasked by the Communist League with composing a manifesto for the tiny but vibrant communist movement in Europe. Engels composed the first draft; Marx's complete overhaul became the most notorious articulation of anticapitalism ever recorded. Marx had a straightforward objective: to drag communism out of the shadows and announce it as a force for revolution. Until then communism had only existed as a murky conspiracy. As he put it with his memorable first sentence: "A spectre is haunting Europe—the spectre of communism." Marx wanted to make material what had been an apparition.[14]

The Communist Manifesto failed to achieve its immediate goal. Few people read it at the time, and hardly anyone outside the movement began thinking about communism as a viable alternative to the status quo. And yet, the text remains crucial because of its eventual fame, and because it represents a decisive threshold in Marx's thought.

Before 1848, Marx fumbled for a durable theory to illuminate the incredible changes taking place before his eyes. *The Communist Manifesto* crystallized those efforts, laying out both a dazzling conception of capitalism and a bracing vision of revolution. Marx was thirty years old when he authored *The Communist Manifesto*. He would change his mind about lots of things over the next thirty-five years. But he never strayed from the basic story of capitalism he first told in *The Communist Manifesto*.[15]

What was this story? To begin with, Marx fastened his particular moment to the long arc of history. "The history of all hitherto existing society," he wrote, "is the history of class struggles." Marx did not mean everything that had happened in the past was part of an existential struggle for power. Rather, Marx sought to separate the forest from the trees. Class struggle shaped the big picture, giving form to every social order and to every revolutionary effort to overthrow the social order. "Freeman and slave, patrician and plebeian, lord and serf, guild-master and journeyman, in a word, oppressor and oppressed,"

Marx wrote, "stood in constant opposition to one another, carried on an uninterrupted, now hidden, now open fight, a fight that each time ended, either in a revolutionary reconstitution of society at large, or in the common ruin of the contending classes."[16]

Class struggle was constant but not static. In attaching the dynamics of 1848 to the long history of class struggle, Marx highlighted the novel antagonisms in "the modern bourgeois society" that had "sprouted from the ruins of feudal society." This society did not end class struggle but rather had "established new classes, new conditions of oppression, new forms of struggle in place of the old ones." The bourgeois epoch had, according to Marx, "simplified class antagonisms. Society as a whole is more and more splitting up into two great hostile camps, into two great classes directly facing each other—Bourgeoisie and Proletariat."[17]

The most lasting conceptual legacy of *The Communist Manifesto* is the idea that capitalism eventually funnels everybody into one of two immense classes: *the bourgeoisie*, the capitalist class, and *the proletariat*, the working class. In this, Marx bestowed an enduring terminology for capitalism as a class system, and for thinking about it as a mechanism for sorting people. Up until then, the term bourgeois was almost solely found in French political discourse as a reference to merchants. Thanks to Marx, it came to personify capital itself. The bourgeoisie was that great class of people who owned the means of production, for example factories, and paid others to make the products they sold for a profit. The word proletarian, which Engels used in his haunting 1845 book *The Condition of the Working Class in England*, came to represent the epitome of human toil. The proletariat was that other great class of people who owned nothing but their own labor, which they had to sell to the bourgeoisie to survive.[18]

Marx's categories were exceedingly abstract. By themselves they were incapable of capturing the full range of human interactions. Yet Marx's scheme has persisted because much of what he wrote in *The Communist Manifesto* has been vindicated by history. Capitalism now has a much longer and more varied history than it did in 1848. Yet it remains true now that capitalism *tends* to push most people into two camps, those who own nothing but their own labor and those who own everything else. There are plenty of people outside this bifurcating framework, but the *tendency* remains intact.

The Communist Manifesto also continues to ring true in its depiction of capitalism as a revolutionary force of world-historical proportions. This aspect of the *Manifesto* demonstrated Marx's perplexing attitude toward capitalism. Yes, Marx hated capitalism, especially for what it did to working people. Not only were the working masses "slaves of the bourgeois class, and of the bourgeois State; they are daily and hourly enslaved by the machine, by the overlooker, and, above all, by the individual bourgeois manufacturer himself." And yet, despite recognition of these horrors, Marx was fully cognizant of the extraordinary transformations capitalism was rushing into existence.[19]

The most telling signal of capitalism's revolutionary force was the quick work it made of feudal society. Capitalism was by necessity an expansionary system and its propulsive qualities, depicted at length in *The Communist Manifesto*, stimulated a dynamism like no other system. "Modern industry," Marx wrote, "has established the world market, for which the discovery of America paved the way. This market has given an immense development to commerce, to navigation, to communication by land. This development has, in its turn, reacted on the extension of industry; and in proportion as industry, commerce, navigation, railways extended, in the same proportion the bourgeoisie developed, increased its capital, and pushed into the background every class handed down from the Middle Ages."[20]

The rapid transition from feudalism, a society premised on lasting obligations between lord and peasant, to capitalism, a system built on fleeting connections between capitalist and worker, had profound cultural consequences. Marx described this process memorably:

> The bourgeoisie, wherever it has got the upper hand, has put an end to all feudal, patriarchal, idyllic relations. It has pitilessly torn asunder the motley feudal ties that bound man to his "natural superiors," and has left remaining no other nexus between man and man than naked self-interest, than callous "cash payment." It has drowned the most

heavenly ecstasies of religious fervour, of chivalrous enthusiasm, of philistine sentimentalism, in the icy water of egotistical calculation. It has resolved personal worth into exchange value, and in place of the numberless indefeasible chartered freedoms, has set up that single, unconscionable freedom—Free Trade. In one word, for exploitation, veiled by religious and political illusions, it has substituted naked, shameless, direct, brutal exploitation.[21]

Marx understood that people in bourgeois society might remain devoted to cherished beliefs, even those that explicitly frowned upon the selfish tendencies of capitalism. He had, after all, read about the United States, where people effortlessly combined belief in God and Mammon. But at bottom such treasured values were toothless in the face of "naked, shameless, direct, brutal exploitation." And yet, for Marx this was not an awful turn of events. At least the horrors of class rule were finally out in the open. Marx expected that once people were stripped of their remaining illusions, they would finally wake up to the unpleasant truth: "All that is solid melts into air, all that is holy is profaned, and man is at last compelled to face with sober senses his real conditions of life, and his relations with his kind." There was nothing special about a life of exploitation.[22]

The Communist Manifesto exemplified the legendary contradiction in Marx's evaluation of capitalism. The world's most renowned anticapitalist thinker commended capitalism, not only for its propensity to liquefy outmoded customs and institutions but also for its predisposition to dissolve itself. Not content with laying waste to the feudal order, the bourgeoisie summoned forces that would eventually spell its own demise. Capitalists produced their "own grave-diggers." The logic of capital reigned supreme to the same degree that the working class grew in numbers. And as the proletariat ballooned, it came together, ready to battle its oppressors. Marx contended "the proletariat alone is a really revolutionary class."[23]

 Marx devoted the rest of his life to theorizing proletarian political power. To his dying breath he believed human emancipation depended on the working class. Only the working class could bring socialist revolution and thus liberate people from exploitation and alienation. Only the working class was positioned to rescue democracy from capitalism. But how? Marx sought answers to that question, a determination given life by the poetic passage that concluded *The Communist Manifesto*: "Let the ruling classes tremble at a Communistic revolution. The proletarians have nothing to lose but their chains. They have a world to win. Working Men of All Countries, Unite!"[24]

As Marx put the finishing touches on his outline for revolution, he could hardly have suspected an actual revolution was imminent. Yet, just as *The Communist Manifesto* went to press in February 1848, Parisians took to the barricades, overthrew their monarch, and established the Second Republic, launching a series of insurrections across the Continent. Extending to over fifty countries, the Revolutions of 1848 were the result of a perfect storm of discontent.[25]

A growing urban proletariat was fed up with longer hours of toil combined with declining standards of living. This precarious situation was made worse by a recession that left many unemployed, including, for example, over 10,000 workers in Vienna in 1847. At the same time, rural peasants seethed over famine-like conditions, most horrifically in Ireland. These awful circumstances were exacerbated by enclosures of land that left peasants bereft of communal resources, "a plain enough case of class robbery" in the historian E. P. Thompson's words. Marx, in one of his earliest expressions of indignancy on behalf of the downtrodden, had written a scathing article in 1842 against Prussian authorities who had taken away the Rhineland peasantry's customary right to fallen wood.[26]

Poverty, exploitation, and dispossession were spurs to rebellion. But mounting economic deprivation, no matter how enflaming, was not the sole cause of revolutionary disaffection. Even the relatively unafflicted bourgeoisie was disillusioned with the status quo. The American and French Revolutions were supposed to have ushered in a new era. People were to have become citizens, enshrined with the rights of man, freed from the spiteful power of venal monarchs. And yet, half a century later, Europe remained chained by absolutism. In this context, a heady mix of prodemocratic and antiabsolutist ideologies thrived, including liberalism, republicanism, nationalism, and socialism. The European masses were materially *and* ideologically prepared for revolution.[27]

The Revolutions of 1848 quickly fanned out from Paris. The Belgian monarchy, fearful of antiabsolutist passions, immediately expelled all foreign radicals, starting with Marx, who had been living in exile there. Although this was traumatic for Marx, who along with his wife Jenny spent a night in prison before being expelled, he spotted an opportunity. Perhaps the revolution would give him with a chance to return home and wage a war of ideas against the Prussian ruling class he despised.[28]

Marx's opening came quickly. Less than a month after the Parisian uprising, German insurgents took to the streets, demanding that absolute rule be replaced by constitutional government. Soon after, Marx traveled to Cologne, a working-class city along the Rhine where revolutionary passions ran deep, and where insurgents had swiftly achieved a liberal government that protected freedom of press. Marx was thus able to restart the *Rheinische Zeitung*, the newspaper that first got him into political trouble when he edited it in the early 1840s.[29]

Marx had always wanted to be a crusading newspaper editor. Although renowned for his polemical voice during his first stint at the *Rheinische Zeitung*, his tone was even more piercing the second time around. Emboldened by the revolution in the streets and by many enthusiastic sponsors, including the Communist League, Marx operated the *Neue Rheinische Zeitung* as a platform for broadcasting the two-stage revolutionary strategy he sketched out in *The Communist Manifesto*. While forcefully editorializing in favor of a liberal revolution, the paper also propagandized for an eventual communist revolution against the bourgeoisie.

Transcending capitalism was Marx's ultimate objective. Yet the *Neue Rheinische Zeitung* devoted more ink to the bourgeois stage of revolution than to the communist one, on the premise that workers would have an impossible time achieving power without first winning a liberal order. Andreas Gottschalk, the popular leader of Cologne communists, disagreed, disparaging Marx for advising the proletariat to "escape the hell of the Middle Ages, by voluntarily plunging into the purgatory of a decrepit rule of capital." Conversely, agents of the absolutist Prussian state interpreted even modest demands as incendiary attacks. The authorities violently cracked down on insurgents of all types, whether liberal or communist, including propagandizing newspapermen. Marx was arrested, and he half expected he would be executed for treason. Instead, he was indicted on lesser charges and, after a rousing speech before a bourgeois jury about the promise of democratic justice, he was acquitted.[30]

In early 1849, Cologne liberals won local elections and ascended to regional power. Seeing this as a sign to shift his focus to the second, communist stage of revolution, Marx joined Gottschalk in calling for the creation of a revolutionary workers organization. His timing was not great. That April, liberals offered to allow Frederick William IV of Prussia to keep the crown, but under the umbrella of a new constitutional monarchy. Frederick turned down the offer, telling a confidant that it was a crown "from the gutter," "disgraced by the stink of revolution, defiled with dirt and mud."[31]

As Germans took to the streets in protest that summer, Prussian forces crushed the insurgency with ruthless efficiency. Most of the captured insurrectionists were executed or sentenced to long prison terms. Many liberals in the Rhineland and elsewhere across Europe, increasingly fearful of rising militancy among the working class, reversed course mid-revolution and aligned with the monarchy. This liberal about-face taught Marx a lesson he would never forget.[32]

In the bloody end-phase of the revolution, Marx largely avoided the fray. But he was sent into exile yet again, this time for good. The more martially inclined Engels took up arms against Prussian forces in the Rhineland before fleeing the country. Both Marx and Engels eventually landed in England, alongside many other German refugees. An even larger number of defeated German revolutionaries emigrated to the United States, where they became known as the Forty-Eighters.[33]

THE SECOND AMERICAN REVOLUTION

In the decades following the Revolutions of 1848, hundreds of thousands of Germans immigrated to the United States. A sizable share of them, whether they had fought on the barricades or not, had internalized revolutionary sensibilities. The New York congressman Thomas Whitney labeled such immigrants "Red Republicans, agrarians, and infidels," fretting they were "the malcontents of the Old World" who "stood by the side of Robespierre." Nativists like Whitney had reason to fear. Although most Forty-Eighters expected to return to Germany at some point to finish what they started, they instead became integral to earth-shattering events in the United States. There was no keeping a lid on their desire for a free society.[34]

As Europe's revolutions ultimately failed to bring even limited constitutional rule, many Americans were smugly confident in their sixty-year-old system of constitutional government. Yet the ugly truth of the American system was hidden in plain sight, in the very Constitution that supposedly safeguarded it from tyranny. The United States had been founded on a compromise with slavery. Ever since the first bargain was struck with that "peculiar institution" in 1789, when the Constitution empowered slave states by counting the enslaved as three-fifths human for the purposes of representation, one conciliation after another barely held together an increasingly divided nation.[35]

Compromise with slavery concealed irresistible forces which sparked a brutal Civil War in 1861 that killed half a million Americans. This is what the slaveholder Thomas Jefferson anticipated when he said that "we have the wolf by the ears and feel the danger of either holding or letting him loose." Only by taking the path of violence, it seems, were Americans able to abolish slavery. Only then was a new nation born.[36]

The amount of blood shed during the Civil War was staggering. But carnage had long been the norm for the millions of black people ensnared by centuries of American slavery. Such violence was partly a byproduct of the insatiable demand for unpaid labor. As cotton became immensely profitable by the 1830s, helping power the westward expansion of the slave plantation complex, and as competition heated up on the international cotton market, the enslaved were treated ever more harshly in an effort to speed up production. American slavery underscored Marx's sense that one person's profit was another person's pain.[37]

By the 1850s, an increasing number of Northerners had been swayed by a growing abolitionist movement. Yet the institution of slavery remained relatively safe as long as those who controlled it retained a monopoly on violence. This explains why the abolitionist John Brown took up arms alongside several formerly enslaved black Americans against the Slave Power, the derogatory label given to the enslavers seemingly in control of the national government. It also explains why Brown drove slavers into fits of rage. As a devout evangelical Christian, Brown was in some ways a characteristic creation of the Second Great Awakening, a period of religious intensification. But there was nothing typical about Brown, whose tête-à-têtes with God focused on the imperative to smash slavery by any means necessary. With divine inspiration, Brown and his sons traveled west in 1856 to join the fight against slavery in what became known as Bleeding Kansas. There, they murdered five proslavery settlers in front of their families. After the "Pottawatomie Massacre," slavers knew that abolitionists could match callousness with callousness.[38]

Brown upped the ante in October 1859, when he led twenty-two black and white men in a raid on the federal arsenal at Harpers Ferry, Virginia. In addition to coveting the stockpile of weapons, Brown hoped news of his party's brave exploits would spark insurrection across the South. A company of US soldiers easily defeated Brown's forces, several of whom were killed, including two of his sons. After a hasty trial, Brown and his surviving coconspirators were hanged. And yet, Brown's audacious efforts had a galvanizing effect. Slavers grew convinced the very existence of a menace like Brown meant the nation was no longer hospitable to slavery. On the flip side, Brown's hasty trial and execution enraged many Northerners, who vowed it would hasten the end of the Slave Power.

Brown's botched raid polarized a nation on the verge of civil war, and he became the definitive martyr to the antislavery cause. Union soldiers took the fight to the Confederacy while singing "John Brown's Body," an ode that inspires left-wing Americans to this day. August Willich, a Forty-Eighter who had fought alongside Engels and who later served as a Union general during the Civil War, organized a torchlight parade in Cincinnati to protest the execution of Brown, during which he gave a fiery antislavery speech. One unsympathetic spectator recounted that Willich, widely known as the "Reddest of the Reds," "exhorted his hearers to whet their sabers and nerve their arms for the day of retribution, when Slavery and Democracy would be crushed in a common grave."[39]

Karl Marx also spotted the significance in Brown's raid, observing to Engels that "the most momentous thing happening in the world today is the slave movement: on the one hand, in America, started by the death of Brown, and in Russia, on the other." Brown and his fellow rebels embodied the escalating global revolution against unfree labor that was also evident in the Russian Empire, where millions of wretched serfs were on the verge of emancipation from bondage. Marx noticed "there was a new slave uprising in Missouri, naturally suppressed. But the signal has now been given." Revolution was on the precipice.[40]

Marx finally had reason to be optimistic again thanks to the looming Civil War. The 1850s had not been good to him, politically or personally. As the dark clouds of reaction settled over Europe in the wake of 1848, Marx's hopes for radical political transformation had been dashed. Further, life as a refugee in the hurly-burly of London crushed his personal prospects, as he and his family suffered from poverty, hunger, disease, and the deaths of three children. After such a grim decade, the incipient threat to the Slave Power brought Marx joy and refreshed his drive to make the ruling classes tremble.

Marx wrote some of his most memorable prose during the dark days of the 1850s. *The Eighteenth Brumaire of Louis Bonaparte*, one of his most celebrated pieces, was written in direct response to the 1851 coup that brought to power a reactionary emperor in France. Originally published in a German-language New York City journal edited by Marx's comrade Joseph Weydemeyer, *The Eighteenth Brumaire* was virtually unknown beyond Forty-Eighters, until an edition was issued in Europe in

1869. Ever since, Marx's essay has impressed readers with its inventive historical analysis, beginning with its unforgettable opening. "Hegel remarks somewhere that all great world-historic facts and personages appear, so to speak, twice," Marx wrote. "He forgot to add: the first time as tragedy, the second time as farce."[41]

For the 1869 edition, Marx added that *The Eighteenth Brumaire* was intended to "demonstrate how the class struggle in France created circumstances and relationships that made it possible for a grotesque mediocrity to play a hero's part." The grotesquerie in question was Louis Napoleon Bonaparte, the nephew of Napoleon Bonaparte. Rather than focus on the transformative power of ideas or personalities, Marx argued history was shaped by material factors, in this case, by class dynamics that had altered the position of the bourgeoisie. "Men make their own history, but they do not make it as they please; they do not make it under self-selected circumstances, but under circumstances existing already, given and transmitted from the past. The tradition of all dead generations weighs like a nightmare on the brains of the living."[42]

What haunted the minds of 1848 revolutionaries was 1789. This, for Marx, was a grave mistake, because material conditions had changed dramatically in the intervening years. "The social revolution of the nineteenth century cannot draw its poetry from the past," he advised, "but only from the future." Whereas the bourgeoisie helped steer the French Revolution because its position as a class was severely limited by an aristocracy, by 1848 the bourgeoisie was wealthier and thus had more to lose. Capitalists were unhappy with the illiberal system that failed to guarantee their inalienable political rights. But that concern paled in comparison to the fear of a radicalized proletariat, which had begun leveraging its precipitous growth to make revolutionary demands on bourgeois property rights. The specter of proletarian power caused capitalists to steer a vastly more conservative path in 1848.

The earlier bourgeoisie had a vexed relationship to the tragedy of Napoleon Bonaparte, who came to power in the bloodless Coup of Eighteen Brumaire. Later capitalists determined they stood to benefit from his farcical nephew's rise to dictatorship. Unlike the capitalists in *The Communist Manifesto* whom Marx celebrated for their revolutionary tendencies, the capitalists in *The Eighteenth Brumaire* were a force for conservatism, even reaction. For this reason, the working class needed to break with the bourgeois past and instead "create for itself the revolutionary point of departure, the situation, the relations, the conditions under which alone modern revolution becomes serious." Socialist revolution was a job for the proletariat.[43]

If Marx was right about the demand for socialist revolutionaries to peer into the future, the situation in the early 1850s did not offer a clear picture of it. Yet, this did not stop Marx from endeavoring to theorize a way forward. He spent a good portion of that decade contemplating the logic of capitalism, compiling piles and piles of notebooks in the process. Marx never shared these mental labors with readers during his lifetime. Some of them were only published posthumously as *Grundrisse: Foundations of the Critique of Political Economy*. Yet his arduous scribbles were the preliminary draft of what became his magnum opus, *Das Capital*. By 1867, Marx had finally grown confident enough to release his voluminous speculations on capitalism for public consumption, due in part to his unceasing attention to American goings-on. The poetry of the future was brought into focus for Marx by the war on American slavery.[44]

During the 1850s, Marx's interest in the United States expanded. Compared to post-1848 Europe, American developments often appeared more promising. Marx's growing attention to the United States was in turn a byproduct of the fascination that many Americans reciprocated toward European political affairs. The *New York Daily Tribune*, an unofficial organ of the Republican Party published by Horace Greeley, was particularly intrigued with the socialist ideas of 1848. When the uprisings began, Greeley sent his editor Charles Dana, who had socialist leanings of his own, to Paris to locate fresh correspondents capable of interpreting events through the lens of this alluring new paradigm.[45]

On the suggestion of a friend, Dana made his way to Cologne to meet with an editor of a radical newspaper who had recently authored an exciting manifesto. By all reports, Dana and Marx got along well during their brief encounter. Impressed by Marx's knowledge and militancy, Dana offered Marx a job as the *Tribune*'s European correspondent. Due to the turmoil that soon landed Marx in London, he was not actually hired until 1853. At that point, Marx commenced working the only steady job he ever had, earning regular paychecks that somewhat improved his family's fraught existence. For the next decade, *Tribune* readers learned about Europe from the world's sharpest socialist thinker.[46]

Students of Marx tend to focus on his programmatic works like *The Communist Manifesto* or his major economic manuscripts like *Capital*. Yet Marx's *Tribune* articles form the largest body of Marx's published work. The newspaper published 487 of his articles, 350 solely written by him, 125 by Engels (as a favor to Marx), and twelve jointly. More to the point, Marx's *Tribune* articles were read by infinitely more people during his lifetime than anything else he wrote (though most were published minus a byline). Greeley's newspaper had more subscribers than any in the world, about 200,000 in 1855, roughly twice that of the *London Times*. Although Marx took pride in the size of the *Tribune* audience, he was more impressed by its quality. *Tribune* readers tended to be open to ideas that expanded the boundaries of republicanism, with its focus on independence, to include socialist ideas, which concentrated on solidarity.[47]

Marx's first appearance in the *Tribune* set the tone of his career as an American journalist. Dana introduced the German as one of "the clearest and most vigorous writers that country has produced—no matter what may be the judgment of the critical upon his public opinions in the sphere of political and social philosophy." That first article was actually written by Engels, but it had Marx's stamp all over it. Titled "Revolution and Counter-Revolution," it pronounced that "the first act of the revolutionary drama on the Continent of Europe has closed. The 'powers that were' before the hurricane of 1848, are again the 'powers that be.'" For Marx and Engels, this sad state of affairs merely represented an interregnum before the climactic final act that would pit the "bourgeoisie" against the "proletariat." Using the terminology of *The Communist Manifesto*, Marx and Engels introduced a strange new vocabulary to a readership more fixated on curbing municipal corruption than digging capitalist graves. And yet something about the article resonated. A friend of Greeley's remarked that the "man goes deep—very deep for me." He then asked, "Who is he?"[48]

Americans have long asked this question. "Who is he?" The answer that Marx was a journalist who wrote for a major American newspaper for nine years has provoked cognitive dissonance. In 1957, the journalist William Harlan Hale summed up his apparent confusion. "During this period Europe's extremest radical," Hale wrote, "sent in well over 500 separate contributions to the great New York family newspaper dedicated to the support of Henry Clay, Daniel Webster, temperance, dietary reform, Going West, and, ultimately, Abraham Lincoln." Hale was dumbfounded that the *Tribune*, that "organ of respectable American Whigs and of their successors, the new Republican party, sustained Karl Marx over the years when he was mapping out his crowning tract of overthrow, *Das Kapital*." Even stranger, it is highly probable that Abraham Lincoln, an avid reader of the newspaper Clarence Darrow labeled the "political and social bible" of all good Republicans, was familiar with Marx's journalism, if not his name.[49]

In 1861, the Civil War forced the *Tribune* to reduce its foreign staff, and Marx lost his job. But not before making European socialism seem a little less strange to Americans raised on republican traditions. In this task, Marx had help from his communist comrades among the Forty-Eighters. Most communist émigrés initially settled in New York City, host to the third largest population of Germans of any city in the world at the time. In 1857, they formed the New York Communist Club, notable for its interracial membership and its fervent abolitionism. Many founders had been affiliates of the Communist League for which Marx and Engels wrote the *Manifesto*, and were veterans of the Revolutions of 1848, including Joseph Weydemeyer, Adolphus Cluss, Friedrich Sorge, and August Willich.[50]

Although myriad European writers, including Marx, had glorified aspects of American life to varying degrees, such a sunny picture did not speak to the experience of these radical German exiles. A more common sentiment was that expressed by Weydemeyer, who told Marx of being "pushed into the American bourgeois shit." But eventually, many German communists warmed to the possibilities of life in

the United States. This change of heart was made possible by the growing antislavery movement, which taught them that Europe was not the
only suitable venue for waging war against the old order.[51]

As sectional tensions rose, many German communists moved west
in search of better opportunities. There they found other working-class
Republicans, like-minded in their hatred of the Slave Power. They also
discovered a growing population of slaves and former slaves who were
becoming bolder in their resistance. Slave uprisings were growing
more common, particularly after John Brown's execution, and everyday forms of slave resistance were more out in the open. Uncompromising German communists like Weydemeyer added fuel to the flames
of this budding insurgency.

As editor of socialist newspapers in Chicago and then in St. Louis,
Weydemeyer tasked himself with mobilizing Forty-Eighters to support
the Republican Party. His fellow communists were lukewarm on the
relatively moderate Lincoln, who as a presidential candidate wanted to
limit the westward expansion of slavery but was against its abolition.
Weydemeyer won many of them over on the grounds that the Slave
Power would construe Lincoln's election as an attack on slavery.[52]

Weydemeyer also pressured Republicans to take a more aggressive
antislavery position. On the western front along the Mississippi, communists joined enslaved people in seeing the deadly sectional conflict
as a fight for emancipation. They were right to think so. The Civil War
was a battle over slavery. As such, it was a struggle over competing
conceptions of labor, over which model would set the parameters of
freedom.[53]

Southern apologists for chattel slavery had long concocted intellectual defenses of their labor system. Whether slavery was divine will or
natural preference, one thing was certain in their eyes: interfering with
it violated the order of things and would only make people less free. In
a speech before the US Senate in 1858, the South Carolina slaver James
Henry Hammond articulated the "mudsill" theory. Hammond said:

> In all social systems there must be a class to do the menial duties, to
> perform the drudgery of life. That is, a class requiring but a low order

of intellect and but little skill. Its requisites are vigor, docility, fidelity. Such a class you must have, or you would not have that other class which leads progress, civilization, and refinement. It constitutes the very mud-sill of society and of political government; and you might as well attempt to build a house in the air, as to build either the one or the other, except on this mud-sill. Fortunately for the South, she found a race adapted to that purpose to her hand. A race inferior to her own, but eminently qualified in temper, in vigor, in docility, in capacity to stand the climate, to answer all her purposes. We use them for our purpose, and call them slaves.

Hammond argued the Northern states were dishonest about the nature of its labor force. Slavery might have been abolished in name in the North, but by necessity it remained in practice. Wage slavery was still slavery. Moreover, Hammond contended Southern slaves were treated better than Northern workers. In the South, people forced to labor were employed for life and never lacked food or shelter. In the North, workers were temporarily hired at pathetic rates and quickly turned back on the streets, begging for food.[54]

In 1859, Abraham Lincoln offered an alternative paradigm to the mudsill theory, rooted in the "free soil, free labor, free men" ideology of most Republicans. Lincoln trusted that social mobility was a fact of life in the United States. The experience of homesteaders like his father, who forged their way west and achieved independence with their own calloused hands, explicitly refuted the notion that society required a permanent class of laborers. Lincoln believed most Americans had the potential to rise up from the ranks of labor and construct independent lives by working hard and gaining an education, as he himself had done. Crucially, Lincoln assumed a society premised on free labor was more just than a slave society because people worked of their own free will. Free labor was also more productive because people were motivated to improve themselves. In contrast, Hammond idealized a society in which refined and clever men did the thinking while strong and dimwitted men and women did the laboring.

The future president's logic doubled as a critique of the communist view of labor, which rejected the very premise of "free soil, free labor, free men." As Marx often argued, there was nothing free about soil, labor, or men under the rule of private property. Many German communists viewed private property as theft because those who owned it had the power to steal the labor of others. This was doubly true when people were held as chattel, when labor itself was property. Thus, Weydemeyer and his comrades were not only struggling for the liberation of the enslaved. They were fighting against the logic of capital and for the freedom of all.

Lincoln's main point of contention with the communist view of labor was the idea at the heart of Marx's theory about the inextricability of labor and capital. As Lincoln said:

> The world is agreed that labor is the source from which human wants are mainly supplied. There is no dispute upon this point. From this point, however, men immediately diverge. Much disputation is maintained as to the best way of applying and controlling the labor element. By some it is assumed that labor is available only in connection with capital—that nobody labors, unless somebody else, owning capital, somehow, by the use of that capital, induces him to do it. Having assumed this, they proceed to consider whether it is best that capital shall hire laborers, and thus induce them to work by their own consent; or buy them, and drive them to it without their consent.[55]

Lincoln was too cautious to run for president as an avowed abolitionist. Yet he firmly believed labor should never be coerced. More to the point, he disagreed with the notion that labor was automatically attached to capital and thus coerced in a capitalist system. Lincoln thought the American system allowed for the possibility that some workers might break free of capital and work for themselves. This, more than anything else, set Lincoln and the Republican Party apart from Marx and the communists.

Lincoln thought the mudsill theory of labor both was wrong and failed to accurately describe the American system of labor outside the slave South. Marx too thought the mudsill theory was a morally repulsive prescription for society because he also believed all humans were capable and deserving of living free. However, unlike Lincoln, Marx believed the mudsill theory got one thing right. In a society dominated by capital, there was no such thing as free labor.

The real question for Marx was not whether capital coerced labor, which was obviously the case, but rather, *who* was to be subjected to unfree labor conditions. "In the Northern states," Marx wrote, "where Negro slavery is in practice impossible, the white working class would gradually be forced down to the level of helotry. This would fully accord with the loudly proclaimed principle that only certain races are capable of freedom, and as the actual labour is the lot of the Negro in the South, so in the North it is the lot of the German and the Irishman, or their direct descendants." The capitalist North needed people to exploit, same as the slave South. As the historian Angela Zimmerman writes, "for Marx and Engels, slavery reveals an economic fact that wages conceal."[56]

Labor in a capitalist system was an indisputable form of exploitation in Marx's view. This did not entail that he believed a capitalist labor system was the moral equivalent of slavery. Indeed, Marx thought slavery was much worse. He also thought that if the Slave Power had its way, it would put working-class people everywhere in literal chains. "Between 1856 and 1860," Marx wrote, "the political spokesmen, jurists, moralists and theologians of the slaveholders' party had already sought to prove, not so much that Negro slavery is justified, but rather that colour is a matter of indifference and the working class is everywhere born to slavery."[57]

Marx's dystopian vision was consistent with Lincoln's criticism of the mudsill theory. Yet, Marx's theory of labor exploitation contradicted the underlying ideology of the Republican Party. For Marx, freedom for the working class was impossible in a capitalist society. That said, in order for the working class to achieve freedom, first slavery had to be abolished. Marx's comrades in the United States thus had a different rationale for fighting the Civil War than did Lincoln and the Republicans, at least at the outset.

After ten states followed South Carolina's lead in seceding to form the Confederate States of America in response to Lincoln's electoral victory in 1860, war seemed likely. When Confederate forces attacked Fort Sumter in the Charleston harbor on April 12, 1861, war became reality. But for what cause? Although Confederate leaders declared secession was a position that they "thoroughly identified with the institution of slavery—the greatest material interest of the world," Lincoln did not intend to wage a war against slavery. Even as Alexander Stephens, the vice president of the Confederacy, avowed the breakaway nation was premised "upon the great truth that the negro is not equal to the white man; that slavery, subordination to the superior race, is his natural and normal condition," the US government sent wave after wave of young men to their deaths not for the great moral cause of abolition but for the simple goal of reunification. In contrast, German communists joined the war effort with the express purpose of destroying slavery.[58]

The radical Forty-Eighters found hospitable grounds for their revolutionary project along the Civil War's western front, joining Union forces under the command of General John C. Fremont. Fremont had a long military history on the frontier in several campaigns against natives and Mexicans. Yet despite his immersion in the nation's genocidal Empire building, he rejected the notion that slavers had a legitimate claim to the West. Rather, Fremont was a quintessential republican. As the party's first presidential candidate in 1856, Fremont had been championed with the alliterative slogan, "Free Soil, Free Labor, Free Men, Fremont."[59]

Fremont set out to deploy Union forces as a hammer to smash slavery. He recruited veterans of the 1848 revolutions to fill out his officer corps. Weydemeyer was among them, and by 1864, having risen to the rank of colonel, he was put in command of forces defending St. Louis. As a rule, Fremont's Forty-Eighters loathed slavery to a degree uncommon among most native-born Union officers. By injecting the western officer corps with a healthy dose of mistrust toward the institution of slavery, Fremont ensured his troops would follow through on his more daring orders, such as his August 31, 1861, declaration that immediately emancipated slaves from "all persons in the state of Missouri who shall take up arms against the United States." Fearing that Missouri and other loyal slave states would join the secessionists as a result, Lincoln reversed the order and removed Fremont from his position. Yet, as enslaved people across the South shared tales of Fremont's exploits—one black conjurer told a Union encampment in Kentucky that "Fremont was in Missouri, freeing all the colored people"—the abolitionist war along the Mississippi endured, with or without Lincoln's endorsement.[60]

The uncompromising struggle being waged by many Forty-Eighters against the Slave Power made Marx proud of his countrymen. Writing to Engels in July 1861, Marx predicted that working-class German immigrants were bound to tip the scales for the Union because they were not so easily intimidated "as the *gentlemen* of Wall Street and the Quakers of Boston." Marx never joined his comrades in their righteous military campaign. Yet he was far from a neutral observer.[61]

Few topics animated Marx more than the American Civil War. In what he described as "the first grand war of contemporaneous history," Marx found the modern social revolution he had been seeking, a conflict pitting the "highest form of popular self-government till now realized" against "the meanest and most shameless form of man's enslaving recorded in the annals of history." This was a turning of the tides away from reaction and toward revolution. Such prospects energized Marx to a degree he had not felt since 1848.[62]

Although the Civil War improved Marx's political mood, it worsened his financial situation. After the *Tribune* cut him loose, Marx took a job with the Vienna newspaper *Die Presse*, writing several articles on the conflict in the United States. Marx's Civil War writings as a whole, consisting of several lengthy articles and countless letters, represented some of the more compelling examinations of the war to be found in Europe or anywhere else.[63]

The most important role Marx played in the crusade against slavery was helping persuade working-class radicals in Europe that the Union cause was theirs as well. Marx's analysis helped crystallize the British working-class perspective in particular. At the outset of the war, many among the British elite desired an alliance with the Confederacy, since the booming English textile industry relied upon cheap, plentiful, slave-picked cotton from the South. Moreover, that elite's unshakable belief in hierarchy translated into tolerance for slavery. Abolitionism among them was often merely a cover for the desire to dominate transatlantic trade. In an 1861 letter, Marx excoriated the British press for echoing this acute hypocrisy. "The whole of the official press in England is, of course, in favor of the *slaveholders*," Marx wrote. "They are the selfsame fellows who have wearied the world with their *antislave trade* philanthropy. But *cotton, cotton!*"[64]

In contrast, the English working class was against the Confederacy. "It ought never to be forgotten in the United States that at least the *working classes* of England," Marx wrote, "have never forsaken them." He observed "that the true people of England, of France, of Germany, of Europe, consider the cause of the United States their own cause, as the cause of liberty, and that . . . , they consider the soil of the United States as the free soil of the landless millions of Europe, as their land of promise, now to be defended sword in hand from the sordid grasp of the slaveholder." Republican visions of "free soil" appealed to even a skeptical communist like Marx.[65]

Marx's war of words with the British press took some surprising turns, even devolving into an argument about the causes of the Civil War. *The Economist*, the archetypical British capitalist publication, described the notion that the war was being fought over slavery "as impudent as it was untrue." To drive home the obvious point that it was, Marx cited the slavers themselves. "The Confederate Congress," he wrote, "boasted that its new-fangled constitution . . . had recognized for the first time Slavery as a thing good in itself, a bulwark of civilization, and a divine institution." By highlighting that the war was about "whether twenty million free men of the North should subordinate themselves any longer to an oligarchy of three thousand slaveholders," Marx had yet again demonstrated that communists and republicans could unite in hatred for the Slave Power. This was a political alliance that might reshape the world.[66]

In general terms, Marx saw the Civil War as an unavoidable consequence of inexorable contradictions. Echoing a speech Lincoln gave in

1858—a "house divided against itself, cannot stand," a nation "cannot endure permanently half slave and half free"—Marx wrote in 1861 that the "present struggle between the South and the North is nothing but a struggle between two social systems, the system of slavery and the system of free labor. . . . The two systems can no longer live peacefully side by side on the North American continent."[67]

Marx and Lincoln had antagonistic viewpoints on the question of labor in relation to capitalist property relations. Yet they shared certain republican sensibilities, which helped convince Marx that Lincoln was the right person to vanquish the Confederacy. But despite his admiration, which grew as the conflict wore on, Marx did not spare Lincoln his typically ruthless criticism. Early in the war, Marx faulted Lincoln for his unwillingness to attack the slave system itself, a reluctance that he believed was both morally questionable and strategically unsound. Marx believed Lincoln's coddling of the border states handicapped the North. For Marx, abolition was the ticket to victory.

Yet Marx was confident the president would eventually grasp the necessity of making the war a war of emancipation. "Events themselves," Marx wrote, "drive to the promulgation of the decisive slogan— *emancipation of the slaves*." Such expectations gave him confidence that the North would win. "There can be no doubt," Marx wrote at the beginning of the war, "that, in the early part of the struggle, the scales will be weighted in favour of the South, where the class of propertyless white adventurers provides an inexhaustible source of martial militia. In the *long run*, of course, the North will be victorious since, if the need arises, it has a last card up its sleeve, in the shape of a slave revolution."[68]

Engels did not share Marx's optimism. After surveying the North's discouraging military record in the summer of 1862, Engels wrote Marx that "unless the North adopts a revolutionary stance, it will get the terrible thrashing it deserves—and that's what seems to be happening." In contrast, Marx trusted the war would inevitably transition from a constitutional conflict, which would merely restore the Union while potentially leaving the institution of slavery intact, into a revolutionary struggle, which would arm the enslaved to fight for their freedom and abolish slavery. Engels focused on military figures like General George McClellan, a Southern-sympathizing Democrat who briefly and disastrously served as Commanding General of the US Army. Marx fixed his attention on characters like the abolitionist Wendell Phillips, who early in the war gave a fire-breathing speech against slavery that Marx called "of greater importance than a battle bulletin" because it signaled rising revolutionary tendencies.[69]

Marx's expectations that the United States would win the war once it evolved into a revolution against slavery were validated by the enslaved themselves. Hundreds of thousands of enslaved black people converted the Civil War into a revolutionary struggle by swamping Union camps and making themselves war "contraband." Lincoln finally got in line with these black freedom fighters—and with Marx—when he issued the Emancipation Proclamation on January 1, 1863. "The fury with which the Southerners are greeting Lincoln's acts," Marx wrote to Engels, "is proof of the importance of these measures," proof that these events "are such as to transform the world."[70]

Marx pondered Lincoln quite a bit in this time. The upshot was a somewhat mixed assessment. Marx's public essays tended to evaluate Lincoln glowingly because he sought to build support for the Union cause. But his private correspondence was more circumspect. There, Marx described Lincoln as an "average man of good will." Yet even such a jab was strangely rooted in admiration. "Never has the New World secured a greater victory than in the demonstration that with its political and social organization," Marx wrote, "average men of good will suffice to do that which in the Old World would have required heroes to do!" Lincoln was a new kind of democratic leader, the antithesis of Louis Napoleon Bonaparte and the other despicable guardians of the Old Order.[71]

Marx judged Lincoln a force for good, not because he thought the American president transcended history, but rather because he believed Lincoln personified powerful democratic forces that promised a new stage in humanity's everlasting pursuit of freedom. After the Emancipation Proclamation, Marx described Lincoln as "a *sui generis* figure in the annals of history." Marx continued:

He has no initiative, no idealistic impetus, . . . no historical trappings. He gives his most important actions always the most commonplace form. Other people claim to be "fighting for an idea," when it is for them a matter of square feet of land. Lincoln, even when he is motivated by an idea, talks about "square feet." He sings the bravura aria of his part hesitatively, reluctantly and unwillingly, as though apologizing for being compelled by circumstances "to act the lion." The most redoubtable decrees . . . flung by him at the enemy all look like, and are intended to look like, routine summonses sent by a lawyer to the lawyer of the opposing party, legal chicaneries, overly complicated *actiones juris*. His latest proclamation, which is drafted in the same style, the manifesto abolishing slavery, is the most important document in American history since the establishment of the Union, tantamount to the tearing up of the old American Constitution.[72]

Marx believed Lincoln embodied democratic revolution, even and especially when he issued earth-shattering decrees in prosaic legalese. This assessment hinged on the fact that Marx saw an emancipatory Civil War as a portent of future socialist revolutions. Marx's notions about Lincoln the revolutionary were on full display in a public letter he wrote to Lincoln on behalf of the International Workingmen's Association, a radical socialist organization Marx helped found in 1864, congratulating him for his reelection that year:

While the working men, the true political power of the North, allowed slavery to defile their own republic; while before the Negro, mastered and sold without his concurrence, they boasted it the highest prerogative of the white-skinned labourer to sell himself and choose his own master; they were unable to attain the true freedom of labour or to support their European brethren in their struggle for emancipation, but this barrier to progress has been swept off by the red sea of civil war.

The workingmen of Europe feel sure that, as the American War of Independence initiated a new era of ascendancy for the middle class, so the American Anti-Slavery War will do for the working classes. They consider it an earnest sign of the epoch to come that it fell to the lot of Abraham Lincoln, the single-minded son of the working class, to lead his country through the matchless struggle for the rescue of an enchained race and the reconstruction of a social world.[73]

It is doubtful Lincoln read Marx's letter. But Charles Francis Adams, the US ambassador to Great Britain, approximated Lincoln's probable reaction when he responded to the International Workingmen's Association in a lawyerly tone. "The government of the United States," Adams wrote, "has a clear consciousness that its policy neither is nor could be reactionary, but, at the same time, it adheres to the course which it adopted at the beginning, of abstaining everywhere from propagandism and unlawful interventionism." Elsewhere, Marx's widely distributed letter was received less fastidiously. German communists in the Union Army read it for inspiration as they advanced on Confederate troops.[74]

Marx supported Lincoln and the Union because he despised slavery. But ultimately his antislavery stance was a product of his firm belief that abolition was an essential step toward working-class emancipation. As he wrote in *Capital*, published two years after the United States crushed the Slave Power: "In the United States of America, every independent workers' movement was paralyzed as long as slavery disfigured part of the republic. Labor in a white skin cannot emancipate itself where it is branded in a black skin." The death of chattel slavery would create conditions more favorable to organizing the working class, since a free labor system would no longer need to compete with a slave one. The liberation of an enchained set of workers would reconstruct the social world. Then, the working class could organize as one, in solidarity, across racial lines.[75]

Marx's Civil War writings reveal that events in the United States had restored his hopes for a socialist future, which had been trounced along with the Revolutions of 1848. But even in the wake of Union victory, Marx knew serious work remained to realize the promise of the Civil War. Reconstruction, the bitter postwar struggle to establish the conditions under which the Confederate states would be readmitted to the United States, a process that included a fight over the status of the formerly enslaved, would ultimately determine whether socialism had a chance. What Marx had referred to as "the reconstruction of a social world" was not merely a reference to the future of the American South. Reconstruction was to prep the grounds for socialist revolution everywhere. If a multiracial working class could rise to power in a place formerly controlled by the Slave Power, one of the most ruthless class of elites in modern world history, then socialism might be possible *anywhere*.[76]

Marx's faith in the transformative potential of Reconstruction informed his initial view of Andrew Johnson, the Tennessee Democrat who became president after John Wilkes Booth assassinated Lincoln on April 15, 1865. Marx immediately wrote a public letter to Johnson, again on behalf of the International Workingmen's Association. "Yours," he wrote, "has become the task to uproot by the law what has been felled by the sword, to preside over the arduous task of political reconstruction and social regeneration . . . to initiate the new era of the emancipation of labour." Marx privately reasoned to Engels that Johnson, as the son of poor whites, should be willing to make the Southern oligarchy pay for its treachery. It was one of the few occasions during the Civil War era that Marx's analysis of the United States missed its mark, in this case by a mile.[77]

Johnson rapidly disabused Marx of the notion that he was a worthy successor to Lincoln. Just a few short months later, Marx wrote to Engels that Johnson's policies were "excessively vacillating and weak." Johnson was content to restore the Slave Power to its position atop the Southern hierarchy, which also meant he was fine with the forceful return of the freedmen to bondage. "The reaction has already set in in America," Marx warned, "and will soon be much fortified if the present lackadaisical attitude is not ended immediately." In thinking about ways to suppress the reaction, Engels contended that immediate black suffrage might be the best course of action. Marx agreed. Working-class people everywhere should support black suffrage in order to bolster their power as a class, which was threatened by Johnson's revanchist turn against black freedom.[78]

Joseph Weydemeyer wrote a three-part article on black suffrage for a German-language socialist paper that captured Marx's position. In Weydemeyer's view, the freedmen were vital to organizing a multiracial working-class movement:

> The modern worker is the direct creation of industry, and his entire existence is inextricably bound up with its development. Although industry oppresses and exploits him, it is only by further developing industry that he can gain the power to destroy these forms of exploitation, as he helped destroy other forms [i.e., slavery] that no longer corresponded to the civilization of our century. What fosters the development of industry thus also fosters his own interests. The more allies he gains for the great fight between labor and monopolizing capital, which we see organized and prepared before our very eyes, the more certain and speedy his victory. But where else in the South will he find these allies, if not among the workers themselves, regardless of what ancestry they have to thank for their skin color?[79]

When Americans repudiated Johnson in 1866 by voting in Radical Republicans, who took firm control of Congress and would soon impeach Johnson, Marx saw interracial working-class solidarity at work. "The workers of the North," he wrote to Engels, "have at last fully understood that white labour will never be emancipated so long as black labour is still stigmatized," a phrase he repeated almost verbatim in *Capital*, published a year later. Marx grew more optimistic after Radical Republicans created laws that endowed black Southerners with basic civil rights and, even better, when they expressed a desire to redistribute land and wealth. Basic rights like voting were crucial, as Marx and his comrades had made clear. But the ultimate problem that Reconstruction needed to solve, in the words of the abolitionist Wendell Phillips, was that "the black man has no capital." As Marx wrote in the preface to *Capital*:

> Mr. Wade, vice-president of the United States, declared in public meetings that, after the abolition of slavery, a radical change of the relations

of capital and of property in land is next upon the order of the day. These are signs of the times. . . . They do not signify that tomorrow a miracle will happen. They show that, within the ruling classes themselves, a foreboding is dawning, that the present society is no solid crystal, but an organism capable of change, and is constantly changing.[80]

CAPITAL AND THE WORKING CLASS

As Americans were struggling to bring about the foreboding dawn, on the other side of the Atlantic Marx was doing his part to make the ruling classes tremble by helping to form the International Workingmen's Association. Founded in London on September 28, 1864, the International, as it was known, was intended as an institutional framework for the international working-class movement upon which Marx rested his political hopes.

As the organization's intellectual sage, Marx authored its most famous pronouncements, such as its congratulatory letter to Lincoln, and also designed its programmatic statements. This included its "Inaugural Address," which declared the group's central objective was "the emancipation of labor." A decade prior, such a goal would have been fantasy. But recent events, including the Civil War, had changed Marx's mind. Closer to home, Marx was energized by recent legislation in Parliament restricting the length of the working day, describing it as "the first time that in broad daylight the political economy of the middle class succumbed to the political economy of the working class." Marx concluded the address with familiar words, transported from an earlier moment of revolutionary hope: "Proletarians of all countries, Unite!"[81]

The revolutionary developments to which Marx lent his considerable programmatic talents during the 1860s motivated him to return to his desk and write the earth-shattering *Capital*. Long in the making, *Capital* finally came together in 1867, thanks in part to things Marx had learned from the Civil War. The slaves who struggled to free themselves during the war, and the Forty-Eighters who fought to transform the conflict into a war of liberation, and the English workers who supported emancipation for the enslaved while also battling for their own shortened working day, all informed a key point of Marx's argument in *Capital*. People are only free if they have autonomy, over their lives, over their time, over their bodies.

Workers trapped in a slave economy had no autonomy. Workers ensnared in a capitalist economy were better off, but autonomy for them was also elusive since they were never their own masters while at work, where they spent most of their waking hours. In this way, *Capital* connected the abolition of slavery to the movement to shorten the working day. As Marx wrote in *Capital*: "A new life immediately arose from the death of slavery. The first fruit of the American Civil War was the eight hours' agitation, which ran from the Atlantic to the Pacific, from New England to California, with the seven-league boots of the locomotive." The abolition of slavery was not the destination but an imperative landmark, much like the eight-hour day, on the long road to liberating the working class. Marx mapped out this road in *Capital*.[82]

Marx intended *Capital* as a ten-volume project. Yet he only managed to see one volume published during his lifetime (Engels oversaw the posthumous publication of two more). The first volume of *Capital* is over one thousand sometimes grueling, frequently thrilling pages about how capital profits by exploiting labor. In its first part, Marx focused on the crucial role of the commodity form, which helped capitalists realize profits while hiding their shameful basis, labor exploitation. The section nicely set up the crucial tenth chapter, "The Working Day," which grew out of Marx's intensifying awareness that capitalism stripped workers of autonomy.

In his analysis of the working day, Marx poignantly demonstrated that the political fight over its length was a crucial site of class struggle, a zero-sum battle between capitalists seeking to maximize profits and workers seeking to minimize their own exploitation. The more time workers were compelled to work for the same or less in wages—the more the working class was exploited—the more capitalists profited. Vice versa, the more capitalists were compelled to pay in wages for the same or less time—the less the working class was exploited—the less capitalists profited.

Marx showed that the very same class struggle also shaped the working day for slave laborers in the fully capitalist American system of slavery. In response to intense international competition that rendered cotton less profitable in the decades approaching the Civil War, slavers sought to recoup losses by brutally enforcing a quicker pace of work on their plantations. Marx explained this general process in some detail, writing that "as soon as people, whose production still moves within the lower forms of slave labor, corvée labor, etc., are drawn into the whirlpool of an international market dominated by the capitalistic mode of production, the sale of their products for export becoming their principal interest, the civilized horrors of overwork are grafted on the barbaric horrors of slavery, serfdom, &c." He continued with a more specific point about slave labor in the United States:

> Hence the Negro labor in the Southern States of the American Union preserved something of a patriarchal character, so long as production was directed to immediate local consumption. But in proportion, as the export of cotton became of vital interest to these states, the over-working of the negro and sometimes the using up of his life in seven years of labor became a factor in a calculated and calculating system. It was no longer a question of obtaining from him a certain quantity of useful products. It was now a question of the production of surplus labor itself.[83]

Marx saw that capitalism was transforming labor relations on both sides of the Atlantic. He thus placed the rising savagery of English factory work alongside the mounting brutality of American slavery. "While the cotton industry introduced child-slavery into England," Marx wrote, "in the United States it gave the impulse for the transformation of the earlier, more or less patriarchal slavery into a system of commercial exploitation. In fact the veiled slavery of the wage-labourers in Europe needed the unqualified slavery of the New World as its pedestal." Abolish slavery, and labor exploitation writ large might crumble.[84]

The specter of American slavery haunts many important sections of *Capital*. The years Marx dedicated to understanding the United States in general, and the Civil War in particular, helped him grasp the tight connection between labor and freedom. Marx's crystal-clear explanation of that close relationship—the opening salvo of the Marx-America dialectic—is ultimately what made *Capital* a book for the ages. Marx's argument that freedom could not be achieved in a society in which some people were coerced to toil, whether by threat of the whip or fear of starvation, has rallied millions to the causes of communism, socialism, and social democracy.

In making the case against coerced labor, and in making that argument the cornerstone of his overarching philosophy, Marx did not deny that people had to perform some work in order for society to function. But in the more equal world he envisioned, the amount of time spent working would be limited to "necessary labor." Each individual would make an essential contribution to society, which would in turn guarantee people the things they needed to make their lives comfortable and rewarding. Or as Marx famously phrased it a few years after the publication of *Capital*: "From each according to his ability, to each according to his needs." In such a society, four-hour workdays might have been sufficient to keep things running smoothly. Of course, the actually existing society in which Marx lived, dominated by the logic of capital, was far from the egalitarian existence of his imagination. "Under the capitalist mode of production," Marx wrote, "this necessary labour can form only a part of the working day; the working day can never be reduced to this minimum." In subordination to the profit motive, people worked well beyond what was necessary.[85]

In the eyes of capitalists, no amount of labor was beyond necessary, except the minimal time workers needed to eat and sleep. By that logic, what was the correct length of the working day? Marx had an answer: "At all events, it is less than a natural day. How much less? The capitalist has his own views of this point of no return, the necessary limit of the working day. . . . The time during which the worker works is the time during which the capitalist consumes the labour-power he has bought from him. If the worker consumes his disposable time for himself, he robs the capitalist." Capital must always be in motion. Since only workers can put capital in motion, the working class must be made to work as much as possible. "Time for education, for intellectual development, for the fulfillment of social functions, for social intercourse, for the free play of vital forces of his body and his mind, even the rest time of Sunday (and that in a country of Sabbatarians)—what foolishness!"[86]

Marx's close study of the "voracious appetite" of English capitalists, who willfully ignored the English Factory Law of 1850 by forcing their workers to toil for longer than the legally prescribed workday because resulting profits far exceeded the cost of fines for violating the law, led him to compare such "monstrous outrages" to "the cruelties of the Spaniards to the American red-skins." Nineteenth-century capitalists, like some of history's other monsters, would have worked their labor force to death if given the opportunity. Indeed, they often did, since such cruelty made for good business, especially when the ranks of the working class swelled with people desperate to be exploited as an alternative to starvation. The capitalist was a lot like the slaver in this regard. As Marx wrote: *Mutato nominee de te fabula narrator* (The name is changed, but the tale is told of you!) For slave trade, read labour-market, for Kentucky and Virginia, Ireland and the agricultural districts of England, Scotland and Wales, for Africa, Germany. We have heard how over-work has thinned the ranks of the bakers in London. Nevertheless, the London labour-market is always over-stocked with German and other candidates for death in the bakeries." The reserve army of labor was a precondition for exploitation, whether in Montgomery or Manchester.[87]

Marx's sense that capitalist labor relations created a desperate situation for most people explains his attention to the length of the working day. After the war to defeat the Slave Power, Marx considered the fight to shorten the working day the next front in "a protracted and more or less concealed civil war between the capitalist class and the working class." Even as the working class won a few battles in the midst of this larger class war, Marx cautioned that "the vampire will not let go," given the high stakes. What was needed was a world-historical victory that might forever alter the terrain, "an all-powerful social barrier by which they can be prevented from selling themselves and their families into slavery and death by voluntary contract with capital." A new Magna Carta, favorable to the laboring masses, was in order.[88]

By the time *Capital* went to print in 1867, the movement for the eight-hour day had been gaining momentum in the United States. In 1866, the newly formed National Labor Union resolved that the greatest priority in the aftermath of the Civil War was "to free labor of this country from capitalist slavery." The best way to achieve such an objective, it asserted, was "the passing of a law by which eight hours shall be the normal working day in all States." With this in mind, Engels implored one of his comrades in the United States "to bring Marx's book to the attention of the German American press and of the workers. With the 8-hour agitation that is in progress in America now," Engels continued, "this book with its chapter on the working day will come at just the right time for you over there."[89]

Although it would take decades for the eight-hour day to become the norm in even a modest number of industries, and although it was many years before *Capital* was translated into English and thus made widely accessible in the United States, the crusade for a shortened working day further endowed Marx with hope that the future was socialist. This was especially the case because the movement developed so quickly on the heels of the victory over the Slave Power. Revolutionary tides seemed to be cascading. But the predictable backwash of reaction dampened Marx's hopes.

RECONSTRUCTION, REVOLUTION, REACTION

Reconstruction made some revolutionary strides before reactionaries put a stop to such progress. Once Radical Republicans sidelined President Johnson in 1867, the US Army returned South, not as conquerors but rather as guarantors of civil rights for newly freed black people. Northern occupation forces, to take one decisive example, were charged with protecting the freedmen's right to vote. As a result, black people were elected to serve in positions at all levels of government, from town sheriff to US senator. Anecdotes abounded about a world turned upside down, as men who had been enslaved a mere two years prior suddenly found themselves elected officials with stern duties, such as settling property disputes involving their former enslavers. This all went according to plan in the eyes of Marx, who predicted that black voting rights would rapidly transform Southern social relations. Of course, he might also have anticipated the ensuing escalation of violence, as paramilitary organizations like the Ku Klux Klan emerged to expressly kill Reconstruction.

Those who terrorized Reconstruction were brazen white supremacists. But because Reconstruction at its most radical represented both black civil rights *and* a threat to property relations, the Southern counterrevolution was also a defense of capitalism. Radicals who openly advocated for redistributing Confederate land to the formerly enslaved, often in the form of "forty acres and a mule," were deemed threatening, and not just to the former Slave Power. Many among the Northern elite worried that if radicals and freedman had their way in the South, they would make similar demands elsewhere. As the historian Heather Cox Richardson writes, "mainstream Northerners increasingly perceived the mass of African-Americans as adherents of a theory of political economy in which labor and capital were at odds and in which a growing government would be used to advance laborers at the expense of capitalists. For these Northerners, the majority of ex-slaves became the face of 'communism' or 'socialism.'" Property rights were property rights, whether in Mississippi or Massachusetts, and propertyless black people represented a menace to such rights.[90]

As Reconstruction came to be associated with communism, more and more Americans grew familiar with Marx's name. Radicals like Benjamin Butler, the US congressman from Massachusetts whose popularity peaked immediately after the Civil War, were linked to Marx and communism—and thus to unwelcome land redistribution. As the historian Eric Foner writes: "The juxtaposition of Butler and Karl Marx as advocates of 'spoilation' of property occurred more frequently in the reform press than the modern reader might imagine."[91]

Reconstruction was eventually killed, and so too was the short-lived alliance between republicanism and communism, between the Butlers and Marxes of the world. Consequently, the Republican Party grew less and less radical. The ideals of free soil, free labor, and free men, for which millions risked their lives in a gruesome war, narrowed, permitting white supremacists to redeem themselves. Marx no longer looked to the United States with as much hope for its socialist prospects. Perhaps he turned his attention away too soon, since even in his private correspondence he mostly quit writing about American developments after 1867, long before Reconstruction was officially put to rest. Of course, events in Europe once again began to inspire him.

In the midst of the fatal assault on Reconstruction, an equally remarkable social experiment came alive on Marx's side of the Atlantic, as revolutionaries took control of Paris in March 1871. The Paris Commune, like Reconstruction, was the child of war, in its case the Franco-Prussian War that terminated the Second French Empire and ended the reign of Louis Napoleon Bonaparte. As Paris was besieged by foreign troops, the government relocated south to Tours, thus leaving a power vacuum that anticapitalist partisans gladly filled by establishing a government by and for the Parisian proletariat. The Paris Commune, like Reconstruction, was a demonstration of working-class self-determination. Yet it was even shorter-lived than Reconstruction as it, too, suffered a violent death at the hands of well-armed reactionaries. Regular French military forces, under command of the newly established Third Republic, retook Paris, and in the process massacred 20,000 Parisians. And yet, despite its brief two-month existence, the Paris Commune inspired revolutionaries around the world. This included Marx.[92]

After its demise, Marx authored *The Civil War in France*, a widely circulated analysis of the Paris Commune on behalf of the International. Marx was confident the Paris Commune, in its efforts to revolutionize the state "to serve as a lever for uprooting the economical foundation upon which rests the existence of classes, and therefore of class rule," set socialists on the correct path. Particularly, in Marx's eyes the Commune had achieved something that eluded radicals in the Reconstruction South. They had actually realized, if only for a dreadfully short period of time, working-class rule. "If the American Civil War was the answer to the failures of the revolutions of 1848," Angela Zimmerman writes, "the Paris Commune, for Marx, was the answer to the disappointments of Reconstruction. Revolutionary politics remained, for Marx and Engels, an innovative and experimental form." The Paris Commune, Marx wrote, was "the form at last discovered."[93]

Even as Marx expressed glowing admiration for the Paris Commune, he was compelled to reckon with one glaring problem: it survived only two months. Marx did not blame the Communards for the violent counterrevolutionary assault that ended the beautiful experiment. That would have been akin to impugning the freedman for the destruction of Reconstruction while letting the Ku Klux Klan off the hook. And yet, Marx thought the Communards might have taken better steps to protect their revolution from its eventual conquerors. Future socialist revolutions would need a centralized organ that could make rapid decisions to consolidate working-class power. Returning to the language of the *Manifesto*, Marx called for "a dictatorship of the proletariat." Thanks to the murderous resolve of capital, anything less was revolutionary suicide.[94]

Marx projected his hopes onto the Paris Commune as a symbol of a better future, and he was not alone. Revolutionaries around the world came to see the Commune as a model for a socialist future. American radicals were no exception. The abolitionist Wendell Phillips, who took up labor as his main cause after the Civil War, sought to convince Americans that the Commune was at the other "end of the telegraph wire of Liberty." "There is no hope for France," Phillips proclaimed, "but in the Reds." His fellow abolitionist Theodore Tilton announced that the "same logic and sympathy—the same conviction and ardor—which made us an Abolitionist twenty years ago, makes us a Communist now."[95]

American partisans of the Paris Commune barely made a dent in the overarching narrative, solidified by extensive negative coverage in newspapers across the United States, that it represented a menace to civilization. In fact, the Commune set off what might be described as the nation's first red scare. If something so disruptive could happen in Paris, it could also happen in New York and Chicago, where the International had established a foothold. Paranoia reached a fevered pitch when the *Chicago Tribune* blamed the catastrophic 1871 Chicago fire on the International.[96]

As Americans battled over the meaning of the Paris Commune, they also fought over the implications of Karl Marx. Because Marx was mistakenly considered the mastermind of the Commune, Americans who began to utter his name rarely did so without also mentioning the Commune. His initial, limited reception was thus mixed at best. Some Americans hailed Marx as a revolutionary hero. The *National Anti-Slavery Standard* likened him to a William Lloyd Garrison for a new age of labor struggle. As a result of this attention, more Americans read Marx for the first time. In 1876, *The Socialist*, a publication of the brand-new Socialist Labor Party, printed an English version of *Capital* in thirteen installments.[97]

Other Americans viewed Marx as an evil genius bent on chaos and destruction. With this trope in mind, a few intrepid American reporters traveled to London to interview Marx. One from the *Chicago Tribune* was impressed and even intimidated by Marx's learnedness. "A man can generally be judged by the books he reads," the journalist wrote, "and you can form your own conclusions when I tell you a casual glance revealed Shakespeare, Dickens, Thackeray, Moliere, Racine, Montaigne, Bacon, Goethe, Voltaire, Paine." Still the reporter spent most of the interview inquiring about several conspiracies that Marx had supposedly hatched, including the Paris Commune.[98]

Another American reporter set an even more dramatic scene for his interview with Marx. "Yes, I am tête-à-tête with the revolution incarnate," he intoned, "with the real founder and guiding spirit of the International Society, with the author of the address in which capital was told that if it warred on labor it must expect to have its house burned down about its ears—in a word, with the apologist for the Commune of Paris." Marx was finally becoming known in the United States, thanks, ironically, to the Paris Commune, for which he could take no credit. But Marx's initial bout with American fame did not result in *Capital* becoming a bestseller. Rather, Marx was on his way to becoming a set piece in the vivid narrative that Americans told themselves about the furious rise of industrial capitalism. For the first of many generations of anti-Marxists, Marx represented a warning about an alternative American future.[99]

EARLY VARIETIES OF AN AMERICAN MARX

If such an alternative were to be ushered in, the International would undoubtedly be to blame. Or so thought many American elites, who treated the International as a band of revolutionaries hell-bent on overthrowing American institutions. No doubt some people joined the International hoping that it would live up to such hype. But in reality, it was weak and riven by divisions. Such disunity was partly a consequence of how the American branch of the International was structured. Organized into sections by national origins, rival factions had conflicting notions about what was to be done.

The most powerful section of the American International was Section One. Led by Marx's Forty-Eighter comrade Friedrich Sorge and composed mostly of German émigrés, Section One had a stable theory of socialism its members had learned during what the historian Timothy Messer-Kruse describes as "intense theoretical discussions of *Das Kapital*." Sorge later wrote that among the hundreds of German communists in New York City, there "was hardly one who had not read Marx." Section One worked from Marx's basic premise that capitalism relied on the exploitation of labor and thus the only way to defeat it was to empower the proletariat. Section One thus sought to mold the International into a vehicle for working-class power, and in 1871 the International led a huge march for the eight-hour day in New York City. Members distributed thousands of leaflets containing excerpts of Marx's working-day chapter from *Capital*. In this way, Section One gave the first American expression of Marx's labor theory of value.[100]

Section Twelve of the American International, led by Victoria Woodhull and Tennessee Claflin and made up almost entirely of native-born Americans, was more anarchic—and doomed. The Yankee radicals who joined Section Twelve seemed at first like a good fit. Marx had

been arguing with Section One that the International needed an in-
flux of American-born members if it was going to make serious inroads
in the United States. By the same token, Woodhull and Claflin used
their considerable wealth to print and distribute thousands of copies
of Marx's *The Civil War in France*. Such symbolic action demonstrated
solidarity with Section One and the cause of labor. But Section Twelve
only supported labor as one of many causes on the road to a more beloved community.[101]

Section Twelve's commitment to nonlabor-based causes, especially women's suffrage, spiritualism, and free love—made explicit in
Woodhall's 1872 campaign for president of the United States—made
them the first representatives of a hybridized American Marx. That
did not sit well with Section One. Engels wrote that Section Twelve
represented an invasion of the International "by bourgeois swindlers,
free-love advocates, spiritual enthusiasts, Shakers, etc." One historian
chalks up such dismissiveness to conservative gender views. Although
Engels himself had views on gender roles that were progressive for the
era, it was indeed true that German socialists tended to possess traditional understandings of gender, sex, and marriage. These perspectives
tracked well alongside views held by most Americans, but they caused
friction with the Chapter Twelve radicals.[102]

German-born socialists did not possess traditional gender views
strictly because they obeyed patriarchal norms. Rather, they adhered
to a working-class romanticism that posited women as the guardians
of the proletarian family. Women served as the glue of working-class
solidarity. But this was ultimately an unequal role since only men could
lead the working class to socialist revolution, only men, the historian
Mari Jo Buhle writes, "possessed a natural path through the trade
union to class consciousness." When German socialist women, "absorbed by childcare and housework, their lives fragmented by inter-
mittent wage labor," dared organize for women's rights specifically,
they were ostracized.[103]

German socialists later came to a more expansive view of gender
relations, not because they accepted feminism but because they recognized that, when it came to exploiting wage labor, capitalism did

not discriminate between men and women. In this they more fully embraced Marx, who had long ago theorized that women's entry into the labor force was an inevitability. Such a view about gender was not necessarily the same thing as feminism, of course, since the latter was concerned with equality for women in a whole range of institutions, not just the workplace. As such, the rift between German American socialism and native-born radicalism did not heal overnight.

Perhaps most crucial to the divide in the International was the belief among Section One socialists that Section Twelve embodied the naive idealism that Marx and Engels had isolated in *The Communist Manifesto*. Yankee radicals, in this view, were akin to the utopian socialists whom Marx and Engels criticized in 1848 for fantasizing that "historical action is to yield to their personal inventive action." In any case, the fissure between those who prioritized class as the defining relation in a capitalist society, and those who included class as merely one of many social categories of equal importance, was irreparable, and it doomed the International.

Ultimately, the schism between sections was born of divergent experiences. As working-class immigrants, being forced into an exploitative situation confirmed for the German-born socialists that American capitalism was far from ideal. In contrast, as relatively well-off professionals, the Yankee radicals disliked many aspects of the American system but did not loathe capitalism with the same intensity as the German reds. While they were all anticapitalists, the two groups of activists were destined to disagree about the things that truly mattered to them as revolutionaries. This fundamental difference even shaped their uneven reactions to Marx.

For the German-born socialists, reading Marx was a revelation. His writings connected their misery to world-historical developments. For the Yankee radicals, Marx was at most one of many interesting thinkers. Section Twelve's well-circulated magazine, *Woodhull & Claflin's Weekly*, as the historian Paul Buhle writes, "had the zest of discovering Marxism for a whole nation (here, *The Communist Manifesto* appeared for the first time in the USA in English), and the superficiality of placing every idea at the same level." Communism was one of many reform movements working to achieve the good life, no better and no worse than, say, free love.[104]

In 1872, the International convened at the Hague to decide its increasingly uncertain future. The European sections were also beleaguered by factionalism. On one side were Marx and his followers, who wanted to continue building an organization with a centralized structure that would challenge the capitalist class for political power on behalf of the working class. On the other side were the Russian anarchist Mikhail Bakunin and his admirers, who wanted a decentralized association that would agitate on behalf of capitalism's "rubbish," those pushed out of society altogether.

Marx decided the best way to marginalize Bakunin was to move the International's headquarters from London to New York City, where his Section One comrades could steer the party in the proper direction. For this reason, Marx consented that Section Twelve should be sidelined, a decision made easier for him by the Yankee radicals themselves when they aligned with Bakunin's faction. Marx also thought relocating to New York was strategically sound because he continued to think the United States would become a seedbed of labor insurgency, as working-class Europeans were arriving on American shores at an increasingly rapid clip. But Marx's hopes were confounded. The German-born socialists took control, yet they were helpless to sustain the organization in the face of a rapidly dwindling membership, which was partly the result of sectarianism. By 1876, the International was dead.[105]

With the demise of the International, coupled with the Republican Party consenting to remove federal forces from the South in exchange for maintaining control of the White House after the disputed presidential election of 1876, a compromise that finished off Reconstruction, Marx probably should have ditched the idea of an American socialism. In fact, by this late stage in his life, Marx was more optimistic about Russia, where he tracked the advance of revolutionary tendencies in that country's large network of communes. But he was not entirely done with the United States.[106]

The Great Railroad Strike of 1877, in which over 100,000 workers across America walked off their jobs to protest dangerous conditions and low wages, renewed Marx's interest in the United States. His German émigré friends had helped found the Workingmen's Party of the United States (WPUS) in 1876 and, amid the railroad strike, helped organize in St. Louis, what Mike Davis has called "the first municipal general strike in U.S. history." These actions, which Marx described as "the first great uprising against the oligarchy of capital which had developed since the Civil War," more closely resembled the Paris Commune than anything the International ever carried out. At least, American capitalists must have thought so, given their ruthless response. Police jailed over one thousand strikers, and clashes between them and workers led to the deaths of over one hundred people.[107]

Placing the Great Railroad Strike in a larger context, Marx wrote in 1879 that "the United States have at present overtaken England in the rapidity of economical progress." Earlier in his life, Marx would have been upbeat about this. But as an older man who had endured countless political setbacks, he no longer assumed capitalist "progress" guaranteed corresponding upticks in working-class solidarity. And yet, he noted, the American "masses are quicker and have greater political means in their hands to resent the form of a progress accomplished at their expense." At the end of his life, Marx retained a flicker of hope for a future American socialism.[108]

MEMORIALIZING MARX

When Marx died on March 14, 1883, finally succumbing to a variety of ongoing, nagging afflictions—tuberculosis chief among them—socialism was nowhere to be found. Certainly not in the United States. But as the life of *Marx the man* was snuffed out, the life of *Marx the idea* had only begun.

Six days after Marx's death, thousands of people streamed into the Cooper Union in New York City to memorialize Marx. The *New York Times* painted a vivid picture of what amounted to the largest memorial held in his name in the world: "A very large mass-meeting of Socialists,

Communists, and working men, to do honor to the memory of Karl Marx, was held last evening. . . . A large portrait of the German Socialist was hung over the stage, and above it was the inscription, 'Vive l'Internationale,' while round both were placed the blood-red banners of the Communists and Socialistic labor clubs."

John Swinton, founder of the fiercely prolabor *John Swinton's Paper*, gave one of the more memorable speeches, comparing Marx to John Brown. Both men made humanity better by combining intellectual genius with "supreme moral qualities," Swinton preached. But both men were also treated shabbily during their lifetimes. John Brown's cause was venerated shortly after his death. Swinton hoped the same for Marx's. Just as Brown's death set off a war against slavery, perhaps Marx's death might inspire a war against capitalism. The Cuban revolutionary José Martí, who also spoke, gave the impression that Marx's death was just the beginning and that powerful men would come to fear Marx's name because "the task of setting men in opposition against men is frightening."[109]

It's true. The name of "the best hated and most calumniated man of his time," as Engels described his best friend during a memorial at Marx's Highgate Cemetery grave in London, inspired fear well after his death. To this day, "Karl Marx" strikes chords of unease, precisely because the name is associated with "the author of the address in which capital was told that if it warred on labor it must expect to have its house burned down about its ears." But the response to Marx's death by the capitalist press at the time did not reveal such fears and anxieties. One California paper danced on his grave, editorializing that Marx's life "was not a success, and at the time of his death he had witnessed the failure of every extensive project on which his hopes had been set and for which he labored with such ability." In the immediate aftermath of the Paris Commune, Marx's name was featured in the first American red scare. Yet when he died a dozen years later, Marx's erstwhile enemies had largely forgotten about him. He was almost just a footnote.[110]

In stark contrast, the socialist newspapers memorialized Marx as a figure of world-shaking consequence. The *New York Volkszeitung*, a German American socialist paper, declared that Marx "is a man who belonged to no nation, no country, no era. His name will live eternally in the human Pantheon—in the purest, noblest temple of fame whose gates will remain closed to the 'great' exploiters of mankind." American socialists kept the Marx-America dialectic alive. For them, the questions Marx raised about what it means to be free in a capitalist society were alive and well.[111]

Those who organized Marx's Cooper Union memorial used the proceeds to publish a new edition of *The Communist Manifesto*. Every union that helped with the event received three hundred copies to distribute to members. Marx was dead. But the specter of Marx? Well, that's another story.

2

WORKING-CLASS HERO

The Gilded Age

[Karl Marx's *Capital*] was the very first to set the "wires humming in my system."

EUGENE V. DEBS

When Karl Marx died in 1883, his legacy appeared secure to the thousands of radicals who attended his raucous memorial in New York City. These working-class militants hailed Marx as the architect of a coming cooperative commonwealth. To the American ruling class, in contrast, Karl Marx was at most an afterthought, buried under the wreckage of the Paris Commune. But Marx's name, and his ideas, did not die. The spirit of Marx remained alive, not because a glorious socialist future came to fruition, but rather because American capitalism itself confirmed his apocalyptic vision of it.

Although rabble-rousing socialists in the mold of Marx held a grim view of capitalism, they were not alone in grasping that a rapidly expanding economy did not benefit everyone. In the United States, where capitalism experienced explosive growth after the Civil War, critics were relatively few but not entirely ignored. In their 1873 novel that gave the era its name, Mark Twain and Charles Dudley Warner depicted a "Gilded Age" marked by grave social problems hidden beneath a shiny veneer.[1]

In contrast, many elites held that the nation had never been more prosperous, never more virtuous. Such was the tenor of the Centennial Celebration of 1876, attended by massive crowds in Philadelphia, where speaker after speaker pronounced on the American penchant for transcending Old World decay. As one declared, "the very scheme of our national life prohibits decline."[2]

Centennial triumphalism was a bit awkward in an economy that had yet to recover from the devastating panic of 1873. Lingering depression meant high rates of unemployment and, for those workers lucky enough to hold onto their jobs, deep wage cuts. These circumstances precipitated the Great Railroad Strike of 1877. Capitalism, in short, had created a setting in which Marx's ideas could flourish. Of course, tinder alone is not enough to start a fire. The contradictions of late nineteenth-century capitalism, which allowed for the accumulation of unparalleled fortunes for a few while millions toiled in humiliating and often dangerous conditions, made it likelier that Marx's words would resonate. But somebody had to light a match. Those *somebodies* were socialists.

On July 4, 1876, the Workingmen's Party of Illinois claimed the centennial for the socialist cause. In a speech before militant workers crowding downtown Chicago, party leader John McAuliffe argued the American Revolution was "inspired by capitalists" who were justified in their complaints about "taxation without representation." But since then, capitalists had seized a monopoly on representation while giving little back to society. By 1876, workers were the exploited class, lacking representation. The Workingmen's Party of Illinois thus demanded a Second American Revolution: "The present system has enabled capitalists to make laws in their own interests to the injury and oppression of workers. It has allowed capitalists to rob mankind of the benefits of progress, by using the grand inventions in labor-saving machinery to still further enslave us, instead of reducing the hours of labor in proportion to the time saved by its use, and thereby giving employment to the thousands whose labor is superseded by machinery." This revised Declaration of Independence encapsulated one of Marx's most enduring ideas: Capitalism expropriates technological advances to make life worse for workers, because the worse workers have it, the more profits there are for capitalists to take.[3]

THE FIRST MARXIST PARTY

After the Chicago rally, socialists agreed to form a new party in Philadelphia later that month. The inaugural meeting of the Workingmen's Party of the United States (WPUS) brought together socialists from several different organizations, including the remnants of the International, which had disbanded just a few days prior. Although the newly formed WPUS had more than its share of debates regarding the proper approach to achieve socialism, it was a Marxist party, the first of its kind in the United States. Or at least, some of its more prominent leaders were Marxists, especially Friedrich Sorge and Adolph Douai.

As "the closest intimate in the later years of both Marx and Engels," according to Marx's son-in-law Edward Aveling, Sorge was arguably more responsible than any other German Forty-Eighter for bringing a Marxist vision of socialism to the United States. After fighting in the Revolutions of 1848 at the age of nineteen, in a regiment led by Friedrich Engels and August Willich, Sorge eventually made his way to London, where he briefly spent time with Marx before sailing for New York City. There, as one of the founders of both the New York Communist Club and Section One of the International, he was a central figure in the construction of a vibrant German American socialist culture. More than that, Sorge led the post–Civil War socialist movement in the United States, serving as general secretary of the International from 1872 until its termination in 1876.[4]

When the WPUS formed, Sorge was arguably better versed in Marx's writings than anyone else in the United States. However, Sorge was more than a bookworm. He and his fellows committed several passages of *Capital* to memory, yet they were also quite adept at organizing the working class. Sorge firmly believed that trade unions, if properly radicalized, would free "labor from the yoke of capital." He thus assumed the WPUS should exclusively commit to organizing labor.[5]

Whereas Sorge's path was relatively well traversed among a particular German immigrant milieu, his fellow Forty-Eighter Adolph Douai's
road was less so. After growing up in poverty in Germany, Douai
worked as a private tutor in Russia and then returned as a schoolmas-
ter to his native city of Altenburg. Radicalized by his struggles as a poor
man under two autocratic regimes, Douai rushed to participate in the
Revolutions of 1848. After that landed him in prison for a year, Douai
emigrated to a small German colony in Texas, a new addition to the
United States taken from Mexico. There, he found trouble again, first
with Catholic elites who detested his freethinking sensibilities, then,
following a move to San Antonio where he started a rebellious newspaper, with slavers who despised his abolitionism. After being driven
from Texas, Douai lived in various northeastern cities, including Boston, New York City, and Newark, where he taught while also avidly
participating in the socialist movement. It was then that Douai read
Marx at a voracious clip.[6]

Douai made a name for himself as the editor of several Marxist newspapers. Like Marx, he believed wage work was "labor of the
most uniform, mind-killing, disgusting, and brutalizing kind," and
that wage laborers had "become slaves of machines." But Douai was
less doctrinaire than Sorge. Due perhaps to his circuitous route to the
movement, he was more willing to compromise over how to achieve
socialism in the United States.[7]

The WPUS only survived for eighteen tumultuous months, from
July 1876 until December 1877. The party was undone by intense internal debates. The struggle was between those who followed the route
outlined by Marx and those who adhered to the views of Ferdinand
Lassalle, the grandfather of German social democracy. While Marx
argued that the state functioned as a "committee for managing the
common affairs of the whole bourgeoisie," Lassalle saw the state as
an empty vessel that socialists might capture. In 1875 Marx knocked
Lassalle's assumption that socialism could be achieved by finding common cause with nonsocialists. Such reformist hopes violated Marx's
revolutionary logic that socialism would be won by an international
movement of workers.[8]

Following Marx, Sorge asserted that the only force capable of challenging capital was an organized working class. As such, the Marxists in the WPUS prioritized trade unionism. Until the working class arose as a unified force, they argued, operating within the capitalist electoral system was a waste of time and energy. In contrast, the Lassalleans, led by such men as the Chicago editor Philip Van Patten, the party's general secretary, presumed labor organizing was doomed to fail because, minus direct state intervention, the laws of capital ensured wages would remain at subsistence levels. The working class could only realize a more dignified existence by building political power within the nation-state.

Whereas Marxists feared that capital would co-opt a socialist movement that engaged in bourgeois politics, Lassalleans thought political alliances, especially with groups that were antagonistic to the system, were a necessary compromise.

Some WPUS members, recognizing that the division between Marxists and Lassalleans was itself debilitating, strove to pursue both unionism and electoral politics. Douai sought to adjudicate between the sides, as did Albert Parsons and a few other party members in Chicago, where Lassalleans otherwise had a stronghold. According to the historian Philip Foner, these fusionists "understood the Marxist fears that an undeveloped and immature labor movement would be easy prey for bogus politicians." But they also grasped "the fears of the Lassalleans that if trade unionism became the only arena of action, the WPUS would become only the political party of the trade unions" and would forgo broader socialist aims. Yet the two sides ultimately saw their differences as intractable.[9]

Why? Why did the Lassalleans ignore the potential clout of organized labor? Why were the Marxists hesitant to work within the political system, especially given that Marx himself imagined socialism would more easily be secured in the United States thanks to working-class access to the ballot box? Indeed, there were many instances when Marx unreservedly supported legislative causes that helped make working-class life less grueling, such as the campaign to codify a shorter working day. This in no way diminishes Marx's deep suspicions of electoral politics within a system dominated by capitalists. But it does raise questions about why many of Marx's American followers were dogmatic about political involvement.

For those Marxists who joined the WPUS after the dissolution of the International, their rejection of electoral politics was partly rooted in experience. German American socialists like Sorge, who had previously formed Section One of the International, likened the Lassalleans to the Section Twelve activists who, in their eyes, had favored bourgeois reforms, radical ideas about gender, and vanity electoral campaigns. Yet this rift does not fully explain the division in the WPUS. Rather, the Marxists worried that if the WPUS dedicated itself entirely to electoral politics, it might morph into a vehicle for anti-Chinese demagoguery in the western United States, where Chinese labor was building the railroads.[10]

The rapid expansion of the railroads across the continent in the decades following the Civil War required tens of thousands of men doing backbreaking labor. Luckily for the East Coast capitalists who underwrote the construction from that direction, there were multitudes of hungry, typically Irish workers desperate enough to take on the arduous task for relatively meager wages. The West Coast capitalists tended to hire Chinese immigrants as their cheap labor source. During an ongoing economic depression, the large presence of Chinese labor triggered a backlash that led to the Chinese Exclusion Act of 1882. It also led to bloodshed, the worst of which came in 1885, when miners in Rock Springs, Wyoming, massacred twenty-eight of their fellow workers for the crime of being Chinese.[11]

The WPUS was not immune to anti-Chinese sentiments, especially in West Coast cities like San Francisco, where a rally metamorphosed into an anti-Chinese mob. WPUS leaders mostly ignored the special plight of racial minorities on the assumption that socialism was a colorblind proposition. This was an ironic oversight since the party's short existence coincided with the precise moment when the federal government abandoned Reconstruction, a tragedy that was both a setback for black people *and* one of the worst blows dealt to the working class in American history. Yet WPUS leaders did in fact organize against anti-

Chinese passions within their own ranks. "We hope our friends," a WPUS newspaper editorialized, "will direct their struggles against the ruling class, not against their victims, the Chinese."[12]

The WPUS campaign of tolerance did not bear much fruit out west, where the working-class exhibited almost knee-jerk anti-Chinese sensibilities, made evident when racist zealots gained control of the Workingmen's Party of California. Its leader, the bigoted firebrand Denis Kearney, concluded his speeches by bluntly stating, "whatever happens, the Chinese must go."[13]

The proliferation of anti-Chinese racism was neither specifically a Marxist nor a Lassallean problem but rather a rank-and-file challenge. But the Marxists worried the Lassallean focus on electoral politics might more easily allow demagogues to run for office as socialists. Avoiding the electoral arena was a tactic for sidelining rabble-rousers like Kearney. Moreover, the Marxists felt that a narrower emphasis on labor organizing would better enable them to make the case that Chinese workers, like all workers, deserved to be treated with dignity. At a more strategic level, they reasoned that organizing Chinese workers alongside all other workers would enhance labor power more broadly and improve the condition of the working class more generally.

These antiracist efforts were ultimately unsuccessful, and the party remained nearly silent on other issues related to the needs of nonwhite working people. That said, the WPUS was home to the nation's first black self-avowed socialist, Peter Clark.

Prior to the Civil War, while traveling across the Midwest campaigning for the Republican Party, Clark met several Forty-Eighters. Settling in the heavily German city of Cincinnati after the war, he was thus familiar with the revolutionary spirit of many locals. There, amid the dour economy, Clark adopted a Marxist perspective and joined the WPUS, becoming a featured speaker at local meetings. "Capital must not rule, but be ruled and regulated," Clark told his fellow socialists. "Capital must be taught that man, and not money is supreme, and that legislation must be had for man." The radicalism of his rhetoric intensified. By the time of the Great Railroad Strike of 1877, Clark was openly advocating the abolition of private property.[14]

Clark's militant rhetoric sounded Marxist. Yet he was recruited by the WPUS Lassalleans to campaign for school commissioner of Ohio, making him the first black American to run for office as a socialist. He lost the election but won a surprisingly high number of votes, mostly in the German and black neighborhoods of Cincinnati, blazing a multiracial trail that many socialists have since followed. Clark was the first of many noteworthy black Americans attracted to Marx's vision of working-class power as a revolutionary force.

Clark was hardly the only worker radicalized by the Great Railroad Strike. With the spirit of revolution in the air, the WPUS grasped the mantle of leadership at the frontline of a brewing class war. A WPUS-led general strike that shut down St. Louis for several days, demonstrating a remarkable degree of working-class solidarity, had the national press talking about a "labor revolution." But the so-called St. Louis Commune was dead on arrival. The city's elite enlisted militias from surrounding states to crush the rebellion. The WPUS, aware that the working class stood no chance against the armed shock troops of capitalism, convinced the strikers to stand down.[15]

A rebellion in Chicago was similarly overpowered. When a large group of striking workers led by Albert Parsons poured into the streets, they were met by police eager to crush the "Chicago Commune." Parsons was arrested and threatened by a lynch mob. Several dozen striking workers were killed. The WPUS headquarters was demolished.

The Great Railroad Strike of 1877 also ended in defeat, with more than one hundred workers killed nationwide, but it altered the way many people thought about the promise of American life. As the *Chicago Tribune* editorialized, "the extremes of wealth and poverty are now to be seen here as abroad; the rich growing richer and the poor poorer, a fact to tempt disorder." For the conservative *Tribune*, the most troublesome aspect of this was clear: "We now have Communists on our soil." Similarly, Allan Pinkerton, creator of the Pinkerton National Detective Agency, the notorious strikebreaking force, said: "We have among us a pernicious communistic spirit, which is demoralizing workmen, continually creating a deeper and more intense antagonism between labor and capital." Pinkerton argued that spirit "must be crushed out completely, or we shall be compelled to submit to greater excesses and more overwhelming disasters in the near future."[16]

The increased notoriety of the WPUS expanded its membership rolls. This prompted Marx to write Engels that they might be witnessing "the point of origin for the creation of a serious workers' party in the United States." Alas, it was not to be. Paradoxically, a taste of success sealed the fate of the WPUS. Owing to widespread working-class disaffection, several WPUS candidates won elections in 1877, especially in Chicago and other midwestern cities, results which cemented the Lassallean conviction that elections were the winning ticket.[17]

At the WPUS convention in December 1877, a Lassallean majority designed a new platform that prioritized elections. Knowing the union cause was lost, Sorge and the Marxists refused to attend the convention, and they quit the party. The Lassallean group eventually became the Socialist Labor Party and had a long life, ironically, as a Marxist party. But the WPUS was dead. As the only Marxist party with a national membership, it would have been reasonably positioned to provide fitting answers to "the Labor Question" that bedeviled American life in the decades ahead.

THE LABOR QUESTION

For capitalists, the Labor Question was simple. How could they compel masses of people to work for little pay and no input over how the workplace was managed? Jay Gould, the railroad magnate and "robber baron," a term that first appeared in 1870 in reference to rapacious capitalists, was often quoted in the labor press for supposedly declaring his ability to "hire half the working class to kill the other half."[18]

For workers, the Labor Question was also clear-cut. In a society that treated them as disposable, how might they achieve a measure of dignity? No matter how straightforward this question, finding feasible answers seemed nearly impossible. The social and demographic makeover of the United States following the Civil War was much more advantageous to capitalists than to workers.[19]

Across the Gilded Age, multitudes of desperate, often hungry people, fleeing rural lives that were being foreclosed upon by the transformations of capitalist production, made their way to burgeoning cities like New York, Chicago, and San Francisco. Hailing from the North American, European, and Asian countrysides, this growing urban proletariat had nothing to sell but their labor. Rapidly expanding industries delivered heaps of jobs but never quite enough of the well-paying sort that might support lives of dignity, much less plenty. Indeed, the very presence of these forlorn masses enabled capitalists to depress wages. Cities became fertile ground for poverty and its accompanying complications, such as crime and disease. Although some well-off Americans were disturbed by these developments, proposed solutions often proved even more worrisome.[20]

The most anxiety-inducing solution for capitalists was the one devised by Marxists, who foresaw a future when workers controlled the workplace. Short of that improbable scenario, Marxists reasoned that workers must combine forces to meet their bosses on a more equal pitch. But capitalists better tolerated wretchedness in their cities than unionization in their workforces. Bourgeois anxieties about proletarian power were evident in the violence consistently used to crush labor unrest.[21]

The capitalist desire to check working-class prospects was palpable in other ways, too. A vivid example is how the ideal of free labor was degraded. Only recently had the idea of free labor motivated countless people to join the Republican Party and wage war against the Confederacy. When millions of people were in bondage, this version of the free-labor ethos had a radical edge to it. Even Marx understood as much. But things changed quickly. The Republican Party that waged war against an oligarchy of slaveowners in the name of free labor was by the 1870s doing the bidding of a new oligarchy of robber barons, also in the name of free labor.[22]

With the abolition of slavery, individual rights were made more concrete. But then a new legal regime emerged that increasingly interpreted *rights* through a lens favorable to capital. Employers enjoyed "freedom of contract," an inviolable right to deal with workers as individuals and individuals only, thus barring outside interference. In *Capital*, Marx mockingly described such a landscape as "a very Eden of the innate rights of man," where, he continued with sarcasm, "both buyer and seller of a commodity, say of labour-power, are constrained only by their own free will. They contract as free agents, and the agreement they come to, is but the form in which they give legal expression to their common will." Of course, employees in the real world were typically denied "freedom of association," or the right to form unions. Indeed, the corrupted legal interpretation of free labor increasingly placed constraints on workers. As a result, not only Marxists contended wage labor was a form of slavery.[23]

Equating "free labor" with "wage slavery" at a time when plenty of workers remained unfree, despite the abolition of chattel slavery, was one of the many glaring contradictions of Gilded Age capitalism. Tens of thousands of black men, mostly in the states of the former Confederacy, were forced into a convict leasing system in which imprisoned men were rented out to employers on the cheap, typically for measly charges like vagrancy. The persistence of bonded labor outraged workers because it distorted the nominally free labor market.[24]

Not everyone embraced the new free labor regime. But this resistance inspired further ideological assaults on working-class consciousness. The most insidious might have been the "gospel of success," an elite outpouring of soaring rhetoric that promoted hard work as an intrinsic good.

The gospel of success was a byproduct of a rapidly expanding industrial economy. Immense growth required lots of factories, but it also required lots of workers. There were plenty of workers, but most of them were rural, preindustrial folk, unconditioned to working six days per week, twelve hours per day, under highly regulated conditions. Such workers were uninterested in becoming yoked to the timeclock. They knew from experience there was more to life than grueling labor under the watchful eyes of the boss, and they were quick to criticize the industrial order as inferior to the agrarian one. Acutely aware of alternatives, many of these workers willingly took action. Between 1880 and 1900, there were nearly 37,000 strikes in the United States.[25]

The gospel of success was impeccably designed for battling with working-class intransigence. The Congregationalist minister Henry Ward Beecher, an abolitionist who later fashioned himself the honorary chaplain of the Republican Party, synopsized this gospel in a July 4, 1876, speech in celebration of the centennial. Beecher preached that prosperity was at hand for anyone willing to work for it and that no man "needs to stand at the bottom of the ladder for twenty years." After that amount of time, if a worker does not own a "household that he can call his home, the sweetest place on earth," then he ought to be "ashamed of himself." Moreover, only workers who dutifully endured deprivation while clawing their way up the social ladder were deserving of something better. As Beecher, never a poor man, said, "the man who cannot live on bread and water is not fit to live." President James Garfield, during his brief tenure, also displayed social Darwinist disdain for those on the lower rungs of society. "Nine times out of ten the best thing that can happen to a young man is to be tossed overboard, and compelled to sink or swim for himself," Garfield stated. "I have never known one who drowned who was worth saving."[26]

The gospel of success was ultimately a dispatch for working-class Americans to build the type of character appropriate to a society of scarcity and competition. Self-mastery was crucial to this character-building project. Only through self-mastery might peasants rein in their brute passions. Beecher was not an ideal role model in this regard, having succumbed to his own basest instincts in a sexual scandal that went national. But the gospel of success was not intended for those like Beecher who spent their entire lives in comfort. It was propaganda for those who lived in austere conditions: that is, workers. *They* were the ones who needed convincing that the daily grind was a positive good rather than a necessary evil. *They* were the ones who needed convincing that breaking their backs was a better option than drinking beer. *They* were the ones who needed convincing that climbing over their fellow workers was a better plan than joining a union.

By the twentieth century, a sizable number of working-class Americans adopted the gospel of success and other elite ideologies as their own. This strange historical development has generated an imperative question: Why have so many American workers internalized assumptions more befitting capitalists? But initially, most late nineteenth-century workers rejected the gospel of success and sought explanations of the world that better matched their experiences. Marxism was one such framework.[27]

It is easy to understand why Marx's ideas were attractive. For starters, he did not blame workers for their own misery. Marx rather offered workers a resonant theory of historical change. He connected their personal struggles to larger impersonal forces beyond their control. And despite the grandiosity of Marx's structural explanation for working-class desolation, he did not leave workers hopeless. Rather, Marx offered a rough blueprint for how they might improve their condition.

Arguably the most remembered aspect of Marx's thoughts on the working class is his notion that workers were destined to be the vanguard of revolutionary change. Once the proletariat overthrows its bourgeois masters, the profit motive will no longer dictate social organization and life will improve tremendously for nearly everybody. But this strain of Marx's thought, a central element of *The Communist Manifesto*, was not what primarily drew American workers to Marx during the Gilded Age. Rather, they were much more attuned to the less ambitious but equally profound argument he made about the working day in *Capital*. By following Marx's logic there, workers would vastly improve their condition by first unionizing, then leveraging their collective power to shorten the workday, and ultimately seizing control of the workplace.

Marx's focus on improving working-class conditions was particularly appealing to workers who had previously championed free labor. Unlike the degraded version of free labor ideology, which paradoxically severely constricted worker autonomy, Marx expanded the realm of self-rule to the workplace, where workers spent so much of their time. Marx thus proposed to apply democracy beyond the ballot box. Workers, who were rapidly becoming the largest chunk of the American population, would never truly be free, would never truly be their own masters, so long as they lived in a labor regime arranged by the dictates of capital.

It took time for a meaningful portion of the workforce to embrace Marx. When the WPUS collapsed at the end of 1877, few Americans were even vaguely familiar with the old Rhinelander. The spread of Marx's ideas was then slowed by the lack of political organization. The Socialistic Labor Party, which had the Lassallean purpose of electing socialists to public office, had extremely limited success. It won a few elected positions in 1878, mostly in Chicago and a few other midwestern cities, but that was it. The Marxists who departed the WPUS, including Sorge, did not fare much better. They joined forces with a few trade unions in the Northeast to form the International Labor Union, which had a decade-long life of little consequence. And yet, despite the lack of a vibrant institutional home, Marx's ideas slowly but surely slipped into the American stream of consciousness.

Not many people in the 1870s and 1880s could have predicted that Marx's framework would eventually gain a foothold in the United States. Marx's philosophy was in competition with a wide and eclectic range of ideas available to those opposed to the increasing might of capital. Many theories were holdovers of the class-free utopianism of the Welsh reformer Robert Owen, progenitor of the short-lived New Harmony, Indiana, colony. Such utopian visions, consistent with long-held Protestant expectations about the persuasive power of moral example, shaped reform movements to such a degree that there was no obvious sense they were on their way out. It was not yet apparent that the seeds had been sown for Marxism to rise above other approaches to confronting capitalism.[28]

Marx and Engels had been critical of what they called utopian socialism since 1848, when they wrote in the *Manifesto* that Owen and his type romanticized that "historical action is to yield to their personal inventive action." Engels developed this idea further in his 1880 pamphlet *Socialism: Utopian and Scientific*. He conceded that early utopian socialists had sought to solve the problem of class that the bourgeois revolutions of the eighteenth century had failed to address. But because they had not anticipated the advances of capitalism as a system that ineluctably drove most everyone into one of two antagonistic classes, they were incapable of seeing the feebleness of utopian communities.

By the 1880s, socialists had no such excuse. They lived in a time when millions of workers manned the machines of capitalism, when simple morality tales lacked the capacity for inspiring revolution.[29]

In the decades following the Civil War, the United States rapidly emerged as an industrial giant. Whereas American industrial output in 1865 paled next to the European economies, by the end of the nineteenth century, the United States was home to the world's largest and most productive industrial economy. A massive expansion of the industrial working class necessarily kept pace with this economic explosion. Before the Civil War, there were fewer than one million industrial wage laborers. By 1890, there were over three million. These shifts were also accompanied by exponential growth of cities alongside the slow yet relentless emptying out of the countryside. As a result, the rural sensibilities that had long demarcated the American political imagination, that had long informed the pastoralism undergirding utopian dreams, were deemed old-fashioned. A tiny socialist city on a hill, no matter how inspirational in its moral clarity, was powerless against historical developments of world-altering proportions.[30]

An urbanizing, industrializing nation, filling up with peculiar people who had recently come ashore from strange lands, was becoming less hospitable to utopianism by the day. But utopianism did not die an immediate death. In fact, its grip on the American imagination served as an obstacle to Marx receiving a wide hearing by the 1880s. What was needed was someone who could dress Marx up in utopian clothing, someone who could render Marx more agreeable to those reform-minded Americans whose old habits died hard.

A MARX FOR AMERICANS

Laurence Gronlund, a Danish-born lawyer, was the first writer to popularize Marx for an American audience. His 1884 book *The Cooperative Commonwealth* interpreted the German philosopher through an easily grasped utopian idiom. Although Engels dismissed *The Cooperative Commonwealth* for its utopianism, several prominent utopian radicals were converted to the Marxist cause by reading it. These included J. A. Wayland, publisher of *Appeal to Reason*, the most widely read socialist newspaper in the United States, and Eugene Debs, the most famous socialist in American history.[31]

Gronlund dedicated a chapter to the component of Marx's thought that most resonated with Gilded Age workers, his theory of surplus value. Gronlund wrote that "workers receive only about half of what they produce, just enough to keep up life and strength and bring up a new generation of laborers, while the other half stealthily passes into the pockets of quite another class of men." Capitalists, in other words, profit from the difference between the value of work done and the amount of wages paid, a feature of the system that Gronlund blamed for "pauperism" and "nearly all modern crime."[32]

Gronlund dismissed the claim often made by capitalism's apologists, and sometimes by utopian socialists, that capital and labor were symbiotic and that noticeable conflicts between the two meant that outside forces were interfering with the natural workings of the system. He argued instead that capitalism was an affront to inherently harmonious human relations. Gronlund maintained that workers did not benefit from working harder in a capitalist economy, in fact quite the opposite since hard labor quickened the deterioration of their bodies. Capitalists, in contrast, profited from their employees working themselves to the bone. This unjust dynamic was the basis for what Gronlund referred to as the "social anarchy" wreaking havoc on humanity. The solution was socialism. "The first lesson of Socialism," Gronlund wrote, "is that the Wage-System, the Profit-System, the Fleecing-System, is utterly unfit for a higher civilization." In equating civilization with order, and by blaming capitalism for the disorder that stood in the way of civilized society, Gronlund put a Gilded Age–inflected spin on Marx's theory.[33]

Gronlund's desire for order was a common impulse in an age of dislocation. It was not uncommon for people to describe their experience with industrial modernity as a case of vertigo. In this, as Debs later noted, Gronlund "worked for a perverse generation." Like many of that era, Gronlund rooted his search for order in nature, or rather, in the scientific authority that informed his sense of the natural. In fact, the most striking aspect of *The Cooperative Commonwealth* is its attempt to enlist Marx not in the utopian cause but into dialogue with scientific discourse. Gronlund was especially motivated to place Marx in conversation with the most significant scientific thinker of the era, Charles Darwin, whose 1859 book *On the Origins of Species* revealed to the world the theory of biological evolution.[34]

Many socialists have categorized Marx's philosophy as "science," often in efforts to make socialism seem inevitable. To cynical denizens of the twenty-first century, such an impulse seems naive at best, tyrannical at worst. But during the nineteenth century, when people across the political spectrum considered science foundational to the good life, such a claim helped an idea gain social acceptance.[35]

Marx himself sometimes related his ideas about political economy to science. As he wrote to Engels upon reading *On the Origin of Species*, "This is the book which contains the basis in natural history for our view." Both Marx and Darwin placed humans squarely in nature. Engels was even more dogmatic about the scientific basis of Marx's theories. (He polemicized about the gulf between utopian socialism and the vastly superior scientific variety.) The second and third volumes of *Capital* that Engels edited after Marx's death converted what Marx often intended as speculative assertion into iron law. Scientific socialism consequently became a synonym for Marxism.[36]

For Gronlund, linking Marx to Darwinian science domesticated Marx for an American readership increasingly accustomed to thinking about both natural *and* human history in evolutionary terms. Marx the scholarly evolutionist was more digestible than Marx the angry revolutionist. Gronlund took this a step further by joining Marx with Darwin's own great popularizer, the English scientist Herbert Spencer. In retrospect, this was a rather bizarre combination, since Spencer used Darwin's theory to justify social hierarchy. Gronlund attached Marx, one of the most egalitarian philosophers, to a man infamous for innovating the deeply inegalitarian theory that became known as "social Darwinism."[37]

Yet there was a logic to linking Marx's work to Spencer's pitiless version of Darwinism. Whereas social Darwinists like Spencer believed hierarchy was biologically predetermined and that class and racial divisions would harden with time, *socialist* Darwinists like Gronlund assumed the inverse: humans were evolving to be more equal. As Marx argued, capitalism increasingly brought workers together into situations where their cooperation posed a serious threat to class rule. The appalling dog-eat-dog present was only temporary. It would soon give way, inevitably, to a more cooperative future.

By the mid-1880s, more Americans than ever, and not just socialists, were organizing to dislodge the rugged form of capitalism that dominated the nation. Prominent among the disgruntled were the Knights of Labor, the largest organization of workers to that point. The Knights sometimes operated as a labor union, and in that spirit, they lobbied for the eight-hour day. But as a fraternal society first and foremost, the Knights focused less on confronting capitalism and more on helping workers cope with life in an industrial order, priorities which Engels disparaged as "little absurdities." Yet Engels also recognized the Knights as "the first national organization created by the American working class as a whole," the "raw material" of an American socialist movement. Their class enemies agreed. Allan Pinkerton denigrated the Knights as "an amalgamation" of the Paris Commune and the Molly Maguires, the militant Irish anthracite miners in Pennsylvania, twenty of whom were hanged for violently confronting their bosses in 1877.[38]

Pinkerton's fevered imagination inflated the degree to which the Knights were a force for revolution. But under the leadership of Terrance Powderly, the group opened its ranks to workers across all trades, thus emerging as the prototypical industrial labor organization, one that included women, black people, and most immigrants, with the notable exception of Chinese workers. The Knights thus signified an important step toward overcoming the divisions that had long foiled working-class solidarity. Boasting an enormous membership of nearly one million by 1886, the Knights had become, if not an existential threat to Gilded Age capitalism, an inconvenience. The Knights were involved in many of the over 1,400 labor strikes that ensued in 1886, a record number for a single year at the time. Yet in working to upend capitalist arrangements, or at least reform them a bit, the Knights were far from alone. Working-class resistance took many forms in 1886. Historians have designated that year "the Great Upheaval."[39]

THE GREAT UPHEAVAL

One notable challenge to the system in 1886 was Henry George's campaign for mayor of New York City. Running on the United Labor Party ticket, the radical journalist finished second but well ahead of the young Republican Theodore Roosevelt. George first made a name for himself with his 1879 book *Progress and Poverty*, which sold more copies in the late nineteenth-century United States than any book other than the Bible. *Progress and Poverty* was George's attempt to answer the perplexing question Marx had tackled: Why did the ranks of the impoverished increase with industrial and technological progress? Instead of focusing on class domination at the point of production, as Marx had, George concentrated on land. As land was developed, its value skyrocketed, which led to rising rents and overall inflation relative to stagnant wages. As a way out, George proposed a "single tax" on land, an elegant solution that attracted followers nationwide and indeed around the world.[40]

Progress and Poverty did not make Marx a fan of George. "Theoretically," he wrote to Sorge, "the man is utterly backward! He understands nothing about the nature of surplus value." Marx argued George had a lot in common with those utopian socialists who "leave wage labour and therefore capitalist production in existence and try to bamboozle themselves or the world into believing that if ground rent were transformed into a state tax all the evils of capitalist production would disappear of themselves." Marx believed *Progress and Poverty* was "simply an attempt, decked out with socialism, to save capitalist domination and indeed to establish it afresh on an even wider basis."[41]

Engels agreed with Marx on most things, including the flaws of *Progress and Poverty*. Yet Engels, who unlike Marx witnessed George's campaign, was optimistic about its meaning. "The Henry George boom," he wrote, was "an epoch-making day" for American socialism. "The first great step of importance for every country newly entering into the movement," Engels continued, "is always the constitution of the workers as an independent political party, no matter how, so long as it is a distinct workers' party. And this step has been taken, much more rapidly than we had a right to expect." Marx interpreted *Progress and Poverty* as an apology for capitalism, but resentful capitalists didn't see it that way. They likened the single tax to an assault on their right to property, and an additional sign that 1886 was a year of rebellion.[42]

That year also saw the mostly forgotten trip across the United States taken by Marx's youngest daughter Eleanor Marx Aveling, a distinguished socialist in her own right. Along with her husband Edward Aveling and the German socialist leader Karl Liebknecht, Marx Aveling took a fifteen-week, thirty-five-stop tour during which the three Marxists spoke before large and receptive audiences along a circuit from New York City to Kansas City. As the Avelings later wrote, "the American people were waiting to hear in their own language what Socialism was." Although most workers appeared skeptical, the three detected an "unconscious socialism" among them. A few workers admitted to the Avelings that hearing their message spurred them to become socialists of the more conscious sort.[43]

The Avelings wrote a book about their travels that included a detailed analysis of working conditions. They found them to be a lot like those in England a few decades earlier, which Eleanor's father had written about in *Capital*. In fact, things were even starker now. "The real division of society into two classes," they wrote, "the labourer and the capitalist, veiled in England and other European countries by the remains of the old systems, by artificial classes of royalty, nobility, and so forth, in America stares one in the face." In their eyes, the situation in the United States confirmed Marx's theory that capitalism obliterated the middle ground between bourgeoisie and proletariat. It also corroborated Marx's impression that capitalism made men into machines.[44]

The event that most evoked the Great Upheaval was the Haymarket Riot of May 4, 1886. Leading up to that infamous episode, militant Chicago radicals, many of whom embraced anarchism, determined

FIGURE 2.1: From left to right: William Liebknecht, Eleanor Marx Aveling, and Edward Aveling, on their trip to the United States in 1886.

that playing by the rules of American democracy was a waste of time. They grew impatient with a system manipulated by the rich, a society where capitalists rigged elections and hired men with guns to snuff out working-class solidarity. Chicago revolutionaries instead embraced what was later called "direct action," a bold strategy for transforming otherwise impervious societies. Direct action meant taking to the streets, sitting down on factory floors, employing human bodies to impede normal operations. It was the tactical equivalent of grinding a machine to a halt by throwing rocks into its gears. Many of the Chicago activists believed that a successful maneuver of this sort would inspire a revolution.[45]

On May 1, hundreds of thousands of workers went out on strike for an eight-hour day. The largest action took place in Chicago, where as many as fifty thousand workers filled the streets, chanting, "Eight hours for work, eight hours for rest, eight hours for what we will!" Albert Parsons, formerly of the WPUS and a recent convert to anarchism, led a large group of strikers down Michigan Avenue. The strike persisted, and on May 3, workers converged on the McCormick Harvesting Machine Company plant to block strikebreakers from entering. In the ensuing melee, police fired into the crowd, killing two striking workers. Outraged activists called for a rally the following day at Haymarket Square, at a busy intersection on the northwest side of downtown Chicago.[46]

On May 4, Parsons, his fellow anarchist August Spies, and the British socialist Samuel Feldon addressed a large gathering there. The crowd remained calm as a large squadron of police looked on. When the speakers wrapped up, police marched in, ordering immediate dispersal. A homemade bomb was tossed at the advancing police and exploded, killing seven cops. The cops responded by firing into the crowd, killing four protestors, and wounding many more on both sides. Eight men, including Parsons and Spies, were arrested and put on trial. Despite a lack of credible evidence tying the defendants to the bombing, the jury returned guilty verdicts for all. Four of the accused were eventually hanged. Another committed suicide rather than face the gallows. Parsons and Spies were among the condemned.[47]

The Haymarket affair became a rallying cry for leftists the world over, a symbol of growing working-class militancy. As Eleanor Marx Aveling declared before a huge crowd in Chicago: Although "these men be murdered, we may say of their executioners, what my father said of those who massacred the people of Paris: 'They are already nailed to the eternal pillory which all the prayers of their priests will not avail to redeem them.'" Engels was saddened by the repression but ebullient about what Haymarket represented. In a letter to the American socialist Florence Kelley, Engels declared that American workers "appear all of a sudden in such organized masses as to strike terror into the whole capitalist class. I only wish Marx could have lived to see it!" Three years later, socialists gathering in Paris to form the Second International declared, in honor of the Haymarket martyrs, the first day of May to be International Workers' Day.[48]

Despite its secure place among the catalog of sacred revolutionary symbols, Haymarket also epitomized the limitations of the Great Upheaval. Due to a steady stream of propaganda published in its aftermath, the public mood soured on working-class radicalism. Indeed, the Haymarket riot produced another mini red scare, much like after the Paris Commune. In Chicago, aggrieved police ransacked the headquarters of anarchist and socialist newspapers.[49]

The red scare, like every red scare, sanctioned a crackdown on working-class radicalism. Capitalists wrested back control of the workplace from unruly workers and momentarily ended the eight-hour struggle. By beating back the Great Upheaval, capitalists cemented what Daniel Bell called "the consolidation of industrial capitalist power."[50]

CORPORATE CAPITALISM AND ITS DISCONTENTS

Capitalism's conquest was consecrated by the Supreme Court in its landmark 1886 decision *Santa Clara County v. Southern Pacific Railroad Company*. The court applied the Equal Protection Clause of the Fourteenth Amendment, ratified in 1868 to ensure freedmen had full protection of the law, to endow corporations with the rights of people. In effect, it armed corporations with constitutional prerogatives, sanctifying developments that had been in motion since the Civil War. Twisting Adam Smith's memorable metaphor for a self-correcting market, the historian Eric Hobsbawm later quipped that during the Gilded Age the "hand was becoming visible in all sorts of ways."[51]

By the late 1880s, the triumph of corporations had come to seem like a fait accompli. Even some of their enemies, like Marx, understood their rise as inevitable, the logical next stage in capitalist development.

But for him, capitalist corporations were not preordained to maintain their grip on society, due to their own scope. As colossal institutions that brought thousands of workers together, corporations had done more to socialize production than any radical movement could. If workers could expropriate these immense institutions, they would transform the system. For Marx, corporations represented an important step in the transition to a better world. This strategic vision came to animate Gilded Age socialism.[52]

Nobody thought transcending corporate capitalism would be easy. Engels made a short trip to the United States in the summer of 1888, his only visit, and came away thinking the American people were "extremely conservative, precisely because America is so purely bourgeois, without any feudal past." It was no wonder corporations ran roughshod. Yet, like Marx, Engels did not imagine corporate capitalism would forever endure. Rather, he believed its harsh inequalities signified that "the last Bourgeois Paradise on earth is fast changing into a Purgatorio." Engels remained optimistic, predicting that socialism might advance further and faster in the United States. "Unless I am greatly mistaken," he wrote to Sorge, "the Americans will astonish us all by the magnitude of their movement." An immense movement of workers, armed with the proper theory, could take control of the seemingly almighty corporations, and redistribute their massive wealth for the well-being of everybody.[53]

Not all Americans looked upon the emergence of corporations with optimism. Those who remained committed to a moral vision in the tradition of Jefferson or Thoreau beheld them with horror. But remarkably, even utopian socialists began to think differently about the trajectory of corporations. Edward Bellamy's 1888 utopian novel *Looking Backward* envisioned a near-perfect future remote from the pastoral imagination.

Bellamy's protagonist Julian West wakes up in the year 2000, after over a century of deep sleep, to a world that Marx might have conjured up. In Bellamy's utopia, industry was organized on a gargantuan scale. But it had also been nationalized and thus under democratic controls. Moreover, whereas workers in 1888 were subject to the dictates of greedy robber barons, not to mention the whims of an unstable, barely regulated economic system, in Bellamy's future workers had come together to form an industrial army. Thanks to working-class solidarity on a grand scale, people's needs were met in a fair and efficient manner.[54]

It is difficult to overstate the influence *Looking Backward* had on a generation of readers. Decades later, John Dewey and Charles Beard, independently, ranked Bellamy's novel second only to *Capital* as the most influential book published in the nineteenth century. Bellamy Clubs popped up all over the nation, sparking a political movement that came to be called Nationalism. Socialism would have been a better term. Bellamy's vision was partly shaped by his having read Gronlund's *Cooperative Commonwealth*. But Bellamy intentionally avoided the word socialism because he wanted *Looking Backward* to have the greatest possible appeal. His strategy worked. The historian Paul Buhle described Bellamy as "a key precipitator of Marxism," as readers of *Looking Backward* came to appreciate "the ethical imperative of Socialism restated in the native lexicon." An avowedly socialist political movement had yet to get off the ground. Yet socialist ideas indebted to Marx were spreading, thanks in no small part to Bellamy.[55]

Despite rising interest in socialism, a political movement of a different kind emerged as the primary threat to the late nineteenth-century corporate order. Populism, a movement that set the western and southern countryside aflame in a furious effort to defeat corporate interests on behalf of small farmers, appealed to many more Americans than socialism did at that time.[56]

Prairie radicalism materialized soon after the Civil War, as a host of impersonal forces, from escalating international competition to agricultural mechanization, led to falling crop prices, which in turn led to crushing debt for small farmers. Discontented rural Americans responded to these worsening conditions as early as 1867, when they established the Grange as a means for promoting the common interests of small farmers. In 1877, a Farmers' Alliance was formed in Texas to foster collective action. But as corporations tightened their grip on the agricultural economy—by buying up half the arable land, by monopolizing the railroads that took harvests to market, and by controlling the banks that loaned to farmers—a more robust political response was needed.[57]

In 1890, furious prairie dwellers formed the People's Party to challenge a two-party system that served corporate power. At its first national convention two years later, the party adopted a broad platform. Populists pledged to nationalize the railroads to curb price gouging; to subsidize grain storage so that farmers might sell their crops only when the price was right; and to expand the money supply by coining silver, reasoning that inflation would benefit them as debtors. They also recommended a graduated income tax to help level rising wealth disparity. Many of these proposals were highly popular, thus revealing the party as a tangible threat to corporate domination.[58]

Populism was mainly a rural phenomenon among small farmers. But, as the only credible challenge to the Democratic and Republican parties, the party also welcomed a diverse group of outsiders, freethinkers, bohemians, and even radical labor unionists. Populist comparisons of corporations to notorious enemies of the people, such as King George III or the Slave Power, resonated widely. Yet populists were not Marxists. They did not think about capitalism in terms of class relations. They did not wish to overthrow the system. Rather, populists desired comparatively mild reforms to the market-based economy. In short, populists favored a smaller regional capitalism. This was a relatively popular program. But it had its limits.

Some populist ideas—like subsidizing farmers to stabilize crop prices—were abundantly forward-thinking. Same goes with progressive taxation and bank and railroad regulation. Yet the populist desire to turn back the clocks on corporate power was also rooted in a yearning for the frontier. During the first century of the United States, when white settlers pushed further and further west, onto lands the US Army had cleared of natives, optimism abounded. Free soil and free labor would indeed produce free (white) men. The frontier appeared to solve problems that normally hindered a healthy society, one in which capitalism and democracy thrived alongside each other. "The constant flow of people to the plains of the Mississippi," Hegel wrote, "overcomes unrest at its principal sources and stabilizes existing conditions."[59]

Hegel's words from the 1820s anticipated the famous paper given by the historian Frederick Jackson Turner at the World's Columbian Exposition in Chicago in 1893. "The Significance of the Frontier in American History" cited recent census figures to claim the western frontier had closed. This was a frightening threshold for Turner, who conceptualized the frontier as endowing Americans with a "buoyancy and exuberance." Turner mourned the death of the frontier as a place of "perennial rebirth." Its end, he maintained, potentially spelled the demise of American democracy. Turner, in effect, placed the populist lament in grand historical terms.[60]

Prairie radicals wanted what an open frontier previously helped make possible: access to cheap, arable land; the freedom to move goods without going into crippling debt; the ability to sustain their way of life independently. These were understandable wishes. But they were also rooted in a tragic irony. The final subjugation of native peoples, whose lives were devastated by the American frontier, also represented the end of that frontier. And in turn, the closing of the frontier nearly extinguished a way of life enjoyed by millions of small farmers who had previously benefited from it. Only corporate capitalism emerged stronger than ever. The entire sordid history gave support to Marx's theory of "primitive accumulation," from *Capital*, where he pointed to the plunder of indigenous peoples and lands as imperative to early capitalism.[61]

Populists often looked to the past while battling the corporate system. Socialists, in contrast, looked to the future, and not just any future. As Marx wrote, a revolution "cannot take its poetry from the past but only the future." Marx did agree with Hegel, and thus Turner, that the frontier steadied American democracy. But for him, such stability was tenuous at best, delusional at worst. By concealing class conflict, Marx thought the frontier masked the very limited freedoms of American democracy. It proved, in his words, that American "bourgeois society is still far too immature for the class struggle to be made perceptible and comprehensible." Marx welcomed the closing of the frontier because it would reveal the true nature of capitalism and thus hasten American workers' understanding of their unfree condition.[62]

Turner, like the populists, wanted a capitalist economy of independent proprietors because it would produce virtuous citizens who thought for themselves. In this vein, an industrial working class was a poor basis for a democratic citizenry because people who worked for wages were dependent on others. Those who dreaded the closing of the frontier ultimately fretted the conversion of proprietors into proles. Marx and his socialist disciples, in contrast, eagerly awaited proletarianization. Only after the frontier was slammed shut forever would the working class realize it had nothing to lose but its chains.

The ideological gulf separating populism from socialism ultimately rested on indisputable differences in interests between farmers and workers. To smooth over these disparities, populists often demonstrated genuine concern for workers. The People's Party platform identified the Knights of Labor as a natural ally and asserted that the enemies of the working class were "identical" to those of small farmers. Yet, aside from western miners, few workers rushed to vote for populist candidates. They rejected the populist plan to expand the money supply, since inflation meant the gradual reduction of their real wages. An increasingly urban and immigrant working class also found it extremely difficult to identify with rural folks. Industrial workers did not believe a small plot of farmland was the only path to dignity.[63]

Although many populists later became socialists, some socialists voiced concern that populism did not speak for the working class. This was particularly true of Marx-attuned socialists, like Daniel De Leon, who blossomed into a renowned Marxist theoretician after he took the helm of the Socialist Labor Party (SLP) in 1890. "Populist farmers are to get their free silver at sixteen to one so that they may pay their debts with depreciated money and thus become capitalists," De Leon said. "The Populist politicians will get the spoils of office, while the Populist wage earners will mop their foreheads and rub their empty stomachs with a glittering generality." De Leon's denunciation of populism was overstated. It was his fashion to exaggerate the distance separating his socialist philosophy from any other political perspective. But he was right that militant American workers, especially those who hailed from Europe, wanted a different program.[64]

IMMIGRANT SOCIALISM

Henry Demarest Lloyd, the muckraking journalist from Chicago famous for exposing the monopolistic practices of the Standard Oil Company, believed a farmer-labor alliance was the only force capable of checking corporate power. Lloyd thus criticized the SLP for its blunt antipopulism. "Our Socialist Labor Party, of German Marxists," he wrote, "has never taken hold of the Americans and never will, for the Americans . . . are not so stupid as to make a class movement of an agitation to abolish class." Lloyd thought Americans were more prone to embrace populism because it was premised on self-reliance. This was a value that corporations had violated and that socialists ignored at their peril. And yet, many workers turned to socialism, as did Lloyd eventually. Up to the 1890s, though, most of those who joined the socialist movement were indeed recent immigrants from Germany.[65]

A sizable chunk of the almost two million Germans who immigrated to the United States in the 1880s and 1890s were socialists already. They were escaping Chancellor Otto von Bismarck's repressive laws that banned socialists from meeting in public, harassed trade unions out of existence, and shut down dozens of socialist newspapers. These immigrants, often fluent in the works of Marx, breathed new life into American radicalism by building socialist institutions in growing industrial cities like New York, Chicago, Cincinnati, and Milwaukee.[66]

Not everyone was enthusiastic about their growing presence. Local elites hated them for helping turn workers against them. Even some who should have seen them as allies, such as Lloyd, believed a Marx-infused socialism was doomed to failure. Marxism, they claimed, did not speak to American problems, and it did not help that those who preached its gospel were rarely native-born. German socialists countered by insisting that they in fact represented the changing face of an increasingly international American proletariat. In this they had a point.[67]

As millions of immigrants poured in from eastern and southern Europe, the face of the American working class was forever changed. So, too, was the face of American socialism, which transformed from a movement mostly of Germans into a much more diverse one. The demographic shifts in SLP membership were indicative. During the 1890s, Jews, mostly from Russia, became its fastest growing group.

As Jewish immigrants streamed into the SLP and other socialist parties, the image of the radical Jew was formed. In 1893, the journalist Ida Van Etten wrote that "thousands of the disciples of Karl Marx may be found among the organized Jewish workingmen." In other words, even though the depiction of the Jewish Marxist became a common antisemitic trope (alongside, strangely, the stereotype of the rapacious Jewish capitalist), there were more than a few grains of truth in the notion. Yet Jewish immigrants rarely disembarked on American shores ready-made Marxists. "Thousands of people, who knew nothing of Karl Marx or his ideas before stepping foot on Manhattan," the historian Tony Michels writes, "were soon marching and striking and educating themselves in his name." Jews found Marx in New York City, the center of global capitalism and by 1900 home to the largest population of Yiddish speakers in the world.[68]

What was it about turn-of-the-century New York City that made so many Jewish immigrants gravitate to Marx? First, most newly arrived Jews took jobs in manufacturing, particularly in the garment industry, placing them alongside each other in less-than-desirable working conditions, a situation that encouraged organization. Second, as Jewish workers began to organize, they found their way into the socialist institutions built by earlier German immigrants. By acculturating into that world, Michels writes, "Russian Jews did not become so much Americanized as German-Americanized." And as they increasingly looked to Marx for wisdom about this new, secular, capitalist world, many gradually turned their backs on rabbinical authority. The Yiddish writer Morris Vintshevsky's short poem captured this shift in loyalty. "In the beginning there is heaven and earth. But in Heaven there is not yet light and on Earth chaos reigns, and darkness is in the abyss. And Marx comes and says: 'Let there be light!'"[69]

The infusion of radical Jews invigorated the SLP. So too did new leadership. Daniel De Leon endowed the party with an aggressive, theoretically attuned brand of Marxism. Having grown up in Curaçao and been educated in Europe, De Leon moved to New York City, where he earned a law degree and was hired as a lecturer at Columbia College. He did not last long, as he was fired in 1886 for his radical politics. Apparently working for the Henry George campaign was a subversive step too far for a university professor. After the 1886 election, De Leon remained with George's United Labor Party for two years, and in 1889 he joined both Bellamy's Nationalist movement and a New York City chapter of the Knights of Labor. In this bustling world of working-class politics, De Leon encountered an eclectic range of radical thinkers and activists, including socialists who introduced him to Marx. There was no turning back.[70]

In 1890, De Leon joined a Socialist Labor Party ripe to be taken in a new direction. He quickly took control and then dedicated the next twenty-four years to making the SLP an engine of working-class radicalism. From the start, De Leon got along with the German socialists. Although he hailed from a tiny Latin American island, and although he loosely identified as a Jew, he had an affinity for German socialists because they knew their Marx. Frequently expressing his debt to "the giant intellectual figure of Karl Marx," De Leon was becoming the high priest of American Marxism.[71]

Known to his enemies as the "Red Pope of Revolution," De Leon's rising popularity among socialists coincided with the Panic of 1893, America's worst depression to that point. This was an economic disaster of such catastrophic proportions that it awakened socialist hopes for revolution. Much as the emergence of the Republican Party ultimately resulted in the abolition of chattel slavery, socialists thought a new, imminent political formation would abolish wage slavery. For many of them, De Leon was their Lincoln.[72]

De Leon's biographer L. Glen Seretan claims the SLP leader found Marx's ideas enticing because their "cosmic sweep" allowed him "to submerge himself in an abstract, generalized conception of the world" that lessened the sting of being an ethnic and religious minority in an age of bellicose nationalism. Marxism permitted De Leon to position himself not as an outcast, but rather as a member of the majority, as a worker doing battle against the capitalist minority, or what he called the "felon class."[73]

No matter why De Leon turned to Marxism, it was evident that, like Marx, he had come to view capitalism as a "steam-roller" that ruthlessly crushed everyone "into one amorphous pulp." He also agreed with Marx's vision of life after capitalism. De Leon wrote that Marx accurately pinpointed a transformed, socialist future, "where democracy prevails, where . . . everything not done for the public—the entire public—is only transitory." Capitalism made people antisocial monsters. Socialism, Marx prophesized, encouraged a social ethic that would heal humanity.[74]

Like most Gilded Age Marxists, De Leon was confident that industrial developments had cleared the path for workers to clutch history by the throat. Using what Daniel Bell described as "a rigor unsurpassed," De Leon theorized that the "time is fast coming when, in the natural source of social evolution, this system, through the destructive actions of its failures and crises on the one hand, and the constructive tendencies of its trusts and other capitalistic combinations on the other hand, shall have worked out its own downfall." Capitalism had both socialized production and subjected society to one crisis after another. It was now up to workers to organize into a collective capable of seizing the means of production, thus ensuring everyone an equal share of the enormous bounty generated by industrial capitalism.[75]

In De Leon's eyes, a worker-led society would be the modern equivalent of what Marx termed "primitive communism," a compassionate order where everyone shared responsibilities and rewards. Such organized compassion entailed, in De Leon's words, "placing the land and all the means of production into the hands of the people as a collective body, and substituting for the present state of planless production, industrial war, and social disorder, the Socialist or Industrial Commonwealth—a commonwealth in which every worker shall have the free exercise and full benefit of his faculties, multiplied by all the modern factors of civilization." This was Marx's vision of the future leavened with the moral vision of Gronlund and Bellamy.[76]

Faith that conditions had prepared the ground for revolution was not enough. The working class had to be convinced of their essential role. De Leon edited the SLP newspaper *The People* with this in mind. In nurturing a vibrant socialist print culture, he consistently positioned Marx's name front and center. Marx helped De Leon nudge the working class toward socialism, and not only by providing the foundation for socialist strategy. Mentioning his name also functioned as a badge that designated someone a socialist in good standing. One member of the SLP rank and file wrote to De Leon that he was soon to be a father and that if he had a son, he was going to name him Karl Marx. Another SLP member, reporting on his work translating Marx into Norwegian, wrote that he deemed "it an honor to be asked to do anything that will encourage my fellow wage-slaves of whatever language to read *The Manifesto of the Communist Party*." "When the children of men come to see their own," he wrote, "they will erect a statue of statesmanship, the central figure of which will be Karl Marx with Thomas Paine on his right and Abraham Lincoln on his left."[77]

De Leon and the SLP helped tilt the American socialist movement toward Marxism. But plenty of American socialists remained of the utopian variety. In fact, as the socialist intellectual Robert Rivers LaMonte wrote, the divide between "Americanizers" and "textualists" defined the movement during the 1890s. For the latter, including De Leon, "the clearness of a comrade could be gauged invariably from the number of ear-marks on his *Manifesto*." Due to this chasm, the late nineteenth century, like so many other eras in the history of the American Left, was marked by factionalism, in this case (as in many others) between those Marxists who centered labor as the driving force of value in a capitalist society, and those who mixed Marx's ideas into hybrid political tendencies. In his fealty to Marx, De Leon was one of the angriest sectarian warriors of the time.[78]

Like many Marxists in the United States, De Leon thought a socialist movement needed to invest all hope in the promise of the labor movement. Under his leadership the SLP sought to capture organized labor. De Leon had sense enough to avoid attempting to penetrate the American Federation of Labor (AFL), an association of unions founded by Samuel Gompers in 1886 as an alternative to the Knights of Labor. As a young immigrant in New York City, working in a cigar factory alongside German immigrants, Gompers could not have avoided the good word about Marx. In fact, he later admitted to learning from Marx that "control over economic power" was the key to political power. Given this, one might have assumed Gompers a natural ally of De Leon. But by the time Gompers had risen to become the most powerful labor leader in Gilded Age America, he was no longer anywhere close to being a socialist.[79]

To the dismay of De Leon and socialists everywhere, Gompers joined forces with renowned robber baron Mark Hanna to form the National Civic Federation, which encouraged cooperation between labor and capital. Gompers thought collaboration was the ticket to the AFL's survival in a capitalist economy. Such an approach had conservative consequences. The AFL's refusal to allow unskilled workers into its ranks pleased the corporate bosses, and seemingly benefited the skilled workers in AFL-affiliated unions. But it also created a labor hierarchy that weakened working-class solidarity.[80]

Rather than target the AFL, De Leon and the SLP decided to bore from within the Knights of Labor. This move had some initial success, as SLP members took control of the Knights' New York assembly in 1893. But in 1895, nonsocialists fought back and removed De Leon from the General Assembly. The fiery Marxist then led the SLP out of the Knights altogether, hastening an end to an organization already in steep decline. In 1896, the SLP formed its own trade association, the Socialist Trades and Labor Alliance, intended to be a revolutionary set of industrial unions that would openly compete with the AFL.

That move was highly controversial. Labor leaders charged De Leon and the SLP with "dual unionism," implying a willingness to destroy the labor solidarity necessary to challenge capital. Nobody disapproved of the Socialist Trades and Labor Alliance more than Gompers, of course, since the AFL had the most to lose to it. But even some within SLP ranks condemned the strategy.[81]

A group of SLP dissidents led by Morris Hillquit revolted in 1899. These "kangaroos," as De Leon loyalists nicknamed them—a nineteenth-century political term of derision for a crook—opposed both dual unionism and De Leon's regime. At the annual SLP meeting, the kangaroos attempted to take physical possession of the party's printing press. A brawl broke out, but the Hillquit group failed to dislodge the De Leon stalwarts. The rebels then took the matter to court, where they sued for the name and property of the SLP, only to lose. De Leon maintained control, but he and the party were damaged by this schism. De Leon and the SLP fell from their perch atop the socialist movement, replaced by Eugene Debs and the Socialist Party of America that formed in 1901.[82]

EUGENE DEBS AND THE SOCIALIST PARTY

If anyone in history personifies American Marxism, it is Eugene Victor Debs. He rallied more Americans to the cause of class struggle than anyone else. Yet Debs was not always a fire-breathing class warrior. The Indiana-born revolutionary started his political career promoting the idea of a "grand cooperative scheme" that would allow people to "work together in harmony in every branch of industry." Rather than a working-class struggle over the means of production, the young Debs called for the creation of utopian colonies modeled on a Christian vision of a city on a hill. The future of socialism, for him at the time, lay in the vision imagined by Robert Owen. Debs believed that a rapacious form of capitalism had betrayed the spirit of brotherhood—a spirit that had long animated Americans—and that the moral example set by the utopian community would help convince others to live up to their highest ideals.[83]

Sinclair Lewis called Debs the John the Baptist of American socialism. Daniel Bell described him as "the man whose gentleness and sweet, passionate anguish touched a chord of goodness in more Americans than probably any other figure in American life after Lincoln." But Debs did not inspire people by invoking the wisdom of Marx, at least not initially. Yet by the end of the nineteenth century, as he sat poised to lead the largest socialist party in the country's history, Debs had fully embraced Marx. He was not alone among labor militants who made this transition during the 1890s, a decade that saw the eruption of furious class warfare.[84]

In 1892, a pitched battle between workers and Pinkerton agents at Andrew Carnegie's steel plant in Homestead, Pennsylvania, led to several deaths. The anarchist Alexander Berkman was so enraged that he attempted to murder the company's chairman, Henry Clay Frick. In the backwash of the Panic of 1893, with unemployment swelling and general misery mounting, one journalist lamented that there were "millions for armories and the military instruction of the young, but not one cent to furnish employment to able-bodied industry in its struggle to escape the terrible alternative of stealing or starving."[85]

Debs dove head-first into the class struggle when he led the American Railway Union (ARU) in a work stoppage at the Pullman Company train-car factory in Chicago in 1894. In response to the depression, Pullman cut wages yet refused to reduce the cost of living in its company town. Pullman workers walked off the job, which precipitated wildcat strikes and boycotts that brought trains across the country to a brief standstill. The mayhem triggered a legal injunction that prohibited Debs from "compelling or inducing" workers to abstain from performing their jobs. It also prompted President Grover Cleveland to send the US Army to Chicago to break the strike. Government repression worked. The ARU failed to win concessions, and Debs was handed a six-month prison sentence in Woodstock, Illinois, for violating the injunction. Yet the Pullman strike made Debs famous. It also, ultimately, made him a Marxist.[86]

The time Debs spent in jail was an important landmark along his road to Marx. Numerous socialists sent him piles of Marxist literature. As Debs later reflected, it was while in prison "that Socialism gradually laid hold of me in its own irresistible fashion. . . . I began to read and think and dissect the anatomy of the system in which workingmen, however organized, could be shattered and battered and splintered at a single stroke." Among the authors who made a mark were Gronlund, Bellamy, and, of course, Marx, who he said guided him "out of darkness into light."

Debs wrote his conversion tale, "How I Became a Socialist," in 1902, eight years after his short stint in prison. That gap obscures the fact that Debs did not emerge from Woodstock a dyed-in-the-wool Marxist. To wit, in 1897, Debs proposed a mass colonization scheme for workers, writing to John D. Rockefeller and asking the robber baron to finance his utopian concoction. But Debs eventually came to embrace a Marxist brand of socialism that emphasized capitalism as a system and class as an antagonism at its heart. He came to believe the nation's salvation was dependent on waging class war against capitalists. Debs said he discovered this in *Capital*, which "set the wires humming in my system."[87]

Debs was partly won over to Marx by the persuasive Milwaukee-based socialist Victor Berger, who had placed *Capital* in his hands. In 1897, Debs led the remnants of the ARU into the newly formed Social Democracy of America, the political machine that Berger had built. Berger was a Marxist in that he believed workers needed power to challenge capitalists. He was also a practical politician who thought the main job of socialists was to make the lives of workers immediately better by offering them municipal reforms like public ownership of utilities. In fact, as part of its inaugural platform, the Social Democracy adopted a reform package of the type that came to be called "sewer socialism," indicating its attention to improving basic local services.[88]

Marxists like Berger were not alone in joining the Social Democracy. So, too, did many utopian socialists. But Berger called them "hazy reformers," and the utopians in turn smeared him and his comrades as "un-American." This divide roiled the party's 1898 convention. Would the Social Democracy build a utopian socialist colony in some remote locale, perhaps rural Tennessee? Or would it focus on class struggle, working in concert with the growing labor movement? Both sides sought Debs's support. He was, after all, a certified working-class hero.

Debs hated being caught between comrades. Sectarian squabbling literally gave him debilitating headaches. He spent the entire convention in his hotel room. Yet just before the meeting closed, Debs hesitantly gave his support to Berger and the Marxists. But the utopians won the majority anyhow and took control of the Social Democracy.

The utopian victory was ultimately pyrrhic. The future of American socialism was with Marx. A faction of the Social Democracy headed by Debs and Berger bolted to form the Social Democratic Party. This new, utopian-free party laid the groundwork for a more mainstream Marx-based socialism. Its inaugural platform, written by Berger, declared that "two distinct classes with conflicting interests" had emerged under capitalism: "the small possessing class of capitalists"; and "the ever-increasing large dispossessed class of wageworkers."[89]

In 1901, the Social Democratic Party merged with disaffected members of the SLP, including Morris Hillquit, to form the Socialist Party of America. Its membership was a combination of urban European immigrants who had learned socialist principles at the feet of Marx and rural American-born radicals who came to socialism by way of political traditions like republicanism, populism, utopianism, and Christianity. The Socialist Party had large memberships in both New York City, where German and Jewish immigrants had created a vibrant Marxist political culture, and Oklahoma, where, after the demise of the People's Party, prairie radicals sought a new anticorporate vehicle. In other words, the ineluctable division in American radicalism, the same one that undermined populism, and that tore apart the Social Democracy, cast a long shadow on the future of the new Socialist Party. Debs might have been the only person alive capable of bridging this chasm.[90]

By this time, Debs had embraced Marxism. But his earlier instincts—republican, populist, utopian, Christian—also remained integral to his socialism. This fact sometimes annoyed his more conventionally Marxist comrades, but it served Debs well as the leader of a diverse party with national aspirations. Debs blended an otherwise contradictory set of sensibilities to form what Paul Buhle calls a "very peculiar socialism." Hundreds of thousands of American workers found a new kind of religion in this peculiar socialism. As the leader of a movement he designated "merely Christianity in action," Debs came to be a Jesus-like figure. Observing the continuities between Jesus, John Brown, and Karl Marx, Debs compared Christ to a martyred member of the working class, or what he termed a "true communist."[91]

As the Socialist Party of America expanded and stabilized, Debs frequently aligned Marxism with his native republicanism, an anti-authoritarian sensibility that ran deep with many Americans. "No man is free," Debs proclaimed, "who has to rely upon the arbitrary will of another for the opportunity to work. Such a man works," he continued, "and therefore lives, by permission." Debs also worked hard to unite socialism with more straightforward American democratic traditions. The Marxists in the party did not always appreciate the appeal of American-centric rhetoric, but Debs knew what he was doing. He was rendering Marx's concept of class struggle in terms more Americans might better relate to. "I like the Fourth of July," Debs proclaimed. "It breathes the spirit of revolution." Debs was an American patriot, but more than that, he was a master of catering to his audience.[92]

When speaking before Marx acolytes, Debs switched up his messaging. "I accept unequivocally the socialist theory," he asserted before one such audience, "that we can only abolish class rule by conquering the capitalist class at the polls." The last bit, about voting capitalists out rather than, say, violently expropriating their property, might have calmed the nerves of those who wanted to keep the revolution within American bounds. But the broader sentiment showed that Debs could speak the international language of Marxist socialism. The historian Melvyn Dubofsky noted that "Debs Americanized and Christianized the socialist movement." But Debs also helped Marxify many Christian workers.[93]

Church leaders certainly recognized something was amiss among their working-class flocks. They routinely expressed grave concerns about the large numbers of one-time congregants who avoided their pews. Religious elites might or might not have blamed socialism for such disobedience. But they unquestionably complained that their erstwhile parishioners worshipped a "historical Jesus" who sought to upend imperial Rome. This Jesus was a lot like Marx in that he supplied the oppressed with a withering critique of the powerful. According to this perspective, Christianity and socialism were two sides of the same coin. Both favored the underdog, for whom heaven became something to achieve in life as in the afterlife.[94]

A few nonconformist preachers agreed with the rabble. These rebels embraced the label Christian Socialism and focused on Jesus as the pivotal socialist prophet. Yet they also venerated Marx. The Congregationalist minister Franklin Monroe Sprague identified Marx in his 1892 book *Socialism from Genesis to Revelation* as "the ablest Socialist and political economist" of the nineteenth century. Sprague praised *Capital*, "the Bible of Socialism," for being a "truly remarkable book." Edward Ellis Carr, a Methodist minister from Danville, Illinois, where he organized a branch of the Socialist Party, said he became a "Marxian, class-conscious socialist" after reading *Capital*.[95]

With Debs at the helm, and with radicals as varied as atheistic Marxists and Christian socialists aboard, the Socialist Party was formidable. Indeed, the party enjoyed exponential growth during the first decade of the twentieth century, what Bell called the "golden age of American socialism." Not only did disaffected workers *and* orphaned populists come together in an anticapitalist political formation, so too did many intellectuals disillusioned by corporate capitalism. Socialism had become "an unbounded dream," as Bell put it. This optimism was bolstered by the over 400,000 people who voted for Debs to be president in 1904, a number that grew with subsequent campaigns. But even as the Socialist Party flourished, and even as Debs attained national stature, many socialists thought they needed to do something more drastic to ensure the working class got a fair shake in capitalist America.[96]

ONE BIG UNION

One such person was William "Big Bill" Haywood, a militant miner from Salt Lake City who became a key figure in the Socialist Party. Haywood's radicalism was born amid the drudgery, desolation, and danger of life in the rock and coal mines of the West. Miners were both more subjugated than the average Gilded Age worker, and more insistent on drastic action. "There was no means of escaping from the gigantic force that was relentlessly crushing all of them beneath its cruel heel," Haywood explained. "The people of these dreadful mining camps were in a fever of revolt. There was no method of appeal; strike was their only weapon." Of course, western mining industrialists, who frequently referred to their workers as simple commodities to be bought and sold, were unyielding in their efforts to crush rebellion.[97]

Mining companies were quick to import strikebreakers. When that tactic failed to wipe out worker solidarity, they turned to the government. This pattern played out in one mining town after another, especially between 1894 and 1904. That struggle, the most violent period of western labor conflict, engendered widespread class resentment among the miners. It also shaped the approach to unionization taken by the Western Federation of Miners (WFM), an international union founded in 1893 that grew more revolutionary every day. The WFM philosophy, familiar to many Marxists, was expressed by the union's founding chief, Ed Boyce: "There can be no harmony between organized capitalists and organized labor. . . . There can be no harmony between employer and employee; the former wants long hours and low wages; the latter wants short hours and high wages. . . . Let the rallying cry be: 'Labor, the producer of all wealth, is entitled to all he creates, the overthrow of the whole profit-making system, the extinction of monopolies, equality for all and the land for the people.'"[98]

The WFM organized several strikes across the Mountain West. The struggle was bitter, victories rare. The WFM represented a significant threat, so capitalists went to extreme lengths to destroy it. Mining companies planted Pinkerton provocateurs, allowing them to keep tabs on and subsequently fire workers who joined the WFM. The companies also paid politicians to do their bidding. On several occasions, Colorado Governor James H. Peabody mobilized the National Guard against the WFM, yet again validating Marx's axiom about the state serving as a committee for the affairs of the bourgeoisie. When Haywood led miners against the Standard Mill Company in Colorado City in 1903, Peabody had striking workers arrested on vagrancy charges

and suspended their habeas corpus rights. A survivor of these wars
wrote a poem, a play on Samuel Francis Smith's patriotic "My Country,
'Tis of Thee," that captured the miner perspective:

> Colorado, it is of thee,
> Dark land of tyranny,
>   Of thee I sing;
> Land wherein labor's bled,
> Land from which law has fled,
> Bow down thy mournful head,
>   Capital is king.

In western states, where mining was the most profitable industry,
the WFM had become public enemy number one. Capital was king,
indeed.[99]

After former Idaho governor Frank Steunenberg was assassinated
in 1905, ostensibly because the populist politician had betrayed mine
workers by inviting President William McKinley to send troops to
crush a strike, the western political establishment thought it had been
gifted a silver bullet with which to destroy the WFM once and for all.
Pinkerton detective James McParland, notorious for infiltrating the
Molly Maguires, was put in charge. He coerced a signed confession
from the assassin Harry Orchard, who claimed to have been secretly
hired by the WFM to detonate the bomb that killed Steunenberg,
among dozens of other bombs on behalf of the miner's union. Orchard
implicated three WFM leaders in the conspiracy to kill Steunenberg:
Haywood, George Pettibone, and WFM president Charles Moyer.

The three union men were quickly extradited from Colorado to sit
trial in Idaho. Two of the nation's most eminent lawyers soon clashed
in a case that became a cause célèbre, as newly elected Idaho Senator
William Borah served the prosecution, and the famous civil libertarian Clarence Darrow stood for the defense. Although the defendants
were found guilty in the court of public approval, thanks to a nonstop
barrage of propaganda from antiunion newspapers like the *Chicago Tribune*, they were found innocent by a jury of their peers. No evidence

beyond the cooked confession existed to tie them to the crime. But the mining industry had sent a powerful message: It would stop at little to destroy the WFM.[100]

Out of this cauldron, the Industrial Workers of the World (IWW) was born. Socialists saw they needed an association that would fight tooth-and-nail for miners and *all* other beleaguered workers, especially those ignored by the AFL. As a result, a diverse group of radicals that included Haywood, Moyer, De Leon, Debs, the renowned agitator Mother Jones, and the anarchist Lucy Parsons met in Chicago in 1905 to charter the IWW. Haywood opened the meeting, the Continental Congress of the Working Class, by imploring the 203 delegates that their undertaking was "to put the working class in possession of the economic power, the means of life, in control of the machinery of production and distribution, without regard to capitalist masters." The Wobblies, as members of the IWW affectionately became known, needed to commit, in Haywood's stirring words, to the "emancipation of the working class from the slave bondage of capitalism."[101]

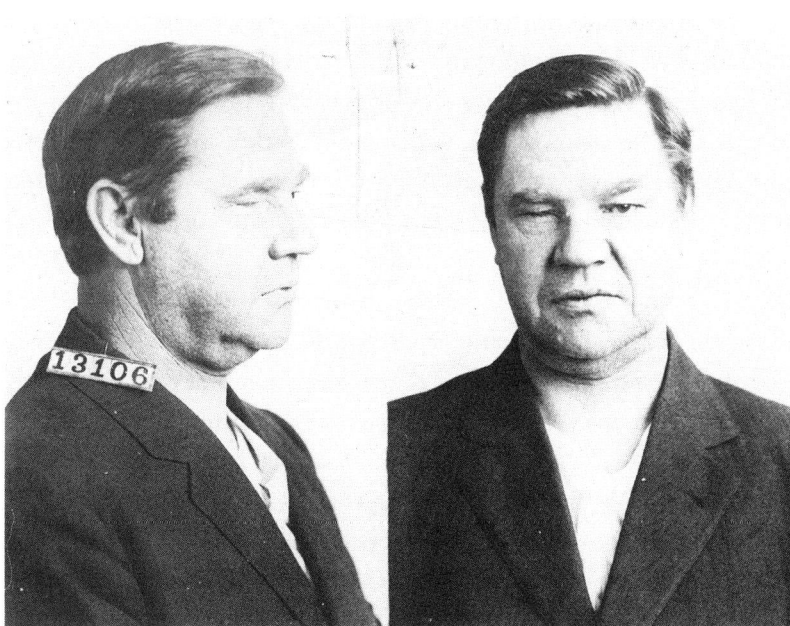

FIGURE 2.2: Big Bill Haywood, Leavenworth Federal Penitentiary, 1918.

The IWW held true to its promise. It organized the most down-trodden among the working class into what it called "One Big Union." Wobblies were a motley assortment of workers, many now nomads, who had been run out of town by antiunion thugs, or pushed off their land, or forced to hit the road in search of work and dignity simply because they were immigrants, black, Mexican, or Chinese. In this, the IWW was the latest incarnation of industrial unionism, presenting workers with a "choice," as Debs put it, "between the A.F. of L. and capitalism on one side and the Industrial Workers and Socialism on the other."[102]

Philosophically, the IWW came closer to representing the Marxist ideal than perhaps any other labor organization. It was unable, however, to entirely avoid regional and demographic divisions, like those between cosmopolitan urbanites who participated in a transatlantic exchange of Marxist ideas, and those on the fringes who simply sought to improve their workaday lives. But unlike many earlier rural Americans, the western workers who joined the IWW thought about capitalism in exceptionally Marxist terms. It was readily apparent to them that capitalism was entirely dependent on their exploitation. They therefore cast their situation in a decidedly Marxist framework, maintaining they needed control of the point of production if they wished to have say over their lives. This fact either demonstrated that Marx's theories tracked with their experience, or that their attitudes had in some fashion been shaped by Marx, likely a mix of both.[103]

Center and periphery came together in the IWW under one big Marxist tent. Yet the distinctions between those who *read* Marx and those who *felt* his truth could be jarring. The New York City socialist August Claessens once recalled that a western miner told him it was unnecessary to read Marx, or *anything* for that matter, in order to be a socialist, since "all a fellow needs to know is that he is robbed." Lots of Wobblies thought this way, including Haywood himself, who supposedly had a habit of saying, "I've never read Marx's *Capital*, but I have the marks of capital all over me."[104]

Hard-scrabble Wobblies identified with Marx. But they were drawn to him less as a philosopher than as an icon, or as one Wobbly called him, a "hobo organizer." In contrast, those who hailed from heavily Marxist urban subcultures remained invested in studying Marx's writings as a guide for their struggle. Claessens was dumbfounded by the notion that a socialist might not need the written word, accustomed as he was to debating comrades all night in Union Square "about the dialectical, historical, materialistic, economic deterministic, Marxian analyses of the exploitation of workers." These were forms of analysis he had largely learned from the written word, especially Marx's.[105]

Despite the IWW's capaciousness, the Wobblies failed to usher in a revolution. The supremacy of capital remained unchallenged, and labor largely remained a disorganized mess. The IWW suffered through an all-too-predictable factional dispute that drove many notable leaders, like De Leon, from its ranks. Never eager to abdicate command of the socialist movement, De Leon had attempted to steer the IWW into becoming a political subsidiary of the SLP. Most Wobblies rejected this plan and ejected De Leon from the organization in 1908. He and his followers then tried to set up their own version of the IWW in Detroit, but it never got off the ground.[106]

Debs also eventually withdrew from the IWW, of his own accord. The Socialist Party leader was an enthusiastic early supporter, even as the moderate Socialists Berger and Hillquit disagreed out of their belief that an alliance with the staid and steady AFL would give the party a better chance of making long-term inroads with labor. Debs was torn between the moderates and Haywood, who had recruited thousands of radicals into the Socialist Party. Debs believed IWW-style industrial unionism was a crucial engine for building a socialist movement. Yet he was wary of Haywood's ultramilitant rhetoric, which had grown increasingly antidemocratic after police attacked workers during the IWW-organized Lawrence textile strike of 1912. After that, Haywood lost all patience with reformist and electoral strategies, believing that direct action and other forms of revolutionary resistance were the only effective methods for combating a ruthless capitalist state.

Debs never chose between reform or revolution. Like many socialists, including Marx, he thought there was room for both. Indeed, he believed reform and revolution were necessarily overlapping pathways to the socialist republic of his dreams. Yet Debs reluctantly aligned with the reformers Berger and Hillquit in their dispute with the revolutionary Haywood. The Socialist Party purged Haywood and his thousands of supporters. At the same moment, Debs parted ways with the IWW, fearing that his presence there would prevent him from making the Socialist Party a national organization. Unfortunately, the split between the Socialist Party and the IWW weakened both organizations. After 1912, it was rare to find anyone who belonged to both. These were tragic results for the Left. Gilded Age working conditions had left the door open for more Americans than ever to discover Marx. Yet the leaders of the biggest Marxist parties were too busy quarreling with one another to take advantage.[107]

The IWW continued organizing the flotsam and jetsam of the working class. Like Marx, the Wobblies conceptualized the working class as the angel of history, destined to end the class system once and for all. As the IWW preamble proclaimed, "the workers of the world organize as a class, take possession of the earth and the machinery of production and abolish the wage system." The Wobblies were not about to quit.[108]

A curious pattern followed the IWW wherever it went. Upon entering a town where workers needed help in their ongoing struggles, Wobblies set up soapboxes from which to preach. They were then hastily arrested and jailed for disrupting the public order. Not to be deterred, more Wobblies would follow in the footsteps of their detained comrades, filling up the jails. The fight, then, became about whether Wobblies had the right to free speech, a right supposedly protected by the First Amendment, even when speech was anticapitalist. This confrontation came to define the legacy of the IWW.[109]

Wobbly songs about their struggles also shaped how the IWW was remembered. The IWW's *Little Red Song Book* circulated among labor radicals long after the union had dwindled into irrelevance. The Swedish immigrant Joe Hill wrote several of the most renowned Wobbly songs. He articulated an intense dislike for capitalism while also capturing the IWW's infamous hatred for capitalism's middlemen— police, politicians, judges, ministers, the Salvation Army. No song portrayed antipathy toward those who abetted the bourgeoisie with more luster than Hill's "The Preacher and the Slave":

> Long-haired preachers come out every night
> Try to tell you what's wrong and what's right
> But when asked how 'bout something to eat
> They will answer in voices so sweet
> You will eat, bye and bye
> In that glorious land above the sky
> Work and pray, live on hay
> You'll get pie in the sky when you die

Hill's lyrical poignancy remained intact even as he was on the verge of being executed by the state of Utah in 1914 for a wrongful murder conviction. Before the men on the firing squad pulled their triggers, he apocryphally gave his comrades around the world instructions: "Don't mourn, organize." Wobbly words, spoken by people whose worldviews had been fashioned in a Marxist context, reverberated into the future, helping shape left-wing American thought during the twentieth century and beyond.[110]

As a declining IWW carried on, so too did a diminished Socialist Party. Debs won nearly a million votes in the memorable 1912 presidential election, which also featured the incumbent Republican president William Howard Taft, the Progressive Party spoiler and former president Theodore Roosevelt, and the Democratic challenger and eventual winner Woodrow Wilson. In 1920, Debs won still more votes, from prison no less. Even though the Socialist Party was weakened in numbers and in the strength of its relationship with a besieged labor movement, Debs remained extremely popular. He was an inspiring and tireless orator, and the socialist message rang true for many people in a society dominated by a ruthless corporate elite.

The Socialist Party legacy, then, is inseparable from a robust collective memory of Debs. Yet that legacy is also inextricably linked to the history of Marx's reception in the United States, a reception made possible not only by Debs or by other famous Gilded Age Marxists like De Leon or Haywood. Socialist Party intellectuals also worked tirelessly to spread Marx's word.

WORKERS OF THE WORLD, READ!

Socialist intellectuals unvaryingly adopted Marx as their teacher. In him, they found a scathing critic of the inhumane economic system that ground American workers into dust. They also discovered a theorist who saw a way out. Algie Martin Simons, an SLP newspaper editor who joined the anti–De Leon faction and thus landed in the Socialist Party like the other so-called kangaroos, wrote in 1906 that Marx taught him to see "in the consolidation of ownership, in the organization of industries, in the trusts, in the concentration of wealth with its merciless inevitable onward movement, but a preparation for collective ownership and control." Capitalism was digging its own grave, out of which socialism would spring forth. As editor of the *International Socialist Review* for the first decade of the new century, Simons showcased Marx's work. He trusted that Marx would help people better understand their world and better change it.[111]

The *International Socialist Review*, like many prominent Socialist periodicals, was published by Charles H. Kerr & Company, described by the historian Allen Ruff as "the most significant English-language publisher and exporter of Marxism in the world between 1900 and 1925." Its namesake founder was the son of abolitionists, and the company started in the early 1890s as a populist mouthpiece. By 1900, it had switched gears and began disseminating accessible translations of important, otherwise unobtainable Marxist texts, what became its renowned Library of Socialist Classics. Headquartered in Chicago, Kerr & Company had in-house translators, many of whom earned a reputation as the best in the business. Ernest Untermann's complete translation of all three volumes of *Capital*, the first full one for an American readership, was a company showpiece.[112]

"Workers of the World, Read!" This Kerr & Company adage became something of a Socialist Party maxim as well. Socialists formed reading groups to cooperatively explore sophisticated Marxist texts. Many of these groups got their start by tackling Untermann's translation of the first volume of *Capital*, published in 1906. Reading *Capital* was no easy task, especially for workers with arduous lives. With this problem in mind, Simons wrote an article about "How to Read *Capital*." He set off a long tradition among Marxist scholars who have sought to help the masses understand it.[113]

Efforts on the part of intellectuals to facilitate wide dissemination of Marx's most important text were somewhat successful in the early twentieth century. Numerous Socialist Party members attributed their ideological transformations to epiphanies they had while reading *Capital*. The Socialist artist Rockwell Kent recounted that he only had to "read but a little way in *Das Kapital* to recognize that here was the truth." It is impossible to know how many of these conversion narratives were literally true, but it is telling that so many people felt compelled to say that Marx inspired them to reject capitalism. Reading *Capital* had become currency in Socialist circles.[114]

Untermann was most responsible for getting Marx into the hands of American socialists. The Berlin-born scholar embodied the life Marx wanted for people "in communist society, where nobody has one exclusive sphere of activity but each can become accomplished in any branch he wishes." Untermann was a lifelong socialist, but he was also a formally trained paleontologist and self-taught artist who later made a name for himself as the composer of several whimsical paintings and murals for Dinosaur National Monument in eastern Utah. As he translated *Capital*, Untermann farmed chickens in Florida, alternating between deciphering German rhetoric about surplus value and warding off the opossums, snakes, and hawks that threatened his livestock. He was fully cognizant of the gravity of both tasks.[115]

In 1907, Untermann wrote *Marxian Economics: A Popular Introduction to the Three Volumes of Marx's "Capital*," also published by Kerr & Company. More than a crib sheet on *Capital*, Untermann's book was also intended to refute "capitalist professors" who propagated false notions about Marx and who could not seem to grasp why anyone would

find Marx relevant. According to Untermann, the very thing these professors most ignored, the ways that Marx connected oppressive conditions in the workplace to the larger operations of the capitalist system, was also what made *Capital* a "working-class Bible." Untermann
bitingly criticized those who willfully got Marx wrong. But he noted
the flourishing genre of bourgeois anti-Marx commentary had a silver
lining. It helped bring Marx to more people. Maybe a few curious souls
would go straight to the source.[116]

Untermann's presentation of *Capital* was clear and compelling. Yet
it is an undeniably strange read in the twenty-first-century. Like Gronlund's *Cooperative Commonwealth*, *Marxian Economics* leavened Marx
with Darwin. Untermann also followed previous socialist thinkers in
rescuing Darwinist analysis from Herbert Spencer's reactionary re-
interpretations. These intellectual moves came easy for Untermann.
His scientific training predisposed him to categorize Marx as an evolutionary thinker. And his socialist background inclined him to dismiss
Spencer's notion that Darwin's "survival of the fittest" applied to human society.[117]

In his refutation of Spencer, Untermann relied upon the American
anthropologist Lewis Morgan's 1877 book *Ancient Society; or, Researches
in the Lines of Human Progress from Savagery, Through Barbarism to Civilization*. Marx had also taken a keen interest in Morgan's findings since
they confirmed his sense that exploitation did not define life before human settlement, a period that Marx termed "primitive communism."
Similarly, Untermann used Morgan's anthropology as a cudgel against
capitalist professors who normalized hierarchy by conflating natural
and human history. He ridiculed such "bourgeois Darwinians" for
their tendency to use evolutionary theory as justification for "human
slavery on the ground that the slaves are of an 'inferior race'" while
conveniently ignoring "the economic causes which alone made slavery
possible." Untermann cited Marx to drive home this point. "In principle," Marx wrote in 1847, "a porter differs less from a philosopher
than a mastiff does from a greyhound. It is the division of labor which
has placed an abyss between the two."[118]

Untermann offered a socialist Darwinist framework as an alternative to social Darwinism. He contended that, just as Darwin provided a roadmap for ascertaining whether life on earth was making "a forward or backward step," Marx supplied the tools for determining whether the cultural norms of a given epoch "represent an evolution or a reaction in the general advance of mankind." Just as Homo sapiens represented a higher stage in the evolution of life, or so early interpreters of Darwin thought, socialism represented an advanced phase in the progression of human relations. Untermann crafted a Marx for early twentieth-century Americans by putting a hopeful, evolutionary spin on his thought.[119]

Efforts to assimilate Marx to the progressive sensibilities of early twentieth-century American political culture did not totally diminish the radicalism of socialist intellectual life. Untermann also fundamentally challenged a basic American assumption when he mocked the common belief that the United States was a meritocracy. "A man becomes a capitalist because he wants to be one," he quipped, "and the others down the billionth generation are poor and dependent through their own fault." As a counter to this and other naive postulations intended to bolster capitalist hierarchy, Untermann presented a heavy dose of unadulterated Marx. Even though Untermann worked hard to accommodate Marxism and Darwinism, he also dedicated large chunks of *Marxian Economics* to promoting a version of straight Marx. In doing so, he focused his attention on *Capital*, the book he wanted everyone to read.[120]

In Untermann's view, *Capital* was a work of pure genius. Marx's magnum opus explained, better than anything else, how workers were thrown together to form an exploited class. Marx also illustrated that it was not always thus. During feudal times, peasants lived coarse lives, but at least they controlled the means of production by virtue of their access to soil. They had some degree of autonomy because they could cultivate food to survive. This narrative drew attention to how the shift from feudalism to capitalism was accompanied by the transformation of peasant into worker, compelling Marx's readers to consider how exploitation was more acute for the worker than for the peasant. "The process," Marx wrote, "that clears the way for the capitalist system, can be none other than the process which takes away from the laborer the possession of his means of production." Bourgeois historians had focused on the liberation of the masses from the endless drudgery of peasant life. Yet they ignored the loss of autonomy—an "expropriation," in Marx's words, "written in the annals of mankind in letters of blood and fire." The class of people who were newly forced to sell their labor to survive, exploited by those who came to control the means of production, in conditions no less drudging, came into existence by use of force. This was what Marx called "the secret of primitive accumulation." It was a story meant to incite revolution.[121]

One notable American inspired by Marx to become a socialist revolutionary was Jack London. Born into poverty in 1876, London lived his early adult years as a vagabond, sometimes riding the rails. In 1894, he marched on Washington, DC, as a member of Coxey's Army, joining thousands of other unemployed in demanding decent jobs. During his time on the road, London spoke with all sorts of down-and-out men. From the more class-conscious among them, many of whom were socialists, he learned that his precarious condition was a feature of the American class system. One militant drifter gave London a tattered copy of *The Communist Manifesto*. Marx "astounded" him, he said. He underlined the *Manifesto*'s famous final passage and recited it in speeches for the rest of his life, even after he became a world-famous novelist. "Let the ruling classes tremble," London repeated. "Workers have nothing to lose but their chains. They have a world to win."[122]

In 1894, London joined the Oakland branch of the SLP. It gave London purpose. However, piecing together a living remained a problem. That, as well as his insatiable desire for adventure meant staying to help build the local SLP was not in the cards. In 1897, London headed north to join the Klondike Gold Rush. London failed to discover gold, like most desperate prospectors. Yet the harsh conditions, only some of which were products of the rugged Yukon landscape and unforgiving climate, taught him even more about the logic of class exploitation. But not quite enough. Returning home, London resolved to round out his hands-on education with book learning. He began furiously reading classic works in political philosophy, with a focus on socialist thinkers, particularly Marx.

London joined other socialists of his generation in reading Darwin and Spencer. Like them, he rejected Spencer's social Darwinism. But London embraced Spencer's dour views on humanity as they pertained to racial difference. London was, in fact, a racist, which sometimes came through in his writing. This did not isolate London, even in a socialist milieu. During the era historians refer to as the nadir period, a low point in the history of American racism, some white socialists framed the world according to a racialist hierarchy despite their otherwise egalitarian sensibilities. Many of London's comrades did find his racist writings repulsive, but his views did not slow his ascent in two worlds, as a man of letters and as a socialist.[123]

Like many SLP members, London joined the Socialist Party in 1901. He wanted to belong to the party of Debs, who inspired him to get more active in the movement. That year, at the age of twenty-five, London accepted the party's nomination as candidate for mayor of Oakland. (He did not win.) But his true callings remained writing and travel. London went to England in 1902 in search of his muse. After six weeks wandering London's East End, where he witnessed human degradation of the type Marx experienced in those very slums, he wrote a book. *The People of the Abyss*, published in 1903, made London renowned among American socialists. That same year he grew more broadly famous, due to the publication of *Call of the Wild*, his short novel about a sled dog's adventures in the Yukon.[124]

After 1903, London's byline regularly appeared in the socialist press, including in J. A. Wayland's *Appeal to Reason*. Philip Foner observed that his "capacity for applying Marxism to American conditions" was on display in both his socialist essays and in his lively correspondence with readers. London's talents as a Marxist thinker were also evident in the numerous lectures he gave. He drew huge crowds, such as the 3,500 students who attended a 1905 speech at the University of California, Berkeley. London was often invited to speak before elite audiences, reveling in telling them that they had "mismanaged the world." He regularly warned his bourgeois attendees that their wealth was on the verge of being expropriated. After a particularly incendiary talk at Yale University, the *New York Times* editorialized that "Mr. Jack London's Socialism is bloody war—the war of one class in society against other classes. He says so. It is a destructive socialism. He glories in it."[125]

London took his socialist-themed writing to new levels with his 1908 book *The Iron Heel*, which Foner described as "the most revolutionary novel in American literature." The protagonist, Ernest Everhard, a blond, Nietzschean Übermensch, is a composite of three illustrious socialists: the charismatic party leader Debs; the brilliant Marxist scholar Untermann; and the daring speaker of truth to power, London himself. The novel is narrated by the hero's wife, Avis Everhard, after Ernest has died in the struggle for a better world. Adding to the novel's allure as a realistic account, London framed Avis's text as only having been discovered seven centuries in the future, long after the victorious socialist revolution. To augment this clever conceit with a veneer of authenticity, London affixed footnotes to what he labeled the Everhard Manuscript. The footnoted manuscript was ostensibly the handiwork of a future scholar who wants to provide readers with context for the ancient names, places, and events in the text.[126]

Early in the novel, Avis, the daughter of a renowned scientist, describes her first conversation with Ernest as a shock to her ears, which had been rendered overly sensitive by a comfy bourgeois upbringing that failed to prepare her for the rough-and-tumble world of class struggle. Avis confesses that "there was much that I did not like" about Everhard, who "laid too great stress on what he called the class struggle, the antagonism between labor and capital, the conflict of interest." But eventually Ernest wins Avis over, and not only because of mutual physical attraction. The airtight logic of his Marxism is too much for her to resist. After one of his many lectures, this one about how the seemingly never-ending capitalist search for places to externalize surpluses would end once capitalist development conquers the entire planet, she admits to being swayed. "It was the first time I had ever heard Karl Marx's doctrine of surplus value elaborated, and Ernest had done it so simply that I, too, sat puzzled and dumbfounded."[127]

Everhard, like the real-life Untermann, makes a living translating Marxist books for a Chicago-based socialist press. Like the real-life London, he enjoys spitting fiery anticapitalist rhetoric to anybody within earshot. "If modern man's producing power is a thousand times greater than that of the cave-man," Ernest asks during a particularly tense speech to a group of angry and defensive capitalists, "why then, in the United States today, are there fifteen million people who are not properly sheltered and properly fed?" Of course, he knows the answer. Echoing London's own speeches, Everhard declares that the "capitalist class has mismanaged." And so would they pay. "It is a struggle of classes," he cautions. "Just as your class dragged down the old feudal nobility, so shall it be dragged down by my class, the working class." Everhard, like London, had been convinced by Marx to pin his hopes on a socialist movement of workers destined to smash the capitalist class. Of course, Everhard and London also knew from Marx, and from experience, that capitalists would not go down without a fight. In the novel, the capitalists put together a counterrevolutionary crusade that London brands the Iron Heel.[128]

The Iron Heel was saturated in evolutionary Marxism. It featured several lengthy, didactic conversations between Everhard, who dutifully represented the Marxist position, and people who stood for other identifiable class positions. One involved Everhard and a group of small businessmen, embodying the petit bourgeois perspective. Contemplating how best to thwart large corporations, the small businessmen argue in favor of fashioning an alliance with the populists as part of a larger antitrust movement. Breaking up monopolistic firms, they contend, is the most effective means for resisting corporate power. In passionately voicing his dissent, Everhard likens the antimonopoly approach to Luddism, which, in its nostalgia, resorts to breaking machines, or in the case of the antitrusters, corporations.

> Let us not destroy these wonderful machines that produce efficiently and cheaply. Let us control them. Let us profit by their efficiency and cheapness. Let us oust the present owners of the wonderful machines, and let us own the wonderful machines ourselves. That, gentlemen, is

socialism, a greater combination than the trusts, a greater economic and social combination than any that has as yet appeared on the planet. It is in line with evolution. It is the winning side. Come on over with us socialists and play on the winning side.

London, in the voice of Everhard, demonstrated a patronizing attitude toward small businesspeople, or really anybody who failed to recognize the inevitable evolution of the class struggle into a battle solely between capital and labor. The evolutionary Marxism of early twentieth-century socialists could be quite rigid. But as a cosmology it could also be quite intoxicating.[129]

The plot of London's novel proceeded according to the teleological expectations of evolutionary socialists. The penultimate act sees the international working class launching a general strike that brings a war between Germany and the United States to a standstill. With a new-found appreciation of its power, the working class battles the forces of reaction, fighting in the streets of Chicago and around the world. Ultimately, one capitalist government after another crumbles. Socialism sweeps the land. "At last was being realized Karl Marx's classic," London wrote in the voice of Avis Everhard. "'The knell of private capitalist property sounds. The expropriators are expropriated.'" Ernest Everhard is mysteriously executed during the revolutionary war. "One of our generalizations," Everhard says in parting, "is that every system founded upon class and caste contains within itself the germs of its own decay."[130]

The Iron Heel's happy ending resonated with American socialists at a time when "Socialism was an unbounded dream," as Daniel Bell sarcastically stated in a more cynical time. The glorious conclusion also tracked with Bell's damning criticism that American socialism was "in but not of the world." Back in reality, the international working class would ultimately prove powerless to stop the wars between capitalist nations, between Germany and the United States. Worse still, socialist parties across Europe willingly joined the global orgy of violence. The Socialist Party of America, notably, did not follow in their footsteps.

For refusing to back the American effort in the Great War, Socialists were persecuted. Debs was thrown back in prison.[131]

The gathering clouds of political persecution did not change the fact that socialism had taken root in the United States, nor did it change the fact that Karl Marx's ideas had found a home in American political culture. Owing to the movements that arose to challenge corporate domination during the Gilded Age, Marx became a hero to many among the American proletariat. Yet plenty more remained attached to political traditions with long-standing resonance, from republicanism to populism and from utopianism to Christianity. The old Rhinelander's centrality to American radical discourse was not guaranteed—that is, until 1917, when Marxist revolutionaries took power in Russia. The Bolshevik Revolution was a galvanizing force for American socialists, a launching pad for the American reception of Marx. Thanks to Vladimir Lenin and his comrades, Marx's name recognition grew by leaps and bounds among Americans of all political persuasions. But the Russian Revolution proved to be both a blessing and a curse to Marx's legacy in the United States, and to those who desired a socialist future for America. To that history we now turn.

3

BOLSHEVIK

The Russian Revolution

Even the most bitter anti-Bolshevik, if he is a socialist, must forget
everything and become filled with love for them when he imagines the
statue of Karl Marx standing in the Kremlin.

ABRAHAM CAHAN

John Reed arrived in Petrograd at the dawn of history. The globetrotting American journalist had traveled to Russia with his feminist wife,
Louise Bryant, as revolution loomed. It was 1917, and Reed had a front-
row seat to the October Revolution. Famous for his vivid firsthand accounts of labor conflict and war, Reed was the perfect writer for the
electrifying story of how Vladimir Lenin, the gifted Karl Marx disciple,
led the Bolsheviks to power in the largest nation in the world.

Ten Days That Shook the World, Reed's celebratory account of the Russian Revolution, has been hailed as an American classic. The Cold War
architect George Kennan praised it as "a reflection of blazing honesty
and a purity of idealism." The former secretary of state Condoleezza
Rice, a Russia specialist, commended Reed for providing "a riveting
and vivid—if not impartial—account of the most pivotal phase of the
revolution, as viewed from the ground."[1]

These are retrospective and even mandarin assessments, but Reed's
triumphalist interpretation of what the Bolsheviks achieved was incen-

diary at the time. In fact, he struggled to find an American publisher willing to incur the wrath of powerful men bent on strangling the Bolshevik threat in its infancy.[2]

In response to the specter of Marxist revolution, American elites intensified a clampdown on radicalism that had been sweeping the nation in the wake of American entry into the First World War. As tens of thousands of socialists, communists, and anarchists were rounded up and jailed or deported during the most severe red scare to that point, the

FIGURE 3.1: John Reed in Moscow, ca. 1920.

nation's leaders juxtaposed "100 percent Americans," as Teddy Roosevelt labeled good men, with "Bolshevists," "red flag socialists," Wobblies, anarchists, "criminals," "bomb-throwers," and "dynamiters."[3]

PROGRESSIVISM VS. SOCIALISM

Roosevelt's language echoed the fire-breathing rhetoric of American reactionaries of the time. Conservative vigilantes likened *any* challenge to corporate power to a Marx-inspired plot. But Teddy Roosevelt was no reactionary. Nor was he a corporate stooge. Rather, after being thrust into the presidency after William McKinley was assassinated by professed anarchist Leon Czolgosz in 1901, Roosevelt jumpstarted reform efforts that gave the Progressive Era its name. McKinley's murder allowed Roosevelt to claim that reform was the "antidote to dangerous and wicked agitation." With one hand, he championed the harsh repression of wicked agitators. With the other, he worked to ameliorate the conditions that cultivated dangerous zealotry in the first place.[4]

The progressive movement encompassed a diverse range of reformers. Some exhibited socialistic sensibilities, including Jane Addams, founder of Chicago's Hull House, a settlement house for working-class immigrants. Addams never joined the Socialist Party, but she maintained that charitable endeavors like hers were poor substitutes for well-paying jobs, decent housing, schools, libraries, and hospitals. She dreamed of a society "reconstructed to the point of offering equal opportunity for all."[5]

Teddy Roosevelt cared about fairness, too, which is partly why he regulated some monopolistic companies. But he also championed reform to undercut "red flag socialists" like the novelist Upton Sinclair, whose 1906 novel *The Jungle* illustrated rampant exploitation in the nation's meatpacking plants. Sinclair's work failed to draw attention to the condition of the working class generally, but it did contribute somewhat to passage of the Pure Food and Drug Act, whose regulations benefited the working class. Roosevelt pushed through the act, which mildly policed the food industry, because he recognized bad food was a real problem. Yet he also hoped this would silence socialist muck-rakers, while not endangering the food industry's profitability.[6]

The language of the act regulating the food industry was mostly written by its representatives. In fact, the National Association of Canned Food Packers had long lobbied for federal inspection and labeling. Pickle tycoon H. J. Heinz Jr. hoped that regulation would endow products with a "stamp of legitimacy," thus easing access to fastidious culinary markets like France. Progressivism wasn't going to bring down capitalism—it injected small doses of socialism to render it slightly more humane, and significantly more effective. By borrowing from socialism, progressivism galvanized a new, mightier form of capitalism.[7]

The distinctions between progressivism and socialism were on display during the presidential campaign of 1912. The Democratic candidate Woodrow Wilson flogged a reform agenda mostly limited to antitrust legislation. Teddy Roosevelt, running as a third-party candidate, forwarded a progressive "New Nationalism." In addition to more regulations, Roosevelt sought a more democratic capitalism that would have included social insurance and a shorter workday. It represented a substantial commitment to the welfare of working-class Americans. But as a radical challenge to corporate capitalism, it paled next to the vision of the Socialist Party's recurring candidate for president, Eugene V. Debs.[8]

Debs campaigned from his train, the "Red Special," promoting Marxist solutions to the nation's problems. "The capitalist system," the Socialist platform pronounced, "has outgrown its historical function, and has become utterly incapable of meeting the problems now confronting society." The platform was largely a recitation of one Marxist premise after another.[9]

Although most Marxists assumed the working class would ultimately overturn exploitative capitalism, Debs and the Socialists wanted action now, like the nationalization of banks and railroads. Their platform was a menace to the corporate order that, in theory, would have instigated a revolution of sweeping magnitude. In practice, Debs and his Marx-infused message struggled to reach American voters.

Debs did his best to draw distinctions between himself and progressives, especially Teddy Roosevelt, whom he called "a charlatan, mountebank, and fraud," and whose promises he described "as the mouthings of a low and utterly unprincipled self-seeker and demagogue." Yet most Americans pulled the lever for gentle tweaks to the system rather than a far-reaching overhaul. Debs only won 6 percent of the popular vote. Roosevelt and Taft outpaced him considerably. But by splitting the Republican vote, they granted Wilson the presidency. The campaign both failed to herald a socialist future and signaled the apex of progressivism.[10]

Most voters preferred the progressive option to the socialist one. Yet nearly a million Americans did pull the lever for an anticapitalist candidate representing a Marxist party. Large crowds gathered along the Debs whistle-stop tour, a spectacle that inspired the socialist faithful. As Debs's running mate Emil Seidel declared, "There is a great giant growing up in this country that will someday take over the affairs of this nation. He is a little giant now, but he is growing fast. The name of this little giant is socialism." Even in the clutch of defeat, socialists remained hopeful their time would come.[11]

THE VARIETIES OF AMERICAN SOCIALISM

Developments beyond electoral politics also gave hope to socialists. People of all types, black and white, women and men, rural and urban, native-born and immigrant, factory worker and farmer, intellectual and vagabond, were busy organizing in the name of socialism. Even though the Socialist Party remained small relative to the growing population, its diversity spoke to its potential as a vehicle for radical change. It also demonstrated the wide-ranging ways in which Marx served as a guide for being a socialist in the United States.

Demography played an ineluctable role in how socialists read Marx. The German-born Marxists who made Milwaukee a socialist stronghold engaged in many of the same debates about Marx and strategy that were then occupying the Social Democratic Party of Germany (SPD), the largest and most powerful socialist party in the world. As a key cog in the Second International, the coalition of socialist and labor parties that formed in Paris in 1889, the SPD adhered to Marxist orthodoxies, for a time.[12]

Orthodox Marxists believed social change resulted from advances in the forces of production, from technological and organizational progress. Revolutionary conditions emerged when social relations failed to keep pace. A Marxist party would seek to take advantage of the contradictions that ensued. Many American socialists observed this Second International line. For example, they fostered the notion that corporations represented a great leap in how humans organized productive forces. "Let us not destroy these wonderful machines that produce efficiently and cheaply," Jack London beseeched anticorporatists. "Let us control them."[13]

The orthodox Marxism of the Second International helped shape Milwaukee socialism. This was hardly surprising since many Milwaukee socialists were SPD members before emigrating to the United States. But just as German socialists in Germany were not single-minded about Marxist theory, neither were German socialists in Milwaukee. The debate about revisionism that rocked the SPD also preoccupied Milwaukee socialists.

Led by Edward Bernstein, who rejected the orthodox position that a revolutionary break with capitalism was a prerequisite to achieving socialism, revisionists in the SPD thought they could obtain power within the existing political system. Revisionists believed socialism would come gradually, through regular bourgeois political channels. In the meantime, Bernstein contended, the primary objective for socialists was to make life tangibly better for the working class. There was no reason to wait for the revolution to help the proletariat.[14]

Some European Marxists, most notably Karl Kautsky, rejected Bernstein's revisionism, as did American socialists who believed in orthodox Marxism. Marx theorized class conflict was relentlessly polarizing. Heightening contradictions would eventually engender a crisis, which in turn would propel a revolution. For many American socialists, the ultraviolent labor conflict, a manifestation of widening class divisions, bore this out. As if by the blueprint, working conditions grew more abject as American capitalists tightened their grip on the forces of production. When workers fought back, capitalists responded with callous violence. Orthodox Marxists thus urged their socialist brethren to prepare for the revolution by recruiting and radicalizing workers.[15]

In contrast, American revisionists emphasized that proworker legislation had improved working-class life. Even if workplace conditions remained wretched, general well-being had been ticking up. Revisionists contended the goal of socialists should be to continue along this path of progress. Marx had to be interpreted for altered conditions. Marx the communist revolutionary was out; Marx the social democratic reformer was in.

In Milwaukee, revisionism won the day. Socialists there were led by Victor Berger, who was sometimes called the "American Bernstein." Berger immigrated to the United States from the Austrian Empire as a young man, eventually making a home in Milwaukee. Berger joined Daniel De Leon's Socialist Labor Party (SLP) and edited two SLP newspapers. Tiring of De Leon's notorious megalomania, Berger quit and helped create three new socialist parties, including the Socialist Party of America in 1901. In 1911, Berger became the first member of the Socialist Party to win a seat in Congress, where he mostly remained until 1929.[16]

Berger personified "sewer socialism," a term coined by revolutionary Marxists to lambaste Milwaukee socialists who bragged about building the best sewer system in the world, instead of preparing for revolution. But sewers were no joke. Berger believed socialism would be achieved one basic service at a time. If socialist politicians delivered concrete reforms, the working class would support them. In a representative democracy, then, the ballot was the best route to socialism. The compound effect of relentless reform would usher in the equivalent of socialist revolution, minus violent upheaval. Berger did not pit reform against revolution. But he did think socialists made themselves most useful fighting for the former while awaiting the latter.[17]

Like Bernstein, Berger thought Marx needed revising. But he did not wish to erase his revolutionary side. Berger asserted Marx had become a social democratic reformer late in life, outspoken in support of the shorter workday and other meaningful improvements, while never ditching dreams of revolution. Marx supported reforms, but he subordinated them to his larger objective of abolishing wage labor. Berger agreed with this general approach, and thanks to his intellectual guidance, the Socialist Party achieved a novel synthesis.

Early twentieth-century Socialists avoided the sectarian debates that tore apart previous Marxist formations such as the WPUS. Rather than debate whether to organize in trade unions or engage in electoral politics, Berger's Socialist Party supported both activities. Every effort to improve the lives of the working class was worthwhile both as an end in itself and for clearing a path to revolution.[18]

Even though a doctrine that offered tangible reforms was easier to market, socialism remained a tough sell. In the minds of many Americans, Marxism remained a dangerously foreign philosophy. This is why American socialists of every generation have attempted to translate Marx's key concepts into American terms. Berger often espoused Marxist ideas in the language of republicanism. "A man is not free," he wrote, "who is dependent upon another for a job—for a chance to make a livelihood."[19]

It was easy enough to make Marx sound like a republican, or like an American. After all, American history had always informed Marxism. Marx's close attention to the Civil War, for example, endowed *Capital* with noticeable republican accents. But there were other impediments to the mainstreaming of Marx. Many native-born Americans were turned off by Marxism because, through the first few decades of the twentieth century, immigrants were often its most eager promoters. At the same time, the United States was a nation of immigrants, and so immigrant Marxists were *American* Marxists. Berger and his Milwaukee comrades, who did as much as anyone to align Socialist Party strategy with Marx, were American Marxists. Even so, they did not have a monopoly on Marx in America.

It should come as no surprise that Socialist Party membership was highly concentrated in cities like New York City and Milwaukee, with large Jewish and German immigrant populations. In contrast, it is astonishing to find so many socialists in heavily rural Oklahoma, mostly populated by American Indians and native-born evangelical Christians. The history of Oklahoma Socialism reveals another approach to reading Marx.

Why did Oklahomans join the Socialist Party? Wretched poverty. The small farmers dotting that desolate landscape were some of the unluckiest souls in the United States. Even those fortunate enough to own small plots of land found survival challenging. Trapped in a vicious cycle of debt, most small landowners mortgaged their humble holdings to the banks, thus joining the growing army of tenant farmers. Due to these long-standing hardships, many Oklahomans got swept up in the prairie radicalism that seized the heartland during the late nineteenth century. The history of Oklahoma socialism has its roots in the Populist struggle for land.[20]

Like their big-city counterparts, Oklahoma socialists read Marx, often with strategy in mind. But neither the orthodox Marxism of the Second International nor the sewer socialism of the Milwaukee Marxists proved relevant to their land-focused struggles. Whereas most socialists conceptualized land reform as anti-Marxist, Oklahoma socialists consistently prioritized it. This insistence helped the Socialist Party of America render Marx more appealing to people whose political dreams began with access to land. At a global scale, such people numbered in the billions and, as Marxists discovered later in the twentieth century, formed the raw material of revolution from China to Cuba.[21]

When Marx defined the working class in *The Communist Manifesto*, he excluded all landholders. Given his focus on European capitalism, this exclusion made sense. The legacy of feudalism meant rural landowners across the continent tended to hail from a powerful class of aristocrats who were well positioned to smoothly adapt to the new capitalist order. The capitalist commodification of land worked to their advantage. Marx thus rejected the notion that restoring precapitalist land rights was a worthy socialist cause. Either way, elites won.

In Marx's later works, which often centered on the global implications of capitalist development, he offered a more nuanced position. In the first volume of *Capital*, Marx argued primitive accumulation, which included theft of land from native peoples by European settlers, was a crucial step in the growth of capitalism. In his later musings on developments in Russia, he conceded that a socialist revolution might emerge from the rural commune movement there. Marx had come to recognize that most people who clung to land were not protocapitalists, and that dispossession was a powerful engine of proletarianization.[22]

There is no evidence that early twentieth-century American socialists engaged with Marx's more complex understanding of the land question. Even if they had, it is doubtful such familiarity would have pushed them to embrace land reform, especially since Marx never argued for reversing the course of proletarianization. The revolutionary poetry of the future was waiting to be written by industrial proles dreaming of progress, not agrarians longing for days past. Yet, the more mature Marx's analysis of land might have left big-city socialists more sympathetic to the plight of their rural comrades.

The more rigid way of reading Marx on the question of land, denying the rights of small landholders, had shaped the Socialist Party of America's position from its founding. In 1908, its national platform promoted collective ownership of land, hardly a way to attract land-starved Oklahomans.[23]

Oklahoma socialists shared Marx's scathing indictment of the capitalist system. But they mixed their Marx with heavy doses of Thomas Jefferson, stressing not just their exploitation but the inherent dignity of working their own small plots. As one said, "Without land, man cannot exist. It is the first necessity of being. It is the exclusion of wage workers from the soil that places them at the mercy of their employers and binds the chains of slavery upon them. There can be no solution of the economic question that does not restore the land to the people." To appeal to small farmers on the dusty prairie, Marxists were compelled to heed Jeffersonian ways of thinking about land and freedom, sensibilities with deep roots in the heartland.[24]

In 1912, the Oklahoma Socialist Party officially endorsed redistributing land to all who toiled on it. This brought it more electoral success than any other branch south of Milwaukee. In staking out a populist position on land, in combination with socialist stances such as nationalizing vital industries, Oklahoma socialists melded two distinct leftist traditions: Marxist socialism and agrarian radicalism. "In these ways," writes the historian Jim Bissett, Oklahoma socialists "rendered Marx's ideas more congruent with the particular experiences of American workers." Marx and Jefferson were not necessarily antithetical.[25]

Many Oklahoma socialists further mixed their Marxism with evangelical Christianity, which was widespread on the prairie. Christian socialism was not uncommon in the period. Yet most Americans who combined Marx and Jesus hailed from liberal Protestant denominations that featured the social gospel, which in telling the story of Jesus emphasized doing good works while on earth. Evangelicals differed in their stringent belief that salvation could only be achieved by devout and frequent worship of Jesus. Some early twentieth-century evangelicals formed communities that prioritized the collective good, meaning everyone there should have the opportunity to achieve redemption. This evangelical notion of collectivity cohered with socialism. Building community with a collective purpose was nearly impossible in the harsh conditions of rural America. Socialism was the solution for many Oklahomans.

The Christian aspects of Oklahoma socialism, as with agrarianism, were alien to cosmopolitan socialists in northern cities. Urban Marxists, even those raised in religious traditions, thought about socialism in secular terms. In this, they agreed with the foes of the Oklahoma socialists, such as a journalist with close ties to the Oklahoma Democratic Party who described socialism as the political embodiment of atheism and labeled Karl Marx "an infidel Jew." Contrast that with the Oklahoma socialist who, after citing Biblical prophecy about a coming messiah, asked, "Who was this man? His name was Karl Marx, born of Jewish parents at Treve, in the province of the Rhone, May 5, 1818." For most Oklahoma socialists, Jesus and Marx were cut from the same cloth, and socialism was "the real Gospel of Christ." A few evangelical pastors were even elected to local and state positions on the Socialist Party ticket.[26]

The Oklahoma Socialist Party enjoyed a brief golden age between 1910 and 1914. In that short window, it outpaced the Republican Party as the Democratic Party's chief rival in the state. In 1914, Oklahoma Socialists won 175 state and local offices. Democrats responded by enacting a law that required that any person who had moved since the prior election had to reregister to vote in the next one; many Oklahoma socialists were itinerant farmers who lacked awareness of this new requirement and thus failed to reregister. Even those more alert peripatetic socialists struggled to have their votes counted, as the registration system operated by Democratic-appointed bureaucrats was incentivized to commit fraud.

The new voter registration process indeed restricted the Socialist vote after 1914. Yet for Democrats this anti-Socialist measure had the added benefit of repressing the growing number of black voters, many of whom were also nomadic tenant farmers. Democrats further established literacy tests and grandfather clauses, time-honored methods for disenfranchising black people. The Socialist Party officially condemned these moves, and many of its members were racial egalitarians. Most Oklahoma socialists criticized racism because interracial solidarity was the only proven way to defeat the enemies of the working class.

But the Socialist Party of America was not without its white supremacists, in Oklahoma and elsewhere. Racists like Jack London made it their political home. Debs was no white supremacist, yet he argued that accentuating racial issues risked dividing the working class. Debs contended that ending the exploitation of workers would end the exploitation of black people, and not only because most black people were working class. Resolving the Labor Question would also be a strike against white supremacy because working-class freedom would obliterate the familiar excuse for racial animosity given by many white workers, that black people were scabs, used by capitalists as fodder for breaking strikes.

Debs helped guide the Socialist Party away from a specifically anti-racist platform. Yet while Woodrow Wilson hosted a private screening of D. W. Griffith's racist movie *The Birth of a Nation* at the White House, Debs helped picket a theater playing the film in Terre Haute. By 1910, a growing number of socialists wanted the party to explicitly fight for the rights of black people, not only because they believed in the justice of the cause but also because they understood black workers needed more reason to join their movement. Their efforts netted some results. A small but appreciable number of black Americans enlisted in the socialist cause.[27]

The West-Indian-born activist Hubert Harrison became one of the more notable black socialists. Harrison only spent three years as a member of a New York City chapter of the party, from 1911 to 1914. But he made his presence felt as a first-rate thinker in the Marxist tradition, with a twist. Harrison used Marxist analysis to help black people make sense of their peculiar conditions. He contended black people were "more essentially proletarian than any other group," not because of the oppressive power of racism per se but because the structural dynamics of class endowed racism with power. This was true during slavery, since "wherever the system was most profitable, the belief that the slave was not human was strongest." And it remained true in his time, when capitalists used black workers "as a club for the other workers."[28]

The Socialist Party hired Harrison as a speaker soon after he joined in 1911. Party leaders viewed the talented orator as ideal for helping them recruit more black people. Harrison did not let them down. In one inspiring speech after another, earning himself the nickname "Black Socrates," Harrison argued before mostly black audiences that socialism, "the emancipation of the wage slaves," would liberate them from the yoke of a hyperexploitative capitalist system.[29]

Harrison's passion for Marxism outlived his time in the Socialist Party. Loathing the party's tight connection with the conservative AFL and frustrated by its failure to dedicate more resources to recruiting black people, Harrison allied with Wobbly firebrands like Big Bill Haywood and Elizabeth Gurley Flynn. Harrison's local branch suspended him for advocating IWW-style direct action to grow the power of the labor movement. In response, Harrison quit the party. By the 1920s, he had given up on Marxism altogether and embraced black nationalism. Nevertheless, Harrison's intellectual biography demonstrates yet another way in which American socialists thought alongside Marx in the early twentieth century. Race-conscious Marxism has served as a powerful hybrid model for many Marxists since.[30]

In addition to German Wisconsinites, rural Oklahomans, and a small number of black Americans, women also added to the diversity of how American socialists interpreted Marx during the Progressive Era. Lots of women joined the Socialist Party, including eminent figures like Helen Keller. Yet socialists struggled to answer the "woman question" which had hounded American Marxists since the schism in the First International. Were women, especially working-class women, best served by exclusively focusing on working-class empowerment? Or should socialists address issues specific to women? As the movement for women's suffrage gained momentum, many socialists acted to resolve this contradiction. Marx's ideas were never far removed from socialist efforts to get to the bottom of the paradoxes of class and sex.

The matter of women's suffrage was surprisingly tricky for the Socialist Party. On the one hand, supporting the democratic aspirations of half the population was a no-brainer for activists who maintained they wanted to strengthen democracy. Moreover, by officially endorsing women's suffrage, the Socialist Party did right by its many members who were suffragists or supported them. On the other hand, socialists were hesitant to line up with the National American Woman Suffrage Association (NAWSA), which led the charge for suffrage. Aligning with what they deemed a bourgeois group was a surefire way to compromise the socialist struggle for working-class autonomy. This choice was especially troubling to socialists in New York City, where elite suffragists had refused to support the militant, women-led labor movement in the garment industry.[31]

On the question whether to work alongside mainstream suffragists, the Socialist Party of America was neutral, leaving the decision to local chapters. In the ensuing debate, some socialists charted a pragmatic path, contending a temporary alliance was reasonable. The socialist Meta Stern recognized class struggle would ultimately liberate humanity. Yet she also thought a cross-class alliance was justifiable in the fight for women's suffrage. "For it is not a class," she proclaimed, "but a sex—the entire female sex—that is disenfranchised in the United States." Other socialists argued against working with bourgeois feminists. Some even hinted the cause might be unworthy, since women

could never be free in a social order arrayed against the working majority. "The country is governed for the richest, for the corporations,
the bankers, the land speculators, and for the exploiters of labor,"
Helen Keller argued. "The majority of mankind are working people.
So long as their fair demands—the ownership and control of their
livelihoods—are set at naught, we can have neither men's rights nor
women's rights."[32]

Keller was not alone. Elizabeth Gurley Flynn, whose fiery soapbox
speeches earned her rousing nicknames like "Rebel Girl" and "East
Side Joan of Arc," also embodied a steadfast Marxist perspective on
women's rights. Flynn was a democrat to her bones. She thought the
good life was possible only for people who ruled themselves. But because Flynn maintained democracy was utterly incompatible with capitalism, she saw the struggle for socialism as paramount. In 1906, the
sixteen-year-old gave a speech on the streets of New York City, encouraging workers to overthrow capitalism. She was arrested that day, the
first time of many.[33]

Flynn never belonged to the Socialist Party. But she lived a quintessential socialist life. Raised by freethinking Irish radicals and card-
carrying Knights of Labor, Flynn recalled being "conditioned to accept
socialist thinking long before we came into contact with socialism as an
organized movement." Yet come into contact they did. After attending
several lectures by German socialists, Flynn's parents joined the party.
Her father grew obsessed with Marx. Flynn later confessed that her
father should have spent more time job hunting and less time reading
Marx. Yet the young Flynn did not alter her own reading habits. She
began reading Marx at the age of fourteen.[34]

Flynn lacked patience for the Socialist Party. The path to socialism
would not be carved out by "professors, lawyers, doctors, ministers,"
middle-strata professionals who might be enticed by bourgeois allures.
Following Marx, Flynn believed an action-oriented, worker-led movement would forge the socialist future. Hunting for a revolutionary conduit to socialism, she joined the IWW in 1906 and rapidly became one
of its most prominent speakers. Each time she stepped onto the soapbox she spoke a socialist future into existence.[35]

FIGURE 3.2: Elizabeth Gurley Flynn, "East Side Joan of Arc," ca. 1910s.

Flynn consistently rejected the bourgeois feminist position that women needed to enter the workforce to achieve equality. She believed freedom for female workers in a capitalist system would remain elusive because, like their male counterparts, they were first and foremost wage slaves. Women-first feminism also rankled Flynn because it presumed women should support one another in the fight for gender equality regardless of class distinctions. "The sisterhood of women, like the brotherhood of man, is a hollow sham to labor," Flynn declared. "Behind all its smug hypocrisy and sickly sentimentality loom the sinister outlines of class war." She maintained socialists should avoid alliances with the mainstream suffrage movement. Equality for *all* people, including women, will only come when the working class wins its war against capitalism.[36]

Flynn's class-first perspective did not prevent her from acting on behalf of women. Along with Big Bill Haywood and Hubert Harrison, she helped the women of the Lawrence textile factories during the "bread and roses" strike of 1912. At the time, mainstream trade unions largely ignored female workers. Women often had to look to peripheral unions with a Marxist bent, such as the IWW, for support. By acting on their behalf, Flynn and her fellow Wobblies demonstrated their fundamental belief in sexual equality, even while it was underwritten by Marxist class analysis.[37]

The Women's Trade Union League (WTUL) also organized on behalf of women workers, seeking to convince trade unions in the AFL to embrace them as equals. Yet Flynn refused to work alongside the WTUL, condemning it for allying with the AFL, and for promoting a women-first alliance. Flynn insisted that most bad things in life, including sexual inequality, were products of an exploitative class system, or at least made worse by it. Defeating capitalism demanded workers—male and female, black and white, urban and rural—come together as one revolutionary class. In this, Flynn identified with Marx, whom she affectionately described as the "mortal enemy of capitalism."[38]

BOHEMIAN MARX

Despite the varieties of socialism materializing across a large and diverse nation, most early twentieth-century Americans either embraced capitalism or reconciled themselves to its mounting indestructibility. Even as Marx had achieved canonical status in socialist circles, his

future among a broader American public was less certain. If the Socialist Party collapsed, who would be left to read Marx? A group of
New York City intellectuals had an answer. The bohemian radicals of
the Greenwich Village salon scene, most of whom wrote for *The Masses*
magazine, fashioned an imaginative anticapitalist sensibility. In this
they helped create a new audience for a modern American Marx.

Founded in 1911 by the Dutch socialist Piet Vlag, *The Masses* was
originally pitched as an arm of the cooperative movement, an effort by
socialists to set up a noncorporate consumer system. But that movement was too demure for the new generation of radicals who walked
the picket lines alongside militant textile workers, and too stuffy for
the bohemian modernists who rejected the Victorian values of their
parents. Few people subscribed. After Vlag ran out of money in 1912, a
group of parlor radicals, sensing demand for a modern socialist magazine, raised funds to keep *The Masses* alive. They conscripted one of their
own as its editor.[39]

The first issue of *The Masses* edited by Max Eastman, a modish intellectual who had studied philosophy with John Dewey, was published in
December 1912. Eastman commissioned reporters to cover major labor struggles, from Lawrence to Ludlow. He also hired writers, poets,
and artists to explore trendy countercultural topics, from feminism to
psychoanalysis to Marxism. His fellow editor Floyd Dell articulated
the magazine's optimistic ethos: "We can have any kind of bloody
world we want."[40]

The world Eastman wanted was one in which the "free-and-easy
mode of life" that he and his Village friends enjoyed was universally available. Eastman recognized such a future required ridding the world "of
classes and class rule." Only then, as Marx wrote, would it be conceivable for everyone, should they choose, "to hunt in the morning, to fish
in the afternoon, rear cattle in the evening, criticize after dinner." Marx
pointed toward an ideal world because he had reconciled science with
poetry. "It was a clash of impetuosities," Eastman recalled, "the thirst of
extreme ideals and the argumentative clinging to facts, which led me to
seize so joyfully upon Marx's idea of progress through class struggle."[41]

The Masses bestowed America with a version of Marx that was serious and playful at the same time. Eastman and his crew knew how to have fun. They were renowned for liquor-soaked dinner parties. But they did not take revolution lightly. At their boozy gatherings, revelry mixed easily with revolutionary discourse. And this was the point. Helping workers of the world unite did not need to be grim business, at least, not always. One historian wrote that *The Masses* "fought the status quo and advocated a revolution of the working classes—'workers of the world unite'—but did so with high good humor and many a hearty guffaw thrown in."[42]

Revolution and fun went well together. More than that, revolution was the best sort of fun. Eastman later confessed that as editor he "was passionately, not to say licentiously, addicted to revolutionary politics." But what did revolution mean for Eastman? In his words, "a radical democratization of industry and society, made possible by the growth of capitalism, but to be accomplished only when and if the spirit of liberty and rebellion is sufficiently awakened in the classes which are now oppressed." In short, Eastman's vision of revolution was underwritten by Marx.[43]

Eastman claimed he never heard mention of Marx during his years working toward a doctorate in philosophy at Columbia University. He only learned about Marx later, in the Village, when his first wife, Ida Rauh, explained to him why Marx was not on reading lists at elite schools like Columbia. "You don't think the people who own the earth," she asked, "are going to give it up voluntarily, do you?"[44]

As a wizened conservative many years later, Eastman colored his conversion to Marxism with a robust shade of cynicism. Marx was convincing, he recollected, because he had suggested "how to move toward an ideally free and just society when human beings, by and large, are more interested in their own advancement than in freedom and justice." This jaded retelling highlighted Eastman's later distrust of human motivation. Yet he had pinpointed a reason for Marx's growing popularity among people who contemplated for a living. Intellectuals discovered that capitalism was the likeliest thing to prevent them from continuing to earn their keep as thinkers, and they applied this deeply personal concern to everyone else.[45]

Individual rights like freedom of expression had become increasingly sacrosanct in the modern era. Yet because most people spent their lives beholden to what Marx described as "the dull compulsion of economic relations," such rights remained remote for the masses. Eastman turned to Marx because he was the only philosopher seemingly capable of solving the problem of the individual ensnared by necessity. "This man Marx," Eastman wrote, "seemed to offer a scheme for attaining the ideal based on the very facts which make it otherwise unattainable." Marx's theory of history, his notion of how revolutions happened when workers banded together, was a solution to an otherwise incongruous puzzle. The best way to enhance individual freedom was through collective action.[46]

The Masses did not really offer a new perspective on Marx. Rather, it articulated an Americanization of Marx that socialists around the nation had long been formulating in words and deeds. *The Masses* joined the broad American socialist movement, from the Forty-Eighters who waged war against the Slave Power, to the immigrant women who battled textile magnates, in thinking that working-class freedom would help fulfill the promise of democracy. Marx was deemed the best guide for liberating workers.

Nobody in Village circles identified with Marx more than John Reed. Nothing in Reed's early biography suggested he would become a renowned radical. Born into a wealthy Oregon family, he discovered his talents as a writer at Harvard. Reed then sought out the bohemia of the Village and began writing profusely. His early essays, observations of extensive wanderings through teeming immigrant neighborhoods, exhibited a cosmopolitan sensibility. But these works were relatively apolitical. By the time he began writing regularly for *The Masses*, Reed had taken an explicit political turn.

Reed's political transformation was ignited by his experience covering the 1913 Wobbly-organized silk workers strike in Paterson, New Jersey. Outraged by the weavers' meager wages, poor working conditions, and the brutal treatment they received from the police, Reed joined their picket line and was promptly thrown in jail. During his four days behind bars, the striking workers engrossed him with stories of despair, engendering a sympathy for the working class that persisted the rest of his life. With financial support from the wealthy art patron Mabel Dodge, Reed dramatized the strike in a pageant he wrote and produced at Madison Square Garden.[47]

Reed quickly became one of the country's best-known radical writers. He established a reputation for fearlessness in pursuit of a good story. After *Metropolitan Magazine* assigned the intrepid twenty-six-year-old to cover the Mexican Revolution in 1914, Reed mailed home remarkable stories of four months eating, drinking, and fighting alongside the peasants who had taken up arms with Pancho Villa. Never one to merely report on his experiences, Reed warned against American intervention in that revolution. Just as spending time with striking silk workers had made him sympathetic to socialism, embedding himself with revolutionary Mexican peasants made him a committed foe of American imperialism. Mexican peasants had a right to determine the fate of Mexico, Americans did not.[48]

Reed's hatred for the capitalist elite mushroomed while he was reporting on the 1914 miners' strike in Ludlow, Colorado, where immigrant coal miners were battling John D. Rockefeller's Colorado Fuel and Iron Company. Rockefeller's mercenaries infamously burned to death two dozen women and children, infuriating labor unionists around the world. As he had in Paterson and Mexico, Reed noticed a gap between what the capitalist press was reporting about Ludlow and what he had witnessed. This rift pushed Reed to conduct in-depth research, making broader connections between the violent repression of the coal miners and their families, and the larger political economy of the mining industry. The more intense the competition for profits, he discovered, the harsher the working conditions. These writings, in the words of Reed's biographer, "marked his growth as a class-conscious writer not easily satisfied with recording his impressions but who must dig deeper into the play of forces behind them." Reed was becoming a Marxist, not because he was hiding away with a stack of books, but because he was bearing witness to the brutality of American class warfare.[49]

His reporting brought Reed a degree of infamy. In 1914, Walter Lippmann wrote a sneering profile of his Harvard classmate, titled

"Legendary John Reed." In Lippmann's estimation, the only principle that Reed stood for was the right to an adventure. Upsetting bourgeois norms was the grandest of all escapades. "Reed is one of the intractables, to whom the organized monotony and virtue of our civilization are unbearable," Lippmann wrote. "You would have to destroy him to make him fit." Even in his condescension, Lippmann was prophetic. Reed's revolutionary passions did indeed destroy him. But in death he became a legend. The same was true of *The Masses*.[50]

WAR, REVOLUTION, REPRESSION

Born as a radical little magazine at a time of optimism among American socialists, *The Masses* died a short time later, the victim of political repression. American entry into the First World War set off a violent new age of fear and reaction that made socialist agitation a much more dangerous business, even for the gregarious gang at *The Masses*.

President Wilson won a second term in the White House in 1916 on the promise that he would keep the United States out of the Great War which had ensnared the European powers. Nonetheless, the nation lurched toward war, largely owing to its abiding commitment to international trade with warring nations, especially England. On April 6, 1917, the United States declared war on Imperial Germany and the other Central Powers, making its implicit alliance with England and the other Allied nations official.[51]

The government took a two-pronged approach to the inconvenient fact that many Americans opposed involvement. First, Wilson established the Committee on Public Information, which hired tens of thousands of public speakers to lecture on the merits of the war. Second, Congress passed the Espionage Act, which made it illegal to obstruct the war effort, effectively criminalizing protest. The new law sanctioned a nationwide crackdown on dissent and empowered Postmaster General Albert Burleson, who believed radicals were working to overthrow the government, to censor the mail.[52]

The Masses strongly opposed American entry into the Great War.

Reed, in Europe, was skeptical of all sides in what he called a "traders' war." He criticized American progressives like John Dewey and Walter Lippmann who supported the war effort out of belief that it would centralize government power and thus make progressive reform more possible. Writing from the ghastly killing fields, Reed argued that the American worker "would do well to realize that his enemy is not Germany." Rather, his adversary "is that 2% of the people of the United States who own 60% of the national wealth, and are now planning to make a soldier out of him to defend their loot." "We advocate," Reed wrote on behalf of *The Masses* editorial staff, "that the workingman prepare himself against that enemy." Or as Eastman candidly suggested, "Turn the imperialist war into a civil war!"[53]

As a result of *The Masses*' blistering stance, the federal government set out to destroy it. Using its new tools of repression, the post office quit mailing the magazine. The government also charged several of its editors, including Eastman and Dell, with violating the Espionage Act by manufacturing a "conspiracy to obstruct recruiting and enlistment." Unable to distribute the magazine and forced to divert precious funds to mounting a legal defense, Eastman terminated publication of *The Masses* in November 1917.[54]

The timing of the death was uncanny. "We closed up the *Masses* office in November 1917," Eastman remembered, "on the very date, almost, of the Bolshevik revolution in Russia. It was as though we had achieved revolution and could now take a rest!" But even in death, new life was promised. Eastman also recalled that "printed in big type on the back cover of the last issue—remains as true a prophecy as ever was penned: John Reed is in Petrograd. . . . His story of the first proletarian Revolution will be an event in the world's literature."[55]

THE BOLSHEVIKS!

It is difficult to overstate the importance of the Bolshevik Revolution. The astonishing fact of communists taking power in a nation that spanned eleven time zones forever changed how Americans thought about their political worlds. Whereas many socialists rejoiced, many more Americans grew increasingly suspicious of communism, socialism, revolution, and even reform. In the pantheon of menacing outside agitators, the Bolshevik was elevated to public enemy number one.[56]

Just as the Russian Revolution disrupted the American political imagination, it transformed how Americans conceptualized Marx, who was inevitably and forever linked to it. Militant American socialists began looking to Marx on how to model their own revolution. Conservative Americans similarly designated Marx the Bolshevik mastermind, a label that became akin to the mark of Satan.

The coincidence that one of the most celebrated Bolsheviks had lived in New York City in the months prior to the revolution further aroused conservative nightmares about the Russian Revolution spreading to America. Lev Davidovich Bronstein, also known as Leon Trotsky, was born into a wealthy Jewish family in 1879 in the westernmost region of the Russian Empire. By 1896, this brilliant young man had embraced Marxist politics. In 1898, he was arrested for revolutionary activity and exiled to Siberia. After escaping in 1902, Trotsky landed in London where he befriended another forceful Marxist theoretician and revolutionary, Vladimir Ilyich Ulyanov, or Vladimir Lenin, the father of the Bolshevik Revolution. Exiled to Siberia once more following the failed 1905 Russian Revolution, Trotsky escaped yet again, spending the next decade on the run worldwide. On January 13, 1917, Trotsky arrived at New York Harbor.[57]

Trotsky had absconded from war-torn Europe on what he called "a wretched little Spanish boat," along with "deserters, adventurers, speculators, or simply 'undesirables' thrown out of Europe," people headed for the capitalist workshops of North America that helped feed the European war machine. Like countless other immigrants, Trotsky looked upon the bright lights and bustle of New York City with wonder, though of a distinctive sort: "Here I was in New York," he wrote, "city of prose and fantasy, of capitalist automatism, its streets a triumph of cubism, its moral philosophy that of the dollar." For Trotsky, New York City epitomized the paradoxes of capitalism.[58]

From the perspective of local socialists, Leon Trotsky epitomized the revolutionary intellectual. This was especially true for Jewish immigrants from the Russian Empire. Tony Michels writes that for "New York's immigrant Jews, . . . the Russian Revolution began with Trotsky's arrival." During his ten weeks in New York, Trotsky exerted an outsized influence, precisely because the renowned Marxist tapped into the substantial Jewish socialist culture.[59]

Trotsky inserted himself into local politics, tirelessly writing articles and giving lectures for large socialist audiences. Trotsky argued American socialists needed to embrace a more revolutionary outlook. He dismissed the Socialist Party as a party of striving "doctors, lawyers, dentists, engineers." Trotsky begrudgingly admitted his admiration for Debs, but with qualifications: "Although he was a romantic and a preacher, and not at all a politician or leader, he was a sincere revolutionary." And yet Debs "succumbed to the influence of people who were in every respect his inferiors," middle-class strivers who sought to dictate the terms of the Socialist Party.[60]

Russian revolutionaries of the non-Bolshevik variety overthrew Czar Nicholas II in February 1917 and established a Provisional Government on a liberal constitutional foundation. The millions of Jews who had come to the United States from the Russian Empire were exhilarated by the news. Socialists celebrated all over New York City, even packing Madison Square Garden to ring in the new day. Morris Hillquit, Socialist Party mayoral candidate, declared that "the fall of Russian absolutism is the doom of political oppression all over the world." Trotsky gave rousing speeches across the city. Jewish socialists hung on his every word.[61]

Trotsky soon returned to Russia, where he helped overthrow the Provisional Government and establish the Bolshevik regime. The Provisional Government had failed to make life better for most Russians, in large part because it refused to withdraw from the deeply unpopular war. Once the Bolsheviks came to power, they promptly did so. These were monumental world events and Trotsky was a hero to New York City Jewish socialists. As the Hebrew writer Reuven Brainin put it: "Leon Trotsky—a few months ago he lived in a poor apartment not far from my street in the Bronx. He made ten dollars a week working for *Novi Mir*. And, behold, today he is the foreign minister of Russia and he stands at the head of government in that country."[62]

Trotsky also stoked the fever dreams of elites. "Because a disreputable alien—Leon Bronstein, the man who now calls himself Trotzky—can inaugurate a reign of terror from his throne room in the Kremlin, because this lowest of all types known to New York can sleep in the Czar's bed, while hundreds of thousands in Russia are without food or shelter," Attorney General A. Mitchell Palmer asked, "should Americans be swayed by such doctrines?" Floyd Dell put a positive spin on things: "To have risen from the obscure position of a Bronxite to the dizzy height of being some sort of Anarchist Despot gives Trotsky a place in the American heart." This would not be the last time Trotsky's name emerged in American discourse about socialism, communism, revolution, and Marx.[63]

Another person who earned his place in the American heart through the Bolshevik Revolution was John Reed, even though *Ten Days that Shook the World*, his self-described "slice of intensified history" had trouble finding an audience at first. "Here by wide acknowledgement," Reed's biographer wrote, "was a great American journalist, an eyewitness to the greatest story of the time, but not an editor outside the tiny radical press would give him an inch of space."[64]

As it became clear that a revolution was on the cusp in Russia, Reed and Louise Bryant had traveled there as quickly as possible. Reed had long been in training for the moment. Yet the only person willing to give Reed an assignment there was Max Eastman. The very reason *The Masses* was eager to publish Reed's account of Bolshevik Revolution also made it difficult to rely upon. While Reed was in Russia, government censors shut it down.

To make matters worse, upon Reed's homecoming in 1918, customs officials seized his trunk full of notes and ephemera, delaying his ability to write the book by several months. Once he retrieved his materials and quickly completed his work, Reed desperately sought a venue to serialize it. The wide-circulation periodicals that had previously published Reed, including *American Magazine*, *Collier's*, *Saturday Evening Post*, and *Metropolitan Magazine*, kept their distance. It took Eastman's new magazine, *The Liberator*, to publish Reed's account of the Bolshevik Revolution. This proved to be an excellent decision.

As a result of Reed's Russia pieces, circulation for *The Liberator* shot up to 60,000 in its very first month, double the peak number of readers of *The Masses*. Seeing this success, the publishing house Boni & Liveright signed a deal with Reed to publish *Ten Days That Shook the World*.[65]

Eastman knew Reed's story demanded an audience. But more than that, Eastman was a big fan of the Bolshevik Revolution. In this, he was not alone. Eugene Debs proclaimed that "from the crown of my head to the soles of my feet I am Bolshevik, and proud of it." Jewish socialists in New York City were even more emphatic. Abraham Cahan, who helped found the Jewish socialist magazine *The Forward*, argued that "even the most bitter anti-Bolshevik, if he is a socialist, must forget everything and become filled with love for them when he imagines the statue of Karl Marx standing in the Kremlin." In the first issue of *The Liberator*, Eastman wrote that the Russian Revolution was "without doubt the most momentous event in the history of peoples." The conclusion to Reed's story in that first issue expressed this mood of exuberance: "Lenin and Trotsky send through me to the revolutionary proletariat of the world the following message: 'Comrades! Greetings from the first proletariat republic of the world. We call you to arms for the international Socialist revolution.'"[66]

Eastman was favorably disposed to the Bolshevik Revolution because he viewed it as an "enactment of ideas born in the mind of Karl Marx over sixty years before," which gave him hope "that intelligence may play its part in every event." His love of Marx made him appreciate the Bolshevik Revolution, and his appreciation of the Bolshevik revolution made him love Marx even more. Marx's ideas, Eastman wrote, had "survived every test and observation throughout this great and bewildering spasm of history." The fact that history supported Marx was, in his words, "the one thing that has ever happened in the political sciences comparable to the confirmation of the hypotheses of Copernicus and Kepler and Newton in the physical sciences." Reed's Russia essays sanctioned the Bolshevik Revolution, which in turn certified Marx's enduring viability.[67]

Ten Days That Shook the World is not an impartial account of the Russian Revolution. Reed described it as the story of how "one hundred and sixty million of the world's most oppressed peoples suddenly achieved liberty." Nevertheless, he was committed to accuracy. "In the struggle my sympathies were not neutral," Reed admitted. "But in telling the story of those great days I have tried to see events with the eye of a conscientious reporter, interested in setting down the truth."[68]

The book got to the heart of the matter precisely because of Reed's class consciousness. While describing the extremely tense situation prior to the revolution, Reed wrote that "to Americans it is incredible that the class war should develop to such a fever pitch." But Reed listened for things others ignored. He heard, for instance, a Russian industrialist vent his frustration with workers and soldiers who were agitating against the Provisional Government. "Winter was always Russia's best friend," the capitalist declared. "Perhaps now it will rid us of Revolution."[69]

Reed and Bryant were everywhere in the delirious early days of the Bolshevik Revolution, bearing witness to several momentous events. Reed wrote a riveting firsthand account of the raucous Second Congress of the Soviets, where the Mensheviks and other moderate groups abandoned the Bolsheviks on the eve of the revolution, hoping to hold together the coalition that had won the February Revolution. Reed captured a dramatic speech by Trotsky following the walk-out. "All these so-called Socialist compromisers, these frightened Mensheviki," Trotsky spoke, "let them go! They are just so much refuse which will be swept into the garbage-heap of history!"[70]

After the Bolsheviks seized the Winter Palace, Reed and Bryant walked through the jubilant streets of Petrograd. They arrived at a Bolshevik checkpoint alongside a group of Mensheviks who were hoping to get into the palace to make one last stand for the doomed Provisional Government. When the soldiers forbade them passage, the Mensheviks threatened to push through, asking, "What will you do to stop us?" One of the soldiers said, "We will spank you!" Reed's record of this interaction became a classic example of the contempt the newly empowered rank and file held for their erstwhile leaders. New day, indeed.[71]

Ten Days That Shook the Earth served as a corrective to the official US government explanation of the Russian Revolution, that a pitiless cabal had conspired to overthrow the Provisional Government. By this logic, the dramatic events of 1917 were better understood as a coup. In contrast, Reed's exciting narrative was consistent with a Marxist understanding of revolutionary change. Millions of Russian soldiers, workers, and peasants, sick and tired of war, hunger, and endless humiliation, came together to make a revolution. "It was against this background of a whole nation in ferment and disintegration," Reed wrote, "that the pageant of the Rising of the Russian Masses unrolled." Lenin, Trotsky, and the other Bolshevik leaders had the courage and the vision to lead the discontented masses, the temerity to step into the breach.[72]

To confirm that the Russian people had agency in the revolution, Reed noted that everywhere he went people were talking politics, history, philosophy. "For months in Petrograd, and all over Russia, every street-corner was a public tribune." This contradicted the assumptions of many Americans, including a correspondent in Petrograd who awkwardly translated a broadside he had seen posted all over the city: "Proletarians of every country, join yourselves together!" The reporter then expressed surprise that such a powerful slogan had "evolved from the brains of ignorant Slavic peasants."[73]

Russia was alive with frightening new words, some of which had long been common in the international socialist movement: class struggle, imperialism, Karl Marx. Some were new, even to longtime Marxists, such as Bolshevik and Menshevik. All of them became commonplace among everyday Russians after 1917. Events in Russia also transformed discourse in the United States. As Eastman later wrote: "The entire esoteric terminology of the Marxian theory . . . suddenly appeared on the front pages of the metropolitan press," terms such as "expropriation of the capitalist," "dictatorship of the proletariat," "international solidarity," and "resistance of the bourgeoisie."[74]

The Bolshevik Revolution fueled political fears. Eastman had the unenviable task of advancing the revolutionary cause while avoiding the vise-like grip of a government increasingly bent on repression. To help *The Liberator* avoid the fate of *The Masses*, he appeased the postmaster general by toning down its political rhetoric. Eastman thought self-censorship necessary because he understood *The Liberator* to have a higher calling: promoting the Bolshevik Revolution when hardly anyone else in the United States would take up that duty. Eastman was not wrong. The very thing that made *The Liberator* a target for repression was what ratcheted up demand for it. Marxists everywhere, including the Italian communist Antonio Gramsci, relied upon *The Liberator* for news about Russia.[75]

Ten Days That Shook the World and its grand American reception were part and parcel of the enthusiasm socialists had for the Bolshevik Revolution. It was no surprise, then, that Reed concluded his account with a note of hope. "I suddenly realized," Reed wrote, "that the devout Russian people no longer needed priests to pray them into heaven. On earth they were building a kingdom more bright than any heaven had to offer, and for which it was a glory to die." That closing line made Reed a prophet of sorts. Not because he forecasted the course of the Soviet Union, which never approximated anything like heaven on earth. Rather, Reed anticipated the ultimate price he would pay for his devotion.[76]

With sedition charges hanging over his head in America, Reed illegally returned to Russia in 1919 as a delegate to the newly created Third International. After the US government prevented him from returning home, Reed fell ill with typhus and, due to a blockade imposed by the capitalist nations, he was unable to receive proper medical treatment in Russia. Reed died in Moscow on October 17, 1920, five days shy of thirty-three. He was buried at the Kremlin Wall Necropolis, the Soviet Union's national cemetery.

BLACK BOLSHEVIKS

Reed and Eastman were the most visible American supporters of the Bolshevik Revolution. But they were not alone. The black socialists A. Philip Randolph and Chandler Owen, who in 1917 founded an important magazine of their own, *The Messenger*, described the Bolshevik Revolution as "the greatest achievement of the twentieth century."

But while they ended up in the same place as Eastman and Reed, they hailed from very different circumstances.[77]

Randolph and Owen were born in the Jim Crow South. As children, they learned the meaning of power and resistance. As a young boy near Jacksonville, Florida, Randolph said, he had an experience "more revolutionary than sitting down and reading Karl Marx." One night, while he and his brother were protected at home by his mother and her loaded shotgun, his father helped a group of armed men set up a blockade at a local jailhouse to prevent Ku Klux Klansmen from lynching a black man.[78]

Randolph and Owen joined millions of black Southerners in the Great Migration north in the early twentieth century. They landed in Harlem, where they became fast friends as students at the City College of New York (CCNY). While Eastman never encountered Marx at Columbia, Randolph was often assigned Marx at CCNY. Those were the "heady days," Randolph remembered, "when the theories of Marx were receiving a respectable examination in the nation's university classrooms." Marx's ideas had begun to be incorporated into some curricula, especially at urban public schools, and in some disciplines, particularly history. Before long, Randolph recalled, he "began reading Marx as children read *Alice in Wonderland*."[79]

Randolph introduced Marx to Owen, who was immediately hooked. This shared passion stoked their comradeship. Beyond their formal education, they learned even more during their endless informal discussions about socialist theory, history, and politics. They also received an education from the Harlem street-corner lecture circuit. Listening to soapbox speeches by Hubert Harrison, Elizabeth Gurley Flynn, Eugene Debs and more brought them into the world of organized socialism.[80]

Randolph and Owen joined the Socialist Party of America, and with its help founded *The Messenger*, dedicated to the "fight for the economic and intellectual emancipation of the workingman." In the first issue, in November 1917, Randolph and Owen denounced the "capitalist origins" of the Great War, echoing Debs, who was traveling the country declaring that "wars of contending national groups of capitalists are not the concern of the workers."[81]

As "the only magazine of scientific radicalism in the world published by negroes," *The Messenger* often turned its lens on racism. It addressed the national panic in the summer of 1917 following a riot in Houston by black soldiers. *The Messenger* did not endorse criminal behavior, yet it proclaimed the black soldiers' violent response was understandable given the persistent brutality they endured at the hands of police. The magazine also highlighted the hypocrisy of the asymmetrical response to the white soldiers who massacred thirty-nine black people in East St. Louis that same summer. While seventeen black men were hanged for rioting in Houston, the white soldiers in St. Louis were let off the hook.[82]

The Messenger came at the problems of American racism from a Marxist perspective. Randolph and Owen situated violent racial clashes in the United States in the larger global context of war and revolution. Dramatic events on the streets of Houston and St. Louis were distant but tangible echoes of developments on the streets of Petrograd.

Black socialists paid close attention to developments in Russia after 1917. The Bolshevik recognition of minority rights made a dramatic impression on them, especially contrasted with the US government's refusal to prosecute lynchers. The Russian Revolution had ended anti-Jewish pogroms at a time when mob violence against black Americans had reached horrible new heights. *The Messenger* also linked the larger plight of Jews to the struggle for black freedom. "Despised and oppressed through centuries," *The Messenger* editorialized, "Jews know what oppression means, and consequently they have always been tender and sympathetic toward the Negroes who have been their companions in drinking the bitter dregs of race prejudice." More than allies, Jews for Randolph and Owen were the "leaders of the radical movement" that they beseeched black Americans to join.[83]

Mostly distributed in northern cities like New York, Chicago, and Detroit, *The Messenger* was more committed to socialism than any magazine published by black Americans at the time. A student in San Francisco expressed a sense of ideological transformation common among its readers. "For the first time," he wrote, "I was being made aware that the study of society and the movement to change it constituted a

THE MESSENGER

A. PHILIP RANDOLPH   CHANDLER OWEN

Editors and Publishers of The Messenger,
President and Executive Secretary
of The Independent Political
Council respectively:

These intelligent, fearless and far-visioned,
young Negro radicals are making a strenuous
fight to elect Morris Hillquit and the
Socialist ticket in New York City.

FIGURE 3.3: Asa Philip Randolph and Chandler Owen in *The Messenger*, which they founded in 1917.

science that had to be grasped if Black America was ever to retain equal rights." *The Messenger* promoted the science of society first devised by Marx, about how labor power was the key to unlocking a better society for the toiling masses. For Randolph and Owen, this was especially true for black Americans, many of whom were among the most down-and-out members of the working class.[84]

In 1918, Randolph and Owen founded the National Association for the Promotion of Labor Unionism among Negroes. A year later, they helped organize the National Brotherhood of Workers, the era's largest organization of black workers. Both groups were premised on the idea that the fortunes of black people, especially black workers in northern cities, would rise and fall with the fate of the entire working class. Solidarity across racial lines was essential. The National Brotherhood asserted that "the combination of black and white workers will be a powerful lesson to the capitalists of the solidarity of labor." Randolph and Owen wished to reverse the historical purpose to which black workers had been subjected. Their new union "will serve to convert a class of worker, which has been used by the capitalist class to defeat organized labor, into an ardent, class-conscious, intelligent, militant group."[85]

Black militancy surged in this era of war and revolution. Race riots became a feature of American urban life. Reactionaries blamed Marxists for spreading Bolshevik propaganda that provoked black people to riot. Randolph responded that disfranchisement, lynching, and grinding poverty were the "true Bolshevik propaganda," without which "the agitator could not exist." Although this was an argument also made by Teddy Roosevelt, few Americans were open to hearing it out of the mouths of a black Marxist. In the context of the red scare that was enveloping the nation, black socialists were given the same scary title assigned to anyone else seeking revolutionary change: Bolsheviks.[86]

THE PLOT AGAINST AMERICA

There was no shortage of conspiracy theories about the specter of Bolshevism after the Russian Revolution. One posited Bolsheviks were

German agents. It was an open secret that German High Command had helped Lenin travel to Petrograd—undoubtedly hoping he would sow chaos in an enemy nation. They could not have predicted that Lenin's arrival at Finland Station in April 1917 would commence a new phase in the revolution. Yet when the Bolsheviks withdrew Russia from the war, the idea that Lenin was a German agent thrived.[87]

American conspiracy theories involving Bolsheviks focused less on the devious plots of foreign adversaries and more on the work of subversives at home. Bolsheviks were familiar if dangerous figures. They were socialists, anarchists, Wobblies, and, for antisemites, Jews. They were threats to the social fabric, responsible for a less predictable, more frightening world. Powerful reactionaries, in control of federal, state, and local police forces, enacted a reign of repression. The brief era when socialism flowered, when the range of American interpretations of Marx multiplied, ended abruptly. The golden age of American socialism was exterminated by a nascent national security state that was anti-Marxist by design.[88]

Soon after the United States joined the Great War, police raided the offices of antiwar groups. The Espionage Act, signed in 1917 and then made even more repressive in 1918, furnished the government with sweeping powers. Police and parapolice forces targeted socialists, anarchists, pacifists, labor activists, foreign and black radicals, anyone deemed hostile to capitalism, war, or a nebulously defined American way. The IWW, a "degenerate organization" in the words of the assistant attorney general, was the obvious first target. Several IWW offices were raided, trashed, burned to the ground. Wobblies were harassed and imprisoned. Almost two hundred IWW leaders, including Elizabeth Gurley Flynn, were arrested. In Arizona and New Mexico, hundreds were herded onto trains at gunpoint and shipped across state lines. A few were murdered. In 1917, IWW organizer Frank Little was lynched in Butte, Montana. The objective was to put the IWW out of business. In this, the forces of reaction succeeded.[89]

The Wobblies were not alone in their militant opposition to American war efforts. Over two hundred tenant farmers in Oklahoma, radicalized by socialism, launched an insurrection against conscription. Calling the military conflict in Europe "a rich man's war, poor man's fight," these farmers threatened to disrupt the draft by bombing bridges and committing other acts of sabotage. They also planned to walk to Washington, DC, recruiting more poor farmers along the way. Labeled the Green Corn Rebellion because they schemed to expropriate and roast green corn to survive their long trip, the movement was crushed by local authorities before it departed. Hundreds were arrested. The Oklahoma Democratic Party used the Green Corn Rebellion as a pretext for routing socialism. Mob violence escalated. Socialists and Wobblies were harassed, beaten, arrested, tarred and feathered. The Socialist Party of Oklahoma never recovered.[90]

The Socialist Party suffered a similar fate at the national level. When the war broke out initially, the party declared it was premised on "imperialist rivalry between the capitalist powers in Europe." It was easy enough to oppose a war its own nation had not joined. Yet the Socialist Party stuck to its principles when the United States did, announcing itself "unalterably opposed to the system of exploitation and class rule which is upheld and strengthened by military power and sham patriotism." Rank-and-file Socialists echoed the party's position. "The idea that Capitalism can end war," one pronounced, "is about as preposterous as that Satan will usher in the millennium." The Socialist Party's unswerving message that war was an extension of capitalism earned it the admiration of resolute Marxists worldwide. Lenin was particularly impressed. Such consistency also rendered the party an enemy of the state.[91]

As socialists filled up the prisons, an aging Eugene Debs felt compelled to speak up, despite the risk. On June 15, 1918, Debs gave a speech before over a thousand people at Nimisilla Park in Canton, Ohio. He began by noting the hypocrisy of a government "fighting to make democracy safe in the world" while imprisoning people for exercising their "constitutional right of free speech." Debs then endorsed socialism, which taught him to treat "every member of the working class without an exception [as] my comrade." He also defended the Bolsheviks, who "by their incomparable valor and sacrifice added fresh

luster to the fame of the international movement." Deb barely men-
tioned the war, but his words touched a nerve.[92]

Most of those who witnessed Debs in Canton were sympathetic. His
speech received a roaring ovation. Yet not everybody there was friendly
to his message. US Attorney E. S. Wertz had dispatched stenographers
to Canton, and from the transcript they produced Justice Department
officials concluded Debs had not quite crossed the threshold for prosecution. An undiscouraged Wertz charged Debs with ten counts of
violating the Espionage Act anyway. After securing a grand jury indictment, Wertz had Debs thrown in jail. During his trial, Debs defended
himself on the notion that the law he violated was unjust. He attempted
to turn the tables by putting capitalism, war, and the repressive state on
trial "before a court of American citizens." An unconvinced jury found
him guilty.

Before the judge issued a sentence, Debs voiced one of the most famous expressions of dissent in American history, words that came to
represent American socialism at its most idealistic. "While there is a
lower class," he pronounced, "I am in it; while there is a criminal element, I am of it; while there is a soul in prison, I am not free." The judge
was moved by his courage, but leniency was out of the question. He

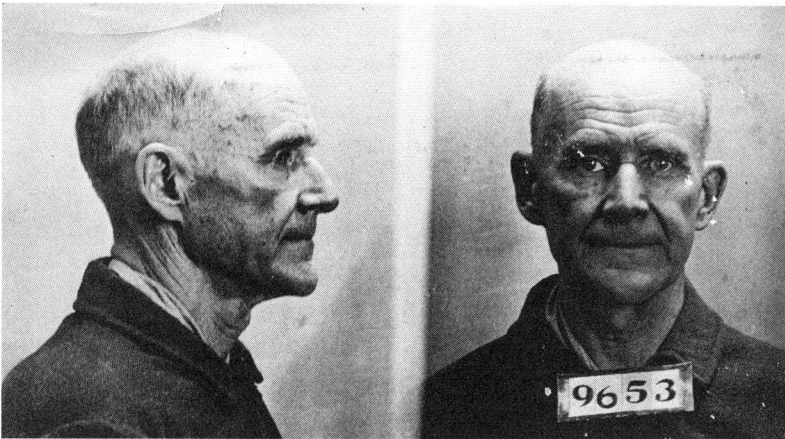

FIGURE 3.4: Eugene V. Debs, Atlanta Federal Penitentiary, 1919.

sentenced Debs to ten years in prison. While there Debs once again ran for president on the Socialist Party ticket in 1920, receiving almost one million votes.[93]

At the time Debs was sentenced to prison, nobody had been acquitted of Espionage Act charges. The editors of *The Masses*, on trial in New York at the same time, should have expected similar results. But the Village bohemians were provided much more latitude to shape the proceedings. Eastman was allowed to give "the jury an education in the principles of international socialism that was more like a postgraduate course at a college than a trial." Morris Hillquit, who served as attorney for the defendants, reflected that "never in the history of American jurisprudence was there a case of this character tried in an American court. It did not seem a trial. It had the appearance of a university for uneducated, unenlightened American citizens." Such grandiose recollections notwithstanding, eleven of twelve jurors were prepared to convict Eastman and his comrades. Luckily for them a single resolute juror refused to believe the socialist intellectuals had committed a crime. The jury was hung.[94]

Frustrated officials arranged another trial, but it turned out much like the first. Eastman worked overtime preparing a defense that doubled as "an exposition of the entire socialist philosophy." He also provided justification for the Socialist Party's "resolution condemning the entrance of the United States into the war." In his speech, widely distributed as a pamphlet under the imprint of *The Liberator*, he told the court that socialism "is a faith which possesses more adherents all over the surface of the earth who acknowledge its name and subscribe to its principles, than any other faith ever had, except those private and mysterious ones that we call religious. It is either the most beautiful and courageous mistake that hundreds of millions of mankind ever made," Eastman continued, "or else it is really the truth that will lead us out of our misery, and anxiety, and poverty, and war, and strife and hatred between classes, into a free and happy world. In either case it deserves your respect." The trial ended in a hung jury once again.[95]

As erudite white men who surely sounded impressive before their peers, Eastman and his crew had a built-in advantage. Most reds ensnared by the state did not fare as well, even after the war. On Armistice Day, with peace finally achieved in Europe, thirteen thousand unlucky American soldiers remained locked in battle with the newly formed Red Army. Wilson had committed troops to northern Russia as part of a western contingent of forces sent to aid counterrevolutionaries bent on reversing the Bolshevik Revolution. Although that effort failed, and although American intervention in Russia was unpopular, the fact that American boys were trading live rounds with Bolsheviks added fuel to the raging fires of the red scare.[96]

Labor militancy also aroused anti-Marxist sentiments. In February 1919, a general strike in Seattle kick-started a wave of strikes nationwide. Many of the sixty thousand workers who threw down their tools in Seattle drew inspiration from the Bolsheviks. They aspired to a Seattle Soviet, or a city run by the working class. Seattle's dockers made a show of solidarity with Russian revolutionaries when they refused to load weapons onto ships headed to Russia. Local elites fought back, of course. Seattle mayor Ole Hanson saw an opportunity to rid the region of labor radicals. Hanson's account of the strike, *Americanism v. Bolshevism*, blamed the entire thing on an ideology that sanctioned "murder, rape, pillage, arson, free love, poverty, want, starvation, filth, slavery, autocracy, suppression, sorrow and Hell on earth."[97]

In an unprecedented time of war and revolution, not to mention the Spanish Flu pandemic that killed millions around the globe, lots of frightened Americans were vulnerable to extravagant claims about a scary foreign ideology. But for many workers committed to organizing for a better life, such rhetoric fell on deaf ears. They were much more concerned about persistent wage suppression, which began as a wartime policy and continued afterward. More than four million workers, twenty percent of the workforce, went on strike in 1919. Of the 3,600 plus strikes that year, the most formidable was the Great Steel Strike in September, of 375,000 steelworkers. Powerful people equated working-class militancy with Bolshevism.[98]

Bolshevism first came to the attention of most Americans in 1917 as a word describing revolutionaries in Russia. By 1919, a Bolshevik was anyone who confronted the interests of capital, or for that matter anyone who challenged accepted wisdom. An astronomer at Columbia University called Albert Einstein's theory of general relativity, about how objects distort space and time, "Bolshevism in physics." Hollywood produced propaganda films about Bolshevism with titles like *Red Viper*. One absurd film, *Bolshevism on Trial*, an adaptation of the novel *Comrades* by Thomas Dixon, who also authored the novel on which *The Birth of a Nation* was based, was about naive young socialists whose dreams of building a utopian commune resulted in a dystopian nightmare.[99]

Bolshevism on Trial made the red scare seem farcical. But the state was deadly serious. In 1917, a Congressional committee was formed to ferret out suspicious Americans. The Overman Committee, named after its chair Lee Overman, was charged with uncovering pro-German subversives. But even before the war ended, the committee became focused on domestic radicalism. Archibald Stevenson, a notorious red hunter, testified that Bolsheviks were German operatives, intent on creating a revolution in the United States. Stevenson submitted a list of nearly two hundred dangerous American reds, including Jane Addams, Eugene Debs, and Elizabeth Gurley Flynn.[100]

The New York state legislature set up a similar committee in 1919 that focused on subversives in New York City. The Lusk Committee, chaired by Clayton Lusk, was the brainchild of Stevenson, who was also its research director. In addition to holding hearings, the Lusk Committee worked closely with police to engineer several high-profile raids. Police ransacked the Russian Soviet Bureau, which had been seeking to convince the United States to officially recognize the new Bolshevik government, and the Rand School of Social Science, founded in 1906 by members of the Socialist Party. Raiders seized reams of documents, forming the basis of a four-thousand-page report edited by Stevenson, titled *Revolutionary Radicalism: Its History, Purpose and Tactics with an Exposition and Discussion of the Steps being Taken and Required to Curb It*.[101]

State repression ticked up considerably in the summer of 1919 when dozens of bombs were mailed to several powerful men, including John D. Rockefeller, J. P. Morgan Jr., and Albert Burleson. One bomb destroyed a wing of Attorney General A. Mitchell Palmer's house.

Prior to that, Palmer's fervor for repressing Marxist revolutionaries had paled in comparison to that of his more ardent underling J. Edgar Hoover, the twenty-two-year-old wunderkind who headed up the War Emergency Division's Alien Enemy Bureau. The attempt on his life changed Palmer's mind about the necessity of state repression.[102]

Congress granted Palmer's request for an additional five hundred thousand dollars to investigate and subdue "ultraradicals or Bolshevists or class-war agitators." Palmer reorganized the Justice Department, founding the General Intelligence Division, also known as the Radical Division, appointing Hoover as head. As a ruthlessly efficient administrator hell-bent on stopping Bolshevism, Hoover compiled a gigantic catalog of thousands of index cards, each one a profile of a radical individual or group.[103]

With Hoover's help, Palmer ordered a series of raids. In the most sweeping one, federal police plundered the New York City offices of the Union of Russian Workers (URW), arresting and deporting 184 members. Along with another sixty-five "alien radicals," they were packed on the USAT *Buford* and shipped to Finland. Most were never charged with a crime.[104]

Once the *Buford* arrived in Finland, the deportees were loaded on a train to the Soviet Union. The press was jubilant. "Just as the sailing of the Ark that Noah built was a pledge for the preservation of the human race, so the sailing of the Soviet Ark is a pledge for the preservation of America," the *New York Evening Journal* reported. The famous anarchist Emma Goldman who, along with her partner Alexander Berkman, was among those deported, remembered the voyage. "For 28 days we were prisoners," she recalled. "Sentries at our cabin doors day and night, sentries on deck during the hour we were daily permitted to breathe the fresh air. Our men comrades were cooped up in dark, damp quarters, wretchedly fed, all of us in complete ignorance of the direction we were to take. Yet our spirits were high. Russia, free, new Russia was before us."[105]

Goldman quickly grew disillusioned with this new Russia. Yet her initial reaction was telling. She and other deportees had originally left the Russian Empire to become American immigrants. Even though their return journey was coerced and unpleasant, being sent to a new and improved homeland was in their eyes a reasonably good outcome. From the perspective of those in power in the United States, all that mattered was that they were gone. Still, the Soviet Ark did not entirely solve the Bolshevik problem.

Powerful men believed Bolshevism had penetrated black political life. In the "Red Summer" of 1919, deadly race riots broke out in cities across the nation. The most lethal ensued in Chicago when a black child who had drifted across the color line at a Lake Michigan beach drowned after angry white men hurled rocks at him from the shore. Two weeks of violence left thirty-eight people dead, over five hundred injured, and over one thousand black people homeless. In response, the *New York Times* ran a story headlined, "Reds Try to Stir Negroes to Revolt," informing readers that "the Bolshevist agitation has been extended among the Negroes." For the *New York Tribune*, the summer of violence confirmed that the "IWW and other agitators . . . financed from Russia . . . are spreading propaganda aimed to breed race hatred." Hoover testified before Congress that "the present attitude of Negro leaders" was due to their association "with such radical organizations as the IWW" and those with "an outspoken advocacy of the Bolsheveki or Soviet doctrine."[106]

Leaders of the Military Intelligence Division assigned a black officer named Walter Loving to figure out why so many black people were defiant. Loving's report rejected the notion that Bolsheviks were to blame and instead identified economic inequality, segregation, police brutality, and lynching as the actual sources of black anger. Unwilling to accept that explanation, no matter how glaringly obvious, government officials stuck with blaming unrest on subversion. This was a common reaction for men conditioned to believe policing was the solution to every social problem. It was easier than seeking genuine answers to pervasive problems like inequality. Better to blame Bolsheviks.[107]

Sometimes federal officials blamed American-born black radicals themselves. Yet they refused to consider that American-born conditions generated black radicalism. Palmer submitted a report to the Senate Judiciary Committee that focused on *The Messenger* as the most dangerous black publication in the nation. Palmer accused Randolph and Owen of fomenting race riots, out of their supposed Bolshevism. The editors leaned into the accusation, writing that they "would be glad to see a Bolshevik government substituted in the South in place of our Bourbon, reactionary, vote stolen misrepresentative Democratic regime."[108]

State repression all but foreclosed upon organized Marxism at the precise moment it began making tentative headway in American political life. This was by design. To be sure, most red baiters, like Hoover, assumed dissident forces indeed threatened the United States. Yet the purveyors of repression had trouble distinguishing between a militant homegrown movement and Bolshevism. In their eyes, perils to capitalism were perils to America. This helps explain how antiradicalism became the animating feature of the national security state once men like Hoover got control of it. From then on, Marx was thought of as anti-American.[109]

THE SECTARIAN ORIGINS OF THE AMERICAN COMMUNIST PARTY

The demise of a broad socialist movement also resulted from self-inflicted wounds. When the state placed socialists in its crosshairs, they would have been wise to circle their wagons. Solidarity was the only realistic defense. Failing to grasp the gravity of their situation, socialists instead fought viciously among themselves. A few short years after the Russian Revolution injected a heavy dose of optimism into the socialist movement, that same event created an almost irreparable rift.

Many American Marxists remained convinced they could replicate the Bolshevik Revolution. Others were circumspect about the prospects of overthrowing the American power structure. The skeptics, who became known as right-wing socialists, maintained American political democracy persisted as a viable conduit for working-class power. In contrast, left-wing socialists were pessimistic about American democracy, which they believed had been permanently corrupted by capitalism, but optimistic about the prospects for revolution.

The rift in the socialist movement came to a head in the summer of

1919. Right-leaning socialists, led by Hillquit, expelled a large group of left-leaners from the Socialist Party. Those purged, most of them Russian and Eastern European immigrants, formed the Communist Party of America. A smaller group of mostly native-born left-wing socialists who had not yet been purged, including John Reed, hoped to take control of the party at its convention in Chicago that summer. After that gambit proved impossible—Hillquit called on police to forcibly remove the leftists—Reed and his comrades founded the Communist Labor Party of America. After three years of struggle over which new communist party would officially represent the United States in the Communist International, or the Comintern, the two combined to create the party that became the Communist Party of the United States of America, or the American Communist Party.[110]

The Socialist Party of America never recovered from the turmoil of those years. It existed well into the twentieth century, but barely. Just as the US government cracked down on the Socialist Party, and just as party leaders purged its most militant and active members, momentum in the world of American Marxism shifted. No longer content to formulate strategy solely with the American working class in mind, the most energetic socialists focused on Russia. "The tremendous prestige of the Russian revolution," the historian Christopher Lasch wrote, "overrode the opposition even of those who supported the revolution but who argued that it was not necessarily the best guide to events in America."[111]

Many socialists had forgotten the hard-won lesson that the choice between reform and revolution did not need to be zero-sum, particularly in America. Reforms that improved life for workers also enhanced their power, thus better positioning their class for revolution. But the immediacy of the Russian Revolution proved too alluring. "For centuries the eyes of the oppressed masses of Europe were turned to the West," a Communist Party newspaper poeticized in 1919. But the future was in the large nation to the East: "In the East is the Red Dawn."[112]

The transition from an inward-focused Socialist Party to an outward-focused Communist Party was not unique to the United States. The historian Eric Hobsbawm wrote that every "Communist Party was the child of two ill-assorted partners, a national left and the October Revolution." In the United States, this partnership was less ill-assorted than elsewhere. In its early stages, many American Communist Party members were immigrants, especially Russian and Eastern European ones. As a result, American Communists were disproportionately attuned to events in Russia. Being Russophiles did not always entail neglecting the goings-on of the American working class. But when many of those workers complied with or even cheered on the repressive aftermath of the war, faith among Marxists in the American working class crumbled. This put American Communists in an awkward position. Without working-class support, igniting an American version of the Bolshevik Revolution, or any kind of Marxist revolution, was a hopeless mission.[113]

THE FIRST COMMUNIST INTELLECTUALS

Some early American Communists strained to solve the puzzle of how to launch a Marxist revolution in an increasingly counterrevolutionary society. Louis Fraina, a Marxist thinker who grew up in an Italian immigrant family deep in the tenements of New York City, made one of the first attempts. In doing so, Fraina expanded the parameters of American Marxism to incorporate an internationalist framework he learned from Marx and Lenin.

Born in 1892, Fraina hated capitalism from a young age. He was only thirteen when his father died, forcing him to quit school and work in a factory to help his family make ends meet. As a militant young worker, Fraina briefly flirted with the Socialist Party, but he never felt entirely comfortable with party culture. Like most Italian leftists, Fraina was a committed atheist and thus felt strange joining a party that appealed to native-born Christians. He also felt removed from Socialists who seemed unserious about Marx. Daniel De Leon's Socialist Labor Party (SLP) was a better home for Fraina, who idolized De Leon as the "Revolution Incarnate."[114]

At the age of seventeen, an SLP newspaper, the *Daily People*, hired

Fraina. Then, as a writer and soapbox speaker, Fraina made a name for himself as a committed but unconventional Marxist. At ease with Marx's published works, Fraina understood that powerful material forces shaped human lives. Yet he also believed people had the collective capacity to change the course of history, and that doing so was imperative for individuals to live free. Fraina's emphasis on collective action made him a Marxist who fit snugly in the SLP, at least until De Leon's death in 1914, after which he left. His attention to individual freedom meant he was also at ease with the bohemian ferment of prewar New York City, and he wrote about modernist culture for the *New Review*. In sum, Fraina rejected the orthodox Marxism of the Second International and its notion that human agency did little to shape the future. He harbored the modernist belief that people had to act. This sensibility set him up nicely to become one of the leading American spokespersons for the Bolshevik Revolution.

Fraina was enamored by the Bolsheviks, who had, in his words, "subjectively introduced the revolutionary epoch of the proletariat." By achieving a society where "Marxism becomes life," the Bolsheviks had given Marxists everywhere a fresh perspective. To express his newfound optimism, Fraina sought out new venues for his writing. In 1917, Fraina took editorial control of the *New International*, run by a Boston-based group of Latvian Marxists. Such language federations formed the bedrock of early American Bolshevism. The Latvian federation took kindly to Fraina's pro-Bolshevik editorial line.[115]

Fraina likewise promoted the Bolshevik Revolution as coeditor of *Class Struggle*, one of the first American outlets to give readers a taste of Lenin, publishing a translation of one of his speeches. Wanting to expose Americans to the full range of Lenin and Trotsky, Fraina also edited and annotated a collection of their works, *The Proletarian Revolution in Russia*. According to James Cannon, fellow charter member of the American Communist Party, Fraina "did more than anybody to explain and popularize the basic program of the Russian Bolsheviks. American Communism owes its first serious interest in theoretical questions primarily to Fraina."[116]

Fraina was more than a popularizer. He was also a first-rate Marxist theorist in his own right. In Cannon's words, Fraina was "the first writer of pioneer American Communism." His 1918 book *Revolutionary Socialism* demonstrated, according to Paul Buhle, "how much intellectual potential American radicals had brought to Bolshevik enthusiasm." *Revolutionary Socialism* delivered a devastating critique of Teddy Roosevelt-style progressivism. Fraina wrote that the concentrated economic power of giant corporations might have seemed efficient to progressives, so long as such companies were held in check by a watchful state. But monopoly capitalism, as Marxists called the economic form that took shape in the early twentieth century, was reliant upon imperial expansion. Fraina termed this new, decidedly unprogressive system "imperialistic State Capitalism."[117]

In making his case, Fraina borrowed heavily from Lenin's 1917 book *Imperialism, the Highest Stage of Capitalism*. Lenin contended that when profits dwindled for firms operating within national markets, they teamed up with banks to invest in underdeveloped economies. Backed by national armies and navies, these newly empowered international cartels reaped huge profits by building empires in Africa, Asia, the Middle East, the Americas. But this form of capitalism led to competition for emerging markets between imperialist nations, which in turn drew them into armed conflict with one another. The First World War was proof of Lenin's thesis.[118]

Fraina built on Lenin to explain that imperialism was a new stage of aggression beyond primitive accumulation. He wrote, "stealing gold, silver, and other precious articles from the natives," who were then exterminated to make room for Europeans, was crucial to the early development of national capitalist economies. But the most powerful imperialist nations of the twentieth century also exported the means of production, in hopes of integrating foreign territories into their economies. "The natives are no longer exterminated to make room for the whites," Fraina wrote, "but are expropriated from the soil and turned into wage-laborers." Non-Europeans had become "human raw material of industry," fodder for "the capitalist mode of production." European workers were sent to slaughter on behalf of imperialists competing to exploit other workers in foreign lands.[119]

The Great War not only killed millions of people. It also scrambled how people perceived their worlds. "Wars, says Marx, are the locomotives of history." In writing those words, the first sentence of *Revolutionary Socialism*, Fraina hoped socialists would realize the unfitness of "the dominant moderate Socialism" in a world where the most powerful capitalists had gone international. Sure, they relied upon the nation-state to enforce the rule of capital to their advantage, which sometimes meant engaging in state-sponsored mass murder, such as when German imperial forces massacred around 75,000 people in what is now Namibia. Yet they imagined their reach spanning the globe. In contrast, most socialists still thought in nationalist terms. In trying to obtain political power within the nation-state, socialist parties abetted the imperialist, warmongering state. Socialists had long dreamed, as Marx had prophesized, that workers of the *world* would gloriously break the chains of exploitation. "Dominant moderate Socialism" had instead consigned workers of the *nation* to ingloriously die for an ignoble cause.[120]

One frustrating thing about socialism's acquiescence to imperialism, Fraina contended, was that such a tragic development happened just as the war demonstrated the supremacy of the proletariat. The most important factor for a nation to successfully wage war was its productive capacity, or the power of its working class. "The proletariat is dominant, economically," Fraina wrote. But labor power, if it was going to reach its full potential and unlock the good life for the masses, needed to be redirected. "All the wealth in the world would shrivel into nothing, and Capitalism collapse, should the proletariat use its economic dominance in its own class interests and against the ruling class." Sadly, workers were being led to embrace—or at least endure—nationalist war. It was no wonder imperialism became the subject Marxists like Lenin and Fraina cared about most during the First World War.[121]

Imperialism, according to Fraina, was propelled by the hunt for low wages and investment opportunities. These twin imperatives had become the engines of capital accumulation. For example, American capitalists had long seen Mexico as a repository of natural resources to be extracted. Yet by the twentieth century, these capitalists began building railroads and factories there. This was a consequential shift. "The export of capital and its investment," Fraina wrote, "immediately develops its ideology—a horror of revolutions, the lamenting of disorders, a Crusader's enthusiasm for making over the country in the image of sacrosanct Capitalism, and the pious desire that the people should live in 'peace' and 'prosperity,' under the domination of a 'superior race' if necessary." American interference in the Mexican Revolution was predicated on this ideology. Fraina convinced the Comintern that because Mexico was a crucially exploited cog in the American Empire, it behooved the Soviet Union to support communist organizing there. In 1921, Fraina moved there himself, helping to organize a Communist Party of Mexico.[122]

Fraina returned to the United States in 1923, having failed to build a communist movement in Mexico. Nor was there much of a movement left to join in the United States. Years of state repression and factionalism had driven the tiny American Communist Party underground. Fraina's writing took on a depressive starkness. The world, he thought, faced a blunt choice: "the collapse of all civilization, or the coming of Socialism." In the shadow of a war of unprecedented horror, and in the wake of a revolution of unmatched significance, this sensibility shaped the Marxist Left. The future would either be socialism or barbarism, as the Marxist philosopher and communist revolutionary Rosa Luxemburg had predicted. Reformism was deluded. Revolution was the only way. And yet, where were the revolutionaries?[123]

A few Marxist revolutionaries emerged from the predominantly black neighborhoods of northern American cities. Harry Haywood, a veteran of the First World War who grew up on the South Side of Chicago, became a dedicated activist after the 1919 race riot there. At first, like many working-class black people of that time, Haywood's politics were black nationalist. But he soon recognized that capitalism was the principal obstacle to black freedom, so he became a socialist. Haywood devoured American socialist masterpieces like *The Iron Heel* and *Ten Days That Shook the World*. He also began digging into Marx and never stopped.[124]

Haywood was enormously inspired by the Russian Revolution. When powerful white people responded to it with hysteria, he decided the revolution must have been a good thing. In 1922, Haywood joined the Chicago chapter of the American Communist Party. He and several of his fellow black communists tried convincing the party to be a force for civil rights. Such efforts would only eventually bear fruit.

In 1925, Haywood traveled to Moscow while evading the suspicious eye of the Bureau of Investigation and its recently appointed director, J. Edgar Hoover. During his five-year stay in the Soviet Union, Haywood studied at the Communist University of the Toilers of the East, a Comintern school designed for revolutionaries from the colonized world, especially Asia. There he explored the Marxist classics as part of a rigorous curriculum that, as he recalled, included "dialectical and historical materialism, the Marxist world concept; the Marxist theory of class struggle as the motive force of human events; the economic doctrines of Marx: value and surplus value, as a key to understanding history by revealing the economic law of motion of modern capitalist societies." Thanks to Soviet efforts to disseminate the gospel of Marx to the world's oppressed peoples, Haywood was molded into one of the foremost American Marxists.[125]

That the Comintern placed Haywood in a university intended for anticolonial revolutionaries was indicative. As oppressed racial minorities hailing from the belly of the beast, black Americans seemed to be obvious candidates to become Communists. Haywood was not the only black American feted by Russian revolutionaries. Bolshevik bigwigs Grigory Zinoviev and Nikolai Bukharin loved having their picture taken with the black American poet Claude McKay, who visited the Soviet Union in 1922.[126]

By building bridges to the nonwhite world, the Comintern facilitated black radical politics in the United States. Many black Americans joined the Communist Party specifically because of the Comintern's formal policy supporting decolonization. Cyril Briggs, founder of the African Blood Brotherhood, had dismissed Marxism as a political philosophy for white people. But when he discovered the Comintern embraced anticolonial struggles in Asia and Africa, Briggs began reading

Marx and joined the Communist Party. Eventually, the Comintern conceptualized a role in the international communist movement for black Americans like the one played by those resisting European colonization. In fact, Haywood was chiefly responsible for shaping the specifics of the Comintern's "black belt thesis," which designated collective black America, especially in the South, as an oppressed nation within a nation, deserving of independence like all nations. Haywood's former black nationalism was put to work for international communism.[127]

Haywood's time in the Soviet Union was eventful. In fact, his entire life as a revolutionary was momentous. In this, he was a lot like another rabble-rousing Marxist, the renowned Wobbly Big Bill Haywood, no relation. In Moscow, Harry met Big Bill, who was in exile, avoiding a prison sentence back home. Harry regularly visited the elder Haywood at his Moscow apartment, because "listening to Big Bill was like a course on the American labor movement." The thing Harry liked most about Big Bill was his hostility toward racism, "which he saw as the mainstay of capitalist domination over the US working class, a continuous brake on labor unity." Big Bill, Harry believed, "obviously understood from his own experience the truth of the Marxian maxim that in the U.S., 'labor in the white skin can never be free as long as in the Black it is branded.'"[128]

Big Bill Haywood succumbed to diabetes in 1928, at the age of fifty-nine. After his body was cremated, half his ashes were shipped back to Chicago for burial at the Haymarket Martyrs' Monument. The other half were buried in the Kremlin Wall Necropolis, alongside John Reed. But Harry Haywood's career as a Marxist revolutionary was just starting. In 1927, he was the first black person admitted to the Lenin School in Moscow. There, he was trained to foment revolution in the United States.

As a key figure in the American Communist Party, Haywood was heavily involved in the party's decision-making process during its heyday in the 1930s. He also worked hard organizing the coal miners of Pennsylvania and West Virginia and the sharecroppers of Alabama. Even after suffering a fate common to countless Communists when he was expelled from the party in the late 1950s, Haywood had done more than enough to earn the nickname "Black Bolshevik," as he titled his autobiography.[129]

The only extraordinary aspect of Haywood's forced departure from the American Communist Party was how late it was. Most Americans in the party either left of their own volition or were purged well before the 1950s. The American Communist Party was the most powerful left-wing political organization in the United States during the 1930s. Yet it also bequeathed a legacy of sectarianism, a less violent cousin of the murderous factionalism that plagued the Soviet Union. Some of the more noteworthy founders departed even before the party emerged from the underground. James Cannon, for instance, was crucial to the early formation of American Communism. Yet by 1928, he was outside the party, looking in.

Cannon was born in 1890 in Rosedale, Kansas, near Kansas City. He had socialistic tendencies from an early age due to his working-class Irish father. Yet Cannon found his way to the world of organized socialism through the printed word. Thanks to a well-worn public library card, he lost himself in novels by Upton Sinclair and Jack London. He also became an avid reader of *Appeal to Reason* and the *International Socialist Review*. At the age of eighteen, Cannon joined the Socialist Party. He also became a regular attendee at a Kansas City Sunday lecture series on Marxism.[130]

In 1911, Cannon joined the IWW. He was twenty-one-years old and his "life was decided," committed to working-class revolution. Cannon traveled the country by rail, performing fiery soapbox speeches while helping striking workers along the way. Like all good Wobblies, he spent time in jail for his actions, and not for the last time.[131]

When the Socialist Party and the IWW arrived at their strategic impasse, Cannon sided with the Wobblies. In his view, the Socialist Party was too committed to its own health, which demanded too much devotion to electoral politics. That focus sapped the revolutionary passions of the most militant socialists, particularly compared with the IWW and its strategy of "organizing the workers and striking and overthrowing the capitalist system." Cannon thought he had things figured out.[132]

But the Russian Revolution shook Cannon to his core. As he put it, "everybody had to start all over again." Much of what Cannon learned about the revolution came from *Ten Days That Shook the World*. Cannon insisted the Russian Revolution "awakened and reeducated" American socialists, making them more inclined to familiarize themselves with Marx. This was also when American Marxists like Fraina grew more influential. After the Bolshevik Revolution, Cannon became an avid reader of Fraina's newspaper, *Class Struggle*.[133]

In addition to intensifying his Marx studies, Cannon rejoined the Socialist Party. This was due to his "revelation" that the Russian Revolution "had been led by a party," "a great blow to the simplistic" IWW notion that "you didn't need any party," just direct action. Cannon teamed up with Reed to try to transform the Socialist Party of America into a revolutionary party like the Bolsheviks. When that failed, the two joined the Communist Labor Party.[134]

Beginning in 1919, Cannon served for a short time as editor of the Communist organ *Worker's World*. One of his first articles violated a court order that forbade support for striking coal miners. Cannon spent sixty days in jail for that transgression, one act amid a widespread government repression that drove a traumatized American communist movement underground for the next decade.[135]

A SPLINTERED LEFT, AN UNDERGROUND MARX

The red scare almost derailed the American Communist Party before it got on track. It also made Americans wary of Marx. With militant working-class movements on the run, with conservatives like Warren Harding and Calvin Coolidge back in control of the state, and with the capitalist economy booming alongside a flourishing consumer culture that provided workers with goods and entertainments like never before, the American reception of Marx flagged during the 1920s. There were exceptions, of course. The iconoclastic conservative thinker Henry Adams saw in Marx a way to criticize modernist sensibilities wrought by capitalism. But for the most part, many of those who read Marx in the 1920s were American Marxists who were taking their cues from the Bolsheviks.[136]

That an American Left decades in the making took on a Bolshevik cast is a bizarre trajectory. What did revolutionaries from Russia, where capitalists were weak and political institutions crumbling, have to offer Marxists in the United States, where capitalists were strong and political institutions stable? In retrospect, not much. At the time, however, the progression seemed normal. The Bolsheviks were, after all, the only Marxists to have successfully conquered the commanding heights of a nation-state.

Bolshevism was never a good fit in the United States. The American proletariat had the potential to take power, even in the face of an unprecedentedly formidable bourgeoisie. The American working class was massive, but workers remained mostly unorganized, their immense ethnic, racial, regional, and ideological diversity difficult to wrangle into solidarity. Organizing the working class required a huge socialist labor movement, not a small vanguard party awaiting an impeccable revolutionary moment.

Sectarian infighting overtook American Marxism in the 1920s. Rampant state repression was a major contributing factor because it provoked paranoia. But American quasi-Bolsheviks did not help matters. Pursuing the correct path to revolution, American communists, like American fundamentalists detailing the correct path to heaven, formed entrenched sects. Worse still, when Bolsheviks in Russia descended into murderous sectarianism themselves, factionalism worsened among American Marxists. Being communists in the world's most powerful capitalist society was hard enough. Minus solidarity, it was nearly impossible.[137]

The most consequential internal strife in the young Soviet Union involved Leon Trotsky, who was cast out by Joseph Stalin in the aftermath of Lenin's death in 1924. He soon led a rival international communist movement, with Trotskyist parties around the world sharing his premise that the Soviet Union had become a "degenerated workers' state" controlled by an authoritarian bureaucracy. Stalinist Russia had betrayed the legacy of Marx. Anti-Stalinist leftists rallied to Trotsky's Fourth International, which sought to replace the Comintern as the true heir to Marx.[138]

Hardly any American Marxists were safe from the devastating sectarian struggles of the 1920s. But few were more central to them than James Cannon. In 1922, Cannon traveled to Moscow, where he spent seven months serving on the presidium of the Comintern, learning from his fellow members, including Bukharin and Zinoviev. In 1925, Cannon and his wife Rose Karsner Cannon helped establish the International Labor Defense (ILD), which conducted legal advocacy at the behest of the American Communist Party and the Comintern. The ILD took on several high-profile cases, such as that of Nicola Sacco and Bartolomeo Vanzetti, Italian anarchists accused of armed robbery and murder. They failed Sacco and Vanzetti, who were executed by the commonwealth of Massachusetts in 1927, yet the ILD had earned the gratitude of leftists around the world. For its legal activism supporting the anti-lynching movement, the ILD also won the appreciation of many black Americans.[139]

In sum, Cannon was a key figure in early American communism and the American Communist Party. In 1928, he attended the Sixth World Congress of the Comintern in Moscow. Trotsky was not there, understandably, but an anti-Stalinist declaration he wrote circulated among attendees, claiming that the Soviet Communist Party was no longer the vanguard. "The banner of Marx and Lenin," Trotsky declared, "is in the hands of the opposition," by which he meant himself and his followers. Cannon found Trotsky convincing and thus was expelled from the American Communist Party.[140]

In 1929, Cannon helped found the first Trotskyist party in the United States, the Communist League of America. He also took on editing duties for the party newspaper, *The Militant*. Cannon proved an effective chaperone of the Trotskyist movement, or what Trotsky took to calling "the American Opposition." Trotsky, like Marx before him, believed Americans would play a crucial role in the forthcoming socialist revolution. "The work to be achieved by the American Opposition has international-historic significance," Trotsky declared, "for in the last historic analysis all the problems of our planet will be decided upon American soil." In 1937, Cannon also organized the Socialist Workers Party as a new vehicle for American Trotskyism.[141]

Cannon remained a Trotskyist until he died in 1974. He was arguably the most significant first-generation American Trotskyist and therefore an important figure in the American reception of Marx. He did not endow the world with a novel analysis of Marx, but Trotskyism would have a tremendous impact on the ways Americans used Marx in the 1930s and after. Cannon himself did leverage Marx for keen insights about a variety of topics, including human nature, that category of knowledge preventing countless Americans from thinking socialism was an actual possibility.[142]

Many Americans, like people elsewhere, have long believed humans are inherently selfish and thus easily corruptible. If children have been naive to this fact it is because they have been sheltered from the harsh realities of life. A proper education would reveal to young people the truth about their nature-bound self-centeredness. More importantly, it would teach that capitalism suits human nature. Reflecting on the appeal of Marxism, Cannon inverted this conventional wisdom. Selfishness, he contended, is "only human nature under a given set of material conditions and a given structure of society."[143]

Cannon believed in the malleability of human nature. He assumed humans were free to change. "Given a different social environment," Cannon said, "I think we'll see different aspects of human nature." In addition to owing this theory to Marx, who wrote that "the whole of history is nothing but the progressive transformation of human nature," Cannon emphasized his indebtedness to Trotsky by paraphrasing the banished Bolshevik's thoughts on how humans had been transformed in the early, revolutionary Soviet Union. "When man learns to conquer and control his own social system and does away with its worst aspects, he'll begin for the first time to turn his attention to the improvement of himself," Cannon said.[144]

Cannon expressed these thoughts in 1974. Even at death's doorstep he remained a true believer in Marx's great cause of liberating the toiling masses and remaking humanity. And yet, Cannon's theory of human nature also owed to his experience as an *American* leftist. During the 1930s, speculation about human pliability blossomed in American political and philosophical discourse. In response to the immense crisis of the Great Depression, left-wing thinkers widened their use of Marx to apply to topics including ideology, culture, literature, and ways of contemplating eternal questions, including about human nature. Even the American Communist Party began to expand beyond its narrow Bolshevism.

In crisis, opportunity was born. As the 1920s crashed into the 1930s, leftists had an unprecedented opportunity to have a say about the future of the United States. Would they be up to the challenge? Thanks to catastrophic economic collapse, Marx was about to be given his widest hearing yet. Would Americans embrace his teachings? Would the United States go the route of the Bolsheviks?

4

PROPHET

The Great Depression

Wherever social injustice rests heaviest upon the worker, wherever he is most completely disinherited, . . . he expresses himself in the creed of the unadulterated and unrevised Marx.

REINHOLD NIEBUHR

Capitalism almost went bust in the 1930s. It was arguably the worst crisis the mighty economic system had known since its advent in the English countryside some three centuries prior. In the United States, the richest and most industrialized nation on the planet, 25 percent of workers were without jobs by 1933. Whole industries were on the brink of destruction. Automobile manufacturers shed over half their workforces. Small farmers, already beleaguered by falling prices and the perils of international competition, were forced off their land and conscripted into the rapidly multiplying armies of the unemployed. Breadlines and soup kitchens popped up to feed the hungry in city after city, where the homeless constructed shanty towns they christened "Hoovervilles" in honor of a president who would not help them. Hobos rode the rails in search of work, sleeping in boxcars and begging for a bite to eat from one stop to the next. Stories of babies dying of hunger in the arms of their mothers were not uncommon. Neither were food riots.[1]

The calamity of the Great Depression left millions of Americans wounded. Cesar Chavez, who grew up to become one of the nation's most powerful labor organizers, remembers the hardships his family suffered. In 1934, when Chavez was six years old, his family's farm in Yuma County, Arizona, was foreclosed on by a local bank owned by a man who had his sights set on the Chavez land. Before the family could load their few precious belongings into their Chevy, a tractor sent by the bank tore down their beloved horse stable.

The Chavez family left Arizona for California, where they became migrant farmworkers. Many years later, Chavez told the oral historian Studs Terkel that his father never stopped longing to call a small patch of land his own again. But the family's precarious existence as migrant pickers crushed this dream, as rapacious labor contractors cheated them time and again. "Anywhere we stopped," Chavez recalled, "there was a labor contractor offering all kinds of jobs and good wages, and we were always deceived by them." Who or what was to blame? Greedy, racist predators, no doubt. But so too were the impersonal forces of international capitalism at fault. Chavez never forgot that lesson.[2]

The horrors of the depression fueled the imagination of indignant American writers. In 1931, the critic Edmund Wilson wrote a moving essay that contrasted the remarkable technological dynamism of American capitalism with the human suffering it caused. He highlighted the dark side by telling the story of a Yugoslavian immigrant millworker who, having lost his job and more thanks to the Depression, had killed himself and his three sons. "Now poor Mrs. Dravic," Wilson wrote, "who yesterday had a family that played trios in the evenings has nothing but four corpses for whom the cheap undertaker has done his best to patch up heads blown out with pointblank pistol shots."[3]

This world of harsh inequality would have been familiar to Karl Marx. In London, he and Jenny had lived in grinding poverty. They and their three young children, with a fourth on the way, packed into a tiny house on the West End, which was populated by refugees from the Irish famine and other similarly miserable creatures. In that wretched section of the richest city in the most industrialized nation in the world, sewage flowed in the streets. Cholera epidemics were commonplace.

Four of the Marxes' eventual seven children died young, victims of sicknesses regularly afflicting the poor. Marx knew who, or rather what, was to blame. He had a name for a system that produced both agony and opulence. Marx also had a theory that made sense of its workings.[4]

In the United States during the Great Depression, countless Americans discovered the name for the system that was to blame for their troubles. Many also learned about the theory of that system advanced by the nineteenth-century bearded philosopher from Trier. Marx toiled at his desk for decades because he dreamed another world was possible. The United States of the 1930s was far removed from that dream, but more Americans than ever began reading, thinking, and writing about Marx. An economic catastrophe of epic proportions had created a golden age for Karl Marx in America.

CAPITALISM CRASHES

When Herbert Hoover was elected president of the United States in 1928, few could have anticipated the stormy four years ahead. After eight years of "normalcy" and laissez-faire approaches to the economy, Hoover thought he would reap the political rewards of prosperity. Enthusiasm for capitalism was boundless. Surely the "roaring twenties" would gently transition into the "thriving thirties." But as the stock market crash of October 1929 made abruptly and painfully clear, Hoover's presidency was not destined for smooth sailing. Neither was capitalism.[5]

The Wall Street Crash of 1929 was unprecedentedly devastating. Billions of dollars were lost in a matter of hours on October 24 and again on October 29 ("Black Tuesday"). Only 25 percent of Americans had a stake in the stock market, but the factors that led to the crash—including falling demand, overproduction, and rampant speculation—combined with its effects, ensured millions felt deep economic pain into the early 1940s.[6]

Because intellectuals and policymakers from a variety of political perspectives came to view the Great Depression as a structural problem endemic to capitalism, it generated an unprecedented degree of macroeconomic analysis. Many such inquiries started with the ideas of the twentieth-century British liberal economist John Maynard Keynes, especially his theory that capitalist economies functioned best when the state engaged in countercyclical fiscal policies. During a recession, the state should spend into a deficit to make up the difference. Some open-minded policymakers grew particularly enamored with this premise because it empowered them to spend money to effectively reverse the economic downturn. But Keynes was not the only economic thinker Americans turned to. Intellectuals and activists, observing that economic inequality might have had something to do with the Great Depression, also looked to Marx for guidance.[7]

A synthesis of the causes of the Great Depression goes roughly as follows. By the late 1920s, due in part to a chilling climate for labor that had its roots in the red scare, wages for most American workers had begun to stagnate, which meant demand fell for automobiles and other mass-produced consumer goods that had powered rapid economic growth. Falling demand led to workers being laid off; workers with even less money bought even fewer things, further depressing demand.[8]

At the same time, in the business-friendly 1920s the richest Americans were accumulating gobs of wealth that they were compelled to invest, sensibly or not. Wild speculation became the norm, especially on the underregulated stock market. Even the biggest banks joined the party. So when a speculative bubble inevitably burst, an already unsound economy came crashing down hard. Legitimate concerns about the banks' solvency resulted in a series of runs on them. Many hundreds of thousands of Americans lost their life savings.

Things were worst in the countryside. The sudden economic catastrophe, alongside chronic problems suffered by most rural Americans, created a perfect storm of deprivation. Small farmers had long been plagued by both falling prices and rising international competition; those challenges had fueled the rise of populism several decades prior. Now, plummeting demand and widespread soil exhaustion made things even harder for millions.[9]

Related to that poor land management, a drought from Texas to the

Dakotas led to debilitating dust storms that made farming impossible. Hundreds of thousands of "Okies" migrated to California in search of agricultural work, but much of what they found there was grossly exploitative. John Steinbeck's 1939 novel *The Grapes of Wrath* detailed the struggles of one such family, the indefatigable Joads. Steinbeck's depiction of capitalism as a pitiless system that ground up little people, and his portrayal of big farmers as rapacious vampires, spurred the Associated Farmers of California to denounce his novel as "communist propaganda."[10]

With the nation's unemployment rate soaring, voters ushered Herbert Hoover out of the White House in resounding fashion. Hoover actually had a history with progressive and humanitarian efforts, such as the food relief programs in Eastern Europe that he administered during the First World War, and the US Food Administration, a classic progressive effort to centralize authority and improve efficiency which he headed up. But Hoover believed in the inevitability of the capitalist business cycle. He assumed the economy would bounce back. Hoover also believed the business class would voluntarily share the pain of a bad economy, and that religious and charitable organizations would provide a safety net for the newly unemployed. None of these assumptions held true, and Hoover came to symbolize elite indifference to the suffering of millions. Franklin Delano Roosevelt easily defeated him in the 1932 presidential election.[11]

Given the unparalleled scope of the economic devastation, it was no wonder the man in charge of the nation fell from power, his legacy forever stained. It was also no wonder more Americans than ever turned to Karl Marx to help them understand their woes. He had, after all, innovated a convincing theory explaining how and why capitalism was always creating crises.

MARX THE PROPHET OF CAPITALISM'S CRISES

The scale and scope of the Great Depression did not catch Marx's epigones entirely unaware. They had been pointing to inescapable blockages in the flow of capital that engendered cycles of boom and bust. They believed these cycles were ever-intensifying, evident in the fact that the scope of the 1930s depression far outstripped the 1893 downturn, which far surpassed the 1873 panic, and so on. For many, a crisis tremendous enough to bring down the whole system seemed inevitable.[12]

In explaining the systemic weaknesses of capitalism, most Marxists began with Marx's theory that the rate of profit tended to fall. Indeed, some Marxist economic thinkers in the 1930s became obsessed with this theory, the fullest elaboration of which was in volume 3 of *Capital*, which Engels had edited from Marx's notes and which Ernest Untermann had translated into English in 1909.[13]

At its most basic, Marx's conception assumed that as rates of profit necessarily fell over time, capitalists would reduce the cost of labor by stifling wages. This response might stem losses in the short term, but it would damage future profits. This vicious feedback loop appeared to have played out during the early 1930s, when masses of workers had their wages slashed or were fired even as capitalist profits plummeted. Marx seemed like a prophet.

Marx had long contemplated the role of crisis in a capitalist economy. The undeniable fact that capitalism was often thrown into crisis—such as in 1857, a panic Marx thought might spark revolutionary energies dormant since the failed Revolutions of 1848—was the key to its eventual demise. Marx believed that a general theory of crisis would make it easier to pinpoint when the time would be ripe for revolution.[14]

In the *Grundrisse: Foundations of the Critique of Political Economy*, a series of notebooks Marx filled in 1857 and 1858 but which went unpublished anywhere until 1939, he called the tendency of the rate of profit to fall "the most important law of political economy," one that political economists from Adam Smith to David Ricardo had tried in vain to decode. By the time he scribbled the notes that went into volume 3 of *Capital*, Marx had more fully fleshed out his thoughts. Indeed, he believed he had worked out the inner mechanism of capitalism's contradictions. He also remained steadfast that these contradictions would usher in the system's downfall. Marx likened his theoretical breakthrough, in a letter to Engels, to "one of the greatest triumphs" in the history of political economy. Marx's ego was on firmer ground than capitalist profits.[15]

How exactly did Marx's theory work? First, he posited the value of "constant capital," his term for the machines of production, would increase by default because capitalists invested in technologies devised to speed up production, a process that later became known as automation. Second, Marx argued the rate of profit would at the same time decrease. When "the same number of workers operate with a constant capital of ever-growing scale," Marx argued, then profits fall because it becomes more expensive to make things.[16]

But what about when fewer workers are required to operate the ever-increasing magnitude of hardware, the very reason for the growing scale of constant capital? Does this not create an equilibrium that allows profits to hold at previous rates? Indeed, what Marx termed "variable capital," meaning the cost of labor, falls in relation to the increase of constant capital, exactly because of automation. As Marx put it: "the growing use of machinery and fixed capital generally enables more raw and ancillary materials to be transformed into products in the same time by the same number of workers, i.e. with less labor."[17]

Since automation was designed precisely to prevent falling profits, what exactly is the process that cut into profits? When Marx layered these trends—the increase in constant capital alongside the decrease in variable capital—upon the labor theory of value, which maintained that only labor could produce new value, he concluded rates of profit must eventually decline. In short, the accumulation process demands labor exploitation. Less labor means less value, which means less profit. This law spoke to general tendencies in capitalism, not to trends in specific firms or even specific industries, because Marx's labor theory of value concerned the accumulation of labor over time. Relative to the buildup of constant capital, labor power would decrease exponentially. The decrease in labor power would mean the precipitous loss of profits, which would lead to crises and, eventually, perhaps, capitalism's demise.

Marx's theory of the falling rate of profit has proven contentious for several reasons. There have been many people, especially in the United States, who have defended capitalism. For some, the idea that capitalism was necessarily headed over a cliff was at best, wishful thinking, at worst, dangerous. There have also been many, often the same people, committed to the notion that capitalism conforms to human nature and is thus the pinnacle of social organization. From this perspective, Marx's theory that capitalism will come to ruin, and that the time of its collapse can be predicted, is absurd. But beyond such ideological objections, Marx's theory has also proven controversial at a conceptual level.[18]

Skeptics, especially those who rejected Marx's labor theory of value, pointed out that labor-saving technologies had balanced out the growth in the expense of machinery, thus stemming profit losses. Marx anticipated this objection when he argued that finding creative ways to cut labor costs "can certainly check the fall in the profit rate, but it cannot cancel it out." Yet he never clarified how or why this would work other than by reference to his labor theory of value, which was unconvincing to critics. Marx's theory of the tendency of the rate of profit to fall seemed unprovable, or at least, not fully conveyed. How, then, could it help make sense of the Great Depression, capitalism's greatest calamity?[19]

The Marxist economist Lewis Corey, previously known as Louis Fraina (he changed his name to distinguish between his past as a communist activist and his future as a public intellectual), had an answer. Corey enriched Marx's theory, making it a workable explanation for the Great Depression, by using it to criticize the idea that state intervention to promote consumerism could rescue capitalism from its tendency to generate crises. In this, Corey argued for Marx's relevance while also criticizing Keynes. (Conservatives, too, doubted Keynes's consumerist remedy.)

Corey worked out his ideas in the early 1930s. At that time, he did not have the benefit of access to Keynes's most important book—namely, *The General Theory of Employment, Interest, and Money*, published in 1936. But Keynes's main ideas about consumption had been in the discourse since the 1920s. To make sense of Marx's theory of the falling rate of profit as an explanation for the Great Depression, Corey examined Keynes's notions about the centrality of consumption in several articles and in his 1934 book *The Decline of American Capitalism*, which the economist Louis Hacker called "a brilliant appendix, drawn entirely from the American experience, to Marx's *Capital*."[20]

Keynes was not the first economist to formulate an overarching scheme about consumption. The theory of underconsumption, or the notion that capitalism only works well when production and consumption levels are roughly equal, has a long history. In volume 2 of *Capital*, Marx offered a stinging criticism of the idea that capitalism reached equilibrium when production and consumption were held in balance. In this, Marx contrasted the theory of underconsumption with his theory of the tendency of the rate of profit to fall. Because labor was the source of all value, and because capitalists, lacking a long-term vision, sought to replace labor with machinery, efforts to stimulate consumption would only temporarily halt capitalism's tendency toward crisis. Production, not consumption, was what mattered. To the notion that propping up consumption was not a long-term solution to the cyclical problems of capitalism, Keynes had a clever response. "In the long run we are all dead."[21]

In rejecting Marx's production-side economics, Keynes rebuffed Marx's labor theory of value. A capitalist economy could maintain profitability, and more importantly for Keynes, stability, so long as the products of capitalism had buyers. Labor was not the source of value upon which the whole edifice rested. The circulation of goods and services was ultimately what mattered. The Great Depression seemed to prove Keynes correct.

We have no idea how Marx would have responded to the challenge of Keynes. Nor do we have any sense of whether or how Marx might have revised his theory of economic crisis in response to the dramatic historical transformations that came after his death. But Lewis Corey's analyses of American capitalism did engage with both men's work.[22]

Corey highlighted the most basic implication of Marx's theory: that efforts to maintain profitability led capitalists to cut labor costs. This was hardly controversial. In fact, since the 1920s American intellectuals had been obsessing about automation, "the displacement of men by machines," as a means of preserving competitiveness. For Corey, the mass layoffs of industrial workers in the 1930s completed this trend. But where Marx's theory got sticky was when he argued profit would continue to fall despite such labor-saving measures. Profits did indeed crumble during the 1930s, but that could easily have been attributed to other factors, especially cratering demand. Thus, any convincing explanation of the economic crisis had to address the role of consumption. This was where Keynes, whom Corey snidely referred to as "the economist of capitalism in extremis," came in handy.[23]

Corey argued that cutting labor costs might have worked in a vacuum, but it weakened consumer power, which also ate into profits. Thus, Keynes's ideas on consumption and aggregate demand allowed Corey to square Marx's attempt to theorize the vicious feedback loops that caused capitalism to tumble from one crisis into another. Corey needed Keynes as a supplement to Marx. Or so it seemed.

Corey thought Marxism allowed him to take consumption *more* seriously than Keynes. He wrote that Keynes, as a "bourgeois economist," fundamentally believed there could be no prosperity, no consumption, without profit. In contrast, Corey thought consumption was independent of profit and, indeed, that consumption could be more widely distributed if it was delinked from profit. Corey argued capitalism, inextricably tied to the profit motive, "is unable to develop freely and fully the conditions of consumption." This in turn meant that "crises and depressions are inherent in the capitalist relations of production, they can be avoided only by the abolition of those relations."[24]

Any solution to capitalism that did not include its abolition was no solution at all. Had Keynes followed his theoretical path to its logical end, he would have concluded capitalism stood no chance. In sum, Corey read Marx through Keynes, and Keynes through Marx, in a way that left Corey optimistic that capitalism was on death's doorstep and that communist revolution was just around the corner. Of course, one did not have to be a Marxist economist to deduce as much. In the 1930s, hundreds of thousands of Americans joined the American Communist Party on the assumption that capitalism was getting what it deserved.

THE ZENITH OF AMERICAN COMMUNISM

When the stock market crashed in 1929, the American Communist Party was a tiny configuration of mostly foreign-born radicals who typically lived in northeastern cities, especially New York City. But during the 1930s, the party rapidly expanded to become the most powerful and significant left-wing organization in the United States.

The chief factor in the Communist Party's swift growth was its sincere commitment to building the labor movement. Marx envisioned the working class as the agent of revolution. The Communist Party endeavored to put that vision into action. A small but growing number of American workers were responsive to the party's revolutionary objectives. Many more welcomed anyone willing to help them achieve more dignified, less desperate lives.[25]

In the early 1930s, Communists worked to unionize some of the most difficult to organize sectors of the American workforce. Communists led noncraft workers, largely ignored by the AFL, including textile workers in North Carolina, lettuce pickers in California, autoworkers in Detroit, miners in Pennsylvania, Ohio, West Virginia, and Kentucky, into strike after strike. Despite a savvy public relations campaign—the party sent prominent intellectuals like Theodore Dreiser and John Dos Passos to "Bloody" Harlan County, Kentucky, ensuring that violent labor action became a cause célèbre—its efforts to mobilize labor power were unsuccessful, at least in the short term. Communist-led unions were forced to disband. Large numbers of striking workers were arrested. Some were killed. But in the long term, the Communist Party's strategy was instructive to the larger labor movement. By organizing workers previously deemed unworthy of unions, Communists established the model that eventually proved triumphant at winning workers a larger share of the nation's immense wealth.[26]

The 1920s had been a low point for working-class militancy. After 1929, strikes grew more frequent and more intense with each year, peaking in 1934, a year of labor upheaval unlike any other. Wave after wave of workers joined picket lines in Toledo, Minneapolis, San Francisco, and elsewhere. Four hundred thousand textile workers went on strike from Maine to Alabama. The historian Mike Davis called 1934 "the highwater mark of the class struggle in modern American history." Picket signs reflected the revolutionary exuberance in the air with a simple, American-themed numerical message: "1776–1865–1934."[27]

This uprising of the working class might not have translated into tangible material gains if a national organizational structure had not developed. None of the assorted unions striking that year could claim to be a nationwide movement with the power necessary to challenge the capitalist class. This void was filled by the Congress of Industrial Organizations (CIO), which formed in 1935 under the leadership of John Lewis of the United Mine Workers. The CIO provided a newly confrontational working class with a vehicle for its collective anger. Communists enlisted in large numbers in the CIO, where they proved themselves as some of the most effective labor organizers.[28]

Unlike the AFL, the CIO expanded the reach of the labor movement beyond craft unionism—a carpenter's union for carpenters, a painter's union for painters, etc. Instead, it organized workers by industry. All workers in the automobile industry, regardless of skill or trade, joined one big autoworker's union. This structure of solidarity endowed unions with more leverage, especially with the threat of a strike. In 1936 and 1937, members of the United Automobile Workers (UAW), a CIO affiliate, shut down the General Motors plant in Flint, Michigan, with a sit-down strike. This collective action resulted in a 5 percent pay increase for autoworkers, a remarkable achievement in a shrunken economy. Even more notable was the legitimacy this successful action conferred upon the UAW, the CIO, and the American Communist Party.[29]

The rise of the CIO, which organized white, black, and brown workers in factories, fields, and mines—almost anywhere workers amassed in an industrial economy—was affirmation of the Marxist idea that class solidarity could move the world. Marx's ideas had gained an implicit place in the American labor ecosystem. With the rise of the American Communist Party, it also became clear that a growing number of Americans more explicitly avowed the wisdom of Marx. "The Communist Party is armed with the teachings of Marx," as it liked to state in its literature.[30]

The role Communists played in the labor movement has sometimes been overshadowed by a lurid fascination with the party's ties to Moscow. Was the party heir to the long-standing American tradition of labor radicalism from the Workies to the Wobblies? Or was it a clandestine cover for a cell of traitors operating at the behest of a foreign enemy? The battles over these two oversimplifications elided what historian Leo P. Ribuffo more accurately described as "the complexity of American Communism."[31]

On the one hand, it was indeed true that American Communist Party leadership took orders from the Comintern, an appendage of the Soviet Communist Party and its general secretary, Joseph Stalin. American Communist Party functionaries, unlike their Soviet counterparts, had no reason to fear death by firing squad. But failure to heed Moscow's directions carried risk, including expulsion from the party. Thus, party leaders tended to comply with orders from abroad, even those they disagreed with.[32]

But a narrow focus on Soviet machinations ignores that American Communist Party objectives were shaped by a persistent struggle between its national leaders, who tended to heed Moscow's orders, and its rank-and-file members, who viewed the party as a vehicle for grassroots activism. The party's role in building the labor movement is the most obvious example of the rank and file dictating its agenda.

Of course, sometimes there was no conflict between Moscow's orders and grassroots priorities. In the early 1930s, the party started to fight racial discrimination in the United States. Inspired by Marx's dictum that "labor in a white skin cannot emancipate itself where it is branded in a black skin," and by black party members like Harry Haywood, many Communists believed overcoming the divisions among the victims of capitalism—like those caused by racism—was key to achieving socialism. Party hierarchy did not need convincing that eradicating racism was a worthy goal since it meshed with the Comintern's "black belt thesis," which designated collective black America an oppressed nation within a nation.[33]

Working-class black Americans did not need help grasping the connection between racism and capitalism. Black sharecroppers certainly appreciated that their lack of civil rights made them more vulnerable to exploitation by large landowners. Likewise, black industrial workers undoubtedly recognized that a racialized division of labor discouraged collective action, thus allowing their bosses to depress wages overall. A. Philip Randolph, who in the 1930s exchanged the nickname "Black Lenin" for "Mr. Black Labor," riffed on Max in saying that "no black worker can be free so long as the white worker is a slave and by the same token, no white worker is certain of security while his black brother is bound."[34]

Some working-class black Americans in the 1930s were responsive to the anticapitalist logic of the American Communist Party, especially once the Party explicitly joined the struggle against racial discrimination. The Party gained even more legitimacy in the eyes of black Americans when it marshaled an international movement in defense of the Scottsboro Boys, nine black teenagers falsely accused of raping a white woman in Alabama. From there, Communists helped organize militant black sharecroppers in Alabama to improve their wretched conditions. They worked with civil rights groups in Los Angeles to desegregate public swimming pools. Communists forged durable bonds of solidarity with black Harlemites by helping them improve local schools, including pressuring the city to build two new schools there. "No socialist organization before or since," according to the historian Mark Naison, "has touched the life of an Afro-American community so profoundly."[35]

In sum, the American Communist Party was regarded as a reliable partner in the fight for black civil rights. Yet massive numbers of black Americans did not join the party. Nor were black Americans chief among Marx devotees. To be sure, there were notable black Marxists in the 1930s, such as the novelist Richard Wright. But mostly, Marx remained an icon for the Eastern European immigrant families, often Jewish, that had flocked to New York City, Chicago, and other large, northern metropolitan hubs. As Vivian Gornick writes about her parents' generation of Jewish immigrants: "The idea of socialist revolution was a dominating strand woven through the rich tapestry of unassimilated Jewish life. When millions of Jews crossed the Atlantic Ocean in the first years of this century, packed in among the pots and pans and ragged clothes were the Talmud, Spinoza, Herzl, and Marx." Although many left-wing Jewish immigrants learned their Marx in the socialist milieu German Americans had created in New York City, those Jewish Americans who joined the Communist Party in the twentieth century considered knowledge of Marx a feature of their identity with almost ancient roots.[36]

Marx's ideas gave Gornick's parents a method for placing their provincial lives "within a context that had world-making properties." Gornick continues: "They were not simply the disinherited of the earth, they were proletarians. They were not a people without a history, they had the Russian Revolution. They were not without a civilizing world view, they had Marxism." Working together to build class consciousness gave poor immigrants in shabby Bronx tenements an identity. "The instrument of consciousness for them was Marx. Marx and the Communist Party and world socialism. Marx was their Socrates, the party was their Plato, world socialism their Athens."[37]

Marx also served as an intellectual gateway for hard-working people beyond northern cities who had never encountered the intoxications of European philosophy. They were often nomads of the west, where populist, socialist, and syndicalist traditions passed down through oral histories and folk songs. One such person, who grew up a dirt-poor vagabond riding the rails of the west before joining the Communist Party in the early 1930s, described "the sheer intellectual joy of reading Marx" for the first time. In Marx, he discovered a deep appreciation for human intelligence, which he compared to "fireworks exploding" in his head. "God, I have never felt so free in my life as I did in those first days when I discovered Marx and the existence of my own mind at the same time." When Communists imagined people waking up to class consciousness, they envisioned them struggling their way through *Capital* in a dingy apartment or dusty tent, after a hard day's work in factory, field, or mine. Marx's magisterial ideas sprang from the pages and affixed themselves in the minds of workers.[38]

The image of working-class Americans reading *Capital* by candlelight might seem overly romantic. But such optimism about working-class reading habits was apiece with the sanguine assumption held by many

Communists that revolution was right around the corner. Anticipating capitalism's demise, and believing that class consciousness mirrored social conditions, the Communist Party maintained that American workers were on the precipice of becoming full-fledged communist revolutionaries.

William Z. Foster, the Communist Party's presidential nominee in 1932, wrote a book that year, *Toward Soviet America*, on the premise that revolution was impending. Among American "workers, farmers, Negroes," Foster maintained, "there are sufficient potential revolutionary forces to put an end to capitalism." He believed that "the deepening capitalist crisis will revolutionize" these groups, and that the Communist Party was positioned to lead them to the promised land. Such expectations were enshrined as Communist Party doctrine during its so-called third period, from 1929 until 1934. During this time, Communists labeled anyone to their right "social fascists," including liberals and socialists. With revolution on the horizon, those advocating mere reform were thwarting it and were thus no better than fascists.[39]

In retrospect, such grandiosity and sectarianism came to seem like a symptom of Communist naivety, or megalomania, or both. But no matter where someone stood on the question whether revolution was imminent, and whether the American people were undergoing ideological transformation in response to the Great Depression, almost everyone interested in these problems turned to Marx.

A MARX FOR AMERICA?

During the 1930s, several notable American intellectuals hid themselves away in libraries, only occasionally joining picket lines or attending party meetings, in an obsessive effort to redefine Marx for America. As Max Shachtman wrote: "There was more writing about Marxism—favorable, though not very perceptive, in many cases—during these years than at any other time in American history." Leaving aside whether such writing was perceptive, one thing is certain: A variety of American thinkers believed that if the genius of Marx could be unlocked—and if it could be made to fit America—all the difficult questions about capitalism and revolution might be answered.[40]

Americans who engaged with Marx in the 1930s often started with the premise that capitalism was on its deathbed, and that the United States, the nation most committed to capitalism, was ideally situated for the transition to socialism. Marx famously theorized that communism had to emerge from capitalism. Capitalism created its own gravediggers—the proletariat—who also happened to be the architects of the future. Marx thus thought socialism might come early to the United States, the first fully realized bourgeois country, where people believed "work is the key to wealth, and wealth the only object of work." Even Marxists who came of age in the shadow of the Bolshevik Revolution, which seemingly disproved the idea that communism had to go through capitalism, since prerevolutionary Russia had been a feudalistic backwater, believed the United States was poised to transition to socialism. The corporate form that had taken root in the United States was the key to this assumption.[41]

Corporations had done more to socialize production than any revolutionary party ever had. If the working class could expropriate those enormous institutions, it would transform a system of socialized production into a system of socialized ownership and socialized control. American Marxists had been making this case for decades. The task seemed straightforward on its face. But powerful vested interests stood in the way, including the state, which worked at the behest of corporations. Were the American people ideologically conditioned to the titanic mission of taking on capitalists and their formidable government agents? Were the toiling masses on the threshold of revolutionary consciousness?[42]

American intellectuals of the Marxist variety, growing in number by the early 1930s, dedicated themselves to closing the gap between revolutionary conditions, which were demonstrable, and revolutionary consciousness, which was lagging. Indeed, the task of forging a Marx for America was seen as the key to unleashing the revolutionary spirit that lurked beneath the surface of working-class consciousness.

This project to Americanize Marx was helped along by those who had long been pushing Marxist ideas in the public square, even during the conservative 1920s. Many of the writers and artists who published with *The Masses* and *The Liberator* continued promoting Marxism well after those magazines went silent. By the 1930s, such Marxist intellectuals had grown more adamant than ever that they had a crucial part to play in making a new American revolution. Their role was to help the American proletariat see their true interests. The Hungarian American artist Hugo Gellert was one key cog.

Like most American socialists, Gellert belligerently opposed American entry into the First World War. He grew even more committed to the antiwar cause, and to Marxist principles more broadly, after his brother was shot dead while imprisoned for refusing to fight in the war. Geller infused his art with these strongly held political beliefs. Throughout the 1920s, his artwork doubled as scathing anticapitalist criticism for *New Masses*, a magazine founded in 1926 and sponsored by the American Communist Party. Gellert believed "being an artist and being a communist are one and the same." He thus joined the party.

To spread the message that art and communism went hand-in-glove, and to pay tribute to his late friend John Reed, Gellert helped found John Reed Clubs, Marxist writing groups with close ties to the Communist Party. "The heroism of the American revolutionary vanguard, the doffed struggles of the workers and farmers in spite of jail, teargas and bullets," Gellert declared, "are the source of a new, vigorous art movement in America worthy of the tradition of John Reed—poet and brilliant journalist—a pioneer in American working class culture, a hero and a martyr of the victorious Russian worker's revolution." Gellert's greatest contribution to this "vigorous new art movement in America" was his 1934 book *Karl Marx's Capital in Lithographs*, which contained excerpts from volume 1 of *Capital* accompanied by sixty-two of Gellert's most inspired illustrations.[43]

The first volume of *Capital* has widely been considered brilliant in its analysis, even by people who have vigorously disagreed with its main thrust. Over the years, many readers have deemed the book beautiful in composition. But plenty of others have found reading *Capital* a rough slog. *Karl Marx's Capital in Lithographs* offered a tempting alternative to

KARL MARX

CAPITAL
IN PICTURES

HUGO
GELLERT

FIGURE 4.1: Hugo Gellert, "Frontispiece," *Capital in Pictures*, 1934.

the long march through the original text. Gellert hoped "that in this abbreviated form the immortal work of Karl Marx will become accessible to the Masses: To the huge army of workers without jobs and farmers without land; to the workers in mills and mines, to all who toil with brain or brawn."[44]

In putting together the book, Gellert selected passages most relevant to the times and sketched illustrations that captured the force of Marx's ideas. Alongside a poignant passage about what Marx termed "primary accumulation," "the expropriation whereby the countryfolk were divorced from the land," Gellert placed a drawing of a distressed peasant woman holding a baby. Although Marx's analysis focused on the centuries-old enclosures in the English countryside that forced peasants off their land and signified the birth of capitalism, these developments persisted into the twentieth century. During the Great Depression such incidents occurred with great frequency in rural

America, as Cesar Chavez discovered firsthand. The photojournalist Dorothea Lange portrayed the trauma of landless labor with her heart-rending 1936 photograph of migrant pea-picker and mother of seven, Florence Owens Thompson. Together, Gellert's sketch and Lange's photograph encapsulated the drama experienced by individuals caught up in sea changes of world-historical consequence.[45]

Another Gellert drawing commented on how capitalists amassed wealth by exploiting the labor of others. In a subsection of *Capital* about the "Purchase and Sale of Labor Power," Gellert did with evocative imagery what Marx had done with sardonic words. Gellert depicted a

FIGURE 4.2: Hugo Gellert, "Primary Accumulation: The Expropriation Whereby the Countryfolk Were Divorced from the Land," *Capital in Pictures*.

FIGURE 4.3: Dorothea Lange, "Migrant Mother," 1936.

capitalist as a literal "Moneybags," Marx's mischievous name for someone with enough cash to purchase labor like it was just another commodity. In contrast, Gellert portrayed the worker as a beaten down,
slavish figure who had no choice but to submit to Moneybags and sell
his labor as a means of survival.[46]

FIGURE 4.4: Hugo Gellert, "Transformation of Money into Capital: Purchase and Sale of Labor Power," *Capital in Pictures.*

Gellert focused the core of his book on Marx's labor theory of value. In this, Gellert's Marx was the labor-centric Marx, the version that carried the most cachet during the Great Depression. In emphasizing that labor is the source of all value and that capital inherently exploits labor, Gellert animated Marx's concept of surplus value. "The rate of surplus value," Marx wrote, "is a precise expression for the degree of the exploitation of labor power by capital, or of the exploitation of the worker by the capitalist." Put another way, a worker might only need to work for, say, six hours to produce value enough to sustain his or her life. But, since the larger system requires workers to work for, say, twelve hours, to be paid enough wages to live, the value equivalent to six hours of work is surplus accumulated by Moneybags. For Marx, then, the working day was a battleground in the class struggle. If workers could compel capitalists to pay them the same wages for fewer hours of labor, that would be a victory. To illuminate this crucial message, Gellert drew a hand manipulating a clock.[47]

Marx's theory of labor value did more than pinpoint a never-ending cycle of exploitation. It also offered a way out. If labor was the source of all value, then labor, organized collectively, could bring capital to its knees. The American labor movement of the 1930s certainly saw things this way. As industry after industry shed costs by reducing wages, firing workers, and breaking unions, often violently, hundreds of thousands joined militant mass labor organizations.

Like most Communists then, Gellert was prone to overestimate the likelihood of revolution. But he was not entirely wrong in asserting that

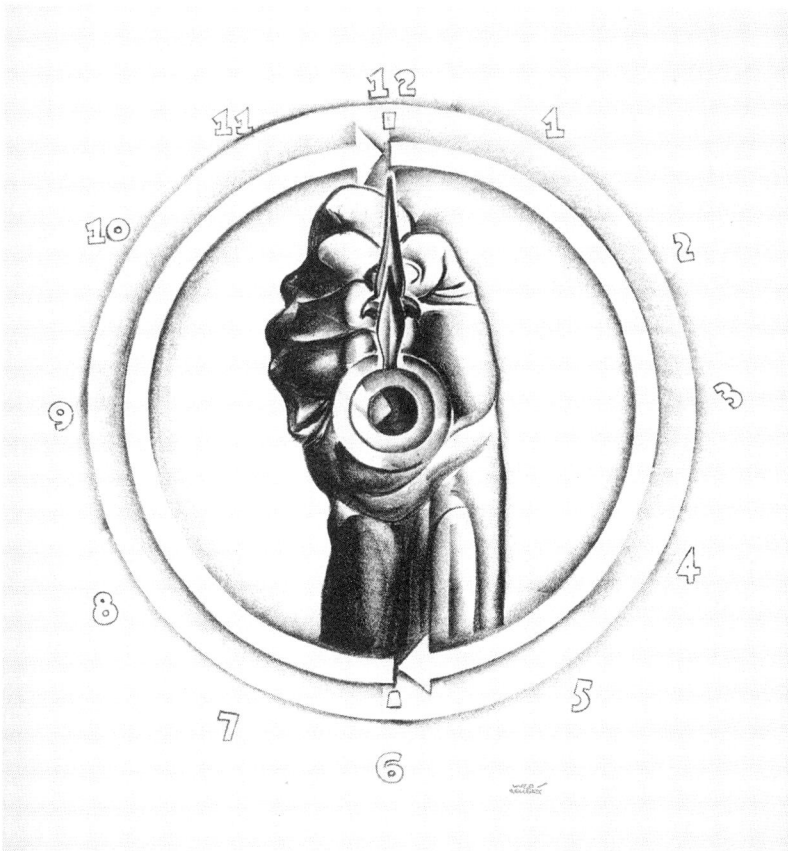

FIGURE 4.5: Hugo Gellert, "Degree of Exploitation of Labor Power," *Capital in Pictures*.

Marx inspired many among the "disinherited of the Earth." "They gain strength and courage and strike out for that higher form of society— the New World: plenty for all, a place in the Sun for everybody."[48]

The person who did arguably more than anyone during the Great Depression to point to this "New World," the thinker who did more than anyone to reconceive Marx for America, was the philosopher Sidney Hook. Just as Corey jostled with Keynes to update Marxian economics as an explanatory scheme for the crisis of capitalism, Hook used the ideas of his teacher John Dewey, the leading theorist of the quintessentially American philosophy known as pragmatism, to renovate Marxian philosophy as a way to think anew about socialist revolution.

A PRAGMATIC MARX

Hook's 1933 book *Towards the Understanding of Karl Marx: A Revolutionary Interpretation*, published on the fiftieth anniversary of Marx's death, was described by a reviewer as "the most significant contribution to Marxism which has as yet appeared in America." Of course, not everyone agreed with this glowing assessment. Max Eastman, also a student of Dewey's who had been rethinking his earlier Marxism and who had an epic public debate with Hook about Marxism in the early 1930s, joked that Hook's book would have been better subtitled, "Sidney Hook's Day-Dream of What Karl Marx Would Have Thought Had He Been a Student of John Dewey."[49]

The American Communist Party demonized Hook for writing a book that interpreted Marx through the lens of Deweyan pragmatism, which they saw as a philosophical apology for the status quo. Party intellectuals likened pragmatism to what they labeled "instrumentalism," a crude term for a crude philosophy about how ideas should be made to work more efficiently regardless of ends, even when those ends were propping up a ruthless status quo. Because he had cleverly mixed pragmatism, a philosophy of the bourgeoisie, with an informed but ultimately bastardized version of Marxism, the party treated Hook's book as contraband. As one party writer put it: "Dr. Hook, who is well-versed in both Marxism and Instrumentalism, is one of the most dangerous neo-revisionists in America. Dewey is less harmful in this respect because he is almost completely ignorant of Marxism. Max Eastman is altogether harmless because he is ignorant of both Marxism and Instrumentalism."[50]

Hook was to gain international fame as an anticommunist during the Cold War. But, like so many of his demographic—born in 1902 to Jewish immigrants in Brooklyn—Hook's first political commitment was to the Socialist Party of Eugene Debs. In the 1920s, he dedicated himself to studying philosophy. Like many serious philosophy students of that era, Hook spent time honing his craft in Berlin. He also studied at the Marx-Engels Institute in Moscow, which helped his makeover into a Marxist theorist. By the early 1930s, as a newly hired professor at New York University, Hook "was almost certainly," in the words of the historian Christopher Phelps, "the only openly Marxist academic philosopher in the United States."[51]

Hook never joined the American Communist Party. But, until 1933 he moved in party circles. His first wife, Carrie Katz, was a party member. In addition, Hook sought to cultivate connections with the party because it was the centrifugal force of Marxism in the era. To be useful to the larger movement, to be taken seriously as a Marxist philosopher, he had to be in the party's good graces. Thus, in 1932 he joined a group of left-wing writers who endorsed the Communist Party's presidential ticket of William Z. Foster, longtime party bigwig, and James W. Ford, the first black American so nominated in the twentieth century. Even after party functionaries panned *Towards the Understanding of Karl Marx*, Hook tried to make nice. But when an article on Soviet education he submitted to the American Communist Party's *Daily Worker* in 1933 was rejected for being too highbrow, Hook wrote to a friend: "Sad days! I guess they don't read *Capital* anymore. The only people I know who are studying Marx these days are people out of the Party." The Communist Party was never as monolithic as its critics have long maintained. Yet, in the early 1930s it withheld its stamp of approval to all but a narrow range of interpretations.[52]

Being a nonmember, even while in the party's orbit, allowed Hook a measure of independence that enriched his eclectic philosophical explorations of Marx. Hook consistently wanted to understand Marx on American terms. But seeking a new angle on Marx did not entail a selective reading of him. Indeed, it seemed nobody in the United States had read more Marx than Hook, especially since his German fluency unlocked texts that had not yet been translated into English. This breadth and depth enabled Hook to take Marx in directions that cut against the grain.

Hook applied insights from overlooked and untranslated texts, such as "Theses on Feuerbach"—eleven short notes from 1845 that outlined the book that became *The German Ideology*—in which Marx argued, in Hook's words, for "a reconstruction of philosophy as a method of approaching the practical problems of men." Hook aligned this with the thinking of Karl Korsch and György Lukács, fellow party heretics who theorized that Marxism was first and foremost a "philosophy of social action." Taken together, these lessons set the stage for Hook's pragmatic, Dewey-inflected Marx.[53]

Invented in the late nineteenth century by a ragtag group of American thinkers, chief among them Charles Sanders Peirce, William James, George Herbert Mead, and Dewey, pragmatism was conceived, in the words of the historian James Kloppenberg, "as a modernist discourse of democratic deliberation in which communities of inquiry tested hypotheses in order to solve problems."[54]

Dewey's chief philosophical contribution to pragmatism was to build on Hegel, by unmasking the long-standing divide between a fixed law of nature and freedom of subjective action as a false dichotomy. Subject and object are not mutually exclusive entities. And yet, Dewey's pragmatism was not hyperrelativist. Truth, so to speak, is possible, but for something to be true, it must be tested, it must be experienced, it must work. Truth is both malleable and grounded. Hook took this lesson to heart and applied it to Marx's ideas, insisting they had to be tested in the context of the American experience. In the process, new truths about Marx, new truths about the American experience, might emerge.[55]

Hook fundamentally agreed with Dewey's epistemology, but he just as vehemently disagreed with his middle-class reformism. Dewey had concluded that collectivism, a trendy term in the 1930s to describe a society of cooperation, was a superior form of modern social organization. But in focusing on reform and education to bring about collectivism, at the expense of revolution, Hook thought Dewey was ignoring his own precepts. If pragmatism was taken to its logical conclusion, Hook maintained, then revolution had to be in play. As he wrote of Dewey: "The only quarrel one can have with him is his failure to appreciate the instrumental value of class struggle rather than class collaboration in effecting the transition from Corporate America to Collective America."

In this way, Hook followed a path blazed by another Dewey student, Randolph Bourne, who in 1917 argued against American entry into the First World War, and against Dewey's support for of it, from the perspective of a pragmatism that appreciated that "vision must constantly outshoot technique." It might have been that revolution was more pragmatic than reform.[56]

As Hook sought to show that Marxism was the only political philosophy up to the pragmatic challenge of solving the crisis of the Great Depression, the Protestant theologian Reinhold Niebuhr invoked Marx to dismiss Dewey's pragmatic approach to politics altogether. Hook and Niebuhr were, in this way, just a few of the many American intellectuals who ruminated on Marx in the 1930s. Both Hook the academic philosopher and Niebuhr the pastor and theologian envisioned a better society for the working masses. But their theories for achieving such a society were at odds. Not incidentally, so too were their perspectives on Marx.[57]

Niebuhr's 1932 book *Moral Man and Immoral Society* offered a quirky perspective on Marx that doubled as a brief against Dewey. Niebuhr also put Marx to work as a cudgel to bludgeon the social gospel, a theological movement closely associated with pragmatism and other reform-based, progressive ideologies. Social Gospelites, a younger Niebuhr among them, assumed better pedagogy could ameliorate social evils. In contrast, an older Niebuhr, who grew cynical after he witnessed the misery capitalism brought to bear on his working-class congregants in Detroit, argued that social evils were manifestations of power. The working class did not need reformers to persuade their bosses to quit exploiting them, and they certainly did not need progressive educators to teach them how to better get along in a capitalist society. They needed power. It was as simple as that.[58]

The American working class needed a less naive, more cynical theory for how to achieve power than that offered by progressives. For this, Niebuhr turned to Marx, who saw morality as a rationalization of class hierarchy, who understood the proletariat had to *take* power from the bourgeoisie. A Marxist framework was consistent with Niebuhr's larger intellectual project. Morality and ethics were reasonable lenses through which to think about individuals. But groups of individuals— societies—had to be considered through the lens of politics. With regards to the working class, inheritors of a world of grinding poverty and exploitation, Niebuhr judged Marx a more sensible guide than Dewey. He wrote that "wherever social injustice rests heaviest upon the worker, wherever he is most completely disinherited . . . he expresses himself in the creed of the unadulterated and unrevised Marx."[59]

Even as Niebuhr appreciated Marx's moral cynicism, as "the antidote which is needed for the toxin of the hypocrisies by which modern society hides its brutalities," he expressed skepticism about Marxist revolution. Marx argued the interests of the working class represented universal human interests. Working-class victory was to be a victory for humanity writ large. "When the proletariat claims the dissolution of the existing order of things," Marx wrote, "it is merely announcing the secret of its own existence, for it is itself the virtual dissolution of the order of things." The coming to power of the proletariat would entail the socialization of the means of production—and private property more generally—and therefore an end to exploitation. "To make the degradation of the proletarian the cause of his ultimate exaltation," Niebuhr wrote, "to find in the very disaster of his social defeat the harbinger of his final victory, and to see in his loss of all property the future of a civilization in which no one will have privileges of property, this is to snatch victory out of defeat in the style of great drama and classical religion."

Despite the appeal of its dramatic telling, Marx's theory of revolution violated Niebuhr's sense of human nature. It is in the nature of humans to form groups, and groups perpetually struggle against one another for power. Can human nature be transformed? Niebuhr had his doubts. "Whether the reorganization of society will reform human nature sufficiently to make an approximation of the ideal possible," he wrote, "is a question which only history can answer, and which sober reason would certainly not answer with as confident an affirmative as the Marxian enthusiast gives." Foreshadowing the tragic sense of realism that later made him famous as America's veritable Cold War theologian, Niebuhr's appreciation of Marx's critical methodology was qualified by his sense that Marx's conclusions defied natural limits.[60]

Niebuhr's lack of faith in the theology that underpinned Marxist revolution should not be mistaken as a lack of faith in the capacity for religious belief to reshape the world. Hook, a secular Jew, also recognized that power when he wrote that "the system of thought associated with Karl Marx differs from all other social theories and methodologies in that it is a fighting philosophy of the greatest mass movement that has swept Europe since the rise of Christianity." But unlike Niebuhr, Hook was a pragmatist. He was more interested in Marx's method than in his conclusions.[61]

In contemplating Marx's usefulness to socialist possibilities in the United States, Hook focused on Marx's "naturalistic, historical and empirical" framework and downplayed his theology of proletarian revolution. More than anything, Marx wanted to account for how things had come to be. To imagine a future devoid of any connection to past and present, unhinged from the material world, was to fantasize alongside metaphysicians, utopianists, millenarians, and romantic daydreamers. The potential of a political project, including revolution, could only be gauged by close attention to powerful historical and social forces that checked the range of possibilities. Marx believed deep structures shaped us to our very cores. Our position in capitalist social relations was crucial in determining the kind of lives we lived, and how we thought about them. And yet Marx, according to Hook, was not a determinist.

One of the long-standing complaints about Marx, lodged by people from a variety of political persuasions, has been that his theory is overly deterministic. Marx left no room for freedom of human action. This criticism shaped Max Eastman's complaint against Hook's interpretation of Marx. For Eastman, no longer a Marxist, Marx's theory of revolution was a "consoling" or "wish-fulfilling" system that failed the test of modern science. "A revolutionary science would study the material world with a view to changing it according to some practical plan," Eastman wrote. "Marx studied the world with a view to making himself believe that it is in process of change according to his plan." Eastman thought Hook, in espousing such an unscientific theory, had betrayed Dewey's pragmatism.[62]

Hook thought Eastman got Marx all wrong. He maintained that for Marx there were no "musts" in history but rather "conditioned probabilities." "Men make their own history," Marx wrote in *The Eighteenth Brumaire*, "but they do not make it as they please; they do not make it under self-selected circumstances, but under circumstances existing already, given and transmitted from the past."

Marxism was a swapping back and forth between historical restraints and human agency. The two went together in any revolutionary philosophy. Those who focused solely on empirical observation, without regard for how the world ought to be, were apologists for the status quo. But those who concentrated entirely on their wishes for the world, without attention to it as it was, were utopian dreamers. Marxism, in the hands of Hook, balanced a lucid understanding of social conditions with a revolutionary desire for a better world. In that balance, a better future could be discerned as a goal. This is what became known as praxis.

Against the idea that Marxism was deterministic, Hook accentuated the action side of Marx that Korsch and Lukács had also highlighted. Hook translated a passage from the "Theses on Feuerbach" in support of the idea that Marxism was a philosophy of social action.

"The materialistic doctrine that men are products of their environment and education, different men products of different environment and education," Marx wrote, "forgets that the environment itself has been changed by man and the educator himself must be educated." As Marx worded this sentiment in *Capital*: "By acting on the external world and changing it, man changes his own nature."[63]

Hook stood opposite Niebuhr in arguing that there is nothing static, nothing final, about being human, since, as Marx said, "the whole of history is nothing but the progressive transformation of human nature." As humans go to work on their social context, both they and it are altered forever. In Hook's hands, far from being deterministic, Marx was profoundly pragmatic, profoundly within an American intellectual tradition going back to Thomas Paine, who famously wrote in 1776 that "we have it in our power to begin the world over again."[64]

Hook's action-oriented Marx, further articulated in his 1936 book *From Hegel to Marx*, stood in emphatic contrast with the dark, deterministic Marx of the anti-Marxist imagination. Yet a fatalistic Marx had shaped a certain orthodox segment of Marxism since the Second International. Orthodox Marxists believed Marx predicted the coming of the good life, and that his prophecy would come true whether they helped it along or not. Hook wrote sneeringly of this perspective. "Socialism is coming! If you welcomed it," he wrote, "well and good—it might come a little sooner. If you did not, it would come anyway—perhaps a little later. In neither case would your attitude make a difference—or much of a difference."[65]

The expectation that socialist revolution was an inevitable byproduct of capitalism was, according to Hook, a misreading of Marx. The old Rhinelander made assumptions about the likelihood of capitalism's demise, but he was also consistently adamant that humans had a say about their future. "It cannot be too strongly insisted upon that Marx did not conceive *Das Kapital* to be a deductive exposition of an objective natural system of political economy," Hook wrote, "but a critical analysis—sociological and historical—of a system which regarded itself as objective." Capitalists and the political economists who studied capitalism were the real determinists, not Marx.[66]

Confusion about Marx's intentions originated with the fact that Marx was influenced by Hegel, who can more easily be seen as a determinist, or with Engels, who assigned too much determinism to Marx's theories when editing the second and third volumes of *Capital*. But more than Hegel or Engels, Hook blamed the German Social Democrats, for whom a deterministic Marx bolstered a reformist agenda from the 1880s through the First World War. Why work outside the system to bring about socialist revolution, a high-risk, low-reward gambit, when socialism was coming into existence regardless? More proximate to Hook's concerns, and coming from a different perspective, the American Communist Party in the 1930s forwarded a deterministic Marx to sustain confidence in its expectations for the coming revolution, and in its self-selected role as its vanguard.

THE PROBLEM OF REVOLUTIONARY CONSCIOUSNESS

Although Hook spent much of the 1930s using Marx to think through the problem of socialist revolution in the capitalist United States, and although he settled on a theory of social action, he failed to solve the dilemma of ideology. There would be no socialist revolution in the United States if Americans did not think of themselves as socialist revolutionaries. Unlike the American Communist Party, Hook was never overly optimistic about the prospects of the American working class developing a revolutionary consciousness.

Hook was not alone in this pessimism. A variety of leftists in the 1930s had the same worry. By mid-decade, even Communists were forced to confront the harsh reality that American workers were not, in fact, morphing into revolutionaries. Communists could not fail to realize that even the economic misery of the Great Depression wasn't enough to transform people into Bolsheviks.

The concern about class consciousness had long been present in Marxist thought. In 1859, Marx wrote that it "is not the consciousness of men that determine their existence, but, conversely, their social existence which determines their consciousness." This single sentence, one of his most cited, was often taken as canon, meaning that a disciple of Marx was to assume that a person's worldview was a direct reflection of their class position. Workers were to recognize themselves as antagonists to capitalism and, under the right conditions, as revolutionaries destined to usher in a more humane existence.[67]

What was novel in the 1930s was the intensity Marxists brought to this topic. The stakes seemed higher than ever. Nobody in the United States focused more on revolutionary ideology in the 1930s than the Marxist impresario V. F. Calverton. Born in Baltimore in 1900, George Goetz began writing under the pseudonym Victor Francis Calverton to evade city officials on the lookout for radical young teachers like himself.

Calverton decided he was a Marxist after reading "Marx's three volumes twice." Marx taught him that humans in capitalist society suffered from the illusion that they were individuals unto themselves instead of social beings, an ideological deception that he believed was the greatest obstacle to human fulfillment. "The world is suffering today," Calverton wrote, "from the Nemesis of the age-long accumulation of its unveracities." In short, a wide gap existed between reality and a collective consciousness gripped by structural untruths, and more so in the United States than anywhere else.[68]

Calverton's main contribution to closing that gap was to publish a little magazine, *Modern Quarterly*, from 1923 until his untimely death in 1940. It became the go-to venue for high-minded leftist discourse. While Calverton wanted the magazine to abet the larger project to Americanize Marx, he invited serious disagreement into its pages. For example, *Modern Quarterly* hosted the renowned debate about Marx between Hook and Eastman.[69]

Like Hook, Calverton read Marx through the lens of American intellectual traditions. He believed socialism was nothing less than a deepening of democracy, even as he tempered expectations about what socialist democracy might look like. "The people," Calverton wrote, "may make a mess of things, but at least they will have made it and not the bankers and industrialists, and it is always better to suffer and die for something you have done yourself than for something that has been done to you." Despite such a seemingly American view of socialism, Alfred Kazin described Calverton as a "remarkably unsubtle Marxist critic." Edmund Wilson, who briefly served in 1934 on the editorial board, demanded, without success, that Calverton remove "Marx" from all editorial statements because "the very labeling of anything as Marxist seems to produce a theological odor."[70]

Calverton never joined the Communist Party. Like Hook, he eventually found himself the target of Communist attacks for minor deviations. But Calverton was indeed a committed Marxist who brought his Marxism to bear on problems of ideology and culture. He believed literature, like all cultural forms, was a direct expression of social forces, part of the superstructure that sat atop the economic base. "Ideals or ideas thus become the result of material conditions, the froth on the stuff of life," Calverton wrote, "but not a distinctive entity." This sociological approach to literature appeared more deterministic than pragmatic, at least on the surface. But Calverton's literary criticism led him to some insightful, even pragmatic thoughts about Marx in the American context.[71]

Calverton first developed his ideas about literature during the "lit wars" of the 1920s. These heated debates about the purpose of literature took place in the shadow of "Proletkult," an institution founded in the Soviet Union to explicitly connect cultural production to the values and aims of revolution. Attention to Soviet cultural developments opened important questions for American critics. Should avant-garde writers and artists persist in pushing formal boundaries without regard for content, "art for art's sake"? Or should their work serve socialism, "art as a class weapon"?[72]

By the early 1930s, most Marxists came out in favor of "art as a class weapon." John Reed Clubs popped up around the country to promote revolutionary literature. Talented writers like Joseph Freeman, Granville Hicks, and Mike Gold transformed *New Masses* into an unapologetic advocate for an American "proletcult." Freeman expressed this mission well in writing, "Communists not only deny that art is something apart from the social structure, they further deny that artists are 'above the battle.'" Gold fired the first shot in the American "lit wars" in 1921, arguing that only working-class writers were positioned to create literature that advanced socialist revolution. All other literature was reactionary. Gold announced he was done with modernist "form-searchers" like Marcel Proust, "the master masturbator of the middle class."[73]

Historian Alan Wald contends Gold, born Itzok Granich on New York's Lower East Side in 1893, did more than any single person in "forging the tradition of proletarian literature as a genre in the United States." "All who came after Gold," Wald writes, "would stand on the shoulders of his legacy." Gold not only advocated for proletcult in the *New Masses*, which he edited from 1928 until 1930, and in the *Daily Worker*, where he had a weekly column titled, "Change the World." He also put his theory into practice with his 1930 semiautobiographical novel *Jews Without Money*, about the horrors of capitalism inflicted upon a working-class Jewish family in New York City.[74]

The protagonist of *Jews Without Money*, a young Gold composite, overcame depression through communism, to which he turned after hearing a fire-breathing soapbox speech by an Elizabeth Gurley Flynn–type figure. In Gold's words, his book and other "proletarian novels" that flourished in the early 1930s were "a fighting art, a Marxist art and frankly a weapon in the class struggle then raging so openly." Proletcult was to be the poetry of the future.[75]

In the 1920s, Gold and Calverton fought on the same sides in the lit wars. In a glowing review of Calverton's 1925 book *The Newer Spirit: A Sociological Criticism of Literature*, Gold asked: "Who else was there with guts and Marxist wisdom to write for American revolutionists?" Calverton returned the favor, consistently praising Gold's work. This bond was shattered in 1932, when the American Communist Party declared Calverton an enemy of the revolution. The *Daily Worker* labeled Calverton a "social fascist" who diluted Marxism with reactionary philosophies such as pragmatism. Calverton's name became something of a trope, a marker of deviation deserving denunciation. The Marxist literary critic Kenneth Burke, after he himself came under attack from Communists, joked that he got his ideas "from Calverton."[76]

The 1932 split between Calverton and Gold ruined an alliance, but it

did not signal a new approach to culture. Rather, it brought old differences to the surface. Calverton had long theorized literature grew out
of social forces, and moreover, that aesthetic greatness was measured
not by political content but rather by how well art spoke to a particular age. Gold had a more didactic view that literature could be judged
only by its potential to advance the revolution. For Gold, nothing had
aesthetic value in and of itself. Calverton was more nuanced in his aesthetic appreciation. Such nuance, Calverton believed, was not a rejection of Marxism but rather a truer reading of Marx.

Calverton's notion that literature was "great" if it genuinely represented the concerns of its era suggested a theory of cultural change.
Due to historical shifts in class relations, all literature eventually outlived its relevance, outdistanced its "greatness." Calverton believed
even Shakespeare was destined to melt into air. He posited that many
of the concerns of the 1930s remained proximate to the concerns of
Shakespeare's time—"the tribulations of a king and the ambitions of a
lord"—which explained why people continued to appreciate the excellence of Shakespeare. American sensibilities in the 1930s were not far
removed from the feudal sensibilities that had fetishized aristocratic
foibles. Building on Marx's aphorism that the past weighed like a nightmare on the brains of the living, Calverton contended people were un-
consciously beset by remnants of previous social arrangements.[77]

Calverton's 1932 magnum opus *The Liberation of American Literature*
applied his theory of cultural lag in systematic fashion. He argued early
American literature was an aesthetic failure because it represented a
narrow slice of American life that looked backward to Europe. Westward expansion changed this, endowing the nation with a literature
that it could authentically call its own. Because the material conditions of westward expansion rewarded "individual initiative, energy,
strength, courage, and a willingness to work rather than a willingness
to live on the work of others," the ideology of individualism gained, in
Calverton's words, "a foothold that it never acquired in any other country." Thanks to the social forces of the American west, individualism
became a civil religion, as expressed in literature.[78]

The literature of the American West was decidedly nonrevolutionary. Gold found nothing useful in it. Neither did Calverton rest his political hopes in it. But Calverton, unlike Gold, felt that a writer like Mark Twain could be appreciated precisely because his words expressed a zeitgeist. This sociological theory of literature was also a way to gauge the political temperature. Calverton contended literature in the 1930s America revealed that "proletarian ideology had not wedged its way far enough into the mind of the masses to develop a cultural force." If American literature was any indication, the masses were nowhere near ready for revolution. This was the type of thinking that led the Communist Party to excommunicate Calverton.[79]

Calverton's literary theory evolved alongside his conception of Marxism. In contrast with one of his correspondents, who attacked "the Marxian approach for being a religious-minded, stereotyped, authoritarian affair," Calverton described Marxism as a "dynamic realistic method which is tested every day in the field of social fact." Marxism of this sort, consistent with Hook's pragmatic Marxism, was perfect for the project of transforming, in the words of the *Modern Quarterly* mission statement, "radical action from something foreign into terms of the American experience." In practice, this meant Calverton had tired of predicting revolution in an ideologically unprepared nation.[80]

Even though conditions were objectively ripe for socialist revolution, too many Americans remained blinded by the fog of individualism. American workers, Calverton wrote, thought "of themselves as potential capitalists rather than inevitable proletarians." In essence, Calverton posited a theory of American exceptionalism, following in the footsteps of countless left-wing thinkers who have long wondered, alongside Werner Sombart, "why is there no socialism in the United States?" For Calverton, the answer was found in ideology—the lack of revolutionary consciousness. The time was *not* ripe for socialist revolution.[81]

The autodidact Kenneth Burke, one of the most influential Marxist literary critics in the 1930s, was, like Calverton, a proletcult skeptic who eventually found himself out of favor with the Communist Party. Yet Burke spent the decade industriously developing a Marxist theory of ideology that was meant to help overcome the barriers to socialist revolution. He wanted to understand not only how people came to believe things, but also how their beliefs might be transformed.[82]

In his breakthrough 1935 book *Permanence and Change*, which the historian Michael Denning describes as "one of the classics of western Marxism," Burke wrote that "the mere fact that something is to a man's interest is no guaranty that he will be interested in it." For example, most Americans ignored proletarian literature and instead read escapist fiction. To this problem Marx was not exactly a guide, since he "tended to confuse the is and ought to be, so that we sometimes feel that class consciousness is inevitable, and at other times feel that it must be coached." But the problem was not just Marx. For Burke, such confusion was embedded in the very logic of political consciousness. Did our ideas emerge organically from our social situation, or did we need to be taught how to think? Burke believed there was a place for pedagogy. "Class morality may rise spontaneously," he wrote, "but class-consciousness must be *taught* by accurate appeal to the class morality." Intellectuals had a role in the revolution after all.[83]

In a 1935 lecture, Burke declared that "the people" ought to be adopted as the essential symbol of revolutionary agency. He believed the term would be politically potent in a country that had a long history of referring to those in need of political redress as "the people." The Communist Party, which in the early 1930s had anointed "workers" or "the masses" the subjects of revolution, harshly rejected Burke's suggestion. Rather than clarifying the lines of class struggle, "the people" clouded them. But Burke believed terms had different meanings in different contexts. In his 1937 book *Attitudes Toward History*, Burke argued political symbols were often stolen "back and forth" and took on new meanings as "frames of acceptance" shifted.[84]

Burke believed Marx had laid the foundations for a vast new frame of reference. Marx opened new ideological terrain that allowed people to imagine a broader framework by "organizing the individual mind to confront a present imperfect world by the coordinates of a subsequent better world." Of course, new coordinates did not register with everyone equally. "Capitalism shouted to Marx until the annoyance gave him a diseased liver," Burke wrote, "but it seems to sing a cradle song

for some." In other words, not everyone had developed a properly revolutionary class consciousness.

The problem of false consciousness was one that Burke believed
writers, poets, and educators could solve. "If we are to revise the productive and the distributive patterns of our economy to suit our sound-
est desires, rather than attempting to revise our desires until they suit
the productive and distributive patterns," he wrote, "it would surely be
in the region of poetry that the 'concentration point' of human desires
should be found." For Burke, poetry was not merely a literary form. It
was something that could be expressed in political actions. Burke believed communism was an expression of poetry in that "we must realize the highly humanistic or poetic nature of its fundamental criteria."[85]

Why did so many Marxist thinkers exert so much energy on culture
in general and literature in particular, especially since Marxists were
known to believe cultural expression was merely window dressing for
what Marx described as the "dull compulsion of the economic"? Perhaps they participated in knock-down, drag-out fights over "the froth
on the stuff of life" because Marxism relied upon the working class
as revolutionary subject. Intellectuals, rarely categorized as working
class, were often insecure about their role. But more important, Marxist intellectuals were forced to reckon with the empirical fact that the
working class lacked revolutionary consciousness despite seemingly
revolutionary conditions. Either there was something wrong with
their theory, or there was something wrong with the working class.

Many Marxist intellectuals concluded their theory was wrong, and,
as we shall see, ditched Marxism. But for others, including Calverton and Burke, the chasm between objectively revolutionary conditions and working-class consciousness became an intellectual problem. Their efforts to solve it led them to hybrid cultural theories that
melded Marx with American intellectual traditions. Burke focused on
the power of language. Calverton, editor of the *Anthology of American
Negro Literature*, turned his attention to African American thought and
culture.

Calverton contended the contributions of black thinkers "constitute
a large part of whatever claim America can make to originality in its

cultural history." Such ingenuity, he maintained, was the product of a culture that emerged from the unique historical context of American slavery. Calverton came to think Marxism might only take root in the United States if it meshed with black cultural forms.[86]

MARX AND BLACK HISTORY

Two of the most original thinkers in American intellectual history were black men who wrote masterpieces of Marxist historical scholarship in the 1930s: W. E. B. Du Bois, author of *Black Reconstruction in America*, published in 1935; and C. L. R. James, who wrote *The Black Jacobins: Toussaint L'Ouverture and the San Domingo Revolution*, published in 1938. Both books were about race, class, slavery, capitalism, and revolution, and were forged with comparable purposes. Du Bois and James wanted their historical insights about revolutions past to speak to revolutions future.[87]

Du Bois, the first black American to receive a PhD from Harvard, author of the landmark book *The Souls of Black Folk* (1903), and founder of the National Association for the Advancement of Colored People (NAACP) in 1909, wished for his trailblazing analysis of the Civil War and Reconstruction to inform the coming movement for black rights in the United States. James, a Trinidadian living in London when he wrote *Black Jacobins* before moving to the United States, where he helped lead various Marxist groups until he was deported in 1953, hoped his remarkable inquiry into the Haitian Revolution would speak to the emerging anticolonial movements in Africa.[88]

Both Du Bois and James wrote with Marx on their minds. *Black Reconstruction* and *The Black Jacobins* were groundbreaking at least in part for their Marxism, however eclectic. Marx and the Marxist tradition helped Du Bois and James achieve remarkable historiographical accomplishments. But Du Bois and James also expanded upon Marx and the Marxist tradition in ways that gave readers a new understanding of capitalism, one that more fully accounted for the plunders of slavery, colonialism, and genocide, what Marx called "primitive accumulation."[89]

The Communist Manifesto mostly focused on capitalism as a system upending European feudalism. But Marx also thought of capitalism as a globalizing system. He often extended his analysis of capitalism beyond Europe. In *Capital*, when seeking to understand the rise of industrial capitalism, Marx wrote: "The discovery of gold and silver in America, the extirpation, enslavement and entombment in mines of the indigenous population of that continent, the beginnings of the conquest and plunder of India, and the conversion of Africa into a preserve for the commercial hunting of blackskins, are all things which characterize the dawn of an era of capitalist production. These idyllic proceedings are the chief moments of primitive accumulation."

Focusing on slavery and race, Marx conceptualized capitalism as a brutal imperialist system reshaping the planet. He thus anticipated the analytical turn made by Du Bois and James. But Marx also argued that as capitalism expanded its reach across the globe it would render slavery and other forms of primitive accumulation to the dustbins of history. Capitalism for Marx was at once both horrible and progressive. This paradox was evident in Marx's Civil War writings.[90]

For Marx, the United States represented the forces of capitalism, which meant that capitalism was progressive insofar as it was attached to the destruction of American slavery. Not only evil in and of itself, slavery was also bad because it inhibited the expansion of a capitalist labor system and the related development of socialist consciousness among the working class. If Marx was limited in his consideration of the Civil War in relation to capitalism, it was because he barely accounted for the role of newly freed black people. Marx did argue the enslaved were ultimately responsible for making the Civil War into a revolutionary war for liberation. He might have assumed the formerly enslaved would take their rightful place alongside the white industrial working class as heirs to revolution. But he failed to spell this out and thus left a lot open to interpretation. Into this void came Du Bois.[91]

Black Reconstruction in America amended US history in several ways.

FIGURE 4.6: W. E. B. Du Bois at the grave of Karl Marx, Highgate Cemetery, London, September 1958.

Most obviously, in his effort to transform how people thought about the Civil War and Reconstruction, in telling his story "as though Negroes were ordinary human beings," Du Bois ran headlong into a generation of white historians known as the Dunning School, after the Columbia University professor William Archibald Dunning. Those historians posited Reconstruction as the most calamitous and corrupt period in the nation's history because imperialistic Radical Republicans empowered subhuman blacks to rule over the respectable white South. This racist interpretation, popularized by *The Birth of a Nation*, functioned as a rationale for stripping Southern black people of their rights.[92]

In addition to treating black people as human beings, another innovative aspect of Du Bois's book was his Marxist exploration of the relationship between capitalism, slavery, and emancipation. Du Bois began exploring Marx and Marxist texts in the early 1930s. He sent a letter to the black Marxist scholar Abram L. Harris in 1933 requesting a list of the "books that the perfect Marxian must know." Du Bois wrote *Black Reconstruction* while running a *Capital* seminar for his graduate students. His attention to Marx showed in his language choices, such as in his contention that black emancipation was "one of the most extraordinary experiments of Marxism that the world, before the Russian Revolution, had seen."[93]

In a 1933 essay, Du Bois admitted his reverence for Marx. "There are certain books in the world which every searcher for truth must know," he wrote, "the Bible, the *Critique of Pure Reason*, *The Origin of Species*, and Karl Marx's *Capital*." He saw in Marx "a colossal genius of infinite sacrifice and monumental industry, and with a mind of extraordinary logical keenness and grasp." Du Bois argued Marx's theories were relevant in the 1930s, even though deep knowledge of Marx was not required to recognize that "there is something radically wrong with an industrial system that turns out simultaneously paupers and millionaires and sets a world starving because it has too much food."[94]

In *Black Reconstruction*, Du Bois argued that "black labor became the foundation not only of the Southern social structure, but of Northern manufacture and commerce, of the English factory system, of European commerce, of buying and selling on a world-wide scale." Put more poetically, he wrote: "Out of the exploitation of the dark proletariat comes the Surplus Value filched from human beasts which, in cultured lands, the Machine and harnessed Power veil and conceal." In this, Du Bois built upon Marx, who wrote that, "without slavery, there would be no cotton, without cotton there would be no modern industry. It is slavery which has given value to the colonies, it is the colonies which have created world trade, and world trade is the necessary condition for large-scale machine industry."[95]

The growth of global capitalism in the nineteenth century was predicated on the blood, sweat, and tears of enslaved black people in the Americas. The enslaved, then, were for Du Bois an important element of the proletariat that was positioned to free the entire world of the horrors of chattel slavery, and maybe even capitalist enslavement as well. Put simply, black slaves had agency.

Du Bois placed the Civil War in the context of a global class struggle. He saw it as "a war to determine how far industry in the United States should be carried on under a system where the capitalist owns not only the nation's raw material, not only the land, but also the laborer himself; or whether the laborer was going to maintain his personal freedom, and enforce it by growing political and economic independence based on widespread ownership of land." In the Civil War, enslaved black people represented the proletariat vanguard.[96]

Du Bois insisted the enslaved emancipated themselves during the Civil War by resisting work on Confederate plantations and by swamping approaching Union lines. This argument had a long pedigree, starting during the war among Union radicals, many of whom were German 48ers fighting along the western front. But Marxist Du Bois went one step further, arguing that when enslaved blacks freed themselves they not only destroyed the American system of chattel slavery but revolted against global capitalism. Du Bois provocatively labeled black resistance during the Civil War a "general strike," like the West Coast Waterfront Strike of 1934 that made headlines while he was writing *Black Reconstruction*. By rebelling against slavery and capitalism, the enslaved had created a proletarian revolution within a bourgeois republic.[97]

Some Marxists criticized Du Bois's ideas as apostasy. They argued slavery might have played an important role in precapitalist developments, but capitalism proper was predicated on industrial production and wage labor. Slavery was a vestige of a precapitalist system, not part and parcel of capitalism itself. Therefore, no matter how unjust their situation, enslaved people were not revolutionaries. The Civil War and Reconstruction era was not a revolutionary moment but rather a period of capitalist consolidation.

Abram Harris, who reviewed *Black Reconstruction* for the *New Republic*, rejected Du Bois's "general strike" framework, too. He argued "the general strike implies a real consciousness not only of the class issues that make its use necessary but also of the ends deliberately sought by those who use it. The Negro slaves' so-called general strike grew out of no such consciousness of the issues or of the significance that their 'escape to freedom' would have upon the ends of the war."[98]

Historians have since largely sided with Du Bois, showing that many of the enslaved were indeed self-conscious about their role in defeating the Confederacy. Enslaved men and women who withheld their labor had an implicit understanding of Marx's labor theory of value: the power of the Confederacy resided in their labor; without it, secession was powerless. Moreover, slave rebellion taught Marx a lesson he applied in *Capital*: the question of labor was a question of autonomy. To be free required control over one's own labor. The slave system denied such freedom absolutely, but so too, to a lesser degree, did the capitalist system.[99]

Du Bois also applied Marxist terminology to his analysis of Reconstruction, which he referred to as a "dictatorship of the proletariat," since some of the black former enslaved suddenly had real power over their white former enslavers. In a letter to Benjamin Stolberg, a black journalist and labor activist who had deep knowledge of Marxism, Du Bois defended his terminology. Knowing some traditional Marxists would lambaste him for it, Du Bois contended it was merited because "there were distinct evidences of determination on the part of black laborers to tax property and administer the state primarily for the benefit of labor." This was particularly true in South Carolina, the most proslavery state prior to the war, where some black judges decided property disputes in favor of black claimants, sometimes against their former enslavers. A white South Carolinian lawyer summed up the situation nicely: "We have gone through one of the most remarkable changes in our relations to each other, that has been known, perhaps in the history of the world."[100]

Stolberg did challenge Du Bois on using the "dictatorship of the proletariat" formulation. He argued that prior to Lenin no such thing existed, since other classes had always maintained some degree of power even in revolutionary situations such as the Paris Commune. Du Bois forged ahead despite such warnings.[101]

Du Bois asserted the Civil War and Reconstruction had overturned class relations to such a radical degree that poor whites began exercising their rights for the first time. He also claimed Reconstruction had the potential to remake American class relations beyond the South. In this he followed Marx, who wrote in *Capital*: "In the USA, every independent movement of the workers was paralyzed so long as slavery disfigured a part of the republic. Labor cannot emancipate itself in the white skin where in the black it is branded. But out of the death of slavery a new life at once arose. The first fruit of the civil war was the eight hours agitation that ran with the seven-leagued boots of the locomotive from the Atlantic to the Pacific."[102]

Class struggle went both ways. Reconstruction was "America's unfinished revolution." It failed to fulfill its promise because northern capitalists realized it had gone too far. Du Bois argued northern capitalists had only joined with the abolitionist forces of democracy out of a temporary convergence of interests. The Slave Power had to be killed because it threatened the rapid westward expansion of capitalism that was more reliant on wage labor than slave labor. But once the interests of capitalists inevitably parted with the interests of those who wanted to extend "the full logic of democracy," Du Bois's terms to describe socialism, the alliance shattered.[103]

If policies forwarded by free blacks and Radical Republicans had been implemented, especially regarding land and wealth redistribution, what was to stop working-class Northerners from making similar demands? Moreover, there remained the problem of labor in the South, which had been one of the key engines of American capitalism. Northern capitalists had an interest in ensuring the formerly enslaved returned to work the land on the cheap. In short, a national elite killed Reconstruction because it needed a chastened labor force. The revolution was smashed when black labor once again came under planter control, which corresponded to the northern army of liberation's desertion of the South in 1877.

Related to his historical analysis of Reconstruction, Du Bois argued the capitalist elite turned the white working class against the black working class. This had the mutually reinforcing effect of dividing the working class while also consigning black people to a new serfdom that emerged in the forms of sharecropping and, eventually, Jim Crow. As opposed to class solidarity, white workers acted on what Du Bois termed a "a public and psychological wage" of whiteness.[104]

In his 1933 essay on Marx, Du Bois wrote that "Negro labor in America suffers because of the fundamental inequities of the whole capitalistic system," but that the worst of the indignities came at the hands of white workers. "It is white labor," Du Bois argued, "that deprives the Negro of his right to vote, denies him education, denies him affiliation with trade unions, expels him from decent houses and neighborhoods, and heaps upon him the public insults of open color discrimination." Du Bois applied this analysis to the potential for revolution in the 1930s. Even though he was somewhat favorably disposed to the American Communist Party, which he later joined, he also believed "the communists cannot even get a respectful hearing in America unless they begin by expelling Negroes." "No soviet of technocrats," he wrote, "would do more than exploit colored labor in order to raise the status of whites."[105]

Du Bois believed Marxism had to account for the special intensity of American racism if it was to be a workable theory in the United States. Class and race mattered in thinking through capitalism and revolution. Racism prevented socialism.

Harris was highly critical of Du Bois's pessimism about class solidarity across racial lines. Harris thought Du Bois had taken the wrong lessons from Marx. "He is a racialist," Harris wrote, "whose discovery of Marxism as a critical instrument has been too recent and sudden for it to discipline his mental processes or basically to change his social philosophy." Harris had a point, since it was indeed impossible to imagine a socialist future without working-class solidarity across racial lines. But in the details, *Black Reconstruction* revealed some degree of optimism about the promise of such a future, about the promise of Marx. Du Bois argued part of the problem was not enough American workers were familiar with *Capital*, which explained why so many of them "did not know that when they let the dictatorship of labor be overthrown in the South they surrendered the hope of democracy in America for all men." The failure of Reconstruction reverberated across the land.

FIGURE 4.7: C. L. R. James, 1938.

But perhaps Americans in the 1930s would learn from those failures. Perhaps they would read Marx! C. L. R. James had a similar hope.[106]

The Black Jacobins, like *Black Reconstruction*, is explicitly grounded in Marx. In fact, James had spent more time with Marx than Du Bois had. Yet at times *The Black Jacobins* seems less Marxist than Shakespearean, a tragedy in the theatrical sense. But one of the appeals of Marx to many twentieth-century thinkers was the drama of his theory of history.[107]

In the form of class struggle, Marxist theory captured the drama of history. Vivian Gornick described American Communists in the 1930s as a generation "whose lives were formed by political history as were no other American lives save those of the original Revolutionists. Their experience embodies the relation between spiritual need and historical context as does the experience of almost no other Americans. History is in them, they are in history." Toward the end of *The Black Jacobins*, as the narrative of Toussaint and the Haitian Revolution reached its climax, James wrote: "There is no drama like the drama of history."[108]

Beyond endowing historical narrative with a dramatic structure,

Marx's theory of history was also a compelling way to think about the interplay between events and people. *The Black Jacobins* toggled between competing assumptions about events determining humans, and vice versa, humans determining events.

Toussaint was a great man. Born enslaved, he made himself into arguably the greatest revolutionary in an age of revolution. And yet, as James wrote, "Toussaint did not make the revolution. It was the revolution that made Toussaint." So, it seemed the Marxist emphasis on social relations spoiled heroic individualism. But perhaps not. James continued with a curious qualifier: "And even that is not the whole truth." James's seeming uncertainty about causality might have been his way of pivoting between the Marxist tradition, which emphasized historical and social embeddedness, and what later came to be known as the "black radical tradition," which focused on black resistance to structures of oppression. Of course, as so many thinkers of the time had shown, one did not have to dump Marx to place value on human agency, especially of the revolutionary sort.[109]

In describing his theory of history in the introduction to *The Black Jacobins*, James hewed closely to Marx's approach, as laid out in *The Eighteenth Brumaire of Louis Bonaparte*. "Great men make history," James wrote, "but only such history as it is possible for them to make. Their freedom of achievement is limited by the necessities of their environment. To portray the limits of those necessities and the realization, complete or partial, of all possibilities, that is the true business of the historian."[110]

James attended to the ways in which larger forces created the conditions for revolution in very Marxist fashion, even if his Marxism might have seemed revisionist to the more orthodox. "The slaves worked on the land, and, like revolutionary peasants everywhere, they aimed at the extermination of their oppressors," James wrote. "But working and living together in gangs of hundreds on the huge sugar-factories, . . . they were closer to a modern proletariat than any group of workers in existence at the time, and the rising was, therefore, a thoroughly prepared and organized mass movement." Nonetheless, conditions were not always ripe for revolution.[111]

In the same way that Du Bois showed how the Civil War made a general strike among slaves possible, James showed how larger historical forces made the Haitian Revolution possible. The French Revolution not only created chaos that served as an opening for the enslaved within the French Empire. It also generated an ethos of liberty that found its way across the Atlantic. If the French masses could overthrow a venal monarchy, then the enslaved could overthrow a debased planter class. The French Revolution could not be cordoned off at the borders of France proper. "Revolution, says Karl Marx, is the locomotive of history. Here was a locomotive that had travelled at remarkable speed," James wrote.[112]

James made clear the connective tissue between home country and empire was not unidirectional. He argued "the slave trade and slavery were the economic basis of the French Revolution." As the French bourgeoisie grew rich from the slave trade and related industries, it asserted its newfound confidence relative to the aristocracy, which ironically precipitated a revolution that eventually spread to the French masses and the enslaved in Sainte-Domingue. Just as Du Bois showed the Civil War was not the end point of struggle, James demonstrated the same for the French Revolution and the slave uprising in Haiti. The French merchant class ultimately conquered the democratic masses and sought to do the same in Sainte-Domingue.[113]

In a hopeful projection, James contended the class question in Paris ultimately determined how France would approach the colonial question. When the radical masses were in power, they saw the revolutionary black people of Haiti as their allies and republican countrymen. But when the bourgeoisie took power, France sought the restoration of slavery in Sainte-Domingue. Thus, Toussaint's hopes that Haiti would be a crucial component of a republican France were dashed. As he withered to his death in a French prison, a war for independence raged and ultimately turned into a racial war of annihilation.

That the Haitian Revolution devolved into a race war was a tragedy in James's eyes, not because the immensely cruel Sainte-Domingue whites were wiped out—they had that coming—and not necessarily because Toussaint died before he could witness a free Haiti. But rather, the Haitian Revolution ended in tragedy because Toussaint's dream of an interracial, republican Sainte-Domingue was crushed. James was less sanguine than Toussaint about the possibilities of interracial democracy in a nation born of slavery. But that did not make the results less tragic. Nor did it put Haiti on a less perilous path.

In the end, Toussaint failed because his idea of revolution was European. James argued capitalism made the black slave a revolutionary just as it had made the industrial worker one. But whereas the industrial worker's culture was shot through with bourgeois norms, the revolutionary culture of the enslaved emerged from its African roots. Haitian Voodoo was a thoroughly antibourgeois and anti-European revolutionary culture. This was an innovation on Marxism, and one that Du Bois had similarly made when he contended the black slave revolt against the planter class took the form of syncretic religious fervor. "This was the coming of the Lord," Du Bois wrote. "This was the fulfillment of prophecy and legend. It was the Golden Dawn, after chains of a thousand years." It turns out "one of the most extraordinary experiments of Marxism" was predicated on a culture of religious belief that had roots in Africa.[114]

This was Marx at the margins—the American margins. On the one hand, the analytical move made by Du Bois and James diminished the explanatory power of Marx, since revolutionary consciousness seemingly emerged from sources that had nothing to do with class in the classic Marxist sense. But on the other hand, it also showed the capaciousness of Marxism. It was a political tradition that, in the hands of black thinkers in the United States, could contribute to a hybrid approach to understanding the modern world. The impulse to revolt against the master class was not limited to the imagination of a nineteenth-century German philosopher. But that very same philosopher was nonetheless helpful in fleshing out the historical forces that gave rise to revolution, whether in factories at the imperial core, or in fields on an empire's edges.

In the early years of the Great Depression, when capitalism crashed down on itself, more Americans than ever turned to Marx. He was the prophet of capitalism's catastrophes, the sage of revolution. But as American capitalism steadied itself, as international political crises reached unbelievable new heights, and as the Soviet Union committed horrible crimes in the name of Marx, a growing number of people grew disillusioned with the nineteenth-century philosopher. Rather than prophetic, Marx's ideas increasingly came to seem flat out false. To that history we now turn.

5

FALSE PROPHET

Midcentury Liberalism

Quite the contrary to Marx's prediction that the most advanced industrial countries would be the first to make the transit from capitalism to socialism and beyond to communism, this most advanced of all such countries has never been insulated so thickly against the appeals of Marxism nor ever behaved in so thoroughly un-Marxist a fashion.

CLINTON ROSSITER

In the 1930s, some Americans regarded Karl Marx a prophet of capitalism's demise. But many more turned to a living savior. Franklin Delano Roosevelt was elected president of the United States in 1932, and three more times, because he promised a government that would ease the suffering caused by the Great Depression. He called this government "a new deal for the American people."[1]

The scion of a wealthy Dutch family from Hyde Park, New York, that included in its lineage William Henry Aspinwall, a prominent nineteenth-century merchant, and Theodore Roosevelt, the twenty-sixth president of the United States, Franklin Roosevelt belonged to an exclusive stratum of the American bourgeoisie. But as Democratic president, Roosevelt was deemed a traitor to his class by many of the capitalists who had thrived on the economic policies of his Republican predecessors.[2]

Roosevelt's political sensibilities were influenced by his wife, Eleanor.

As he worked his way up through the Democratic Party, she carved out a life as an activist. Heavily involved in the Women's Trade Union League, Eleanor welcomed a steady stream of trade unionists and socialists into the family home. Roosevelt received a political education from these houseguests quite unlike the one he obtained during years of elite private schooling. The crash course in American working-class history that Eleanor and her comrades gave Roosevelt compelled him to rethink the meaning of democracy.[3]

Roosevelt's refashioned political philosophy was on display as early as 1912, when, in the New York State Senate, he spoke about the need to prioritize the "struggle for liberty of the community rather than liberty of the individual." This speech inaugurated Roosevelt's habit of grounding his political vision in American history. In arguing that Americans needed to emphasize community over the individual, Roosevelt did not deny the legitimacy of the Jeffersonian vision of democracy, which lauded the independent yeoman farmer precisely because his self-sufficiency was a bulwark against special interests. Rather, in the highly complex, interdependent society that arose from the twin transformations of urbanization and industrialization, Roosevelt believed individualism had outlived its virtues.[4]

To the degree that individualism had come to be the watchword of a competitive society that benefited the capitalist class and degraded the working class, it was particularly outmoded as a democratic ideology. As Roosevelt's contemporary John Dewey argued, idealizing individualism had become "an unnamed form of insanity which is responsible for a large part of the remediable suffering in the world." For both Roosevelt and Dewey, such suffering was the direct result of an unjust economic system that individualism undergirded.[5]

In 1921, Roosevelt contracted an incapacitating disease that bound him to a wheelchair for the rest of his life. Losing the use of his legs made Roosevelt even more empathetic to the downtrodden. It also made him more sensitive to the fact of human interdependence, a theme he hammered home in his inaugural speech in 1928 as the governor of New York. Roosevelt declared himself proud that New Yorkers had "grown to realize the interdependence on each other which modern civilization has created."[6]

Interconnectedness was not mere rhetoric for Roosevelt. It had material consequences. It meant society was obliged to "guard the toilers in the factories and to ensure them a fair wage." It meant the necessities of modern life, such as running water and electricity, should be made available to everyone as public utilities. It meant an end to "rich man's justice" in the application of law. Roosevelt had translated interdependence into political terms, putting into action a theory of democracy befitting the complexities of modern society. For democracy to work for everyone, it had to be socialized to an extent never before seen in the United States.[7]

Roosevelt had the instincts of a reformer, not a radical, and certainly not a Marxist. His attention to community as the source of political organization rejected what he called the "ancient disease known as 'class consciousness.'" But when the Great Depression steamrolled the American economy, Roosevelt came to believe a thorough restructuring of capitalism was necessary. As governor of New York, he did what he could to relieve suffering, but he recognized that combating an economic crisis of such a magnitude required massive changes at the national level. Half-measures would not suffice. "There is no question in my mind," Roosevelt said, "that it is time for the country to become fairly radical for at least one generation."[8]

In 1932, as Roosevelt was gearing up to run for president, he proposed dramatic, even radical measures, including wealth redistribution and "a larger measure of social planning." Roosevelt observed that the Great Depression was not caused by a natural disaster. It was rather the result of an economic system made by humans. Attributing the economic calamity to human failure was sobering but also liberating. Any system made by humans could also be unmade, or better yet in Roosevelt's eyes, remade to work better.[9]

American capitalism, Roosevelt conceded, had the productive capacity to provide every American with a secure and decent life. The problem, though, was that as configured it left millions behind. "This is the awful paradox with which we are confronted," Roosevelt said, "a stinging rebuke that challenges our power to operate the economic machine which we have created." Capitalism would only truly thrive if government intervened to level the playing field.[10]

Roosevelt believed a laissez-faire version of capitalism generated instability that threatened to lay waste to the whole system. This made the Republican defense of unfettered capitalism that much more infuriating and, in Roosevelt's eyes, unprincipled. Republicans wanted an economy, Roosevelt said, that prioritized "the favored few" in the half-hearted expectation "that some of their prosperity will leak through, sift through, to labor, to the farmer, to the small businessman." "That theory," he lamented, "belongs to the party of Toryism, and I had hoped that most of the Tories left this country in 1776."[11]

As president, Roosevelt remained unsparing of those who obstructed his efforts to bury the Tory theory of economics. In a speech in 1936, he chastised the "economic royalists" who spared nobody in carving out "new dynasties" of wealth and privilege. Roosevelt lamented that the "whole structure of modern life," "corporations, banks and securities, new machinery of industry and agriculture, labor and capital," had been pressed into serving greedy capitalists. The only solution was a democratic revival—and the New Deal was the vehicle to make it happen.[12]

SAVING CAPITALISM FROM ITSELF, SAVING AMERICA FROM MARX

Roosevelt's 1936 speech might have made Marx proud with its evocations of "mercenaries" who "sought to regiment the people, their labor, and their property." He gave voice to working-class anger, speaking on behalf of a New York City woman who had written Eleanor to emphasize that Roosevelt had "a mandate from the people . . . to redistribute wealth" and to warn that "anyone who trifles with the people at this time had better be careful." Roosevelt also spoke for a Columbus, Georgia man who had thanked him for government aid, because he had been evicted from his home after being fired from his job for having "the nerve to ask or 'demand,' better working conditions." Another man let Roosevelt know that "all of the working men are for you." "Saint Roosevelt," as his working-class admirers often called him, gave hope to the forgotten Americans who had been beaten down by capitalism. He became a symbol of hope, even revolution.[13]

But was Roosevelt a revolutionary? Was the New Deal a dramatic move toward socialism? Had Marx been snuck into the corridors of American power? Or, did Roosevelt save capitalism from itself? Did the New Deal sop up revolutionary energies that had seemed so promising, that had given life to such a robust reception of Marx? Answers to these questions help illuminate the fate of Marx in mid-twentieth-century America.

Roosevelt was not a Marxist. But his political philosophy rhymed with Marxism, signifying a brief convergence between Marxism and liberalism. Out of this conjunction a new type of liberalism was born.[14]

The liberalism that Roosevelt adopted as his own bore little resemblance to that practiced by nineteenth-century Europeans who promoted the liberalization of market forces. It also went beyond Teddy Roosevelt's progressivism, which empowered the state to shield corporate capitalism from its worst excesses. Roosevelt's liberalism was premised on the idea that an activist government was ultimately responsible for guaranteeing an economy that worked for everyone, including the working class. Although this liberalism was underwritten by the assumption that the state should sit atop the commanding heights of the economy, it was not anticapitalist. Rather, it was expected government would intervene when market forces alone failed to ensure the general welfare. When Roosevelt challenged the economic royalists, he did so in the name of liberalism, not Marxism.

The fundamental difference between liberalism and Marxism in the Age of Roosevelt was that, whereas liberals wanted to reform the economic system, which implied the persistence of capitalism in some form, Marxists desired a socialist revolution, which inferred an end to capitalism. Historians and political theorists sometimes downplay the distinction between reform and revolution because lines between the two are blurry. But Roosevelt was crystal clear about what the difference meant to him, and to the future of the United States.

Roosevelt believed it was his job to save the nation from revolution by offering what he described as "a workable program of reconstruction." He was not alone in holding this view. In 1933, just as the New Deal was kicking into action, John Maynard Keynes told Roosevelt that he had made himself "the trustee for those in every country who seek to mend the evils of our condition by reasoned experiment within the framework of the existing social system." Gardiner C. Means, part of Roosevelt's vaunted "brain trust," the collection of clever policymakers charged with tinkering a way out of the Great Depression, said in retrospect that "there was no question in our minds we were saving the country." Rex Tugwell, another Roosevelt aide, later wrote that had it not been for Roosevelt the United States "might have succumbed to a dictatorship." In an era of global turmoil, when nations were capitulating to the communist Left or the fascist Right, Roosevelt sought a middle ground.[15]

The New Deal was Roosevelt's middle course between communism and fascism. It was a calculated effort to save capitalism from itself, and without kowtowing to capitalists. Roosevelt understood that the state had to assume more control over the direction of American business, a posture that Marx himself had once described as "a committee for managing the common affairs of the whole bourgeoisie." But Roosevelt was no fan of Marx.[16]

By diverting the United States from Marxist revolution, Roosevelt also helped defuse the broad fascination with Marx that had taken hold during the Great Depression. While other significant factors would contribute to the midcentury disavowal of Marx, nobody did more to stifle Marx's influence in the United States than Roosevelt. There was irony to this. After all, Roosevelt, like Marx, understood that a free society afforded dignity to its toilers. Yet the American political tradition was far less characterized by a positive conception of what it was than by what it was not. It was *not* in alignment with Marx. Renouncing Marx helped give the American political tradition meaning—as did the fact that the American economy not only survived the Great Depression, but thrived soon after. Put another way, the American political tradition was a midcentury invention made possible by the fact that Roosevelt saved capitalism.

Saving capitalism from itself was not an easy task. When Roosevelt entered the White House in 1933, after a landslide victory that inaugurated decades of Democratic domination, he was confronted with several seemingly intractable problems that appeared inherent to capitalism. The system was stuck. Working class exploitation, in the form of anti-unionism and other strategies that depressed wages, reached new levels of harshness even as the labor force had become more productive than ever. This led to a vicious cycle of underconsumption and overproduction. Under the leadership of Hoover, the state had been both unwilling and unable to act. Roosevelt's simple promise was that he would do something, *anything*, to alleviate the pain felt by millions.

Roosevelt possessed an overarching understanding about what needed to be done to end the Great Depression. He wanted to restructure American society to lessen rampant inequality. But, the immediacy of the situation demanded an experimental approach. Roosevelt's famous "First 100 Days," during which he and Democratic majorities in Congress passed a record number of laws, was premised less on a single blueprint and more on an ad hoc set of strategies. This legislative landslide is known as the First New Deal.[17]

Much of this legislation was straightforward enough in aiming to inject a measure of stability into the faltering economic system. The Glass-Steagall Act, a crucial piece of legislation regulating the banking and financial sectors, created the Federal Deposit Insurance Company (FDIC), which underwrote savings deposits at failing banks. Glass-Steagall also put into effect an important new regulation that separated retail from investment banking, forbidding banks from using depositors' funds for high-risk investments. Similarly, the Agricultural Adjustment Act sought to stabilize the nation's agricultural system, plagued as it was by overproduction, by paying farmers *not* to plant.[18]

The First New Deal also employed millions of Americans, which alleviated crushing unemployment while improving the nation's public works. The new Civil Conservation Corps put over three million young men to work on rural infrastructure, building or refurbishing bridges, roads, foot trails, dams, camps, parks, fisheries, and more. The Tennessee Valley Authority hired hundreds of thousands of Americans to build dams that controlled floods and connected a huge region of the South to electrical grids for the first time. These measures did not end the Great Depression. But they were relatively popular programs that were the first steps toward better days. Other early measures taken by Roosevelt did not fare as well.[19]

One of the most pressing issues that confronted Roosevelt concerned the enormity of corporate power. Colossal corporations felt free to act in ways that benefited their immediate profit margins while also severely damaging the health of the larger economy. Industrial recovery thus required that the state compel corporations to change their behavior. Roosevelt did not fear this task, but his administration was divided over the best approach to it.[20]

One faction, the antitrusters, thought that big corporations should be broken up. The other faction, the corporatists, believed runaway competition was the obstacle to a stable economy. They contended the solution was to allow a select number of corporations to gain an even larger share of the market, but under the watchful eye of the state. Roosevelt's brain trust concluded that the corporatist resolution struck the right balance.[21]

The National Industrial Recovery Act (NIRA), which became law on June 16, 1933, was the result. The law empowered a new agency, the National Recovery Administration (NRA), to oversee wage, price, and production targets for nearly every industry. More than a method for taming the chaos of unrestrained competition, this legislative linchpin of the First New Deal was an attempt to overhaul American capitalism. The historian Ira Katznelson writes that "nothing like this comprehensive restructuring of market capitalism by a national state had ever been tried before in a constitutional democracy."[22]

NIRA came under fire almost immediately. Former president Hoover, speaking on behalf of conservative critics, contended that its empowerment of the state mirrored that of the rising European dictatorships. NIRA indeed indicated that policymakers were willing to go to extreme lengths to save capitalism, even looking to the example set by Italy under the fascist dictator Benito Mussolini. Of course, the Roosevelt administration insisted its version of corporatism differed; NIRA was created "on American terms for American purposes." Donald Richberg, general counsel for the NRA, argued that the law did not grant dictatorial power to the state, but rather provided incentives that would encourage a more disciplined "self-government of industry." The New Deal corporatist solution was, in Richberg's view, "a democratic and a truly American solution" that distinguished it from the "the socialist doctrines of Karl Marx."[23]

If the purpose of the New Deal was to save capitalism, and if "the socialist doctrines of Karl Marx" were anathema, then NIRA was promising. To wit, most of the new regulatory codes were written by agents of the very corporations that were the intended objects of regulation, and industry representatives were charged with coordinating price levels and production targets. Not all capitalists benefited equally from these arrangements. Large firms, which combined into even larger companies thanks to NIRA's alleviation of antitrust regulations, captured the regulatory state to their advantage, weakening smaller firms, or those with fewer connections to New Deal bureaucrats.[24]

The Roosevelt administration was primarily focused on the management side of the corporate order when it crafted NIRA. But the law included a tiny subsection about labor, section 7(a), which stipulated that workers would be granted "the right to organize and bargain collectively through representatives of their own choosing." This seemingly inconsequential stipulation, which some industries lobbied for because they thought unions would help them regulate against ruinous competition, was barely an afterthought for the Roosevelt brain trust. Yet section 7(a) permanently reshaped labor relations in the United States. Workers interpreted it as an instruction from the president to join a union. Angry about increasingly miserable working conditions, American workers reveled in the fact that Roosevelt seemed to be on their side. For the first time, the US government, which had until then reflexively aligned with capital against labor, would guarantee workers the right to form independent unions and collectively bargain. The working class interpreted NIRA as a call to arms.[25]

Although some members of the business elite benefited from NIRA, or what the historian Gabriel Kolko termed "political capitalism," many others thought it unfair, un-American, socialist even. Chief among the latter group were the wealthy industrialists who formed the American Liberty League in 1934 to challenge Roosevelt's program. A conservative Supreme Court, in alignment with the Liberty League, unanimously ruled in its 1935 landmark decision *A. L. A. Schechter Poultry Corp. v. United States*, that NIRA violated the Constitution by overstepping the powers granted to Congress by the Commerce Clause. More than a limited ruling in favor of an aggrieved chicken farmer, *Schechter* invalidated the Roosevelt administration's efforts at economic coordination on the grounds that such intervention allowed for collusion between some firms to the detriment of others. It also nullified section 7(a) on the notion that unions were analogous to such unwarranted market associations. By the standards set by the economic royalists, workers were not entitled to form unions.[26]

The Supreme Court ruling was a setback for the working class in the short term. But in the long arc of organized labor's growth in the 1930s, the decision barely registered as a hiccup. To begin with, the short-lived NIRA regime was hardly a golden age of government-labor relations. Uneven federal enforcement of section 7(a) meant most businesses refused to recognize labor's newfound right to organize. More important, there was no turning back the clock on working-class militancy, which continued to spread like wildfire, with or without Supreme Court approval. Rather than idly wait for government support where none was coming, workers revolted. This was the larger political context that made 1934 the year of the strike.

It is not surprising that the zenith of Marx's reception in the United States happened while the American working class rebelled against the economic and political elite. But at this historical moment, when proletarian revolution appeared within the realm of possibility, Roosevelt found a way around the Supreme Court and embraced the working class. Roosevelt's Second New Deal did what his First New Deal had failed to do. It dissipated the radical energies that made Marx such a powerful symbol.

Although Roosevelt was incredibly popular during his first few years as president, and although a majority supported his First New Deal, not everyone believed his administration was doing enough to end the suffering. Sundry "voices of protest" held Roosevelt's feet to the fire and ensured that his Second New Deal of 1935 was farther-reaching than his first. The Louisiana politician Huey Long's "Share Our Wealth" program, premised on a radical redistribution of wealth and massive public works spending, pushed Roosevelt to embrace more audacious approaches. This included the Works Progress Administration, which went even further than Roosevelt's earlier public works projects in putting millions of the unemployed to work on infrastructure. The California doctor Robert Townsend's activism helped shape Roosevelt's 1935 Social Security Act, which codified Townsend's idea for old-age insurance. In sum, the Second New Deal was transformative in response to demands made by energized and radicalized American citizens.[27]

This was especially true with regard to the rapidly growing and increasingly militant labor movement, which compelled passage of the National Labor Relations Act (NLRA). Also known as the Wagner Act, after Senator Robert Wagner of New York, the NLRA was a more forceful version of section 7(a). It forbade employers from interfering with employee efforts to form unions, and it included mechanisms to enforce this.

The Wagner Act should be understood in two ways. On the one hand, it was an unparalleled victory for the American working class. Organized labor gained legitimacy in the eyes of the state, and with legitimacy came protection, which enabled its immediate expansion. The percentage of unionized workers in manufacturing tripled by 1940. On the other hand, the NLRA was also a clear means of reducing labor militancy. It brought an unruly working class into the fold of the Democratic Party. In 1936, organized labor assisted Roosevelt's landslide reelection and helped the Democratic Party achieve even larger majorities in Congress. In this way, the Second New Deal, even in its most prolabor form, was by no means Marxist. The president had no intention of handing over control of the means of production to workers. Roosevelt was both challenging capitalists on behalf of workers and saving capitalism for future capitalists. No wonder he was a source of such cognitive dissonance for Marxists.[28]

Plenty of people on the left admired Roosevelt. The British Marxist historian Eric Hobsbawm wrote fondly, "Roosevelt was passionately loathed and denounced by American big business, that is to say by the very people who more than any others represented the evils of capitalism to us." Hobsbawm echoed the sentiments of many American leftists at the time. The Trinidadian-American Marxist sociologist Oliver Cromwell Cox wrote in 1948 that "the charge of the capitalist politicians that Roosevelt was a communist is in its essence correct." Cox continued in this counterintuitive vein:

> His policies and actions had the potentialities of taking the economy step by step, inch by inch, out of the hands of the bourgeoisie and of turning it over to the people as a whole; and this is exactly what is meant by communistic activities. The logical conclusion of such a trend must necessarily result in the overthrow of the capitalist order. There has probably been no individual in the history of the United States who has done so much to bring about democracy and therefore communism in the United States as President Roosevelt; and there has been no individual so much beloved by the people and so much hated by the bourgeoisie as he.[29]

Not everyone on the Left remembered Roosevelt with such affection. The Marxist activist Fred Thompson recalled that the Industrial Workers of the World depicted Roosevelt as "hated by those he had helped and loved by those he had harmed." Thompson lamented that Roosevelt's "unionism by permit" policies co-opted working-class militancy, symbolized by union banners that read: "The President Wants You to Join the Union." The Marxist intellectual James Burnham labeled the Wagner Act a "a class collaborationist device" meant to restrain working-class militancy "firmly within the framework of the bourgeois state." Burnham noted capitalists hated the Wagner Act because it was indeed a significant "concession" to the working class. But he contended such opposition was short-sighted, especially since the law, which Roosevelt described as "ambiguous" in structure, could be manipulated to their advantage. Indeed, such manipulation would eventually come to pass. But not before another wave of labor radicalism.[30]

One of the most powerful demonstrations of labor solidarity began when United Automobile Workers (UAW) kick-started a sit-down strike at the General Motors plant in Flint, Michigan on December 24, 1936. Autoworkers occupied the plant to protest poor wages and shoddy treatment by management that including forbidding them from talking during lunch breaks. As one participant later portrayed the working conditions: "You might call yourself a man if you was on the street, but as soon as you went through the door and punched your card, you was nothing more or less than a robot. Do this, go there, do that." Even after the government had sanctioned their right to unionize, workers persisted to struggle for dignity and autonomy.[31]

In the spring of 1937, over 400,000 workers staged 477 sit-down strikes across America. This was a major headache for Roosevelt at a time when he was also being pressured by Southern conservatives in his own party who were growing increasingly worried that federal intervention might upset their system of racial segregation and class hierarchy. Since Roosevelt had already made major concessions to workers, and since union leadership had promised to support him in exchange, the administration determined something had to be done about persistent working-class stubbornness. Labor leaders like John Lewis, head of the CIO, worked closely with New Deal officials to curtail the wave of strikes.[32]

In short, the New Deal state both enabled and captured the radical labor movement. And if that wasn't paradox enough, Roosevelt had the help of the American Communist Party in taming working-class militancy. The history of the American Left is rife with such ironies. By 1935, the party had moved away from its "third period" policy of tarring anyone to its right as "social fascists." The Comintern ordered the American Communist Party to moderate its position with regard to trade unions and other liberal democratic institutions. That this shift took place at precisely the moment Roosevelt moved left on labor issues precipitated a left-liberal coalescence known as the Popular Front.[33]

THE POPULAR FRONT AGAINST MARX

It is important to note the international dimension of the Popular Front, which was an uneasy alignment between the Soviet Union and liberal democracies against fascism. The domestic and international components of the Popular Front went hand-in-glove for American Communists. The historian Maurice Isserman notes that support for the Soviet Union allowed Communists to retain their Marxist credentials even as "they immersed themselves in reform-oriented day-to-day politics," rather than revolution. In this era, the American Communist Party acted as the left-wing of the labor movement and as a junior partner in the New Deal coalition.[34]

As the Communist Party made tenuous peace with American liberalism, it underwent an ideological shift represented by party leader Earl Browder's slogan, "Communism is Twentieth Century Americanism." When intellectuals like Sidney Hook sought to Americanize Marx in the early 1930s, Marx's ideas remained in the forefront of such efforts. America served as backdrop or context. But Popular Front impulses downplayed Marx and elevated America.[35]

The midcentury erasure of Marx is typically assumed to have been a byproduct of political repression. For example, Kenneth Burke, for new editions of his 1930s books published during the 1950s red scare, removed traces of Marx. But the Popular Front anticipated this development at a time when such self-censorship had little to do with repression. Rather, the de-emphasizing of Marx was a consequence of the Popular Front's compulsion to Americanize, and its desire for mainstream influence. For the radical children of Eastern European immigrants, "Communism is Twentieth Century Americanism" was a ticket to assimilation. The motto connected the socialism their parents first discovered in faraway lands, in books authored by exotic philosophers, to the millions of progressive Americans who supported the New Deal. Such Americanization, as with all cultural assimilation, was a two-way street.[36]

Just as foreign radicals adapted to American political culture, so too was America transformed. What, people soon asked, was America? The field of American studies, which emerged in the 1940s, was part of an ideological project that sought to define American culture as distinct from Marxism yet still vital, even revolutionary. Its early years are often characterized as being dominated by a nationalist strain, as embodied in Daniel Boorstin's classic trilogy *The Americans*. In the hands of Boorstin and other midcentury liberal scholars, the study of America became a study in American exceptionalism. The United States was exempt from the laws of history to which Europe was bound. As the liberal historian Henry Steele Commager wrote: "By some alchemy, out of the blending of inheritance, environment, and experience, there came a distinctive American character."[37]

But American studies originated as a Popular Front project, intertwined with the leftist suppression of Marx. The Popular Front intellectual F. O. Matthiessen sought a usable past not in European letters—not in Marx—but rather in nineteenth-century American writers like Emerson, Thoreau, Whitman, Hawthorne, and Melville. The men of the American Renaissance, in the words of Matthiessen, "felt that it was incumbent upon their generation to give fulfillment to the potentialities freed by the Revolution, to provide a culture commensurate with America's political opportunity." Their body of work represented nothing less than the "undiminished resources" of American democracy. Even more, "their devotion to the possibilities of democracy" could help build a world that would provide dignity to all Americans, including workers. But such a revolutionary world, if it were to come into being, had to be first be imagined in an American dialect. Emerson, not Marx.[38]

Despite its patriotic tilt, or perhaps because of it, the Popular Front became the object of harsh criticism by those with equal claims to

American patriotism. The so-called New York Intellectuals who wrote for little magazines like *Partisan Review* were the first to undertake such a rhetorical attack. Their animus toward the Popular Front was partly political, since most members of "the family," Murray Kempton's apt designation for that disputatious tribe, learned the art of polemics during years spent in the City College of New York cafeteria's celebrated Alcove No. 1, where young Trotskyists waged ideological warfare against the Communist students who occupied Alcove No. 2. New York Intellectuals, erstwhile Trotskyists, loathed the Popular Front for what they deemed its schlocky patriotic cover for Stalinism.[39]

TROTSKYISM AND THE MARXIST DIALECTIC

The intellectual history of Trotskyism is crucial to understanding the full range of the American reception of Marx in the twentieth century. This is especially true when considering the Popular Front, since both formations backed away from Marx in their own unique ways, an illustration of powerful historical forces at work.

Many American intellectuals were attracted to Trotskyism and its American vehicle, the Socialist Workers Party, because it allowed them to reconcile Marxism and anti-Stalinism. Since the sclerotic dogmas of the American Communist Party seemed a byproduct of obeisance to Stalin, being a Trotskyist allowed more intellectual wiggle room to theorize Marx in an American context. Trotskyism often seemed a movement of free-floating Marxist intellectuals. Some of the most renowned American Marxists came through the Trotskyist movement, including Sidney Hook, C. L. R. James, A. J. Muste, Dwight Macdonald, Max Eastman, Irving Kristol, Raya Dunayevskaya, Grace Lee, James Burnham, V. F. Calverton, Hal Draper, Gertrude Himmelfarb, Irving Howe, and Max Shachtman, to name but a few. This intellectual lineage explains the formative connection between Trotskyism and the New York Intellectuals. It also makes clear why the latter launched a vicious and sustained critique of the Popular Front.[40]

Whereas the New York Intellectuals saw themselves as avant-garde agents of cosmopolitan modernity, they deemed Popular Front writers as populist peddlers of nationalist romanticism. There was irony in this distinction. New York Intellectuals projected their ideas in a dour, antirevolutionary register they believed better connected with American culture, even as they often used European thought, including Marx, as a window onto such pessimism. In contrast, Popular Front writers like Matthiessen were much more attentive to American letters and yet were mocked for their characteristically American optimism. This paradoxical division in left-wing American intellectual culture had a profound impact on Marx's role in that culture. The optimistic Popular Front types increasingly ignored him. The pessimistic New York Intellectuals concentrated on him through the lens of their disillusionment. Either way, Marx quit being a source of revolutionary inspiration even as he remained a specter haunting all sides.[41]

Almost all the major figures who entered the Trotskyist movement in the 1930s abandoned it by the end of the decade. Most, though not all, also grew dissatisfied with Marx, Marxism, and the Left more broadly. Many such people traveled the well-worn path from Trotskyism to liberalism. Several high-profile ex-Trotskyists, including Kristol, Hook, Eastman, and Burnham, went even further on the political spectrum and landed on versions of conservatism. But they held onto habits of mind that they developed in their Alcove 2 days. Long after they had eschewed political Marxism, they maintained the Marxist tendency of diagnosing problems in relation to root causes, internal logics, and overarching structures. They espoused universal understandings of the world, and believed any problem, no matter how provincial, should be related to larger forces. Try as they might, many former Marxists could not escape the grip of Marx. Thus, our very understanding of America as it developed across the twentieth century is underwritten by a subterranean Marx.[42]

James Burnham's intellectual biography is indicative of Marx's hidden influence on postwar American political thought. Burnham began his academic career in 1929, taking a position in the New York University Philosophy Department, where he hoped to pursue literary criticism. But the Great Depression wreaked havoc on his worldview, and in 1930 he began reading Marx. Sidney Hook, his colleague in the Philosophy Department, was determinative in this regard. But it was ultimately Trotsky who converted Burnham to full-throated Marxism. Burnham came to Trotsky's style of Marxist analysis after reading his 1932 book *The History of the Russian Revolution*. Burnham was particularly influenced by Trotsky's emphasis on dialectical materialism.[43]

The dialectic, in generic terms, is shorthand for the method Marx had appropriated from Hegel to explain how capitalism was generating contradictions that were paving the way for communism. Revolution would spring forth from the conditions of capitalism that had cast people into antagonistic classes, the bourgeoisie and the proletariat. Hegel theorized that, in the unfolding of history, a time was fast approaching in which a rational, absolute ideal—something like divine truth—will have revealed itself in the progressive development of human consciousness as manifested in philosophy, specifically in the mind of a genius philosopher like Hegel. Marx flipped this on its head. Marx, too, had a teleology, or a sense of where the future was headed based on the direction of history. But the endpoint for Marx was found not in human consciousness but in social relations, in the material world. Hegel, right side up.[44]

In the hands of Soviet theorists and some orthodox Marxists, what came to be called dialectical materialism rationalized the Bolshevik Revolution. This total theory provided the Soviets with powerful ideological vindication. Their revolution was foretold, and thus any action they took to defend it was historically necessary. But in the hands of Trotsky, 1917 was not the culmination of dialectical materialism. Trotsky took issue not with Soviet grandiosity but with its parochial view of the dialectic. For Trotsky, socialism could never survive in one country alone, much less in an economic backwater like Russia. The revolution had to be permanent, and it had to be brought to the rest of the world, especially rich countries like the United States. Trotsky's version of dialectical materialism remained in motion, and it included a role for Americans.[45]

From 1933 through 1939 Burnham was a respected member of the Trotskyist movement that sought to build an anti-Stalinist Left in the

United States. Although never a committed organizer, his intellectual output, his string of clear-headed criticisms of American capitalism, Soviet Communism, and the American Communist Party, captured the spirit of Trotskyism in the United States. But in 1940, in the midst of debates about the "Russia question," Burnham quit the Trotskyist movement and declared he was no longer a Marxist.

The debate about the Russia question was actually an argument about a series of questions. Was the Soviet Union a worker's state? Or was it ruled by a tiny, brutal elite that represented the proletariat in name only? Was Stalinism a deformation of the Russian Revolution? Was it a betrayal of Marx? Or was Stalinism the logical conclusion of Marxism? Trotsky's position, and thus the position of the entire Trotskyist movement, was that Stalin and his inner circle had wrested control of the revolution and centralized its authority over the proletariat. Stalin had betrayed the revolution, and Stalinist Russia had devolved into what Trotsky labeled a "degenerated workers' state."[46]

At first, Trotskyists like Burnham accepted that formulation, since it allowed them to effortlessly combine Marxism with anti-Stalinism. But when Trotsky argued the Soviet Union, no matter how fallen, remained a workers' state that demanded support in the face of imperialist aggression, Burnham and several other American Marxists began to peel away, quitting the Socialist Workers Party. Backing the Soviet Union grew even less tenable in the wake of Stalin's show trials, a series of rigged trials in Moscow between 1936 and 1938 against Trotskyists and the "right opposition," not to mention the Nazi-Soviet Pact and the ensuing Soviet occupation of Eastern Europe and Finland. Given that Stalin coveted putting Trotsky on trial in Moscow, Trotsky's persistent defense of the degenerated workers' state was rather remarkable. Given that an agent of Stalin murdered Trotsky in 1940 by sticking an ice pick in the back of his skull also made such a defense a tragic irony.[47]

In the context of the Nazi-Soviet Pact, Burnham broke with Trotsky. More than that, he theorized that the Soviet Union didn't need protection from imperialist powers because it was in fact barely different from them. In making this break, Burnham declared in 1940 that he

was no longer a Marxist. He contended the Marxist dialectic, in predicting a coming socialist revolution, was a lousy way to think about
the United States, where the New Deal had stabilized capitalism.

Dismissing the Marxist dialectic as a flimsy philosophy led to a
snide yet comical exchange with Trotsky. "Burnham does not recognize the dialectic," Trotsky wrote, "but the dialectic recognizes Burnham." Burnham responded in kind: "Comrade Trotsky, I will not
match metaphors with you. In such a verbal tournament, I concede
you the ribbon in advance. Evidence, argument, proof: these only are
my weapons."[48]

Such polemics have a storied place in Marxist discourse that is partly
the result of the sectarianism that marks the history of Marxism. Sectarian discord has often been viewed as irrational, especially since it
has given aid and comfort to the capitalist enemy. But as with other
schismatic traditions, such as Protestant Christianity, rhetorical attacks, no matter how vicious, often spoke to authentic points of disagreement over significant issues. Just as a correct theory about how
to enter heaven has been a grave matter to Christians, a correct theory
about how to achieve socialist revolution has been a weighty issue to
Marxists.

Marx himself was famous for his brow-beating style, even when
jousting with left-wing comrades. At an 1846 meeting of the League
of the Just in Brussels, comrades witnessed Marx's verbal pugilism.
With communism growing in popularity across Europe, the "tailor-
agitator" William Weitling had emerged as leader of those German
workers attracted to this new political ideal. Unimpressed, Marx
publicly reprimanded Weitling for endorsing spontaneous revolt,
since those who heeded his call became targets of state repression.
Such recklessness, Marx yelled, was due to Weitling's lack of a well-
considered theory of revolution. Humiliated, Weitling responded that
action was better than analysis. To which Marx exploded: "Ignorance
has never helped anybody yet!"[49]

This was not the first time Marx had callously dismissed an erstwhile ally. Nor would it be the last. He and Engels spent several months
at a time writing harsh, book-length takedowns of their fellow social-

ists. "Ruthless criticism of everything existing," as Marx had once de-scribed the role of the philosopher, had a purpose. Socialist revolution was a matter of high stakes. It was important to get it right.[50]

It was particularly important, it seems, for Trotskyists to get the Russia question right. One might have thought an advantage of not being a Communist Party member would have been the freedom to ignore Moscow-centric discourse. But because Trotsky was Stalin's most prodigious irritant-in-exile, anti-Stalinism was Trotskyism's raison d'être. And because Trotskyism was arguably the foundational political sensibility of the New York Intellectuals, their persistence in focusing on the Russia question, even well after Burnham and other leading American Trotskyists left the movement, has a certain logic.

Trotskyists like Burnham were predisposed to distrust the Soviet Union. Unlike devout members of the Communist Party, or even Pop-ular Front thinkers like Kenneth Burke, Trotskyists were much more inclined to believe the horror stories coming out of Stalinist Russia. But when the full scope of Stalin's murderous regime became apparent, even *they* were traumatized. As a result, many Trotskyists grew increas-ingly disillusioned with Marxism and the entire left-wing project more generally. Trotskyism came to be a wellspring of Marxist disenchant-ment that helped shape American liberalism and American political culture more broadly.[51]

Developments external to Trotskyism also contributed to the dogged insistence that what happened in Moscow mattered in New York. The world was at war yet again, only this time, more so than the last, the lines of demarcation seemed more clearly drawn. While the United States had not yet entered the war, the Second World War was to be a war between dictatorship and democracy. But even with such clarity, the Russia question remained murky.[52]

Would the Soviet Union align with the forces of dictatorship, as many anti-Stalinists assumed, and as the Nazi-Soviet Pact seemed to confirm? Or would the Soviets side with the beleaguered democracies, a testament to the Popular Front that became a reality when Hitler's armies invaded the Soviet Union? Even after that, many Americans were hesitant to accept the Soviets as partners. Harry S. Truman, then a US senator, declared a pox on both houses. "If we see that Germany is winning we ought to help Russia," Truman said, "and if Russia is winning we ought to help Germany, and that way let them kill as many as possible."[53]

Burnham also lumped together the Soviet Union and Nazi Germany. In 1941, a year removed from quitting Trotskyism and declaring Marxism wrong, Burnham wrote his most famous book, *The Managerial Revolution*. Burnham argued the economic means of production were now controlled by a technocratic elite headed by world leaders such as Stalin and Hitler. He called this new form of political organization "bureaucratic collectivism." For the growing number of Americans like Truman who conflated communism and fascism, so far, so good. But Burnham included Roosevelt among this new ruling elite.

The United States, he said, had succumbed to the new antidemocratic system that had overtaken Germany and Russia. Like Marx, Burnham offered up a grand theory of historical change. But he pronounced Marx wrong. The future was here, the future was not socialism. Yet even as he left the Marxist dialectic behind, Burnham retained a teleology indebted to a Marxist theory of power. Whoever controlled the productive forces also controlled the political forces. The American government had once been in the pocket of capitalist kingmakers like John D. Rockefeller. Now, New Deal technocrats, neither capitalist nor socialist, managed both the economy and the government. This placed them in the same historical class as Nazi administrators and Soviet bureaucrats.[54]

Burnham protested too loudly when he rejected Marx. The historian Jack Diggins astutely described *The Managerial Revolution* as "an answer to Trotskyism and a farewell to Marxism as a philosophy of history and as a program of hope—but not as a mode of analysis." Burnham's unsentimental theory of power, in which he argued democracy had become a facade for power, owed to his Marxism. For Marx, what people called democracy was a formal system easily manipulated by the bourgeoisie. For Burnham, American democracy was a useful sham that legitimized managerial government. This connection explains why C. Wright Mills later named Burnham "A Marx for the Managers." Burnham claimed to be done with Marx. Marx was not done with Burnham.[55]

Burnham's trajectory is one example of widespread intellectual ferment that owed to events of world-historical proportion. On the heels of the great dislocations of the 1930s came the cataclysmic Second World War, which killed seventy-five million people and is remembered for death camps and mushroom clouds. That calamity was followed by the Cold War, yet another international crisis, this one pitting the capitalist superpower against its communist counterpart in a deadly global struggle for material, ideological, and nuclear supremacy. Put simply, the middle of the twentieth century is characterized by unprecedented mass trauma. It was predictable that so many people radically altered their worldviews.

INVENTING THE AMERICAN POLITICAL TRADITION

It was also somewhat inevitable that so many American intellectuals turned away from Marx, whose theories seemed increasingly implicated in the chaos that had inundated the world. But midcentury American intellectuals could not simply ignore Marx, especially those who had long engaged his ideas. Rather, to make clear their disillusionment, they had to perform an exorcism. Marx had to be reinterpreted for the demands of a drastically altered world. Over the course of a decade, a vastly different Marx appeared on the American scene. Marx the prophet was replaced by Marx the false prophet. The fact that this stark transformation was not only a phenomenon in the larger intellectual culture, but also occurred in the minds of individual thinkers, speaks to the power of twentieth-century historical forces.

The project of rethinking Marx helped define midcentury liberal thought. As we have seen, a lot of this had to do with Roosevelt's New Deal, which successfully supplanted Marx in the minds of many American radicals. But it also had a lot to do with the Cold War. In fact, midcentury liberal thought, for better or worse, is known now as simply Cold War liberalism. Cold War liberals used Marx as an integrative force for calibrating their views to a world in flux. But they did not use Marx as a source of positive inspiration. Rather, Marx became their bête noire.

It is difficult to pinpoint when exactly this project began, or whom it began with. The liberal anti-Marx project began in fits and starts before expanding into an avalanche. One plausible starting point might be the publication of Isaiah Berlin's acclaimed 1939 biography *Karl Marx: His Life and Environment*.[56]

Although not an American, Berlin was a quintessential Cold War liberal, in part because of his biography. He was born in Latvia in 1909, but as a young boy moved to Petrograd, where he witnessed the Bolshevik Revolution. In 1922, Berlin's family fled Russia, which was being torn apart by the civil war that had raged since the revolution. They landed in London, where Berlin earned entrance to Oxford University. Berlin eventually joined the faculty there. He became a liberal theorist renowned for his pluralist contention that the "necessity and agony of choice" was a prerequisite of freedom. But before gaining fame as a liberal philosopher, Berlin authored a lively little Marx biography.[57]

Berlin introduced his book by recognizing the reach of Marx's influence. "No thinker in the nineteenth century," Berlin wrote, "has had so direct, deliberate and powerful an influence upon mankind as Karl Marx." He also begrudgingly praised *Capital*, as "the most formidable, sustained and elaborate indictment ever delivered against an entire social order, against its rulers, its supporters, its ideologists, its willing slaves, all whose lives are bound up with its survival." But these admissions masked Berlin's true task.[58]

Berlin sought to prove Marx's fallibility and undermine the essential components of his historical theory. For Berlin, Marx was a hidebound determinist who was "convinced that human history is governed by laws which, like the laws which govern nature, cannot be altered by the intervention of individuals actuated by this or that ideal." Even worse than his humorless obliteration of human agency, Marx's gravest offense was his evasion of ethics.[59]

In his laser-like focus on prophesizing the coming revolution, Marx had ignored a more significant moral problem. Would the revolution be a good thing? Berlin likened Marx's fanatical insistence on the coming revolution to the totalitarian zealots whose armies were now marching across Europe and Asia. "His faith in his own synoptic vision of an orderly, disciplined world, destined to arise out of the inevitable self-destruction of the chaotic society of the present," Berlin wrote, "was of that boundless, absolute kind which puts an end to all questions and dissolves all difficulties."[60]

Berlin's rendering of Marx overlooked important aspects of his thought. Marx had a more flexible understanding of human agency in relation to social forces than Berlin gave him credit for and was thus less deterministic than Berlin made him out to be. Furthermore, in placing human autonomy at the center of his larger theory of capitalism, Marx was more ethical than Berlin imagined. Berlin's critique of Marx was better understood as a critique of the orthodox Marxism that had particular purchase in the Second International and in the Soviet Union during Berlin's time. But the publication of Berlin's book was perfectly timed since it coincided with a growing sense that Marx was dangerously wrong. At the end of the 1930s, such emergent sentiments did not yet represent a full-fledged liberal creed. It took more than a slim Marx biography from an obscure Latvian-English philosopher to accomplish such an ideological overhaul. The exorcism of Marx was just getting started.

Another crucial beginning was the publication of Edmund Wilson's 1940 book *To the Finland Station*, a dramatic narrative history of socialism from the storming of the Bastille until that fateful moment when Lenin arrived at Finland Station in St. Petersburg to lead the Bolsheviks to power. Unlike Berlin, Wilson was already a well-known left-wing essayist when his book was published. During the 1930s, Wilson had grown disgusted with capitalism, and it showed in his prose. But by 1940, disillusion with the world's most famous critic of capitalism also began to seep into Wilson's writing.[61]

More than a narrative history of socialism, *To the Finland Station* was an investigation of the life and ideas of leading socialists, Marx foremost among them. Even though Wilson later described the book as a critique of Marx, it was understated, especially compared with

Berlin's. That said, Marshall Berman overstated the case when he later contended that Marx was the "tragic hero of Wilson's story." Rather, Marx is an ironic if central figure on the long and winding road to the Finland Station.[62]

In his single-minded quest to slay the horrible beast known as capitalism, Marx himself became a beast of a man. Wilson, ever the clever stylist, used Marx's friendship with Engels as a literary device for exploring this paradox. Marx, the calculating rhetorician, endowed the world with metaphors that surgically captured the sweep of history. Engels, the more compassionate figure, added human texture to Marx's abstract structures. Whereas an unsentimental Marx thundered on about the means of production, Engels showed basic human decency when he wrote about the Manchester working class "being shoveled into the mines and the mills like so much raw materials for the prices their finished products would bring, with no attempt even to dispose of the waste."[63]

Wilson's distinction is exaggerated. Marx often wrote movingly of working-class conditions. The novelist F. Scott Fitzgerald insisted to his daughter that she read "the terrible chapter in *Das Kapital* on The Working Day, and see if you are ever quite the same." Moreover, although Engels had indeed written sympathetically about the working class, he was also the person chiefly responsible for whittling down Marx's theories into abstractions. Nevertheless, distinguishing between Marx and Engels in this way helped Wilson make a point that would become central to how Cold War liberals framed Marx.[64]

The portrait of Marx as an unsparing exponent of rigid abstractions foregrounded Wilson's criticism of the Marxist dialectic. The dialectic was to his mind rock-solid proof that Marx was a determinist. Socialist revolution, as the myth of the dialectic had it, would spring forth from the conditions of capitalism. Wilson argued Marx never really worked out the precise nature of causal relations in this system. Marx never dealt effectively with the relation between human will and the web of material conditions in which humans are situated. How did Marx reconcile the existence of himself as a revolutionary philosopher with a materialist conception that human consciousness was constrained by social relations? Wilson contended Marx's apparent failure to solve this contradiction was grounded in his inability to escape his German roots:

> Karl Marx, with his rigorous morality and his international point of view, had tried to harness the primitive German Will to a movement which should lead all humanity to prosperity, happiness and freedom. But insofar as this movement involves, under the disguise of the Dialectic, a semi-divine principle of History, to which it is possible to shift the human responsibility for thinking, for deciding, for acting— and we are living at the present time in a period of decadence for Marxism—it lends itself to the repressions of the tyrant. The parent stream of the old German Will, which stayed at home and remained patriotic, became canalized as the philosophy of German imperialism and ultimately of the Nazi movement.[65]

American socialists, in Wilson's view, should have discarded the dialectic and instead embraced a less deterministic, more humanistic form of socialism. Marx leavened with Emerson. In a world where Stalinism existed as a blood-soaked legacy of the Marxist dialectic, such a proposal was not uncommon nor unreasonable. But it was based on a misreading.

The most important thing to know about the Hegelian dialectic is that for Hegel history was a process of unfolding in which, as Louis Menand writes, "every paradigm contains the seed of its own undoing." The unfolding of contradictions conserves the past and reembodies it in the future. Just as we detect some semblance of the present in the past, we seek to detect some semblance of the future in the present. Yet this does not mean that the future is more of the same. Nor does it mean there is a definitive path to the future, or that humans have no role in carving such a path. In both the Hegelian and Marxist dialectics, humans do not sit idly by awaiting the unfolding of history. Humans *are* the unfolding of history.[66]

The idea that the Marxist dialectic erased human will and was thus a deterministic forerunner to totalitarianism seemed a solid paradigm for explaining a world on the precipice of being conquered by Hitler and Stalin. Wilson was hardly alone in espousing such thoughts. Max Eastman's 1941 book *Marxism: Is it Science?* was a similar, piercing attack on the Marxist dialectic. The key to understanding the Marxist dialectic, according to Eastman, like Wilson, was to understand Marx's inability to overcome his German roots.

Eastman recognized that Marx traded Hegel's idealism for materialism. But in Marx's assertion that the working class has "only to release the elements of the new society which the collapsing bourgeois society carries in its womb," Eastman argued he retained a central Hegelian idea that there was an internal logic to historical development that tended in a specific direction. Given this, Marx had no choice, wrote Eastman, "but to present the conditions which make his plan possible as causes which make its success inevitable." The Marxist dialectic was a feedback loop premised on an unprovable tautology. Marx predicted his preferred future was coming into being due to ironclad laws that he had discerned. "That is why," Eastman argued, "Marx's blueprints of the proposed society are so sketchy, and yet are laid down as though Marx had prophetic insight and was able to write a history of the remote future of the world." Marx spent his life laboring over a grand theory of capitalism that amounted to little more than magical thinking.[67]

Eastman explained his contention that Marxism lacked a scientific basis and was better thought of as theology by pointing to national origins. In contrast with the German and Russian minds, which remained firmly in the grip of metaphysics, the Anglo-American mind manifested a scientific sensibility, he said. Eastman elevated these national differences into normative claims. He argued the Anglo-American approach to knowledge was more mature than the German and Russian methods, and that such maturity was a byproduct of a more advanced Anglo-American economic system.

Eastman's grandiose claims were dripping with irony, and he took notice. "Marx regarded England as a model of the mature workings of that capitalist system that he analyzed, and he would regard present-day America as a supermodel," Eastman wrote. "Nevertheless, it is just in England and America that Marxism never found a home." A scientific, positivistic, pragmatic culture could not welcome Marx. American intellectuals were not abstract world-builders. Rather, they began with the world as it actually existed. If they determined the world needed improvement, they would search for scientific solutions. This was because Anglo-American intellectual culture had transcended the religious sentiments structuring German thought.[68]

It had long been thought Marxism threatened religious belief. Marx, after all, had infamously dismissed religion as the "opiate of the masses," or "illusory happiness." But for Eastman, Marx was less a threat to religion and more a substitute for religious thought. "Marx banished the spirit," Eastman argued, "but retained in his material world the now still more extraordinary gift of being in sympathy with his ideals." To midcentury liberals obsessing over the pluralist underpinnings of democracy, the religion of Marxism came to seem incompatible with America.[69]

Not all liberal intellectuals had concluded by the end of the Second World War that Marx had endowed the world with a quasi-theology. Refashioning Marx remained a work in progress, and alternative interpretations vied for attention. Reinhold Niebuhr advanced one with his 1944 book *The Children of Light and the Children of Darkness*. Niebuhr is a paradoxical figure in the history of liberals rethinking Marx. His premises originated from a vastly different place, yet he came to similar conclusions. The charge that Marx was wrong because he was too theological did not carry much weight with Niebuhr since he himself had a theological view of politics. Niebuhr believed a Christian perspective accorded with democracy because proper Christians recognized humans were capable of evil. Yet despite this rather important difference, Niebuhr was one of several American intellectuals whose favorable view of Marx had soured.

The Children of Light and the Children of Darkness retains the main theme of Niebuhr's 1932 book *Moral Man and Immoral Society*. Liberal naivety remained a grave problem in the face of evil. But the later Niebuhr was much harsher in his assessment of Marx. In 1932, Niebuhr affirmed his appreciation for Marx's understanding of power, which led Marx to a suitable cynicism regarding liberal platitudes like justice. In 1944, Niebuhr included Marx among the "children of light," those naive dupes who believed in the goodness of human nature. This was a severe charge, since Niebuhr argued incredulous progressives had enabled the "children of darkness" to run roughshod over the planet. "Stalin will probably have the same relation to the early dreamers of the Marxist dreams," he wrote, "which Napoleon has to the liberal dreamers of the eighteenth century."[70]

Marx's grim theory of class struggle hardly made him a likely candidate for children of light status. But in Niebuhr's view, Marx's ideas were premised on the prospect that humanity is perfectible. "Marxism expects men to be as tame and social on the other side of the revolution," Niebuhr wrote, "as Adam Smith and Jeremy Bentham thought them to be tame and prudential on this side of the revolution." For Niebuhr, there was no such thing as a tame and orderly humanity. The children of light, whether Marxist or liberal, misunderstood human nature.[71]

What was the appropriate response to the dangers posed by the children of darkness? For Niebuhr, people committed to democracy had to recognize that humans were capable of dragging us all into the pits of hell. But they also had to acknowledge that free and creative individuals could transcend seemingly inexorable social forces. Marx obscured human potential, which was another way of labeling him a determinist. Both Niebuhr the Christian and Eastman the secularist had ultimately concluded Marx was a false prophet. Anti-Marxism had become a powerful and capacious ideological tendency among liberal thinkers of a wide variety.

Dwight Macdonald, the writer, editor, and ex-Trotskyist, took an even more circuitous path to a comparable conclusion. Unlike Eastman, who thought Marx was not scientific enough, Macdonald believed Marx was too scientific. In this, Macdonald was closer to Niebuhr. He believed freedom hinged on people becoming sensitive to "the tragic element in man's fate not only today but in any conceivable kind of society."[72]

Macdonald, the former editor of *Partisan Review*, had become one of the nation's leading pacifists. His opposition to war was grounded in hostility to the instrumentalism that had embedded itself in Enlightenment thought. For Macdonald, Marxism was "the most profound expression" of this type of thinking, "the belief that the advance of science, with the resulting increase of man's mastery over nature, is the climax of a historical pattern of Progress." Breaking with the false idol of Progress mandated banishing Marx. Macdonald's 1946 book *The Root Is Man* was written precisely with this goal in mind.[73]

Before severing ties with Marx, Macdonald had a nasty breakup with Trotsky. Macdonald joined the Socialist Worker's Party in 1939. But he was too independent to be a disciplined member of the Fourth International. When a controversy arose in Trotskyist circles about the Kronstadt rebellion, a 1921 uprising by anarchist Russian sailors who were easily crushed by the Trotsky-led Red Army, the feisty Macdonald could not help but interject.

The exchange that ensued was overheated, like many other instances of intra-Left polemics. But, also like other such debates, it addressed an issue of enduring significance. To what extent should revolutionaries resort to violence? Trotsky was adamant the Kronstadt rebels represented a grave threat to the Bolsheviks, who had barely maintained their hold on power in the midst of an ugly civil war. The rebels got what was coming to them. When the French philosopher Simone Weil asked Trotsky in 1933 why he gave the order to crush the Kronstadt uprising, he asked her if she was from the Salvation Army—implying that those who questioned the necessity of defeating the rebellion were similarly unwitting tools of capitalism.[74]

Macdonald saw in Trotsky an authoritarian strain that all too often characterized Marxism. Trotsky deployed his typical acerbic wit in responding to Macdonald. "Everyone has a natural right to be stupid, but beyond a certain point it becomes an intolerable privilege." The longtime Trotskyist James Cannon piled on, calling Macdonald a "political Alice in Wonderland." Macdonald wore such invective as a badge of honor. "Alice is presented," Macdonald wrote, "as a normal and reasonable person who is constantly amused, bewildered or distressed by the fantastic behavior and logic of the inhabitants of Wonderland." Macdonald quit the movement in 1940.[75]

Macdonald's rejection of Trotsky sowed the seeds of his eventual rejection of Marx, and his embrace of pacifism and anarchism. It helped him conclude that any ethical approach to the world had to begin with the individual, and that this "ethical dynamic comes from absolute and non-historical values, such as Truth and Justice, rather than from the course of history." When Trotsky ordered the slaughter of the Kronstadt sailors, he believed he was fulfilling a larger purpose. Marx had endowed him with a sense of historical inevitability. A couple thousand sailors could not stand in the way. Just as a couple million peasants could not stand in the way of Stalin's march to destiny. Running roughshod over the individual was indefensible to Macdonald no matter how compelling the historical logic.[76]

The plight of the individual, trapped in a web of the masses, was a postwar liberal trope informing a range of bestselling books, including David Riesman's *The Lonely Crowd* (1950) and William H. Whyte's *The Organization Man* (1956). *The Root of Man* pointed forward to those books. But it also pointed backward to Burnham's *Managerial Society*. Like Burnham, Macdonald failed to shed Marxist habits of mind even as he explicitly rejected Marxist goals and conclusions.[77]

Macdonald theorized capitalism had been transformed into something else, and that a different class of people dictated the terms of the new social order. "The external process is working out," Macdonald wrote, "but the inner spirit is the reverse of what Marx expected." He wrote that "private capitalism is indeed decaying and the bourgeoisie are being expropriated, but the agency is not the proletariat but rather a new political ruling class which is substituting its rule for the old ruling class in the time-honored way." The old capitalist elite had been replaced by a new managerial elite. This transformation had resulted not in liberation for the masses but in an even ghastlier enslavement.[78]

As evidence for this extravagant claim, Macdonald pointed to the history of organized labor. In the early years of the Great Depression, the labor movement was infused with the spirit of anticapitalism.

Unions not only demanded better working conditions, but also control over the workplace. Workers wanted power relative to the means of production. But as the New Deal order came into being, labor unions trimmed such ambitions and became, according to Macdonald, "an integral part of capitalism rather than a force for labor's emancipation from capitalism." Opposite Marx's expectations, the proletariat in a highly developed nation like the United States had not become revolutionary. Capitalist wealth had not engendered socialist consciousness. To the contrary, the only successful communist revolution at that time had occurred in a country that was largely considered an economic backwater.[79]

Macdonald's observations highlighted a dilemma for Marxists that grew more acute across the second half of the twentieth century. Where communist revolution had been successful, in the Soviet Union and later in China and other poorer nations, life remained miserable for many. Where communist revolution might have made life better for many people, such as a nation like the United States where there was wealth enough to go around, it never happened, and those who would have benefited the most from such a revolution rejected it. The failure of socialism in highly capitalistic countries informed those who grew disillusioned with Marx. For the same reason there was no socialism in the United States, Marx was deemed a false prophet.

MIDCENTURY LIBERALISM AGAINST MARX

The idea that America signified a powerful alternative to Marx was a bedrock assumption of midcentury liberalism. The historian Arthur Schlesinger Jr. beat people over the head with this idea in his widely read 1949 book *The Vital Center: The Politics of Freedom*. In carving out the center, Schlesinger attacked both right and left. As a liberal Democrat, Schlesinger scorned conservatives like the Republican senator Robert Taft, who rejected the New Deal and opposed the interventionist foreign policy demanded by the Cold War. But Schlesinger saved his most indignant prose for "Doughface progressives" like Henry Wallace, who protested Truman's uncompromising stance on the Soviet Union by organizing a third-party campaign for president in 1948.[80]

Taking his cues from Niebuhr, Schlesinger mocked the progressive belief that humans were basically good. Wallace was the perfect foil in this regard because his naivety led him to assert that cooperation with the Soviets was possible, and also allowed his campaign to be infiltrated by Communists. Luckily, Schlesinger argued, the aberrant ideologies of right and left were on the wane in the United States, where the "vital center" had become the political norm instead.

What did it mean for Schlesinger that the United States was a centrist nation? It meant it was a "New Deal country," which also meant it was best positioned to fight off totalitarianism. Because the New Deal ran "contrary to Marx's prediction of increasing proletarian misery," because it "vastly increased the wealth and freedom of the ordinary worker," the United States was best able to ward off utopian ideologies like Marxism.[81]

Schlesinger liked hard-boiled political rhetoric, which was ironic coming from a bow-tied Harvard professor. In the eyes of millions of people, Marx was nothing if not tough with his talk about class struggle. But for Schlesinger, Marx was yet another doughface progressive whose utopian dreams unwittingly ushered in dystopian nightmares. "Marx's dream of a classless society," Schlesinger wrote, "dissolves into the harsh realities" of life under communist rule. Marx was the roadmap to the Soviet Union, where, in the words of Dostoevsky, "all are slaves and all are equal in their slavery."[82]

In equating communism and slavery, Schlesinger compared Marx to a nineteenth-century American champion of slavery, George Fitzhugh. Like Marx, Fitzhugh noted the chaos sown by capitalism. Fitzhugh theorized socialism would emerge as a way to tame the vertiginous experience of capitalism. But the price people would have to pay to end such disorder would be to give up their freedom. "Socialism proposes to do away with free competition; to afford protection and support at all times to the laboring class; to bring about, at least, a qualified community of property, and to associate labor. All these purposes," Fitzhugh wrote, "slavery fully and perfectly attains." Socialism was slavery, and slavery was socialism. Schlesinger agreed with Fitzhugh's premise, calling him a wiser and more honest thinker than Marx while declaring that modern-day communism was far worse than "a relatively amiable, mid-Victorian" slave plantation. If Fitzhugh was the apologist of slavery's past, Marx was the prophet of slavery's future.[83]

In the early 1930s, plenty of Americans thought Marx presented them with an avenue to freedom. By 1949, many more Americans agreed with Schlesinger that Marx represented the road to slavery. Nothing demonstrates this midcentury transformation like the makeover that took place in the mind of Sidney Hook. The juxtaposition between Hook's 1933 book *Towards the Understanding of Karl Marx* and his 1955 book *Marx and the Marxists: The Ambiguous Legacy* is palpable.

Whereas the younger Hook appreciated Marx's optimism about humanity's future, the later Hook argued that Marx lacked a sense of the tragic. "After all, if even angels revolt in the City of God who can be sure of human behavior in the City of Man?" The two decades between Hook's Marx books were a time of unparalleled horror. Auschwitz, Hiroshima, and the gulag made people consider the tragic foundations of history. But Hook's altered perspective on Marx owed as much to dramatic political and intellectual developments in his own life.[84]

Hook's unorthodox Marxism meant he could never find a place in the Communist Party. The Trotskyist movement served as his political home throughout much of the 1930s. But Hook's disgust with events in the Soviet Union eventually morphed into disgust at international Marxism writ large. In 1939, Hook helped John Dewey found the Committee for Cultural Freedom, which promoted democratic reforms in fascist and communist nations. The committee played an important role in convincing American liberals that communism and fascism were two sides of the same totalitarian coin. This conflation, which hardened into Cold War liberal dogma, informed the 1950 formation of the international Congress of Cultural Freedom (CCF). Hook was also heavily involved in that organization. So too was the Central Intelligence Agency (CIA), which secretly funneled cash to the CCF in an effort to convince left-wing European intellectuals to reject the Soviets.[85]

Hook took anticommunism to new heights with his 1953 book *Heresy, Yes—Conspiracy, No!* where he advocated barring Communists from government employment, including teaching positions. He argued party membership alone was proof of conspiracy, and that people who conspired against the state could not be trusted to work for it nor with impressionable young minds. Hook grew renowned as a fierce anticommunist.[86]

Hook wrote *Marx and the Marxists* to banish the specter of Marx. Even more, he wrote it to extinguish his own past. Hook no longer wanted to be associated with his earlier favorable perspective on Marx. He forbade publication of a new edition of *Towards the Understanding of Karl Marx*, whose pragmatic interpretation of Marx had positioned him well within American intellectual traditions. Instead, with *Marx and the Marxists*, Hook gave readers a Cold War–inflected evaluation of Marx, which cast Marx well outside such traditions.[87]

The 1955 Hook offered up the twentieth century as definitive evidence that Marx was wrong about capitalism's future trajectory. "Marx vastly underestimated the regenerative power of capitalism to overcome its own periodic crises," Hook contended. Marx's argument that capitalism would immiserate workers, who would then turn to socialism out of desperation, miscalculated "the pressure labor could exert through the extension of political democracy on the distribution of wealth and on social security."[88]

The rise of social democracy, including the New Deal but especially the more robust European variants, did serious damage to Marx's reputation as capitalism's greatest critic. Social democracy softened capitalism's edges, proving that in some nations workers could live in relative comfort even as capitalists accumulated wealth and power. Indeed, during a period that Eric Hobsbawm refers to as the "Golden Age" of capitalism, from 1947 until 1973, capitalism stabilized in unprecedented ways. Like never before or since, the system benefited the working class, at least in the developed nations of North America and Western Europe.[89]

This historical development did as much as the Cold War to compel liberal intellectuals to reevaluate Marx. "British, American, and

Western-European economies show features almost as profoundly different from those Marx predicted as inescapably involved in the development of capitalism," Hook wrote, "as are the characteristic features of Soviet economy from those Marx expected to follow upon the disappearance of capitalism." Such certainties about Marx's failures were every bit as rooted in the 1950s as Hook's earlier certainties about Marx's prescience were rooted in the 1930s. If Marx confused the nineteenth-century variant of capitalism with the system's universal form, Cold War liberals mistakenly believed the New Deal had forever solved capitalism's contradictions. They mistakenly believed social democracy had forever proven Marx wrong.[90]

Hook pointed to other twentieth-century developments as discrediting Marx. He argued it was "noteworthy that neither Marx nor Engels nor any leading protagonist of historical materialism predicted the rise of Fascism in any of its varieties." Hook attributed this lack of foresight to Marx's disregard of powerful nonmaterial historical forces like nationalism. Marx's theory of class struggle presumed an international proletariat would overthrow the bourgeoisie. Marx did not envision a Herrenvolk amassing to conquer Europe and murder as many Jews as possible.

The charge that Marx ignored the irrational side of human political behavior overlooks some of Marx's most famous work, such as *The German Ideology* and *The Eighteenth Brumaire*, in which the irrational featured large. But either way, it is not very surprising, nor interesting, that a nineteenth-century thinker, even one widely admired for his foresight, got a lot wrong about the twentieth century. What *is* interesting is that so many twentieth-century thinkers thought the fact that a nineteenth-century thinker misjudged the future was proof of him being a bad thinker. Cold War liberals subjected Marx to unprecedented scrutiny precisely because his ideas spawned mass movements across the world, which they increasingly interpreted as threats to an American way of life they had increasingly come to appreciate. Marx's legacy was thus in need of undoing.[91]

In the same way that Cold War liberals employed the twentieth century as proof that Marx's theories were wrong, they also used American history as a definitive counterexample. Nobody did this more force-fully than the political scientist Louis Hartz, author of the renowned 1955 book *The Liberal Tradition in America*.

For Hartz, any analysis of American political thought had to begin with what he termed the "storybook truth about American history": the United States had no feudal past. This helped explain why the United States, unlike Europe, lacked both "a genuine revolutionary tradition" and "a tradition of reaction." The philosopher who embod-ied American political thought was not Marx, nor Edmund Burke, but rather John Locke. Neither class struggle nor aristocratic distinction shaped American political sensibilities. Rather, the idea that animated American politics was Locke's theory that government was socially contracted to protect the natural rights of the individual, and that property was one such right.[92]

Hartz recognized there were historical exceptions, most glaringly the political philosophy of the Slave Power, which Hartz called "an alien child in a liberal family." But over time, the liberal tradition crushed all that stood in its way. Whereas both a reactionary like Fitzhugh and a revolutionary like Marx were, in Hartz's words, "crucified by the Amer-ican general will," liberals like John Dewey "flourished in consequence of their crucifixion." The liberal tradition thus represented an Ameri-can consensus.[93]

Most midcentury liberals came to believe a liberal consensus was one of the defining features of American history, and that this con-sensus was a key aspect of what distinguished American history from European history. This distinction also functioned as the bedrock of American exceptionalism, the idea that the United States had never been beholden to the historical constraints that shaped Europe. In the hands of some American cold warriors, American exceptionalism was an ideology of national superiority. Not only was America different, it was better. But there was nothing inherently nationalistic about the notion that American history was defined by consensus.

As the liberal historian Richard Hofstadter argued, the idea of an American consensus "owed almost as much to Marx as to Tocqueville." Hofstadter wondered how "any realistic Marxist historian could fail to be struck at many points by the pervasively liberal-bourgeois character of American society in the past." Arguably, neither was there anything inherently nationalistic about American exceptionalism, at least as a theory. As a point of fact, although Alexis de Tocqueville had posited a version of American exceptionalism, modern usage of the phrase owed to left-wing sectarianism. In 1927, when the American Communist Jay Lovestone argued the United States was not ready for socialist revolution due to the unique power of American capitalism, Stalin accused him of "the heresy of American exceptionalism."[94]

Although Stalin undoubtedly thought he was defending Marxist doctrine, Marx himself put forward a concept of American exceptionalism. Marx wrote that American capitalism developed "as in a greenhouse," and he described the United States as the first fully realized bourgeois country because its people were conditioned to the idea that "work is the key to wealth, and wealth the only object of work." More remarkable to Marx was that even though the United States had become an industrial giant, it had not yet developed fixed class distinctions. In Marx's view, this was largely because the United States was able to avoid the pathologies of a feudal past, including class hatred. Marx, in other words, anticipated Hartz.[95]

To most midcentury liberals, American exceptionalism proved that Marx's theory of capitalism did not stand up to the evidence. But Marx had anticipated such objections. Tocqueville argued America represented Europe's future because Europe was inexorably transforming into a postfeudal, democratic society of the American type. Marx argued instead that Europe was America's future. American exceptionalism was a temporary condition.

Marx attributed the exceptional nature of American class consciousness to the fact that there did not yet exist a surplus population in the United States as there did in Europe. He assumed that with massive European migration, a persistent fact for much of Marx's life, the United States would soon boast one. Foreshadowing Frederick Jackson Turner's famous "frontier thesis," Marx also contended that as the American frontier closed, European immigrants would no longer be welcomed with land and the autonomy that came with land ownership. The nineteenth-century equivalent of the American dream would soon be dead. Workers would be obligated to work for wages as part of a blossoming proletariat. If American exceptionalism was the negation of Marx's theory of socialist revolution, Marx negated the negation. He applied his dialectical mode of thought to America.

The Marxist dialectic posited that labor in a capitalist economy would become more and more degraded while at the same time workers would become more and more conscious of the ways in which they are repressed. Cold War liberals vehemently disagreed with this idea, as well as most of Marx's theories about labor. But Marx's rather more prosaic idea that labor is the essence of human experience—that labor is our *species being*—was not one many liberals engaged. The German Jewish émigré philosopher Hannah Arendt was unique in this regard. In her 1958 book *The Human Condition*, Arendt forwarded a withering critique of Marx's theory about labor's essence, arguing that it pointed toward totalitarianism.

Nobody did more than Arendt to shape American understandings of totalitarianism. Her widely read 1951 book *The Origins of Totalitarianism*, focused on the ideological phenomena that gave rise to Nazism. But *Origins* also made the more generic point that totalitarianism "claims to transform the human species into an active unfailing carrier of a law." In the Cold War context, many readers assumed Arendt had Marx in mind here. But at that time, Arendt's familiarity with Marx was limited. Subsequently, she systematically read Marx, and *The Human Condition* was the result.[96]

Arendt's criticism of Marx was built on the ancient distinction between labor and work. Labor was defined by human activity that was necessary to ensure the reproduction of human life, such as raising crops. Work was defined by the crafting of objects that had some permanence, like a chair or a marble statue or a philosophy book. Both labor and work could be arduous, backbreaking, even soul-wrenching. But only labor was thought of throughout human history as degrading, as something animals did. Indeed, Arendt argued the universal desire to evade labor had been crucial to defining the parameters of human freedom for millennia. Ancient Athenians enslaved people to avoid the unfreedoms they associated with labor. The degradation of labor and the freedom that accompanied its avoidance were intrinsic to the human condition. Slaves were less than human because they were forced to spend their lives doing tasks otherwise reserved for animals.[97]

Marx ignored the distinction between work and labor, and elevated labor as that which "distinguished man from other animals." He conceptualized labor as humanity's species being, as the essence of human nature. But, perplexingly, he also hoped that labor could be eliminated altogether. Marx argued humans had always been laboring beings even as he envisioned a future "in which this greatest and most human power is no longer necessary." He theorized, in Arendt's words, that "only when labor is abolished can the 'realm of freedom' supplant the 'realm of necessity.'"[98]

Arendt highlighted this apparent contradiction as a way to advance her argument that Marx had dodged the very terms of life itself. The pain and suffering involved in labor are the modes that make life legible to us as humans. "Man cannot be free if he does not know that he is subject to necessity," Arendt wrote, "because his freedom is always won in his never wholly successful attempts to liberate himself from necessity." By arguing that humans would be free when they transcended necessity, Marx ignored that humans will always find meaning in the toggling between necessity and freedom. We cannot have one without the other, now or in the future. Arendt believed Marx's theory of labor obliterated the plurality of ways in which humans experienced life. Its singular focus had destroyed the pluralism necessary to democratic politics. This made Marx a totalitarian thinker.[99]

Arendt's close philosophical attention to totalitarianism, and especially her conclusion that Marx was totalitarian, resonated with the broader currents of Cold War liberalism. But not everything about her ideas rested easily in postwar American culture. Arendt's notion that necessity would always define the human condition was not only at odds with Marx. It also went against the grain of the more optimistic, even utopian, ideas about modern development advanced by many American social scientists. In a way, this is not surprising since such theories were often structured in explicitly Marxist terms even as they were sold as the opposite. Take the theory of modernization forwarded by the liberal economic historian Walt Whitman Rostow.

Rostow explicitly pitched his hugely influential 1960 book *The Stages of Economic Growth* as the antithesis to Marx. His purpose was made abundantly clear by the subtitle: *A Non-Communist Manifesto*. Yet Rostow's ideas about economic development, in a strange way, owed a debt to Marx. Rostow believed historical patterns revealed iron laws. In this he was not unlike Marx. Where Marx and Rostow differed was in the utopian conclusions to their teleological dreams. Marx theorized history was developing in the direction of communism. Rostow believed liberal capitalism was the end of history.[100]

Rostow's background was similar to others in the New York intellectual milieu. Born in 1916, he was raised in Brooklyn by Jewish immigrant socialists. Rostow was a gifted student, and he won a scholarship to Yale University after graduating from high school at age fifteen. While at Yale, Rostow discovered Keynes, which he described as lifechanging. He also discovered Marx, which was equally lifechanging for different reasons. After reading Marx, Rostow determined he would dedicate his life's work to unlocking the mysteries of economic history, the mysteries of Karl Marx. "Marx raised some interesting questions," he wrote in his personal journal, "but gave some bloody bad answers." Rostow vowed to one day answer "Marx's theory of history."[101]

In 1958, Rostow, by then a professor of economic history at the Massachusetts Institute of Technology, won a Carnegie Corporation grant to spend a year at Cambridge University developing what would become *The Stages of Economic Growth*. During that year, Rostow wrote to the two-time Democratic presidential nominee Adlai Stevenson: "As an eighteen-year-old Yale undergraduate, much disliking the pretentious nineteenth century Germans," Rostow reflected, "I promised to produce an alternative to Marxism as a theory of modern history; and I have used my sabbatical to make my bid." In another private letter, Rostow wrote that he was working to "uproot the bad works of that angry, old man Karl Marx." In short, Marx weighed heavily on Rostow's mind as he wrote *The Stages of Economic Growth*, a book once described as "Marxism without Marx."[102]

Just as Marx had theorized historical phases that passed from feudalism through capitalism and concluded with communism, Rostow had a teleology of five historical stages that began with a traditional society, the equivalent of feudalism, and ended with American-style liberal capitalism, or what he termed "the age of high mass-consumption." Rostow argued his theory of development was superior because, unlike Marx, he did not reduce human motivations to economic incentives. Paradoxically, Marx pitched his work as a challenge to bourgeois political economists for believing just such a thing.

Marx was forever intent on exploding the myth of *Homo economicus*. But Cold War liberals ignored such an inconvenient detail because their reinterpretation of Marx offered them a flattering contrast. Rostow's economic model, not Marx's, accounted for complex motivational factors and was thus appropriate to pluralist, democratic politics. Indeed, this is how Rostow made the case that liberal capitalism was the platonic ideal. Liberal capitalism, not communism, affords individuals a range of choices in their lives, from the jobs they choose to work, to the automobiles they choose to drive. Rostow's end of history thus presented immeasurable psychological rewards.[103]

After reading *The Stages of Economic Growth*, Stevenson wrote Rostow. "Is the future Rostowism vs. Marxism?" Stevenson asked. "If so, I am ready to vote now." There was no doubt which lever Stevenson would have pulled. Like Marx, Rostow had created a confident model for future development. But unlike Marx, Rostow's future had a happy ending that liberals like Stevenson could appreciate. The world was inexorably coming to look more and more American. Rostow's work was part of a much larger project to make Americanism into a normative conception of the good life. Marx was the convenient "other" to this project.[104]

It goes without saying that Cold War liberal teleology had many unhappy endings. In Vietnam, three million people died as a result of American efforts to remake that country in accordance with liberal designs. Rostow personified this tragedy. The author of the archetypal utopian theory of liberal development was also one of the policymakers responsible for the dystopian war in Vietnam. Rostow's trajectory from

FIGURE 5.1: From left to right: Francis M. Bator, economist; George E. Christian Jr., White House press secretary; Walt W. Rostow, special assistant to the president; Secretary of Defense Robert S. McNamara; and President Lyndon B. Johnson, in the Oval Office in June 1967.

social theorist to war strategist exemplified the ideological ossification of Cold War liberalism. As evidence mounted that perhaps not everyone wanted liberal capitalism after all, Cold War liberals dug in their heels. In an irony of epic proportions, they also declared the death of ideology. For them, an ideology was a rigid system for understanding the world, something only other people had. And by other people, they meant Marxists.[105]

THE END OF (MARXIST) IDEOLOGY

When Cold War liberals declared ideology dead, what they really meant was that Marxism had died. Daniel Bell's famous 1960 collection of essays *The End of Ideology: On the Exhaustion of Political Ideas in the Fifties* was largely an examination of how Marx had lost his grip on American political culture.[106]

Bell, a luminary of the New York Intellectual scene who became a Harvard University sociology professor, had been writing about Marx and American socialism for years. In his 1952 book *Marxian Socialism in the United States*, Bell argued Marxists acted as if they were "*in* but not *of* the world." Conservative Christians often used this expression to describe their difficult task of living in a fallen world with full knowledge they were destined for a better place known as heaven. Bell used this saying to describe Marxists who lived in a degraded capitalist world with full knowledge they were destined for a better future known as socialism. For Bell, such expectations showed Marxists did not take the world as it actually existed seriously. "Socialism," Bell wrote, "was an unbounded dream." But the dream died.[107]

Bell admitted socialism was not the only ideology worth considering. "America, too, was an unbounded dream," he wrote. Indeed, socialism failed to take root in America precisely because "Americanism, with its creed of egalitarianism, was a surrogate of socialism." During the 1930s, when a growing number of Americans confronted capitalism's greatest crisis by turning to Marx, all the various Marxist movements ultimately collapsed because "the New Deal, like the earlier ideology of Americanism, had become a somewhat different surrogate for socialism." But if the New Deal was the apotheosis of Americanism, it also represented its end as an ideology. "From the sixteenth-century chiliast, burning with impatient zeal for immediate salvation," Bell wrote, "to the twenty-century American labor leader, sunning himself on the sands of Miami Beach, is a long, almost surrealist jump of history."[108]

President Dwight Eisenhower recognized how Marx missed this jump when he addressed union leaders in 1955. "The Class Struggle Doctrine of Marx was the invention of a lonely refugee scribbling in a dark recess of the British Museum," Eisenhower declared. "He abhorred and detested the middle class. He did not foresee that, in America, labor, respected and prosperous, would constitute . . . his hated middle class."[109]

By the 1950s, ideology in either its Marxist or Americanist forms had been seemingly rendered obsolete by an affluent society where even the working class lived in relative luxury. When the system worked well for everybody, ideology was no longer necessary. Midcentury liberals believed ideology took hold of people who needed answers to intractable problems. Marxism emerged as an answer to the seemingly knotty problems related to capitalism. "Out of the immanent, convulsive contradictions of capitalism," Bell wrote, doing his best Marx impersonation, workers "would inherit the world." But because Marxism's solutions were "*in* but not *of* the world," it was no better than a secular religion. Marx was God, and God was dead.[110]

When Bell put the final nail in the coffin of ideology, he placed the final nail in Marx's coffin. Another book published in 1960, Clinton Rossiter's *Marxism: The View from America*, was an even more overt attempt to bury Marx. It compiled the many ways in which Marxism "never had a chance in America." In outlining his case, the Cornell University historian covered well-trod ground.[111]

Americans rejected Marx's philosophy of misery because they had largely been happier, healthier, and wealthier than people elsewhere. Rehashing Werner Sombart's formula, Rossiter wrote that socialism foundered "on the shoals of roast beef and apple pie." Thus, the success of the New Deal made postwar America even less inviting for Marx than at any time in American history. "Quite the contrary to Marx's prediction that the most advanced industrial countries would be the first to make the transit from capitalism to socialism and beyond to communism," Rossiter wrote, "this most advanced of all such countries has never been insulated so thickly against the appeals of Marxism nor ever behaved in so thoroughly un-Marxist a fashion."[112]

Rossiter's book was an argument against Marx. But it was also an argument *for* the American tradition. These two objectives went together. Marx was the archetypal foil that helped Cold War liberals come to grips with the American political tradition. "The American tradition has no Marx," Rossiter wrote, "its essence is pluralism, which means that each of its children is encouraged to make his own interpretation of its principles; and it is, after all, the product of centuries of unplanned accretion rather than of a few years of imperious dogmatizing."[113]

Marx's half-baked determinism pointed toward totalitarianism. The American tradition's hard-won pragmatism pointed toward democracy. Unlike Marxism, which reduced social and historical change "to a single determining principle," the American tradition was "permissively pluralistic." In this, Rossiter made a common error of his time: Pluralism had never really been a defining feature of American history, but liberals badly wanted it to be so. They confused their aspirations for reality. They lived *in* but not *of* the world. In their eagerness to discredit Marxism as a religion, midcentury liberals were blind to the fact that they had created a secular religion of their own. "The new man of Marxism," Rossiter wrote, "is a dream in which a line of tough-minded thinkers from John Adams to Reinhold Niebuhr has forbidden us steadily to indulge." The new man of Marxism stood in contrast with the new man of Americanism. But each presented the world with a utopian ideal. And each had its founding heroes.[114]

Rossiter's Marx was an extreme caricature even by the standards of Cold War liberalism. At least as far back as Isaiah Berlin's 1939 Marx biography, liberals had been in the habit of selectively interpreting Marx. By Rossiter's time, this habit had become a full-blown addiction. Rossiter's imagined Marx was stripped of all nuance and complexity. The Marx of *Capital* who grappled with the intricate relationship between capitalism and slavery was nowhere to be found. The Marx of *The Eighteenth Brumaire* who struggled with understanding how the forces of reaction captured the popular will had disappeared. Instead, Rossiter presented a rigid Marx that gave the world Stalin. "In pulverizing the barriers to political power, in sneering at the instruments of 'mere formal freedom,' in stripping the family of its private character," Rossiter wrote, "Marx opened the way to the dynamic, all-pervading collectivism of Soviet totalitarianism."[115]

Rossiter's contribution to Marx studies doubled as Cold War apologia. "What we come down to in the end is a fundamental conflict between two bodies of principle, two faiths, two ideologies, a conflict so severe that peace between them has always been and remains today impossible to achieve." Rossiter was talking about the conflict between Marx and the American tradition. But he might also have been talking about the conflict between the Soviet Union and the United States. In his eyes, they amounted to the same thing.[116]

From the late 1930s until the early 1960s, Marx's reception tracked alongside liberalism's narrative arc. As assorted left-wing and liberal intellectuals grew disillusioned with Marx, they slowly grew enamored with America, and not just any America. Liberals came to love the America they imagined. This America was not merely a military powerhouse that could stand up to Soviet aggression; it also represented an antitotalitarian political culture. The America of the liberal imagination was a beacon that endowed the world with a pluralist political philosophy. But liberal pluralism, even if more prescriptive than descriptive, more aspirational than actual, was marred by an enormous chasm.

BLACK MARXIST AS COUNTERFACTUAL

Midcentury liberalism largely overlooked race in its political philosophizing. When liberalism did attend to race, it held that black Americans simply should act as other ethnic groups in American history, like the Irish, had. The liberal celebration of pluralism commenced against the backdrop of Jim Crow, which denied basic civil rights to black Americans, especially in the South, at a time when the United States was trying to convince nonwhite people across the globe to align with it in the Cold War. This hypocrisy is only one reason why black Americans were generally less than eager to embrace Cold War liberalism. It certainly explains why some black thinkers bucked powerful intellectual trends by sticking with Marxism, even at risk of their freedom.[117]

W. E. B. Du Bois was far from alone among major American intellectuals when he used Marx to help him interpret history and society in the 1930s. But during the 1940s and 1950s, as former Marxists like Hook and Burnham zigged right, Du Bois zagged left. In 1961, after years of being hounded by the federal government for his left-wing activities, he joined the Communist Party. With this symbolic act, the ninety-three-year-old Du Bois told America to go to hell.

Another major black intellectual who never grew out of love with Marx, even at the cost of his political freedom in the United States, was C. L. R. James, dubbed the "Black Plato" by the *New York Times* in 1980. As a prominent Trotskyist who broke with that movement in 1940, James might have joined the likes of Burnham and Hook in their travels away from Marxism. But living in America as a black man was a radically different experience that led to a radically different trajectory.

Being a black man in Europe had already made James a different sort of Marxist, one who brought black and colonized peoples into a mostly European framework. After moving to the United States in 1938, and especially after traveling across the country on a bus, James undertook to do the same with American culture. This would not be an easy task, although he was well suited to it. As James wrote: "From the first day of my stay in the United States to the last, I never made the mistake that so many otherwise intelligent Europeans made of trying to fit that country into European standards. Perhaps for one reason— because of my colonial background—I always saw it for what it was, and not for what I thought it ought to be. I took in stride the cruelties and anomalies that shocked me and the immense vitality, generosity and audacity of those strange people."[118]

James was fascinated by America. He not only staved off disillusionment with Marx, but he also managed to remain somewhat optimistic about the strange country he called home for fifteen years. James's unique perspective led him to produce an unknown masterpiece. *American Civilization*, which James wrote in 1950 but which went unpublished until 1993, represents a compelling counterfactual. How would the study of America have been different had midcentury liberalism not exorcised Marx?

James was convinced that bringing Marx and America together was crucial if the United States was going to have any chance at a socialist future. More than that, he thought it was necessary for a fuller understanding of the United States. He thus accepted the challenge posed by

Charles and Mary Beard in their 1942 book *The American Spirit: A Study of the Idea of Civilization in the United States*. "The utterly alien nature of Marxism was illustrated by the fact," the Beards wrote, "that neither foreign born nor native Marxists produced any significant contributions to thought in relation to American history or economy." James wanted to prove the Beards wrong.[119]

The overriding concern James expressed in *American Civilization* was with capitalist automation and what this meant for freedom. James argued American civilization had reached a threshold unlike any since the Civil War. Modern industrial relations had curtailed individual freedoms to an almost unprecedented degree. Like some of his fellow ex-Trotskyists, James stressed that the horrors of totalitarianism were not limited to people in far-off lands like Russia. The workplace, due to advances in mechanization, was a totalitarian institution. "The modern worker is a cog in a machine," James argued. "All progress in industry consists of making him more and more of a cog and less and less of a human being." These developments represented a civilizational threshold because of the vast gulf that separated liberal democratic expectations from the experience of work in a capitalist economy. James wrote:

> Upon a people bursting with energy, untroubled by feudal remains or a feudal past, soaked to the marrow in a tradition of individual freedom, individual security, free association, a tradition which is constantly held before them as the basis of their civilization, upon this people more than all others has been imposed a mechanized way of life at work, mechanized forms of living, a mechanized totality which from morning till night, week after week, day after day, crushed the very individualism which tradition nourishes and the abundance of mass-produced goods encourages. The average American citizen is baffled by it, has always been. He cannot grasp the process by which a genuine democracy escapes him.[120]

Workers were alienated not because of low wages or lack of access to consumer goods. Rather, the American working class lacked autonomy. What this spelled for the future, other than working-class anger that might express itself in a range of unpredictable registers, was left an open question. James assumed the issue of automation would become a problem of almost existential proportions. Perhaps he was wrong about that. But James wrote about American society through the lens of Marx, who conceptualized human happiness as deeply bound up with autonomy. People who lack control over their own labor remain unfree. This was the logic that undergirded *Capital*, and the logic that structured *Black Jacobins*. Being a black Marxist who had closely studied the history of slavery and slave rebellion helped James make these connections. When midcentury liberalism jettisoned Marx from the American imagination, such logic became almost entirely absent from the study of America.

The repression of Marx and Marxists would only get more severe. James learned this the hard way in 1953, when the US government deported him to London, where he would live the remainder of his life in exile. A lot like Marx.

6

RED MENACE

Postwar Conservatism

The seeds of Marx's theory took hold when the story of Virgin Mary
was doubted.

GERALD L. K. SMITH

In the years following the Second World War, a red scare of unprecedented force swept over American political culture. Red baiting became a national pastime across nearly all political persuasions. Liberals helped stoke a climate of fear in subtle but powerful ways. In 1947,
President Harry Truman issued Executive Order 9835, known as the
Federal Employee Loyalty Program, designed to root out subversives
in the federal government by empowering loyalty oath boards. This instigated an epidemic of finger-pointing. Countless Americans accused
erstwhile friends and colleagues of various transgressions, including
the high crime of reading Karl Marx.[1]

Although American liberalism contributed to the postwar red
scare, and although the red scare helped shape the liberal invention
of the American political tradition, the anticommunist crusade is
more closely associated with American conservatism. Red baiting as
a method of political repression became synonymous with the right-
wing Republican senator from Wisconsin, Joseph McCarthy. The red
scare was more than McCarthyism, but the label does highlight two

salient facts. First, people throughout American history have fiercely opposed social levelers of all kinds—abolitionists, socialists, anarchists, communists, Marxists, feminists, civil rights activists, and so on—and these opponents of equality, like McCarthy, are best described as conservative. Second, the postwar red scare, as with all red scares, mostly benefited conservatives, who leveraged the repressive mood not only against leftists but also against liberals, their main political foes. Conservatives of all types, from elitist snobs to populist demagogues, conflated leftism and liberalism in their efforts to discredit both.[2]

The specter of Marx haunted the New Deal from the beginning. In the conservative imagination, Marx was its architect, with Franklin Roosevelt merely his unwitting dupe. Roosevelt's trusted advisers often declared their intention to save capitalism. Conservative critics saw it otherwise. Elizabeth Dilling, a right-wing activist committed to rooting out Marxism, believed that "Roosevelt is following Marx nicely." In her 1934 encyclopedia *The Red Network: A 'Who's Who' and Handbook of Radicalism for Patriots*, Dilling mapped out a subversive web connecting communists like Marx and Lenin to liberals such as Roosevelt and John Dewey. She regarded *The Communist Manifesto* as seed of Roosevelt's mantra about the "forgotten man."[3]

Dilling's 1936 follow-up *The Roosevelt Red Record and Its Background* undertook a step-by-step comparison of the New Deal to *The Communist Manifesto*. "Marx and Engels wrote ponderous tomes," she wrote, "awesomely regarded by followers because of their pompous polysyllabled words and pedantic style, perhaps deliberately obscure." And yet somehow *The Communist Manifesto* provided a blueprint for the New Deal—whose agenda, she said, was the "abolition of property," "a heavy or progressive graduated income tax," "centralization of the means of communication," and "equal liability of all to work."[4]

In seeing the New Deal as dictatorial at heart, Dilling aligned with the American Liberty League, which was started by a group of capitalists in 1934 to resist the alleged New Deal threat to property. In this historical moment, conservatives began to coalesce against what they considered unwarranted government interference in the affairs of capitalism. This was yet another example of how the 1930s crisis of

FIGURE 6.1: Elizabeth Dilling, addressing the Senate Judiciary Committee, January 11, 1939.

capitalism acted as an ideological sorting machine. Americans oriented themselves to an emerging right-center-left political spectrum based on their positions relative to capitalism, the New Deal, and, yes, Marx.[5]

For the unapologetic defenders of capitalism, Roosevelt had taken the United States down a road to ruin paved by Marx. Some of his fellow Democrats even felt this way—even Al Smith, the party's 1928 presidential nominee. The publishing baron William Randolph Hearst also deserted the Democratic Party, bemoaning that it had become the "imported, autocratic, Asiatic Socialist party of Karl Marx and Franklin Delano Roosevelt."[6]

For a sizable number of American conservatives, especially those on the Far Right, Marx menaced more than capitalism. As the demonic face of modernity, he also threatened other bedrock institutions upon which they believed the American nation rested. Dilling lamented that Marx wanted to end not merely capitalism but religion and the family as well. The Far Right Christian Gerald L. K. Smith declared that "the seeds of Marx's theory took hold when the story of Virgin Mary was doubted." By the logic of this conspiracy theory, Marx asserted that religion was the "opiate of the masses" not simply because he was an atheist but also because he believed communism would only take hold after people lose faith in God. Smith applied this logic to his analysis of New Deal bureaucrats, who "hatched from the snake nest of atheistic Marxism. They are predicated on the abolition of the church, the philosophy of the anti-Christ, and the reduction of the individual to regimented slavery and bureaucratic tyranny."[7]

Father Charles Coughlin, the Catholic priest who boasted a national radio audience rivaled in size only by Roosevelt's fireside chats, placed Marx at the center of a vast conspiracy. That Marx was a Jew was hardly incidental since Coughlin's theory traveled a well-worn antisemitic path. In 1933, Coughlin was friendly toward Roosevelt's efforts to curb predatory capitalism and believed the New Deal might in fact save the United States from Marxism. But in 1936, Coughlin denounced the New Deal as communistic. In 1938, he blamed Jews for the Marxist infiltration of American government, and he reprinted the antisemitic hoax *The Protocols of the Elders of Zion* in his periodical *Social Justice*. In 1940, Coughlin praised his fellow opponent of "Jewish Marxism," Adolf Hitler. When the Roosevelt administration threatened to charge Coughlin with sedition in 1942, and when it indicted thirty American fascists in 1944—what the historian Leo P. Ribuffo termed the "brown scare"—it confirmed in the eyes of the Far Right that the government was indeed beholden to Godless Marxism.[8]

After Allied troops liberated the German death camps at the end of the Second World War, revealing the full scale of Nazi atrocities, explicit antisemitism persisted in the United States only on the extreme right-wing fringe. But conspiracy theories about Marx's dastardly influence still abounded among American conservatives. That Marx's ideas shaped American liberalism became a staple of mainstream conservative thought, even among the sober-minded brahmins who sneered at Far Right crackpots.

Historians of the postwar conservative movement often emphasize the distinctions between its diverse components. American conservatism included people who promoted tradition, and those who hyped liberty. But when it came to Marx, there were few differences. Conservatives who focused on the Marxist threat to capitalism were not far apart from those who concentrated on the Marxist threat to tradition presented by liberalism.[9]

The postwar red scare brought the nadir of Marx's American reception. His name was invoked frequently, but rarely sympathetically. Even among the millions of Americans who had never read Marx, most knew his ideas were dangerously anti-American.

Liberals and conservatives alike contributed to defining Marx as anti-American. But whereas liberals argued the New Deal proved Marx wrong, conservatives contended it was his brainchild. Liberals maintained Marx's ideas would never work in America. Conservatives asserted they were already at work within liberalism. Conflating Marx with liberalism made liberalism seem duplicitous in the eyes of millions of Americans. This was an intended consequence.

CHASTENING THE LABOR MOVEMENT

Marx's ideas were indeed at work in American life, but not in the government institutions that executed the New Deal. Rather, Marx was alive, if not well, among the labor movement's rank and file. Surveys in 1945 and 1946 confirmed that autonomy in the workplace—independence from supervision by management—was the single most common desire of unionized workers. American workers intuited

Marx's notions about exploitation and freedom. Capitalist exploitation is above all predicated on expropriating value from work, on stealing time and controlling bodies. Marx's socialism sought to extend
freedom to the workplace, which is where most people in a capitalist
society spend the majority of their waking hours. But control over
the workplace was precisely what American capitalists were loath to
concede.[10]

As the historian Nelson Lichtenstein argues, America is indeed
exceptional relative to other capitalist nations, but not in the ways
normally cited. Rather, America is exceptional in the intensity of capitalist hostility toward industrial democracy, under which workers
control their own fates. Because American corporations developed
into continent-wide organizations in the nineteenth century, when
government regulation was weak at best, American capitalists had long
maintained supreme disdain for state guidance or worker interference.
The Great Depression unsettled this equation, forcing capitalists to
submit to the New Deal regulatory state. Worse yet for the business
elite, a powerful labor movement compelled a degree of deference to
unions. But as capitalists emerged from the Second World War with
renewed self-assurance, they sought a return to what they considered
the natural order of things. The business elite, with help from sympathetic politicians and opportunistic labor leaders, waged a frontal assault on the militant elements of organized labor. Any semblance of
Marxism that had taken hold of the labor movement during the 1930s
was stamped out.[11]

During the war, most unions signed no-strike pledges in a show of
patriotic duty. But in 1945 and 1946, a wave of strikes paralyzed several
industries, as workers sought to regain leverage and recoup lost wages.
In response, antiunion sentiment grew among the business class. *Fortune* magazine editorialized that the labor movement "carried with it
the echoes of the class struggle and Marxian dogma." Politicians joined
capitalists in working to weaken an intransigent rank and file. President Truman sought to end a United Mine Workers strike in 1946 by
seizing the mines. He also urged Congress to pass a bill that would au-
thorize the President to draft striking workers into the military. That

measure never became law. But when Republicans took control of both houses of Congress in 1946, antilabor legislation became a certainty.[12]

The coalition that elected Roosevelt four times and ushered in the New Deal regime was always somewhat unstable. Its commitment to organized labor was even less durable. The main reason for this fragility was the coalition's reliance on elite southern white Democrats who benefited from a strict system of race and class domination. These Southern Bourbons supported massive New Deal projects that improved southern infrastructure, but on the condition that the federal government overlook their ruthless enforcement of regional labor hierarchy, whether in the textile mills of the southern Piedmont or the cotton fields across the former Confederacy.[13]

Unions had long recognized the strategic importance of organizing the South, since as a cheap labor market it weakened the bargaining power of organized labor elsewhere. In 1946 the CIO launched Operation Dixie, a massive union drive in twelve southern states. But the CIO underestimated the Bourbon opposition, who charged that communists had to be behind any effort to alter southern social arrangements. By 1953, Operation Dixie had failed.[14]

Demonstrating the national consequences of southern antiunionism, in 1947 southern Democrats joined with conservative Republicans in Congress to pass the antilabor Taft-Hartley Act. The law constrained working-class solidarity by placing limits on the right to strike, by outlawing secondary boycotts, and by prohibiting the closed union shop, which created large "right-to-work" zones, mostly in the South and West. Taft-Hartley also compelled union leaders to sign federal loyalty oaths.[15]

Although the compulsory loyalty oaths were a sop to anticommunist conservatives, many union leaders welcomed them. Philip Murray, president of the CIO since 1940, declared that "we have no classes in this country; that's why the Marxist theory of the class struggle has gained so few adherents. We're *all* workers here. And in the final analysis the interests of farmers, factory hands, business and professional people, and white-collar toilers prove to be the same." Murray appreciated loyalty oaths not only because he was anti-Marxist, but also because they allowed him to firm up control over workers who demanded rights in the workplace that might be deemed Marxist, which in turn eased his access to the corridors of power. Capitalists were always more amenable to working with an autocratic union than with one responsive to an unruly rank and file.[16]

Militant unionism of the Marxist variety, in which capital-labor relations were understood as an oppositional struggle, had been replaced by what the sociologist C. Wright Mills characterized as pliancy and subordination. Guided by "the new men of power," as Mills labeled postwar labor leadership, unions reconciled themselves to their subservient position in American capitalism. The supposed social compact forged by the "Treaty of Detroit," in which the UAW signed a contract with General Motors that increased wages in exchange for control over the shop floor and a no-strike pledge, was not an agreement between equals. It was a manifestation of labor's newfound position of deference.[17]

The Taft-Hartley Act helped create these arrangements by softening labor's radical edges. Purging reds from unions also expelled Marxist ideas from the labor movement, one of Marx's last refuges in American life. These developments were part of a larger pattern of Cold War consolidation that helped conservatives regain their footing after nearly two decades in the wilderness. With Marxist ideas quarantined, conservative ideas had more room to grow. An international fear of Marxism also made such advances possible.[18]

RAISING THE IRON CURTAIN

In broad terms, the Cold War was a global struggle between the capitalist West, under the leadership of the United States, and the communist East, under the leadership of the Soviet Union. American politicians committed to the struggle with gusto, especially Truman. In his taking a hard line with the Soviets after of the Second World War, Truman followed the lead of the staunchly anticommunist policymaker George Kennan.[19]

A junior Foreign Service Officer stationed in Moscow in 1946, Kennan was asked to explain why the Soviets refused to cooperate with American designs for European economic integration. He responded with a "long telegram" that explained the Soviet fear of "capitalist encirclement" rooted in a "neurotic view of world affairs." Kennan argued such neuroses had a long and deep history. Earlier confrontations with the more advanced nations of Western Europe created a national inferiority complex that left "backward" Russia ripe for Marxist infection. Kennan wrote:

> It was no coincidence that Marxism, which had smoldered ineffectively for half a century in Western Europe, caught hold and blazed for first time in Russia. Only in this land which had never known a friendly neighbor or indeed any tolerant equilibrium of separate powers, either internal or international, could a doctrine thrive which viewed economic conflicts of society as insoluble by peaceful means. After establishment of Bolshevist regime, Marxist dogma, rendered even more truculent and intolerant by Lenin's interpretation, became a perfect vehicle for sense of insecurity with which Bolsheviks, even more than previous Russian rulers, were afflicted. In this dogma, with its basic altruism of purpose, they found justification for their instinctive fear of outside world, for the dictatorship without which they did not know how to rule, for cruelties they did not dare not to inflict, for sacrifice they felt bound to demand. In the name of Marxism they sacrificed every single ethical value in their methods and tactics.[20]

Kennan's long telegram, published in *Foreign Affairs*, became the intellectual rationale for the policy of containment in which the United States, under Truman's leadership, committed to constraining the spread of communism. But Kennan's strange historical brew, peppered with a generous dash of psychological reductionism, was not enough to convince many Americans that the Soviet Union represented an existential threat that required major sacrifices. For that purpose, Truman had to up the ante.[21]

In March 1947, in a speech before a joint session of Congress, Truman asked for $400 million, mostly to aid Greek nationalists in their civil war with communists, or as he put it, to avert the imposition of "totalitarian governments." "Nearly every nation must choose between alternative ways of life," Truman warned. Such stark rhetoric was intended to frighten the American public into supporting a highly expensive interventionist policy—the Truman Doctrine—in a time of apparent peace. It worked, and the grounds for Marx's reception grew more hostile than ever.[22]

The Truman Doctrine had a domestic counterpart in Truman's loyalty oath program, which resulted in the firings of thousands of federal employees. The executive order allowed for "reasonable grounds for dismissal," which was interpreted broadly as an excuse to fire people for transgressions ranging from being gay to reading left-wing magazines. Although federal loyalty oath boards never uncovered proof of espionage or subversion, thirty-nine states employed similar loyalty boards. The most frequent targets of state boards were college professors and public-school teachers. After organized labor, education was the last institution where Marx's ideas maintained a small degree of traction. The postwar red scare closed that off as well.

The national mood of fear removed lingering domestic obstacles to an even more pronounced interventionism that came to fruition in 1948 when the United States earmarked twelve billion dollars to rebuild Europe. The plan, designed by Secretary of State George Marshall, represented a massive commitment to helping Western European nations recover as trade partners, important as part of a larger American mission to avoid another depression. The Marshall Plan also made sense to policymakers fearful that communists might take advantage of European instability. This security concern was made real by large French and Italian communist parties that seemed poised to take power.[23]

The Marshall Plan was a success. American aid stabilized recipient nations, thus rendering them less amenable to communism. But the plan also ratcheted up what the historian William Appleman Williams called "the diplomacy of the vicious circle," whereby every move to shore up American power in Western Europe had the intended effect of alienating the Russians. The Soviet Union was obliged to reject the Marshall Plan because it could not agree, as each receiving nation was required to, to reveal its economic strengths and weaknesses. Kennan admitted that the Marshall Plan put the Soviets "over a barrel" since opening up their books amounted to giving up a degree of sovereignty.[24]

The 1949 creation of the North Atlantic Treaty Organization (NATO), which many Western European nations joined alongside the United States and Canada, represented another turn of the diplomatic screw. The stated intention of NATO was to serve as a collective security arrangement against potential Soviet *and* German aggression. But in 1955, the Federal Republic of Germany, or West Germany, joined NATO itself. This compelled the Soviet Union and Eastern European nations to create a similar defense treaty, the Warsaw Pact. Winston Churchill's admonition that an "iron curtain" had descended across Europe was hyperbole when he said it in 1946. By 1955 this description had become fitting. Tensions between the capitalist West and the communist East had grown increasingly fraught by the year. Marx was caught in the crosshairs.[25]

These monumental geopolitical developments occurred against the backdrop of a nuclear arms race that began during the Second World War. After the United States invented atomic bombs and demonstrated their power by dropping them on Hiroshima and Nagasaki in August 1945, the world entered an era where nations could destroy whole cities. After the Soviets developed their own bomb, American fears shot up. The power of God was in the hands of a godless enemy.[26]

The year 1949 was ominous for American cold warriors. A few months after the Soviets got the bomb, Mao Zedong's communist forces seized power in mainland China. Republicans blamed Democrats for "losing" China to the reds. Marxist-leaning Foreign Service Officers, Republicans charged, had convinced Democrats to take a wait-and-see approach to the Chinese Civil War. These "China Hands" were eventually purged by red-baiting conservatives, with Senator McCarthy taking the lead. Anyone with even a tiny trace of Marxism in their background could not be trusted to craft American foreign policy.[27]

The next year communists once again marched in Asia when North Korean troops invaded South Korea. This time, Truman demonstrated his anticommunist mettle by waging war in the name of containment, originally a strategy specific to Europe. The war did not go well, particularly after Chinese forces entered the fray. The fighting ended in a 1953 armistice that left North and South Korea divided to this day. Five million people died, including forty thousand Americans.[28]

Worse still in the minds of vigilant anticommunists, several American prisoners of war returned home brainwashed. The Chinese had figured out a new way to control minds, so the story went. Edward Hunter, an Office of Strategic Services (OSS) agent during the Second World War, told government officials the Chinese had developed experts in the use of "drugs and hypnotism." Hunter warned Marxist brainwashing would make Americans "subjects of a 'new world order' for the benefit of a mad little knot of despots in the Kremlin." Right-wing conspiracy theories of this type have enjoyed a long and illustrious career in American political culture. World-historical events of the 1940s and 1950s aroused the right-wing conspiratorial imagination, which had the effect of exacerbating the red scare.[29]

The generation of Americans who fought fascism to then be confronted with another implacable, totalitarian foe believed the fate of civilization rested on its shoulders. People interpreted that responsibility differently depending on ideological orientation. Liberal intellectuals responded by working to solidify a modern philosophical rationale for American democracy that starkly contrasted not only with Soviet Communism but with Marx's socialism. Conservative intellectuals varied in their response, at least on the surface.

Traditionalist conservatives rejected modernist political projects altogether, including liberalism and Marxism, as part of their effort to bring older, often religious-infused principles back into fashion. Libertarian conservatives rebuffed not liberalism in toto, but rather twentieth-century versions of liberalism, as part of their endeavor to let market forces shape society. But traditionalism and libertarianism overlapped in one highly significant way. Both schools of thought saw contemporary liberalism as perilously similar to Marxism. And both blamed America's problems on that convergence. The notion that liberalism and Marxism were two sides of the same anti-American coin became a conservative consensus.

UN-AMERICAN ACTIVITIES

For it to hold true that liberals were crypto-Marxists, it also had to hold true that liberals sought to subvert American democracy—since in the conservative worldview Marxism was inherently anti-American. Maintaining such a view about millions of Americans who called themselves liberal was extreme. But a series of sensational spy cases, revealing the existence of actual communist espionage, made such a view seem somewhat less extreme, and made repression of internal enemies seem necessary.[30]

Congress named a prominent committee on the premise that anti-communism was a vital expression of Americanism, and inversely, that communism was a vital expression of anti-Americanism. The House Un-American Activities Committee (HUAC), created in 1938 for the ostensible purpose of uncovering anti-American people of all sorts, came into its own as a persecutor of leftists during the second red scare. HUAC used its power to subpoena people and hold perjurers in contempt of Congress to pressure hostile witnesses to furnish it with information, particularly names of Communist Party members. The famed Hollywood Ten—movie producers, directors, and writers called before HUAC in 1947—went to prison and were blacklisted by the film industry after being found guilty of contempt for refusing to name names.[31]

Targeting left-wing cultural producers had a higher purpose than mere harassment. An exchange between Robert Stripling, lead HUAC investigator and author of *The Red Plot against America*, and the German émigré playwright Bertolt Brecht, was revealing. Stripling asked: "Have many of your writings been based upon the philosophy of Lenin and Marx?" Brecht replied: "I do not think intelligent plays today can be written without such study. Also, history written now is vitally influenced by the studies of Marx about history."[32]

Brecht was defiant, but rather than face prison time he fled the country, the one that had given him respite from the Nazis, to return home to the eastern region of Germany, which had since become part of the Soviet Bloc. HUAC achieved its objectives. By essentially purging Brecht, by imprisoning and blacklisting the Hollywood Ten, and by intimidating countless other writers, directors, and actors, conservative vigilantes stamped out Marxist cultural production—and intimidated who knows how many potential left-wing activists. Ritualistic red baiting reinforced the lines dividing Marx and America. It also threw into question on which side of the Marx-America ledger to locate liberalism.

Liberalism itself took center stage in 1948, when the consummate New Dealer Alger Hiss was accused by former Communist Whittaker Chambers of having been a member of a secret Communist cell in the 1930s. After a dramatic and consequential trial, Hiss was convicted of perjury and was sentenced to five years in federal prison. But the Hiss trial was about more than Communist espionage. It was an expression of conservative unhappiness with American liberalism, allowing them to claim smoking-gun evidence that the New Deal had always been tainted by Marx.[33]

In case there was any question about winners and losers in the spectacle, Hiss went to prison and Chambers became a literary star with his bestselling 1952 autobiography *Witness*. Part psychological confession, part philosophical contemplation, part spiritual meditation, *Witness* resonated with millions of right-leaning Americans, ensuring enshrinement in the conservative canon. Ronald Reagan committed passages of *Witness* to memory.[34]

Witness registered the existential drama of history so common to Marxist thought in the 1930s. It was apparent Chambers had internalized some of the habits of mind he inculcated as a Communist. Addressing his children in the book's foreword, Chambers wrote: "In nothing shall I be so much a witness, in no way am I so much called

FIGURE 6.2: Whittaker Chambers, 1948.

upon to fulfill my task, as in trying to make clear to you (and to the world) the true nature of Communism and the source of its power, which was the cause of my ordeal as a man, and remains the historic ordeal of the world in the 20th century."[35]

Witness provided an important service to conservative readers by defining communism in terms they could understand. Doing so first required disposing of common misunderstandings. Communism "is not simply a vicious plot hatched by wicked men in a sub-cellar," Chambers wrote. "It is not just the writings of Marx and Lenin, dialectical materialism, the Politburo, the labor theory of value, the theory of the gene-

ral strike, the Red Army, secret police, labor camps, underground conspiracy, the dictatorship of the proletariat, the technique of the coup
d'état." Rather, a single, famous sentence Marx wrote in 1845 captured
the essence of communism: "Philosophers have explained the world;
it is necessary to change the world." In this way Chambers equated
Marxists to Christians as "that part of mankind which has recovered
the power to live or die—to bear witness—for its faith." But there was
one difference that meant everything to Chambers. "The Communist
vision is the vision of Man without God."[36]

Communists renounced faith in God's heaven and replaced it with
faith in their ability to make heaven on Earth. Marxist faith filled a
great personal void for the younger Chambers, as with many others, by
soothing his existential anguish. "The evidence is strong," wrote conservative sociologist Robert Nisbet in 1953, "that the typical convert to
communism is a person for whom the processes of ordinary existence
are morally empty and spiritually insupportable." Marx offered Chambers a modern solution to this eternal problem of the human condition.
But it was a false solution, he decided: Christianity offered the correct
path to redemption because it presumed that humans are imperfect.
Marxists would go to any length, commit any atrocity, to achieve the
impossible, to realize perfection on earth. For Christians, such utopian
visions were only reachable in the afterlife. Heaven was a distant place
that could only be attained by those with faith in Christ and the grace
to be good people while living within earthly constraints.[37]

Liberals criticized Marxism because it was too much like a religion.
Conservatives criticized Marxism because it was atheism masquerad-
ing as religion. Conservatives also thought they more fully grasped the
danger Marxism posed because they better understood the passion
that religious faith inspired, whether a true faith like Christianity or a
false one like Marxism. Religious conservatives also appreciated that
devotion relied upon adherence to original text. For them, of course,
it was the King James Bible; they assumed *The Communist Manifesto* was
the Marxist equivalent.

When American Communist Party members were put on trial

during the 1950s for violating the Smith Act, which outlawed advocating the violent overthrow of the government, Marx's words were often used as evidence of guilt. Party members were found guilty by association with *The Communist Manifesto*, a century-old text that envisaged "the violent overthrow of the bourgeoisie [laying] the foundation for the sway of the proletariat." This clear violation of their First Amendment rights was rectified to some degree in the 1957 Supreme Court case *Yates v. United States*, which overturned fourteen Smith Act convictions. Yet in writing for the majority, Justice Hugo Black argued the greatest problem with the Smith Act convictions was that witness testimony was "comparatively insignificant" compared to what Marx "wrote or advocated as much as a hundred years or more ago." The real guilty party was Marx.[38]

Joseph McCarthy rose to national prominence in 1950 on behalf of conservatives who imagined a zombie Marx pulling the strings of a treacherous, atheistic communism nested within American liberalism. In using the specter of communism to attack Democrats in that year's political campaigns, McCarthy made one absurd allegation after another. The first accusations came on February 9, when he charged the Truman administration with "traitorous actions." "I have here in my hand a list of 205 names," McCarthy said. "A list of names known to the Secretary of State as being members of the Communist Party and who nevertheless are still working and shaping policy."[39]

The list was a fabrication, but McCarthy became an instant media sensation. Republicans, seizing their chance to inflict damage on Democrats, allowed him to lead numerous Senate hearings on communist infiltration. McCarthy weaponized indiscriminate and unsubstantiated charges and crossed boundaries few were willing to traverse. He remarkably went after establishment figures Dean Acheson and George Marshall, labeling the former "Red Dean" and accusing the latter of aiding and abetting communists.[40]

McCarthy's fans appreciated his no-holds barred rhetoric. "A true American," McCarthy declared, "detested Communists and queers" and "egg sucking liberals." For all his bluster, however, McCarthy's ideas tracked well with the larger conservative sense that Marxism threatened all that was sacred about America. McCarthy articulated this in his initial anticommunist speech. "The great difference between our western Christian world and the atheistic Communist world is not political," he declared, "it is moral."[41]

For McCarthy and conservatives at large, the fundamental distinction between communism and capitalism "lies in the religion of immoralism," which was "invented by Marx, preached feverishly by Lenin, and carried to unimaginable extremes by Stalin." McCarthy feared that if Marxism triumphed "this religion of immoralism will more deeply wound and damage mankind than any conceivable economic or political system." McCarthy dipped into a semi-fictitious version of Marx's biography to illustrate his point. "Karl Marx," McCarthy wrote, "expelled people from his Communist Party for mentioning such things as love, justice, humanity or morality. He called this 'soulful ravings' and 'sloppy sentimentality.'" Marx's cold, calculating ways set an example for his epigones. Without God as a check on morality, Stalin was free to murder millions of people in the name of communism. Nobody ever accused Stalin of "sloppy sentimentality."[42]

McCarthy's name is forever tied to the second red scare. However, J. Edgar Hoover, director of the Federal Bureau of Investigation (FBI) from its inception in 1924 until his death in 1972, truly embodied the anticommunist crusade. "Communism," Hoover believed, "is an evil and malignant way of life. It must be quarantined as any infection must be." Hoover never quit invoking the success of Lenin and the Bolsheviks as a warning against complacency. Testifying before HUAC, he noted that "in 1917 when the Communists overthrew the Russian government there was one Communist for every 2,277 persons in Russia. In the United States today there is one Communist for every 1,814 persons in the country." The past wasn't even past.[43]

Hoover had nearly unchecked power to mold the domestic national security apparatus to his view of what constituted a threat to America, which led to systematic abuses of people merely for their political beliefs. Beyond actual Communist spies like Julius Rosenberg, who was

executed in 1953 alongside his innocent wife Ethel for passing atomic
secrets to the Soviets, social levelers of all sorts were deemed threats to
Hoover's America. This included Martin Luther King, Jr., whose FBI
files were thicker than any others.[44]

Although Hoover wielded most of his power behind the scenes, he
also worked to shape public opinion. His 1958 book *Masters of Deceit:
The Story of Communism in America and How to Fight It*, was a bona fide
hit, selling well over two million copies. *Masters of Deceit* was researched
and written by the FBI's Domestic Intelligence Division, yet it was a
thorough distillation of Hoover's views. Given that Hoover personified the FBI, employees had enough sense to stay true to his vision,
summed up in a single sentence in the introduction: "International
communism will never rest until the whole world, including the United
States, is under the hammer and sickle."[45]

Masters of Deceit dug into Marx's biography to illuminate the historical origins of malignant communism. It portrayed Marx as a man
of few redeeming qualities beyond a sharp mind. "A few years before
the American Civil War," Hoover's agents wrote, "'scientific socialism'
stemmed from the mind of an egotistical, crabby, stubborn man who
from student days showed no interest in productive labor to support
his family and who used to pawn his overcoat in the middle of winter
to buy a few loaves of bread."[46]

Hoover's researchers judged Marx a colossal hypocrite, and Engels
a class traitor. "It is a bitter irony of history, indeed," they wrote, "that
the founder of communism should be literally kept alive by a wealthy
industrialist, and that a 'capitalist's' son, turned communist, should become the second 'father' of this revolutionary movement." They went
on in this vein: "No wonder a remark, attributed to his mother, was
made that instead of writing about capital it would have been better
if Karl had made some." Hoover and his assistants assumed Marx's
choice to dedicate his life to anticapitalism, even as his family went
hungry, was morally bankrupt. Only a depraved individual, with a "per-
verted and biased" mind, could have conjured up a debauched political
philosophy like communism.[47]

THE THREAT TO TRADITION

In Hoover's view, the most malicious aspect of Marx's philosophy was its atheism. Since Marx believed that "man is walking dust, without spark or image of his divine Creator," humans had nothing to inspire them to moral conduct. Echoing conservatives everywhere, *Masters of Deceit* worked from the premise that people brought low by atheism were predisposed to communistic and other nihilistic ideologies. Godlessness and Marxism went hand in hand. So too did Godliness and Americanism.[48]

Americans could not be faulted for thinking that Marx was obsessed with religion, for his atheism was endlessly discussed. It is of course true that he was a nonbeliever. But very little of Marx's voluminous written work, published or unpublished, focused on religion. A short essay from 1844, "Introduction to *A Contribution to the Critique of Hegel's Philosophy of Right*," in which he briefly conveyed his thoughts about religion, became the go-to source for ruminations about his atheism. It was there Marx infamously proclaimed that "religion is the opium of the people."[49]

Taken out of context, this quote has served anti-Marxists well because it sounds elitist. But when read in context, the meaning of that phrase changes. "Religious suffering," Marx wrote, "is, at one and the same time, the expression of real suffering and a protest against real suffering. Religion is the sigh of the oppressed creature, the heart of a heartless world, and the soul of soulless conditions. It is the opium of the people." Marx recognized that religion was more than a mere symptom of an oppressive society. Religion comforted the afflicted. Opium made people feel better, at least temporarily. But Marx also believed religion, like opium, clouded people's judgments about earthly matters, such as how to reduce suffering. This is what Marx meant when he wrote that the "critique of religion is the prerequisite of every critique."[50]

Even when understood in its full context, Marx's analysis of religion could never please conservatives. Marx's heartfelt appraisal might have refuted the image of him as heartless, but his atheism remained a radical challenge. For Marx, religion was a decisive foundation in the exploitative social structure he wished to upend, the very structure that conservatives wished to preserve. "The abolition of religion as the illusory happiness of the people," Marx wrote, "is a demand for their true happiness. The call to abandon illusions about their condition is the call to abandon a condition which requires illusions. Thus, the critique of religion is the critique in embryo of the vale of tears of which religion is the halo." The first step toward liberation was to do away with religion. Then humans will be free to "think, act, and fashion" a better world. "Thus," Marx argued, "the criticism of Heaven turns into the criticism of Earth, the criticism of religion into the criticism of law, and the criticism of theology into the criticism of politics." Marx's atheism was predicated on his desire that people get free on earth. In this way, conservatives were right. Marx's atheism *was* meant to be a Trojan horse for communism.[51]

Most American conservatives during the Cold War saw Marxism as the primary threat to religious and other cherished traditions. This informed their rabid anticommunism. It also helps clarify why the postwar red scare was mainly limited to the United States, the most religious and conservative nation among the Western capitalist ones.

By extension, many conservative Americans also believed the New Deal, as a Marx-inspired scheme, imperiled the nation's Christian heritage. To the more honest conservative intellectuals, Christianity safeguarded what they saw as the natural order of things, including hierarchy. As the conservative sociologist Ernest van den Haag wrote in 1950: "Religion is useful, even a necessary opiate—a sedative protecting us from excessive anxiety and agitation and from those who, like Marx, thrive on agitation and therefore hate the sedative and would replace it by the murderer's hashish." In this way, the American traditionalist project blended a robust defense of Christian order with a vigorous campaign on behalf of natural law, a body of unchanging moral principles that guided the United States from its founding. This project came into focus for postwar conservatives precisely because they felt the New Deal's leveling ambitions contravened nature, thus flouting the founders.[52]

Russell Kirk's 1953 book *The Conservative Mind*, which according to the *New York Times* "gave American conservatives an identity and a genealogy and catalyzed the postwar movement," arguably made the best case for natural rights as a Christian American inheritance. *The Conservative Mind* focused on the right-wing British and American thinkers who, since the French Revolution, had invented conservatism. In this reading, England and the United States were the only Western nations to escape violent upheavals since the French Revolution (somehow ignoring the US Civil War), thus freeing people there to think in nonrevolutionary registers. Edmund Burke, author of the 1790 counterrevolutionary masterpiece *Reflections on the Revolution in France* is the hero of Kirk's book. Burke expressed modern conservatism's ethos when he wrote that "the levelers only change and pervert the natural order of things."[53]

Kirk outlined several "canons of conservative thought" that had come to define the conservative temperament since Burke. Among them was belief in the divine, as well as the "conviction that civilized society requires orders and classes." Kirk continued: "The only true equality is moral equality; all other attempts at levelling lead to despair, if enforced by positive legislation." All humans are equal in the eyes of God. But from an earthly perspective, from the standpoint of law, politics, economy, and society, inequality was necessary, and good. On these grounds, Kirk opposed liberal reforms, including New Deal policies, which he depicted as "a deadening collectivism masked as liberal humanitarianism." Equality meant reducing everyone to a collective mass of brutish mediocrity.[54]

Marxism appalled Kirk as the authoritative philosophy of leveling that all other egalitarian-minded theories, including New Deal liberalism, took their cues from. Marx was the definitive defiler of natural rights. To support this claim, Kirk attributed a fabricated sentence to Marx. "In order to establish equality," Marx allegedly wrote, "we must first establish inequality." Kirk described this line as the single "most significant sentence in *Capital*," despite it not appearing there. In Kirk's eyes, Marx intended people to recognize that there was nothing natural about inequality. Natural law and similar such theories of timelessness were constructs of the mind that rationalized exploitation. Unmasking natural law at an intellectual level might help people see the reality of their material conditions. It might help people achieve equality. For Kirk, Marx's dismissal of nature was destined to turn the world upside down, and not for the better. "The clever, the strong, the industrious, the virtuous," Kirk wrote, "must be compelled to serve the weak and stupid and slack and vicious." The submission of nature to socialism and other leveling projects foretold the death of cleverness, strength, industriousness, and virtue.[55]

Like most conservatives, Kirk believed Marx's ideas had burrowed into twentieth-century American liberalism. This was not a good thing. But Kirk begrudgingly admired Marx for seeing clearly that liberalism, with its unimaginative trust in the political and moral virtues of science, was a bankrupt political philosophy. Comparing Marx to his contemporary, the British conservative Benjamin Disraeli, enabled Kirk to show that liberalism was ill-fated, and that conservatism was the better alternative to it. Kirk wrote: "Two Jews introduced the new conservatism and the new radicalism: Disraeli and Marx. For three decades, though poles apart in society, they inhabited the same London. . . . These two children of Israel, either the son of a Jewish father who had divorced himself from the old orthodoxy, perceived that the liberal society was doomed to suicide. Marx proposed to efface the whole extant social order and substitute a collectivistic life shaped upon a thorough materialism; Disraeli was determined to resuscitate the virtues of an older order."[56]

How should we think about Marx in relation to liberalism? Marx's thought hailed from at least three distinct philosophical traditions: German idealism, French utopian socialism, and British political economy. He criticized all three traditions, often harshly, but never in the spirit of destruction; rather, he did so with a mind toward creation. He started with ideas of those who came before him, to go to places they could not have gone.

In Marx's late, more mature works, including *Capital*, which he produced in London, Marx tended to focus on British political economy. He criticized and built upon ideas first developed by Adam Smith and

David Ricardo, among other British political economists. This meant that, as with many other nineteenth-century liberal thinkers in the British realm, including intellectuals ranging from Jeremey Bentham to Charles Darwin, Marx was obliged to express his study of capitalism in scientific language. He even came up with mathematical equations that were supposed to have calculated things like the degree of labor exploitation. This empiricism might have made Marx seem like a liberal thinker, though he was one of the most scathing opponents of political liberalism.[57]

Kirk knew better than to mistake Marx for a liberal. "Despite Marx's formal adherence to Utilitarian concepts of argument and proof, despite his belligerent determination to be scientific," Kirk wrote, "his influence has been that of a man of imagination—an imagination begrimed and fettered, true, but still participating in the world of ideas, superior to the tyranny of particular facts." Kirk implied that even the late Marx persistently grappled with German idealism, particularly Hegel, and French utopian socialism. More than mere empirical calculations, Marx's writings were imaginative projections of a postcapitalist world. More than a mere technocrat, Marx was a world-builder in the prophetic sense. As such, it was not worth debating whether Marx was right or wrong about this or that point. Kirk quoted the Scottish poet and economist Alexander Gray: "when we consort with Marx we are no longer in the world of reason or logic. He saw visions—clear visions of the passing of all things, much more nebulous visions of how all things may be made new. And his visions, or some of them, awoke a responsive chord in the hearts of many men."[58]

Kirk's fellow traditionalist Russell Weaver made a similar case for communism in his 1948 book *Ideas Have Consequences*. Following Marx, the Bolsheviks recognized that appeals to material reality were not enough to inspire people. Measuring mountains did not move mountains. Weaver wrote that Marxism, "despite its ostensible commitment to materialism, has generated a body of ideas with a terrifying power to spread." He warned of the "paradox of materialist Russia expanding by the irresistible force of idea, while the United States, which supposedly has the heritage of values and ideals, frantically throws up barricades of money around the globe."⁵⁹

Conservatives like Kirk and Weaver despised Marx yet they also displayed a hint of jealous admiration for a man who awoke the world to a powerful set of ideas. Conservatives sought to do the same, but with ideas—order, tradition, nature—of a much different type. This is why Kirk elevated venerable conservatives like Burke and Disraeli. He hoped their model would inspire a new generation of conservatives.

Both Marx and Disraeli hated what industrial capitalism did to people. But whereas Marx loathed it for engendering economic misery, Disraeli detested it for begetting spiritual impoverishment. For Kirk, this distinction was decisive. "The vast majority of men have always been poor," he wrote, "but perhaps never, since the triumph of Christianity, had they been so bored and hopeless, condemned to monotonous labor in the grimiest and grittiest of hideous towns, in a milieu philosophically dedicated to material success and moral individualism."⁶⁰

Both Marx and Disraeli recognized that class divided nineteenth-century English society. Marx hoped abolishing capitalism would create social equality, obviating class divisions. Disraeli, in contrast, wanted people to accept their class position rather than rebel against it. He "abhorred the idea of equality" as the enemy of order, and order was the guarantor of the good society. No wonder Disraeli joined Burke atop Kirk's conservative pantheon.⁶¹

Closer to home, American conservatives discovered a stealth defender of the ancient order in Leo Strauss, the German émigré and University of Chicago philosopher. Strauss was perhaps most famous for spawning a whole coterie of followers, men like Allan Bloom, who popularized reactionary dissent against all things modern. As a proponent of classical wisdom, as a believer that humankind had not improved upon Plato and Aristotle, Strauss disdained modernity, especially its propensity for leveling. In this Strauss hated Marx, the quintessential leveler, with as much passion as a classical philosopher could muster. But Strauss never stooped to write much about Marx, leaving such distasteful tasks to his students. It was Bloom, not Strauss, who battled the abomination known as Friedrich Nietzsche. Likewise, Strauss left the burden of condemning Marx to his student Joseph Cropsey.[62]

Cropsey taught political philosophy at the University of Chicago, while serving as the associate director of the John M. Olin Center, a conservative foundation. Cropsey authored the authoritative Straussian criticism of Marx in the textbook that he coedited with Strauss, *History of Political Philosophy*. This unorthodox 1963 production consisted of thirty-eight intellectual biographies of canonical Western thinkers ranging from Plato to Dewey.[63]

Cropsey's twenty-six-page Marx chapter focused on the problem of Marx's relativism, which traditionalist conservatives saw as a specter that haunted conventions of timeless value, whether those of natural law, ancient wisdom, or Christianity. Traditionalists across the twentieth century likened the liberal philosopher John Dewey to the second coming of Marx because he dispensed with certainty in his deeply contextual quest for truth-like knowledge. In his surprise 1987 bestseller *The Closing of the American Mind*, Allan Bloom's biggest complaint was with "indiscriminateness," or the cancerous idea "that truth is relative." As proof of the gravity of the situation, Straussians needed only to point to moderns' veneration of "Mick Jagger tarting it up on stage."[64]

Cropsey argued Marx, like most modern thinkers, had a deeply relativistic theory of how the world worked, which was fatal. Marx wrote in his 1847 book *The Poverty of Philosophy* that "the hand-mill gives you society with the feudal lord; the steam-mill, society with the industrial capitalist." The ways in which people are ruled are relative to the ways in which they are made to work. Such relativism was indeed an important feature of Marx's historical materialism. Marx theorized that social structures, political institutions, and conceptions of the world all correspond to the predominant modes of production. "He asserts," Cropsey wrote, "that all morality, philosophy, religion, and politics are the result of the conditioning of men by their environment—their manmade environment which is the expression of the mode of production."[65]

Marx's deeply contextual theory obliterated the idea that humans have natural tendencies, or that ethics exist independent of situation.

It was no wonder Marxists cavalierly rejected the idea inscribed in the Declaration of Independence that people have "inalienable, irreducible rights." "The sanctity of those rights," Cropsey wrote "thought by writers like Locke to be the ground for guaranteeing the freedom and thus the humanity of men, is rejected by Marx because he views the assertion of those rights as the course of, surely the expression of man's dehumanization." This illustrated the dire threat that Marx posed to what Cropsey called "the ruling principles of Western constitutionalism." Marx's war against nature was a war against America.[66]

Cropsey framed the war between Marx and America as a battle between the philosophical concepts of *becoming* and *being*. Since Marx believed humans were malleable, he also believed that, together, people could become something better. Or in Cropsey's rendering of Marx's vision: "the state or political order will wholly wither away, and homogenous mankind will live socially under the rule of absolute benevolence—from each according to his ability, to each according to his needs." In contrast, Cropsey believed human nature was fixed, and that conflict among people, no matter the larger context, was inevitable.[67]

Straussians believed philosophy of the classical sort allowed capable people to unlock universal verities, especially the timeless truth that humans needed politics to mediate their natural tendency to feud with one another. And for those people incapable of grasping such a crucial philosophical insight, religion would serve: people did not need to understand the logic of nature to obey it. This formulation was elitist, but Straussians have long argued that by keeping the order of things, ancient absolutes better led to justice, especially in contrast with Marxism.[68]

As Cropsey contended, Marx had swapped philosophy for history, politics for economics, and religion for society: a total, unshakable, and tragic relativism. "We begin to suspect the soundness of the antiphilosophic historicism of Marx," Cropsey wrote. "Observing its weakness prepares us to concede that history can make room for spiritually impoverished societies: the viability of Marxist nations is a sign not of the soundness of Marx's prophecy but of the unsoundness of the sanguine historicism on which he based it." Marx placed his trust in the power of history to reshape humankind. Or as Cropsey wrote, "We have every right to conclude that history is the opiate of the masses."[69]

Traditionalist conservatives rarely questioned capitalism, even Straussians who invoked an ancient order that predated capitalism by millennia. Tradition had been weaponized in the service of a mighty economic system that, to paraphrase Marx, profaned all that was holy, including cherished traditions. *Especially* cherished traditions. A select few conservative thinkers discerned these facts about capitalism.

The poet and historian Peter Viereck, a self-styled "true" conservative, argued that the "pseudo-conservatives" who had come to be identified with American conservatism, such as the right-wing publisher William Buckley Jr., who supported libertarian economic policies, endangered the "historic content of conservatism." By defending an unfettered version of capitalism, pseudo-conservatives had turned their backs on the tried-and-true practices that set American political culture apart, namely "organic unity and rooted liberty." By indulging libertarianism, or what Viereck called "Manchester liberalism," pseudo-conservatives empowered an unchecked form of capitalism that destabilized society. Marx, who knew a thing or two about Manchester liberalism, captured this phenomenon with his pithy observation that "all that is solid melts into air."[70]

Viereck contended pseudo-conservatives were making Marx into a prophet by goading Americans into "behaving exactly as Marxism says we behave." This was a dubious irony. The United States had confounded Marxist conceptions of society when it held firm to traditional American values. Organic unity and rooted liberty acted as prophylactics against political ideologies like Marxism that flourished alongside chaos and repression. But by "putting our capitalist profit motive over all religious, ethical, and cultural ties," libertarian-sodden pseudo-conservatives had made Americans into the equivalent of "Marxist economic determinists." Nothing mattered more than profit, not democracy, not Christianity, nothing. In this Viereck was echoed by Whittaker Chambers, whose ferocious essay about libertarian novelist Ayn Rand concluded that "Randian Man, like Marxian Man, is made the center of a godless world." The conservative embrace of libertarianism, which resonated with the antilabor thrust of the American right, was an unfortunate turn of events for Viereck, who thought Marx's predictions had otherwise been proven "almost 100 per cent wrong," thanks to the New Deal. "Capitalism has benefitted from democracy's capacity for peaceful self-correction," Viereck wrote, "a capacity ignored by Marx."[71]

Viereck might have called himself a conservative. But his support for the New Deal placed him closer to midcentury liberalism on the American political spectrum. Whereas conservatives agitated against the New Deal, lumping it together with Marxism, Viereck described New Deal policies as "the mildest, revolution-preventing reforms, passed by *both* parties." The New Deal was democracy at its best, not a Marxist machination. "No New Deal conspiracy was needed to make Americans cushion their capitalism with social security laws," Viereck wrote. "If there was any conspiracy, it was one that occurred nineteen centuries ago in Bethlehem. In our ideals we happen to be a Christian nation, not a nation of capitalist or Marxist materialism."[72]

Perhaps traditionalists should have seen things Viereck's way. There was a certain logic to his argument that a proper defense of American traditions required support for the New Deal. The Great Depression, capitalism's greatest catastrophe, was not advantageous to order. Roosevelt's reforms helped stabilize both the economy and the social fabric. But libertarian conservatives could never have supported the New Deal, and they were much more concerned with the threat Marx posed to capitalism than the danger he presented to Christianity. For this reason, libertarians were much more adamant than traditionalists that the New Deal was Marxism in liberal guise. Libertarian enmity for all such attempts to reform capitalism knew no bounds.

THE THREAT TO LIBERTY

The two most influential libertarian thinkers of the twentieth century, Friedrich Hayek and his teacher Ludwig von Mises, were Austrians who, along with like-minded colleagues assembled in Geneva in the 1920s and 1930s to plot a self-described "neoliberal" revolution. Geneva School economists sought to shelter capitalist markets from the meddling hands of government planners. This did not mean they were against state intervention itself. Rather, they wanted to create institutions that would allow capitalist markets to operate unimpeded. Capitalism had to be privileged, they said, because it was the only economic system that did not spawn tyranny.[73]

For Geneva School thinkers, capitalism was *the* priority, much more so than democracy. In fact, they saw democracy as often a barrier to liberty because people in their infinite shortsightedness tended to choose socialism, which entailed restrictions of one sort of another. Inequality and hierarchy, then, were not causes for alarm but rather necessary byproducts of capitalism and, weirdly enough, freedom. Libertarians and traditionalists arrived at the same destination by different means: Social leveling was a malignancy, whether because enforced equality contravened nature, as traditionalists had it, or because it interfered with capitalism, as libertarians believed. Marx, the social leveler par excellence, was the enemy of all conservatives.

Both Hayek and Mises fled Nazi-occupied Europe for the United States. Hayek, who eventually established a beachhead for neoliberal economic doctrine at the University of Chicago, first took America by storm with his 1944 book *The Road to Serfdom*. Max Eastman arranged to have *Reader's Digest* publish it in serial form. Hayek's argument that most government interference in the economy necessarily devolved into authoritarianism found a receptive audience among American conservatives seeking ammunition against the New Deal. Hayek's theory challenged the popular Marxist argument that fascism emerged as a reaction to socialism. Instead, Hayek argued that fascism—and modern authoritarianism in general—were outgrowths of socialism, a term he applied to all forms of centralized economic planning.[74]

Writing in London in 1943, Hayek pitched *The Road Serfdom* as a response to Nazism. If Great Britain wanted to avoid the disaster that had befallen Germany, it had to abandon the idea that the state should manage the economy. But Hayek's book better registered with Cold

War Americans because it showed how Marxist ideas wormed their way into popular understandings of how the world works. Hayek wrote that Marx's "direct influence on current affairs" was perhaps negligible. "But when his ideas have become common property, through the work of historians and publicists, teachers and writers, and intellectuals generally, they effectively guide developments."[75]

As an example, Hayek cited popular support for progressive taxation. In *The Communist Manifesto*, Marx and Engels contended that a "heavy progressive or graduated income tax" was necessary to help the proletariat wrest power from the bourgeoisie. But mid-twentieth-century liberal reformers shunned the language of class warfare, advocating for progressive taxation on the grounds that it greased the wheels of consumer capitalism by granting the working class more money to spend on consumer goods. Liberals thought they looked to Keynes, not Marx; Hayek felt that the true influence had merely been concealed by the distance of a century.[76]

Hayek believed Marx's ideas had also secretly distorted how people understood the history of capitalism. This included most economic historians, whose socialism had blinded them to the truth of the past. The "supreme myth" that most bothered Hayek was that capitalism's emergence created of a class of miserable people whom Marx called the proletariat. Whereas Marx's theory presumed that peasants had been ripped from their land and thrown into factories, becoming more miserable as a result, Hayek contended to the contrary that the working class was made up of people who would not have survived had it not been for capitalism.[77]

Early capitalism's workers, Hayek believed, were born without tools or land and often lacked the means for survival. As such, they would have been among feudalism's victims. "Although it was certainly not from charitable motives," Hayek wrote, capitalism "still was the first time in history that one group of people found it in their interest to use their earnings on a large scale to provide new instruments of production to be operated by those who without them could not have produced their own sustenance." Hayek, like Marx, understood that the relationship between owners and workers was central to capitalism.

But Hayek, unlike Marx, assumed this relationship was mutually beneficial. Libertarians believed that capitalism, if unleashed, would benefit
all humans, of all classes.[78]

Mises never achieved Hayek's degree of notoriety. Although he was
appointed to a professorship at New York University, subsidized by a
wealthy American businessman, Mises never landed a prestigious position like Hayek's, and he never wrote a bestseller. But as an unparalleled enthusiast for capitalism, Mises did manage to attract a group of
extremely devoted right-wing followers.[79]

Mises is best remembered by libertarian economists for taking a
technical calculation about the price mechanism and elevating it into a
meditation on capitalism's moral superiority. He argued that capitalist
pricing translated subjective human desires into objective information,
thus ensuring a rational allocation of resources that satisfied the greatest number of people. In socialist economies, by contrast, the state
controlled the means of production, thus distorting the price mechanism and leading to an irrational system of distribution. Markets were
all knowing. People, in contrast, were ignorant, even when they made
collective plans. Marxism, then, was at best irrational. More than that,
for Mises, Marx's evil system brought misery to millions.[80]

Part of the appeal of Mises to Far Right libertarians was the purity
of his hatred for all things Marx-related. In 1952, Mises gave a series of
nine lectures titled "Marxism Unmasked: From Delusion to Destruction." Mises outlined all the ways Marx had been bad for the world.
Like Hayek, Mises believed Marx's ideas were dominant beyond what
people were ready to admit. He called Marx "the most powerful personality of our age," his ideas the most "widely accepted today, even
by many who emphatically declare that they are anti-communist and
anti-Marxist." Mises argued that "without knowing it, many people
are philosophical Marxists, although they use different names for
their philosophical ideas." Mises hoped that by unmasking all the ways
Marx's ideas had come to shape American thought, and by shining a
light on the hazards presented by them, Americans might yet right
the ship.[81]

One of the most dangerous Marxist concepts that had infiltrated the

American subconscious was class. Hayek did not necessarily deny the existence of class, but Mises thought all political philosophy began and ended with the individual. Class was an illegitimate category of analysis. This was made evident by the fact that Marx had never worked out a feasible theory of class, even as class was the "fundamental concept of *The Communist Manifesto*."[82]

"According to Marx," Mises said, "everybody is forced—by the material productive forces—to think in such a way that the result shows his class interests." People who thought or acted against their class interests had been suckered into a false consciousness that kept them in fetters. Such a theory empowered governments to dictate the terms of living to large groups, with brutal, even genocidal results. Free societies thus would have to start from the premise that individuals are unique, not clay in the hands of Marxist planners.[83]

Free societies also presumed that individuals required free will, and that the best way to express free will was as consumers, not as workers. Consumers had agency in capitalism, something Marx failed to understand. Indeed, many of Marx's gravest errors stemmed from this. Mises declared:

> What really destroyed Marx was his idea of the progressive impoverishment of the workers. Marx didn't see that the most important characteristic of capitalism was large-scale production for the needs of the masses; the main objective of capitalists is to produce for the broad masses. Nor did Marx see that under capitalism the customer is always right. In his capacity as a wage earner, the worker cannot determine what is to be made. But in his capacity as a customer, he is really the boss and tells his boss, the entrepreneur, what to do.[84]

Marx did not live to see consumption emerge as a primary category of economic analysis. But by the time Mises gave his Marx lectures, consumption was arguably *the* category of analysis *and* debate. Keynesians dominated the debate with their argument that government had an obligation to flood the economy with cash that working people could spend. By stimulating consumer demand, government would prevent another depression, and in the process win the allegiance of working people to it.[85]

Libertarians also claimed to speak for the consumer. But they vehemently disagreed with the Keynesian approach because they correctly assumed government-funded consumer demand required a tax on capital. It required redistribution, or social leveling. "We must realize," Mises argued, "that every governmental measure that lowers the amount of profit successful enterprises can make or which taxes away their profits is a measure that weakens the influence of the consumers over producers." By intruding on the market-based price mechanism, taxes had the effect of distorting the information feedback loop between producers and consumers. Taxes also empowered the state to control the price mechanism and a whole host of other human transactions. Mises made his displeasure with the New Deal explicit: "If this tax system is continued, it could lead finally to complete government control." Liberty was an all-or-nothing proposition for Mises. Marx was clearly on the wrong side of the ledger. So too was the New Deal.[86]

Frank Chodorov, the editor of conservative magazines like *The New Freeman* and *Human Events*, was perhaps the most forceful proponent of the case linking the New Deal to Marx. The eleventh son of Russian Jewish immigrants, Chodorov grew up on the Lower East Side of Manhattan, in coffee shops frequented by passionate communists. "The customers, or habitués," he remembered, "seemed to be less interested in eating and drinking than in arguing the metaphysical notions of Karl Marx." Chodorov lamented the disappearance of these Marxists. "There is nobody to argue with," he wrote, "and all the hours I put into *Das Kapital*, for the purposes of dialectic, now seem to have been wasted."[87]

Chodorov longed to joust with the communists of his childhood because he believed he was equipped to beat them. He had come to the ironclad conclusion that Marx's ideas were patently false. "Capitalism, without benefit of a theory," Chodorov wrote, "and operating solely on the mundane profit motive, has disproven Marx on every point." As one example, Chodorov noticed that "capitalism has raised wages, not lowered them, as Marx predicted. So much so, that the worker with a washing machine and an automobile has lost every vestige of 'working-class consciousness.' He even plays golf."⁸⁸

Chodorov echoed the Geneva School economists by emphasizing the role of the consumer. Putting Mises's ideas about the price mechanism in more basic terms, Chodorov claimed that when people wanted something, it was made and sold at a price people would pay for it. When people did not want something, it was not made, simple as that. "It took capitalism almost a hundred years to demolish 'scientific' socialism by the pragmatic method," Chodorov wrote, "but it did so thorough a job of it that *Das Kapital* has been laid to rest without a requiem."⁸⁹

Chodorov related Marx to the New Deal in unique fashion. "In America," Chodorov wrote, "it is the so-called capitalist who is to blame for the fulfillment of Marx's prophecies. Beguiled by the state's siren song of privilege, the capitalists have abandoned capitalism." Chodorov contended that much of what Marx listed in *The Communist Manifesto* as steps toward communism had already been fulfilled by the New Deal, without the help of communists. The Federal Reserve Bank, the Interstate Commerce Commission, the Federal Communications Commission, the Tennessee Valley Authority, the income tax, the inheritance tax, "government schools with compulsory attendance and support," all of these were Marxist projects made possible by the American people, few of whom considered themselves disciples of Marx. "Government ownership and government controls have come to America because we the people have demanded them," Chodorov wrote, "not because the communists brought them from Russia."⁹⁰

Marx argued that the state was only exploitative when it worked for capitalists, or the ruling class in any form. This was the only type of state Marx had witnessed during his lifetime. In contrast, he famously welcomed a "dictatorship of the proletariat," a phrase that sounded much worse in the 1950s than it had in the 1840s. For Chodorov, "dictatorship" was just the right term since the state was always an engine of repression, whether it worked for the bourgeoisie or the proletariat or anyone else. This was especially true regarding taxes and other forms of wealth redistribution, which he likened to theft. "If the state takes from the capitalist to give to the worker, or from the mechanic to give to the farmer, or from all to better itself," Chodorov wrote, "force has been used to deprive someone of his rightful property."[91]

When American politicians levied taxes to fund New Deal projects, they acted in the spirit of the Spanish conquistadores who stole gold from the Indians, or in the spirit of ruthless Soviet bureaucrats who expropriated Kulak land. All were guilty of extreme forms of coercion that violated individual rights. There was no redeeming the New Deal for a libertarian like Chodorov. There was certainly no redeeming Marx.

The unrestrained hostility of libertarians to Marx overlooked the profound irony that they understood a crucial aspect of capitalism similarly. For both libertarians and Marx, capitalism was a system of constant revolution. And for both, its revolutionary capacities were largely beneficial, although for vastly different reasons.

Libertarians liked that capitalism constantly innovated to expand and improve consumer choice. This made capitalism a rational system that, if properly cared for, should persist indefinitely. In contrast, Marx appreciated in a roundabout way that capitalism compelled capitalists to maximize profits, because this in turn demanded they innovate ways to exploit workers—and that that ratcheting up of exploitation would also hasten the revolution. "What the bourgeoisie, therefore, produces, above all," Marx wrote, "is its own grave-diggers."

Joseph A. Schumpeter, another Austrian economic thinker who landed at a prestigious American university, in his case Harvard, exemplified how libertarian thought rhymed with Marxism. Schumpeter's 1942 landmark book *Capitalism, Socialism, and Democracy* echoed Marx in concluding that "capitalism is being killed by its achievements."[92]

Marx argued that capitalism would bring workers together to take control of the means of production. Marx further theorized that when capitalists predictably unite to elude proletarian power, they would throw the whole system into crisis. Put another way, their compulsion to relieve themselves of an unruly human workforce, via automation, would ultimately result in capitalism's demise, since profits derive from the exploitation of labor. No labor, no profits.

Schumpeter, in contrast, contended that, because capitalism required some firms thrive as others die, the state would inevitably intervene to stop the destruction, demolishing capitalism in the process.
The very logic that propelled capitalism, as Marx and Schumpeter var-
iously understood it, would kill it. And both Marx and Schumpeter
believed capitalism would be succeeded by socialism.[93]

Although Schumpeter would have recoiled at being compared to
Marx, he credited Marx as a "great" thinker, made evident by the way
he perpetually connected with modern people. In a secular age where
positivism had replaced religious faith, God was pronounced dead
alongside other beliefs that could not be empirically verified. And yet,
Schumpeter argued, people everywhere longed for faith. Marx served
as a siren amid modernity because he offered the perfect mix of analysis
and prophecy. People turned to him to satisfy their desire for theology
in a world of hyperempiricism. "Panting with impatience to have their
innings," Schumpeter wrote of such people, "longing to save the world
from something or other, disgusted with textbooks of undescribable
tedium, dissatisfied emotionally and intellectually, unable to achieve
synthesis by their own effort, they find what they crave for in Marx."[94]

Characterizing Marx as a religious thinker was hardly a form of
praise, as Schumpeter considered his own prediction about capitalism's demise less prophesy than cold calculation. He theorized that
in a capitalist economy, firms were forced to innovate lest they be destroyed, and that when one firm developed a successful innovation all
others had to follow. The upshot was the replacement of older forms of
production with newer forms, older products with newer ones. This sequence, which created more consumer choice—more freedom—was
the lifeblood of capitalism.[95]

Capitalist innovation, Schumpeter wrote, "incessantly revolution-
izes the economic structure from within, incessantly destroying the
old one, incessantly creating a new one. This process of Creative Destruction is the essential fact about capitalism." Without creative destruction, capitalism withers. But people would try to thwart capitalism's destructive tendencies. In rich nations like the United States, the
immense wealth generated by creative destruction could be turned

against capitalism. Indeed, for Schumpeter, these were the exact factors that led to the New Deal, an expensive welfare state reliant upon the wealth generated by capitalism.[96]

The New Deal wreaked havoc on capitalism because it diminished the role of the entrepreneur, whom Schumpeter saw as responsible for the innovations that engendered the cycle of creative destruction. Crucially, an entrepreneur only innovated when threatened with failure. But the New Deal state's regulatory and welfare functions diminished risk to minuscule levels, thus driving a stake through the heart of entrepreneurship. Schumpeter argued that capitalism would not die from its failures, or from its ever-intensifying cycles of boom and bust that Marx had identified. Rather capitalism's very success undermined the conditions that allowed it to thrive. Schumpeter was convinced socialism was destined to replace capitalism for this very reason. The New Deal, an expression of hostility to capitalism, was the harbinger of that transition.[97]

Marx was cognizant of capitalism's cycle of creative destruction even if he had different words to describe it, and divergent expectations about how it would unfold. "Marx saw this process of industrial change more clearly and he realized its pivotal importance more fully than any other economist of his time," Schumpeter admitted. The bourgeoisie, Marx wrote, "has played a most revolutionary role in history. It cannot exist without constantly revolutionizing the instrument of production, and thereby the relations of production, and with them the whole relations of society." But Schumpeter felt Marx did not have the right words to accurately analyze the contradictions of capitalism.[98]

Lacking an "adequate theory of enterprise," Marx had failed "to distinguish the entrepreneur from the capitalist." According to Schumpeter, capitalists used their immense wealth and power to shield themselves from the threat of destruction that entrepreneurs faced regularly. Capitalists, in other words, were risk averse. Entrepreneurs, unlike capitalists, hazarded ruin, which meant they were the driving force of innovation. Schumpeter implied that capitalist wealth was unearned. Capitalists lived high on the hog of entrepreneurial innovation. Marx was more explicit in his insults even as he readily demonstrated his admiration for the ways in which the "bourgeoisie, during its rule of scarce one hundred years, has created more massive and more colossal productive forces than have all preceding generations together." Marx frequently used pejoratives like "Moneybags" to signify what he described as the "vampire-like" qualities of the bourgeoisie.[99]

Marx lumped all capitalists together. Capitalists were the ruling class. Even if they had created the conditions for universal liberation, such liberation could only be achieved by unmercifully destroying them as a class. In contrast, Schumpeter distinguished between capitalists and entrepreneurs to highlight the fact that capitalism was based not on exploitation but on creativity. That distinction became a core feature of conservative discourse in postwar America.

So long as the Great Depression weighed on the minds of conservative Americans like a nightmare, celebrating free enterprise was effective marketing, much better than talk about a "vampire-like" capitalism. Schumpeter usefully endowed conservatives with a heroic figure, the plucky entrepreneur, the latest representative of rugged American individualism. The entrepreneur was a vastly more alluring figure than the dour totalitarian man who had come to represent Marxism. The entrepreneur was also more appealing than the faceless white-collar cog in the corporate machine that was the focus of so much postwar social criticism. Fixating on the entrepreneur allowed conservatives to draw attention away from the less attractive features of capitalism. Libertarianism in this way turned Marxist frameworks upside down to reach decidedly un-Marxist conclusions.[100]

MARXISM OF THE MASTER CLASS

Libertarian thought grew influential in the second half of the twentieth century primarily because of the Cold War. More to the point, libertarianism became an ideological weapon in the war of ideas against Marxism. It sought to match Marxism in its revolutionary claims about freedom while also refuting Marxism's ability to carry through on its promises. Some libertarian thinkers were more explicit about

this project than others. Mises made it clear that his aim was to debunk Marx while offering the world a better mode of thinking about
freedom.

The American libertarian theorist James Buchanan was straightforward about wanting to counter Marxism. He was one of the originators
of public choice theory, an influential approach to thinking about the
role of the state. Since politicians acted out of self-interest, Buchanan
contended, the state was incapable of governing on behalf of the public interest. In fact, he maintained, there was no such thing as a public
interest. At most, it was a vague, even meaningless term that papered
over the inexorable will to power of politicians. Buchanan proclaimed
public choice theory unmasked the "normative delusion" central to
Marxism and all Marxist offshoots, including midcentury liberalism,
that "the state was, somehow, a benevolent entity and those who made
decisions on behalf of the state were guided by consideration of the
general or public interest." Investing authority in the state, in the name
of an abstraction like the public interest, represented the slippery slope
to totalitarianism.[101]

Buchanan converted to neoliberalism—generally speaking, the notion that markets better serve people than the state—while studying at
the University of Chicago, which became a sort of Geneva School West.
Yet Buchanan's unique spin on libertarianism was spawned in the petri
dish of 1950s Virginia politics. Libertarianism was not only a response
to the Cold War but also a philosophical rationale for resistance to social leveling. Libertarianism worked to protect hierarchies even of the
most objectionable sort, such as the racial hierarchy in the Jim Crow
South. As an economics professor at the University of Virginia, where
Buchanan established a cadre of like-minded economists, he developed
ideas to aid state legislators in hamstringing school desegregation efforts in the wake of the Supreme Court's decision in *Brown v. Board of
Education* (1954).[102]

Buchanan proposed that Virginia could finesse compliance with
Brown and avoid the impression that the state wished to maintain Jim
Crow. His innovative solution was school vouchers, which would em-
power parents to send children to schools of their choice on the public

dime, while also abetting white and affluent populations in restricting broader cross-racial access to state-financed education. He contended a voucher system was the best allocation of educational resources because it would compel schools to compete for students and resources, which would lead to educational improvement on the consumer choice model. On paper, at least, Buchanan advocated a market-based, seemingly race-neutral policy solution. In effect, however, it allowed for the perpetuation of segregation. Virginia's Prince Edward County shuttered its public schools in 1959 while doling out vouchers to private schools that only accepted white children. As a result, black children in Prince Edward County went without formal education for more than five years.[103]

By enlisting in the policy frontlines of Virginia's massive resistance to civil rights, Buchanan launched a long and productive career of tailoring economic ideas to serve reactionary forces. He codified this work in the 1962 book that kick-started public choice theory, *The Calculus of Consent*, coauthored with Gordon Tullock, another University of Virginia economist. *The Calculus of Consent* took neoliberal economic theory and applied it to government. Libertarians had long posited that people trade with one another because they have different needs and interests. Trade was a rational way to fulfill needs that ensured the greatest amount of human freedom. Buchanan and Tullock wondered why such a common-sense theory of individual difference— known as rational choice theory—had not yet been applied to political behavior.[104]

In doing so, Buchanan and Tullock discovered an ironic incongruence: whereas self-interest played out beautifully in the market, self-interest in government, although unavoidable, had disastrous consequences. The key to unraveling this seeming paradox lay in the logic of state coercion. The market was the fairest allocator of resources because individuals were always best positioned to make decisions for themselves about what to buy and sell and for how much. Adam Smith was right to hymn the mysteries, and the majesty, of the "invisible hand" of the market. In contrast, politicians distorted the natural rhythm of the market, also out of self-interest. Legislators who needed votes for reelection enacted policies that won over majorities. This had the perverse market-distorting effect of overproducing public goods like education or healthcare, goods that libertarians believed were better left to market forces to supply even if democratic majorities thought otherwise.[105]

Buchanan and other libertarians began referring to such forms of government-produced advantage as "rents," an idea with a distinctly smash-the-state underdog connotation. After all, Buchanan and his followers reasoned, government advantage was by definition unfair to those not protected by the state. A libertarian might argue that if an upstart company was unfairly accused of fraud by federal agents, it could well be because the federal government was beholden to a more established company. But most often, such theorizing targeted New Deal social leveling. Government healthcare subsidies to the poor and elderly were rents—that is, illegitimate fees imposed on the market— that distorted the market for healthcare. State funds to public universities, a sop to voters, were rents that distorted the market for higher education. And so on.[106]

Public choice theory, as an avowed contrast with Marxism and other theories of social leveling, was a twentieth-century innovation. But it also had deep roots in American political thought going back before *The Communist Manifesto*. As the libertarian economists Alexander Tabarrok and Tyler Cowen note, John C. Calhoun, the fire-breathing South Carolinian defender of slaveholders' rights, favored "public choice" avant la lettre. Calhoun, like Buchanan later, had theorized that majority rule tended to repress a select few. Both Buchanan and Calhoun aimed to protect an aggrieved if privileged minority. And just as Calhoun argued that laws should only be approved by a "concurrent majority," which would grant veto power to a region such as the South, Buchanan posited that laws should only be made by unanimous consent. As Tabarrok and Cowen put it, these two theories had "the same purpose and effect": they oblige people with different interests to unite. Should interested parties fail to achieve unanimity, government is paralyzed—for the good.[107]

In marking Calhoun's political philosophy as the crucial antecedent of public choice theory, Tabarrok and Cowen confirmed what critics have long maintained: libertarianism is a political philosophy shot through with class rule. Public choice theory, a technical language nominally about human behavior and incentives, helps prevent social leveling. Just as Calhoun developed his novel political philosophy in response to the growing fear that a northern majority might seek to abolish slavery, Buchanan's public choice theory was an innovative approach to resisting federal enforcement of civil rights and the New Deal.

But public choice theory was also a creative method for countering Marxist and Marx-adjacent concepts like class. For Buchanan, as with most libertarians, a Marxist abstraction like class was even worse than a vague progressive concept like the public interest. In *The Calculus of Consent*, Buchanan and Tullock articulated their opposition to "any theory or conception of the collectivity which embodies the exploitation of a ruled by a ruling class." Buchanan thought class was an especially wrongheaded way to think about the United States, where market exchange, backed by contract law, distributed power so that people remained free agents unencumbered by false solidarities like class. Such, at any rate, was their ideal. And the great ideological premise of public choice theory was to highlight this ideal against Marxism and other forms of creeping collectivism.[108]

During the Cold War, Marxism was caricatured as a theory of collectivism. This caricature was lent considerable credence by the Soviet Union, the first nation to proclaim itself Marxist, while vesting all power in an authoritarian state. In contrast, public choice was a theory of freedom that portrayed the state as the embodiment of repression. What gets lost in this formulation is Marxism's actual role as a theory of freedom that saw the state as an engine of repression. As Marx and Engels famously asserted, "the executive of the modern state is but a committee for the affairs of the bourgeoisie." Or as Buchanan and Tullock recognized, Marxism "incorporates the polity as one means through which the economically dominant group imposes its will on the downtrodden." For Marxists, socialist revolution entailed liberation not only from capitalism but also from the capitalist state.[109]

Marxism was antistatist from the beginning, though this was hard to remember during the Cold War, since some communists fetishized Soviet state power. Marx's own words also seemed to belie the idea. His infamous "dictatorship of the proletariat" phrase ostensibly gave totalitarians the perfect excuse to crush liberty. But Marx's conception of a dictatorship did not carry all that baggage (and of course he wrote not knowing of the Soviet Union). Rather, he understood the state as an expression of class power. In capitalist nations, even in a nominal democracy like the United States, the state was a dictatorship of the bourgeoisie. Marx referred to the Paris Commune as a dictatorship of the proletariat, even though it sought to establish universal suffrage. Marx's infamous phrase does not disprove that he pushed a critical theory of the state.[110]

When Marx died in 1883, one of his New York City eulogists decreed that "now it is the duty of true lovers of liberty to honor the name of Karl Marx." Marx believed, in the words of the political theorist William Clare Roberts, that "only the defeat of this servile and violent state can establish the conditions of emancipation." This was especially true in the later sections of *Capital*, where Marx discussed primitive accumulation. Marx wrote that capitalists "employ the power of the state, the concentrated and organized force of society, to hasten, hot-house fashion, the process of transformation of the feudal mode of production into the capitalist mode, and to shorten the transition. Force is the midwife of every old society pregnant with a new one. It is itself an economic power." The state, for Marx, was a brutal and repressive agent of the epoch-making transition to capitalism.[111]

In sum, public choice theory and Marxism rhymed. Buchanan and Tullock recognized as much even as they bent over backward to explain such resonances away. "The class-dominance approach to political activity," they wrote, "is acutely related to our own in an unfortunate terminological sense. By historical accident, the class-dominance conception, in its Marxian variant, has come to be known as the 'economic' conception or interpretation of State activity." This Marxist approach, Buchanan and Tullock fretted, "has caused the perfectly good word 'economic' to be used in a wholly misleading manner." Public choice theory turned the Marxist theory of the state on its head. As opposed to wishing to free the masses from a state controlled by the capitalist elite, Buchanan wished to free the capitalist elite from a state controlled by the unruly masses. This returns us, suitably enough, to John C. Calhoun.[112]

Richard Hofstadter's 1948 book *The American Political Tradition: And the Men Who Made It* included the essay "John C. Calhoun: The Marx of the Master Class." Hofstadter wrote that Calhoun foreshadowed Marx in that he "had a keen sense for social structure and class forces." Calhoun "placed the central ideas of 'scientific' socialism in an inverted framework of moral values and produced an arresting defense of reaction." In Calhoun's words: "There is and always has been in an advanced stage of wealth and civilization, a conflict between capital and labor. The condition of society in the South exempts us from the disorders and dangers resulting from this conflict, and which explains why it is that the political conditions of the slaveholding states has been so much more stable and quiet than that of the North."[113]

Marx made a similar argument in his writings about the Civil War—except that he reversed the basic terms of Calhoun's appraisal of the South as a paternal model of quasi-feudal social peace. Marx welcomed the destruction of slavery because he believed that would create conditions more favorable to organizing the working class, since a free labor system would no longer need to compete with an unfree one. The disorder Calhoun feared, which would bring power to people of the lower order, was precisely the disorder Marx welcomed. Calhoun is an analog to Marx, in other words, in the same way that public choice theory is an analog to the Marxist theory of the state. Public choice theory is the Marxism of the master class.

The Cold War conservative reception of Marx was nothing if not paradoxical. Libertarians claimed to love liberty even as they proposed various antidemocratic ways to unleash capitalism. Marx proposed a dictatorship of the proletariat even as he dreamed of liberty and justice for all. Conservatives opposed social leveling of all sorts, from Marxism to the New Deal, often in the name of freedom, even if it required state repression to prevent leveling.

During the early Cold War, conservatives meant to bury Marx. With the help of the postwar red scare, they nearly succeeded. But in an irony of epic proportions, right-wing attention to Marx, even in its most conspiratorial form, helped his ideas persist, if through a dark mirror.

In the eyes of the few remaining Marxists in postwar America, Marx persevered as a clear-eyed, foundational theorist. For them, so long as the ultimate conundrum of modernity endured, the person who did more than anyone else to flesh out this conundrum would continue to matter. Until the freedom of some no longer required the unfreedom of others, Marx would carry on, no matter how intently his enemies tried to erase him.

7

HUMANIST LIBERATOR

The New Left

The United States has not proved that Marx was wrong.

WILLIAM APPLEMAN WILLIAMS

In the decades following the Second World War, American capitalism became the most powerful economic system the world had ever seen. In 1960, Americans accounted for 7 percent of the earth's population but generated 40 percent of the world's income. Yet at that very moment, when Marx's predictions about capitalism's overwhelming tendency to expand had come to fruition, his reputation was hanging by a thread in the nation that had been the principal engine of the system. Marx was almost dead in America—*almost*.

During the second red scare, a few brave souls kept Marx alive in the United States. Included among them were the intrepid editors of the lively independent socialist magazine *Monthly Review*. Founded in 1949 by the Marxist economists Paul Sweezy and Leo Huberman, with money seeded by F. O. Matthiessen, *Monthly Review* bridged an Old Left that orbited around the Communist Party in the 1930s and a New Left that emerged in the 1960s among antiwar young people. In the *Monthly Review* milieu, Marx was no less helpful in explaining America's insatiable postwar expansionism than he had been in articulating the reasons for capitalism's prewar implosion.[1]

A BRIDGE BETWEEN THE OLD AND NEW LEFTS

Sweezy was the foremost intellectual force behind *Monthly Review*, perhaps surprising given that he grew up among the eastern bourgeoisie.
His father was a New York City banker, his mother graduated from
an elite liberal arts college, and he attended Phillips Exeter Academy
and then Harvard University, where he graduated summa cum laude
in 1932. But Sweezy was joined by other products of East Coast privilege who became renowned Marxists, including James Burnham and
Dwight Macdonald. Like them, Sweezy was radicalized by the Great
Depression. Also like them, Leon Trotsky's *History of the Russian Revolution* served as the final push onto his leftward arc. But unlike Burnham and Macdonald, he did not join the Trotskyist movement. Attracted to Soviet-style state planning, Sweezy was a fellow traveler of
the Communist Party, though never a card-carrying member.[2]

Sweezy's introduction to Marx's ideas came in 1932, when he studied with the left-leaning Joan Robinson at the London School of Economics. From then on, he was sold on the wisdom of Marx. In a 1949
centennial essay on *The Communist Manifesto*, Sweezy designated the
fabled text as "one of the most important documents in the entire history of the human race." He never changed his mind about this.[3]

After a year in England, Sweezy returned to Harvard and took a doctorate in economics under the tutelage of Joseph Schumpeter. After
Sweezy became a Harvard instructor in his own right, he and Schumpeter clashed in several public debates. Two of the greatest economic
minds of their generation faced each other, underscoring crucial midcentury distinctions between Marxism and libertarianism.[4]

Sweezy agreed with Schumpeter that innovation in a capitalist economy was necessary. But Sweezy strongly disagreed with Schumpeter's
claim that innovation resulted from entrepreneurial genius. Rather,
the capitalist, no matter how creative, was merely "a tool of the social
relations in which he is enmeshed and which force him to innovate on
pain of elimination." Drawing from Marx, Sweezy maintained that
profit, not innovation, was the motor force of capitalism. "From this
standpoint," he wrote, "the form of the profit-making process itself

produces the pressure to accumulate, and accumulation generates innovation as a means of preserving the profit-making mechanism and the class structure on which it rests." Innovation was the result of a social process, not vice versa, and the profit motive, not entrepreneurship, powered the constant motion of a highly destructive capitalist system. In making this distinction, Sweezy juxtaposed a Marxist framework to the libertarian tendency of highlighting the behavior of individuals to explain structural economic phenomena.[5]

Schumpeter feared democratically elected officials would create enough disincentives to discourage entrepreneurs from innovating and thus end capitalism. Sweezy, in contrast, welcomed the demise of capitalism and the advent of socialism. For Sweezy, a planned socialist economy in which the state oversaw the distribution of goods and services did not preclude innovation, which might be warranted for more equitable allocation. What such an economy *did* prevent was the profit motive, the ultimate root of social breakdown. In sum, Schumpeter pointed to a less regulated capitalism, while Sweezy advocated a command socialist economy. Sweezy envisioned a socialism that was both innovative and nondestructive, a system not of creative destruction but of creative production.[6]

Monthly Review persistently promoted socialist planning. Such advocacy was not beyond the pale of acceptability in the aftermath of the Great Depression and amid the Second World War, when many nations, including the United States, enforced centralized planning regimes for vital products and resources. Marxist support for planning was entirely consistent with Old Left preoccupations that emerged in an era of acute economic deprivation. But *Monthly Review* also anticipated New Left anxieties about state capitalism, or what came to be called corporate liberalism.[7]

Sweezy's 1942 book *The Theory of Capitalist Development: Principles of Marxian Political Economy* argued that the state was an agent of capital. The most horrific result of this cozy relationship was war. Modern warfare, the argument went, mostly resulted from government efforts on behalf of profit-seeking capitalists to break into new markets.[8]

Writing during the Second World War, Sweezy agreed with liberal economists that transitioning out of a wartime economy might cause another depression unless the state replaced military spending with social spending. But he also argued the elite would resist spending on social programs. Most policymakers assumed money was better spent on weapons than on public housing. Sweezy wrote that "the only forms of massive government spending which are acceptable to the capitalist class are those which have imperialist expansion and war preparations as their aim." Sweezy's Marxist theory of imperialism helped connect Old Left concerns about capitalism's inevitable demise with New Left concerns about capitalism's ineluctable expansion. This type of Marxist thinking reverberated across the 1960s, when the violence of American Empire building became an overriding concern to millions of people.[9]

Writing in the 1940s, Sweezy was upbeat about the possibilities for socialism. This set him apart from beleaguered Communists and dispirited Trotskyists. But then red baiters targeted Sweezy. In 1954, New Hampshire State Attorney General Louis Wyman, empowered by a state antisubversion law, investigated Sweezy and demanded that he give up the names of his Communist associates. Wyman also commanded that Sweezy reveal his notes from a recent lecture on socialism. Sweezy refused both orders and was found guilty of contempt. He appealed, and his case climbed to the Supreme Court, which ruled in 1957 that the state had violated Sweezy's right to due process. Although the majority opinion in *Sweezy v. New Hampshire* was founded on narrow legal grounds, the decision implicitly established a more robust legal precedent for academic freedom. *Sweezy v. New Hampshire* also represented one of many strikes against McCarthyism, as a rising generation of activists began to fight back against red baiting.[10]

Despite such a notable victory, Sweezy grew despondent about socialism's prospects. Living as a fervent Marxist in a profoundly anticommunist nation eviscerated his hopes for the American working class. By the 1950s, the working class upon which Marxists had once pinned their hopes had come to seem less and less revolutionary. But not all was lost. Desperate peasants ninety miles south of Florida restored Sweezy's faith in a Marxist future. By overthrowing the

American-backed Batista dictatorship and by implementing sweeping socialist reforms, Cuban revolutionaries earned the admiration of leftists across the planet.

Sweezy visited revolutionary Cuba in 1960. He returned home a zealous champion of Fidel Castro's experiment in socialism. Revolutionary agency was to be found no longer among the urban working class in the West but in the sugarcane fields of Cuba. This fed a major shift in how Americans thought about Marx.[11]

Leftists in the 1930s placed Marx on a pedestal, towering over all revolutionary thinkers. Leftists in the 1960s tended to foreground blistering tribunes of anti-imperialism like Che Guevara, Mao Zedong, and Frantz Fanon. These additions to the Marxist canon, however, did not crowd out the original. In fact, after rough treatment during the postwar red scare, when Marx was regarded as the ultimate American taboo, the grandfather of communism resurfaced as a fresh symbol of youthful militancy.[12]

FIGURE 7.1: *Monthly Review*'s trip to Cuba, from left to right: Paul Sweezy, Paul Baran, Fidel Castro, Leo Huberman, 1963.

Marx's resurgence can perhaps best be explained simply by the fact that the New Left was critical of capitalism. Marx was, after all, the pre-eminent anticapitalist thinker. However, in the 1960s, even with the Left reemerging on the American political scene, Marx's return was counterintuitive. Contrary to Marx's expectations about the immis-eration of the proletariat, the American working class had never been wealthier. The labor theory of value in *Capital* no longer resonated with workers who increasingly identified as "middle class." But a powerful historical convergence was also at work.

Marx's most recognizable writings had served the Left well during the economic catastrophe of the 1930s. Monumental texts like *Capital* forecast the ways the profit-making imperative both exploited the pro-letariat and threw the whole capitalist system into crisis. This argument did not ring as loudly in the postwar years, when the system had recov-ered and indeed was *thriving*. But there were many layers to Marx's writ-ings. Marx persisted as a revolutionary touchstone because his analyses and prophesies cannot be limited to any one era, context, or people.

Marx's ideas were certainly applicable to the 1960s. The first volume of *Capital* included a key section on the relationship between capital-ism and the brutal subjugation of the noncapitalist world, which Marx termed "primitive accumulation" and mocked as "the rosy dawn of the era of capitalist production." This analysis resonated with a New Left increasingly attuned to the relationship between capitalism and im-perialism. Primitive accumulation encompassed a variety of imperial practices, such as the ruthless taking of land and labor, and the forc-ing of people into the proletariat. Although twentieth-century Ameri-can imperialism differed from earlier variants of European conquest, young leftists found a comrade in the Marx who lamented "conquest and looting" at the margins of the capitalist metropole.[13]

DISCOVERING THE YOUNG MARX

But Marx the anti-imperialist was ultimately not the Marx who won the hearts and minds of 1960s activists. The Marx that laid claim to the Age of Aquarius was the eloquent bard of alienation found in his early writings, which finally made their way to American readers after the Second World War. This young Marx, who theorized less about surplus and accumulation and more about how capitalism estranged us from our true natures, found a kindred spirit in a young Tom Hayden, who authored the Port Huron Statement, the founding document of Students for a Democratic Society (SDS). Writing in 1844, the young Marx worried about how labor "estranges from man his own body, as well as external nature and his spiritual aspect, his *human* aspect." Writing in 1962, the young Hayden fretted about how he and his peers were "looking uncomfortably to the world we inherit." For both, that world was pitilessly hostile to the human spirit.[14]

Young Marx was restlessly seeking to break free of constraints of all sorts. This included the philosophical restrictions imposed upon him and others by the towering figure of Hegel. The Hegelian dialectic was positively liberating to people coming of age in an era of growing complexity. Marx persistently recognized Hegel's genius in establishing an approach that seamlessly stitched past, present, and future into an organic whole. But the political implications of some of Hegel's most famous postulations, such as his contention that the state is the manifestation of collective human will, were impossibly conservative for a revolutionary like Marx. In Marx's eyes, the repressive Prussian regime he grew up under was simply one class of people keeping another down. Marx broke with Hegel at an early age because he began to see class struggle as the engine of world history.[15]

Marx's *Economic and Philosophic Manuscripts of 1844* are the articulations of a gifted dreamer awakening to the deepening misery that was enveloping modern society. Never published during his lifetime, the *Economic and Philosophic Manuscripts* were Marx's first sustained examination of capitalism as a system of class exploitation. As he argued, capitalism makes the worker miserable in a material sense. Workers find sustaining life for themselves and their families increasingly difficult. But capitalism also makes workers psychologically miserable. It both immiserates and alienates the proletariat because, ironically, it is so productive. In capitalism, Marx wrote, the "worker becomes all the poorer the more wealth he produces, the more his production increases in power and size." He put this contradiction in pithy terms: "The *devaluation* of the world of men is in direct proportion to the *increasing value* of the world of things."[16]

Capitalism elevates the status of commodities even as it grinds the humans who make them into dust. This was what Marx meant in calling estrangement one of capitalism's defining features. It is natural for humans to make things they need. It is also natural for humans to take pride in the things they make for their own use. But it is unnatural when humans work to make things that are then separated from them. It is even less natural when those things take on lives of their own as commodities. Commodification, integral to capitalism, is premised on human alienation. Humans in capitalist society are alienated from the products of their labor, alienated from themselves, alienated from one another. In his twenties, Marx had isolated the tragedy of modern human existence. He spent the rest of his life agonizing over a way out.[17]

The *Economic and Philosophic Manuscripts* were first published in 1932 by the Marx-Engels-Lenin Institute in Moscow only to be subsequently suppressed by Stalinist theoreticians who deemed the young Marx insufficiently scientific—that is, they failed to adhere to the correct Stalinist line. That Marx was too searching, too sensitive, for the iron-fisted Stalin, whose subjects might have been experiencing alienation of the type Marx identified. But these texts slowly made their way into the hands of eager readers elsewhere. In the 1930s, a few American Marxists who read German found their insights productive. The young Sidney Hook drew upon the young Marx to help him reconstruct Marxist "philosophy as a method of approaching the practical problems of men." For Hook, these writings seemed a useful conduit to his larger project of theorizing a new philosophy of freedom by blending Marxism, which offered a revolutionary critique of capitalism, with pragmatism, which suggested a realistic and humane means to revolutionary ends. But this Marx remained unknown to most American intellectuals and activists until the 1940s and 1950s, when they became readily available in English.[18]

The person most responsible for translating the young Marx for

FIGURE 7.2: From left to right: Diego Rivera, Raya Dunayevskaya, Leon Trotsky, Mexico City, 1940.

an American readership was Raya Dunayevskaya, one the most important if overlooked twentieth-century American Marxists. Born Raya Shpigel in 1910, in the part of the Russian Empire that became Ukraine, Dunayevskaya's family emigrated to the United States in 1922. Always the radical, thirteen-year-old Dunayevskaya led a strike against her draconian Chicago public-school principal. She joined the Communist Party as a teenager, but at eighteen she was expelled and thrown down a flight of stairs after proposing to her comrades that they read Trotsky's response to Stalin after he was purged.[19]

Nevertheless, Dunayevskaya remained a committed Marxist activist. She participated in the San Francisco general strike of 1934 and taught classes on Marxism in Los Angeles. In 1936, she moved to Washington, DC, where she worked with the National Negro Congress on behalf of sharecroppers. In the late 1930s, she joined the Trotskyist movement, and served for a time as Trotsky's personal secretary in Mexico City. In 1940, Dunayevskaya parted ways with Trotsky over his persistent defense of the Soviet Union as a workers' state.[20]

Unlike several Trotskyists who moved right on the political spectrum after breaking with the movement, Dunayevskaya remained a committed, independent Marxist. Indeed, her unconventional brand of Marxism, which relied upon the *Economic and Philosophic Manuscripts*, was the hinge of a new philosophy. Dubbed Marxist Humanism, Dunayevskaya's theoretical innovation was well timed. The young radicals of the 1960s are remembered for wanting to bring down the system that their elders had built. But many of them also sought to imagine what came next. Dunayevskaya, helped by young Marx, offered just such a vision.[21]

MARXIST HUMANISM

Dunayevskaya did not invent Marxist humanism alone. Such theoretical tendencies already existed alongside other strains of Marxism. Dunayevskaya was familiar with a wide variety of Marxist thinkers including those like György Lukács, Walter Benjamin, and Herbert Marcuse who worked in a more humanistic vein. But two of her close comrades, the inventive C. L. R. James, and the talented Grace Lee, were more important in shaping her Marxist humanism.[22]

Dunayevskaya and James met in the Socialist Workers Party before leaving it together amid the debate over the Russia question, in favor of

Max Shachtman's Workers Party. As two of the formative theorists of state capitalism, the idea that capitalism and the state were mutually reliant upon one another, Dunayevskaya and James coauthored a book in 1950 alongside their comrade Grace Lee. *State Capitalism and World Revolution* was equally critical of Soviet tyranny and American workplace despotism. To help make this connection, James and his colleagues looked to the early Marx. The fight against "the man," whether he was propping up racism or capitalism or imperialism, was a fight against the estrangement that a brooding young Marx had pinpointed.[23]

Despite their commitment to a theory that put state capitalism in an international context, Dunayevskaya and James were never fully happy in a Marxist organization that focused more on events on the other side of the planet than on struggles closer to home. As such, they formed a dissident circle within the Workers Party known as the Johnson-Forest Tendency, based on their pseudonyms J. R. Johnson (James) and Freddie Forest (Dunayevskaya). Joined by Lee, who wrote as Ria Stone, the Johnson-Forest Tendency focused its considerable theoretical talents on the problem of race in America.[24]

The trio formed one of the more remarkable groups of Marxist thinkers in America. Dunayevskaya brought her immense philosophical

FIGURE 7.3: The Tendency, from left to right: Raya Dunayevskaya, C. L. R. James, Grace Lee, ca. late 1940s.

knowledge and her passion for civil rights and women's liberation. James contributed his vast reservoir of historical wisdom along with his acute sense of where Marxist theory meshed with political activism. Lee added her philosophical and linguistic talents as she, with Dunayevskaya, translated sections of the *Economic and Philosophic Manuscripts* into English in the 1940s. As the daughter of Chinese immigrants and eventual spouse of the black autoworker and labor organizer James Boggs, Lee also helped push the Tendency to emphasize civil rights.

Dunayevskaya, James, and Lee melded a Marxist analysis of capitalism with a humanistic focus on the problem of racism in the American context. This approach proved increasingly relevant by the 1960s. It is not surprising that it took three immigrants, two of whom were women and two of whom where people of color, to revise and multiply the ways in which American leftists thought about Marx. Sometimes position shapes perspective in productive ways.

Dunayevskaya's 1958 book *Marxism and Freedom* put Marxist humanism on the map. Dunayevskaya spent several years traveling the world talking about the book, which was translated into several languages. With it, she wanted nothing less than to reclaim Marx from the Soviet Union. In 1956, two events ensured her message would resonate widely, especially in Eastern Europe, where her book circulated as samizdat. In February, the Soviet leader Nikita Khrushchev famously divulged Stalin's crimes. These were not revelations to the Soviet Union's critics, but it was the first time a Soviet leader had admitted to them. The speech sent shockwaves through the worldwide communist movement, and countless people in the United States and elsewhere quit the party in disgust. This even included many longtime defenders of the Soviet Union.[25]

In October of 1956, Soviet tanks rolled into Budapest and crushed a revolution that aimed to build an independent, democratic, socialist Hungary. This violent act of repression also disgusted people worldwide, including many on the Left. Some among the dwindling number of socialists began to search for a revolutionary program untainted by the Soviets. Enter the young Marx, who had contended that we "should especially avoid establishing society as an abstraction opposed to the individual. The individual *is* the social entity." Dunayevskaya pointed to the stark contrast between that sentiment and Soviet Communism. "Today, in the face of the constant struggle of man for full freedom on both sides of the Iron Curtain," she wrote, "there is a veritable conspiracy to identify Marxism, a theory of liberation, with its opposite, Communism, the theory and practice of enslavement." She aimed "to re-establish Marxism in its original form, which Marx called 'a thoroughgoing Naturalism, or Humanism.'"[26]

Dunayevskaya had two objectives with *Marxism and Freedom*. First, she wanted to present Marx as a critic of capitalism *and* as a beacon of human freedom. Second, she sought to uncover the American roots of Marx's ideas. Indeed, her book's subtitle—*From 1776 until Today*—signaled the centrality of American history to her effort. "Marxism," Dunayevskaya wrote, "is the theoretical expression of the instinctive strivings of the proletariat for liberation." The American proletariat, struggling against the most formidable bourgeoisie the world had yet seen, inspired Marx, and if Dunayevskaya had her way, would continue to stir Marxists to action.[27]

Although Dunayevskaya accentuated Marx's early writings, she insisted that no clear line of demarcation existed between the young and more mature versions of Marx. The young Marx speculated in the abstract about what alienated humans. The mature Marx merely got more specific.

Dunayevskaya contended that *Capital*, the apex of Marx's mature thought, built upon Marx's lifelong conceptualization of what it would take for people to be free. Moreover, she argued Marx's fully fleshed-out vision of human freedom owed to the fact of his attention to the American proletariat. This was particularly noticeable in his focus on the working day. The enslaved who revolted during the Civil War helped overthrow a system that had maintained total control over their working day. This act of defiance demonstrated to workers everywhere that they could have more autonomy over their time and labor. As the influential German émigré and Marxist Herbert Marcuse wrote in the preface to *Marxism and Freedom*, "A socialist society is a society in which free time, not labor time is the social measure of wealth and the dimension of individual existence."[28]

The Marx who advocated for individual freedom and more leisure time might have appeared strange to people who linked Marx with the repression and drudgery of life in the Soviet Union. Correcting this misconception was precisely why Dunayevskaya wrote *Marxism and Freedom*. It was also why she used the United States as a canvas for her analysis. The young Marx's conception of labor alienation had come alive for an American working class that, due to automation, had been separated farther than ever from the products of their labor. As James wrote about the *Economic and Philosophic Manuscripts*: "the great masses of the American workers feel and think in a way that invest these century-old essays with a meaning and significance." The American working class taught Dunayevskaya and her fellows something about Marx they could not have learned from his words alone.[29]

The Tendency's interpretation of rising proletarian radicalism, which it attributed to the coherence of working-class attitudes with the early Marx's yearnings for freedom, cuts against the grain of the narrative that the American working class had by the 1960s grown more contented, more conservative. Such conventional wisdom is at least partially true, but only insofar as the working class is defined as white men. But Dunayevskaya and her comrades had a much more expansive definition that included women and nonwhite people. Even more important, they enlarged the revolutionary class to include students and national liberation movements. Dunayevskaya placed special emphasis on the civil rights movement. Her Marxist theory of revolution was tailored for the 1960s.[30]

While Dunayevskaya and her comrades were formulating theory for a new revolutionary age, most Americans were blissfully unaware of the militant Marxists among them. Mainstream American culture in the 1950s was largely defined by political consensus over big-ticket items like the Cold War and the legacy of the New Deal, and a stifling cultural conformity regarding gender and race relations. The United States was the richest and most powerful nation, and many of its citizens prospered. It would have been a gigantic leap for most Americans

to imagine let alone desire an alternative to a system that seemingly
worked so well.

THE RISE AND FALL OF LIBERALISM

John F. Kennedy's election to the White House in 1960 might have
seemed like a harbinger of change. With his youthful good looks and
soaring rhetoric, Kennedy inspired young Americans who desired a
more just nation. In reality, his presidency embodied stasis. A moderate Catholic from a wealthy Massachusetts political family, Kennedy
was hardly a portent of a radical New Left on the precipice of advancing
revolutionary change.

Most Cold War liberals lined up behind Kennedy, but he was at best
a tepid liberal, especially next to Franklin D. Roosevelt. Kennedy styled
himself a foreign policy president, and his administration bogged
the nation down in international crises from Cuba to Vietnam. For
Marxists, American imperialism of this type was almost preordained,
whether liberals or conservatives were at the helm.[31]

On November 22, 1963, Kennedy was assassinated. Vice President
Lyndon Baines Johnson, quickly sworn in as Kennedy's replacement,
was the beneficiary of a grieving nation's goodwill, which enabled him
to push through transformative legislation, including the 1964 Civil
Rights Act. The Johnson presidency was the peak of midcentury liberalism. After crushing Arizona conservative Barry Goldwater in the
1964 presidential election, Johnson advanced a robust liberal agenda.
The Great Society included civil and voting rights for black Americans, health care for the elderly, federal money for public schools, food
stamps for the hungry, national parks, improved transportation, enforcement of labor rights, job training programs, and support for mu-
seums and other cultural institutions. The Great Society, a suitable heir
to the New Deal, was designed to benefit all Americans.[32]

Liberals were flying high not only in the corridors of power. In the
early- to mid-1960s, liberals also attained the pinnacle of intellectual
authority. Liberal thinkers were never more confident, especially in

their dismissal of both conservatism and Marxism as atavistic remnants of a bygone era. As late as 1964, the historian Richard Hofstadter was on seemingly safe footing when he claimed that the "angry minds" of the American right could never win an electoral majority. Right-wing Americans had always possessed a "paranoid style," Hofstadter argued. The same applied to left-wing Americans, who had never recovered from Henry Wallace's humiliating 1948 presidential campaign. Liberal intellectuals could be forgiven for discounting right- and left-wing prospects. But the center did not hold.[33]

American liberalism experienced dramatic decline beginning in the second half of the 1960s. In the long term, conservatives were the main beneficiaries of liberalism's falloff. But in the short term, the Left was able to come in from the wilderness. A growing number of Americans, especially young people, rejected the liberal center and joined the various radical movements that collectively came to be called the New Left. Liberal intellectuals had not predicted the degree to which the Jim Crow regime and the war in Vietnam were radicalizing millions.[34]

Black Americans had resisted Jim Crow since its emergence in the late nineteenth century. But a powerful national movement began to coalesce only after the Supreme Court ruled school segregation unconstitutional in 1954. Legal change alone was not enough to extinguish Jim Crow. Southern white supremacists organized a counterrevolutionary crusade known as "massive resistance." They saw the civil rights movement as a conspiracy of outside agitators—specifically, communists, whom they alleged sowed racial discord to weaken America.[35]

Yet the black freedom movement was not communist led, nor was it Marxist. Guided by southern black people themselves, the movement was a moral crusade for dignity and equal rights, not a revolutionary struggle against capitalism. But the movement did set off a wave of radical activism that carried well beyond the states of the former Confederacy.[36]

A line can be drawn connecting the civil rights movement to the emergence of a New Left, and even to the reemergence of American Marxism. Dunayevskaya recognized as much when she compared the victorious Montgomery Bus Boycott to the Paris Commune for how

it made ideas concrete through action. For Dunayevskaya, the boycot-
ters sought to make the promises of 1776, 1844, and 1871 reality. She
cited Marx, who wrote that the "great social measure of the Commune
was its own working existence." "So too," Dunayevskaya contended,
"for the Montgomery Bus Boycott, the movement that launched over
a decade of revolutionary activity on the part of African Americans and
their allies."[37]

Martin Luther King Jr. emerged as the face of the civil rights movement after leading the Montgomery Bus Boycott. King, who held a
PhD in theology from Boston University, where he studied Gandhi
and Thoreau, helped solidify nonviolent civil disobedience as the movement's strategy of choice. With images of white police brutalizing black
activists with batons, water cannons, and German shepherds airing
around the world, it seemed King's approach was a winning one. The
effectiveness of nonviolent civil disobedience was made even clearer
by the young activists who sat at segregated lunch counters across the
South, enduring harassment and arrest to draw negative attention to
Jim Crow. The civil rights movement, more than perhaps anything
else, exposed the rottenness at the core of the American system. It sent
people in search for answers. Many, including the young radicals of the
New Left, found Marx.[38]

The Vietnam War, which rivaled the civil rights movement as fuel
for the New Left, also drove people to Marx. The war was initially popular with an American public conditioned to Cold War propaganda.
But between 1961 and 1973, over 59,000 American soldiers and about
three million Vietnamese soldiers and civilians died. As the dead piled
up, with no American victory in sight, the largest antiwar movement
in the nation's history rose in resistance. In 1965, an antiwar gathering on Boston Common drew five thousand people; in 1971, a similar demonstration drew hundreds of thousands. Many young people
undoubtedly joined the antiwar movement because they did not want
to be drafted, but a growing number of people saw the need to resist
the warmongers. For many, mobilizing the planet's deadliest military
machine against impoverished people who never threatened American
lives was a crime against humanity. Millions saw the war simply as a

moral stain on the nation, a critique that grew increasingly poignant as American soldiers committed atrocities like the March 1968 massacre of three to five hundred unarmed men, women, and children at the village of My Lai. Upon their return home, veterans shared gruesome descriptions of many more such bloodbaths.[39]

In the face of the nation's clear capacity for evil, many young activists gave up hope that it could be saved. In addition to Marx, they turned to Che, Mao, and Fanon for inspiration overseas. But even those who still hoped for America to be just had grown more receptive to increasingly radical ideas, including Marxist ones. For many new leftists the war was no longer a tragic mistake but an inevitable product of the imperialism that grew from capitalism.[40]

One Marxist group described the war as "a key part of American imperialism's offensive against the world revolution, whose axis during the past two decades has been in the colonial areas." They contended that the "goals of U.S. imperialism in Vietnam are to crush the national liberation struggle and, if possible, overturn the North Vietnamese workers state, thus dealing fatal blows to the socialist revolution in all Southeast Asia." Some young anti-imperialists took to flying the Viet Cong flag during antiwar demonstrations. Such irreverence, even disloyalty, came to define the New Left.[41]

One explanation for the New Left's willful disobedience is its youth. Its nucleus was on college campuses. The university system grew in size and significance as millions of baby boomers came of age. Nearly four million students enrolled in colleges in 1960. By 1970, that figure had more than doubled. Students were a new demographic force to be reckoned with. When Mario Savio stood on a police car on December 2, 1964, and loudly proclaimed the existence of himself and his fellow Berkeley protestors—"We're human beings!"—he not only gave voice to the Free Speech Movement, he embodied the alienation of a generation.[42]

For Marx, alienation was pervasive but also a particular product of capitalism. New leftists like Savio were no fans of capitalism. But they articulated a more general alienation. Yes, they lacked connection to a society that provided them with little more than soul-crushing jobs, cheap commodities, and trivial entertainments. But young radicals were also estranged from a political system that was structured to make meaningful participation feel impossible for all but the privileged few. Elaborations on alienation filled left-wing political discourse. Fanning out from a specifically Marxist interpretation of life in a modern capitalist society, criticism of alienation morphed into sweeping calls for liberation from the many repressive institutions.[43]

Not only did young people rail against a state that conscripted them to kill and die for imperialism. Not only did courageous activists overthrow the appalling system of racial apartheid and rebel against the deeply entrenched racism of many American institutions. Natives renewed their centuries-old resistance to occupation and genocide. Young women revolted against a patriarchal society. Gays and lesbians rejected the dehumanizing constraints of heteronormative culture. People of all sorts struggled against alienation, and even more, against coercion. They revolted against the straitjacket of cultural conformity that prevented them from simply being themselves.[44]

During the 1960s, liberation movements often mixed with Marxism. Take for example Cesar Chavez, who earned international renown for organizing, along with Delores Huerta, Mexican American farmworkers, some of the most exploited people in the United States. Chavez's National Farm Workers Association (NFWA), founded in 1962, became a symbol of Mexican American resistance. The union's slogan, "Sí se puede" (Yes, we can), announced the emergence of Chicano power. The NFWA was also a union of working-class people across ethnic, racial, and national lines. Its members stood in solidarity with Filipino farmworkers by arranging a boycott against the hyperexploitative growers of table grapes in California.[45]

Chavez knew from his precarious childhood in the 1930s that it was difficult to be an itinerant worker and doubly difficult to be a brown one. By the 1950s, he also understood that powerful white people saw his organizing efforts as communist subversion. By the 1960s, Chavez recognized from his immersion in the history of the American labor movement that power in a capitalist society was about economic leverage. "We have to make the grower spend fifty dollars to our one dollar,"

Chavez declared. "We affect production and costs and profit. And if we hold out, we can win."[46]

The best way to help brown workers, or any workers, was to organize power over production. Chavez was not alone among major figures in the various liberation movements in thinking that labor struggle was the key to unlocking freedom for oppressed peoples. Martin Luther King Jr., who was sympathetic to Marx's critique of capitalism because he found the "gulf between superfluous wealth and abject poverty" wrong, understood as much. King was assassinated in 1968 while supporting striking sanitation workers in Memphis. The Civil Rights Act had passed four years prior, yet King knew that the dignity of black workers was still best secured through labor struggle.[47]

Marx might seem irrelevant to the concerns of the 1960s now, but people at the time saw things differently. Of course, the Marx that emerged in the 1960s was unique to the concerns of that era. Marx's reception across American history has been far from linear. There were boom periods in the 1930s and 1960s, but few Americans read Marx with any seriousness in the 1940s and 1950s. Those left-wing thinkers who persisted in grappling with Marx, such as Dunayevskaya, spoke to tiny audiences, until the 1960s, when history caught up to their ideas. That said, this narrative of decline and renewal misses an important if subterranean development in the American reception of Marx: the influence of those émigré Marxist intellectuals who collectively came to be known as the Frankfurt School.[48]

THE FRANKFURT SCHOOL

During the 1930s, a determined group of imaginative theorists fled Germany before the vise of Nazism closed in on them, moving the Institute for Social Research, which they founded in Frankfurt in 1923, to Columbia University. Max Horkheimer, Friedrich Pollack, Erich Fromm, Leo Lowenthal, Theodore Adorno, and Herbert Marcuse, among others, pioneered a type of Marxism they termed critical theory. This creative and rigorous framework was much less optimistic about the possibilities for revolution than earlier forms of Marxism. Critical theory, wrote the historian Martin Jay, was "permeated more with a sense of loss and decline than with expectation and hope."[49]

Two developments contributed to this "dialectic of defeat." First, Frankfurt School thinkers had to grapple with the withering away of the revolutionary working class. They had to come to terms with the sobering fact that lots of workers embraced fascism during the 1930s and 1940s. Second, Frankfurt Schoolers recognized that the rough edges of capitalism had been blunted by powerful cultural forces, such as mass-produced entertainment. Living in America, the epicenter of what Horkheimer and Adorno called the "culture industry," thus exacerbated their pessimism about the revolutionary potential of the working class. The culture industry had engineered working-class passivity.[50]

Yet the Frankfurt School expanded the theoretical terrain of Marxism. Rather than a systematic approach to political economy like Marx's late work, critical theory was an antisystem of sorts that mixed sociology, philosophy, and psychology. Such heterogeneity was consistent with the Frankfurt School's larger mission to lay bare the sweeping logic of capitalism. Any sphere of capitalism, from its predatory economic features to its anesthetizing cultural characteristics to its constraining political form, was fair game for withering critique, precisely because all aspects of capitalism had contributed to human alienation.

In dissecting the causes of alienation, Frankfurt School thinkers inventively mixed Marx with other European philosophers of modernity like Max Weber. Marx's observation that capitalists used their extraordinary wealth to capture the state jelled with Weber's notion that bureaucratic power over society was akin to an "iron cage." The enigmatic operations of bureaucracies were bad enough. But Kafkaesque bureaucracies working at the behest of concentrated wealth and power was truly a nightmare.[51]

Such theoretical promiscuity elevated the libertarian side of Marx. This was crucial to ensuring Marxism's relevance in the noncommunist world during the Cold War. Combining Marx and Weber also endowed Frankfurt School theorists with a powerful lens for examining how modernity had radically reshaped social organization. The new source of power that had to be properly understood and ultimately confronted was what they called "state capitalism."

State capitalism, a term that made its way into left-wing discourse in the 1960s because it succinctly pointed to the combination of forces responsible for American imperialism in Vietnam, had its roots in the anti-Stalinist Left. The paradigm advanced in the Johnson-Forest Tendency's 1950 book *State Capitalism and World Revolution* had a lot in common with critical theory. For both the Tendency and the Frankfurt School, modernity was the figurative equivalent of a prison cell. But because James, Dunayevskaya, and Lee worked within the labor and the civil rights movements, they forwarded an antiauthoritarian version of Marx that retained its revolutionary optimism about a multiracial American working class. In contrast, the Frankfurt exiles functioned in elite institutions that afforded them little contact with activists, or ordinary working people for that matter. That aloofness contributed to their pessimism.

Frankfurt School thinkers might have been detached from activist groups—at least, until the late 1960s when Marcuse became a New Left guru of sorts—but they had no trouble getting along with social scientists. Critical theory influenced a generation of elite American social scientific thought. Frankfurt pessimism about the working class resonated profoundly with liberal intellectuals who blamed McCarthyism on the ill-informed and conspiracy-prone masses. While most American intellectuals, especially liberals, were deeply anticommunist, they desired better company than Joseph McCarthy and his disreputable rabble.[52]

The Authoritarian Personality, a 1950 book coedited by Adorno, represented the apotheosis of the Frankfurt School's clout with elite American intellectuals. The book insisted a new species of human personality, "the authoritarian type of man," had surfaced. They argued the authoritarian personality comfortably blended new, sometimes enlightened ways of knowing that had emerged alongside industrial society, with an antirational, superstitious belief system like what plagued earlier epochs. It is difficult to overstate the degree to which this overarching paradigm shaped liberal thought in the ensuing decades. To this day, when a right-wing figure makes a ludicrous claim, pundits trot out Hofstadter's contention that American history has always been afflicted by a "paranoid style," a notion that owed an undeniable debt to *The Authoritarian Personality*. For the liberal elite, political expressions that challenged their pragmatic and technocratic centrism had to be rooted in a primal inability to adjust to modern society.[53]

Agonizing about the unwashed masses also seemed consistent with the Frankfurt School's turn to Sigmund Freud, who believed people are governed by unconscious impulses that made them prone to violence, authoritarianism, and paranoia. But reading Freud alongside Marx, especially early Marx, could feel liberating. The young Marx's analysis of how capitalism alienates us was complemented by Freud's theory that our actions are guided by hidden compulsions. Both the larger system *and* our individual psyches keep us separated from our true selves, and from our fellow humans. Moreover, these divisions require unmasking, which was the overarching rationale for critical theory.

In short, Frankfurt School reception did not have a predictable political configuration. In its pessimism about the working class, it cohered with Cold War liberalism. But in its ultimate belief in the possibility of human freedom, no matter how unlikely, critical theory inspired a new generation of left-wing radicals.[54]

Erich Fromm, a psychoanalytical thinker, Marxist, Frankfurt Schooler, and professor at major institutions like Michigan State University and New York University, was ideally suited to bringing the young Marx into conversation with both Freud and America in a way that promoted the cause of human liberation. Fromm's 1961 book *Marx's Concept of Man* included the first complete translation of Marx's *Economic and Philosophic Manuscripts*. (Dunayevskaya and Lee only ever translated pieces of them.) Just as notable, the book situated that work squarely in the twentieth century.[55]

Like Dunayevskaya, Fromm accentuated Marx's humanism—specifically his avowal that freedom is the ultimate horizon of humanity yet only achievable in the context of social relations. We will only ever realize our full potential as humans when we emancipate ourselves from a system in which some people control the labor of others. This basic premise endured throughout Marx's work. As he wrote in 1875, "From each according to his ability, to each according to his needs." Nothing less, nothing more.[56]

For Fromm, Marxist humanism was a superior alternative to both Western capitalism and Soviet communism. But for it to become a compelling social vision for Americans, Fromm wrote, we "must discard the ignorant and distorted picture of Marxism which is current in American thinking today." This was a tough job, since "this ignorance and distortion of Marx are to be found more in the United States than in any other Western country." *Marx's Concept of Man* was Fromm's counterattack.[57]

One myth Fromm sought to dispel was the notion that Marx's philosophy was a "wish for uniformity and subordination." This Cold War stereotype was often associated with the misconception that Marx was a determinist. In contrast, Fromm painted a picture of a Marx whose ideas were surprisingly flexible. Marx, in Fromm's words, "claims that the way man produces determines his thinking and his desires, and not that his main desires are those for maximal material gain." Marx was an enduring critic of the assumption that humans are naturally acquisitive. "Marx's whole criticism of capitalism," Fromm maintained, "is exactly that it has made interest in money and material gain the main motive in man, and his concept of socialism is precisely that of a society in which the material interest would cease to be the dominant one."[58]

Fromm assumed capitalism had a nearly overwhelming hold on us, so powerful that it had obliterated the boundary between individuals' social and the psychological realms. These provinces had been knit together so tightly that people could not distinguish between individual desire and the compulsions of capital. People "are increasingly satisfied with a life regulated and manipulated," Fromm wrote, "by the state and the big corporations and their respective bureaucracies; they have reached a degree of conformity which has wiped out individuality to a remarkable extent." Borrowing from Marx, Fromm claimed that most people had become "commodity men," or *Homo economicus*. Capitalism had colonized our innermost psyches. And we had offered up little resistance.[59]

Fromm's pessimism was consistent with the larger Frankfurt School project. But, thanks to Freud, Fromm retained a sliver of optimism. The young Marx, like Freud, believed "that the true mainsprings of man's actions are unconscious to him." People are oblivious to the origins of their desires. "According to Freud," such desires "are rooted in man's libidinal strivings; according to Marx, they are rooted in the whole social organization of man which directs his consciousness in certain directions and blocks him from being aware of certain facts and experiences."

In capitalism, human consciousness is false because the system prevents us from seeing our true circumstances. But Marx exposed the ideological facade that kept us shackled. By demonstrating *Homo economicus* was a recent species, Marx showed that it might be temporary. In working to transform society, humans would also transform themselves. Building socialism would be akin to rising from the ashes of our contemporary inferno.[60]

Fromm's optimism helped shape how the New Left put Marx to use. So too did the work of a growing number of homegrown American thinkers whose sympathetic readings of Marx were integral to their rejection of Cold War liberalism. Take the radical sociologist C. Wright Mills. Before his untimely death in 1962, Mills authored several pioneering books that explored the dynamics of power and class in American society. Frankfurt School readers would have found several themes in them familiar.

MARX IN THE AMERICAN NEW LEFT IMAGINATION

In *White Collar: The American Middle Classes* (1951), Mills depicted the United States through a dystopian lens, beholden to the iron cage of government and corporate bureaucracy. In his 1956 book *The Power Elite*, Mills similarly applied a Weberian lens to the institutional structures of the American elite, "those political, economic, and military circles which as an intricate set of overlapping cliques share decisions having at least national consequences."[61]

Much like critical theory, Mills saw power in the United States as intensely hierarchical. He therefore, like the Frankfurt exiles, was often pessimistic. Although the self-styled renegade cut a starkly different image next to a prim aesthete like Adorno, Mills had internalized Frankfurt School wisdom. Indeed, one of his foremost teachers was the Frankfurt émigré Hans Gerth. And yet, unlike others in the New York intellectual milieu who were shaped by the Frankfurt School, the Columbia University sociologist's gloomy outlook did not lead him down a conservative path. Liberal intellectuals embraced the Cold War state. Mills rejected American imperialism.[62]

In his 1960 book *Listen Yankee*, which sold over 400,000 copies, Mills asserted that the United States should keep its hands off the Cuban Revolution, which he confidently assumed was developing "a human socialism," not the authoritarianism of the Soviet Union. The United States did not heed his advice. Yet Mills also grew skeptical that Castro's Cuba was on a humanist path, despite early progress in literacy and healthcare. Still, he remained confident in Marxism's liberatory potential.[63]

Mills's final book *The Marxists*, published posthumously in 1962, offered an undoctrinaire overview of Marx and Marxism for American readers. Mills was never a member of the Communist Party, nor any other left-wing organization. He was consistently unsympathetic to the Soviet Union and left-wing authoritarianism. But Mills was also deeply critical of American capitalism, and intensely disapproving of American Cold War policies. Mills wanted to transcend the Iron Curtain. In this, Mills did more than serve up harsh takes on Soviet and American policies. He also sought a political philosophy that would bridge the expanding chasm between liberalism and Marxism.

Mills argued liberalism and Marxism had hardened into crude ideologies, a predictable outcome once nation-states adopted these political philosophies as dogma. Liberalism in the United States had become a defense of an unjust status quo. Marxism in the Soviet Union had become a rationalization of a repressive system. This was ironic, since both philosophies emerged from a humanist tradition that valued insurgency. But that tradition was in the throes of a crisis. The best way to confront it, and one of the most effective methods for breaking free of the iron cage of Cold War logic, was a thorough reexamination of Karl Marx. This was because Marx took nineteenth-century liberal ideals like freedom and liberty more seriously than liberals did, because Marx extended these ideals to "the lower depths of liberal society." In the hands of Marx, liberal values could be made to work for all.[64]

Mills understood the appeal of Marx to working-class and poor people, those whom Marx said would "be exploited as long as capitalism prevails." But many who did not hail from "the lower depths," including many relatively comfortable Americans, also found Marx's ideas brilliant and relevant—"a specter that at once haunts and attracts." Mastering Marx's work, Mills wrote, "is to experience in our own intellectual development the central themes of social and political thinking developed in the last hundred years."[65]

Mills contended most American intellectuals, including many social scientists, lacked awareness of how deep historical structures shaped their lives. In contrast, Marx was the master of big-picture thought. "Each epoch is a new type of society," Mills wrote, describing Marx's structural theory. "It creates new types of men and women, and neither the society nor the men can be understood in terms of the old epoch."[66]

By helping people connect their "personal troubles to public issues," by showing them that their individual identities were forged by social and historical processes, Marx pioneered what Mills called the "sociological imagination." Those who viewed the world through this lens never mistook their individual circumstances for a universal condition.[67]

Mills especially appreciated Marx's epochal framework. "Any man can think only *within* his own times," Mills wrote, "but he can think *about* the past and the future, thus attempting to expand 'his' time, constructing out of its materials the image of an epoch. That—to a brilliant extent—is what Karl Marx did."[68]

Still, Mills was not uncritical of Marx. Like his liberal counterparts, Mills acknowledged that Marx's theory that capitalism amplifies working-class economic misery had been proven wrong, at least in wealthy capitalist societies like the United States. Liberals reveled in this refutation, convinced it had discredited Marx altogether. Mills had a more complex position, recognizing that the American capitalist economy had stabilized in large part due to exorbitant military spending. For an anti-imperialist, this was hardly worth celebrating.

That debate aside, Marx's thoughts on psychological alienation remained relevant. Marx theorized that workers grew more miserable in a capitalist society in a material sense *and* at a psychological level. American workers might have been doing relatively well in material terms. But thanks to automation and the increasingly specialized division of labor, American workers had less autonomy, which caused alienation. Workers might have been wealthier than ever. But this does not mean they were happier or more fulfilled than ever. Capitalism remained a problem for most people, and thus Marx remained relevant. But there was a catch.[69]

When workers suffer from economic misery, they are prone to rebellion. But as Mills contended, alienation of the psychological variety does not produce revolutionary impulses. "The psychological alternatives for men in capitalist society are no more polarized than is the class structure," Mills wrote. "Not conservatism *or* insurgency, proletarian *or* bourgeois, but social apathy, a developed and mature political indifference, is often the determining psychological condition. Such apathy is not readily explained in terms of Marx's rationalist model of ideological forms and class consciousness, or by its conception of alienation." The twentieth century proved people rarely did what was in their best interests, at least by Marxist standards. Alienation does not engender revolution. Just more alienation.[70]

Mills was not quite right about this. He did not live to observe the growing number of young people overcome with revolutionary impulses despite relative prosperity. In fact, this historical reality was central to distinguishing the New Left from the Old Left. Marxists in the 1930s saw economic exploitation and deprivation everywhere. Marxists in the 1960s had to look harder to find it (although it obviously existed, as Michael Harrington showed in his 1962 study of poverty, *The Other America*). Yet, they saw misery everywhere, and they wanted a theory that explained it. Thus, the New Left too turned to Marx, but a different Marx. This divergence helps us understand the contours of the New Left relative to the longer history of the American Left.[71]

In 1961, Eleanor Hakim, one of the founding editors of *Studies on the Left*, a journal of radical thought, cleverly used a softball game (The Maoist Maulers vs. The Flying Bolsheviks) as a metaphor for the growing rift between the Old Left and New Left. "It does seem," Hakim wrote to Marxist historian Eugene Genovese, "the old left must resort to more and more blatant tactics, and strong-arm methods as skills diminish and as they get more and more on the wrong side of History!" Indeed, *Studies on the Left* epitomized a crossing of the threshold between the Old and New Left. The magazine's reading of Marx illuminates this historical transformation.[72]

Studies was founded by a group of University of Wisconsin graduate students—mostly in the history department—that included Hakim, James Weinstein, Michael Lebowitz, Saul Landau, Steven Scheinberg, Martin Sklar, and Dale Lewis. The editorial board eventually came to also include Genovese, Staughton Lynd, and Tom Hayden. Despite conventional wisdom that the New Left had no use for anyone over the age of thirty, the young intellectuals of *Studies* respected their elders, which they demonstrated by taking Marx seriously, by adhering to the socialist label, and by publishing essays by a veritable "who's who" of seasoned leftists, including Marcuse, Mills, Herbert Aptheker, Noam Chomsky, Philip Foner, Langston Hughes, Jean-Paul Sartre, and William Appleman Williams. Such gravitas might have had something to do with the initial enthusiasm for the journal. Its first issue sold all three thousand copies in just a few weeks, and soon thereafter leftists from all over the world were submitting manuscripts.[73]

But the *Studies* youngsters were also at times irreverent. In 1961, when a French academic submitted an article on literature, Hakim indicated that it was "barbarically oversimplified" and "stoopid!" "The prose is a mass of clichés," she continued, "French academic clichés (which are perhaps pardonable) and existentialist clichés (which are unforgivable!)" Another editor wrote a scathing review of a manuscript by black budding intellectual Harold Cruse, which *Studies* eventually published after several intense rounds of editing. The reviewer determined that Cruse's prose was replete with "the circular verbiage (rhymes with garbage) of nationalism." W. E. B. Du Bois, ninety years old, submitted a pamphlet he had prepared for the Nigerian government. Although Sklar showed Du Bois the proper admiration in his reply—"it gives us no little cause for feeling pride and honor that you should have thought of *Studies*"—the editorial team rejected the submission.[74]

Such chutzpah typified the New Left. These young people were not about to reflexively bow down to their elders. But *Studies* also worked against some New Left qualities, such as a lack of theoretical rigor bordering on anti-intellectualism. Its editors attempted to fashion an Americanized Marx that would cohere with the sensibilities of a movement dominated by young people.

Like many other Marxists of the era, the *Studies* thinkers came to Marx by way of the Frankfurt School. The University of Wisconsin–Madison, where Hans Gerth taught, was a good place to go for Frankfurt School studies. Gerth assigned Adorno and Fromm in addition to Marx and the Italian Marxist Antonio Gramsci. Thanks to Gerth and an eclectic range of thinkers open to reading Marxist texts, a rarity in the early Cold War, the history and sociology departments were hotbeds of intellectual ferment. This reputation was cemented when William Appleman Williams, who had taken classes with Gerth, was hired in the History Department. Williams quickly became the favorite teacher of the *Studies* editors. Williams was grounded in Marx; but his approach to history and politics was also rooted in American traditions like republicanism. As a result, the journal's editorial vision was a heady mix of Frankfurt School pessimism and Williams's more optimistic native radicalism. This combination made for a rich theoretical contribution to the history of American leftist thought.[75]

The *Studies* editors were serious about using sophisticated Marxist theories to analyze American politics and history. Sklar encouraged Marcuse in 1962 to contribute to *Studies*, since it sought to "revitalize interest in, and analysis of, dialectics as it relates particularly to epistemology and to ideology taken broadly as a world view," no matter how difficult this would be "in the practicalist-positivist intellectual circles of the United States." Sklar's letter conveyed his fluency in the argot of critical theory. It also demonstrated that *Studies* wanted to bring Marxism of the most rigorous type to bear on American problems. More specifically, Sklar indicated he wanted the journal to take up the Frankfurt School's question about why the working class was averse to socialist revolution.[76]

Its aspirations to be an organ of erudite Marxist philosophy often put *Studies* at odds with fellow radicals who tended toward an antitheoretical moralism. This moralist leftism, grounded in an uncompromising love of justice, had deep roots in the American Left going back to the abolitionist movement and, more pertinent to American Marxism, back to Section Twelve of the First International. These roots overlapped with the history of American liberalism. But moral leftism was not identical to liberalism. The former had a much more expansive view of the good life that included justice for workers at the workplace, women in the home, farmers on the prairie, black Americans everywhere. Also, whereas liberals tended to trust in the law to remedy injustice, moral leftists believed in the edifying power of the dramatic deed. But the moral Left and liberalism had one crucial commonality. Both were suspicious of the Marxist class struggle paradigm. Neither hinged its politics on Marx's labor theory of value.[77]

In *The Communist Manifesto*, Marx and Engels criticized utopian socialists like Robert Owen for fantasizing that "historical action is to yield to their personal inventive action." In this, they might as well have been censuring the moral Left. But the editors of *Studies* did not explicitly partake in such sectarian bloodletting, which had long defined the Marxist tradition. In fact, they worked to include voices in the moralist tradition. For instance, the radical historian Staughton Lynd, who was far likelier to invoke Henry David Thoreau than Karl Marx, became a contributing editor in 1963. The moralist Lynd was described by Weinstein, a Marxist through and through, as nonetheless "a prototype of the radical young intellectuals we would like to have associated with *Studies*."[78]

Embracing non-Marxists and hybrid Marxists was never easy for the labor-centric Marxist editors of *Studies*. In 1962, Lynd submitted an article, "The Admirable Radical: Henry Thoreau," which Hakim trashed as "poorly written" and "unacceptable." Yet Hakim was alone among the editors in thinking Thoreau was relevant to contemporary radicalism. "I am afraid that the kind of radicals on the Board of *Studies on the Left*, getting their impetus from Marxist political and economic approaches," Hakim warned, "fail to appreciate or even recognize the validity of the radical of conscience." She continued: "Lynd is certainly correct, in my view, to characterize the new radicalism as being essentially moral in impetus and action oriented." In her defense of Lynd and Thoreau, Hakim sought to tear down the walls between a theoretically refined European Marxism and the plainspoken moralism of homegrown American radicalism.[79]

Hakim was not alone among leftist thinkers in desiring to bring Marx together with a radicalism of conscience. The leftist historian Howard Zinn was another. As author of an acclaimed book about the Student Nonviolent Coordinating Committee—*SNCC: The New Abolitionists*—Zinn had his finger on the pulse of left-wing social movements. He observed that the New Left was already combining the best of Marx with the best of moral leftism. He contended that the practice of stirring "pragmatism, empiricism, and existentialism into Marxist theory goes straight back to the *Theses on Feuerbach* and straight ahead to the spirit of the New Left." The *Theses*, eleven short philosophical musings Marx wrote in 1845, memorably mandated that "philosophers have hitherto only *interpreted* the world in various ways; the point is to *change* it."[80]

Action-oriented New Leftists like Zinn accentuated Marx as a tribune of socialist revolution while largely downplaying his abstract theorist side. "To 'act out' the Marxian approach is to remind ourselves," Zinn wrote, "that much of what is called 'intellectual history' is the aimless dredging up of what is and was rather than a creative recollection of experience that points to the betterment of human life." Marx was useful only insofar as he was an immediate and practical guide along the path to a better world. In this, Zinn proposed a hybridized, moralized, Americanized Marx.[81]

To reinforce a pragmatic Marx, New Leftists would have benefited from reading Sidney Hook's 1933 book *Towards the Understanding of*

Karl Marx. But by the 1960s, Hook was known less as a brilliant Marx scholar and more as a cranky neoconservative. Hook himself foreclosed on the likelihood that young activists would read his imaginative take on Marx by forbidding new editions of his book. Activists hungry for a usable Marx had to turn elsewhere. Many of them looked to Dunayevskaya, who pointed them to the young Marx.

Studies frequently grappled with Marxist humanism. In 1962, it published a long review of Dunayevskaya's *Marxism and Freedom*. The reviewer championed it as the signature book to reclaim Marx for a humanistic vision of the world, highlighting Dunayevskaya's emphasis on how modern technologies, as part of the capitalist machine, made people into "fragments" of human beings. This argument resonated in an era of unprecedented economic growth. Marx's theory of immiseration might have been proven wrong, at least for the time being. But Marx's insistence that capitalism made workers less human—more alienated—remained true.[82]

Zinn was one of many left-wing thinkers in the 1960s who read Marx's *Economic and Philosophical Manuscripts of 1844* and concluded that its articulation of estrangement spoke to young people. Marx, in the words of Zinn, "talked of men who produce things that are alien to them, that become (so to speak) monsters that are independent of them (an anticipation, perhaps, of our automobiles, television sets, skyscrapers, and even our universities)." This tracked with the broader logic that shaped the New Left. "We find ourselves living a life," Zinn wrote, "that is different from the one we really want to live."[83]

A devotion to the young Marx helped the Marxist-inclined New Left establish genuine links with a moralist Left that prioritized abstract objectives like justice and freedom. But even as this commitment helped submerge sectarian divisions that otherwise might have extinguished the New Left before it got off the ground, it is worth noting that zeal for the young Marx was nonetheless zeal for Marxism, not liberalism. In a 1961 essay that expressed dismay that the playwright Bertolt Brecht's newfound popularity among American critics was predicated on a disavowal of his left-wing politics, Hakim made clear this distinction. Hakim, the foremost proponent of the homegrown radicalism of conscience among the *Studies* Marxists, directed her anger specifically at Eric Bentley, who published an English translation of several Brecht plays yet excised crucial political content from them.[84]

In his translation of *The Good Woman of Setzuan*, a play about a prostitute who tries to live a good life, Bentley expunged Brecht's politically motivated epilogue. In the original script, Brecht had the actors confront the audience about how revolution is the only solution to the play's dilemma, that a good woman is forced to do bad things. "For your great, godly deeds, I was too poor, too small," the woman proclaimed. As Hakim wrote, Bentley's translation obscured Brecht's larger irony, that "in a just world, there are no such great, godly deeds."[85]

Individual heroism is necessary in a world torn asunder by capitalist social relations. A truly free society does not require remarkable feats by individuals. Whereas liberals countenanced a world in which heroism is necessary, Marxists insisted that freedom is social. Nobody is free in a system that exploits the many for the benefit of the few. No solidarity, no freedom. This lesson, which was the key to Marx's writings across his entire life, was the most important point that Americans might take from Marx. It was also the most threatening to a system that pitted people against one another.

Hakim's capacious reading of Marx, which was designed to allow inroads with the moral Left while remaining true to the core implications of Marx's theory of capitalism, represented *Studies* at its nonsectarian best. Its commitment to building a broad-based New Left meant sustaining patience for some non-Marxist political traditions, even those that had kinship with liberalism. Such forbearance, however, did not also entail tolerance for the liberal political tradition itself. That was a bridge too far. *Studies* nurtured the New Left hatred for liberalism.

Sklar, who did more than anyone to chart the *Studies* editorial course, developed a theory that helped give shape to New Left antipathy for liberalism. He argued that liberalism had become the politics of the corporate class. Sklar coined the term "corporate liberalism," which became arguably the New Left's definitive contribution to conceptualizing the postwar American state. In this view, rather than a justice-oriented political philosophy, liberalism had become little more than ideological window dressing for corporate domination.[86]

Sklar's corporate liberalism was a close conceptual cousin to C. L. R. James's "state capitalism." Both theories presumed that a robust, interventionist state existed to ensure the basic functions of a capitalist economy. Liberals dismissed the idea, pointing to the good that the New Deal state had done for average working people, often against the wishes of capitalists. But Sklar backed up his assertion with compelling historical evidence.

In an influential article, Sklar contended Woodrow Wilson's famed idealism helped rationalize the material interests of American corporations. Like most early twentieth-century progressives, Wilson fitted his vision of moral uplift to the new political realities in which massive corporations dominated the American economy. He believed the regulatory state needed to focus less on boosting the competitiveness of small firms and more on abetting corporations. Wilson's task, Sklar argued, was not to dissolve corporations but to ensure they acted in the public interest, at least as Wilson defined it. The liberal state was to work hand-in-glove with corporations to guarantee a moral economy, not only for the United States, but for the whole planet. In this way, said Sklar, Wilson oversaw the consolidation of corporate liberalism.[87]

Liberalism became the New Left's principal ideological foe during the 1960s. *Studies* dedicated many more pages to confronting corporate liberalism than to criticizing conservatism. This made for strange bedfellows. *Studies* published the libertarian Murray Rothbard, who, like Friedrich Hayek, thought the New Deal was a stalking horse for authoritarianism. Rothbard's perspective, despite being partly shaped by Hayekian conservatism, meshed well with the journal's full-throated attack on corporate liberalism. In one counterintuitive piece, Rothbard reasoned that "the Hooverian new economics was remarkably similar to the Roosevelt New Deal." Rothbard chalked up commonplace assumptions that Herbert Hoover represented the last gasp of laissez-faire capitalism and that Roosevelt was the first president to do battle with economic royalists, to liberal folklore. Both Hoover and Roosevelt sought to empower the state to protect the corporate elite. Their differences were a matter of degree, not kind. In this, Rothbard aided the *Studies* mission of presenting corporate liberalism as a monolith that had overwhelmed the twentieth-century American state.[88]

Antistatism was not a libertarian invention. Marxism has a long tradition of antistatism, because Marx often saw the state as a barrier to freedom. This strain of Marxism informed the writings of the Italian communist Antonio Gramsci. Imprisoned by the fascist leader Benito Mussolini, Gramsci theorized that the ruling class uses the state and other institutions to establish ideological power over the working class. This form of power, which Gramsci termed "hegemony," is especially insidious because the working class identifies with the state even as it serves capitalists. In a 1967 *Studies* article, Genovese argued that Gramsci pointed to a more realistic reading of American history. "We need to face the fact," Genovese wrote, "that an identification between bourgeois and general interests exists and has existed . . . throughout American history." The notion that the elite secured mastery because their ideas were accepted even by those whom they dominated undergirded the theory of corporate liberalism.[89]

The concept of corporate liberalism resonated because it offered a plausible account for a new form of class domination. It was also convincing because an extraordinarily volatile economic system had at long last been stabilized by a centralized state of unprecedented size and scope. As throughout the history of capitalism, Marx had written words that spoke to these developments. Writing in *Studies* in 1967, Martin Nicolaus highlighted a way to read Marx that aligned Marx with the fact that capitalism had stabilized itself. Nicolaus discovered this side of Marx while working on an English translation of Marx's gargantuan, unpolished notes known as *Grundrisse: Foundations of the Critique of Political Economy*. Written between 1857 and 1861, *Grundrisse* ("floor plans") amounted to a rough draft of *Capital*. In it, according to Nicolaus, Marx dispensed with his erstwhile attachment to the Hegelian dialectic. This shift made him more useful to Marxists in the 1960s who were thoroughly convinced that corporate liberalism had foreclosed on proletariat revolution.[90]

Many of those scholars and activists, including Dunayevskaya, maintained there was continuity between the young and old Marx. But some thinkers, Nicolaus among them, stressed discontinuity, because they believed the older, reformed Marx was more relevant to their situation. Prior to writing *Grundrisse*, Nicolaus noted, Marx was prone to a "Hegelian leap of faith, to assume that the contradiction between capital and labor would continue to develop and unfold in this manner until the two classes confronted each other." Marx would only be valuable to 1960s readers if they ignored this insistence on the dialectical paradigm. The twentieth century had shown that proletarian revolution was far from imminent and the Hegelian choreography was false. According to Nicolaus, "the most industrially advanced capitalist nations typically have the most quiescent, noninsurrectionary proletariats."[91]

There was merit in arguing that throughout his life Marx worked on the singularly important problem of how humans might push through capitalism to a social system that would better allow people to flourish as free individuals. This thrust was important to reclaiming Marx for a capitalist world that associated Marx with communist authoritarianism. But there was also value in recognizing that some of Marx's emphases had shifted over his life. If Marx was wrong about some things, and if he made course corrections, then we could surely do the same.

As translator of the *Grundrisse*, Nicolaus was better positioned than anyone to judge that Marx's floor plans had dispensed with Hegelian teleology. It was in *Grundrisse* where Marx first worked at length on his famous theory of "labor power" that would be one of the focal points of *Capital*. Marx theorized that in early capitalist development the bourgeoisie derived surplus value from labor power by forcing the proletariat to work longer hours. But when this approach to maximizing profits reached its limits—when workers died young, or worse yet, when they unionized—mechanization enabled capitalists to continue to derive surplus value from a fixed working day.

Marx later wrote, in what became the third volume of *Capital*, that capitalism was prone to crisis precisely because it sought to suppress the labor force. But as a stand-alone theory, Marx's "labor power" innovation helped New Leftists explain the stability of corporate capitalism. This is why Nicolaus found the *Grundrisse* so poignant. Automation enabled large corporations to survive demands for higher wages because large-scale investment in mechanization, of the type that only large corporations could undertake, ensured profits above and beyond the squeezing of the labor force. In this way, exploitation in its strictly Marxist terms—profit derived from labor power—could go on into infinity even as working-class standards of living continued to rise. Such a reading of Marx was like Genovese's reading of Gramsci because it suggested that corporate capitalism was accompanied not by the immiseration of the proletariat but by its acquiescence.

During this golden age of capitalism, several influential Marxists in Europe speculated that even if the social democratic state did not necessarily work in the interests of every capitalist, which were varied and often in conflict, it did indeed work to buttress capitalism's long-term sustainability. In their efforts to tame an explosive economic system, state actors were often forced to make hard decisions that some individual capitalists found unappealing. The purpose of the state was pacification of the forces that threatened capitalism, even if specific measures offended some capitalists.[92]

Sklar's theory of corporate liberalism was an American version of this antistatist Marxism, an elaboration on earlier criticisms of Roosevelt and the New Deal. In Sklar's view, in any corporate stabilization process, elites conspired to maintain an ironclad grip on power. While many Americans unwittingly consented to this arrangement, the few had all the power at the expense of the many. Democracy, in any sense of the term meaningful to young leftists, was a farce.

The idea of corporate liberalism explained the persistence of capitalist power in the context of New Deal government. Yet the theory might have fallen on deaf ears had it not been for the deadly imperialist war on Vietnam launched by American liberals. The New Left increasingly thought of corporate liberalism as the political philosophy of the capitalist war machine. As the violence peaked in 1968, Zinn hoped that the war would at least shift attitudes about American power. As he wrote: "In America, liberalism and radicalism alike were beguiled into cheering for state power because under F.D.R. it seemed beneficent: it enacted various economic reforms and it waged war against Hitler. The New Left, we must hope, will continue to recognize that a state cannot be trusted, as a 'liberal America' could not be trusted to carry reforms far enough or to drop bombs only on Nazi invaders and not on Asian peasants in their own countries."[93]

As young people joined the burgeoning movement to stop the Vietnam War, they came into contact with some of the Marxist ideas about capitalism and imperialism. Although at its core the antiwar movement put forward a simple, yet powerful message—stop the war, bring the troops home, end the draft—many activists saw the war as the logical outgrowth of American capitalism. The Marxist tradition had a long history of this style of conjecturing, dating back to Marx's thoughts about primitive accumulation, and after that, to Lenin's explanation of the causes of the First World War.[94]

MARX AGAINST AMERICAN EMPIRE

Motivated by the Vietnam War, some left-wing thinkers expanded upon Marx and Lenin to account for twentieth-century American imperialism. Harry Magdoff's *The Age of Imperialism*, published in 1969, sold over 100,000 copies because it fed a New Left readership hungry for Marxist theories about the subject.[95]

Born in 1914 in Brooklyn to Russian Jewish immigrants, Magdoff first read Marx at the age of fifteen. "It blew my mind," Magdoff recalled. "His view of history was a revelation . . . that got me started reading about economics." Magdoff took a degree in economics from New York University, after which he became an economic statistician with the federal government, first with the Works Progress Administration, and then with the War Production Board. During that time, Magdoff grew optimistic that socialism might be achieved through state planning. But after his experience on the doomed Henry Wallace campaign, Magdoff's optimism about the American state dimmed (his

confidence in state planning never diminished). He committed himself
to Marxist studies to figure out the tight grip that capitalism had on the
American state.[96]

The Age of Imperialism contended that the United States was at the
forefront of a new kind of imperialism. Earlier imperialist nations
were most concerned with competition from other imperialist nations.
But postwar imperialist nations focused on reversing the contraction
of the imperial system as a whole. This was particularly the concern of
the United States, which emerged from the Second World War as the
unchallenged capitalist superpower, made evident by the fact that its
share of total world investments mushroomed to over 59 percent by
1960. As people across the planet won freedom from the European
empires, some also fought for independence from the oppressive fetters of a new American-led international system. The United States
interpreted these movements as direct threats to its interests—direct
threats to the empire of capitalism—and thus sought to crush freedom
movements across the planet. For Magdoff, this explained American
interventions in Guatemala, Iran, Cuba, and Vietnam.[97]

As instrumental as Magdoff's account was for many in the antiwar
movement, nobody did more to shape New Left thought about American foreign policy than the heterodox left-wing historian William
Appleman Williams. After an injury forced him to give up a career in
the military, Williams pursed a career in history at the University of
Wisconsin–Madison, first as a student and then as a professor popular among leftist graduate students. While a graduate student himself,
Williams came under the guidance of several progressive historians
who had absorbed Charles Beard's hypereconomic analysis of American history. This sensibility, deeply intertwined with the moral Left
tradition, indelibly marked Williams. His most renowned book, *The
Tragedy of American Diplomacy*, first published in 1959, was written from
a hybrid Marxist perspective that adopted a moral leftist tone. The title
included the word *tragedy* because Williams believed American foreign
policy had taken a wrong path due to its leaders' ideological blinders.
But these blinders were in part the result of structural connections to
capitalism.[98]

Tragedy held that American foreign policy had always been expansionary but became explicitly so on a global level only with Secretary of State John Hay's Open Door Notes, a series of missives written in 1899 and 1900 in response to European nations carving up spheres of influence in China. The philosophy that informed the Open Door Notes, Williams asserted, shaped *all* American diplomacy. Policymakers assumed all nations should be granted equal access to markets everywhere in the world, irrespective of borders, imperial claims, or trade deals.[99]

An open-door policy was tragic in Williams's eyes because it defined trade in straightforward imperialistic terms, as "markets for our surplus products and control of raw materials for our factories." More to the point, this diplomatic imperative implied the United States had a right to dominate markets anywhere and everywhere, a right that policymakers were eager to defend with force. *Tragedy* thus offered a ready-made explanation for American military intervention in Vietnam even though Williams wrote it well before the escalation of that war.[100]

FIGURE 7.4: William Appleman Williams, ca. 1960s.

In tandem with his critique of American diplomacy, Williams imagined an alternative foreign policy for the United States. In contrast with the dictates of the Cold War, he dreamed the nation might "evolve and adopt a program that will encourage and enable the communist countries to move in the direction of their own utopian vision of the good society as we endeavor to move in accordance with our own ideals." Williams called this doctrine "an open door for revolutions." The first step was to arrange American society in a more just manner. Only then might the United States help other societies achieve their own ideals. Such a foreign policy, which paid more than lip service to the concept of self-determination, would have truly been anti-imperialist. It was also a prophecy grounded in the moral Left tradition. Whereas Marx and Lenin argued capitalism cannot abide limits, Williams implored Americans to accept them.[101]

To say that Williams drew from the moral Left tradition is not to contend that he ignored Marxism. In the 1960s, an uneasy truce settled over the century-long sectarian battle over a leftist vision for the future. This ceasefire allowed for an apprehensive coexistence between the moral Left tradition and a labor-focused Marxism. Williams personified this brief period of left-wing harmony. On the one hand, in the spirit of moral prophets from Henry David Thoreau to Edward Bellamy to Martin Luther King Jr., he envisioned a community premised on justice, equal opportunity, and brotherhood. Yet on the other, Williams also found wisdom in Marx's more pitiless foresights about class struggle and revolution. Indeed, in 1964 Williams wrote a weird little book highlighting how Marx was useful to understanding American society and history: *The Great Evasion: An Essay on the Contemporary Relevance of Karl Marx and on the Wisdom of Admitting the Heretic into the Dialogue about America's Future*.[102]

Williams was committed to battling the American propensity to avoid unpleasant truths. In *The Great Evasion* Williams argued that "of all the evasions in which Americans have indulged themselves, the most serious one is very probably their persistent flight from any intellectual and moral confrontation with Karl Marx." Americans were achieving economic prosperity, but they remained estranged from meaningful lives. "This deepening crisis of increasing alienation, deprivation, and frustration was forecast over a century ago by Karl Marx." Marx's humanist focus corresponded with Williams's desire for a beloved community. "Marx was concerned," he wrote, "with the way man defined himself and his relationships with other men, and how he used his creativity once his basic needs had been satisfied." This Marx resonated with many New Leftists. But to those more attuned to the Marx of the Old Left—the Marx focused on class and labor—the Marx of the New Left was a horrible distortion.[103]

Eugene Genovese's staunch Old Left views had softened to a degree, but he nonetheless took issue with Williams's rendition of Marx. Genovese criticized Williams's imprecise use of a concept like "community," highlighting that plenty of non-Marxists, including fascists, saw community as a solution to alienation. Moreover, in emphasizing community, Williams ignored class struggle, the most revolutionary element of Marx. It was difficult to reconcile community with class struggle since the latter almost precluded the former. Without a full-blown anticapitalist revolution, how could people come together when divisions spawned by capitalism kept them apart? Such criticism aside, Genovese appreciated that Williams knew that the costs of capitalism went well beyond the immiseration of the working class. Genovese wrote: "The destruction of community solidarity alone condemns capitalism." For Williams, Marxism was a classical call to human freedom.[104]

In his effort to convince Americans to grapple with Marx, Williams reconciled his moralistic notions of American foreign policy with a Marxist conceptualization. Like Magdoff, Williams described American imperialism as the extension of American economic power. "From the seventeenth century to the present," he wrote, "the capitalist commitment to expanding the marketplace has guided and set limits upon American foreign policy." But Williams also attributed such expansionism to more idiosyncratic rationales. In discussing how the closing of the frontier had led the United States to shift its imperial gaze overseas, Williams wrote: "The world itself became the room required to swing the American Ego." The American need to assert itself across the planet fulfilled deep-seated psychological desires.[105]

Williams was intent to show that American imperialism had proven Marx correct about the ineluctable expansionary forces of capital. But he was also insistent on fitting Marx into his utopian vision of a beloved community, writing: "The alienation of millions of human beings— from each other, from their society, and from their own humanness— has been and remains an inherent part of the development process involved in the informal empire of the United States." Americans would only relinquish violent empire building, would only forgo primitive accumulation, would only quit swinging their ego around the world, after they found a more humane, more peaceful existence within their own national boundaries.[106]

Ultimately, Williams believed that a confrontation with Marx would compel Americans to recognize that their history was not exceptional, that like people everywhere, they were passengers on the locomotive of history. Marx would have found nothing unique about twentieth-century American expansionism. He would have seen it as distinct from previous European imperialism only in that it conformed to a new type of capitalism, namely corporate liberalism. In sum, Williams wrote, "the United States has not proved that Marx was wrong."[107]

Unlike Cold War liberals who contended postwar American capitalism had rendered Marx obsolete, Williams thought at most it had achieved a "high-level stalemate with the internal forces that Marx identified as driving capitalism toward breakdown." Williams recognized that that stalemate was specific to time and place. He appreciated that American capitalism was sustained by imperialism, and he understood that imperialism was a fickle beast. The American tendency to export its social problems was unsustainable.[108]

THE CHALLENGE OF BLACK POWER

The most identifiable American social problem during the 1960s, as with most times, was racism. It was only logical, then, that Black Power militants often linked racial oppression at home to American aggression abroad. Black Panther Party activists stirred a heady mix of black nationalism and Marxism in connecting their struggles on the streets of America to the fighting in the jungles of Vietnam. As Fred Hampton, chairman of the Chicago chapter of the party, told a rapt audience in November 1969, a month before the state murdered him: "The liberation of the oppressed people of Vietnam or the oppressed people of Babylon's freedom . . . has to be founded on the land that is fertilized by the bones and blood of these aggressive pig dogs that come into our communities and occupy our communities like troops occupy a foreign territory and go into Vietnam and fight and struggle relentlessly against the people in Vietnam to have a right to self-determination. We don't care whether anybody likes it or not. That's our line. It's a Marxist-Leninist line."[109]

Hampton's poignant lecture illuminated an important development in New Left thought. Largely due to the solidarity extended to non-white victims of American imperialism abroad by nonwhite victims of American capitalism at home, a forceful internationalist sensibility had reemerged on the Left. Marxism thrived in such an environment precisely because Marx framed his anticapitalism as necessarily international. "Workers of the *world*, unite!" In aligning themselves with the Viet Cong, many Black Power activists turned to the Marxist tradition. But in other ways, Marxism did not sit well with the Black Power movement.

Harold Cruse emerged as a forceful critic of Marxism from a Black Power perspective. Cruse came to this position through personal struggle. As a former member of the Communist Party, he was scorned by doctrinaire Marxists who robotically rejected race-focused political thought. When Cruse first starting writing about black nationalism, he half expected approval from New Left comrades who, like him, rejected Old Left nostrums. But squaring black nationalism and Marxism would prove to be almost impossible.[110]

In 1961, Cruse submitted a long article to *Studies*, titled, "Cuba, Marxism, Nationalism, and the American Negro." Cruse argued black Americans could learn more from Cuban revolutionaries by focusing on their nationalism, not their Marxism. This provoked serious intellectual soul-searching among the young Marxist editors. They had

enough difficulty finding common ground with proponents of Thoreau. Now they were also being asked to see the value of a social philosophy based on the ideas of Marcus Garvey and Malcolm X. But, sincere
in its effort to forge a capacious New Left, *Studies* published Cruse's
polemical call for nationalism. However, that act of solidarity was not
enough to convince Cruse that his political vision had a future with the
American Left.[111]

With the 1967 publication of his mammoth book *The Crisis of the Negro Intellectual*, Cruse quit the Left in favor of a heterogeneous form of
black nationalism. Cruse argued that the "individual Negro has, pro-
portionately, very few rights indeed because his ethnic group (whether
or not he actually identifies with it) has very little political, economic or
social power (beyond moral grounds) to wield." Black Americans would
never achieve freedom without first building their own institutions.[112]

In declaring this, Cruse meant more than political and economic
institutions. He also argued that black freedom required independent black cultural institutions—theaters, newspapers, schools—and
that black intellectuals from the Harlem Renaissance on had failed to
develop them. By working in racially integrated cultural settings and
institutions—or worse, by working for white cultural patrons—black
intellectuals had been unable to attain the cultural independence that
was a necessary precondition of black freedom.[113]

Insofar as *The Crisis of the Negro Intellectual* was a mandate for building racial solidarity in order to achieve power, Cruse's book was consistent with the Black Power literature of the era. Stokely Carmichael and
Charles Hamilton's *Black Power: The Politics of Liberation*, also published
in 1967, hinged on the idea that "group solidarity is necessary before a
group can effectively form a bargaining position of strength in a pluralistic society." What distinguished *Crisis* was Cruse's willingness, like
Marx, to "ruthlessly criticize everything existing," including the white
American Left and American Marxism. He argued that the Marxism
pitched by the American Communist Party, including the Party's black
members, was based on ideas alien to the American masses. Marx,
Cruse contended, had no purchase on American political life.[114]

In this contention, Cruse was influenced by one of his intellectual

FIGURE 7.5: Harold Cruse, ca. 1970s.

heroes, V. F. Calverton. In the 1930s, Calverton argued that European Marxism was ill-suited to building a Left in the United States. Building on Calverton, Cruse contended that if effective socialist theory was going to sprout in America, it had to be planted by black intellectuals. Cruse quoted W. E. B. Du Bois: "We who are dark can see America in a way that white Americans cannot." Only the most exploited people could truly understand American capitalism. "It evidently never occurred to Negro revolutionaries," Cruse wrote, "that there was no one in America who possessed the remotest potential for Americanizing Marxism but themselves." Cruse was dour on the prospects for an

American Marxism, unless black intellectuals redefined Marxism for that context. Many on the Left came to a similar conclusion.[115]

The historian Christopher Lasch wrote a sympathetic review of *Crisis* for *The New York Review of Books*, the most widely read New Left publication in the late 1960s. Lasch fundamentally agreed with Cruse about the need for separate black institutions. "American history seems to show," Lasch wrote, "that a group cannot achieve 'integration'—that is, equality—without first developing institutions which express and create a sense of its own distinctiveness."[116]

Lasch also appreciated Cruse's frustration with black radicals for mindlessly joining the white American Left, or for "mistakenly conceiving collective action in class terms which are irrelevant to the Negro's situation in America." Given its anti-Marxist implications, this was a strange position to stake out in a left-wing magazine. It seems to anticipate Lasch's own eventual rejection of the Left, as he later gained renown as an opponent of all progressive ideology, including Marxism. But as a leftist at the time, his review foreshadowed a crucial development in leftist thought. By the late 1960s, many American leftists began embracing what became known as "identity politics," black nationalism included. This trend had serious implications for the American reception of Marx beyond the 1960s. *Crisis* thus was an important transition point.[117]

Cruse believed racial solidarity was a more effective way to achieve political power than class solidarity, in part because he believed race was a more authentic form of belonging. Building on this, he contended that even ostensibly class-based political groupings centered on race or ethnicity. He made the provocative argument that the American Communist Party was a vehicle for Jewish power. In fact, Cruse declared Karl Marx was the first to cloak Jewish Power behind the facade of class struggle. Accordingly, he criticized black Communists for inadvertently enhancing Jewish power. Cruse asserted that "the great brainwashing of Negro radical intellectuals was not achieved by capitalism, or the capitalistic bourgeoisie, but by Jewish intellectuals in the American Communist Party." In the zero-sum game of ethnic politics,

Cruse believed black Communists unwittingly worked to derail the Black Power project.[118]

If Cruse's stark black nationalism represented a bellwether for a post-1960s American Left, it appeared Marxism would be forced to take a backseat. If identity politics and other non-class-based forms of political analysis were in the driver's seat, it seemed the American reception of Marx was on the verge of yet another down period. Yet some key thinkers toiled to yoke Marx to the new sensibilities, whether shaped by black nationalism, feminism, or the counterculture. Herbert Marcuse was especially up to this task.

PHILOSOPHER OF THE NEW LEFT

Marcuse, who made his mark as one of the Frankfurt School's most prolific writers, came of age during the heyday of the Old Left. But more than most Old Leftists, and more than most of his fellow critical theorists, Marcuse tolerated efforts by young activists to drastically transform left-wing priorities. At a time when the left was riven by generational conflict, epitomized by Adorno calling on police to remove student protestors from a university building, the intellectually curious Marcuse embraced the changes taking place. No wonder the *New York Times* dubbed him the "Philosopher of the New Left."[119]

Marcuse's writings spoke to New Left inclinations well before the 1960s. In his 1955 book *Eros and Civilization*, one of the earliest and most persuasive fusions of Freudian psychoanalysis with Marxist dialectics, Marcuse theorized that sexual repression, as a form of alienation, was an effect of capitalism. In this, Marcuse spoke to the countercultural impulses of young leftists who thought sexual revolution went hand-in-glove with anticapitalism. When Marcuse opened a 1967 speech before a group of Berlin students by summoning "flower power," mirroring the antiwar movement's "make love, not war" mantra, he truly meant it as a call to revolution. The counterculture was the antidote to alienation.[120]

Marcuse was an earnest theorist of the counterculture. But he was also updating Marx for an era of working-class deradicalization. Marcuse's 1964 book *One-Dimensional Man* theorized that the pacification of the revolutionary working class was both material and ideological. On the one hand, American capitalism had purchased the loyalties of working-class Americans. On the other, the needs of the powerful came to represent seemingly universal values, or in Marcuse's words, "the whole appears to be the very embodiment of Reason."[121]

The contradictions that seemed so transparent to Marx—the ones that would usher in communist revolution—no longer appeared self-evident in an era marked not only by affluence but also by total administrative control. Like his liberal contemporaries, Marcuse observed an American consensus—what he called one-dimensional man. But unlike Cold War liberals, who saw consensus as a democratic ideal that could only be achieved within the ingenious American political tradition, Marcuse saw the one-dimensional society as a Kafkaesque nightmare. "A comfortable, smooth, reasonable, democratic unfreedom prevails in advanced industrial civilization," he wrote.[122]

Marcuse's bleak description resembled Sklar's pessimistic rendering of corporate liberalism. For both, the conflicts seemingly inherent in capitalism had been ironed out. Marcuse wondered whether this equilibrium was fleeting, "in the sense that it does not affect the *roots* of the conflicts which Marx found in the capitalist mode of production (contradiction between private ownership of the means of production and social productivity)." But he also pondered whether the balance was premised on a more fundamental "transformation of the antagonistic structure itself, which resolves the contradictions by making them tolerable." Like Sklar and many other New Left Marxists, Marcuse judged that the latter scenario was likelier. The structure of capitalism had been altered to such a degree, he believed, that conflicts previously thought inevitable had been entirely suppressed.[123]

In Marx's epoch, the working class imagined a utopian socialism as the flipside to their wretched existence. In Marcuse's era, the working class was too comfortable, too ideologically confused, to imagine something beyond capitalism. This was a tragic development. "The slaves of developed industrial civilization are sublimated slaves," Marcuse wrote, but nevertheless, "they are slaves." Workers did not realize their condition of servitude.[124]

Despite giving up on the belief that workers were destined to be revolutionaries, Marcuse remained a Marxist. He remained committed to figuring out how to get free from capitalism, even if that meant transcending novel material and ideological constraints that Marx could never have foreseen. As such, *One-Dimensional Man*, despite its weighty pessimism, concluded on a note of hope. Marcuse posited that a "New Historical Subject" might arise to set people free:

> Underneath the conservative popular base is the substratum of the outcasts and outsiders, the exploited and persecuted of other races and other colors, the unemployed and unemployable. They exist outside the democratic process; their life is the most immediate and the most real need for ending intolerable conditions and institutions. Thus their opposition is revolutionary even if their consciousness is not. Their opposition hits the system from without and is therefore not deflected by the system. . . . The fact that they start refusing to play the game may be the fact which marks the beginning of the end.[125]

Marcuse looked beyond the traditional working class to find a revolutionary subject among victims of the system who were not overly attached to it. If there was going to be an anticapitalist revolution, it would be led by those whom Frantz Fanon called the "wretched of the earth." In the United States, this meant people who were marked by oppression, especially black Americans, who "see America in a way that white Americans cannot." It also meant women.[126]

THE CHALLENGE OF FEMINISM

The mainstream feminist movement that emerged in the 1960s desired for women to have the same opportunities as men. But otherwise, mainstream feminism did not make many demands on capitalism.

Yet, any movement serious about achieving equality was compelled to consider a whole range of constraints on it. Many feminists quickly learned that even equal opportunity, a seemingly modest objective, was nearly impossible to accomplish within the existing system. A more radical demand, such as equality of outcomes, was even more difficult to imagine. Some feminists thus turned to Marxism. They concluded, as the social critic Barbara Ehrenreich put it, "there is no way to understand sexism as it acts on our lives without putting it in the historical context of capitalism."[127]

If some feminists discovered Marx due to the limitations of mainstream feminism, many more Marxists discovered feminism due to the limitations of the Left. Robin Morgan's political transformation was indicative of this trajectory. Morgan began writing for New Left publications in 1962, principally dedicated to ending the Vietnam War. But in 1967, she expanded her activism to include women's liberation, helping to found New York Radical Women, which protested the Miss America Pageant in 1968. Soon after, Morgan's notions about radical politics changed. "No matter how empathetic you are to another's oppression," she wrote, "you become truly committed to radical change only when you realize your own oppression." In a 1970 essay, "Goodbye to All That," Morgan publicly severed ties with the Left: "We have met the enemy and he's our friend." Morgan had grown incredulous that so many self-avowed Marxists persisted in avoiding women's issues, which they denounced as "bourgeois." In contrast, Morgan contended that patriarchy was the world's "primary oppression," an argument made by women weary of being relegated to secretarial duties in a movement supposedly seeking universal freedom.[128]

Just as lots of left-wing women rejected subordinate roles in male-dominated New Left organizations, several radical intellectuals came to recognize that Marxism failed to properly address sexual inequality. As feminists created organizations dedicated to women's liberation, they also committed themselves to explicitly feminist theory. The British feminist Juliet Mitchell blazed this theoretical trail with her highly influential "Women: The Longest Revolution," a 1966 essay which, in her words, "arose out of my involvement with Marxism and my dissatisfaction with any economist understanding of the position of women." Mitchell's analysis built on the works of groundbreaking feminist thinkers like Simone de Beauvoir and Betty Friedan—but not before addressing the weaknesses in the prototypical Marxist analysis of the question of women, Friedrich Engels's *The Origins of the Family, Private Property and the State*.[129]

First published in 1884, just a year after Marx's death, *Origins* was one of Engels's many elegies to his comrade. Engels was the sole author of *Origins*, yet the idea of the book owed to Marx's detailed notes on the American anthropologist Lewis Morgan's 1877 book *Ancient Society; or, Researches in the Lines of Human Progress from Savagery, Through Barbarism to Civilization*. Both Marx and Engels believed Morgan's findings confirmed their theory of historical materialism, in particular their sense that shifting class relations prompted other social changes, including relations between the sexes.[130]

Morgan's close study of indigenous culture revealed to Engels that hunter-gatherer societies, what Marx called "primitive communism," were both nonacquisitive and matrilineal, and that these two qualities were inextricable. Engels likened the "overthrow of mother right," or the death of matrilineality, to "the world-historic defeat of the female sex." He also noted that this transformation occurred, not coincidentally, precisely when property laws came into existence. As property became sacrosanct, the patriarchal family came to operate as a property claim. Bourgeois men relied upon the patriarchal family structure as a source of inheritance. The nuclear family unit was not a feature of proletarian life because the working class had no property claims, but because sex was embedded in property, many working-class women turned to prostitution as a means of survival. Women were caged by men, either in the family as wives or in society as sex workers, because everyone was enslaved by capitalism. Since patriarchy was an extension of capitalism, Engels implied, the coming of socialism would kill both capitalism and patriarchy.[131]

In contrast with Engels, Mitchell believed a proper understanding of women's oppression required examining sexual relations "as a specific structure" separate from capitalism. "This will mean," she wrote, "rejecting the idea that woman's condition can be deduced derivatively from the economy or equated symbolically with society." Most feminist thinkers came to agree with Mitchell, including the Canadian-American feminist activist and writer Shulamith Firestone, whose 1970 book *The Dialectic of Sex: The Case for Feminist Revolution* built on Mitchell's argument.[132]

Firestone, like Mitchell, dismissed Marx's theory of class struggle as a useful explanation for the exploitation of women. But unlike Mitchell, who maintained an appreciation for Marx as a theorist of capitalism, Firestone believed her theory of history was more comprehensive and more radical than Marx's because she was "dealing with a larger problem, with an oppression that goes back beyond recorded history to the animal kingdom itself." Due to the biological necessity of reproduction, which required that men protect women and children, men had wielded power over women since the beginning of human history. Patriarchy was the first form of oppression and underwrote all others. Historical cruelties that Marx and Marxists had assigned to capitalism—sexism, racism, imperialism—should in fact be attributed to male supremacy. For Firestone, a theory about how women might get free needed to account for the timelessness of patriarchy. *Any* theory of political freedom had to begin with the everlasting problem of sexual domination.[133]

Firestone's notion about the ongoing war between the sexes was markedly different from Marx's idea of perpetual class struggle. Where Firestone accentuated the timeless nature of patriarchy, Marx highlighted the contextual characteristics of class rule. Marx was well known for declaring the "*history* of *all* hitherto existing society is the *history of class struggles*," a seemingly ahistorical paradigm. But he consistently demonstrated that class dynamics were interwoven with historical context. The feudal class system, for example, was enormously different from the capitalist class structure. Firestone, in contrast, downplayed shifting arrangements between the sexes, even as she likened her theory to dialectical materialism.

One of the advantages of a contextual theory of history like Marx's was that it made change seem possible, even likely. If capitalism was merely the latest era in the long history of humanity, if capitalist class arrangements only recently came into existence, then it was easier to imagine an alternative, postcapitalist, perhaps even socialist future. In contrast, it was difficult to envision a way out of an oppressive patriarchy if that condition was an enduring mark of humanity. This was a troubling outcome of Firestone's theory given its liberationist aspirations. And yet, Firestone was optimistic that sexual revolution was possible in the late twentieth century. "Humanity has begun to outgrow nature," she wrote, such that "we can no longer justify the maintenance of a discriminatory sex class system on grounds of its origins in Nature." Due to revolutionary circumstances that were made possible by technological advances, sexual distinction was no longer necessary to human reproduction. The mechanisms of reproduction, such as conception, and the maintenance of childhood, such as childcare, could be socialized, thus obliterating the rationale for patriarchy. There was no longer any biological compulsion for women to live under the yoke of men.[134]

Although Firestone disagreed with Marx about history, their visions of the future converged. Firestone wrote that "just as the end goal of socialist revolution was not only the end of economic class *privilege* but of the economic class *distinction* itself, so the end goal of feminist revolution must be . . . not just the elimination of male *privilege* but of the sex distinction itself." This would spell the death of all oppressive systems. Firestone believed she had turned Marx and Engels right side up. Marx and Engels thought socialism would usher in a world free of all oppressions, patriarchy included. Firestone contended rather that feminism was the fulcrum of revolution.[135]

Firestone's case was bolstered by the sexism within New Left Marxist circles. Ellie Hakim, the sole woman editor of *Studies on the Left*, was subjected to sexist treatment by many of her male colleagues and correspondents, some of whom referred to her as "honey." When the Trotskyist historian George Rawick discovered Hakim had existentialist leanings, he wrote that she was "given like most women to some sort of idealist mystical nonsense." Though such misogyny eventually contributed to her departure from *Studies*, Hakim held the journal together in its early years with her voluminous, thoughtful, and witty correspondence. And she did so because she ultimately believed Marxist analysis was the correct method for bringing about a revolution that would liberate everyone, women included.[136]

Hakim was not alone among feminists who put forward Marxist forms of analysis, even as Marxism grew less popular among feminist intellectuals following the 1960s. Angela Davis, who emerged as a brilliant feminist thinker and liberationist theorist, has also been one of the world's most renowned Marxists. Davis put Marxism to use, even when she was articulating a philosophy of women's liberation.

Raised by leftist parents in Birmingham, Alabama, Davis met Marcuse while she was an undergraduate student at Brandeis University. Marcuse impressed upon her that it was possible to be both an academic philosopher and a radical activist, indeed, that the two roles went well together, and she followed in his footsteps by studying in Frankfurt, Germany. Although hyperattentive to the civil rights movement from a young age, Davis was unimpressed by black nationalism, expressing frustration when she heard Stokely Carmichael reject communism as a "white man's thing." Davis became a member of the American Communist Party, joining the Che-Lumumba Club, a black group within the Party. Marxism became the guiding intellectual and political force of her life.[137]

After earning advanced degrees from the University of California, San Diego, where Marcuse had moved from Brandeis, and Humboldt University in East Berlin, Davis accepted a position at the University of California, Los Angeles (UCLA) in 1969. Amid urban unrest across the nation, Davis was fired at the urging of Governor Ronald Reagan, for her Communist Party membership and for her Black Power activism. This did not slow her advocacy, especially on behalf of black political prisoners. A warrant for Davis's arrest was issued in 1970 when a gun that belonged to her was used in a botched effort to free prisoners at a courthouse that resulted in the deaths of four people, including a judge. Davis spent sixteen months in prison, during which time "Free Angela Davis" became a rallying cry for leftists across the world.[138]

During her time in prison, Davis wrote a dense and insightful Marxist analysis of sexual inequality, "Women and Capitalism: Dialectics of Oppression and Liberation." Such a lofty theoretical accomplishment was unsurprising to the people most familiar with Davis's mind. Marcuse considered her his best student ever. The historian Mike Davis (no relation) said she was the only person in the California branch of the American Communist Party who knew Marx's work intimately. He only lamented that she was too busy to teach Marx to the rest of them.[139]

Davis made her familiarity with Marx readily apparent in "Women and Capitalism." Her purpose was to bring the discourse around women's liberation back to Marx's "theoretical reconstruction of history" in order "to specify the ways in which the subjugation of women and their ideological relegation to the sphere of nature were indissolubly wedded to the consolidation of capitalism." Davis disagreed with more mainstream feminist theory, which posited that the roots of sexism were independent of capitalism, and that "capitalism, imperialism, and racism are symptoms of male supremacy." For Davis, twentieth-century male supremacy could not be attributed to patriarchy immemorial but rather to a more recent iteration of patriarchy that was inextricable from the mighty advances of capitalism.[140]

FIGURE 7.6: Herbert Marcuse and Angela Davis, 1970.

Where many feminists blamed sexual oppression on natural differences, Davis contended that the belief that women were "firmly anchored in nature's domain" was itself an effect of capitalism. The naturalization of sexism was a "recurring ideological motif" that helped rationalize "the epoch of bourgeois rule." Prior to capitalism, men and women had seemingly natural roles to fulfill, as men partook in hunting, fishing, and farming while women gathered, reproduced, and cared for children. But as men grew to be cogs in the industrial machine and were thus severed from nature, women remained in that realm, as caregivers.[141]

Women's consignment to the realm of nature grew crucial to upholding the capitalist order as nature became something that men were meant to master. Davis wrote: "The hypostasized notion that woman, as contrasted with man, is only a creature of nature, is blatantly false and a camouflage for the social subjugation women daily experience. But even in its falsity, there is also a hidden truth: the real oppression of women today is inextricably bound up with the capitalist mode of appropriating and mastering nature." Humanity was compelled by capitalist logic to conquer nature, and in a shadow move, men were pushed to subjugate women.[142]

As with sex-determinist feminists like Firestone, Davis trusted in the possibility of a future free of male supremacy. But unlike Firestone, Davis believed the stumbling block to all liberation was capitalism. This did not mean sexual inequality could be ignored until after the revolution. Rather, fighting sexism was integral to the struggle against capitalism. In this, Davis drew on the Marx who "construed the male-female bond to be a central ingredient of the social complex which must be overturned and remolded by the revolutionary process." Davis believed, like Marx, that human nature was malleable, even seemingly intractable aspects of it like sexual relations. "The woman-man union," she wrote, "is very much mutable and always subject to social transformation." Davis also assumed, like Marx, that capitalism inhibited a better human nature, arguing that "as long as social production takes place within the fetters of capitalist relations—as long as the appropriation of nature means the exploitation of human beings—this union between the sexes remains stunted and misshapen." Capitalism's crimes against human nature fed patriarchy's crimes against women.[143]

The idea that women were exploited because they were considered part of the natural world had Marx's theory of alienation written all over it. But Davis must have known her conceptualization was too abstract to inform feminist activism. She thus supported it with a powerful illustration. Because capitalism kept workers from enjoying the fruits of their labor, they had to take solace in other pleasurable activities, especially sex. But the problem with sex as a salve against alienation was its essential animality. Humans were social beings, so freedom from alienation demanded a social solution. Only that, ironically, would get humans closer to their actual nature.

And while sex failed to liberate men, for women it was often yet another form of subjugation. Women suffered from double alienation. Davis wrote: "Compelled to make only minimal contributions, or none whatsoever, to social production—not even in and through the alienated patterns of work—she is effectively reduced to the status of a mere *biological* need of man." This is what Davis meant in arguing that relegating women to the realm of nature ensured their oppression. Women, like trees, were things to be used, and often abused. Davis, following Marx, wanted to recalibrate the relationship between humans and nature, between men and women, and thought anticapitalist revolution was the way to do it.[144]

In emphasizing what capitalism did to relations between the sexes, Davis went beyond focusing on how capitalism shaped the bourgeois family. As Engels argued, the family arose as a capitalist institution to protect property. The woman's role within it was to cultivate and protect children as future inheritors. But Davis included the working-class family, which she argued had gained in importance as the only place where working men found a sense of self-mastery, albeit superficial.

If the role of women had become "inseparably anchored to the fabric necessary for the maintenance of the worker as individual," if the working-class family had become a haven in a heartless world, then women had also become central to the preservation of capitalism. The imperatives of capitalism, not nature, kept women in their chains. This, according to Davis, signified the contradiction at the heart of capitalist sex relations. Women were rigidly categorized as natural even as they served the social function of keeping the family together, and thus upholding the capitalist system.[145]

The revolutionary implications of Davis's analysis were clear. The debate about whether to prioritize women's liberation or socialism was based on a faulty premise. Freedom from patriarchy was unachievable without freedom from capitalism, and vice versa. This would become doubly clear in the latter decades of the twentieth century, as the nuclear family began to fall apart, victimized by neoliberal economic attacks.[146]

Marcuse agreed with Davis. By the early 1970s, he had come to believe women's liberation was one of the most promising revolutionary movements. Marcuse acknowledged that "women are not a class in the Marxist sense" and that "there can be discrimination against women even under socialism." But even as Marcuse conceded that "the male-female relationship cuts across class lines," he also posited that "the immediate needs and potentialities of women are definitely class-conditioned to a high degree."[147]

Women had been oppressed for thousands of years. But capitalism funneled women into specific subservient roles. Men worked outside the home as exploited cogs. When women worked outside the home, they did so for less pay than men. But more crucially, to maintain the larger system, women were also required to work within the home. As such, women's domestic work had value by the standard Marxist formula, yet because they went unpaid for it, it was measured exclusively as surplus. It accrued in its entirety to the larger capitalist system. In short, women's unpaid labor helped enrich the bourgeoisie. For Marcuse, then, if the women's liberation movement was to succeed, if the patriarchy was to be defeated, capitalism had to be destroyed. Any feminism true to its word had to be Marxist.

Both feminism and Marxism decayed after the 1960s, as the Left all but disappeared from the American political spectrum. New Deal liberalism also entered a period of steep decline when a powerful conservative movement began a steady ascent. With that rise came a new consensus about the relationship between the state and capitalism. The state was no longer expected to placate the working class by managing capitalism. Instead, the US government geared up to unleash capitalism upon the entire planet. The capitalism of Marx's imagination returned like a repressed memory. But a revolutionary working class failed to reemerge in kind. The contradictions of capitalism pinpointed by Marx did not reveal themselves, at least, not right away. It took decades for the Marxist dialectic to reappear in plain sight. Yet Marx remained alive in America—on life support, but alive.

As the liberation movements of the 1960s faded, a residue of Marx persisted. Marx no longer resonated in the union halls, as he had in the 1930s. He no longer reverberated among young radicals, as he had in the 1960s. Nevertheless, Marx remained alive in academic journals and graduate seminar rooms. In this way, the American reception of Marx became a highly specialized affair. No longer a totem of social movements, Marx became a symbol of cosmopolitan erudition. This was a Marx befitting an age of neoliberalism.

8

THEORIST

Academia in the Age of Reagan

I confess to being so infuriated by the contemptuous ignorance which
mainstream academics and opportunistic politicians display toward
Marx that I want to make a gesture of solidarity with a dead man who
can't defend himself.

MICHAEL HARRINGTON

In 1975, a member of the Front de Libération Nationale politburo told
the economist Branko Milanovíc, then a student working in Algeria,
that they had a problem. "All students we send to the United States
come back to Algeria as Marxists. All students we send to the Soviet
Union come back as anticommunists. So, we should do the reverse of
what we want to achieve."[1]

The Algerian apparatchik's fable underscored the divergent paths
Marxism had taken on opposite sides of the Iron Curtain. The Soviet
Union had originally hosted some of Marxism's most groundbreaking
thinkers, namely Lenin and Trotsky. But after several decades of rigidly enforced party dogma, Soviet Marxism had desiccated, now less
a theory for understanding and changing the world, more an apology
for Soviet power.[2]

Something different happened in the United States. Owing to the liberationist sensibilities of its intellectual culture after the 1960s, Amer-

ican Marxism was infused with an eccentric range of enthusiasms that transformed it into a multitudinous academic tool for analyzing not only capitalism but also history, culture, ideology, race, gender, slavery, colonialism, and almost any other aspect of American life. Marx continued to thrill American readers. Yet as Marxism flourished in an academic register, Marx had very little purchase on American political life.

The American reception of Marx grew weird after the 1960s. Even as most Americans persevered in blissfully ignoring Marx, and even as some persisted in demonizing his ideas, many notable intellectuals grappled with him in novel ways. In a nation increasingly devoted to a "neoliberal" brand of capitalism that annihilated the regulated New Deal version, a thousand Marxes bloomed. Marxism's detachment from political channels allowed it to develop in creative ways. History never stops provoking ironies. Especially when Marx is involved.

DEBATING KARL MARX ON THE EVE OF NEOLIBERALISM

If you had asked Michael Harrington, it was not supposed to be this way. The longtime socialist and author of *The Other America*, the 1962 bestselling book about poverty amid plenty, believed conditions remained ripe for a Marxist *political* renaissance. Harrington's 1972 book *Socialism*, yet another bestseller, was a political and philosophical manifesto that argued "man has socialized everything except himself." This claim was heavily reliant upon Marx. Yet Harrington also took the old Rhinelander's analysis a step further.[3]

Harrington agreed with Marx about capitalism's tendencies. Enormous organizations had brought people together across vast distances to ensure extraordinary productivity, which in turn yielded unprecedented wealth. Harrington also concurred with Marx that these proclivities pointed toward socialism. "It is men who create wealth," Harrington wrote, paraphrasing Marx. "In doing so, at a certain historical point they become so productive that they must create a just society, for the old orders of domination are no longer capable of containing their ingenuity."[4]

Harrington's admiration for Marx's achievement was boundless. "*Das Kapital*," he wrote, "is nothing other than a magnificent analysis of 'socialized man' and, in particular, how productivity grows enormously through the application of science to a cooperative, interdependent process of production. And its conclusion is, of course, that man must recognize, and organize, these powers of his as *social* powers." Humans must gather up their collective power of production and transform their societies. This theme in Marx's work, Harrington argued, was "more relevant today than when he wrote *Das Kapital*."[5]

Although Marx's prophecies about production and wealth proved true, Harrington also recognized these developments were riddled with contradictions. Prosperity for some was accompanied by destitution for others. Marx pinpointed these paradoxes. But because Marx "mistook the rise of capitalism for its decline," he wrongly assumed the socialization of capital would quickly follow the socialization of labor. At the time of *Socialism*'s publication, more than a century after *Capital* was published, a tiny elite maintained an iron grip on capital. Meanwhile, misery endured for millions. Harrington called this "socialization without solidarity." Proper socialization required a redistribution of wealth and power to the vast majorities who lacked both. For Harrington, *democracy* required just such a redistribution.[6]

By the 1970s, Harrington had become arguably the most influential socialist in the United States. As a committed radical from an early age, the St. Louis–born Irish Catholic moved through various left-wing groups, from Dorothy Day's Catholic Worker's Movement to Norman Thomas's Socialist Party. In 1973, Harrington helped found the Democratic Socialist Organizing Committee, which became the Democratic Socialists of America (DSA). His vision of socialism was grounded in the idea that revolutionary aims could be achieved through reformist means. Harrington thought a mass movement might use the mechanisms of political democracy to radically transform society. Americans could socialize themselves, without the violence and authoritarianism that had bedeviled socialist revolutions elsewhere.[7]

Harrington believed socialism and democracy were unachievable in isolation from each other. To support this claim, he relied upon Marx.

FIGURE 8.1: Michael Harrington, 1978.

Whereas most Americans had been conditioned by the Cold War to think of Marx as the wily paterfamilias of totalitarian dictatorship, Harrington saw him as a champion of democracy. The idea of a democratic Marx provoked cognitive dissonance among those who shared Ronald Reagan's sense that he had spawned the Evil Empire, Reagan's label for the Soviet Union. "How do you tell a Communist?" Reagan quipped. "Well, it's someone who reads Marx and Lenin. And how do you tell an anti-Communist? It's someone who *understands* Marx and Lenin."[8]

Harrington saw claiming Marx for the democratic socialist project as "a contemporary political act, an attempt to restore his genuine memory to the future." This was a demanding task given Marx and Engels were wrongly "seen by most people as the fathers of totalitarianism and as materialistic simpletons who taught that economic interests neatly determine the entire course of society." Yet as Harrington wrote, Marx "regarded democracy as the essence of socialism." Marx knew that "socialism cannot be decreed for the masses, it must be won by them."[9]

Harrington thought there was one democratic Marx, from his earliest writings to his last. Unlike those who believed the young, humanist Marx was invested in overcoming alienation out of love for democracy, only to have been replaced by a craggier, more cynical Marx, whose unyielding determinism left no room for democratic aspirations, Harrington argued "democracy and the self-emancipation of the working class is central to all of Marx's writings." In fact, Harrington believed Marx grew more, not less, attuned to democracy over time. With the eventual emergence of organized labor, "Marx became the first Marxian revisionist," Harrington wrote. "He analyzed the prevailing situation, developed a new strategy and in the process prepared the way for one of the most decisive events in the history of socialism: its identification with the labor movement." In doing so, Harrington argued, this version of Marx, the "Unknown Karl Marx," "marked the rise of democratic socialism."[10]

The Unknown Karl Marx was palpable in how he sought to guide the First International. In his activism, Marx articulated a "political economy of the working class" that formed the bedrock of democratic socialism. In the process, Harrington contended, Marx offered "answers to a perennial problem for radicals: What is the relationship between immediate reform and ultimate revolution?" In teasing out these answers, Harrington focused on the famous debate Marx had in 1872 with the anarchist Mikhail Bakunin.[11]

After escaping from a Siberian prison, where he was sent for his role in the 1848 Revolutions, and after evading Russian authorities across Europe, Bakunin landed in London, where he built up a base of supporters poised to take control of the International from the Marx contingent. Bakunin believed the revolutionary future of socialism was found not in the working class, which was integral to capitalism, but rather in those discarded by the system—a class of people Marx called the "lumpenproletariat." The Marx-Bakunin exchange, Harrington wrote, "counterposed proletarian and lumpenproletarian so-cialism, and even more important, concerned the ultimate vision of socialism."[12]

Harrington brought attention to the Marx-Bakunin debate pre-cisely because its contours remained relevant to an American Left swimming in the backwash of 1960s revolutionary fervor. Just as Marx opposed Bakunin, Harrington disagreed with thinkers such as Herbert Marcuse, who dismissed the revolutionary potential of organized la-bor in favor of the urban black masses that had seemingly been in open rebellion since the Watts riot of 1965.[13]

"Marx had great compassion for the lumpenproletariat," Har-rington wrote. But he also had "great suspicion of its political predis-positions." Because the lives of the wretched "were so precarious and fluid, its activists tended toward a Bohemian personal life and a politics of conspiracy and insurrection." Sometimes conspiracy and insurrec-tion worked toward socialism. But more often, they stood in its way. In *The Eighteenth Brumaire*, Marx observed that the lumpenproletariat joined reactionary forces to help bring Napoleon III to power. Har-rington extended this "shrewd insight" to make sense of more recent history. The Nazis "had just such a wing in their movement and one writer even called them the 'armed Bohemians.'"[14]

The situation in the United States in the 1970s was vastly different from that in France in the 1850s or in Germany in the 1930s. The white working class was more easily co-opted by reactionary forces than any group that might be considered a lumpenproletariat, especially urban black Americans. Richard Nixon was reelected in a landslide in 1972, the same year *Socialism* was published, partly because many white work-ers rejected the growing prominence of black people in the Democratic Party coalition.[15]

In Harrington's defense, he was fully cognizant of the situation. In fact, his analysis of the nineteenth-century struggle between social-ists and anarchists was motivated by his twentieth-century concern that a democratic socialist future was rapidly evaporating in the face of an emboldened conservatism. He believed ultra-left-wing rhet-oric that championed lumpen insurrection made matters worse by de-emphasizing the correct path to socialism that Marx had shown. "Marxian socialism," Harrington wrote, "based itself not upon the good will of capitalists nor upon the destructive rage of the lumpen-proletariat, but upon the self-consciousness of the workers."[16]

Harrington read Marx as arguing that democratic reforms which galvanized workers were steps toward revolution. He cited Marx's consistent support for the efforts of workers in the United States and England to codify shorter working days as evidence of his recognition that reform did not obstruct revolution. Socialists did not feel compelled to choose between reform *or* revolution. On this point, "history has confirmed the judgment of Marx against that of his rivals." This was a Marx that would have been more at home with liberal New Dealers than with the radical young activists of the 1960s who wanted to burn the system down.[17]

Harrington was aware that his version of Marx might seem unrecognizable, a projection of his own politics. This could not be helped. If Marx assisted Harrington in making sense of his world, then Marx was worth rethinking, even if fitting Marx's ideas to his agenda required coloring outside the lines. By endowing Americans with a Democratic Socialist Marx comfortable with New Deal–style reformism, Harrington succeeded on his own terms. But by envisioning a New Deal Marx at the moment when the New Deal itself was on the precipice of being obliterated, Harrington's success was rather limited in scope.[18]

When New Left revolutionary aspirations sputtered, a growing number of Marxists embraced an academic Marx that concentrated more on theory and culture. Those who carried on reading him through the lens of politics-qua-politics, in contrast with Harrington, tended to be highly critical. They tended to be conservative.

Some right-wingers evoked the specter of Marx as a gauche scare tactic. Like Reagan. Yet not every conservative critic was a demagogue. Of note, the Polish intellectual historian Leszek Kolakowski offered a learned, conservative analysis of Marx and Marxism in his monumental, three-volume masterpiece *Main Currents of Marxism: Its Rise, Growth, and Dissolution*, first published in English in 1978. Kolakowski's perspective resonated with American readers hungry for an intelligent way to connect Marx to the failures of twentieth-century communism.[19]

As a younger man, Kolakowski had been a Marxist who believed there was something profoundly democratic in Marx's work, even if it could not be found in actually existing socialist states. By the time he wrote *Main Currents*, Kolakowski had rejected Marxism altogether. The first volume, a close reading of Marx's oeuvre, doled out a stinging rebuke. But Kolakowski's criticism was fair and sophisticated, a far cry from the ad hominem attacks so common to anti-Marxist discourse.[20]

Kolakowski did not outright blame Marx for Soviet atrocities. He stressed that political movements are shaped more by social forces than by ideological traditions. And yet, even if Marx could not be held liable for events after his lifetime, his *ideas* were somewhat implicated. The purpose of *Main Currents* was "to analyze the strange fate of an idea which began in Promethean humanism and culminated in the monstrous tyranny of Stalin."[21]

Religious conservatives employed the term "Promethean humanism" as a slur because it referenced the elevation of humans above God. Kolakowski did not use the term in this pejorative sense, but it did stress that Marx believed in the power of humans to create the world anew. "The Promethean idea which recurs constantly in Marx's work," Kolakowski wrote, "is that of faith in man's unlimited powers as self-creator, contempt for tradition and worship of the past, history as man's self-realization through labor, and the belief that the man of tomorrow will derive his 'poetry' from the future."[22]

Despite accentuating human agency, Marx did not concentrate on individual activity exclusive of larger environment. Marx also attended to the powerful structures that inhibited agency. But for Kolakowski, it was crucial to demystify the dialectical relationship between structure and agency, the connection in Marx's mind between subject and situation, to understand the transition from Promethean humanism to communist despotism. Kolakowski drew attention to how Marx connected parts to whole. He wrote that Marx "sought to create instruments of thought or categories of knowledge that were sufficiently general to make all human phenomena intelligible." Even as humans had some degree of control over their own fate, their agency was inextricably tangled up in historical processes. This basic assumption was central to everything Marx ever wrote.[23]

In devising an explanatory framework that related fragments of human experience to the total package, Marx attached specific class formations to grander historical forces that were inexorably trending in the direction of revolution. Kolakowski referred to this aspect of Marx's thought as his revolutionary eschatology. The *proletariat*, as one part of the larger class system in a capitalist society, embodied *everyone's* revolutionary future.

There were vastly different ways to evaluate Marx's revolutionary eschatology. Harrington downplayed inevitability and focused instead on the democratic possibilities of working-class politics. In glaring contrast, Kolakowski saw totalitarian potential in the theoretical embodiment of one class of people over another. That two such clever thinkers should come to polar-opposite readings demonstrates the perplexities of Marx reception. More conspicuously still, both Harrington and Kolakowski, unlike many Marxologists, saw consistency across Marx's oeuvre.

Like Harrington, Kolakowski did not split the young Marx from the more mature version. But unlike Harrington, Kolakowski considered Marx's unswerving intellectual trajectory a problem. It's true Marx's late works concentrate more on the mechanics of capitalism, with an emphasis on how class struggle shaped its historical development, while focusing less on the revolutionary eschatology that Marx had prioritized in his youth. But Kolakowski insisted the older Marx's analysis of capitalism only made sense with his earlier concerns as backdrop. Rooting his theory of value in the primacy of labor, and then resting his understanding of the larger capitalist system on this notion of value, was only possible because Marx had previously oriented the working class toward a communist horizon. The working class was the contradiction at the heart of capitalism. Whether this contradiction engendered alienation, as the young Marx argued, or whether it provoked systemic crises, as the older Marx contended, these were equivalent problems demanding a singular solution: socialist revolution.

Kolakowski sniffed a whiff of totalitarianism here. One of his chief concerns was that Marx had obliterated the distinction between human consciousness and social change. Marx imagined that socialist revolution was baked into capitalism, and he also posited that recognition of this revolutionary trajectory would necessarily accompany the social transformation. For Marx, wrote Kolakowski, the revolutionary philosopher comes to the fore "when the subject and object coincide, when the difference between educator and educated disappears, and when thought itself becomes a revolutionary act, the self-recognition of human existence."[24]

That Marx's eschatology set Kolakowski on edge was understandable. Living under a regime that couched its terror in the rhetoric of inevitability was bound to make Marx's prophesies seem chilling. Yet Kolakowski knew that "Marx's socialist programme did not, as his opponents have often claimed, involve the extinction of individuality or a general levelling for the sake of the 'universal good.'" Rather, in Marx's view, "socialism represented the full emancipation of the individual by the destruction" of capitalism, the system that estranged humans from their neighbors, from their work, from themselves. "Marx's ideal," Kolakowski continued, "was that every man should be fully aware of his own character as a social being, but should also, for this very reason, be capable of developing his personal aptitudes in all their fullness and variety." Unlike nineteenth-century liberals and twentieth-century libertarians, who defined freedom as the lack of interference by the state, Marx conceptualized freedom as "the voluntary unity of the individual with his fellow men."[25]

That was all fine at the level of theory. But Kolakowski knew that, in practice, there was nothing voluntary about unity. He argued that Marx's implicit belief that class conflict would dissolve in a postcapitalist society "is not wholly innocent." Marx's revolutionary eschatology shaped the practices of those who enacted communism in the twentieth century. "As, by definition," he wrote, "the proletariat's aspirations were embodied in the proletarian state, those who failed in any way to conform to the new unity deserved destruction as survivals of bourgeois society." None of this was predestined. A Marxist politics

could have taken several different avenues. But one route, Kolakowski contended, was despotism. "And thus Prometheus awakens from
his dream of power, as ignominiously as Gregor Samsa in Kafka's
Metamorphosis."[26]

For conservatives, and many liberals, Kolakowski advanced the definitive statement on Marxism. His unpacking of its inner workings
confirmed long-standing beliefs. William Buckley Jr. praised *Main
Currents* for clarifying "the connection between Marxist theory and
Stalinist reality." But not everyone agreed. Harrington argued that
Main Currents misread Marx and Marxism. In doing so, Harrington
persisted in arguing that Marx was an antiauthoritarian democrat
who would have been appalled by the states that organized under the
banner of his name. Harrington furthermore rejected Kolakowski's
assertion that Marx "thought that there would be a time of 'absolute
knowledge' in the Hegelian sense, when the essential would be on the
very surface of social life." Again, Harrington and Kolakowski could
not be further apart in how they interpreted what they both had read.
Harrington wrote that Marx "rejected that notion of the total recon-
ciliation between subject and object, humankind and world, individual
and society."[27]

At a less speculative level, Harrington emphasized the explicitly
democratic political positions Marx took. Harrington cited Marx's
1875 *Critique of the Gotha Programme*, the closest thing to a manifesto
he had written since his more famous 1848 one, focusing on the "democratic section" where Marx criticized German socialists for proposing to make schooling a function of the state. Harrington noted that
Marx unfavorably contrasted the German socialist approach with
the American system of local control. Marx wanted the state to keep
its hands off schools, hardly the attitude, Harrington observed, of a
protototalitarian.[28]

Harrington forgave readers who might have thought him excessively
protective of Marx. But Harrington's defense was a product of his belief that Marx best articulated the most pressing problems confronting
modern humans. The record needed to be set straight because the real
Marx continued to matter. Could humans have socialization *with* sol-

idarity? Could they socialize power and wealth alongside production? Could humanity move from capitalism to democratic socialism? Could Americans? Marx's formulation of these problems remained "a profoundly relevant point of departure" in what Harrington called "stagflationist, Jimmy Carter America."[29]

Harrington hoped to keep his version of Marx alive in the face of conservative headwinds. This freedom-loving Marx had long existed in American political culture, as someone many people counted on to help them deepen democracy. But by the 1970s, Harrington's Marx was in danger. Instead of Democratic Socialist Marx, who encouraged the working class to consciously rise up and take control of its future, Americans were likelier to be confronted by Gulag Marx, more closely associated with barbed wire than with liberation.

Americans were also more apt to encounter Cultural Theorist Marx, who explained the peculiar sensations of capitalism at a time when political transformation was off the table, or even Dead White Man Marx, whose nineteenth-century European male biases made him a poor guide through the thickets of a diverse nation founded on the sins of slavery, patriarchy, and genocide. The version of Marx who might help Americans organize against capitalism was on the edge of oblivion at a time when capitalism was being unleashed to a degree unforeseen even by Marx.

THE NEOLIBERAL CONTEXT

In the 1970s, the stable, regulated version of capitalism that had supposedly proven Marx wrong began its death spiral. That system, forever linked with the New Deal reforms that helped usher in capitalism's golden age, was supplanted, piece by piece, by a highly volatile variety of capitalism that came to be called neoliberalism. It is perhaps best to consider neoliberalism as a philosophy that has reshaped the political economy of capitalism since the 1970s. Neoliberalism's signature principle is that capitalist markets better serve people than government and thus government should serve capitalist markets. Neoliberalism relegated the public-good ethos that had reluctantly shaped American governance since the 1930s to the ash heap of history.[30]

In its resemblance to the pre-welfare-state capitalism of the nineteenth century, Marx would have recognized several features of neoliberal capitalism, especially the neoliberal state's brazen alliance with capital and the system's cruel disregard for working-class and poor people. In this, perhaps neoliberal capitalism was a return to normalcy; perhaps welfare-state capitalism was an outlier. But there is no single historical form of capitalism, and there was nothing inevitable about the neoliberal conquest of New Deal capitalism.

Various historical contingencies laid the foundation for the neoliberal upheaval, two related factors in particular. First, international economic turbulence destabilized the balance struck in the middle of the twentieth century between capital and labor. Second, a conservative movement rose to power in the United States that worked tirelessly at the behest of capital to crush labor.

Richard Nixon was a contradictory figure in the transition away from the New Deal. Nixon was elected president in 1968, and again in 1972, partly because he spoke for those Americans who rejected demands for black freedom. Representing reaction was not wholly inconsistent for him. Nixon, after all, first made his name as Alger Hiss's topmost prosecutor. But as centrist Dwight Eisenhower's loyal vice president for eight years, Nixon's reactionary image had been toned down. By proclaiming he would dedicate his presidency to establishing "law and order," Nixon gave a coded nod to white backlashers. Yet Nixon also frustrated the growing number of anti–New Dealers whose libertarian desires had yet to find political expression in the upper echelons of government. Rather, as global economic trends destabilized the economy, Nixon responded with policies that paired well with his apocryphal quote that "We're all Keynesians now."[31]

Nixon was not against conservative policies. He favored cuts in social spending. But he mixed such cuts with Keynesian policies intended to stimulate employment. As the novel economic condition of stagflation, a combination of stagnation and inflation, threw the American economy into its first full-fledged crisis since the 1930s, Nixon took dramatic steps with his New Economic Policy (a moniker that was quickly dropped when it was discovered Lenin had coined the same name for Soviet reforms in the 1920s). To curb inflation, Nixon placed controls on prices and wages. He also broke up the international currency system by delinking the dollar from gold, allowing currencies to float on an open exchange. This resulted in a dramatic devaluation of the dollar, which Nixon hoped, along with a newly instituted import surcharge, would enable American companies to better compete with international rivals. Nixon's maneuvers were intended to strengthen American manufacturing and put Americans back to work.[32]

Nixon's approach to capitalism represents a waystation between the New Deal and neoliberalism. Nixon, for all his conservatism, was fine with popular New Deal–style reforms. In this, he has been called "the last liberal president." More to the point, Nixon was content doing whatever it took to stabilize a topsy-turvy economy, even if he angered conservatives. And anger them he did. Dogmatic libertarians who put their faith in the self-correcting wisdom of capitalist markets bemoaned Nixon's Keynesian approach to employment. They contended such policies enhanced the power of labor and impeded the free flow of capital. In the eyes of business conservatives, Nixon's misplaced effort to placate voters made the situation worse.[33]

Did they? In the short term, economic indicators slightly improved, contributing to Nixon's landslide reelection in 1972. In the long term, Nixon's stopgaps failed, but not in the way libertarians predicted. Rather, stagflation returned because reversing the ongoing transformations that underwrote the toxic combination of recession and inflation proved extremely difficult. In fact, if the Watergate scandal had not toppled the Nixon presidency, endemic economic troubles very well might have bogged it down.[34]

Worsening conditions of stagflation guaranteed a rocky presidency for Gerald Ford, who succeeded Nixon. Unemployment crept up to 9 percent by 1975, the highest since before the Second World War, thanks to unrelenting international competition, automation, and new policies that allowed American companies to relocate jobs to other countries without penalty. Inflation also persisted, even with millions of Americans out of work, due largely to skyrocketing oil prices that shocked the global capitalist system. In sum, the postwar capitalist system, the stability of which had ostensibly proved Marx wrong about capitalism's future, was unraveling. Capitalism was again seen to be crisis prone and inherently precarious.[35]

Ford took his cues from the conservative-minded Business Round-table, founded in 1972 and comprising CEOs of major corporations. Profit-hungry capitalists found high unemployment useful. Having on hand what Marx referred to as a "reserve army of labor" was perfect for depressing wages. In contrast, though, capitalists balked at inflation, since it precipitously reduced the value of their investments. Ford made fighting inflation his top priority.[36]

Ford's anti-inflation efforts, what he called Whip Inflation Now, or WIN, were predicated on a consensus that slowly emerged from the wreckage of stagflation: combating inflation demanded deregulation, or a different type of economic regulation that was more favorable to big business. Ford's economic guru Alan Greenspan advised Ford to deregulate major industries such as air travel and trucking in order to increase competition and lower prices. Soon, liberated corporations had returned to pre–New Deal levels of profit, exploitation, fraud, scandal, and, ultimately, calamity.[37]

Ford proved willing to dish out pain to the proletariat at the behest of the bourgeoisie. And yet his efforts to curb inflation were unsuccessful. He lost the 1976 election to the Georgia governor and peanut farmer Jimmy Carter. Though the working class was hopeful that a Democrat in the White House would stop the bleeding, help was not on the way. Carter's political profile did not make him a likely champion of the New Deal. As a midlevel agricultural businessman who distrusted big government, he was better suited to carrying on the emerging neoliberal consensus.[38]

For the American working class, the historical shift to neoliberalism had grave implications. The postwar social compact, signified by the 1950 Treaty of Detroit in which reluctant capitalists gave up a greater share of profits in exchange for outright authority over the workplace, was by 1980 on the precipice of crumbling. After decades of expansion, unionization began a steep decline. The percentage of the American workforce that was unionized went from well over 20 percent in 1980 to well under 10 percent four decades later. The once mighty labor movement upon which working-class prosperity rested—upon which overall systemic stability rested—was put on the defensive.

Organized labor during the 1970s was not a spent force, but it was deeply divided. Young workers fought for the age-old Marxist objective of autonomy, putting them at odds with union leaders, who discouraged rank-and-file radicalism in order to preserve the Treaty of Detroit. That structure had served workers well in strictly bread-and-butter terms. By the 1970s, the American working class had higher wages, more generous benefits, and better overall economic security than ever. But young workers also wanted compensation that could not be measured in dollars and cents. They aspired to a degree of independence from managers, who had grown increasingly tyrannical due to the immense pressure placed upon them to speed up production.

The 1972 wildcat strike at the General Motors plant in Lordstown, Ohio, was indicative of the implacable fissure in organized labor. Ignoring union leadership, a radicalized rank and file walked off increasingly automized assembly lines. The Lordstown Strike failed to win tangible changes, but it represents the ironic repositioning of labor relations. The leaders of the national unions, and many of their older members who remembered leaner times, were satisfied with the Treaty of Detroit. But both young working-class militants *and* capitalists sought to smash that truce. As Michael Harrington wrote of the era, Americans were moving "vigorously left, right, and center at the same time."[39]

The generational gulf was not the only division among the labor movement. Another rift grew from racism and sexism. Inspired by the liberation movements of the 1960s, lots of young workers, especially nonwhite and women workers, sought racial and gender equality in the workplace. Many older, white male workers, firmly entrenched in the upper echelons of union hierarchy, showed little interest. This was a serious dilemma for the Marxist Left. Herbert Marcuse wrote that the white working class had become a "counterrevolutionary force." But Marcuse also argued that "the transformation of the social system" remained dependent on winning over the entire working class, including hidebound white workers.[40]

Developments related to race within the labor movement were consistent with national political trends. More and more working-class white people rejected the Democratic Party that promoted civil rights, even though the party also had a history of protecting labor rights. They turned instead to a Republican Party that increasingly defended white privilege at the symbolic level while attacking labor rights at the material. As capital's attacks on labor grew in ferocity, organized labor sadly proved unwilling to widen its circle of solidarity.[41]

Forces were arrayed against Carter as he sought reelection in 1980. The Republican Party carried on peeling off working-class whites. Stagflation persisted. Lines to fill up gasoline tanks were longer than ever. This was not a recipe for electoral success. Making Carter's reelection even less likely, his opponent Ronald Reagan was tailor-made for the moment. The charismatic former Hollywood actor was uniquely suited to the emerging era of neoliberal government. Reagan's convincing victory, more than merely a thorough repudiation of Carter, demonstrated the fragility of a New Deal coalition once believed indestructible.[42]

The New Deal coalition had always relied upon a high degree of working-class solidarity. Reagan put a nail in the coffin of that coalition by winning more white working-class voters than any Republican since before Roosevelt. Many such voters, "Reagan Democrats," switched parties for explicitly race-related reasons. But a good number of them voted for Reagan as part of a larger revolt against taxation, a rebellion that surfaced in 1978 when Californians amended their constitution to forbid their state government from raising taxes without a popular referendum. Reagan positioned himself as the antitax, antigovernment candidate, declaring in 1980 that "government is not a solution to our problem, government is our problem."[43]

Reagan cast his first ballot for president in 1932, pulling the lever for Roosevelt that year, and three more times. But he had long since declared himself an enemy of the New Deal. His move to the right began in Hollywood. As president of the Screen Actors Guild, he testified against the Hollywood Ten because he thought communists had no place in American life. By the early 1960s, Reagan was traveling the country as a spokesperson for General Motors, preaching against unions, socialized medicine, anything that seemed to him like a Trojan horse for Marxism. By the time he was elected governor of California in 1966, Reagan was the darling of the conservative movement.[44]

Reagan's campaign against government was attractive because lots of Americans sought to lessen their tax burden to recoup their standard of living in the face of declining wages and inflation. The Great Depression had radicalized many working-class people in the 1930s. But the 1970s downturn had a much different effect on working-class politics. The American working class in the 1930s responded to the economic crisis somewhat similarly to the French bourgeoisie in 1789 by embracing radicalism. The American working class in the 1970s, however, responded similarly to the European bourgeoisie after the 1848 revolutions, by rejecting radicalism. Whereas most workers in the 1930s sensed they had little to lose, workers in the 1970s, particularly white ones, felt they had everything to lose.

Reagan Democrats got more than they bargained for. Reagan quickly distinguished himself as one of the most aggressive advocates for capital to occupy the presidency. He embraced his role as the nation's unapologetic defender of wealth from day one, signaled by the $25,000 gown First Lady Nancy Reagan wore to an inaugural ball. Reagan immediately followed through on his promise to slash federal taxes with a 25 percent overall cut. The biggest beneficiaries were the wealthiest Americans, as the marginal tax rates on incomes above $200,000 were reduced from 70 percent to 24 percent. Reagan's supply-side tax policies, also known as "trickle-down" economics or "Reaganomics," redistributed wealth upward into the hands of the richest Americans.[45]

The working class did not fare as well. When Reagan crushed the Professional Air Traffic Controllers (PATCO) strike of 1981, he showed that the federal government was no longer a neutral arbiter between capital and labor. PATCO had gone on strike for better wages and shorter workweeks, which the air traffic controllers saw as warranted due to the stressful nature of their job. As federal employees, it was technically illegal for them to strike, but other sectors of the federal workforce had previously done so without reprisal. PATCO thought it had leverage because its members were highly skilled workers essential to the nation's gigantic, intricate air travel network. But PATCO overplayed its hand.

With wages in decline, public opinion was tilted against PATCO for making demands most workers could not. Moreover, the resurgent conservative movement was out for blood. Thus, Reagan declared the strike a "peril to national safety." He threatened to fire every air traffic controller who failed to immediately return to work, and then did fire over 11,000 out of 13,000 total PATCO members. Reagan replaced them with qualified military personnel, who kept planes from colliding until new controllers could be hired and trained. He then punished the fired workers by barring them from federal employment for the rest of their lives (a ban that was eventually lifted).[46]

As Reagan turned back the clock on how the government treated labor, he also strained to reignite the Cold War, which had grown far less tense in the 1970s. In addition to provocatively labeling the Soviet Union an "Evil Empire," Reagan sounded the alarm about communist revolutions in the nation's backyard, warning that Marxists in Central America were "closer to Houston, Texas, than Houston is to Washington, D.C."[47]

MARX IN THE CULTURE WARS

Reagan's renewal of Cold War tensions had a cultural dimension. Popular culture in the 1980s had what the journalist Sidney Blumenthal called "the neokitsch aesthetic," a pastiche of the 1950s. This was a nostalgic, irony-free celebration of traditional American greatness, when John Wayne was king and the Cold War was a battle between good Americans and evil Marxists. Illustrative films included the 1984 *Red Dawn*, which depicted scrappy teenagers waging guerrilla war against invading communists, and the 1985 *Rocky IV*, which matched the plucky working-class boxer Rocky Balboa, icon of rugged American individualism, against the robotic Ivan Drago, representative of Marxist collectivism. Harrington observed that the future of American culture was likely to be in the mold of Disney World, "a reactionary and very modern future in the fantastic costume of a dead past."[48]

Still, the aesthetic was not hegemonic. *Reds*, a 1981 John Reed biopic, won critical acclaim for Warren Beatty, who wrote, directed, and starred in the film. *Reds* was not pure hagiography. Beatty was critical of Reed's prioritization of communist revolution over the woman he loved, Louise Bryant. Beatty's Reed was hell-bent on justice, leading him to momentary lapses of judgment and temporary bouts of dogma. Yet overall, the portrait of Reed was deeply sympathetic, and the Russian Revolution was cast as a noble tragedy.[49]

Hollywood was not the only cultural institution that sometimes challenged Reagan's America. Radical ideas of various kinds thrived in universities. Some of these ideas were explicitly Marxist. Even more of them were ideational outgrowths of the liberation movements that sprouted in the 1960s, from Black Power to feminism to gay liberation. Not longing for heroic white men of lore, liberationist academia pushed forward a transgressive sensibility that criticized the dominant culture's implicit biases, whether rooted in race, gender, or sexuality. Fashionable academic theories multiplied from the Black Power leader Stokely Carmichael's criticism of the "white power structure" that had bottled up black freedom for centuries, from the radical feminist Robin Morgan's efforts to smash patriarchy in the name of a future "genderless society," and from the gay liberation activist Martha Shelley's declaration to Americans that she will "never go straight until you go gay." Sixties liberation movements shook up normative America.[50]

Of course, right-wing Americans vigorously rejected such efforts. This antagonism came to be called the culture wars. But even as they raged, and even as liberationist Americans won many of the battles, especially over control of the academic curriculum, capital continued its unstoppable consolidation. Neoliberal capitalism was easily adaptable to the new spirit of liberation, made evident when companies like the

global fashion brand the United Colors of Benetton adopted a superficial version of cultural liberation to help them hawk their goods.

Some conservatives saw the culture wars as a continuation of the
Cold War. Liberation, in this view, was a transparent scheme for sneak-
ing Marx into American culture. Surveying American universities in
1985, the *Washington Times* columnist Arnold Beichman concluded that
Marxism was "*the* growth industry of the American campus." "Despite
the bloody history of Marxist praxis," Beichman wrote, "it is in the U.S.
university where Marxism has become a regnant philosophical theme
among academics who teach the social sciences and humanities." Similarly, the conservative art critic James Cooper described modern art
as "the purveyor of a destructive, degenerative, ugly, pornographic,
Marxist, anti-American ideology."[51]

Allan Bloom, author of the bestselling 1987 book *The Closing of the
American Mind*, held Marxism partly responsible for the widespread
relativism that he thought was wiping away centuries of Western standards. Bloom believed the whole world was divided between those who
followed Marx and those who followed John Locke. Americans had
long favored Locke. But too many were falling into Marx's footsteps.[52]

Blaming Marxism for the liberationist ideas sweeping the cultural landscape was perplexing given that most of those ideas were
not explicitly Marxist. Few liberationist thinkers looked to Marx for
inspiration. In their 1967 book *Black Power*, Carmichael and Charles
Hamilton argued in favor of what they called "group solidarity," not
Marxism, as a realistic political program for black liberation. Conceptualizing political power as racial or ethnic unity, an increasingly popular move in the aftermath of the 1960s, took the focus away from the
Marxist concern for working class solidarity.[53]

For Marx and Marxists of the labor theory variant, a person's position relative to the forces of production was the single most important factor in determining where they stood in a capitalist society.
Marxists rarely denied that race was a crucial aspect of such positioning. Black people were underrepresented among the bourgeoisie and
overrepresented among the proletariat. But by Marxist logic this did

not change the fact that, if the goal was to improve the material conditions of working-class people, racial unity was a poor substitute for working-class solidarity. Workers only had leverage against capitalists as a class.[54]

The conceptual differences between black nationalism and Marxism did not make them mutually exclusive. The American Communist Party at one time embraced black nationalism as an appendage of its larger revolutionary efforts. Likewise, the Black Panther Party adopted Marxism in its quest for racial freedom. Carmichael exemplified this strange ideological brew when he argued that Marxism had its roots in the traditional communalistic societies of Africa. Nevertheless, it was nearly inevitable that tension would surface.[55]

Angela Davis was something of an outlier in combining Marxist, feminist, and black liberation thought. Davis desired a socialist and feminist future. Yet she argued such a future could never be achieved without the support of black women. They had a special part to play because, going back to the era of slavery, when their bodies were explicitly commodified, black women had long occupied a position of extreme oppression amid patriarchal capitalism. "If the quest for black women's liberation is woven into the larger bid for female emancipation," Davis wrote, "if the women's movement begins to incorporate a socialist consciousness and forges its practice accordingly; then it can undoubtedly become a radical and subversive force of yet untold proportions. In this way the women's liberation movement may assume its well-earned place among the current gravediggers of capitalism." For Davis, accounting for black women was crucial to a Marxist approach to feminism.[56]

In connecting race, class, and sex, Davis anticipated the trajectory of liberationist thought. In this she was joined by the Combahee River Collective, formed in 1974 in Boston by Barbara Smith and other activists who identified as black lesbians. The group came together because it wanted to fight for feminism outside racist feminist organizations, and for black freedom outside sexist and homophobic civil rights groups. In 1978, Smith and her comrades issued the Combahee River

Collective Statement, considered the founding document for identity politics, "a politics that grew out of our objective material experiences as Black women." This approach to liberation owed a debt to Davis. Yet whereas Davis foregrounded Marx as indispensable to understanding life in capitalist America, including for black women, the Combahee River Collective was more circumspect.

The Combahee intellectuals called themselves socialists, agreeing with "Marx's theory as it applied to the very specific economic relationships he analyzed." But, as part of their belief that Marx's "analysis must be extended further in order for us to understand our specific economic situation as Black women," the Collective tended to see class as only one of several overlapping identities. Whereas Davis stretched Marx to fit almost any situation, Combahee's vision of Marx was far less flexible.[57]

The Combahee River Collective pushed the envelope of liberationist thought. Soon after its statement, innovative ideas about the intersectionality of identity, from race and ethnicity to gender and sexuality, grew in importance in academic spheres. People from unprecedentedly diverse demographic backgrounds stormed the gates of higher education using liberationist epistemologies that questioned the legitimacy of white, patriarchal, heteronormative norms. Yet in this transformational moment in American intellectual history, Marx was left behind. Or rather, the explicitly political, expressly revolutionary Marx that had long informed leftist thought in the United States was tamed. In his stead came a highly theoretical, highly cultural Marx that better fit the times. Marx was alive, but this variant would have been unrecognizable to previous generations of Marxist revolutionaries.

Coming on the heels of the radical 1960s, when Marx was among the symbols of revolution, some people expected Marx's star to continue to rise. Vintage Books, one of the foremost publishers of trade paperbacks, issued a new translation of *Capital* in 1977 on this plausible assumption. In 1978, the philosopher Bertell Ollman created the board game Class Struggle, a Marxist variation on Monopoly. Moreover, Marx's popularity on campuses did continue to grow, as he was cited more than Shakespeare and "God himself." Yet these favorable trends did not translate into political relevance of the type Marx enjoyed in the 1930s and 1960s.[58]

The philosopher Marshall Berman argued that in the selective reading of Marx in America after the 1960s "what gets left out is what is most alive and exciting, Marx's vision of the world as a whole." What made *Capital* such a great book, in Berman's eyes, was that it told the truth about capitalist society. Ironically, Marx's truthfulness might have been the very cause of his perplexing late twentieth-century reception. At a time when many Americans were either championing reactionary politicians who angrily scorned Marx, or adopting liberationist sensibilities that covertly elided Marx, the hollowness of their Marxes was predictable.[59]

The academic turn in Marx reception was a move away from a politically relevant or revolutionary Marx. Yet not all academics at the heart of this transition can be labeled nonpolitical. Many of them saw themselves as working to not only understand the world, but also change it. And many of them were highly successful, at least in the former pursuit. Marxist academics helped make history, but "not in self-selected circumstances." Rather, they did so in a neoliberal moment, when the labor movement and other left-wing organizations were in rapid decline, and when the radical energies of the New Left were being sucked up by cultural institutions, especially universities. This wider context helps to unravel the contradiction at the heart of Marx reception in late twentieth-century America. How was it that so many academic Marxists viewed themselves as revolutionaries, albeit armed with books and papers rather than bricks and revolvers, at a time when Marx's message was losing its revolutionary edge?

MARX AND THE HISTORIANS

The Marxists in higher education who arguably did the most to keep Marx's revolutionary torch alive were historians. Left-wing American historians took their cues from the Communist Party Historians

Group, made up of several groundbreaking British Marxist historians, including Eric Hobsbawm, Christopher Hill, and E. P. Thompson. With its mode of writing "history from below," the Communist Party Historians Group reshaped historiography throughout much of the world, including in the United States. The watershed work in this milieu was E. P. Thompson's *The Making of the English Working Class*, a massive 1963 book which filled in Marx's theory of class struggle with more flesh and blood than even Marx himself had supplied. Using archival ephemera that historians had previously discarded, including popular songs and union membership cards, Thompson not only uncovered the formation of the English working class in the late eighteenth and early nineteenth centuries. He also revealed how English workers, in establishing the first ever anticapitalist labor movement, saw themselves as politically conscious agents. Ultimately, *The Making of the English Working Class* had two big takeaways. First, class is a relation, not a structure. Second, class consciousness does not automatically surface from a given historical situation, rather workers actively shape it for themselves. The working class, "present at its own making," has agency.[60]

Thompson's book intervened in a long-standing Marxist debate about how socialist revolution is made. Rather than patiently awaiting the inevitably correct moment to strike for revolution, it was up to the working class to make itself into a revolutionary force. American historians were deeply impressed by this spin on Marx's theory of class struggle, no surprise since their sensibilities tracked with Thomas Paine's Promethean 1776 missive about how "we have it in our power to begin the world over again." Given that Ronald Reagan was fond of quoting this particular Paine passage, it should be obvious in retrospect that the concept of human agency did not trend in any single political direction. But after the 1960s, left-leaning American historians were confident that agency was the foundation of radical transformation. This was especially so for the new social historians.[61]

In its unearthing of peoples long neglected by a discipline over-attuned to political and economic elites, social history was indeed a revelation. Social historians sought to prove that oppressed peoples helped determine the warp and woof of history. Gary Nash's 1974 book *Red, White, and Black: The Peoples of Early America* argued that the histories of natives and enslaved black people were more than merely byproducts of forces set into motion by European settlers. Rather, they actively participated in the forging of a new world. "Africans were not merely enslaved. Indians were not merely driven from the land," Nash explained. "To include them in our history in this way, simply as victims of the more powerful Europeans, is no better than to exclude them altogether. It is to render voiceless, nameless, and faceless people who powerfully affected the course of our historical development as a nation."[62]

Social historians like Nash built upon Thompson's work. In the process, they revised American history dramatically, a remarkable achievement. But they also unintentionally diluted the explicitly Marxist implications of Thompson's work. They moved away from his specific interest in how working-class radicalism formed in the hothouse of industrial production to focus intently on American slavery. Did enslaved black people form a collective consciousness as an exploited labor force? Did the enslaved have agency? Were they revolutionary in the Marxist sense? Although Du Bois had powerfully argued that, yes, enslaved black people indeed had revolutionary agency as a class of workers, particularly after the Civil War afforded them the opportunity, for social historians these questions were far from settled. And Marx did not offer clear-cut answers.

Eugene Genovese, perhaps the most important Marxist among American historians, wrote several pathbreaking books, most notably his 1974 work *Roll, Jordan, Roll: The World the Slaves Made*, which challenged the central premises of social history in at least three ways. First, although he granted that slave agency was real insofar as enslaved black people built their own protocultural institutions, Genovese argued that such agency was *deeply* constrained. Second, Genovese contended that Southern slave society was paternalistic rather than capitalistic: whereas the master-slave relationship was premised on reciprocal obligations, the capitalist-worker relationship was grounded in cash alone. Third, Genovese argued the Southern master class had developed a complex, anticapitalist ideology that social historians neglected to appreciate because, as liberals, they failed to understand how power works.[63]

Genovese, who grew up in a working-class family that hailed from Sicily and settled in Brooklyn, joined the Communist Party in 1945 at the age of fifteen. Although he was expelled five years later for "having zigged when [he] was supposed to zag," Genovese had by then discovered Marx, and there was no taking that away from him. "When I came across some Communists at age fifteen and read *The Communist Manifesto*," Genovese recalled, "I suddenly had a precise focus for my hatred." While Genovese was a promising undergraduate at Brooklyn College, one of his history professors suggested he combine his hatred for the ruling class and his passion for historical study by researching the slave South, which exemplified "how a ruling class really rules."[64]

Genovese completed his graduate work at Columbia University, where he began his trek to becoming the preeminent historian of the antebellum South. Although he remained committed to Marxism, he did not immediately reveal this predilection, later telling Du Bois that he framed his master's thesis in Weberian terms since, "discretion being the better part of valor, it [was] best to omit direct mention of Marx." Such reticence quickly faded. During a 1965 teach-in at Rutgers University, where he taught, Genovese generated a wave of controversy. "Those of you who know me know that I am a Marxist and a Socialist," he declared. "Therefore, unlike most of my distinguished colleagues here this morning, I do not fear or regret the impending Viet Cong victory in Vietnam. I welcome it." This comment was not well received.[65]

Genovese's second book, *In Red and Black: Marxian Explorations in Southern and Afro-American History* (1968), argued that a Marxist historical framework was the best way "of seeing history as a process." "Marxism," he wrote, "maintains that the root of the great qualitative leaps in social development are to be sought in the rise, development, and confrontation of social classes."[66]

If history was forged in the crucible of class struggle, then Southern history was made by the master-slave dialectic. "Masters and slaves shaped each other," Genovese wrote, "and cannot be discussed or analyzed in isolation." Although this theory of history bound human agency to the chains of context, Genovese rejected determinism. If he took anything from the social historians, it was their attention to black culture as a distinct response to slavery. In fact, Genovese wrote at length about black agency in *Roll, Jordan, Roll*. But unlike the social historians, he did not contend that slave culture was a form of resistance, or that exploitation was an ineluctably radicalizing experience. Exploited classes were much more likely to accommodate themselves to oppression than revolt against it. If the enslaved had agency, they demonstrated it by cultivating ways to lessen their misery, especially distinct religious practices. Genovese's lengthy analysis of black Christianity, the basis of the world the slaves made for themselves, came close to concluding that it was the opiate of the enslaved masses.[67]

Genovese attributed the lack of resistance among the enslaved to Southern paternalism. In making this, his most renowned argument, Genovese relied upon Antonio Gramsci. When Gramsci was imprisoned in 1926 by Mussolini, the prosecutor in Gramsci's case declared that "for twenty years we must stop his brain from functioning." Gramsci never again experienced freedom. But luckily for the world of Marxist theory, his brain never quit functioning, as he wrote over three thousand pages of Marx-inspired theory and history. Gramsci's *Prison Notebooks* offered a rigorous account of the role culture played in fortifying a class society. In this, Gramsci expanded upon the concept of "hegemony," about how violent coercion is not the sole means by which a ruling class gains the consent of the ruled. A class society, no matter how oppressive, secures legitimacy when the oppressed class identifies with the beneficiary class and accepts the rationale for unfair social arrangements.[68]

Genovese contended that the paternalistic Southern slave society perfectly illustrated Gramsci's theory of hegemony. Genovese never claimed slaves relished their condition. He recognized and described some of the brutalities of American slavery. Yet, building on Gramsci, he also maintained that slaves identified with their masters, and that this identification made it more difficult for them to come together as a class to overthrow the system. "Wherever paternalism exists," Genovese wrote, "it undermines solidarity among the oppressed by linking them as individuals to their oppressors."[69]

In making this argument, Genovese compared master-slave relations favorably to capitalist-worker relations. Whereas slaveowners were obligated to feed, clothe, and house their slaves, however poorly, capitalists were not compelled to provide anything to workers beyond payment for their labor. Genovese thought his analogy was less a defense of slavery than an indictment of capitalism. Yet in making the case that slavery was not as harsh as the capitalist labor system, he replicated a flawed defense of slavery made by the master class itself. As the historian Manisha Sinha writes: "There are no known instances of wageworkers, no matter how degraded their condition, selling themselves and their posterity into slavery." Wage labor was no picnic, but it was better than slave labor.[70]

Genovese's semidefense of American slavery distinguished him from the social historians. They depicted slavery as one of the worst of all possible societies, and slaveowners as tyrants. Yet their portrayal of capitalists was not that different from their depiction of Southern slaveowners. Capitalists ruthlessly exploited workers to amass riches and build empires.

Social historians tended to put their historical subjects into two categories. Slaves and workers, in addition to women and immigrants or really anyone hailing from an oppressed group, were "the people," and the people were good. Slaveowners and capitalists, and those who did their dirty work, like slave patrols and Pinkerton agents, were against the people, and therefore were bad. In making this moral distinction, social history had a populist sensibility, even a Popular Front quality. For Genovese, who was something closer to a Stalinist, or what he described as a "law and order Marxist," this was exactly the problem. Like their Popular Front forerunners, who were less Marxists than liberals in pink clothing, social historians did not understand the way power worked. Their historical categories looked more like caricatures.[71]

Genovese insisted that social historians were blind to the South's actual makeup, which had compelling features. He sought to cultivate an appreciation for the South's antiliberal culture, which in his estimation represented a real threat to liberal capitalism. It was the Southern apologists, "especially in the brilliant polemics of George Fitzhugh but also in the writings of Calhoun, Holmes, Hughes, Hammond, Ruffin, and others, who questioned the assumptions of liberal society, denounced the hypocrisy and barbarism of the marketplace, and advanced a vision of an organic society and a collective community." In championing Fitzhugh and some of slavery's most notorious proponents as the most skillful critics of capitalism, Genovese thought his analysis was the towering Marxist examination of the South. But Genovese ignored that those Southern apologists hated democracy more than anything else, which hardly made his position an appropriately Marxist one.[72]

Marx, of course, was also a brilliant critic of capitalism in Genovese's view. Yet Genovese hated Marx's Civil War writings, likening them to the drivel of the social historians. "It was proper for Marx to hate slavery and throw his efforts into organizing the European proletariat against it," Genovese wrote. But "it was neither proper nor necessary," he continued, "for him to permit his partisanship to lead to a gross underestimation of the slaveholding class and to an ambiguous assessment of the origins of the war." Genovese particularly disliked Marx's description of the South as "neither a territory strictly detached from the North geographically, nor a moral unity. It is not a country at all, but a battle cry."[73]

Marx, in Genovese's assessment, believed the South seceded merely because its master class wanted to continue to exploit its enslaved workforce. In this way, Genovese believed that Marx viewed the slave South as a particularly savage extension of the larger capitalist system, rather than as a society with its own internal dynamics. "Ironically," Genovese wrote, "to criticize Marx and Engels on this particular question, as on some others, means to criticize certain features of American liberal dogma." Marx, like liberal social historians, seemed to think slaveowners had created an ideological defense of the South merely as a cover for capitalistic plunder. For Genovese, that master class ideology, as an authentic defense of its position, had produced an authentic critique of capitalism. Ultimately, Genovese thought a Marxist analysis of the American South was impossible without a systematic analysis of the slaveholders as a class. He implied that he, *the* historian of the master class, was better prepared than Marx, and certainly better prepared than social historians, to offer a Marxist explanation of slavery and the Civil War.[74]

Social historians of slavery wondered how Genovese could consider himself a Marxist in good standing when he refused to support the liberationist aspirations of the enslaved and other oppressed peoples. Genovese and his wife, Elizabeth Fox-Genovese, responded with an article that argued social historians practiced bad history and lousy Marxism because they projected revolutionary consciousness onto their subjects. Historical scholarship, they maintained, must do more than demonstrate "that the 'people' have always resented being abused." The Genoveses opposed the social historians' tendency to conceptualize historical subjects as extensions of their political selves. They wrote that liberationist-minded historians "had no theory of society, no theory of social change, and no understanding of the nature and promise of socialism." History needed to be understood as "primarily the story of who rides whom and how." The social historians ignored this edict.[75]

This debate revealed the waning influence of Marx on American historiography. Genovese might have won the battle for the soul of Marx, even over Marx himself, but his victory was pyrrhic. His acute pessimism about American prospects for revolution led him to reactionary antimodernism, ultimately rendering his Marxism politically irrelevant. Just as racism helped weaken organized labor as the international forces of capital were coalescing against the working class, Genovese's illiberal brand of Marxism ultimately diminished the political Marx at the worst possible time. By the 1990s, Genovese rejoined the Catholic Church in which he was raised and embraced conservative traditionalism. For many of his critics, and even some of his friends, this turnabout was entirely predictable. As his student Leo Ribuffo said: "I liked to tease Gene that he had always hated liberalism more than he loved socialism."[76]

On the other side of this debate were the social historians, inheritors of the Popular Front, whose capacious embrace of "the people" as inherent revolutionaries demonstrated a curious understanding of power. In their evasion of a specific theory about class dynamics in relation to historical change, in their liberationist assumptions that oppressed peoples formed an unbroken chain of resistance from some epochal date like 1492 or 1619 to the present, the social historians lost the war for Marx but ultimately conquered the historical discipline. Between a Marxism that dead-ended in Southern reaction and an embrace of liberation that eschewed Marx, the choice was an easy one. Going the liberationist route provided historians with the sense that they were contributing to a better world.

Was it mere coincidence that the long ascent of liberationist thought commenced alongside the steep decline of the revolutionary Marx? Was the ease with which liberationist thought eventually meshed with neoliberalism related to Marx's fall into political oblivion?

MARX AND THE CULTURAL THEORISTS

Cultural theory, an influential avenue of liberationist thought, and an important transmission point in the decline of a political Marx, arose as arguably the trendiest academic discourse of the 1980s and 1990s. Cultural theorists were not individually at fault for the fact that Americans mostly quit looking to Marx as a political guide in the labyrinth of neoliberalism. As with historians—as with everyone—cultural theorists forged ahead in a world not of their own making that shaped their ideas in unforeseeable ways. But cultural theory as a collective was not blameless in Marx's near erasure from revolutionary discourse. Some cultural theorists renounced Marx outright. But they alone were not the cause of Marx's decline as a political sage. Even Fredric Jameson, arguably the preeminent Marxist cultural theorist, had a hidden role in this ironic development. Jameson has given us the tools for grasping the elusive relationship between human consciousness and historical time, and for recognizing that people do not always know what they do, including Jameson himself![77]

Jameson's 1971 book *Marxism and Form: Twentieth-Century Dialectical*

Theories of Literature was an introduction to the ideas of Western Marxists like Lukács, Benjamin, Adorno, and Sartre, among others. More than a précis on non-Stalinist Marxist thought, *Marxism and Form* was a polemic against Anglo-American empiricism, a venerable branch of liberalism that Jameson believed operated as an alternative to Marxism. Jameson disliked "the anti-speculative bias of that tradition, its emphasis on the individual fact or item at the expense of the network of relationships in which that item may be embedded." He considered Anglo-American empiricism a mode of analysis that encouraged submission to the status quo because it prevented people from making "otherwise unavoidable conclusions" about capitalism. In contrast with empiricism, the "the dominant ideology of the Western countries," Jameson sought to cut through the multiplying mystifications of capitalism.[78]

Jameson believed literary criticism was the best method of political inquiry, with one major qualification: only if it was Marxist. Jameson's most famous methodological pronouncement, the first sentence of his 1981 book *The Political Unconscious*, represented his approach. "Always historicize!" Jameson meant that the "object of study is less the text itself than the interpretations through which we attempt to confront and to appropriate it."[79]

Marxism, as applied to criticism, was a method for connecting texts to larger interpretive frameworks. More than that, Marxism was a metainterpretation that transcended other interpretive forms because it related both texts *and* modes of interpretation to an all-encompassing world. Marx had pointed the way forward in this regard. By establishing that our collective understandings of capitalism are constitutive of capitalism itself, Marx had endowed the world with a framework for deciphering the deep, inexorable connections between text and context, form and content, consciousness and history. If literature was an expression of human consciousness, then criticism was a way to interpret history.[80]

Marxism for Jameson was a methodology for understanding the world. It was also an opportunity to change the world, because only Marxism could capture the urgency of our cultural symbols, an urgency born of "the collective struggle to wrest a realm of Freedom from

a realm of Necessity." Jameson counseled that texts should be interpreted as if they gave us insight into class struggle, because they did. He
also advised that cultural symbols should be theorized as if deciphering
their political content was more difficult than ever, because it was.[81]

Jameson hailed from a long line of Marxist literary critics who saw
their work as critical to socialist revolution. If the masses were going
to be won over to socialism, affairs of the mind mattered. But Jameson
also believed that theorists of the 1930s had had it easier because they
lived in "a world in which social conflict was sharpened and more
clearly visible, a world which projected a tangible model of antagonism
of the various classes toward each other." By the 1970s, the contours of
the struggle had lost focus. Jameson observed that:

> For the most part, and particularly in the United States, the develop-
> ment of postindustrial monopoly capitalism has brought with it an
> increasing occultation of the class structure through techniques of
> mystification practiced by the media and particularly by advertising in
> its enormous expansion since the onset of the Cold War. In existential
> terms, what this means is that our experience is no longer whole: we
> are no longer able to make any felt connection between the concerns
> of private life, as it follows its own course within the walls and con-
> fines of the affluent society, and the structural projections of the system
> in the outside world, in the form of neocolonialism, oppression, and
> counterinsurgency warfare. In psychological terms, we may say that as
> a service economy we are henceforth so far removed from the realities
> of production and work on the world that we inhabit a dream world of
> artificial stimuli and televised experience: never in any previous civi-
> lization had the great metaphysical preoccupations, the fundamental
> questions of being and the meaning of life, seemed so utterly remote
> and pointless.[82]

Although Jameson articulated these thoughts in 1971, when the
breakup of the postwar social compact was not yet foreseeable, the
basic insight about what he later called "postmodernism, or the cultural logic of late capitalism," held. Capitalism had incapacitated the

critical faculties of its subjects. People could no longer grasp the big picture. For that, they needed Marx, more than ever. But Marx's grand historical narrative resonated less and less. The cure for the disease was ignored because ignorance of the cure was a symptom of the disease.[83]

To peel away the obfuscations of late capitalism, Jameson turned his attention to a section in the first volume of *Capital* where Marx explained "the fetishism of the commodity and its secret." This section became canon to cultural theorists. One of Marx's basic projects in *Capital* was to clarify how capitalism came to seem like a naturally occurring phenomenon; how a product of human relations came to seem like something beyond human control. His theory about commodity fetishism was a case in point.[84]

The value of a commodity, a good or service bought and sold for an agreed-upon price, was thought to be related to the thing in itself. (This is what Marx called "commodity fetishism.") In contrast, Marx held that a commodity's actual value resulted from the labor required to get it to market. The value of an oak table might seem intrinsic to its existence as a sturdy piece of furniture, but in fact its value in a capitalist economy is the result of labor: humans chopping down an oak tree, fastening the wood into the form of a table, and then trucking the table to market, not to mention the labor that went into the necessary tools and machinery.

Marx further showed that the value of a commodity is shaped by the fact that labor is itself a commodity. In fact, labor is *the* central cog in a system that only functions when capitalists profit from other people's labor, and when workers sell their own labor in order to survive. All commodities are valuable because they are products of this intricate web of human relations. Commodities are historical, not natural.

But how, then, did commodity fetishism work? Marx explains:

It is nothing but the definite social relation between men themselves which assumes here, for them, the fantastic form of a relation between things. In order, therefore, to find an analogy, we must take flight into the misty realm of religion. There the products of the human brain appear as autonomous figures endowed with a life of their own, which enter into relations both with each other and with the human race. So it is in the world of commodities with the products of men's hands. This I call the fetishism which attaches itself to the products of labor as soon as they are produced as commodities, and which is therefore inseparable from the production of commodities.[85]

For Jameson, and many cultural theorists to follow, Marx's notion of commodity fetishism was applicable as a "basic insight into the structure of the modern world." Modern humans enter networks that are historically constructed upon edifices of oppression. But these social relations, no matter how unequal, appear to them as natural. As Marx wrote, when people equate "their different products to each other in exchange as values, they equate their different kinds of labour as human labour. They do this without being aware of it." Jameson, like Marx, identified this paradoxical situation as integral to capitalism. The "illusion of objectivity," Jameson wrote, "forms the very existential fabric of our lives, which are characterized by *belief* in this reified appearance (fetishism is a form of belief) and which are wholly absorbed with the acquisition and consumption of commodities in general." Human consciousness about life in capitalism stood in stark contrast with the "reality of social life," which "lies in the labor process itself, in the transparency of human work and action which is ultimately responsible both for the commodities produced and for the very social mode in which commodities form the principal category of production."[86]

Jameson's approach was predicated on Marx having been right about capitalism, both in its social reality and in how humans misapprehended that reality. Capitalism is a system of labor exploitation created by humans. It thrives because its very structure blocks people from making sense of its workings. The "truth of social life is concealed," and according to Jameson, "can be made visible only mediately through critical analysis." In other words, literary criticism, if Marxist, might bridge the gulf between consciousness and history. For Jameson, this project was "doubly historical: not only are the phenomena with which it works historical in character, but it must unfreeze the very concepts

with which they have been understood, and interpret the very immobil-
ity of the latter as historical phenomena in their own right." A properly
Marxist criticism would deliver a profound "epistemological shock"
that would create newly self-aware subjects. Once the truth of social
life was unmasked, once people saw the system for what it really was,
capitalism would be in trouble.[87]

Such an undertaking would not be easy, of course. Any criticism designed to break through the ideological logjam of commodity fetishism would by design be difficult. Given that Jameson saw criticism as
a weapon in the class struggle, given that he thought defeating capitalism would require Herculean efforts, he also thought studying Marxist
criticism should be a demanding task. In contrast with the challenge
presented by reading Marxist theory, Jameson likened American reading habits to commodity fetishism. Simple texts of the type favored
by an American readership, he claimed, were ideological devices "intended to speed the reader across a sentence in such a way that he can
salute a ready-made idea effortlessly in passing, without suspecting
that real thought demands a descent into the materiality of language
and a consent to time itself in the form of the sentence." There was no
quick and easy way to confront capitalism, and this extended to the
experience of reading.[88]

Reading Marx was no simple task either. But the difficulty rested
less in Marx's prose, which was clear enough and often quite clever,
than in the complexity of the concepts. If capitalism was mystifying,
then a simple explanation of it would not suffice. Reading a challenging text like *Capital*, then, was purposeful; a remade consciousness
awaited those who accomplished the feat. For many cultural theorists,
however, challenging prose became less a means to an end and more an
end in itself. Cultural theory made a fetish of difficult language.

Many of the most influential cultural theorists couched their insights in burdensome language. Revolutionary thinkers like Judith
Butler contended that new ideas demanded new words. Those words,
however, were not necessarily new; often they were expropriated concepts from European philosophy. Yet most American cultural theorists
(Jameson excepted) skipped over Marx and went straight to Michel

Foucault. Although Marx's theory about the hidden forces of capitalism was a starting point for much continental philosophy in general and Foucault in particular, the French theorist's concept of power was an important point of departure.[89]

Marx saw power in places nobody had previously thought to look. But with the correct theoretical lens, power could be revealed, as a force wielded by one class against another. Power extended to many realms of human experience, including consciousness, as Marx made clear with his theory of commodity fetishism. Yet power was an expression of capitalist social relations, which meant that it emanated from the point of production, which in turn meant that it could be directly challenged by a revolutionary working class. Marx in this way had a materialist understanding of power. Gaining control over the means of production, over the material necessary to sustain life in a modern society, was a route to overturning capitalist power.

Power for Foucault, in contrast, was a diffuse force that injects itself into everything we experience. Power not only structures our institutions, especially our prisons and schools, it also shapes the words we use, and even, disturbingly, our thoughts. For Foucault, power was at once everywhere and nowhere, which meant there was no enemy for the working class to overthrow. The enemy was within, and there was no escaping it. For French theory, as it came to be known in the United States, modern humans were destined to live with what amounted to totalitarian conditions, or what Foucault likened to a permanent panopticon in which not only are we surveilled but we internalize and impose discipline upon ourselves. In such a world, there is no foreseeable route to revolution. Foucault in this way had a post-Marxist understanding of power. Gaining control over the means of production was akin to shuffling deck chairs on the *Titanic*.[90]

American cultural theorists put Foucault to work in the culture wars raging in higher education. Whereas Foucault theorized that seemingly objective standards, such as laws, only had claims to truth, and thus power, within institutional contexts, his American devotees reduced this concept to a more immediately applicable formulation. The "truth," so-called, represented the interests of the powerful. The

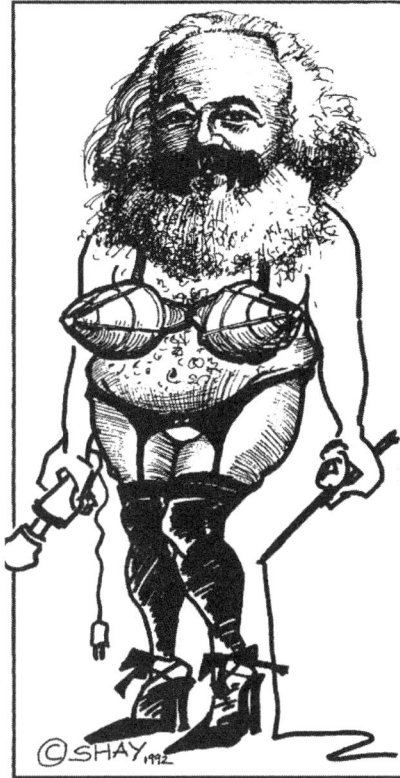

FIGURE 8.2: Political cartoon which appeared in the May 1992 issue of *Heterodoxy*, a conservative magazine edited by David Horowitz and Peter Collier that focused criticism on academia.

Western canon, for example, was the embodiment of white male supremacy. American cultural theory, taken to its logical conclusion, had reduced Marx, the most famous and arguably the most insightful critic of capitalism, to the status of yet another dead white male underserving of our continued attention.[91]

A BLACK MARX?

Many attempts to knock Marx off his world-historical pedestal came across as cartoonish. But not all. Some of the academic criticism of

Marx that emerged in the 1980s was based on a sophisticated reading of him against alternative paradigms. Cedric Robinson's 1983 book *Black Marxism: The Making of the Black Radical Tradition* is the best example. Robinson distinguished Marxism from what he called the "black radical tradition," a framework he located in African and syncretic forms that, according to Robin D. G. Kelley, "confounded Western social analysis." In making this distinction, Robinson revised the conventional narrative about Marxism's global implications, arguing instead that it was a doctrine specific to the nineteenth-century European middle class and was thus unhelpful in grasping the historical dimensions

FIGURE 8.3: Cedric Robinson, 2006.

of racial oppression. Robinson offered up his own theory of capitalism, or as he preferred to call it, "racial capitalism," instead.[92]

Marx identified capitalism as a system that arose in Europe and that destroyed the feudal order. He also predicted that as capitalism spread it would demolish all ancient regimes, including race-based slavery. Robinson challenged the idea that capitalism broke from an older order. He argued instead that capitalism inherited crucial elements of the old order, particularly a well-defined racial hierarchy that placed black Africans at the bottom. For Robinson, capitalism did not create racism. Europe had long before been racist.[93]

In Robinson's paradigm, capitalism as defined by Marx was little more than an abstraction. Racial capitalism as defined by Robinson, in contrast, was a global system reliant upon slavery, imperialism, and genocide. The history of how people profited from capitalism cannot be understood apart from the history of how millions of nonwhite people were enslaved and murdered. The sociologist Oliver Cox, an influential forerunner to Robinson, declared that Marx's concept of primitive accumulation was "none other than fundamentally capitalist accumulation."[94]

Robinson believed that Marx largely ignored the racial side of capitalism, that he explained away slavery as a vestige of an older order, because the racial aspects of capitalism did not fit with his conception of how the system produced its own gravediggers. For Marx, socialist revolution was bound to happen first in the advanced nations of Europe because there capitalism had primed an industrial working class to throw off its chains. For Robinson, this was evidence of Marx's provincialism; Marx should have concentrated on the European empires. For this reason, Robinson thought W. E. B. Du Bois and C. L. R. James offered necessary correctives to Marx with their respective books *Black Reconstruction* and *Black Jacobins*. Du Bois and James personified the black radical tradition, by fostering revisions of Marx superior to the original.[95]

Although Du Bois understood *Black Reconstruction* as a Marxist work, Robinson argued Du Bois's analysis depended upon a conception of *racial* capitalism. The strength of the industrial revolution in

Europe and North America was, for Du Bois, heavily reliant upon the Southern system of slavery. One did not happen without the other. Robinson also highlighted Du Bois's contention that the black slave revolt against the planter class during and after the Civil War took the form of religious fervor rather than class consciousness. "This was the coming of the Lord," Du Bois wrote. "This was the fulfillment of prophecy and legend. It was the Golden Dawn, after chains of a thousand years." It turns out "one of the most extraordinary experiments of Marxism," Du Bois's description of slave insurrection, was predicated on religious beliefs rooted in Africa. For Robinson, this was evidence that Du Bois had actually unshackled himself from Marxism and embraced the black radical tradition.[96]

Robinson interpreted *Black Jacobins* similarly. Not only did James analyze the Haitian Revolution by placing it in the context of racial capitalism, not Marx's Eurocentric version. He also adhered to the black radical tradition by recognizing that resistance to European enslavement in Sainte-Domingue was rooted in Haitian Voodoo, a thoroughly antibourgeois, anti-European revolutionary culture. "This was a complete departure from the way in which Marx and Engels had conceptualized the transformative and rationalizing significance of the bourgeoisie," Robinson wrote. "It *implied* (and James did not see this) that bourgeois culture and thought and ideology were irrelevant to the development of revolutionary consciousness among Black and other Third World peoples."[97]

Black resistance had nothing to do with Marx's materialistic understanding of history, and everything to do with a culture of struggle going back to Africa. The black radical tradition, like feminist theories that emphasized the timelessness of patriarchy, was transhistorical in that it originated the day the first ill-intentioned European set foot on the African continent. Racism, like sexism, marked capitalism from the beginning.

Robinson's argument that Du Bois and James expanded upon Marx in crucial ways was spot-on. Du Bois and James indeed fleshed out Marx's preliminary thoughts on the role that slavery and colonialism played in the historical development of capitalism. In this they nicely represented an Americanized, hybridized version of Marx even as they remained true to Marx's revolutionary aims. As *Black Marxism*'s stature as a significant book flourished, so too did the reputations of *Black Reconstruction* and *Black Jacobins*. This should have come as a welcome development for those invested in the revolutionary Marx. But the favorable reevaluation of these two powerful books was shaped by a contradiction. *Black Reconstruction* and *Black Jacobins*, written with the explicitly Marxist aim of socialist liberation, and published in the revolutionary phase of American Marx reception, ultimately achieved fame during the reign of cultural theory, when liberation and Marxism were seemingly at odds. In the eyes of his disciples, Robinson had successfully separated Du Bois and James from Marx, just as he successfully split the black radical tradition from Marxism.

In addition to being right about how Du Bois and James added breadth and depth to Marx's writings on primitive accumulation, Robinson was also correct that Marx had developed his theories in the context of nineteenth-century Europe and that this fact should weight the value of Marxism in other times and places. The nineteenth-century European working class was perhaps not the best model for a black man in the United States in the 1980s. But just as Marx's theories were constrained by context, so too were Robinson's. His framework for criticizing Marx from the vantage point of a black radical tradition was rooted in the nationalistic sensibilities that had arisen in the 1960s alongside the Black Power movement.

From Robinson's perspective, of course Marx's pretensions to having innovated a universal theory about a global system were patently absurd in that they covered over Marx's own position as a white man in nineteenth-century Europe. But was Marxism any less particular than the black radical tradition? Marxism at least forwarded a historicist framework that sought to account for changing contexts, a potentially self-correcting feature. The black radical tradition operated from the assumption that societies formed by Europeans were irredeemably racist, and that those who stood against racism there formed an unbroken chain of resistance going back to the original sin. White supremacy and black resistance were mutually reinforcing, though hardly dialectical given their immutability. The only thing that might upend the everlasting cycle was a revolution that overthrew racial capitalism. But, from the vantage point of the black radical tradition, it was difficult to imagine such a revolution in the United States given the racist white majority's seemingly eternal grip on power.

It should come as no surprise that Robinson's provocative revision of Marx was popular at a time when dead white men represented the opposite of liberation in many academic circles. Yet some of Robinson's central claims were premised on a blinkered reading of Marx. The theory of revolution Marx laid out in *The Communist Manifesto*, where an industrial working class would lead the world to socialism, might have seemed like something only a nineteenth-century European man could have dreamed up. Robinson's counter to this—that most people have identified themselves not in terms of class but rather in relation to nation, ethnicity, and race—was true to a large extent. Indeed, the gory histories of racism and nationalism have seemingly refuted the Marxist emphasis on class. But Robinson's reading conveniently ignored Marx's writings that specifically addressed racism and nationalism, often in ways that anticipated the very framework from which Du Bois, James, and yes, Robinson operated. Marx had a much more capacious theory of capitalism, based on a much grander scale of world history, than he was given credit for by Robinson and other liberationist thinkers.[98]

Marx wrote about the role of nationalism in some of his lesser-known texts, such as in his letters about the "Irish Question." Unlike most forms of nationalism, which he considered deleterious to the working class, Marx thought the role of Irish nationalism was salubrious because he saw Irish resistance to British imperialism as an expression of anticapitalism. Marx might have thought the same about black nationalism in the United States had he witnessed its rise. Indeed, many Marxists contended as much across the twentieth century.[99]

Marx's work on the American Civil War should also have given Robinson pause. Beyond Marx's unwavering support for the Union and his open hostility toward slavery, his recognition that slavery propelled the rule of capital should have been evidence that Marx was, at least, atypical among European thinkers. Du Bois and James certainly thought as much. They understood themselves as working well within the Marxist tradition, even when they were going beyond Marx. This is what Angela Davis meant in proclaiming that Marxism "has always been both a method and an object of criticism." Despite generally supporting Robinson's work, Davis failed to "see the terms 'Marxism' and 'Black Marxism' as oppositional."[100]

It was one thing when conservatives and liberals dismissed Marx but quite another when scathing critics of capitalism like Robinson had unfavorable views. Expressions of liberation premised on race and nation complicated Marxist formulations about capitalism as a class system, turning potential comrades into adversaries. This antagonism was not new in the late twentieth century, but it grew in intensity, as seen among black nationalist thinkers like Robinson, and even more, among indigenous intellectuals like Ward Churchill and Russell Means.

AN INDIGENOUS MARX?

Churchill, a scholar who focused on the US government's barbaric treatment of American Indians, was a veteran of the Vietnam War who in the 1960s had been active in the New Left before taking a position at the University of Colorado. An outspoken proponent of indigenous causes, Churchill became a scathing critic of the American Left and its "reliance on adaptations of theories advanced by Karl Marx well over a century earlier, in Europe." His 1983 edited collection *Marxism and Native Americans* gave voice to an indigenous critique of Marxism as yet another Eurocentric philosophy that rationalized Western domination over non-Europeans. Churchill contended Marxism was "as genocidal in its implications as anything by Manifest Destiny imperialism or heathen-crushing Christianity." "Native Americans are irrelevant to the course of World History," he wrote, "they constitute a minor sideshow on the stage of World Revolution."[101]

The Oglala Lakota and American Indian Movement activist Russell Means similarly argued that Marxism could not "be separated from the rest of the European intellectual tradition. It's really just the same old song." Means contended Marx was yet another enabler of European conquest because Marx, like many others, sought to connect *being*, or the human spirit, to *gaining*, or the material world. By this framework, Means wrote, "satisfaction is measured in terms of gaining material—so the mountain becomes gravel and the lake becomes coolant for a factory and the people are rounded up for processing through the indoctrination mills Europeans like to call schools." Means argued Marx's theory about how labor defines humans as a species implied manipulating the natural world, including people native to that world. Indigenous philosophy, in contrast, focused entirely on *being* as separate from *gaining*. Material acquisition, environmental degradation, and human exploitation were spiritually deficient in the eyes of natives.[102]

From such a vantage point, Marx was yet another tribune of European "progress." Marxism might have been good for working-class Europeans in that it proposed to better spread wealth among Europeans. But "the real nature of a European revolutionary doctrine" should not be judged "on the basis of the changes it proposes to make within the European power structure and society." Rather, Means contended, a European theory of revolution should be evaluated relative to "the effects it will have on non-European peoples." By speeding up industrialization, Marxism helped make imperialism an even more efficient killing machine. Even though none of the primary imperialist powers, including the United States, were ever governed by Marxist regimes, Means thought of Marxism as constitutive of the genocidal effort against native peoples.[103]

As an alternative to Marxism, Means posited "the traditional Lakota way." This route to liberation worked from the native supposition that "humans do *not* have the right to degrade Mother Earth, that there are forces beyond anything the European mind has conceived, that humans must be in harmony with *all* relations or the relations will eventually eliminate the disharmony." Means suggested that the European faith in science was equivalent to believing "that man is god."

Unlike indigenous peoples, who revered the natural world because they knew their way of life depended on it, Europeans searched for a flesh-and-blood messiah, "whether that be the man Jesus Christ or the man Karl Marx."[104]

Means articulated what might be called a native radical tradition. Like the black radical tradition, the native version combined revolutionary anticapitalism with antimaterialist spiritualism. In its anticapitalist zeal, the native radical tradition outpaced Marx and most Marxists. Yet in its spiritualism, which was underwritten by its antipathy toward Promethean humanism, indigenous radicalism had more in common with conservative traditionalism. Both Russell Means and Russell Kirk hated the Marxist elevation of man, whether over nature or over God.

Marxism and Native Americans contained a response to Means written by a Revolutionary Communist Party (RCP) collective. Although Churchill published this response as a courtesy that he claimed his Marxist foes never extended to him, he stacked the deck because the RCP was one of Marxism's worst representatives. The RCP had assumed the personality of its paranoid chairman Bob Avakian, who founded it as a Maoist sect in 1975. Its writers played to type when they charged that Means had arrayed "the *most backward* ideas" against Marxism, "*the most advanced* ideas represented in the political struggle." As Churchill and Dora-Lee Larson described this condescendingly racist attitude in their own reply, "it could hardly have gone further in reinforcing virtually every point posited by Means, even if Russell had drafted the Party paper itself."[105]

The RCP made itself into an easy target with its doctrinaire arrogance. Yet readers patient enough to wade through a thicket of dogma were confronted with one compelling point: Means, in distinguishing himself from European thinkers like Marx, had assumed the "noble savage" identity, an invention of the bourgeois imagination used to describe premoderns who shunned modern industrial life. The most famous literary characterization of this type came in the form of a heroic European. Robinson Crusoe personified premodern self-mastery for having survived twenty-eight years as a castaway. As Marx wrote in the *Grundrisse*, self-reliant individuals like Crusoe existed "as an ideal whose existence belonged to the past. Not as a historical result, but as history's point of departure. Not as arising historically but as posited by nature."[106]

The noble savage trope sprung from the bourgeois imagination as respite from capitalism, which degraded a romanticized notion of human nature. Marx, in contrast, thought humans were never entirely at one with nature, and that this disjunction is what made humans unique as a species. Means imagined that native peoples were at one with nature, at least prior to European invasion. Thus, the RCP alleged that Means had capitulated to "insipid fantasies of the bourgeoisie."[107]

This was an unfair accusation. For one, Means was correct that native ways were less destructive to both humanity and the environment. Moreover, life was indisputably better for indigenous peoples prior to European invasion. And yet, the question remained: Given there was no going back to life before European conquest, did the native radical tradition offer a way forward?[108]

Churchill and Larson suggested the native radical tradition was superior to Marxism in its "abandonment of faith in the fundamental role of production." Production was simply too destructive, to people and the environment, even when the working class obtained control over its means. Yet Churchill and Larson hoped that Marxism's "dialectical methodology" would allow it "to transcend its own intellectual/theoretical stalemate." Marx's approach to knowledge allowed for new concepts to emerge out of novel contexts. Perhaps a syncretic methodology, a combination of Marx's criticism of capitalism as a system of exploitation with the native radical tradition's insistence on spiritual resistance, would be the key to unlocking anticapitalist revolution. This was what Churchill and Larson meant in saying that the "only valid point of departure for American Marxists is with the cultural knowledge of *Native* Americans."[109]

The Laguna Pueblo writer Leslie Marmon Silko's sprawling 1991 novel *Almanac of the Dead* was such a point of departure. A story about dozens of eccentric, mostly native, brown and black characters strewn across the American and Mexican borderlands joining forces in resistance against the capitalist war machine, *Almanac of the Dead* promiscu-ously mixed Marxism with native spiritualism in its scathing portrayal of American history. The anthropologist Amanda Walker Johnson la-bels Silko's approach "Native American Marxism."[110]

The experience of reading *Almanac of the Dead* was for some like digging into a novel written by Marx. As the writer Larry McMurtry worded it, "if Karl Marx had chosen to make *Das Kapital* a novel set in the Americas, he might have come out with a book something like this." Silko did not shy from this comparison, calling *Almanac of the Dead* "her tribute to Marx." Silko mirrored Marx in showing how the state was a tool of capital, and how the powerful hid their evildoings behind the veil of civilization. Although most of her characters exist in tension with the law, the boundaries in the book between illicit and legitimate are blurry to nonexistent. In Silko's world, drug runners and sex workers have a lot in common with politicians and corporate ti-tans, except people in the underworld commit crimes far less harmful to humanity than do the elite.[111]

By using fiery images and blood-soaked metaphors to expose the workings of capitalist power, *Almanac of the Dead* echoed *Capital*. Yet, true to her grounding in the native radical tradition, Silko also por-trayed a timeless world of native resistance. The main object around which Silko's characters organize their resistance is an ancient almanac that prophesizes a native reclamation of the Americas. By calling on the power of indigenous experience drawn from the distant past, the almanac represents a native mysticism that bends time in defiance of Marxist historicism. And yet, Silko's native-infused anti-imperialism remained tied to Marx, and not only because his concept of primitive accumulation perfectly matched the gringo exploitation that served as a backdrop to Silko's epic story. *Capital* is characterized in *Almanac of the Dead* as an ancient text with mystical powers in its own right.

As a proxy for her own encounters with Marx, Silko deployed a strong-willed, revolutionary character dubbed La Escapía. Reminiscing about her discovery of Marx, La Escapía reflects on boring Marxist ed-ucational sessions she had attended. But then her Cuban instructors began reading directly from *Capital*. "La Escapía had felt it. A flash! A sudden boom! This old white-man philosopher had something to say about the greed and cruelty. For La Escapía it had been the first time a white man had ever made sense. For hundreds of years white men had been telling the people of the Americas to forget the past; but now the white man Marx came along and he was telling people to remember."

Silko's Marx understood that a timeless chain of resistance was necessary to defeat the ageless forces of evil. "This man Marx had understood that the stories or 'histories' are sacred; that within 'history' reside relentless forces, powerful spirits, vengeful, relentlessly seeking justice." The Marxist dialectic was an angel of history sent to redeem.[112]

Silko was not alone among those who contrived a messianic Marx, thus inverting the terms of dialectical materialism. The Frankfurt School theorist Walter Benjamin, who combined Marxism with a Jewish mysticism amid the Nazi conquest of Europe, also conceptualized history as a metaphysical force over the present. "The only writer of history with the gift of setting alight the sparks of hope in the past," Benjamin wrote in 1940, "is the one who is convinced of this: that not even the dead will be safe from the enemy, if he is victorious." For these mystical dialecticians, tales of past deeds surpassed projections of the future.[113]

The messianic Marx conjured up by Benjamin and Silko was a peripheral conception that came from the marginalized perspectives of an indigenous novelist and a German Jewish philosopher. It was also a religious way to conceptualize Marx, which was a touch strange in an American context where Christianity dominated religious thinking. Outside of a few socialists sprinkled across American history, Christian thinkers rarely conceptualized Marx with any degree of sympathy, much less originality. The black Christian philosopher Cornel West was a notable exception.

A PROPHETIC CHRISTIAN MARX?

In the 1990s, West became one of the most famous intellectuals in the United States. While holding academic positions at various elite universities, including Yale, Princeton, and Harvard, West was regularly featured on television and radio, and even made cameo appearances in two of the blockbuster *Matrix* films. But as a young scholar, West had written an analysis of Marxism, eventually published in 1991 as *Ethical Dimensions of Marxist Thought*. West expressed appreciation for Marxism, yet he also proclaimed he was not a Marxist. Despite being a charter member of Harrington's DSA, West maintained that his commitment to Christianity prevented him from being a Marxist.

West found Marxism valuable precisely for the reason he, as a Christian, could not subscribe to it. "The Marxist tradition," he wrote, "is silent about the existential meaning of death, suffering, love, and friendship owing to its preoccupation with improving the social circumstances under which people pursue love, revel in friendship, and confront death." West shared the Marxist concern for bettering society, but he believed people needed an everyday philosophy with more spiritual depth. "Marxist thought," he wrote, "does not purport to be existential wisdom—of how to live one's life day by day. Rather, it claims to be a social theory of histories, societies, and cultures. Social theory is not the same as existential wisdom." West found wisdom in Christianity, even as he recognized that Marxism helped him understand the conditions under which people might discover such wisdom. Aided by Marxism, West articulated a Christian radical tradition, or what we might call a prophetic Christian Marxism.[114]

West was turned on to Marx as a young man because he was more interested in internationalism than black nationalism. In this his views were consistent with the Black Panthers, who promoted Marxist internationalism "over what Huey Newton called 'porkchop nationalism.'" But as West's Christian socialism deepened, he grew absorbed with cultivating a democratic culture that might be enjoyed by all Americans, including black and other historically subjugated peoples. By that point, he had come to recognize Marxism's weaknesses, not only in its failure to fill an existential void but also in its lack of a sufficient framework for solving the problems associated with racism. And yet, reading Marx remained crucial because all such problems had to be solved in the context of capitalism.[115]

West believed understanding Marx could help Americans from

diverse backgrounds, including black Americans, better come to terms with living in the United States, because Marx linked the plight of individual freedom to a larger context. West highlighted how Marx had located a "fascinating tension between the moral conviction of the flowering of individuality under wholesale democratic socioeconomic and political conditions and the theoretical concern of explaining scientifically the dynamics and tendencies of profit-driven capitalist societies that foster a narrow individualism and a truncated political democracy." West thought this aspect of Marx's thought was imperative to making sense of an increasingly complex and unjust world. As he wrote:

> Despite its blindness and inadequacies—especially in regard to racism, patriarchy, homophobia, and ecological abuse—Marxist thought is an indispensable tradition for freedom fighters who focus on the fundamental issues of jobs, food, shelter, health and childcare for all. One of the major ironies of our time is that Marxist thought becomes even more relevant after the collapse of communism in the Soviet Union and Eastern Europe than it was before. The explosion of capitalist market forces on a global scale—concomitant with open class conflict, aggressive consumerism, rapacious individualism, xenophobic tribalism, and chauvinistic nationalism—makes Marxist thought an inescapable part of the weaponry for present-day freedom fighters.

West, in short, had a realistic assessment of Marx's persistent usefulness. One could find aspects of Marx pertinent without adopting Marxism whole cloth.[116]

That West had a selective approach to Marx was consistent with his background as a philosophical pragmatist who leaned heavily on John Dewey and Sidney Hook, two American thinkers who stressed that ideas were only truthful insofar as they were helpful. Indeed, one of the primary reasons West found Marx persistently relevant was because elements of Marx's thought anticipated aspects of pragmatism.[117]

In tracing Marx's intellectual development, West argued that as Marx grew disillusioned with the quest for certainty, he adopted a radical form of historicism of the sort pragmatists later embraced. "My basic claim," West wrote, "is that Marx's turn toward history resembles the anti-foundationalist arguments of the American pragmatists." Marx acquired a deeply contextual understanding of consciousness such that, like the pragmatists, he thought forms of knowledge were only verifiable within particular times and places. But to a degree unmatched by the pragmatists, Marx retained just enough certainty about enduring concepts like justice and nature to build a theory of social change. For West, this powerful cocktail of historicism and conviction was born of Marx's political activism.[118]

In West's view, the more a thinker delved into specific political struggles, the more they were forced to reckon with the need for objective moral standards. This realization came to Marx early in his career as a journalist, when he investigated impoverished German peasants who had been stripped of their right to gather wood. In figuring out how best to convey the issues at stake, Marx had to become more cognizant of the contingencies of power, of the particulars that compelled a local elite to enclose upon a common good, without losing sight of the injustice being done to a disempowered class.

Marx served for West as a model of the ethical philosopher because he was also an activist. "Societal possibilities can be realized only when the philosopher-critic digs for them," West wrote. "This digging consists of heightening people's awareness of the actual struggles they engage in." West concluded his 1991 book with a call for Marxist philosophers to be more like Marx. "The failure of the Marxist philosophers," he wrote, "is that they ultimately remain philosophers, whereas Marx's radical historicist metaphilosophical vision enables him to stop doing philosophy and to begin to describe, explain, and ultimately change the world."[119]

West appropriated the radical historicist, metaphilosopher Marx as an ally in the intellectual battles of the late twentieth century, juxtaposing him with that particular "moment of epistemic skepticism, explanatory agnosticism, political impotence (among progressives), and historical cynicism." Marx's modern vision of social change was vastly superior to the postmodern "disciples of Jacques Derrida and

Michel Foucault who talk about subtle relations of rhetoric, knowledge, and power, yet remain silent about concrete ways in which people are empowered to resist and what can be gained by such resistance." Within historical constraints, Marx offered a reasonably hopeful vision of change. Postmodernists, in contrast, pointed toward quietism at best, nihilism at worst. Of course, even as he highlighted the guarded optimism baked into Marxism, West made clear that a Marxist interpretation of the world offered no guarantee of a better future. Capitalism would not easily be overcome and no Marxist worth their salt ever thought otherwise, nor for that matter did any sensible Christian socialist. Yet West, following Marx, thought capitalism had certain weaknesses that might eventually lead to its demise. Given that, people might as well plan for a better future.[120]

West's version of Marx reinforced his confidence in the human capacity for social change. It also reinforced his confidence in Marx as a philosopher of freedom. Only someone who believed in human freedom could trust humans to change their situation. Such a freedom-loving Marx comported with the essential question that Americans had long asked: What does it mean to live free? Marx had valuable answers. The problem, though, was that few late twentieth-century Americans seemed willing to listen. Sidney's Hook's earlier version of Marx was not that different from West's, yet in the 1930s many more Americans were willing to entertain Marx as a proponent of both democracy and revolution. By the 1980s, Americans tended to either despise Marx from a conservative perspective, or discount him from a postmodern standpoint. For postmodernists, Foucault was the king of theory; Marx was an antiquated curiosity. But unbeknownst to them, Marx was also a ghost in the American machine.

A POSTMODERN MARX?

As Marxist forms of academic analysis fell out of fashion, the French philosopher Jacques Derrida's postmodern theory of "deconstruction" became all the rage. Deconstruction focused on the inherent tensions and dualisms of human life. It offered a new theoretical elocution of the growing sense that metaphysical oppositions, such as between mind and body, were false binaries. The point in deconstructing fallacious dualisms was not to unveil some imaginary, preexistent whole, or to suture mind and body together, but rather to understand the perpetual human compulsion to drive wedges. If deconstruction forwarded a criticism of Marxism, it was that human existence had forever been marked by alienation. Every human condition, including alienation and even language itself, was structured into infinity by self-contradiction and paradox—what Derrida called *différance*. Alienation was unresolvable. The key was to learn to better live with it.[121]

Although deconstruction contained an implicit critique of Marxism from the first, Derrida intentionally avoided writing about Marx for most of his life. As he said in 1989, "I meant to read Marx my way when the time came." That time came at the end of the Cold War, when Derrida decided a reading of Marx would finally be useful and gave a two-part keynote at a 1993 conference at the University of California–Riverside on the topic "Whither Marxism." Those talks formed the basis of his 1994 book *Specters of Marx*.[122]

Specters of Marx appeared as intellectuals around the world were rethinking basic categories, following the demise of state communism. For Derrida and others, the fall of the Berlin Wall and the collapse of the Soviet Union did not make Marx less relevant, in fact, quite the opposite. But how might Marx help cultural theorists make sense of the moment? Derrida claimed there "will be no future without Marx, without the memory and inheritance of Marx." He argued there were many specters of Marx, or many surprising ways that Marx spoke to the present and future. Derrida's ideas about Marx's significance were as ethereal and ambiguous as his prose. His notorious lack of clarity, a feature of his theory about the incommensurability of language, carried over into his book on Marx. But uncertainty also spoke to the political moment, which some, remarkably, referred to as the end of history. Rather than digging their own graves, as Marx prophesized, capitalists had buried communism. This made rethinking Marx a necessity for some. For others it meant interring him once and for all.[123]

Francis Fukuyama, a conservative political philosopher and student of Leo Strauss, fell into that group of thinkers. In his bestselling 1992 book *The End of History and the Last Man*, Fukuyama declared capitalism's victory over communism, or rather, he wrote that liberal democracy had "conquered rival ideologies like hereditary monarchy, fascism, and most recently communism." As capitalism and democracy advanced across the planet, Fukuyama asserted that "all the really big questions had been settled." Liberal democracy of the American type was the "end point of mankind's ideological evolution," the "final form of human government," the "end of history." (Whatever Derrida thought of Marx, he rejected the concept that anything ever ends.) Fukuyama did not presume the rest of the world would willingly or peacefully embrace liberal democracy. Rather he believed history had progressed such that "the *ideal* of liberal democracy could not be improved upon." By history, Fukuyama meant "history understood as a single-coherent, evolutionary process, when taking into account the experience of all peoples in all times."[124]

Fukuyama, like Marx, followed Hegel in his belief that social contradictions gave way to social transformations. He also went along with Hegel and Marx in assuming one final, grandiose contradiction would emerge that, once resolved, would bring an end to history. Fukuyama of course highlighted where the two dead German philosophers parted company. "Where Marx differed from Hegel," he wrote, "was over just what kind of society emerged at the end of history." Hegel thought liberal democracy solved the riddle of human alienation by offering people the possibility of freedom. In contrast, according to Fukuyama, "Marx believed that the liberal state failed to resolve one fundamental contradiction, that of class conflict, the struggle between the bourgeoisie and the proletariat." Marx assumed "that in liberal societies man remains alienated from himself because capital, a human creation, has turned into man's lord and master and controls him." The end of history for Hegel was democratic capitalism. For Marx, communism would put a stake in history. Fukuyama left little doubt about which of the two visions he aligned with.[125]

The cultural theorists who gathered to discuss Marx in Riverside did so under the shadow of a Cold War triumphalism exemplified by Fukuyama. *The End of History* answered in the affirmative that, indeed, Marxism was waning. Of course, speculation about Marx's decline did not originate with the collapse of the Soviet Union. During the middle of the twentieth century, anti-Stalinists obsessed over this question. During the 1950s Derrida and his comrades had wrestled over Marx's pertinence. In fact, Derrida claimed it was there he formulated deconstruction as an exit from the false choice between Stalinism and capitalism. Deconstruction was a method of interpretation that helped people imagine what it meant to live a more bearable life in a world of bad choices.

But where did this leave Marx? For most of Derrida's public life, Marx seemed to be hidden away. Yet as a "quasi paternal figure" Marx was far from forgotten. Derrida was not alone in this. As people everywhere sought to bury Marx, the old communist returned again and again, like a repressed desire. "At a time when a new world disorder is attempting to install its neo-capitalism and neo-liberalism," Derrida wrote, "no disavowal has managed to rid itself of all of Marx's ghosts." In a direct challenge to Fukuyama's apology for capitalism, Derrida contended neoliberalism was too destructive to ensure its ideological victory, and that this, more than anything, explained why Marx continued to haunt the collective imagination. Capitalism cannot kill Marx because its horrors call him into existence: Marx, the keeper of its history.[126]

Given that many American cultural theorists had spent many years criticizing Marxism as a totalizing philosophy that did violence to pluralistic understandings of the world—understandings that attended to differentiating identities like race, gender, ethnicity, or sexuality—the fact that a cultural theorist of Derrida's standing had called for a return to Marx was potentially encouraging news for the few committed Marxists left. But Derrida's observation that Marx would persist so long as capitalism endured was not a new point. Moreover, the one seemingly novel contribution Derrida made to Marxist discourse, that Marxism should be deconstructed like any other master narrative, was an opaque observation that bordered on banality. In this, the intellectual historian Russell Jacoby hit the mark when he wrote that *Specters of Marx* "reads like Derrida satirizing Derrida." But in a larger sense, Derrida should be understood less as an agent of postmodern esotericism and more as a symptom of the intellectual Left's abandonment of material concerns in favor of disembodied cultural and textual interests.[127]

Derrida's nebulous analysis of Marx should also be considered a by-product of a general confusion about the state of the world at the end of the Cold War. As Jacoby noted at the time, "even the most learned Marxists are puzzled. Eric Hobsbawm closes his new book, *The Age of Extremes*, admitting the century is winding down with 'a global disorder' whose nature and resolution are 'unclear.' This is surely right." Jacoby took this analysis further in definitively declaring that "a Marxism that celebrates incoherence or renounces materialism and the effort to grasp the whole has renounced itself." No matter how much Derrida protested that he, too, was a Marxist, deconstruction was by definition a renunciation of Marx.[128]

In a transformative yet confusing time in the history of capitalism, Marx was needed more than ever. The vague Marx of cultural theory, a limited Marx who could be deconstructed in some ill-defined discursive project, was not what was needed. Rather, the more radical Marx popular in earlier eras, a revolutionary Marx who expanded the horizons of our political imagination, would have been more appropriate to the vast problems associated with the neoliberal capitalism that was storming the planet. Yet American intellectuals in the 1980s and 1990s were mostly ill-equipped to ruminate on the revolutionary implications of Marx. Luckily for those dreaming of a socialist future, this situation was not permanent.

A NEW MARX FOR A NEW CAPITALISM

Few left-wing intellectuals offered new and compelling reflections on Marx during much of the 1990s. It was a quiet time for political radicalism in the United States. But amid the era's intensifying exploitation, there was an obvious need for rethinking the key philosopher of exploitation and capitalism. Identifying this demand, the University of Chicago social theorist Moishe Postone wrote *Time, Labor, and Social Domination: A Reinterpretation of Marx's Critical Theory*. Postone's 1993 book set Marxist studies on a new course, one seemingly befitting an era marked by an emboldened capitalist class, at a time when more and more people were concluding that work sucks.[129]

Postone's major revision of Marx doubled as his analysis of how exploitation worked in modern societies. Postone contended Marx's social theory was about the historically unique configuration of social domination that shaped the modern era writ large. More to the point, Postone believed that exploitation typified modern industrial labor regimes whether in a capitalist society or a communist one. This was because the predominant form of exploitation in modern societies was labor, regardless of who was coercing it. Simply put, being compelled to work, arguably the common feature of all modern industrial regimes, amounted to having one's mind, body, and time dominated, all in the pursuit of *value*. Postone believed a proper understanding of domination would help people more accurately visualize revolutionary possibilities, especially as the modern industrial world gave way to something different, if equally exploitative.

Postone focused on overlooked passages of the *Grundrisse* about how surmounting capitalism required overcoming labor. The "ultimate object," Marx wrote, was "the suspension not of distribution, but of the mode of production itself." It was not enough to merely redistribute wealth. Freedom required abolishing production. Postone wrote: "Overcoming capitalism, according to Marx, entails a fundamental transformation of the material form of production, of the way people work." This for Postone was the key to social theory at the time.[130]

Postone also rethought conventional understandings of Marxist politics, questioning whether workers had the power to overthrow capitalism. Postone departed from the more orthodox conception of the working class that was ironically held by Communist Party theorists and Frankfurt School thinkers alike, despite their dramatically different conclusions about the political direction and composition of the working class. Communist Party thinkers painted a picture of workers

heroically lifting the world up to a better place. Frankfurt School theorists portrayed the proletariat as a defeated class that not only failed
to fulfill its historic role but worse yet turned to reactionary politics as
a result. Postone, in contrast, contended the political trajectory of the
working class was irrelevant.[131]

Postone was building a Marxist theory of capitalism he considered
more appropriate to the post–New Deal world. He wrote:

> The contours of this new phase are not yet clear, but the past two
> decades have witnessed the relative decline in importance of the in-
> stitutions and centers of power that had been at the heart of state-
> interventionist capitalism—a form characterized by centralized
> production, large industrial labor unions, ongoing government in-
> tervention in the economy, and a vastly expanded welfare state. Two
> apparently opposed historical tendencies have contributed to this
> weakening . . . : on the one hand, a partial decentralization of pro-
> duction and politics, and with it the emergence of a plurality of social
> groupings, organizations, movements, parties, subcultures; and on
> the other, a process of the globalization and concentration of capital
> that has taken place on a new, very abstract level, far removed from
> immediate experience and apparently, for now, beyond the effective
> control of the state.[132]

Twentieth-century capitalism had been radically transformed. Yet
the obligation humans had to spend their lives working persisted.
Thus, people continued to be dominated by those in control of production. The fact that many things had dramatically changed yet exploitation persisted had to be considered in theorizing a better future.
Exploitation transcended any one form of capitalism. Whether the
state intervened to distribute wealth more equally, a feature of mid-
twentieth-century capitalism that had been growing less common, was
ultimately less important than finding a way to minimize the burden
of labor.

In updating Marx for the neoliberal world, Postone emphasized
Marx's work on machine automation, which had become more preva-

lent than ever. For Marx, machines were troublesome in that they disciplined labor to an even greater degree by speeding up production. But machines also created openings for transcending labor. At least, this is how Postone read Marx. In the *Grundrisse*, Marx hinted that his labor theory of value was on the precipice of obsolescence due to mounting machine use. As the theory became anachronistic, so too would the industrial process of production. Postone thought this might spell the end of capitalism. Or, as Marx imagined, anticipating the twenty-first-century American obsession with a machine-controlled dystopian future:

> It requires no great penetration to grasp that, where e.g. free labour or wage labour arising out of the dissolution of bondage is the point of departure, there machines can only *arise* in antithesis to living labour, as property alien to it, and as power hostile to it; i.e., that they must confront it as capital. But it is just as easy to perceive that machines will not cease to be agencies of social production when they become e.g. property of the associated workers. In the first case, however, their distribution, i.e., that they *do not belong* to the worker, is just as much a condition of the mode of production founded on wage labour. In the second case the changed distribution would start from a *changed* foundation of production, a new foundation first created by the process of history.

By getting control of the machines, people could profoundly alter production and thus end the regime of industrial labor. Of course, it could also go horribly wrong. The choice between socialism or barbarism had never seemed more palpable.[133]

In discerning from Marx's social theory that production prevented humans from flourishing, Postone believed Marx pointed to "the possibility of every person existing as a full and richly developed being." Freedom from domination, freedom from labor, was the very definition of freedom writ large. Postone believed his analysis allowed for the possibility of social transformation because it presumed multiple forms of revolutionary consciousness might emerge within capitalism, and not only from a narrowly defined working class. This proposition carried weight at the close of the twentieth century, when concerns about capitalist production came to the fore of not only the labor-centric Marxism but also the hybrid forms that had taken their cues from feminism and the black and native radical traditions.[134]

Marx argued the proletariat offered the key to revolution precisely because it was the force capable of halting capitalism at its very point of production. If this is true, then surely organized labor factors into any postcapitalist future. But Postone downplayed this aspect of Marx's theory. And in an era when people were increasingly despondent about work and production, not only as a method of social domination but also as a form of planetary exploitation, Postone's argument resonated. In the twenty-first century, when capitalist production threatens the very survival of the planet, more and more people are grasping for anything that might save them. A growing number of people are even, once again, turning to the nearly forgotten revolutionary Marx.

9

SPECTER HAUNTING

Twenty-First-Century Capitalism

Don't you wonder: why is it necessary to declare me dead again and again?

"KARL MARX" IN *MARX IN SOHO* BY HOWARD ZINN

Not unlike countless people in this book, I turned to Karl Marx to try to make sense of the world and possibly change it. Indeed, my motivation for researching and writing this book has been somewhat selfish: I want to place myself in the long line of socialists who, owing partly to Marx, clearly see capitalism for the exploitative system it is.

While I am far from unique, once Marx became fundamental to who I am, I began to feel out of step with my generation. Born in 1972, I missed out on the rediscovery of Marx in the 1960s that accompanied the rise of a New Left. And I came of age well before the 2008 financial collapse, the most catastrophic crisis of capitalism since the Great Depression and the wellspring of our current Marx revival.

Hardly any Americans of Generation X, who like me who grew up in the shadow of Ronald Reagan, turned to Marx as a source of wisdom. Our formative years were marked by celebrations of capitalism and an ideological assault on Marxism. Few Gen Xers emerged from that cauldron devotees of Marx. Yet pockets of Marx-infused resistance were there all along.[1]

One of my earliest introductions to Marxist political expression came by listening to Rage against the Machine, a rock band out of Los Angeles. I fell in love with the group's infectious mix of heavy metal, funk, and rap, particularly the primal noises of Tom Morello's electric guitar. The militant lyrics by Zach de la Rocha, grandson of a Mexican revolutionary, urged millions of alienated young fans to wake up and resist the corporate war machine.[2]

Rage provided listeners with a hip-hop-ish version of Marxist history. As de la Rocha hollered in the 1996 song, "Down Rodeo": "A thousand years they had the tools, we should be takin' 'em; Fuck the G-ride, I want the machines that are makin' 'em." Rage appreciated Marx's theory that power derived from command over the means of production.[3]

Rage offered listeners a gateway to a world of revolutionary thought. In the liner notes of their second album, *Evil Empire*, was a photo of books spread across a table. I steadily worked my way through the Rage reading list, beginning with iconic missives like Frantz Fanon's *The Wretched of the Earth* and Che Guevara's *Guerrilla Warfare*. Yet *The Marx-Engels Reader* edited by Robert Tucker, which became the standard Marx collection soon after its 1972 publication, wasn't one I got to. I picked up a copy, but, at that initial stage in my left-wing education, I was not quite ready to fully dig into Marx. I got there soon enough.

A PEOPLE'S MARXIST

The most formative book of my early intellectual development, Howard Zinn's *A People's History of the United States*, was surprisingly not shown on Rage's table. Yet it was impossible to avoid. *A People's History* has done more to popularize a leftist version of American history than any other book. Selling more than two million copies and counting, Zinn's magnum opus is an alternative to nationalistic textbooks that narrate stories of elite-driven progress. *A People's History* is told from the perspective of the downtrodden. Zinn's haunting portrayals of suffering—by the dispossessed, the enslaved, wage laborers, victims of American wars—were meant to evoke sympathy for the subjugated. *A People's History* also emphasized Americans who resisted injustice, Zinn's "people." Writing a history from their vantage point planted the seeds of an alternative American future.[4]

In the early 1990s, the book was well on its way to prominence. In addition to becoming a fixture in history classes, it was becoming a pop culture icon. In a pivotal scene in the 1997 film *Good Will Hunting*, the working-class prodigy character played by Matt Damon (who grew up next door to Zinn), asks his therapist: "You wanna read a real history book? Read Howard Zinn's *A People's History of the United States*. That book'll knock you on your ass." In a 2002 episode of *The Sopranos*, mafia boss Tony Soprano's son AJ reports he learned at school that Christopher Columbus was a murderer. In response to his Italian American father's fuming objection, AJ assures him "it's not just my teacher—it's the truth. It's in my history book." "You finally read a book and it's bull shit," Tony retorts.[5]

Conservatives have long despised *A People's History*, bemoaning that a book written by an "unreconstructed, anti-American Marxist," as one right-winger labeled Zinn, has had such reach. Claims that Zinn was a Marxist have fueled efforts to censor *A People's History*. After Zinn died in 2010, the Republican Indiana governor Mitch Daniels investigated the possibility of removing his book from public universities there.[6]

Yet Michael Kazin, a left-leaning historian, rejects the notion that Zinn was a Marxist. Zinn posited a "transhistorical" ruling class, unchanged "from the days when its members owned slaves and wore knee-britches to the era of the Internet and Armani." Kazin pointed out that the "old Rhinelander never took so static or simplistic a view of history." Zinn himself rejected the label, often repeating the apocryphal line Marx purportedly told a young admirer, "*Je ne suis pas un Marxiste*" (I am not a Marxist). Yet Zinn's life and work illustrated the time-honored Marx-America dialectic.[7]

A People's History is not a doctrinaire Marxist text. Rather, Zinn's book exhibits the sensibilities of a moral leftist who identified with an eclectic mix of radical movements that included socialism but also abolitionism, pacifism, and anarchism. He would have been at home in Section Twelve of the International. His commitment to a big-tent American Left, one that prizes Thoreau as much as Marx, is evident throughout *A People's History*. Even so, Marx's fingerprints are distinct. As the historian Nick Witham argues, Zinn's book "represented a multi-generational and deeply American approach to Marxism."[8]

Zinn's analysis of labor relied on Marx, or on labor historians heavily dependent on Marx in their own right. In this way, *A People's History* fashioned a fresh narrative of American labor history that synthesized the twentieth-century American reception of Marx. In his treatment of the rent strike that shook the Hudson Valley in the 1840s, for example, Zinn owed his overarching conclusion to Henry Christman's classic 1945 book *Tin Horns and Calico*. Zinn wrote: "The farmers had fought, been crushed by the law, their struggle diverted into voting, and the system stabilized by enlarging the class of small landowners, leaving the basic structure of rich and poor intact." Zinn described this as "a common sequence in American history."[9]

Zinn's interpretation of the American state borrowed from the New Left evaluation of corporate liberalism, itself an offshoot of Marxism. The US government behaved, Zinn wrote, "almost exactly as Karl Marx described a capitalist state: pretending neutrality in order to maintain order, but serving the interests of the rich. Not that the rich agreed among themselves; they had disputes over policies. But the purpose of the state was to settle upper-class disputes peacefully, control lower-class rebellion, and adopt policies that would further the long-range stability of the system."[10]

Marx had been in Zinn's life since 1939, when the seventeen-year-old from a working-class Jewish immigrant family first read *The Communist Manifesto*. Zinn recalled the "profound effect" the *Manifesto* had on him. The circumstances of his youth "seemed to be explained, put into historical context, and placed under a powerful analytical light." Three years later, while working in a shipyard, Zinn devoured *Capital*, ultimately typing up forty-one pages of notes on it. As a longtime professor at Boston University, he consistently assigned a variety of Marx texts in his courses.[11]

The Marx piece Zinn found "most profound" was the *Economic and Philosophic Manuscripts*, where the Marxist humanists had also found inspiration. Echoing Raya Dunayevskaya, Zinn declared the Soviet Union had betrayed Marx when it smashed the Hungarian uprising in 1956. He went further, proclaiming Marx would have agreed with Emma Goldman's criticism of the early Soviet Union. "If I can't dance," Goldman purportedly asserted, "I don't want to be part of your revolution."[12]

Like Goldman, Zinn embraced a heady mix of Marxism and anarchism. He often cited a quote about Marx's nemesis, the anarchist Mikhail Bakunin. "He called me a sentimental idealist, and he was right," Bakunin said. "I called him vain, treacherous, and morose, and I was right." Zinn loathed the infighting that had plagued the Left since well before Marx and Bakunin went toe-to-toe for control of the International. He sought to forge a middle ground between Marxism and anarchism, where "the people" might unite to overthrow a rapacious ruling elite.[13]

In 1995, Zinn wrote a one-man play, *Marx in Soho: A Play on History*, as a new vehicle for advancing his vision of the world. *Marx in Soho* appeared at a time, he said, when "Marx was truly dead," even though his critique of capitalism remained "fundamentally true," "corroborated every day in newspaper headlines." Zinn wanted to reintroduce the revolutionary Marx to an American audience because the times called for revolutionary solutions.[14]

Marx in Soho was performed in select theaters in North America and Europe. The play begins with Marx addressing the audience. "I've been reading your newspapers," he tells them. "They are all proclaiming that my ideas are dead! It's nothing new. These clowns have been saying this for more than a hundred years. Don't you wonder," the old Rhinelander asks, "why is it necessary to declare me dead again and again?" Zinn's Marx likes asking rhetorical questions. "Did I not say, a hundred and fifty years ago, that capitalism would enormously increase the

FIGURE 9.1: Left, Bob Weick (playing Karl Marx in *Marx in Soho*); right, Howard Zinn, Boston, 2006.

wealth of society, but that this wealth would be concentrated in fewer and fewer hands?" Marx reads from a newspaper: "Giant merger of Chemical Bank and Chase Manhattan Bank. Twelve thousand workers will lose jobs. . . . Stocks rise." He looks up at the audience with a sly grin. "And they say my ideas are dead!" Zinn might have denied he was a Marxist, but his play sought to convince audiences Marx's ideas were relevant. His actions betrayed his words.[15]

The most important idea Marx gave the world, the devastating notion that capitalist wealth is predicated on exploitation of workers, is the reason Zinn raised Marx from the dead. "Just last week," Zinn's fictional Marx says, "I was reading the reports of the United States Department of Labor. Your workers are producing more and more goods and getting less and less in wages. What is the result? Just as I predicted. Now the richest one percent of the American population owns forty percent of the nation's wealth. And this in the great model of world capitalism, the nation that has not only robbed its own people, but sucked the wealth of the rest of the world." Zinn joined a long line of American Marxists who interpreted Marx for a domestic audience. He wanted his play to inspire people to discover Marx for themselves.[16]

THE NEW ERA OF ENCLOSURES

Marx in Soho was produced in the midst of one of capitalism's most unremitting phases of expansion and consolidation. Marx conceptualized capitalism as a world-conquering system as early as 1848. "Modern industry has established the world market," he wrote, "for which the discovery of America paved the way." And yet, even Marx might have been surprised by the rapid rate of capitalist expansion in the 1990s. The biggest barrier to its reach during the twentieth century had been the communist states which controlled a third of the earth's land mass. But after the Berlin Wall fell in 1989, after the Soviet Union collapsed in 1991, and after the Chinese Communist Party introduced reforms that unleashed markets in the world's most populous nation, capitalism was sprung free. The "discovery of America" went global.

Late twentieth-century capitalism resembled the system at its birth. In the early modern period, nascent capitalists deprived English peasants of access to common lands. In the postmodern era, globetrotting capitalists dispossessed the world's workers of basic necessities. The word for these new enclosures was *privatization*. In the formerly communist world, publicly owned, state-run systems of distribution, which often met people's essential needs, were sold off to the highest bidders. As Western capitalists and a burgeoning class of local oligarchs got fat off the public trough, the economies of Russia and Eastern Europe shrunk dramatically. In the United States, which never had as robust a public sector, privateering capitalists targeted water systems, hospitals, pension plans, schools, police forces, prisons, military forces, parking meters, and more.[17]

In this new era of enclosures, what Eric Hobsbawm labeled an "ultra-extreme market fundamentalism" became an enforced way of life. In the poor nations of Asia, Africa, and Latin America, which had amassed enormous debt, austerity was deemed the solution. Augusto Pinochet, a ruthless general who came to power in Chile in 1973 after the United States helped him remove the democratically elected socialist president Salvador Allende, enacted deep cuts to the Chilean welfare state, often on advice from neoliberal economists trained at the

University of Chicago. Pinochet and like-minded autocrats elsewhere privatized state-owned assets, including basic necessities like fresh water. When local tyrants proved unhelpful or unobtainable, international organizations controlled by the United States stepped in to ensure compliance. Obey the World Bank, International Monetary Fund, and World Trade Organization, or suffer the wrath of capital flight, a fate worse than austerity.[18]

Resistance to the neoliberal order was minimal during the 1990s. This was especially true in the United States, where the political system was increasingly arrayed against the working class. The Republican Party had long pushed policies inimical to the interests of workers. These commitments grew more fervent after the party adopted Ronald Reagan as its lodestar, signaling its support for a brand of capitalism that accelerated the downward spiral of working-class conditions. The Democratic Party had been friendlier to workers since 1932, when Franklin D. Roosevelt's election ushered in the New Deal order. Yet by the time Bill Clinton was elected president in 1992, neoliberalism had slain the New Deal. "The true test of a political order," the historian Gary Gerstle writes, "is when the opposition acquiesces to an order's ideological and policy imperatives." Clinton "facilitated that acquiescence," Gerstle notes, actions befitting "America's neoliberal president par excellence."[19]

As a Yale law student in 1972, Clinton managed George McGovern's presidential campaign in Texas. The South Dakota senator's prolabor bona fides were impeccable, yet McGovern lost many white working-class voters unhappy with the Democratic Party's (uneven) support for black people. Clinton observed Richard Nixon's thrashing of McGovern as a sign that Democrats would need to move rightward on the political spectrum. Clinton gauged the political winds correctly. As governor of Arkansas during the 1980s, Clinton became identified as a "New Democrat," one of the rising stars in a party shifting to embrace post–New Deal capitalism. In 1992, Clinton ran for president promising to "end welfare as we know it," a position the Republican incumbent George H. W. Bush refused to adopt for fear of seeming too cruel.[20]

Anti–New Deal tendencies shaped Clinton's eight years in the

White House. His signature piece of neoliberal legislation was the North American Free Trade Agreement (NAFTA), which became law on January 1, 1994. A pact between the United States, Mexico, and Canada, NAFTA empowered corporations to conduct business more freely across North America by wiping away a host of pesky regulations and prohibitive tariffs. A windfall for profits, NAFTA was a disaster for the American working class. Union contracts were rendered moot as companies relocated production south of the border, where a more ruthless form of exploitation prevailed. Sending jobs abroad, or off-shoring, was not new. Policies that eased restrictions on this practice were first enacted in the 1970s, and Mexico was hardly the only cheap labor market where corporations turned to maximize profits. China alone absorbed a massive proportion of the world's manufacturing jobs. But NAFTA represented the final nail in the coffin of New Deal–style support for the proletariat.[21]

Neoliberal capitalism fueled a return to Gilded Age levels of economic inequality. With steadily fewer people enjoying stable employment, precarity was normalized. Beginning in the 1980s, hunger and homelessness proliferated. Drug addiction, gun violence, depression, and suicide all reached epidemic levels. By 2020, with an opioid crisis ravaging the nation, over one hundred thousand Americans were dying of drug overdoses each year.[22]

Things were worse in many other parts of the world, as over a billion people are now warehoused in what Mike Davis called a "planet of slums." The rich often shield themselves from such wretchedness, only bearing witness to the world's many pest-ridden favelas and sewage-drenched shantytowns from helicopters. Yet they cannot entirely avoid the mounting turbulence sending shock waves through their system. For the first time since the 1930s, as one economic catastrophe after another rocked the global economy to its core, Marx's theory about capitalism's inevitable propensity to spawn crises became germane again. Marx reemerged, like a specter, foretelling the trajectory of an undead capitalism.[23]

In the late twentieth century, few outside academia turned to Marx. As state communism expired, there seemed little point in spending time with the philosopher who inspired a losing way of life. And yet, as capitalism's champions were celebrating their grand triumph, more judicious minds cautioned that capitalism might have been *too* successful. As the system subjugated the entire world to its logic, it recapitulated the patterns and problems Marx had long ago identified.

THE RETURN OF KARL MARX

In 1997, the *New Yorker* published an article titled, "The Return of Karl Marx." The author, John Cassidy, began with a truth: "Hardly anybody reads Marx these days." And yet. "Many of the contradictions that he saw in Victorian capitalism," Cassidy wrote, "have been reappearing in new guises, like mutant viruses." Marx's observation in 1844, that "money is the alienated essence of man's work and being," and that this "alien essence dominates him," was, according to Cassidy, truer than ever. Marx would have recognized a world where magazine racks were lined with titles like *Money* and *Fortune*, where a profit-hungry media "regularly lionized" billionaires such as Warren Buffett and George Soros.[24]

In 1999, *The Economist* concurred, designating Marx "The Prophet of Capitalism." At the dawn of a new millennium, globalization had revealed an undeniable truth. Marx had been onto something.[25]

Most leftists had never doubted Marx's lasting pertinence. Yet even they began taking fresh interest. In 1998, the left-wing publisher Verso celebrated the 150-year anniversary of *The Communist Manifesto* by issuing a new edition and by hosting an event at Cooper Union in New York City. Enticed by emails declaring the meeting would "not be the first time that the spirit of Karl Marx has been present at Cooper Union," a reference to the memorial for Marx held there in 1883, a crowd of nine hundred gathered to hear literary luminaries like Tony Kushner and Amiri Baraka read from the *Manifesto*. Frances Wheen, author of a 1999 Marx biography, wrote that the more he "studied Marx, the more astoundingly topical he seemed to be." The seeds of a new Marx boom were on the verge of sprouting.[26]

And then they leaped off the page and into the streets. On November 30, 1999, over forty thousand protestors disrupted the annual conference of the World Trade Organization, a supranational institution that worked on behalf of neoliberal capitalism. Nourished by its surprising success in Seattle in bringing attention to the problems of capitalism, a ragtag group of social justice activists, trade unionists, environmentalists, and anarchists coalesced to challenge the globalization of neoliberal capitalism. Declaring "another world is possible," the antiglobalization movement staged several additional protests against what they labeled, in a nod to American hegemony, "the Washington consensus." In April 2000, a large demonstration targeted the chief enforcers of this consensus, the World Bank and International Monetary Fund, at their headquarters in Washington, DC. Perhaps a revolutionary Left was waking up from its long slumber.[27]

The antiglobalization movement showed its ability to organize flashy demonstrations. Setting down roots among the working class proved more difficult. Activists were not completely at fault for this. Few American workers were in a radical frame of mind. Yet rather than taking their cues from Marx, who believed the best way to gain leverage against capitalists was for workers to organize at the point of production—autoworkers at automobile factories, teachers at schools, restaurant workers at restaurants—activists followed the lead of Subcomandante Marcos, the masked voice of the Zapatistas, indigenous revolutionaries from Chiapas, Mexico.

On January 1, 1994, the Zapatistas had asserted their liberation from both the Mexican state and neoliberal capitalism. Chiapas, the southernmost region of Mexico, was to be an autonomous zone. That the Zapatistas declared independence on the very day NAFTA became law was no coincidence. Subcomandante Marcos, the nom de guerre of Rafael Sebastián Guillén Vicente, who studied Marxist theory at university, was a public relations maestro. He recognized the symbolic power of linking the Zapatista rebellion to a treaty that codified corporate supremacy.[28]

Marcos also understood how to generate sympathy from American leftists. "Marcos is gay in San Francisco," he proclaimed, "black in South Africa, Asian in Europe, Chicano in San Isidro, Anarchist in Spain, Palestinian in Israel." This conception of solidarity, in which Marcos embodied the world's "exploited, marginalized, oppressed minorities," is what the historians Howard Brick and Christopher Phelps brand a "left episodic." Protest a lumber company here, a trade organization there, police brutality here, Israeli settlements there. Meanwhile, capitalism does what it does, mostly unabated. In this way, the American Left at the turn of the millennium displayed sensibilities rooted in a moral Left tradition going back to abolitionism. The noble goal of the moral Left, to pinpoint and uproot oppression of all types, has sometimes been achievable. But in confronting neoliberal sovereignty, moral leftism has proven poorly equipped.[29]

Although the antiglobalization movement hardly threatened the neoliberal order, its symbolic anticapitalism represented an important step for a Left wishing to reclaim relevance. The French Marxist Daniel Bensaïd contended the movement symbolized the return of history. It likewise signified a transition point in the American reception of Marx. Bensaïd argued that research inspired by Marx "only has a genuine future if, rather than seeking refuge in the academic fold, it succeeds in establishing an organic relationship with the revived practice of social movements—in particular, with the resistance to imperialist globalization." Unleashed from the academic seminar room, Marx had regained his revolutionary footing.[30]

Or had he? Engaging with the antiglobalization movement in this time made me realize I had not yet spent enough time with Marx's writings, which undergirded so much of it. In 2001, I began graduate studies at the George Washington University. As a Marxist in Washington, DC, I felt like I was living in the belly of the beast—especially after the terrorist attacks of September 11, 2001, effectively finished off the short-lived antiglobalization movement. A few weeks after the attacks, the mood at a demonstration against the World Bank and IMF was subdued, and a touch fearful. Yet, movement or not, I persisted.

Others did, too. *Empire*, by Michael Hardt and Antonio Negri, was the trendiest book in Marxist studies at the time. Viewed by the mainstream literary press as an antiglobalization manifesto, the Marxist authors were more ambitious than that. Hardt and Negri wanted *Empire* to do for 2000 what *Capital* had done for 1867. They wrote what they thought was an all-encompassing philosophical examination of how the world worked.

THE BIRTH OF EMPIRE

Hardt the American literary theorist and Negri the Italian political philosopher, who wrote his portion of *Empire* while imprisoned for alleged crimes in the 1970s as a member of the Red Brigades, depicted global arrangements at the turn of the millennium through an eclectic set of philosophical lenses. Marx served as a theoretical anchor for *Empire*, but he was only one of its many foundations, which included the sixteenth-century Italian philosopher Niccolò Machiavelli and the twentieth-century French theorists Gilles Deleuze and Félix Guattari. *Empire* was a postmodern response to the global consolidation of capitalism. Just as bricolage was the preferred style of postmodern architects, Hardt and Negri borrowed promiscuously from a diverse range of perspectives to demonstrate that capitalism had entered a new phase, and that resistance must take novel forms.[31]

In contending that the imperialist phase of capitalism, dominated by a few powerful nations that exploited large swaths of the planet, had given way to a qualitatively different phase, Hardt and Negri took their cues from Deleuze and Guattari. In two works from 1972 and 1980, collectively titled *Capitalism and Schizophrenia*, Deleuze and Guattari identified a world where power was organized in nonlinear fashion, like botanical rhizomes, interconnected but without a core and without a periphery. These new capitalist arrangements, what Hardt and Negri called empire, meant that everyone was chained to a matrix—everyone was exploited—but no central power, no single nation, not even the United States, controlled the system. This kind of empire had displaced imperialist sovereignty. In such a world, resistance might have seemed futile, at least as a colonized people or as a working class. Yet another world was possible! A better world could be forged by the *multitude*, Hardt and Negri's term for a new agent of revolution. They contended that every form of resistance, no matter how small, made a difference. Every person was their own prince.[32]

Marx hardly seemed necessary to help make sense of the world depicted in *Empire*. Yet he was invoked time and again. The Marx in *Empire* was a weird one, residing somewhere between the academic Marx and the revolutionary version. Despite their fluency in academic argot, and despite their insistence that Marx's angel of history had fallen, Hardt and Negri traced their revolutionary optimism to Marx. In the 1970s, Negri had participated in the generational rethinking of basic Marxist categories. His 1979 book, *Marx Beyond Marx: Lessons on the Grundrisse*, argued that Marx himself had toyed with the idea of expanding the revolutionary subject beyond the classically defined working class to include a whole range of alienated people. At a time when workers were moving to the right, Negri found revolutionary hope in the dispossessed. The seeds of the multitude had been planted.[33]

Hardt and Negri invoked Marx's dialectical sensibilities as support for their belief that empire opens new avenues to liberation. "We claim," they wrote, "that Empire is better in the same way that Marx insists that capitalism is better than the forms of society and modes of production that came before it." Marx's "well grubbed old mole," a metaphor he used to describe working-class struggle in nineteenth-century Europe—a mole surfaces in times of conflict then submerges to dig new holes in preparation for the next contest—had been replaced by a snake. "Today's struggles slither silently," unable to communicate with one another. This might have seemed like a problem if communication was a prerequisite of solidarity, and solidarity a prerequisite of revolutionary organization. But for Hardt and Negri, communication was overrated. Since empire existed everywhere, since power dwelled at every node, empire was vulnerable anywhere. "Empire creates a greater potential for revolution than did the modern regimes of power because it presents us with an alternative: the set of all the exploited and the subjugated, a multitude that is directly opposed to Empire, with no mediation between them." Anybody, anytime, could become one with the multitude.[34]

Empire tossed aside left-wing pessimism. Unlike those academics who viewed Marx as a paradigm provider rather than as a rebel prophet, Hardt and Negri drew inspiration from the revolutionary Marx. Yet they believed capitalism had outlived the Marxist paradigm. Their Marx had been ripped from the material that made his ideas pertinent. *Empire* is a byproduct of the antiglobalization movement's detachment from working-class politics. Hardt and Negri's assumption that resistance anywhere strikes a tiny blow against the system was consistent with the Left's sporadic approach to organizing. As Gopal Balakrishnan wrote, this narrow idea of resistance owed to "the politics of the society of spectacle, in which the masses seek only the most immediate experiences of empowerment and agency, even if these are only ever episodic." *Empire* was written by professed Marxists. But its analysis was steeped in moral leftism.[35]

Hardt and Negri argued the masses migrating from poor to rich nations represented the potential power of the multitude. Because empire is heavily reliant on the productive capacities of a migrant labor force, even as it represses it, the migratory multitude has immense revolutionary potential. Balakrishnan scoffed at that notion, contending that "the desire to live, work and raise families in more affluent lands arguably finds its true manifesto in the inscription at the foot of the Statue of Liberty, holding out the promise of entirely prosaic freedoms." Balakrishnan dismissed *Empire* "as *The Lexus and the Olive Tree* of the Far Left," referencing the *New York Times* columnist Thomas Friedman's 1999 love letter to globalization. Hardt and Negri placed too much faith in their idea that countless tiny acts of resistance, even migration, would aggregate to a revolution from below. Such a notion was hardly less pie-in-the-sky than Friedman's preposterous fantasy that unleashing capitalism around the globe had empowered innumerable tiny actors. Neither the globalization of capitalism nor the globalization of a repressed multitude was a force for democratization.[36]

Yet *Empire* was exhilarating in a bleak time. Learned Marxists were announcing the world had never been riper for revolution. And in thrilling, manifesto-like prose! Hardt and Negri concluded their lengthy book by affirming "the irrepressible lightness and joy of being communist." Such "theoretical ecstasy," as Balakrishnan described it, was intoxicating, but Hardt and Negri's theories and prophesies have not stood the test of time. Their effort to join the pantheon of Marxist philosophy fell short. *Capital* is timeless, still; *Empire* is dated, already. Yet *Empire* is a telling artifact of that brief moment when the antiglobalization movement seemed like the antidote to neoliberalism.[37]

Empire is a revealing source for the history of Marx's American reception due less to its presentation of Marx and more to its rendering of *America*. Although Hardt and Negri are communists, their roadmap to achieving communism was arguably more reliant upon the American political tradition than it was on Marxism. Empire transitioned away from imperialism because its animating spirit was an outgrowth of the republicanism codified by the US Constitution. Harkening back to liberal intellectuals like Frederick Jackson Turner and Louis Hartz, Hardt and Negri argued the frontier enabled people to create lives free from the long-standing hierarchies that had shaped Europe. "Tocqueville and Marx, from opposite perspectives, agree on this point," they wrote. "American civil society does not develop within the heavy shackles of feudal and aristocratic power but starts off from a separate and very different foundation."[38]

As the American frontier swamped European traditions, before flooding the entire planet, empire overtook imperialism. More than that, the expansion of the American political tradition provided an opening for revolution. The postmodern equivalent of the frontier, found in recent patterns of human migration, called the multitude into existence. Hardt and Negri cited Hegel to support their claim that American republicanism was the key to unlocking a communist future. "America is the country of the future, and its world-historical importance has yet to be revealed in the ages which lie ahead," Hegel wrote. "It is the land of desire for all those who are weary of the historical arsenal of old Europe." Whereas most critics of capitalist globalization bemoaned the Americanization of the planet, Hardt and Negri welcomed it, all while dismissing the idea that the United States was an imperialist nation, much less *the* imperialist superpower. This was a curious position for left-wingers to take.[39]

AMERICAN IMPERIALISM STRIKES BACK

Hardt and Negri's notion that the United States had developed into something significantly different from the European imperialist powers was bound to blow up in their faces. The verdict came swiftly. A year after *Empire* was published, twenty-two members of Al-Qaeda, a militant Sunni Islamic organization led by Osama bin Laden, launched terrorist attacks on symbols of American imperialism: the World Trade Center and the Pentagon. The White House may well have been a target as well. Within weeks, the United States invaded Afghanistan, which had sheltered bin Laden, and soon thereafter declared a Global War on Terror. On March 20, 2003, the George W. Bush administration launched Operation Iraqi Freedom, kicking off a brutal and lengthy occupation of a nation that had nothing to do with the September 11 attacks.[40]

The invasion of Iraq might have led to a Marx renaissance. Many Americans had turned to Marx in the 1960s because Marxist accounts of imperialism helped make sense of the war against Vietnamese independence. The war on Iraq had similar trappings.[41]

Because Vietnam was not rich enough to plunder, that war required a sophisticated understanding of the link between capitalism and imperialism. In the 1960s, Marxist scholars like Harry Magdoff held that after the Second World War the United States sought to reverse the contraction of the imperial system, thus making Vietnamese independence a threat. In 2003, such nuance was not required. The crudest of all versions of Marxism pointed to oil, the crudest of all commodities, as the war's chief motivating factor. Iraq had massive oil reserves, the third largest in the world. On February 15, 2003, tens of millions of people in over six hundred cities around the world marched against the imminent war, many with the simple slogan "No blood for oil."[42]

Ensuing events did not disprove the blood-for-oil theory. Despite ample evidence that chaos would commence once the United States finished off longtime Iraqi dictator Saddam Hussein's regime, American military forces permitted widespread looting of all kinds. Yet they were extremely attentive to Iraqi oil reserves and somehow proved capable of defending the Iraqi Ministry of Oil.[43]

Oil had long shaped US foreign policy in the Middle East. In 1953, the Central Intelligence Agency helped orchestrate a coup in Iran after its democratically elected leader Mohammad Mosaddegh nationalized oil. Almost half a century later, an energy task force led by Vice President Dick Cheney reported that "Middle East oil producers will remain central to world oil security" and that the Persian Gulf region, including Iraq, would continue to "be a primary focus of U.S. international energy policy." Several years into the Iraq War, British Petroleum, Shell, and ExxonMobil negotiated deals with the Iraqi government for long-coveted access to the nation's oil reserves.[44]

Marx argued in *Capital* that the proven method for expanding capitalism's reach was to violently separate people from their means of subsistence. Marx called this theory primitive accumulation. The American occupation of Iraq was a case study of it. Thus, it might have been expected to lead to a Marx revival, especially since the antiglobalization movement had already planted the seeds. But Marx remained in the wilderness during much of the first decade of the twenty-first century. One reason for this had to do with the lack of a military draft. The threat of conscription awakened young Americans to the Vietnam War's larger context, leading many of them to explore critical perspectives, Marxism among them. But the draft ended in 1973. Soon after Bush sent his all-volunteer military into battle, the antiwar movement fizzled out.[45]

Beyond the particulars of the war, the American population was not primed for a Marx resurgence in 2003. In the 1960s, thanks to the inspiration of the civil rights movement, and as a result of disaffection with the repressive norms that permeated cold war American culture, lots of young people became amenable to radical change. In that context, Marx thrived. But when it came to flirting with revolutionary ideas during the early 2000s, most Americans were somewhere between lethargic and resistant. Even though the economic situation had dramatically worsened for most working Americans, the vast majority had yet to awaken from their neoliberal slumber. Nothing less than economic disaster would be required to shake people out of their torpor. And soon, they got one.

FINANCIAL MELTDOWN

On September 15, 2008, Lehman Brothers, the fourth-largest investment firm in the United States, filed the country's biggest ever Chapter Eleven petition. After several turbulent months for financial markets, the Lehman Brothers bankruptcy represented the climax of a crisis with global implications. Although Lehman Brothers was the only large firm the US government allowed to fail, it was not the only one in distress. In less than a year, several major banks and financial institutions, including Bear Stearns, American International Group (AIG), Countrywide Insurance, Goldman Sachs, Citigroup, Bank of America, and Morgan Stanley all verged on insolvency. The government intervened to save them by insuring bad loans, facilitating acquisitions, bailing them out directly, and in the case of AIG, nationalizing the company.[46]

The origins of the global financial crisis appeared proximate. Due to an overinflated housing bubble that finally popped, big firms were overleveraged with toxic assets. Although this short-term cause was noteworthy, the meltdown was ultimately the result of an unsound economic structure decades in the making. Few people seemed to recognize the problem before it was too late, including former Federal Reserve chairman Alan Greenspan, who admitted he was "partially wrong" to be confident in the neoliberal system he helped construct. To Americans who benefited from neoliberal arrangements, many of whom were largely oblivious to rapidly rising inequality, the economy appeared on sound footing. There seemed enough jobs for anyone who wanted one (never mind their deteriorating quality). Moreover, American companies took the lead in cutting-edge industries like digital technology, which enriched lots of well-positioned people. A favorable investment climate ensured a booming stock market for much of the 1980s and 1990s. For the richest 1 percent, and even for the 10 percent lucky enough to have well-compensated jobs, there was no better time to be an American. But a thriving bourgeoisie did not guarantee a stable economy. In fact, the opposite is often true, as Marx knew well.[47]

Several factors made the crisis nearly inevitable. First, the economic center of gravity had profoundly shifted away from heavy industries like steel and automobile production, and toward finance. At the behest of financial service firms, especially credit card companies, the Reagan administration repealed anti-usury laws that had forbidden hyperexploitative interest rates. At the moment when workers needed credit more than ever to maintain a standard of living, companies began charging as much as 50 percent interest on services previously capped at 10 percent. These escalating rates translated into soaring profits for financial firms. In response, excess capital, of which there was no shortage, shifted from the manufacturing to the financial sector, from Detroit to Wall Street.[48]

With more profits came more power over government. Lobbying vigorously for deregulation of all kinds, the financial industry struck gold in 1999 when the Clinton administration overturned key aspects of Glass-Steagall, legislation passed in 1933 to prohibit bank-holding companies from owning other financial firms. The reason for this was simple. The federal government appointed itself the insurer of last resort for low-risk financial activity, such as simple bank deposits, so people had reassurance that their life's savings would not disappear during a run on a bank. In turn, the Roosevelt administration built a wall between banks and financial service firms, since their combination inexorably led companies to use safe, insurable deposits to bolster unsafe investment portfolios. The repeal of this prohibition generated incentives for risky behavior.[49]

Newly enlarged banks and financial firms began probing for ways to invest the enormous amounts of cash now at their disposal. Wall Street developed newfangled methods for growing revenue. After the rapid rise and fall of internet companies—after the dot-com bubble burst in early 2000—capitalists returned to real estate, that reliably lucrative repository of excess capital. This was a strategy Henry George would have recognized. After the housing market began cooking, banks aggressively inked people to mortgages, including those with little chance of paying them off. Predatory lending became standard practice. Hundreds of thousands, mostly poor Americans, were deceived into taking out subprime loans, affordable for the first few years but impossible to repay once exorbitant balloon payments came due. Banks shielded themselves from the risk presented by subprime mortgages by selling them off to financial institutions like Lehman Brothers, which packaged them for sale on international securities markets. Due to the colossal scale of the whole scheme, to the tune of trillions of dollars, no single financial institution thought itself at risk. They were only partially wrong.[50]

When millions of Americans defaulted on their loans, banks and financial institutions owed ungodly amounts of money to hedge funds, which bet on losses by investing heavily in a derivatives market that shadowed the securities market. The global economy was operating like a giant casino; the entire capitalist system hung in the balance. Millions of American families suffered the hardship and indignity of being evicted from their homes. Yet thanks to the Troubled Assets Relief Program, passed by Congress and signed into law by George W. Bush at the tail end of his presidency, most of the companies at fault were rescued. Citigroup alone received $350 billion in stock buyouts and assets guarantees. Marx's renowned statement that "the executive of the modern state is but a committee for managing the common affairs of the whole bourgeoisie" rang true—yet again. Or to extend the casino analogy, the house always wins. The timing was right for the fourth Marx boom in America.[51]

THE FOURTH MARX BOOM

As the financial crisis spiraled out of control, triggering a steep rise in unemployment, which in one year doubled from 5 to 10 percent, conventional economic wisdom grew increasingly stale. Americans began looking elsewhere for answers. Some found right-wing voices to sooth (or amplify!) their fear and anger. Ayn Rand's 1957 novel *Atlas Shrugged*, which extolled the virtues of selfishness as an antidote to soul-sucking government bureaucracy, enjoyed brisk sales. A conservative movement calling itself the Tea Party emerged to challenge the bailouts and most other forms of government spending. The Tea Party movement hardly represented a challenge to neoliberalism. It was banked by rich and powerful patrons, and it found its stride as the conduit for opposition to Obamacare, President Barack Obama's market-based attempt to make the nation's private healthcare system more accessible to tens of millions of uninsured Americans. Rather, the Tea Party was an angrier version of the economic vision Reagan and Clinton had successfully sold.[52]

Conservative expressions were not the only ones available to Americans who needed words for their discontent. More than a few found Marx. By late 2008, sales of *The Communist Manifesto* on Amazon had increased by over 700 percent. *Capital* also began flying off the proverbial shelves. The old Rhinelander reentered mainstream discourse. Marx, in the words of the historian Timothy Shenk, seemed "original, and daring, to those without a background in Marxism, which happens to include the overwhelming majority of American journalists." The Marxist political scientist Leo Panitch wrote that "Marx had premonitions of AIG and Bear Stearns trembling a century and a half later." Panitch had taken poetic license. But given how flabbergasted mainstream economic commentators were by the extent of the emergency, he can be forgiven. He was correct that Marx would have viewed the 2008 crisis as a case study in the cascading destructiveness of capitalism, like "the sorcerer who is no longer able to control the powers of the netherworld whom he has called up by his spells." Francis Wheen predicted that Marx "could yet become the most influential thinker of the twenty-first century."[53]

Alongside new interest in Marx, the financial collapse spawned a movement against neoliberal capitalism. Kalle Lasn, publisher of *Adbusters*, a glossy anticapitalist magazine, issued a call to demonstrate against the financial institutions that had shattered so many lives. On September 17, 2011, thousands of radicals set up camp in Zuccotti Park, a small public square a few blocks from Wall Street. Occupy Wall Street's slogan, "we are the 99 percent," caught fire, as did the implication that the "1 percent" were to blame for the Great Recession. Activists around the world set up similar public encampments. Their efforts lodged economic inequality firmly in the headlines.[54]

Critics contended Occupy Wall Street failed to exploit its sudden notoriety by refusing to forward a policy-specific agenda. The lack of an explicit program might have owed to the fact that most of the movement's organizers, including the renowned anthropologist David Graeber, were anarchists. Occupy observed a nonhierarchical, consensus-driven decision-making process that seemingly led to paralysis. Indeed, when the New York Police Department cleared Zuccotti Park on November 15, 2011, the movement was incapable of highlighting any tangible victories. But thanks to it, class struggle was back, or at least, class anger was shaping political conversation once again. The words the movement used to depict neoliberal class arrangements, pitting the masses of the "99 percent" against a malicious "1 percent," echoed distant rumbles of a valiant proletariat struggling against a vampiric bourgeoisie.[55]

Occupy Wall Street created an opening for left-wing intellectual life unlike any since the 1960s. There was heightened interest in the work of a host of leftist thinkers, including Naomi Klein, arguably the most prominent intellectual of the antiglobalization movement, and Slavoj Žižek, the controversial Slovenian who brought Marx, Hegel, and the French psychoanalyst Jacques Lacan to bear on contemporary political culture. Graeber's 2011 book, *Debt: The First 5,000 Years*, which argued debt had long shaped institutional forms of hierarchy, became something of a bible to the young Occupy activists enchained by student loans. The return of class analysis also brought attention to Marxists. David Harvey, long renowned in left-wing academic circles as an innovative Marxist geographer, gained fame beyond the ivory tower.[56]

AMERICA'S TEACHER OF MARX

Born and educated in Great Britain, Harvey moved to Baltimore in the summer of 1969 to teach at Johns Hopkins University. In search of a framework to make sense of turbulent times, he began teaching an informal course on Marx's *Capital*, a class he has offered ever since. Harvey's popular *Capital* lectures are now downloadable as videos and podcast episodes. He has likely taught more Americans how to read Marx than anyone else in the long history of Marx reception.[57]

Listening to Harvey speak about *Capital* is exciting. His passion for its merits is contagious. In Harvey's view, Marx's magnum opus remains relevant because it persists in helping readers unravel the tangled workings of capitalism. *Capital* also remains valuable as a masterful literary construction. Harvey advises students to "have a good time talking to the text and letting it talk to you." He takes his own advice by affectionately ridiculing Marx for his "modest" claim to being the first to ever think about certain things. In contrast, Harvey humbly asserts that he learns something new every time he reads Marx's rich text. He also admits to learning from his students. Harvey jokes about the time he offered his *Capital* course to an English department during the heyday of Derrida. Determined to deconstruct every last word, his pupils never ventured beyond the first chapter, a teaching experience he found both edifying and exasperating.[58]

In Harvey's reading of *Capital*, Marx invented a method of analysis that digs beneath the surface of things to uncover root concepts, an approach that enabled Marx to situate everyday experience in a larger structural apparatus. Harvey makes this point to help students grasp Marx's peculiar method of exposition, which demands a high degree of patience. Marx did not organize his thoughts in the "brick-by-brick" style to which twenty-first century readers are accustomed. Marx's unfolding of his system was more akin to peeling an onion. Eventually readers arrive at the core lesson, but Marx did not offer signposts along the way. In this, *Capital* epitomizes Marx's dialectical method. Just as *Capital* the text locates meaning in the transitions, capital the unit of wealth is a process. Marx does not dwell on conclusions because capitalism is constantly in motion. When capital stops moving, the system is thrown into crisis. But even that is not an end, so to speak.[59]

Crises of capitalism tend to exacerbate misery. But crises also create revolutionary opportunity, which is why Marxists have long studied the boom-and-bust cycle of capitalism as a potential roadmap to socialism. Marx empowered this prophetic imagination with some of his more optimistic theoretical longings. As Mike Davis wrote, "It was Marx's

brilliant insight that the spiral of the business cycle periodically opens
and closes the possibilities for proletarian advance." But Harvey contends *Capital* does not leave much room for revolutionary hope since
the point at which capital seemingly reaches an impasse represents the
unfolding of another layer, or a new tension to overcome. Capital, for
Marx, is "perpetually on the road," as Harvey words it. Contradictions
do not indicate an end but rather a new beginning.[60]

Harvey's exhaustive knowledge of Marx positioned him to offer a
resounding explanation of the 2008 financial collapse. His 2010 book
The Enigma of Capital and the Crises of Capitalism, a sweeping examination
of what he calls the "mother of all crises," uses Marx's theory of the
motion-crisis dialectic to determine the roots of the catastrophe. Harvey argues Marx was correct that crises are integral to the operation of
capitalism. Each new crisis seemingly pushes capitalism to the precipice. And yet, the genius of capitalism is that it grows from its mistakes.
As Harvey puts it, crises are "the irrational rationalizers of an always
unstable capitalism."[61]

A crisis of capitalism occurs, according to Harvey, when a surplus
of capital and a surplus of labor exist with "seemingly no way to put
them back together." He uses the Great Depression as an example. After a decade of immense capital accumulation *and* extraordinary labor
productivity, the formula for the unprecedented economic boom of the
1920s, the system went off the rails. Rising economic inequality generated an imbalance between production and consumption which in turn
spawned a situation where both factories and workers sat idle. Millions
of lives were then devastated. But out of the ashes, a bigger, more productive regime of capitalist production arose like a phoenix. Perhaps
something similar was on the horizon after the 2008 collapse? Harvey
knew which nineteenth-century communist philosopher to look to on
this question. The "situation today," he wrote, "may be far closer than
ever before to that which Marx described."[62]

Harvey learned from Marx that "capital cannot abide limits." As
the bearded old communist phrased it: "Every limit appears as a barrier to be overcome." Harvey relies heavily on this nugget of wisdom
in his analysis of the 2008 crisis. Barriers to capital accumulation had

popped up all over the place in the previous forty years. Understanding these obstacles, the crises they caused, and how capital worked to overcome them is the key to comprehending the financial collapse.[63]

Between the end of the Second World War and the 1970s, capitalism experienced a golden age. Crises were few and far between and those that did surface were relatively manageable. But since then, crises have rocked capitalism with increasing frequency and escalating intensity. This is because, according to Harvey, capitalism has struggled since the 1970s to grow at a 3 percent rate, the historical threshold for avoiding a crisis. Such modest growth has proven challenging because most of the world is now part of the capitalist system, creating unprecedented spatial constraints on profitability. Harvey the geographer writes that "only substantial zones of Africa, though thoroughly ravaged by exploitation of their natural resources, along with remote usually interior regions of Asia and Latin America, have yet to be fully colonized by capital accumulation." Capitalism's planetary saturation has limited its capacity to grow at a crisis-proof rate. In response, capitalists have returned to the tried-and-true method of capital accumulation. They have devised better ways of exploiting the proletariat, to ensure workers are "accessible, socialized, disciplined and of the requisite qualities (i.e. flexible, docile, manipulable and skilled when necessary)."[64]

American capitalists were doubly motivated to clamp down on the American working class because international competition cut into their accustomed levels of profits. The problem with the postwar working class was that it had yet to be disciplined to accept austerity. American workers had come to expect too much, in terms of high wages, expensive benefits, generous pension plans, and job security. Capitalists solved their labor problem with, in Harvey's words, "a combination of political repression (including the collapse of communist regimes), technological changes, the heightened capacity for capital mobility and a massive wave of primitive accumulation in (and migration from) formerly peripheral zones." Capital overcame the spatial barrier to accumulation by chastening the working class. This was the crux of neoliberalism.[65]

Harvey focuses on the condition of the working class in his analy-

SPECTER HAUNTING   481

sis, yet he also understands that there are countless potential barriers to the flow of capital. A crisis of capitalism has many possible causes. "When one limit is overcome accumulation often hits up against another somewhere else." For example, whereas the power of labor engendered a crisis in the 1970s, Harvey writes that "these days the main problem lies in the fact that capital is too powerful and labor too weak." With labor power enfeebled, consumer power tumbled. Surplus capital and surplus labor grew apart yet again, with "seemingly no way to put them back together." Efforts by capitalists, Harvey writes, "to alleviate a crisis of labor supply and to curb the political power of organized labor in the 1970s diminished the effective demand for product, which created difficulties for realization of the surplus in the market during the 1990s."[66]

Attempts to overcome weakened consumer demand led to the extension of credit. As Harvey reminds us again, capitalism's "crisis tendencies are not resolved but merely moved around." Financialization, or increased leverage, was the new magic pill. "It was almost as if the banking community had retired into the penthouse of capitalism," Harvey writes, "where they manufactured oodles of money by trading and leveraging among themselves without any mind whatsoever for what the working people living in the basement were doing." Of course, capitalists did ultimately care about the conditions of working people, not out of concern for their welfare but rather because they wanted to keep them subordinate. They were more than happy to extend credit to workers, pitched as a mechanism to reclaim their standard of living in the short run even as, given exorbitant interest rates, it was an instrument of deprivation in the long run. But wages were to remain low no matter what. An untenable mixture of "over-indebtedness relative to income," according to Harvey, prompted a new barrier to capital accumulation in the form of "a crisis of confidence in the quality of debt instruments." This deadly combination of high debt and low pay wrecked the economy.[67]

Well before 2008, uncertainty about an overleveraged market drove capitalists to invest in housing. According to Harvey, ground rent—land, property, housing—is the investment of choice for staving off a crisis because it is a form of fictitious capital. "Like all such forms of fictitious capital," Harvey writes, "what is traded is a claim on future revenues." But sinking capital into ground rent cannot keep a crisis at bay forever. Moreover, crises stemming from investments in the built environment are typically worse and longer-lasting than those that emerge from the stock market because they tend to be "credit based, high-risk and long in the making." Harvey was spot-on about the aftershocks of the 2008 collapse. The Great Recession was long lasting, especially for the millions of people burned by a predatory housing bubble. The irrational rationalizers of an always unstable capitalism, indeed.[68]

Harvey's lifelong engagement with Marx made him one of the early twenty-first century's greatest scholars of capitalism. He was seventy-five years old when *The Enigma of Capital* hit bookshelves. Yet Harvey's Marx-dependent interpretations made him an indispensable resource for a younger generation of newly committed left-wingers clawing their way onto the American political scene.

MILLENNIAL SOCIALISM

For prospective young leftists, 2008 might have convinced them capitalism was rotten. And Occupy Wall Street might have persuaded them they could build a movement. But, as the labor historian Kim Moody insists, longer-term transformations to the makeup of the working class are what cultivated a context for radicalization. While many well-paid blue-collar jobs were being replaced by low-wage service work, many highly coveted white-collar jobs were being diminished in terms of both compensation and conditions. The so-called middle class, the demographic backbone of American prosperity since the Second World War, underwent proletarianization. Young people in the twenty-first century, college-educated or not, joined a labor market designed to make their lives precarious. The millennial generation came to view capitalism with cynicism. Many young people became leftists, forming what has come to be known as millennial socialism.[69]

One of the hallmarks of millennial socialism is its hatred for liberalism. When young leftists think about liberalism, they do not reflect upon Franklin Roosevelt or the New Deal. That version of the Democratic Party is dead to them. When millennial socialists judge liberalism, they are actually evaluating *neoliberalism*. "Much of the culture of twenty-first century socialism is not Marxist in any doctrinaire sense," the historian Tim Jelfs writes, but it does distinguish "leftism from an American liberalism that has in recent decades, and especially since the financial crisis of 2007–2008, failed to deliver any prospect of a more prosperous, healthy, or materially and ecologically sustainable future for many Americans." The young Left's anger at liberalism is understandable. Ever since the Clinton administration, the Democratic Party has done little to mitigate the damages wrought by neoliberal capitalism, and has in fact helped lay waste to the New Deal state that kept capitalism in check.[70]

Yet Marxism is something of an afterthought for many young leftists. The act of referring to Marx is often, as Jelfs puts it, "merely gestural." On May 5, 2018, the two hundredth anniversary of Marx's birthday, millennial socialists flocked to social media to signal their piety to the long-dead philosopher. *Teen Vogue*, which turned leftward following the election of Donald Trump, published an article providing context for the viral outbreak of communist memes. The reporter interviewed the historian George Ciccariello-Maher, who said that Marx's dialectical approach teaches us that "history moves forward not slowly or gradually or bit by bit, but it moves forward through the sort of crushing blows of struggles between generally two opposing ideas or groups or concepts or people." But to older liberals, the idea that *Teen Vogue* finds it necessary to explain Karl Marx offers more proof that millennial socialism is the political equivalent of a toddler's tantrum. Immature young leftists need to accept that liberal capitalism is the best humans can do.[71]

Reducing millennial socialism to a generational tantrum ignores the fact that many young Americans have been pushed leftward by deeply entrenched historical pressures. It also overlooks the equally salient detail that plenty of young leftists engage with Marx and the Marxist tradition in serious fashion. Their interpretations possess generational inflections, of course. But the presence of the old Rhinelander in millennial socialist discourse often runs deeper than the merely gestural. The novelist Benjamin Kunkel, another rare Gen X Marxist, celebrates "a revival of Marxist thought, which might loosely be defined as the collective effort to contemplate capitalism as a whole." Perhaps no venue exemplifies this better than *Jacobin*, a magazine founded in 2010 by the millennial socialist Bhaskar Sunkara.[72]

Jacobin first made its name by picking fights with liberals, including then President Barack Obama. In its third issue, published in 2011, the magazine editorialized that "Obama, and the Democrats generally, have made themselves the instruments of an energized and revanchist ruling class which has seized a moment of economic dislocation and working class disarray to roll back the meager but long-hated social protections of the New Deal and Great Society."[73]

Many young socialists relish the fact that their mere existence annoys liberals. Nobody has done more to represent the churlish side of millennial socialism than the various hosts of the popular podcast Chapo Trap House, who have transformed the act of ridiculing liberalism into comedic art. Founded in March 2016, the show routinely mocks "lizard-brain" conservatives like Trump, but its popularity largely owes to its presentation of liberalism as a cartoonish ideology of ineffectual morons. And yet, more than a hint of Marxism underwrites Chapo's overarching disposition.[74]

At first blush, the most obvious model for Chapo's iteration of left-wing theatrics is the absurdist branch of the 1960s New Left, young activists who also derided their liberal elders. Chapo could easily be mistaken for the Internet Age version of the Youth International Party—the Yippies—who, among other high-jinks, in 1968 playfully advanced a pig for president and advocated group joint-rolling and nude "grope-ins" for peace. On occasion, the Yippies proclaimed themselves Marxists. But they rarely demonstrated engagement with Marx or the Marxist tradition. Their Marxism was merely gestural, or what Hoffman called "Groucho Marxist." The Chapo leftists, in contrast, combine Groucho Marxism with Karl Marxism. This mixture is evident in their 2018 book, *The Chapo Guide to Revolution*, a survey of "the blasted landscape of contemporary American politics and culture through our scientific ideology of irony, half-baked Marxism, revolutionary discipline . . . and posting on the internet."[75]

Coming online in the midst of the 2016 presidential campaign, Chapo launched a scorched-earth rhetorical onslaught against Hillary Clinton and her fellow neoliberals. To Chapo, the role of Clinton Democrats is to administer the decline of the New Deal, not fight for its expansion. Instead of advocating for universal healthcare, Democrats passed Obamacare, a less effective, market-based solution. Instead of helping launch a working-class movement to benefit the masses, the Democratic Party ethos is technocratic and meritocratic. Chapo dedicated an episode to lambasting *The West Wing*, Aaron Sorkin's popular television show that fetishized the liberal view that a smart, dedicated, anti-ideological elite will save the world from right-wing Neanderthals. Chapo contends this is a naive understanding of politics that ignores the crucial role of power. *The West Wing* perspective poisoned the liberal American mind, thus facilitating right-wing domination.[76]

Because Chapo is unrelenting in its rhetorical attacks on liberalism, its hosts have been described as nihilists. Yet these accusations confuse Chapo's mean-spiritedness with a lack of concern. "I'm a Marxist," host Amber A'Lee Frost declares. "You can't be a Marxist and a nihilist at the same time." When Chapo mercilessly mocks the capitalist ethos, which celebrates leisure for the rich while advocating humility for the poor, the show is demonstrating not sociopathy but rather a Marxist concern for human dignity.[77]

Something similar can be said for *Jacobin*. Despite sticking to script in its relentless assault on liberalism, Sunkara's magazine has published volumes of articles that promote Marxism as a positive program. And unlike the esoteric Marxism found in the avant-garde academic journals of the 1980s, *Jacobin* is maximally accessible, in two ways. First, its articles are written in language that most educated readers of English can comprehend. Second, *Jacobin* invites people into its circle by seeking to avoid left-wing sectarianism. Such an approach does not please everyone. But it has been largely successful.[78]

Jacobin published an article in 2012 by the historian Robin Blackburn that exemplified its populist approach. "Lincoln and Marx" patiently told the story of Marx exchanging letters with the Lincoln administration, making the larger point that both men were revolutionaries worthy of imitation. They had different ideas about the relationship between capitalism and the good life, of course. Lincoln held to a republicanism in which the abolition of slavery would unleash a free world of masterless men within capitalism. Marx, in contrast, thought freedom ultimately depended on smashing capitalism. But, Blackburn argued, both dreams died violent deaths when Northern capitalists united with Southern planters to butcher Reconstruction. "The defeat of Lincoln's vision of a unified, democratic, and authoritative republic was a defeat for the socialists too," Blackburn wrote. Socialism had much greater potential for growth in a Lincolnian free republic than in a plutocracy. With this article and many more, *Jacobin* has given millennial socialists a taste of the political world that shaped Marx's thought.[79]

Jacobin's program is to teach young leftists how to use Marxist ideas to advance socialist political power. Sunkara offers a lengthy elaboration of this project in his 2019 book, *The Socialist Manifesto: The Case for Radical Politics in an Era of Extreme Inequality*. According to Jelfs, Sunkara's book drafts a blueprint for a socialism "in which Marx is a distant founding figure, of significant symbolic value, but not all that dominant in relation to more proximate political concerns such as lack of healthcare, stable employment, and the already unfolding climate catastrophe." Jelfs is not entirely wrong in this characterization. Indeed, Sunkara argues leftists should support social democratic reforms like universal healthcare since they would profoundly improve the lives of working people. He also contends robust social democracies like those in the Scandinavian countries are the best societies humans have yet to realize. And yet, to overemphasize the book's reformism is to understate the subtle poignancy of Marx's presence in it.[80]

Sunkara reflects in the preface that, as a middle-class immigrant kid, he "found radicalism through books." Among the writers who most influenced him were Leon Trotsky, Michael Harrington, "and eventually the mysterious Karl Marx himself." Sunkara roots his vision of a socialist future in a usable past shot through with Marx. His book's concise narrative of capitalism, "that accident of history," is indebted to Marx and a host of Marxist scholars. Capitalism at its origin, Sunkara writes, "had conjured a dangerous combination: immense, lucrative industries and a deprived and discontented class of people locked within them." Sunkara is of two minds about capitalism because even though its emergence generated lots of misery, it also brought about the advent of socialist dreams. An epoch defined by vast concentrations of wealth alongside a massive new class of exploited people "was the reality," he wrote, "in which Marxist theory was first constructed."[81]

The Socialist Manifesto includes a lively synopsis of *The Communist Manifesto*, "debated and scrutinized like no other work since the Bible." Sunkara marvels that *The Communist Manifesto*—written by "one of history's great partnerships," the "Jordan and Pippen" of socialist theory—was so prescient about capitalism's propensity to dissolve "all fixed, fast-frozen relations, with their train of ancient and venerable prejudices and opinions." Marx and Engels, he writes, sketched "a better description, perhaps, of what capitalism has accomplished by 2018 than of its record in 1848." That is, its legacy has far outstripped its original purpose because it endowed the world with functional definitions of capitalism, a system in which one class of people constantly transforms social relations in order to better exploit another class, and communism, "an association in which the free development of each is the condition for the free development of all." The immense reach of *The Communist Manifesto* is a product of it being the first socialist text in favor of "galloping forward alongside modernity."[82]

The Socialist Manifesto contemplates how to have a socialist revolution in an ultracapitalist nation like the United States. Sunkara writes that "Marxism provided a framework for understanding why reforms won within capitalism were so hard to sustain and why there was so much suffering in societies filled with abundance." Capitalism constantly threatens hard-won social democratic victories. This is why Sunkara proposes organizing for social democratic reforms in the immediate future while targeting socialist revolution in the long run. Social democracy is both a good in itself, *and* a steppingstone to a more ambitious endpoint. Sunkara's twist is his belief that the inevitable capitalist backlash against social democracy will heighten class consciousness among workers and thus encourage them to build a more thoroughly anticapitalist society.[83]

Sunkara is not the first Marxist hoping to transcend the age-old division between reform and revolution. In this he follows Michael Harrington, one of his intellectual heroes. He also takes his cues from Marx, who "thought socialism came from the struggle of workers, not the plans of a few intellectuals," and who embraced some reforms, such as laws that limited the working day. Sunkara likewise promotes working-class empowerment. In this he walks the "perilous tightrope" that Harrington warned American socialists must travel, in which they remain "true to a socialist vision of a new society" while bringing "that vision into contact with the actual movements fighting not to transform the system, but to gain some little increment of dignity or even just a piece of bread." *Jacobin* stood ready to join, and perhaps gently nudge, any movement for working-class dignity. Luckily, in the wake of Occupy Wall Street, several movements were in the works.[84]

The first movement of consequence to emerge after Sunkara founded *Jacobin* in 2010, and after Occupy Wall Street in 2011, was the Fight for $15, a campaign aiming to raise the federal minimum wage from seven to fifteen dollars an hour. Started in 2012 by fast-food workers in New York City, the Fight for $15 built momentum over the next several years with strikes in a range of industries, from restaurant to retail and healthcare to childcare to higher education. In this, the Fight for $15 represents the chronically unorganized, or "the reserve army of labor," those whose mere presence in the labor market disciplines less exploited workers to get in line. It is the type of reform movement that Marx supported in his lifetime.[85]

Jacobin has striven to transform the Fight for $15 from a movement seeking to secure "dignity or even just a piece of bread," into one that is "true to a socialist vision of a new society." With this goal in view, *Jacobin* published an interview with the labor organizer Jane McAlevey in 2015 that was critical of the movement's approach. According to McAlevey, the campaign had concentrated on mobilizing, a strategy orchestrated by a media firm hired by the Service Employees International Union, to the detriment of organizing, which requires conversations with actual workers. Mobilization is inadequate, she contended, because it merely rounds up support from those who already agree with the cause. In contrast, organizing is designed to grow the movement. Organizing along class lines is effective in particular because it connects people who might otherwise disagree but who share views about economic justice. Such organizing is a necessary precursor to nurturing socialist sensibilities among the masses. As the Fight for $15 began to focus its energies on organizing, *Jacobin* was there to document its successes, including a victory by Seattle airport workers.[86]

Jacobin was also there when Senator Bernie Sanders, the Fight for $15's most enthusiastic advocate among national politicians, ran for president in 2016 and again in 2020. Millennial socialists supported the Sanders campaigns, and *Jacobin* led the charge, publishing hundreds of articles about the self-described socialist's quixotic quest for the White House.

Jacobin saw the Sanders campaign as possibly "a way for socialists to regroup, organize together, and articulate the kind of politics that speaks to the needs and aspirations of the vast majority of people." The socialist magazine also believed the septuagenarian's run for president might "begin to legitimate the word 'socialist,' and spark a conversation around it." In due time, *Jacobin* and millennial socialists came to adore Sanders. In a vacuum, this might have been surprising, given he was essentially a New Deal Democrat in socialist clothing. But, compared to the Democratic Party's neoliberalism, Sanders seemed like Eugene Debs. Whereas Hillary Clinton floated the possibility of watering down Obamacare as a concession to right-wing opposition, Sanders demanded universal healthcare and yelled at corporations standing in the way. In short, Sanders is a class warrior. "If there is going to be class warfare in this country," he posted to Twitter in 2019, "it's about time the working class won that war." By launching a rhetorical attack on billionaires, he heightened the stakes of the political moment.[87]

Sanders had surprising success. In 2016 he finished a close second to Clinton. The Brooklyn-accented Jew became a folk hero to millen-

nial socialists, an avatar for their Marx-soaked hopes and dreams.
When reports surfaced early in his first campaign that "socialism" had
become the most searched word on the internet, and that a majority
of young Americans preferred socialism to capitalism, left-wing optimism reached a frenzied pitch. Then when liberal elites responded with
open hostility, and worse still, when the Democratic Party establishment organized to thwart his chances, a hopeful mood soured.[88]

The historian Matt Karp's lengthy 2020 postmortem documented
how Democratic elites conspired to crush Sanders and how the capitalist press granted powerful liberals unlimited airtime to criticize him.
"Sanders lost," Karp bitterly wrote, using the Civil War as an analogy.
"He waged a five-year war against the billionaire class and the Democratic Party's leadership—a war across six Aprils—and in the end, he
was beaten on both fronts." Bernie's defeat taught millennial socialists a lesson Marx learned from the 1848 revolutions. Powerful liberals,
as members of the capitalist elite, will go to much greater lengths to
trounce a socialist insurgency than they will to slow down advances by
reactionaries. Sanders was viewed as more threatening to the status
quo than Donald Trump.

Karp's article also diagnosed the shortcomings of the Sanders campaign, including its unfulfilled promise to inspire millions of alienated
working-class Americans to vote. That Sanders failed to improve turn-
out among chronic nonvoters was proof, Karp wrote, "that a social-
democratic majority does not yet exist." Yet the Sanders campaign also
showed that "bold social-democratic ideas" are popular. Karp saw the
Sanders campaigns as a starting point, showing socialist ideas could
find a large audience. But they also showed socialism will not build
itself.[89]

Out of the ashes of the Sanders campaigns, many young leftists
joined the Democratic Socialists of America (DSA), fashioning the
largely moribund organization into a vehicle for millennial socialism.
Prior to 2016, DSA had five thousand members and a median age of
sixty-eight. By 2021, it had over ninety thousand members and a median age of thirty-three. The newly invigorated organization pushes
for social democratic reforms that would reduce the power of capital-

ists and improve the lives of workers. DSA also follows the premise of its founder Michael Harrington, who believed organizing for social democratic policies would ignite a class struggle that might eventually propel a mass movement against capitalism. DSA and *Jacobin* are cut from the same ideological and demographic cloth. Together they form the backbone of millennial socialism.[90]

As part of its broad-based strategy to bring socialism to the United States, DSA also dedicates time and energy to educational outreach, which includes offering Marx lessons. DSA sponsors talks by Marx scholars like Hadas Thier, known for her popular "Marxism in a Minute" videos on YouTube, including "What is Marxist Economics?" and "What is the Labor Theory of Value?" Its efforts to promote Marx place DSA firmly in the tradition of socialist political organizations dating to the nineteenth century. It is also another instance of DSA following the approach of Harrington, who believed Marx's work was "more relevant today than when he wrote *Das Kapital*." Millennial socialism is a political formation of young activists whose understanding of Marx is refracted through a lens provided by Harrington.[91]

DSA is not a conventional party. It does not run candidates in elections. But as it has grown, an increasing number of DSA members have been elected to office as Democrats. This includes five US representatives, counting Alexandria Ocasio-Cortez. DSA has cultivated a strong presence in New York City and Chicago, where several of its members have been elected to city offices. But its reach is not limited to large northern cities. In 2021, a DSA slate took control of the Nevada Democratic Party. The organization melds traditional working-class concerns like declining unions with existential unease about global warming. DSA successfully campaigned for the Build Public Renewables Act (BPRA), which became a New York state law in 2023. In addition to reducing energy costs for low-income consumers and bolstering the unionized workforce at utility companies, the BPRA also sets 2030 as the deadline for all public facilities in the state to run on renewable energy. DSA members like Ocasio-Cortez have been some of the foremost advocates of the Green New Deal, a proposed federal legislation package that would transition the nation's energy system away from fossil fuels while also creating well-paying jobs to build clean energy infrastructure.[92]

MARXIST ECOLOGY

Socialists are not alone in being anxious about global warming. As oceans rise, deserts expand, glaciers melt, and wildfires rage, people holding a variety of perspectives have been on edge. But the socialist viewpoint on climate change highlights the tight connection between global warming and capitalism. The principal reason the planet is warming at a potentially cataclysmic rate is because humans have been burning fossil fuels, which socialists argue is a byproduct of capitalism. The field of Marxist ecology has emerged in the last two decades to scrutinize the bond between capitalism and global warming.

Monthly Review has become the go-to venue for the field, thanks to John Bellamy Foster, a sociologist who was named coeditor in 2000, the year his groundbreaking book *Marx's Ecology* was published. There, Foster examined Marx's neglected writings about nature to argue for Marx's concern for ecology. For Marx, according to Foster, the dichotomy that has shaped the modern understanding of the relationship between humanity and the environment, that humans are to history as land is to nature, is false. Rather the relationship between humans and land is dialectical in that both are subject to history *and* nature. "To say that man's physical and mental life is linked to nature," Marx wrote "simply means that nature is linked to itself, for man is a part of nature." This, for Marx, was the materialist way of understanding humans in nature. In *Marx's Ecology*, Foster wanted to persuade environmentalists to be more materialist. Environmentalists had tended to argue that materialist analyses ignore human agency. In Marx's view, since humans and the environment evolve alongside each other, human agency is vital. If humanity is to survive, humans *must* be the agents who slow down global warming. Humans started the fire; they must be the ones to put it out.[93]

The concept that humanity and nature are locked in a dialectical struggle animates the new Marxist environmental history, a close cousin to Marxist ecology, best represented by the Swedish author Andreas Malm and his pioneering 2016 book *Fossil Capital: The Rise of Steam Power and the Roots of Global Warming*. The very first sentence of Malm's book is "Global warming is the unintended by-product par excellence." What he means is that global warming originated alongside the emergence of steam power in eighteenth-century England and therefore alongside the intensification of capitalism.[94]

Capitalism has constantly relied upon a compliant labor force, and so capitalists have constantly invented methods for disciplining them. Early capitalists, Malm writes, "fought the annoying idiosyncrasies of human workers precisely by installing ever more machinery impelled by ever more powerful steam engines, unsuspecting of any particular noxious effects." Prior to the invention of steam power, protocapitalists typically located production near rivers, since naturally rushing water was one of the only workable nonhuman sources of power. Steam power endowed capitalists with more control over labor since they could relocate production to wherever larger, more profitable pools of surplus labor existed. In this way, steam power was both *physical* in its power to move material and *sociological* in its power to dominate humans.[95]

Malm's central historical argument is that fossil fuels were extracted from the earth and made to power machinery so that the bourgeoisie might better manage the proletariat. Fossil fuels, in Malm's words, "are, by definition, a materialization of social relations." Paraphrasing Marx, Malm writes that "scientists have so far interpreted global warming as a phenomenon in nature; the point, however, is to trace its human origins." Global warming is the ultimate tyranny of the past. The process of using machines that require fuel to discipline workers set into motion a Frankenstein-like duality of environmental degradation alongside labor exploitation. Capitalist profits are reliant upon better exploiting labor in order to speed up production, or as Marx wrote, "the pores of time are so to speak shrunk through the compression of labour." Petroleum-powered machines have lubricated this cycle, which represents an ironic twist on the concept of capitalist time. "In fossil fuels," Malm writes, "the time of photosynthesis hundreds of millions of years old is compressed so that living labour can be condensed, their timelessness the material prop for a tyranny of the abstract." Or as C. S. Lewis put it: "Man's power over Nature turns out to be a power exercised by some men over other men with Nature as its instrument." Malm's analysis leads to only one conclusion: In order to tame global warming, humans must smash capitalism. Moreover, if Marxist ecology is correct, then Marx is a crucial guide in the struggle for humanity's survival.[96]

In 2017, one year after Malm published his book, an equally innovative work of Marxist ecology came out, Kohei Saito's *Karl Marx's Ecosocialism: Capital, Nature, and the Unfinished Critique of Political Economy*. Saito is a Japanese Marxist philosopher who completed his doctorate at Humboldt University in Berlin while helping edit *Die Marx-Engels-Gesamtausgabe (MEGA)*, the largest collection of Marx and Engels writings. *Karl Marx's Ecosocialism* originated in German as Saito's dissertation before Foster facilitated an English version for Monthly Review Press. A systematic analysis of Marx's work, the book contends it is "not possible to comprehend the full scope of his critique of political economy if one ignores its ecological dimension." Saito argues against the "popular stereotype" that Marx the Promethean favored unlimited technological progress even at the cost of environmental degradation. Saito believes Marx thought capitalism left humans alienated from themselves *and* from nature.[97]

Saito arrived at a fuller understanding of Marx's ecology after a close reading of the notebooks Marx kept during the last fifteen years of his life, which often fixated on nature. Rethinking Marx in light of new contexts has long been the norm in the history of Marx reception. It makes perfect sense that Marxist ecologists would reexamine Marx's ideas against the backdrop of global warming. But that a profound reevaluation of Marx is also underway because everyone prior to twenty-first century Marxist ecologists seemingly ignored his late notebooks is curious. Marx's ideas, after all, have been picked over perhaps more than anyone else's in the last 150 years. Yet here we are, confronted by a radical revision to Marx that has major implications.

Whereas the Marx of *The Communist Manifesto* was somewhat positive about capitalism, Saito argues the Marx of the late notebooks
"quite consciously abandoned his earlier optimistic evaluation of the
emancipatory potential of capitalism." For Saito, as for the late Marx,
there is no reconciling capitalism and environmental sustainability.
"Indeed," Saito writes, "by attempting to subsume nature, capital cannot help but destroy, on an expanding scale, the fundamental material
conditions for free human development." Viewing capitalism as incompatible with sustainable environmental practices might seem obvious today. But in the 1870s, even to Marx himself, such an assessment
was far from preordained. And yet, according to Saito, Marx judged
the relationship between capitalism and nature in precisely this way.[98]

One reason the young Marx believed capitalism was emancipatory
was because he thought workers in a capitalist society had more freedom than peasants in a feudal land, or at least, could better create the
conditions for freedom. Yet as he soured on capitalism's capacity to
liberate, Marx also reconsidered feudalism. He never romanticized
feudalism, but the older Marx came to believe survival was easier for
peasants than for workers because, whereas peasants had a right to
subsist on the land, capitalist property relations denied workers that
right. "Due to the commodification of land," Saito writes, "the producers in modern society lose any direct connection with the earth
and come to be separated from their original means of production,
whereas serfs were still tightly connected to the land." This had grave
consequences for the landless masses, compelled to permanently sell
themselves into alienation. It also had severe outcomes for environmental sustainability. "When the land becomes a commodity," Saito
writes, "the relationship between humans and land is radically modified and reorganized for the sake of producing capitalist wealth." In
one of his forgotten letters, Marx called this a "metabolic rift." By that
he meant that capitalism is an alien system that separates us from our
true selves, and from nature. Marxist ecology is invested in reconciling
Marx with environmentalism because Marx teaches that environmental sustainability is impossible as long as capitalism reigns supreme.[99]

Saito's second book, *Marx in the Anthropocene: Towards the Idea of*

Degrowth Communism, published in 2023, stakes an even bolder position. By embracing the philosophy of degrowth socialism, Saito joins Marxist ecologists who argue the consumption-based lifestyle cultivated by capitalism is intimately linked with the processes driving global warming. Degrowth socialists reject the idea of a technological silver bullet in combating climate change. The only way to undo the damage done by the "metabolic rift" is to quit burning fossil fuels, and the best way to achieve that is to slow the trajectory of capitalist growth, including technological progress. Marx was onto something late in his life when he developed a sanguine view of precapitalist societies, which had, in Saito's words, "a unique way of communal regulations of land." Marx has been known to dismiss such societies for their backwardness. But he came to appreciate them, according to Saito, because they "imposed various rules on their production and consumption which realized a more steady-state of sustainable production."[100]

Saito's inventive reinterpretation of Marx in the context of a burning planet has catapulted him to surprising fame. His approach has also drawn criticism, and not only from ardent defenders of capitalism. Other Marxist ecologists have been critical of Saito and degrowth socialism. These critics identify with what is called eco-modernism, which believes large-scale technologies can be a part of the solution to climate change as long as capitalists are not in control of them. Matt Huber, a Marxist geographer and leading ecomodernist, has expressed incredulity about Saito's claim that Marx "consciously discarded historical materialism," crucial to Saito's belief that the only way to make the earth sustainable for human life again is to dump capitalist technologies alongside capitalism.[101]

Eco-modernists claim Saito's revision of Marx is a gross distortion that dismisses over a century of Marxist scholarship. They also reject the philosophy of degrowth on the grounds that it would make life worse for working people everywhere. Eco-modernists believe it would be better to harness the means of production as one component of a comprehensive, politically effective socialist strategy. In this way, the Green New Deal is the quintessential ecomodernist project. "A public works plan to vastly expand union jobs and manufacturing alongside guaranteed stable and affordable energy prices for the working class," Huber wrote in *Jacobin*, "could actually create the mass constituency needed to intervene in the real world of capitalist power and climate politics."[102]

Jacobin ultimately aligns with eco-modernism. Its leading science writer Leigh Phillips argues that if degrowth socialists have their way, the standard of living for workers in wealthy nations would undergo an even steeper decline than that of the last four decades. Phillips believes Saito misdiagnoses the problem. "The problem with capitalism is not that it produces too much," Phillips says, "but that it irrationally limits production to what is profitable." The fossil-fuel economy has been extremely profitable for well-positioned capitalists. But evenly distributed economic growth powered by sustainable energy is also possible.

Both sides in the debate within Marxist ecology enlist Marx as an authority. For Saito, Marx became a protodegrowth socialist, for whom the "metabolic rift" was central to his conception of political economy. Phillips, in contrast, sticks with the time-tested notion that Marx was Promethean. "Marx saw the marvels of capitalism and the Industrial Revolution and wondered how much farther humanity could go if production were not restricted to the profit incentive," Phillips says. "We would have so much more than capitalism can produce! This is what he called 'unfettering the forces of production.'"[103]

The spirited rivalry is a symptom of the magnitude of global warming as a concern. The dispute also signals Marx's unrelenting applicability to capitalism. Well-meaning Marxists have long used Marx to support opposing solutions to problems posed by capitalism. The vital debate within Marxist ecology today portends yet another rekindling of Marxism.

BLACK LIVES MATTER

Marx did not offer ready solutions for all problems. What he *did* offer was a powerful method for thinking about capitalism, revolution, and history, which is why he continues to be read and interpreted well after his death. And yet, even people who subscribe to his method disagree about its meaning and implications. This is what Angela Davis meant by proclaiming in 2017 that Marxism "has always been both a method and an object of criticism." Davis was responding to the growing conversation about Cedric Robinson's *Black Marxism*, a book at the heart of another dispute over how to think about Marx. First published but barely noticed in 1983, *Black Marxism* received more fanfare when a second edition was published in 2000, thanks in part to a stirring foreword by the historian Robin D. G. Kelley, a former Robinson student. By the time of a third edition in 2021, five years after Robinson's death, *Black Marxism* had become an almanac for the Black Lives Matter movement.[104]

Black Lives Matter arose as a crusade for racial justice in 2013, after George Zimmerman was acquitted of murdering Trayvon Martin despite damning evidence that he shot the unarmed black teenager without reasonable cause. In the summer of 2014, demonstrations spread like wildfire after police gunned down Michael Brown in Ferguson, Missouri, and after police strangled Eric Garner in New York City. In the summer of 2020, millions of people took to the streets after a video showing the Minneapolis cop Derek Chauvin killing George Floyd by kneeling on his neck went viral. More Americans began focusing their political energies on combating racism than at any time since the 1960s. Many millennial socialists who had joined DSA to push for universal healthcare and the like pivoted to a call for "defunding" the police. This is not to say people were incapable of holding two thoughts in their heads at once. Plenty understood that both race *and* class shaped the American social order in interrelated fashion. But in a world of police brutality and Black Lives Matter, race seemed paramount.[105]

Socialists have always struggled to build working-class solidarity in an intensely racist nation. This held true in the twenty-first century. In the summer of 2015, Black Lives Matter activists disrupted a Bernie Sanders rally about healthcare because they wanted him to focus on fighting racism. In response, Sanders asserted economic inequality and systematic racism were "parallel problems" and declared that he was willing to do something about both. At a rally of her own in the

spring of 2016, Hillary Clinton dismissed the notion that these problems ran parallel. Clinton asked the crowd, "if we broke up the banks
tomorrow," a frequent Sanders demand, "would that end racism?"
Clinton's cynical cooptation of Black Lives Matter to deflect Bernie's
populist rhetoric resonated. This was a time, after all, when a 2014
article making "The Case for Reparations" launched its author, Ta-
Nehisi Coates, into the intellectual stratosphere. By demanding, in the
words of historian Touré Reed, that "we must treat race as a force that
exists independently of capitalism," Coates had become, according to
Reed, "neoliberalism's most visible black emissary." Proving this point,
Coates criticized Sanders in 2016 for prioritizing universal programs
that would help the entire working class, like healthcare and parental
leave, over race-specific issues like reparations.[106]

Not all Black Lives Matter activists neglected the socialist cause.
Some believed anticapitalism and antiracism went hand-in-glove.
Black Marxism was tailor-made for such rebels, endowing them with
a potent vocabulary. Robinson's book empowered activists to situate
their struggle against "racial capitalism" in a "black radical tradition"
dating to the early slave trade. Robinson emphasized racial capitalism
as a direct challenge to Marx's idea that capitalism was a force for upending premodern systems like feudalism and slavery. "Capitalism
and racism," Robin Kelley wrote in an essay about *Black Marxism*, "did
not break from the old order but rather evolved from it to produce a
modern world system of 'racial capitalism' dependent on slavery, violence, imperialism, and genocide." This paradigm was useful to young
radicals who hoped their antiracist work might also count in the anticapitalist ledger. If capitalism had always been intricately connected
to racism, from slavery and dispossession up through police brutality
and mass incarceration, then the fight against one was the fight against
the other. Calls to defund the police or abolish prisons were seen as
integral to the anticapitalist worldview.[107]

As *Black Marxism*'s popularity mushroomed, Karl Marx was pronounced dead yet again. The eulogists this time were people who
agreed with much of what he stood for but rejected him for Eurocentrism. In this Robinson-inspired perspective, Marx's wrongheaded

claim that capitalism would eventually consign race to the dustbins of history was predetermined by the fact that he was a nineteenth-century white European man. Because Marx focused on the workshops of England as the driving force of capitalism, which led him to largely ignore the more determinative dynamics of European imperialism, his work was ill-suited as a theory for grasping the logic of twenty-first-century racism.

Marx was a nineteenth-century white man, but he was also a transcendent thinker whose ideas have had worldwide repercussions. Diminishing Marx as a dead white male is akin to reducing capitalism to a racial phenomenon. Which is why Robinson's mischaracterization of Marx matters. The British socialist writer China Miéville has described the attempt to elevate Robinson's concept of racial capitalism over Marx's theory of capitalism as "unhelpful to the point of calumny." The caricature of Marx as Eurocentric is also unhelpful since, according to Miéville, Marx's well-documented "awareness of racism as a factor impacting the world and the workers' movement" was central to his "commitment to radical change."[108]

To be sure, *The Communist Manifesto* forwarded a unilinear model of historical change of the type that was somewhat unique to nineteenth-century European thought. One of Marx's early essays, in which he hypothesized that British colonialism might ironically be good for India, since he believed it would upend the premodern Indian caste system, has often been cited as explicit evidence of his orientalism. But it should also be noted that Marx dramatically changed his mind about that as he came to appreciate Indian resistance to the British Empire. The Marx scholar Kevin Anderson argues that "the notion of a Eurocentric Marx does not hold up when one examines the whole of his writings across the period from 1841 to 1883, for he was above all a thinker who continued to rework and develop his conceptual apparatus." Marx's writings about Russia in the last decade of his life, for example, demonstrated he had acquired an eclectic, nonlinear notion of historical development. He viewed the rural communes in Russia as a potential base for worldwide revolution, an outlook that contradicted

his earlier theory that socialism would emerge from highly industrialized capitalist nations.[109]

In defending Marx against the charge of Eurocentrism, the point
is not to rescue the long-dead Rhinelander from the enormous condescension of posterity. Rather, if our goal is to make sense of the trajectory of capitalism, confining Marx to nineteenth-century Europe
is counterproductive. Revolutions can come from anywhere, as Marx
learned. They were not predetermined to arise out of advanced industrialized nations like England or the United States. But for a revolution to be truly transformative, it *must* direct its energy at the source
of power, at the foundation of exploitation. Revolutions must target
capitalism, now more than ever. Who else but Marx as a starting point
for such ambitions?

If the communist rapper and filmmaker Boots Riley has his way,
the revolution of the future will emerge from the streets of his home-
town of Oakland. Riley's political identity, as a black man fighting for
racial justice who also happens to be an unreconstructed Marxist,
challenges Robinson's stance that something called "black Marxism"
is distinguishable from straightforward Marxism. As one of the most
imaginative Marxist visionaries of twenty-first-century American culture, Riley is a befitting spokesperson for millennial socialism, despite
being of Gen X. Born in 1971, Riley joined the Progressive Labor Party,
a Marxist-Leninist organization with roots in the Communist Party, at
fifteen. In 1990, Boots founded The Coup, a rap group that effortlessly
merged infectiously funky beats with bitingly hilarious revolutionary
messaging. From the start, The Coup was expert at mocking capitalists. Its first album, released in 1992, was titled *Kill My Landlord*. One
of the group's most popular songs from its critically acclaimed 2001
record, *Party Music*, was called "5 Million Ways to Kill a C.E.O.," which
included the Marx-inspired line, "He workin' you while we happy just
to work a day." In 2006, Riley joined Rage against the Machine guitar-
ist Tom Morello to form Street Sweeper Social Club. One of that band's
most popular songs, "100 Little Curses," remained true to Riley's time-
tested theme of heckling the bourgeoisie:

May your Ferrari break down, may your chauffeur get high
And smash up your stretch Rolls up on Rodeo Drive
Off the breaking backs of others is where you got all your bucks
Till we make the revolution, I just hope your life sucks.[110]

Although Riley's music put him on the map, his most notable Marxist production is *Sorry to Bother You*, a 2018 film he wrote and directed that portrays the dystopian absurdities of neoliberal capitalism in postindustrial Oakland. The protagonist Cassius, or Cash, discovers a path out of grinding poverty by excelling in his job at a call center, one of those ubiquitous factories of neoliberal alienation. There he cashes in on his hidden talent of performing "white voice" so impeccably that it puts even the most hostile customers at ease. This skill rockets Cash up the corporate ladder, tempting him with a life of luxury—as long as he is okay with selling out his fellow workers, not to mention his soul. Cash's white voice, Riley has said, is a commentary on the idea that how we behave, how we conform to dominant cultural mores, determines our standing in the capitalist hierarchy. Yet *Sorry to Bother You* is premised on the notion that political economy, not behavior, determines social arrangements.[111]

Riley's debut film is one of the best cinematic adaptations of Marx's *Capital*. Whereas most workers sell their labor because it is their only means for meager survival, a few lucky proles like Cash are positioned to strike a better bargain. *Sorry to Bother You* thus transports Marx's labor theory of value to twenty-first-century American capitalism. The film also encompasses a surreal representation of class struggle. The sinister Worry Free corporation, which enlists cheap labor for weapons manufacturers, develops a technology that transforms regular people into horse people, or "equisapiens," an enslaved race that will be more compliant and harder working while also serving as a new "other" to divide the working class. Riley resolves this uncanny cinematic illustration of class struggle by having Cash become an equisapien but turn his newfound freakish strength against capitalism by leading a violent protest against Worry Free. In this strange conclusion, Riley resorts to magical realism to convey an otherwise unpalatable message. Collective working-class rebellion is the only escape from our neoliberal hellscape.[112]

A working-class revolution of the sort dreamed up by Marxists like Boots Riley is the stuff of conservative nightmares. Which explains why, any time radicals have gained momentum throughout American history, the right has gathered its strength to slow them down. Upticks in Marxism have consistently been followed by red scares. Our current moment is no different.

A NEW RED SCARE

Right-wing vigilantism has never been entirely rational. Reactionaries blamed Marx for the Paris Commune even though he had nothing to do with it. But conservatives have sometimes plausibly targeted radicals even as they overstated the threat. The 249 anarchists and socialists deported to Russia in 1919 were not about to overthrow the American government. But they would have liked to! In comparison with the anarchist Alexander Berkman, who tried to assassinate the capitalist Henry Clay Frick in 1892, millennial socialists are a decidedly tamer bunch. But this has not stopped right-wingers from sounding alarm bells about the left-wing threat to America. The object of their rage this time, however, is more difficult to pinpoint. Vigilantes have converged on an ill-defined group of carpetbaggers whom they are convinced have indoctrinated a generation in the belief that the United States is irredeemably racist, sexist, imperialistic, anti-intellectual, even fascist. Specifically, the right blames "cultural Marxism," a brand of subversive thought it traces to the Frankfurt School, for keeping Marx alive in the culture.

The premise that the Frankfurt School forced a poison pill known as cultural Marxism on an unsuspecting nation emerged in the late 1980s and early 1990s as an explanation for "political correctness," a right-wing bête noire during that high point in the nation's culture wars. First espoused by followers of the conspiracy-huckstering, perennial presidential candidate Lyndon LaRouche, the theory was popularized by William Lind of the Free Congress Foundation. Lind argued that political correctness, a label to describe an ideological narrowness that swept across American higher education—a narrowness that ignored truth in its efforts to address the long history of oppression—was nothing other than "Marxism translated from economic into cultural terms." The infiltration of the Frankfurt School had remade college campuses, Lind claimed, into "ivy-covered North Koreas."[113]

Lind argued that ever since the First World War, when the workers of the world defied Marx and chose nation over class, Marxists have been reduced to criticizing capitalist nations at the level of culture. Lind pinpointed Lukács and Gramsci as the first of these. Through their theories of reification and hegemony, respectively, Lukács and Gramsci contended workers failed to comprehend their real interests because they had been hoodwinked by the various mystifications of capitalist culture. Lind pointed to the Frankfurt School as a transmission point between cultural Marxism, which developed in early twentieth-century Europe, and critical theory, which spread like a weed in late twentieth-century America.[114]

The cultural Marxism trope, like many Far Right conspiracy theories, has proven attractive to antisemites. When questioned about this, Lind always proclaimed his innocence. But when discussing the dangers posed by the Frankfurt School, he consistently highlighted its members' Jewishness. He also gave a speech about cultural Marxism in 2002 before a group of Holocaust deniers. Infamously overt antisemites like David Duke, former grand wizard of the Knights of the Ku Klux Klan, latched on to the Frankfurt School explanation because it has all the earmarks of their favorite kind of conspiracy theory. Frankfurt School intellectuals were Jews from another land who hawked Marxism as a tool for destroying American society while clinging to their own wealth and property. These wily hypocrites promoted multiculturalism and sexual revolution while retaining their own tight ethnic and family ties. One American antisemite called Frankfurt School thinkers "parasitic Freudian Talmudists."[115]

Paradoxically, renowned Jewish conservatives like Andrew Breitbart and Ben Shapiro have been prominent promoters of this theory. In his

2011 book *Righteous Indignation*, Breitbart described his recognition that the Frankfurt School was to blame for American decline as an "aha moment." He remembered that his "American Studies program at Tulane had far more Adorno and Gramsci and Horkheimer and Marcuse than Twain or Jefferson or Lincoln." When multiplied across college campuses, such reading habits had the effect of unnecessarily pitting Americans against one another. Breitbart's version of the Frankfurt School theory lacked the antisemitic flavor of David Duke's. Yet the way it connected remote dots made it no less conspiratorial. Referring to Herbert Marcuse as the "Jesus of the New Left," he likened Saul Alinsky, the theoretician of community organizing, to Marcuse's "St. Paul." Marcuse was thus indirectly responsible for Hillary Clinton, who wrote her senior thesis at Wellesley College on Alinsky, and Barack Obama, who embodied the Marcuse-Alinsky vision as a community organizer on the South Side of Chicago. Following this line of thought, the right-wing YouTube personality Shapiro declared that "if you ask most Democrats, do you like Karl Marx, most Democrats will say no, even as they're buying directly into his philosophy."[116]

In a world where millennial socialism and Black Lives Matter have become legitimate political forces, the cultural Marxism conspiracy theory appeals to lots of conservatives. In his 2021 bestselling book *American Marxism*, right-wing radio personality Mark Levin credits Marcuse, the "German-born Hegelian-Marxist ideologue of the Franklin (*sic*) School of political theorists," with "hatching the Critical Theory ideology from which the racial, gender, and other Critical Theory-based movements were launched in America." Levin embodies the anti-intellectual conspiracy-mongering of the contemporary Far Right. Following a long line of conservative red baiters, he roots every political expression he dislikes, from feminism to environmentalism to Black Lives Matter, in ideas hatched by Marx and Marxists. The British left-wing writer Richard Seymour calls this type of politics "anticommunism without communism." To paraphrase China Miéville, who paraphrases Marx, "First time as tragedy, second time as farce, third time as debased reality television." And yet, despite his boundless ignorance, Levin is right that American society has in the last sixty years undergone dramatic social change that is mostly anathema to conservatives. He is also correct that Marx has yet to die. Perhaps Levin is subconsciously reacting to a truth revealed by the long history of Marx reception: as long as capitalism persists, Marx cannot be killed.[117]

THE SPECTER OF FREEDOM

The future of capitalism is incredibly uncertain. We may or may not be living in *late* capitalism, a once popular phrase among overly optimistic Marxists. What seems certain is that our current Marx boom has yet to crest.

A fresh wave of political theorists has emerged to double down on the freedom aspect of Marx's philosophy. William Clare Roberts's 2018 book *Marx's Inferno: The Political Theory of Capital* is one of the better examples of this. Roberts, an American-born scholar who teaches in Canada, presents a version of Marx familiar to late nineteenth-century socialists. Premised on the sentiment of a eulogy given at the 1883 Cooper Union memorial—"Now it is the duty of true lovers of liberty to honor the name of Karl Marx"—Roberts wagers that twenty-first-century liberty lovers will come to appreciate Marx if they read him correctly.[118]

The title of Roberts's book unveils the most dramatic element of his thesis, that Marx constructed *Capital* in the mode of Dante's *Inferno*, a poem about a journey through the nine circles of hell guided by the ancient Roman bard Virgil. As Virgil is to Dante, Marx is to the working class. *Capital* is a travel guide for the proletariat's tour through the depths of the "social hell" that is capitalism. Although this analogy might seem overheated, it helps Roberts situate Marx's masterpiece in the context of the working class struggle to be free.

Roberts contends Marx wrote *Capital* from the perspective of a working-class republican who hated arbitrary power like that of both capitalism and the state. Roberts points to the section of *Capital* on primitive accumulation, where Marx argues the state serves capitalist accumulation. "Only the defeat of this servile and violent state,"

Roberts writes, channeling Marx, "can establish the conditions of emancipation." It is debatable whether Marx was technically republican. Whereas republican theory highlighted the human desire to be free from *interpersonal* power, Marx thought capitalism's formidability was a byproduct of its *impersonal* power. Yet Roberts is absolutely correct that Marx believed capitalism inhibits the human yearning to be free, and that, in the twenty-first century, this aspect of Marx matters greatly.[119]

The year after Roberts's creative reinterpretation, another book similarly promoted Marx as essential to the modern quest for freedom, *This Life: Secular Faith and Spiritual Freedom*. Written by Martin Hägglund, a Swedish-born philosopher, *This Life* argues humans must understand life as finite to make meaning of it. We must recognize that our existence ends if we are going to care about what happens while we are living. The common religious belief that our physical finitude is merely a means to an eternal end downgrades the value of life and degrades our political possibilities. Hägglund writes that "climate change and the possible destruction of the Earth cannot be seen as an *existential* threat from the standpoint of religious faith." He instead promotes what he calls "secular faith," the secrets to which "can be found in the work of Karl Marx," "the most important inheritor of the secular commitment to freedom and democracy."[120]

Marx is crucial to thinking about the possibilities of freedom because he possessed the correct premise of "what it means to be *living* and *free*." In making this case, Hägglund follows Marx's labor theory of value. "Insofar as we spend our time working a job that is not fulfilling but merely serves as a means for our survival," Hägglund writes, "our labor time is unfree, since we cannot affirm that what we do is an expression of who we are." While we must perform some labor to stay alive, this is the realm of necessity. The problem is that capitalism demands most people spend the majority of their time stuck in that realm. In order to be free, humans must also spend time in the realm of freedom, where we have autonomy. "What Marx calls the realm of freedom," Hägglund writes, "is opened up by the capacity of living beings to *generate more lifetime than is required to secure the means of survival.*" We do not need to work our lives away in order to survive.[121]

Recognizing the finitude of life is the key to understanding Marx's labor theory of value because it allows us to qualitatively compare the different ways we spend time, between, for example, working a mind-numbing, soul-crushing job and, say, playing basketball or painting or hiking or reading philosophy or napping in the sun. Hägglund argues that Marx's "critique of capitalism makes sense only in light of his commitment to the freedom of social individuals to lead their own lives." An emancipated, socialist society would be organized around the principle of people having more time to do as they wish.[122]

Capitalism, in addition to being hostile to individual freedom, is also against reason. "Under capitalism," Hägglund writes, "all questions of what we need, what we want, and what is durable, must be subordinated to the question of what is profitable." The system's devotion to profit prevents us from improving human life. We cannot universalize healthcare, we cannot wipe out homelessness, we cannot ensure the planet remains inhabitable, because such aspirations are not in harmony with the profit motive.[123]

Capitalism cannot provide freedom to most people because it measures value by how much surplus labor can be wrung from workers. If technological improvements reduce the labor time required to bring precious commodities to people, human logic dictates that people would need to work less to sustain a good life. But the logic of capitalism requires that people sell their labor for some other pursuit. "The very calculation of value under capitalism," Hägglund writes, "is inimical to the actualization of freedom." This is particularly true in the neoliberal era when everything has a price on it. "This vicious circle can be broken only through an overcoming of capitalism," he argues, "which requires a transformation of our conception of value." Hägglund calls himself a socialist because he dreams of a future in which free time will be the actual measure of value. A society of such transformed priorities would be a much less miserable, much less alienated, much happier society.[124]

We are currently a long way from social happiness, especially in the United States, where people spend more hours at work than their counterparts in other developed nations. But recent events have demonstrated that Marxists are not alone among Americans desiring a less exploitative, less desolate future. In the midst of the COVID-19 pandemic, responsible for over one million deaths in the United States, a large number of Americans revealed their true feelings about work in a capitalist society. When authorities closed down businesses in a desperate attempt to slow the spread of the virus, millions of Americans lost their jobs on what was expected to be a temporary basis. Yet when many refused to return to work, even after the risk of death dropped, in an uncoordinated mass action known as the Great Resignation, defenders of the system had a collective meltdown. Conspicuous whining about a lazy workforce reminded that capitalists are above all concerned about losing the upper hand in the never-ending class struggle.[125]

Perhaps capitalists worry for nothing. Once the state quit subsidizing the stay-at-home mandate, most Americans had no choice but to return to work. The bourgeoisie regained leverage over the proletariat. Moreover, thanks in part to a reactionary Supreme Court, legal protections guaranteeing the hard-won right to collective bargaining are eroding.

Yet, even in the face of such daunting forces, workers are not resigned to their miserable fates. A wave of strikes has swept the nation, including at some of the world's most powerful corporations like Starbucks, Amazon, and the big three car companies. Although the current strike wave is nowhere near as big as the one in 1934, working-class consciousness is on the rise. Polls show unions are popular for the first time in half a century. No wonder Marx is booming again. We are witnesses to one of Marx's signature theories playing out in real time. Power in a capitalist society flows from control over people who work at the point of production. Class conflict emanates from this tension. This is the most important lesson to take from the long history of Karl Marx in America.[126]

"Common sense," China Miéville writes in his 2022 book about *The Communist Manifesto*, "is, by definition, generally very powerful." American common sense has it that capitalism is here to stay. Karl Marx and American common sense do not hang together.[127]

And yet.

The surprising story of Karl Marx in America suggests there are other ways to sense the world. As Miéville says, common sense is "also very often wrong, and not infrequently swept aside by history." I cannot predict that history will sweep aside American common sense. But the history of Karl Marx in America might just provide us with an alternative, one necessary to dreaming a better future. A future where people live free. What do we have to lose?

ACKNOWLEDGMENTS

Completing this book has been the most challenging thing I've accomplished in my career. It has been my white whale. And yet, despite the thousands of hours of research and writing that went into the making of this book—research and writing done in solitude—many people helped make it possible.

The most significant person to ensuring publication of this book, and to improving its quality, is Tim Mennel, my editor at the University of Chicago Press. Although the road to publication has been long, winding, and often harrowing, Tim has consistently stood behind me and this project. As an editor, he is unrivaled; as a friend, he is a mensch.

A big part of Tim's job was securing five anonymous reviewers—two for the book proposal, three for the full manuscript—and helping me to make collective sense of their thorough, critical, divergent reports. Even though the final product probably doesn't live up to the lofty standards of these careful reviewers, the book is much better for their advice.

My literary agent, John Wright, passed away while I was finishing the manuscript. I'm sad he will not share in the triumph of publication. I will always remember him fondly for seeing something in me as a potential trade author.

This is the second book I've published with the University of Chicago Press. I'm again impressed by the care its staff puts into making great books. Andrea Blatz, Tim's editorial assistant, made the work of preparing the manuscript for production as painless as possible. Thanks also to Stephen Twilley, my production editor; Olivia Aguilar, my promotions manager; and especially Trevor Perri, my amazing copy editor. I am also grateful to Vaneesa Cook, a fantastic historian in her own right who created this book's highly usable index.

I must express my gratitude to several people at Illinois State University (ISU), the institution that has employed me since 2006. Four chairs of the history department have bent over backward to support this book: Tony Crubaugh, Kyle Ciani, Ross Kennedy, and Richard Hughes. Ross in particular helped me secure a sabbatical and paved the way for my leave when I won a research fellowship in London. I'm also grateful to the consummate professionals who run the history department office and history education program: Ron Gifford, Sara Piotrowski, Monica Noraian, Matt Blue, Sharon Foiles, Tricia Gudeman, Faith Ten Haken, Kali Gordon, and Skyler Reilly.

A heartfelt thanks to Joe Blaney, the person at ISU most responsible for creating a community of writers by organizing Fourth Friday writing days and an annual summer writing retreat. The Office of Research and Sponsored Programs, led by John Baur and Craig McLauchlan, has supported Joe's initiatives, to my benefit. Vanette Schwartz has been the history department's librarian at ISU since my arrival on campus and has always gone out of her way to help me. Other staff in the Milner Library who generously donated time to this book include Karmine Beecroft and Colby Cilento. I love working with my fellow scholars and teachers in the ISU history department. Thanks to them all, especially Touré Reed and Keith Pluymers (our ongoing text thread is the most hilarious Marxist reading group I've been a part of). I also deeply appreciate my fellow ISU historians Issam Nassar, Amy Wood, and Stewart Winger.

Three of my cherished teachers and friends died while I was writing this book: Leo Ribuffo, Marty Sherwin, and Richard King. Each in their own unique way helped me become the historian I am today—and all of them would object to many of this book's conclusions!

Special shout-out to my closest friends in the history business: Ray Haberski, podcast cohost, coeditor, first reader, biggest supporter of my work; Bob Fitzgerald, historian of punk who coaches our sons' basketball team like a punk rocker; Pete Kuryla, who teaches me that the life of the mind is weird; and Kevin Schultz, who always seems to have a book come out at the same time as me!

Several historian friends generously offered feedback on parts of the book, including David Sehat, my most painfully honest reader; Jim Livingston, my most counterintuitively brilliant reader; and Julian Nemeth, my most historiographically informed reader. Thanks also to the wonderful historians Lauren Lassabe Shepherd and Natalia Mehlman Petrzela for helping me write a hopefully enticing and readable introduction.

I am grateful to be among the intellectual community built by my wonderful friends Jennifer Ratner-Rosenhagen and Kevin Schulz (again), who created the Midwest Intellectual History Group, which meets biannually, and an online reading group, which got together monthly during COVID. I submitted parts of my book to both communities and received invaluable comments from Thomas Broman, Katie Brownell, Pete Cajka, Dan Hummel, Patrick Iber, Sarah Igo, Joel Isaac, Tim Lacy, John McGreevy, Michelle Nickerson, Anders Rasmussen, Dan Rodgers, Jeffrey Sklansky, Richard Cándida Smith, Caroline Winterer, and Molly Worthen, among others.

I am forever indebted to those teachers who put me on the path to writing a big book about Karl Marx, beginning with Mr. Roberts, my high school history teacher who assigned *The Communist Manifesto*, and Ms. Keeton, my high school English teacher who gave me something to debate by assigning Ayn Rand's *Atlas Shrugged*. Thanks also to Virginia Scharff, who kept my passion for history alive during my first year as an undergraduate student at the University of New Mexico, and Angela Zimmerman, who generously guided me and my comrades Ariane Fischer and Megan Davis though an independent study on Marx (my very first Marxist reading group).

In the process of teaching two graduate seminars on Marx and Marxism in US history, one at Southern Denmark University and the other at ISU, I learned tons from many hard-working, intellectually curious students. I am grateful to them. I also appreciate my Danish student Peter Roswall, who spent a week of his holiday serving as my research assistant at the British Library. I will never forget such generosity.

Over the last two decades, I've read and discussed Marx and Marxism with several friends and comrades who've enriched my understanding, most notably Peter Henry, Andres Martinez, Salik Farooqi, Roy Olson, Kevin McLeish, Stefen Robinson, and Cem İsmail Addemir. Also remarkably helpful has been discussing this project with some of the smartest historians alive, including Christopher Arnold, Tom Arnold-Forster, Niels Bjerre-Poulson, Jodie Collins, Leilah Danielson, Janine Giordano Drake, Chris Hickman, Nelson Lichtenstein, Joe Malherek, Abdul Mohamud, Bo Peery, Daniel Rinn, Jason Roberts, Alan Wald, Robin Whitburn, Nick Witham, and Jonathan Zimmerman.

The Society for U.S. Intellectual History endows this book a platform that would otherwise not exist. Thanks to those who have made this community of scholars go: Sara Georgini, Robert Greene, Ben Alpers, Sarah Bridger, Andrew Klumpp, Rebecca Brenner, Lora Burnett, Paul Murphy, Dan Wickberg, Mike O'Connor, Lisa Szefel, Claire Arcenas, Glory Liu, Katy Hull, Bill Fine, Paul Kern, Bryn Upton, David Steigerwald, Katherine Jewell, Emily Conroy-Krutz, Benjamin Park, Christopher Nichols, Guy Emerson Mount, David Weinfeld, Ronnie Grinberg, Casey Nelson Blake, Elisabeth Lasch-Quinn, Allison Perlman, Angus Burgin, Christopher Cameron, Jonathan Holloway, Michael Kramer, Nicole Hemmer, Amy Kittelstrom, Ruben Flores, Andy Jewett, and Howard Brick (apologies to those I inevitably missed).

In 2019, I was lucky to win a Fulbright fellowship at the British Library to advance work on this book. Warm thanks to Ana Pereira of the UK Fulbright Commission and Cara Rodway, Philip Hatfield, and Philip Abraham of the Eccles Center for American Studies at the British Library for making my time in London so productive. Special shout-out to my dear friends Mike and Nicky Cochran for allowing me to stay in their spare room, the only way I was able to afford living in London for six months.

While working on this book, I wrote shorter pieces about Marx and would like to thank the editors of those pieces for sharpening my thinking and prose: Chris Lehmann at the *Baffler*; Bhaskar Sunkara and Shawn Gude at *Jacobin*; Michael Kazin and Natasha Lewis at *Dissent*; Christopher Phelps and Robin Vandome, editors of *Marxism and America: New Appraisals* (Manchester University Press, 2021), which includes a chapter I wrote; Michael McGandy, former editor at Cornell University Press, which published a book I coedited with Ray Haberski, *American Labyrinth: Intellectual History for Complicated Times* (2018), and which includes a chapter I wrote; and Tobias Dias and Magnus Møller Ziegler, who published an interview they conducted with me for the Danish journal *Slagmark*.

I've been invited to give several lectures on Karl Marx in America since I began work on this book. Discussing my research with smart and engaged audiences has honed my thinking in immeasurable ways. Thank you to Gleaves Whitney at the Hauenstein Center in Grand Rapids; Antti Lepistö at Helsinki University; Gary Gerstle and Duncan Kelly, who combined the seminars they convene at Cambridge University into one for me (the American History Seminar and the Political Thought and Intellectual History Seminar); Robert Mason and David Silkenat at the University of Edinburgh; Vanessa Mongey at Newcastle University; Randall Stephens at the University of Oslo; David Milne at the University of East Anglia; Lorenzo Costaguta at the University of Birmingham; the Southern Denmark University history department; the British Library; the organizers of the "Marx and Marxism in the United States" conference at the University of Nottingham; the Colloquium on Work, Labor, and Political Economy at the University of California, Santa Barbara; Tim Jelfs at the University of Groningen; Kate Masur and the Northwestern University history department seminar; Shalon van Tine at Ohio University; the History Graduate Student Association at Purdue University; and Christopher Wellin and the ISU Sociology and Anthropology department seminar.

Historical research is impossible without librarians and archivists. I am indebted to so many! I visited numerous libraries and archives but would like to especially thank those who helped me at five where I spent a lot of time: the British Library; the Wisconsin Historical Society; the Hoover Institute; the New York Public Library Manuscripts and Archives Division; and the Tamiment Library and Wagner Labor Archives at New York University.

I am so incredibly grateful to my family. Beyond writing a book, they make life worthwhile. To my parents by marriage Jane Wilhelm, Rich Wilhelm, and Shelly Porges, thank you for supporting me and being proud of me like I'm your own son. To my siblings Matt Hartman and Sarah Hartman, I'm proud to be your older brother. To my dad Tim Hartman, who died before I even began work on this book, I wish you were still here to join me with a celebratory beer. To my mom Karen Hartman, I can't thank you enough for being my biggest fan—I dedicate this book to you.

To my sons Asa and Eli, helping raise you is the most important job of my life, or as Marx would say, my *species being*. Thanks for reminding me that writing a book pales in comparison to that job—by constantly teasing me for not finishing this book! (What do you have to say now?!) Last, thank you, Erica, my love. None of this is possible without you—I dedicate this book to you as well.

NOTES

INTRODUCTION

1 Christopher Hitchens, "The Revenge of Karl Marx," *The Atlantic*, April 2009.
2 Karl Marx, *Capital*, vol. 1, trans. Ben Fowkes (1867; New York: Vintage, 1977). Honoré de Balzac, *The Unknown Masterpiece and Other Stories* (1831; Mineola, NY: Dover Publications, 2011).
3 David Sehat, *The Jefferson Rule: How the Founding Fathers Became Infallible and Our Politics Inflexible* (New York: Simon and Schuster, 2016). Drew R, McCoy, *The Last of the Fathers: James Madison and The Republican Legacy* (Cambridge: Cambridge University Press, 1991). Glory M. Liu, *Adam Smith's America: How a Scottish Philosopher Became an Icon of American Capitalism* (Princeton, NJ: Princeton University Press, 2022). Claire Rydell Arcenas, *America's Philosopher: John Locke in American Intellectual Life* (Chicago: University of Chicago Press, 2022). Seth Cotlar, *Tom Paine's America: The Rise and Fall of Transatlantic Radicalism in the Early Republic* (Charlottesville: University of Virginia Press, 2011).
4 Karl Marx, *Economic and Philosophical Manuscripts of 1844*, Marxists Internet Archive, accessed July 8, 2024, https://www.marxists.org/archive/marx/works /1844/manuscripts/preface.htm.
5 Harold Bloom, ed., *Ralph Waldo Emerson*, updated ed. (New York: Chelsea House, 2007), 127. Henry David Thoreau, *Walden; or, Life in the Woods* (Boston: Ticknor and Fields, 1854), 58–59.
6 Jill Lepore, *These Truths: A History of the United States* (New York: W. W. Norton, 2008), 230–31.
7 John Cassidy, "The Return of Karl Marx," *New Yorker*, October 12, 1997, 248.
8 "Marx After Communism," *The Economist*, December 19, 2002. Karl Marx and Friedrich Engels, *The Manifesto of the Communist Party* (1848), Marxists Internet Archive, accessed July 8, 2024, https://www.marxists.org/archive/marx /works/1848/communist-manifesto/.

9   "Occupy Anti-Capitalism Protests Spread Around the World," *The Guardian*, October 15, 2011.

10   Tim Jelfs, "Will the Revolution Be Podcast? Marxism and the Culture of 'Millennial Socialism' in the United States," in *Marxism and America: New Appraisals*, ed. Christopher Phelps and Robin Vandome (Manchester: Manchester University Press, 2021), 241–63.

11   Stuart Jeffries, "Why Marxism is on the Rise Again," *The Guardian* (July 4, 2012). Michelle Goldberg, "A Generation of Intellectuals Shaped by 2008 Crash Rescues Marx from History's Dustbin," *Tablet*, October 13, 2013.

12   Andrew Hartman, "Marx at 200: Just Getting Started," *Dissent*, May 4, 2018.

13   Phelps and Vandome, *Marxism and America*, 1.

14   The short early biography of Marx that follows is derived from four recent biographies: Mary Gabriel, *Love and Capital: Karl and Jenny Marx and the Birth of a Revolution* (Boston: Back Bay, 2012). Jonathan Sperber, *Karl Marx: A Nineteenth-Century Life* (New York: Liveright, 2013). Gareth Stedman Jones, *Karl Marx: Greatness and Illusion* (Cambridge, MA: Belknap Press of Harvard University Press, 2016). Sven-Eric Liedman, *A World to Win: The Life and Works of Karl Marx*, trans. Jeffrey N. Skinner (London: Verso, 2018).

CHAPTER ONE

1   Robin Blackburn, *An Unfinished Revolution: Karl Marx and Abraham Lincoln* (London: Verso, 2011), 2. August H. Nimtz Jr., *Marx, Tocqueville, and Race in America: The "Absolute Democracy" or "Defiled Republic"* (Lanham, MD: Lexington Books, 2003).

2   For Marx, who died well before 1917, "communism" and "socialism" were often interchangeable terms.

3   Karl Marx, *On the Jewish Question* (1844), Marxists Internet Archive, accessed July 8, 2024, https://www.marxists.org/archive/marx/works/1844/jewish -question/.

4   Marx, *On the Jewish Question*.

5   Karl Marx, "Moralising Criticism and Critical Morality" (1847), in *Marx Engels Collected Works*, 50 vols. (Moscow: Progress Publisher, 1976), 322.

6   Marx, *On the Jewish Question*.

7   Marx, *On the Jewish Question*.

8   Thomas Hamilton, *Men and Manners in America*, 2 vols. (London, 1833), 95–96, 156–57. Sean F. Monahan, "The American Workingmen's Parties, Universal Suffrage, and Marx's Democratic Communism," *Modern Intellectual History* 18, no. 2 (June 2021): 379–402.

9   Die Marx-Engels-Gesamtausgabe (hereafter *MEGA*), 1/6: 598; Thomas Cooper, *Lectures on the Elements of Political Economy*, 2nd ed. (London, 1831 [Columbia, SC, 1829]). Monahan, "The American Workingmen's Parties, Universal Suffrage, and Marx's Democratic Communism."

10   Monahan, "The American Workingmen's Parties, Universal Suffrage, and Marx's Democratic Communism." David Harris, *Socialist Origins in the United States: American Forerunners to Marx, 1817–1832* (Assen: Van Corcun, 1966). Alex

Gourevitch, *From Slavery to the Cooperative Commonwealth: Labor and Republican Liberty in the Nineteenth Century* (Cambridge: Cambridge University Press, 2015).

11 Michael Harrington, *Socialism* (New York: Saturday Review Press, 1972), 114. August H. Nimtz Jr., *Marx, Tocqueville, and Race in America: The "Absolute Democracy" or "Defiled Republic"* (New York: Lexington Books, 2003), 58.

12 Karl Marx, *The Poverty of Philosophy* (1847), Marxists Internet Archive, accessed July 8, 2024, https://www.marxists.org/archive/marx/works/1847/poverty-philosophy/. Nimtz, *Marx, Tocqueville, and Race in America*, 61.

13 Karl Marx, *Wage Labour and Capital* (1847), Marxists Internet Archive, accessed July 8, 2024, https://www.marxists.org/archive/marx/works/1847/wage-labour/. Nimtz, *Marx, Tocqueville, and Race in America*, 52.

14 Robert C. Tucker, ed., *The Marx-Engels Reader*, 2nd ed. (New York: W. W. Norton, 1978), 473.

15 Sven-Eric Liedman, *A World to Win: The Life and Works of Karl Marx*, trans. Jeffrey N. Skinner (London: Verso, 2018), 219–66.

16 Tucker, *The Marx-Engels Reader*, 473–74.

17 Tucker, *The Marx-Engels Reader*, 474.

18 Friedrich Engels, *The Condition of the Working Class in England* (1845).

19 Tucker, *The Marx-Engels Reader*, 479.

20 Tucker, *The Marx-Engels Reader*, 475.

21 Tucker, *The Marx-Engels Reader*, 475.

22 Tucker, *The Marx-Engels Reader*, 476.

23 Tucker, *The Marx-Engels Reader*, 481–82.

24 Tucker, *The Marx-Engels Reader*, 500.

25 Jonathan Sperber, *The European Revolutions, 1848–51* (Cambridge: Cambridge University Press, 2005).

26 E.P. Thompson, *The Making of the English Working Class* (1964; New York: Penguin Books, 1991), 237. Liedman, *A World to Win*, 85.

27 Neil Davidson, *How Revolutionary Were the Bourgeois Revolutions?* (Chicago: Haymarket Books, 2012).

28 Jonathan Sperber, *Karl Marx: A Nineteenth-Century Life* (New York: Liveright, 2013), 215–16.

29 Gareth Stedman Jones, *Karl Marx: Greatness and Illusion* (Cambridge, MA: Belknap Press of Harvard University Press, 2016), 258–63.

30 Sperber, *Karl Marx*, 232–33.

31 Priscilla Smith Robertson, *Revolutions of 1848: A Social History* (Princeton, NJ: Princeton University Press, 1952).

32 Liedman, *A World to Win*, 248–66.

33 Liedman, *A World to Win*, 260–66.

34 Bruce Levine, *The Spirit of 1848: German Immigrants, Labor Conflict, and the Coming of the Civil War* (Urbana: University of Illinois Press, 1992), 5.

35 Paul Finkelman, "How the Proslavery Constitution Led to the Civil War," *Rutgers Law Journal* 43, no. 3 (2015).

36 John Chester Miller, *The Wolf by the Ears: Thomas Jefferson and Slavery* (Charlottesville: University of Virginia Press, 1991).

37 Edward Baptist, *The Half Has Never Been Told: Slavery and the Making of American Capitalism* (New York: Basic Books, 2014).

38   David S. Reynolds, *John Brown, Abolitionist: The Man Who Killed Slavery, Sparked the Civil War, and Seeded Civil Rights* (New York: Vintage, 2005).

39   Boyd B. Stutler, *Glory, Glory, Hallelujah! The Story of "John Brown's Body" and "Battle Hymn of the Republic"* (Cincinnati: C. J. Krehbiel, 1960). Nimtz, *Marx, Tocqueville, and Race in America*, 70–71.

40   Kevin B. Anderson, *Marx at the Margins: on Nationalism, Ethnicity, and Non-Western Societies* (Chicago: University of Chicago Press, 2016), 85.

41   Karl Marx, *The Eighteenth Brumaire of Louis Bonaparte* (1852), Marxists Internet Archive, accessed July 8, 2024, https://www.marxists.org/archive/marx/works/1852/18th-brumaire/.

42   Marx, *The Eighteenth Brumaire of Louis Bonaparte*.

43   Marx, *The Eighteenth Brumaire of Louis Bonaparte*. Angela Zimmerman "From the Second American Revolution to the First International and Back Again: Marxism, the Popular Front, and the American Civil War," in *The World the Civil War Made*, ed. Gregory P. Downs and Kate Masur (Chapel Hill: University of North Carolina Press, 2015), 309–10. Angela Zimmerman, "Guinea Sam Nightingale and Magic Marx in Civil War Missouri: Provincializing Global History and Decolonizing Theory," *History of the Present* 8 (Fall 2018): 140–76.

44   Liedman, *A World to Win*, 341–94. Karl Marx, *Grundrisse: Foundations of the Critique of Political Economy (Rough Draft)*, trans. Martin Nicolaus (New York: Penguin Books, 1973).

45   Adam Tuchinsky, *Horace Greeley's New-York Tribune: Civil War-Era Socialism and the Crisis of Free Labor* (Ithaca, NY: Cornell University Press, 2009).

46   John Nichols, *The "S" Word: A Short History of an American Tradition* (London: Verso, 2011), 77–80.

47   Francis Wheen, *Karl Marx: A Life* (New York: W. W. Norton, 2001), 180–87.

48   William Harlan Hale, "When Karl Marx Worked for Horace Greeley," *American Heritage* 8, no. 3 (April 1957).

49   Hale, "When Karl Marx Worked for Horace Greeley." Nichols, *The "S" Word*, 71–72.

50   Levine, *The Spirit of 1848*, 100.

51   Joseph Weydemeyer to Karl Marx, September 28, 1851, MEGA 2 III/4: 471–72. For this translation, I am indebted to Angela Zimmerman.

52   David Herreshoff, *American Disciples of Marx: From the Age of Jackson to the Progressive Era* (Detroit: Wayne State University Press, 1967).

53   Zimmerman, "From the Second American Revolution to the First International and Back Again."

54   James Henry Hammond, "The 'Mudsill' Theory," Speech to the US Senate, March 4, 1858.

55   Abraham Lincoln, "Address before the Wisconsin State Agricultural Society," Milwaukee, Wisconsin, September 30, 1859.

56   August H. Nimtz, "Marx and Engels on the US Civil War: The 'Materialist Conception of History' in Action," *Historical Materialism* 19, no. 4 (2011): 178. Karl Marx and Frederick Engels, *The Civil War in the United States*, trans. and ed. Angela Zimmerman (New York: International Publishers, 2016), xxi.

57   Nimtz, *Marx, Tocqueville, and Race in America*, 97.

58   "A Declaration of the Immediate Causes Which Induce and Justify the Seces-

sion of the State of Mississippi from the Federal Union," *Journal of the State Convention and Ordinances and Resolutions Adopted in January 1861.* Alexander Stephens, "Cornerstone Speech," Savannah, Georgia, March 21, 1861.

59 Tom Chaffin, *Pathfinder: John Charles Frémont and the Course of American Empire* (New York: Hill and Wang, 2002).

60 "An Act to Confiscate Property Used for Insurrectionary Purposes (the First Confiscation Act)," August 6, 1861, Freedmen & Southern Society Project. Original U.S., Statutes at Large, Treaties, and Proclamations of the United States of America, vol. 12 (Boston, 1863), 319. The conjurer William Webb, *The History of William Webb, Composed by Himself* (Detroit: Egbert Hoekstra, 1873), 32, as cited by Angela Zimmerman, unpublished book manuscript.

61 Marx to Engels (July 1, 1861), in *The Civil War in the United States*, 23.

62 Marx, "The London *Times* on the Orleans Princes in America," *New York Daily Tribune*, November 7, 1861, in *The Civil War in the United States*, 53–54.

63 Blackburn, *An Unfinished Revolution*, 3–4.

64 Eleanor Morecraft, "Antislavery, Elite Men, and the 'Voice of the British Nation': c. 1790–1860," *History Compass* (May 2017). Richard Huzzey, *Freedom Burning: Anti-Slavery and Empire in Victorian Britain* (Ithaca: Cornell University Press, 2012). Marx letter to Ferdinand Lassalle (May 29, 1861), in *The Civil War in the United States*, 20.

65 Marx, "English Public Opinion," *New York Daily Tribune*, February 1, 1862, in *The Civil War in the United States*, 70.

66 Marx, "The American Question in England," *New York Daily Tribune*, October 11, 1861, in *The Civil War in the United States*, 28–29; Karl Marx, "The North American Civil War," *Die Press*, October 25, 1861; Blackburn, *An Unfinished Revolution*, 11.

67 Abraham Lincoln, "House Divided Speech," Illinois Republican State Convention, Springfield, Illinois, June 16, 1858. Marx, "The Civil War in the United States," *Die Press*, November 7, 1861, in *The Civil War in the United States*, 61.

68 Nimtz, *Marx, Tocqueville, and Race in America*, 96. Marx letter to Lion Phillips (May 6, 1861), in *The Civil War in the United States*, 19.

69 Engels to Marx (July 30, 1862); Marx, "Abolitionist Demonstrations in America," *Die Presse*, August 30, 1861, *The Civil War in the United States*, 120, 124.

70 Ira Berlin, *Slaves No More: Three Essays on Emancipation and the Civil War* (Cambridge: Cambridge University Press, 1993). Marx to Engels (October 29, 1862), in *The Civil War in the United States*, 136.

71 Gabriel, *Love and Capital*, 291. Anderson, *Marx at the Margins*, 102.

72 Marx, "Comments on the North American Events," *Die Presse*, October 12, 1862, in *The Civil War in the United States*, 133.

73 Marx, "On Behalf of the International Working Men's Association, to President Abraham Lincoln" (November 22, 1864), in *The Civil War in the United States*, 153–54.

74 Charles Francis Adams, US Ambassador to the United Kingdom, to William Randal Cremer, Honorary Secretary of the International Working Men's Association (January 28, 1865), in *The Civil War in the United States*, 157.

75 Karl Marx, *Capital*, vol. 1, trans. Ben Fowkes (1867; New York: Vintage, 1977), 414.

76   Eric Foner, *Reconstruction: America's Unfinished Revolution, 1863–1877* (New York: Harper & Row, 1988).

77   Marx, " Behalf of the International Working Men's Association, to President Andrew Johnson" (May 20, 1865); Marx to Engels (June 24, 1865), in *The Civil War in the United States*, 165–66, 167.

78   Nimtz, *Marx, Tocqueville, and Race in America*, 141.

79   Joseph Weydemeyer, "On the Negro Vote," 3 Parts, *Westliche Post* (St. Louis), September 8, 13, 14, 1865, trans. Angela Zimmerman, in *The Civil War in the United States*, 174.

80   Nimtz, *Marx, Tocqueville, and Race in America*, 143–44. Karl Marx, *Capital*, vol. 1, 93.

81   Karl Marx, "Inaugural Address of the International Working Men's Association" (October 21, 1864), Marxists Internet Archive, accessed July 8, 2024, https://www.marxists.org/archive/marx/works/1864/10/27.htm. Stedman Jones, *Karl Marx*, 466.

82   Marx, *Capital*, vol. 1, 414.

83   Marx, *Capital*, vol. 1, 345.

84   Marx, *Capital*, 925.

85   Karl Marx, *Critique of the Gotha Programme*, Marxists Internet Archive, accessed July 8, 2024, https://www.marxists.org/archive/marx/works/1875/gotha/. Marx, *Capital*, vol. 1, 341.

86   Marx, *Capital*, vol. 1, 342, 375.

87   Marx, *Capital*, vol. 1, 353, 377–78.

88   Marx, *Capital*, vol. 1, 412–13, 416.

89   Robert Weiner, "Karl Marx's Vision of America: A Biographical and Bibliographical Sketch," *The Review of Politics* 42, no. 4 (Oct 1980): 493–95. Nimtz, *Marx, Tocqueville, and Race in America*, 149.

90   Heather Cox Richardson, *The Death of Reconstruction: Race, Labor, and Politics in the Post-Civil War North, 1865–1901* (Cambridge, MA: Harvard University Press, 2004), 244.

91   Foner, *Reconstruction*, 491.

92   Donny Gluckstein, *The Paris Commune: A Revolution in Democracy* (London: Bookmarks, 2006).

93   Marx, *The Civil War in France* (1871), Marxists Internet Archive, accessed July 8, 2024, https://www.marxists.org/archive/marx/works/1871/civil-war-france/. Marx and Engels, *The Civil War in the United States*, 202.

94   Marx, *The Civil War in France*.

95   Samuel Bernstein, *The First International in America* (New York: Augustus M. Kelley, 1962), 82. Howard Brick and Christopher Phelps, *Radicals in America: The U.S. Left Since the Second World War* (New York: Cambridge University Press, 2015), 11.

96   Samuel Bernstein, "The Impact of the Paris Commune in the United States," *The Massachusetts Review* 12, no. 3 (Summer 1971): 435–46. Bernstein, *The First International in America*, 74.

97   Timothy Messer-Kruse, *The Yankee International: Marxism and the American Reform Tradition, 1848–1876* (Chapel Hill: University of North Carolina Press,

1998), 101. Philip S. Foner, "Marx's 'Capital' in the United States," *Science & Society* 31, no. 4 (Fall 1967): 461–66.

98   "Karl Marx: Interviews with the Corner-Stone of Modern Socialism," *Chicago Tribune*, January 5, 1879; Philip S. Foner, ed., *Karl Marx Remembered: Comments at the Time of His Death* (New York: Synthesis Publications, 1983), 252.

99   "The Curtain Raised, Interview with Karl Marx, the Head of L'Internationale," *New York World* (1871), in Foner, *Karl Marx Remembered*, 242.

100 Messer-Kruse, *The Yankee International*, 133, 75. Bernstein, *The First International in America*, 66–67.

101 Bernstein, *The First International in America*, 63.

102 Engels quoted in Harrington, *Socialism*, 116. Messer-Kruse is the historian most critical of Marx and the German Marxists in the International. Marx and Engels, *Communist Manifesto*.

103 Mari Jo Buhle, *Women and American Socialism, 1870–1920* (Urbana: University of Illinois Press, 1981), 20.

104 Paul Buhle, *Marxism in the United States: A History of the American Left*, 3rd ed (1987; London: Verso, 2013), 37.

105 Bernstein, *The First International in America*, 145–96.

106 Stedman Jones, *Karl Marx*, 582.

107 Mike Davis, *Old Gods, New Enigmas: Marx's Lost Theory* (London: Verso, 2018), 27.

108 Lucia Pradella, "Crisis, Revolution and Hegemonic Transition: The American Civil War and Emancipation in Marx's *Capital*," *Science & Society* 80, no. 4 (October 2016): 460.

109 "The Communists in Mourning; Testifying Their Respect for Karl Marx and his Doctrine," *New York Times*, March 21, 1883. "The Cooper Union Memorial Meeting," *New York Sun*, March 21, 1883. Foner, *Karl Marx Remembered*. Jose Martí, "The Memorial Meeting in Honor of Karl Marx," *La Nación* (Buenos Aires), May 13 and 16, 1883.

110 Foner, *Karl Marx Remembered*, 11, 78.

111 Foner, *Karl Marx Remembered*, 70.

CHAPTER TWO

1   Mark Twain and Charles Dudley Warner, *The Gilded Age: A Tale of Today* (1873; New York: Penguin Classics, 2001).

2   "Day of Days," *National Republican* (Washington, DC), July 6, 1876, Library of Congress Digital Collections.

3   Philips S. Foner, *The Workingmen's Party of the United States: A History of the First Marxist Party in the Americas* (Minneapolis: MEP Publications, 1984), 31.

4   Karl Marx and Friedrich Engels, *Marx and Engels on the Trade Unions*, ed. Kenneth Lapides (New York City: International Publishers, 1990), 209. Franz Mehring, "Obituary of Friedrich Sorge," *Historical Materialism* 11, no. 4 (2003), 301–4.

5   David Herreshoff, *American Disciples of Marx: From the Age of Jackson to the Progressive Era* (Detroit: Wayne State University Press, 1967), 81.

6   Justine Davis Randers-Pehrson, *Adolf Douai, 1819–1888: The Turbulent Life of a German Forty-Eighter in the Homeland and in the United States* (New York: Peter Lang, 2000).

7   Adolph Douai, "Labor and Work," *Workmen's Advocate* 3, no. 17 (April 23, 1887): 1; accessed at the Marxists Internet Archive, accessed July 8, 2024, https://www .marxists.org/history/usa/parties/slp/1887/0423-douai-laborandwork.pdf.

8   Karl Marx and Frederick Engels, *The Manifesto of the Communist Party* (1848), Marxists Internet Archive, accessed July 8, 2024, https://www.marxists.org /archive/marx/works/download/pdf/Manifesto.pdf. Karl Marx, *Critique of the Gotha Programme*, Marxists Internet Archive, accessed July 8, 2024, https:// www.marxists.org/archive/marx/works/1875/gotha/.

9   Foner, *The Workingmen's Party of the United States*, 57–67.

10 Buhle, *Women and American Socialism*. Foner, *The Workingmen's Party of the United States*, 77.

11 Richard White, *Railroaded: The Transcontinentals and the Making of Modern America* (Cambridge, MA: Harvard University Press, 2012). Mae Ngai, *Impossible Subjects: Illegal Aliens and the Making of Modern America* (Princeton, NJ: Princeton University Press, 2004).

12 Lorenzo Costaguta, "'Geographies of Peoples': Scientific Racialism and Labor Internationalism in Gilded Age American Socialism," *The Journal of the Gilded Age and Progressive Era* (2019): 1–22. Foner, *The Workingmen's Party of the United States*, 77.

13 Andrew Gyory, *Closing the Gate: Race, Politics, and the Chinese Exclusion Act* (Chapel Hill: University of North Carolina Press, 1998), 111. Michael Kazin, "The July Days in San Francisco, 1877: Prelude to Kearneyism," in *The Great Strikes of 1877*, ed. David O. Stowell (Urbana: University of Illinois Press, 2008), 136–63.

14 Nikki M. Taylor, *America's First Black Socialist: The Radical Life of Peter H. Clark* (Lexington: University of Kentucky Press, 2013), 142.

15 Walter Johnson, *The Broken Heart of America: St. Louis and the Violent History of the United States* (New York: Basic Books, 2020).

16 Foner, *The Workingmen's Party of the United States*, 85–95. Edward T. O'Donnell, *Henry George and the Crisis of Inequality: Progress and Poverty in the Gilded Age* (New York: Columbia University Press, 2015), xx.

17 Foner, *The Workingmen's Party of the United States*, 95.

18 Matthew Josephson, *The Robber Barons: The Great American Capitalists, 1861–1901* (1934; New York: Horace Brace International, 1962). John C. Cort, *Christian Socialism: An Informal History* (1988; Maryknoll, NY: Orbis Books, 2020), 252.

19 Rosanne Currarino, *The Labor Question in America: Economic Democracy in the Gilded Age* (Urbana: University of Illinois Press, 2011).

20 Jacob Riis, *How the Other Half Lives: Studies among the Tenements of New York* (1890; New York: Kessinger Publishing, 2004).

21 Robert Michael Smith, *From Blackjacks to Briefcases: A History of Commercialized Strikebreaking and Unionbusting in the United States* (Athens: Ohio University Press, 2003).

22 Eric Foner, *Free Soil, Free Labor, Free Men: The Ideology of the Republican Party Before the Civil War* (Oxford: Oxford University Press, 1970).

23   Karl Marx, *Capital*, vol. 1, trans. Ben Fowkes (1867; New York: Vintage, 1977), 280.

24   Alex Lichtenstein, *Twice the Work of Free Labor: The Political Economy of Convict Labor in the New South* (London: Verso, 1996).

25   Frank D. Lewis, "Explaining the Shift of Labor from Agriculture to Industry in the United States: 1869 to 1899," *The Journal of Economic History* 39, no. 3 (September 1979): 681–98. Steve Fraser, *The Age of Acquiescence: The Life and Death of American Resistance to Organized Wealth and Power* (New York: Basic Books, 2016).

26   Debby Applegate, *The Most Famous Man in America: The Biography of Henry Ward Beecher* (New York: Three Leaves Press, 2006). Ward Beecher, Bayard Taylor, and William M. Evarts, *Independence Day Orations and Poems: July 4, 1876* (1876). John Clark Ridpath, *The Life and Work of James A. Garfield: Twentieth President of the United States* (1881; Whitefish, MT: Kessinger Publishing, 2010), 245.

27   Gwendolyn Mink, *Old Labor and New Immigrants in American Political Development: Union, Party and State, 1875–1920* (Ithaca, NY: Cornell University Press, 1990).

28   Carl J. Guarneri, *The Utopian Alternative: Fourierism in Nineteenth-Century America* (Cornell University Press, Ithaca, 1991).

29   Marx and Engels, *Manifesto of the Communist Party*. Friedrich Engels, "Socialism: Utopian and Scientific," in *The Marx-Engels Reader*, 2nd ed., ed. Robert C. Tucker (New York: W. W. Norton, 1978), 683–715.

30   Jonathan Rees, *Industrialization and the Transformation of American Life: A Brief Introduction* (Armonk, NY: M. E. Sharpe, 2013).

31   Solomon Gemorah, "Laurence Gronlund—Utopian or Reformer?" *Science & Society* 33, no. 4 (Fall–Winter, 1969): 446–58. Laurence Gronlund, *The Cooperative Commonwealth*, ed. Stow Persons (1884; Cambridge, MA: Belknap Press of Harvard University Press, 1965). Mark Pittinger, *American Socialists and Evolutionary Thought, 1870–1920* (Madison: University of Wisconsin Press, 1993), 44.

32   Gronlund, *The Cooperative Commonwealth*, 21, 24.

33   Robert H. Wiebe, *The Search for Order, 1877–1920* (New York: Hill and Wang, 1967). Gronlund, *The Cooperative Commonwealth*, 29.

34   Pittinger, *American Socialists and Evolutionary Thought*, 62.

35   David M. Knight, *The Age of Science: Scientific World-View in the Nineteenth Century* (London: Blackwell Publishers, 1986).

36   Gerald Runkle, "Marxism and Charles Darwin," *The Journal of Politics* 23, no. 1 (February 1961), 108–26. Pittinger, *American Socialists and Evolutionary Thought*, 15.

37   Richard Hofstadter, *Social Darwinism in American Thought* (1944; Boston: Beacon Press, 1992).

38   Charles Postel, *Equality: An American Dilemma, 1866–1896* (New York: Farrar, Straus and Giroux, 2019), 173–74, 208.

39   Leon Fink, *Workingmen's Democracy: The Knights of Labor and American Politics* (Urbana: University of Illinois Press, 1983). Postel, *Equality*, 171–272.

40   O'Donnell, *Henry George and the Crisis of Inequality.* Henry George, *Progress and Poverty* (New York: D. Appleton, 1879).

41   Karl Marx letter to Friedrich Engels (June 20, 1881), *Karl Marx and Frederick Engels, Selected Correspondence* (Moscow: Progress Publishers, 1975). Daniel Bell, "The Background and Development of Marxian Socialism in the United States," in *Socialism and American Life*, vol. 1, ed. Donald Drew Egbert and Stow Persons (Princeton: Princeton University Press, 1952), 240.

42   O'Donnell, *Henry George and the Crisis of Inequality*, xxiii.

43   Edward Aveling and Eleanor Marx Aveling, *The Working-Class Movement in America* (1891; New York: Arno, 1969), 9.

44   Aveling and Marx Aveling, *The Working-Class Movement in America*, 14.

45   Paul Avrich, *The Haymarket Tragedy* (Princeton, NJ: Princeton University Press, 1984).

46   Foner, *The Workingmen's Party of the United States*, 111.

47   James Green, *Death in the Haymarket: A Story of Chicago, the First Labor Movement, and the Bombing That Divided Gilded Age America* (New York: Pantheon Books, 2006).

48   Davis, *Old Gods, New Enigmas*, 145. Herbert M. Morais, "Marx and Engels on America," *Science & Society* 12. 1 (Winter, 1948), 18. Kathryn Sklar, *Notes of Sixty Years: The Autobiography of Florence Kelley* (Chicago: Charles H. Kerr Publishing, 1986). Philip Foner, *May Day: A Short History of the International Workers' Holiday, 1886–1986* (New York: International Publishers, 1986).

49   Howard H. Quint, *The Forging of American Socialism: Origins of the Modern Movement* (Columbia: University of South Carolina Press, 1953).

50   Bell, "The Background and Development of Marxian Socialism in the United States," 242.

51   Mike O'Connor, *A Commercial Republic: America's Enduring Debate over Democratic Capitalism* (Lawrence: University Press of Kansas, 2014), 82–116. Eric Hobsbawm, *The Age of Empire, 1875–1914* (New York: Vintage Books, 1989), 54.

52   Paul Sweezy, "Marx on the Significance of the Corporation," *Science and Society* 3, no. 2 (Spring 1939), 238–41.

53   Engels to Florence Kelley-Wischnewtzky (June 3, 1886); and Engels to Friedrich Sorge (August 8, 1887, February 8, 1890, and March 18, 1893), in *Marx and Engels on the United States* (Moscow: Progress Publishers, 1979), 307, 319, 331. Phelps and Vandome, *Marxism and America*, 3–4.

54   Edward Bellamy, *Looking Backward, 2000–1887* (New York: Ticknor, 1888).

55   Cort, *Christian Socialism*, 258. Paul Buhle, *Marxism in the United States: A History of the American Left*, 3rd ed (1987; London: Verso, 2013), 70–71. John Thomas, *Alternative America: Henry George, Edward Bellamy, Henry Demarest Lloyd and the Adversary Tradition* (Cambridge, MA: Harvard University Press, 1983).

56   Lawrence Goodwyn, *Democratic Promise: The Populist Moment in America* (London: Oxford University Press, 1976).

57   Postel, *Equality*, 17–111.

58   Charles Postel, *The Populist Vision* (London: Oxford University Press, 2009). "People's Party Platform," *Omaha Morning World-Herald*, July 5, 1892.

59 Herreshoff, *American Disciples of Marx*, 12. Richard Hofstadter, *The Age of Reform: From Bryan to F. D. R.* (New York: Vintage Books, 1955).

60 Greg Grandin, *The End of the Myth: From the Frontier to the Border Wall in the Mind of America* (New York: Metropolitan Books, 2019), 1–2. Frederick Jackson Turner, *The Frontier in American History* (1893; Plano, TX: Digireads.com, 2010), 26.

61 Roseanne Dunbar-Ortiz, *An Indigenous Peoples' History of the United States* (Boston: Beacon Press, 2015).

62 Karl Marx, *The Eighteenth Brumaire of Louis Bonaparte* (1852), Marxists Internet Archive, accessed July 8, 2024, https://www.marxists.org/archive/marx /works/1852/18th-brumaire/. August H. Nimtz Jr., *Marx, Tocqueville, and Race in America: The "Absolute Democracy" or "Defiled Republic"* (New York: Lexington Books, 2003), 58.

63 "People's Party Platform."

64 Melvyn Dubofsky, *We Shall Be All: A History of the Industrial Workers of the World* (Chicago: Quadrangle Books, 1969), 14.

65 Herreshoff, *American Disciples of Marx*, 119.

66 Vernon L. Lidtke, *The Outlawed Party: Social Democracy in Germany, 1878–1890* (Princeton: Princeton University Press, 1966). Bruce Levine, *The Spirit of 1848: German Immigrants, Labor Conflict, and the Coming of the Civil War* (Urbana: University of Illinois Press, 1992).

67 Buhle, *Marxism in the United States*, 19–57.

68 Tony Michels, *A Fire in Their Hearts: Yiddish Socialists in New York* (Cambridge, MA: Harvard University Press, 2005), 2–4.

69 Michels, *A Fire in Their Hearts*, 5, 10–15, 47.

70 L. Glen Seretan, *Daniel DeLeon: The Odyssey of an American Marxist* (Cambridge, MA: Harvard University Press, 1979).

71 Seretan, *Daniel DeLeon*, 60.

72 Dubofsky, *We Shall Be All*, 75. Bell, "The Background and Development of Marxian Socialism in the United States," 242.

73 Seretan, *Daniel DeLeon*, 60–61.

74 Seretan, *Daniel DeLeon*, 61.

75 Bell, "The Background and Development of Marxian Socialism in the United States," 246. Socialist Labor Party of America Records, Wisconsin Historical Society, Library-Archives Division (hereafter SLP Records), Box 38, Folder 17: "Socialist Labor Party, Platform and Constitution, 1896 (New York City)."

76 Seretan, *Daniel DeLeon*, 66.

77 SLP Records, Box 39, Folder 5: "1904 Convention."

78 Buhle, *Marxism in the United States*, 56.

79 John R. Commons, "Karl Marx and Samuel Gompers," *Political Science Quarterly* 41, no. 2 (June 1926): 281.

80 Julie Greene, *Pure and Simple Politics: The American Federation of Labor and Political Activism, 1881–1917* (New York: Cambridge University Press, 1998). Salvatore, *Eugene V. Debs*, 206.

81 Bell, "The Background and Development of Marxian Socialism in the United States," 243–46.

82 Norma Fain Pratt, *Morris Hillquit: A Political History of an American Jewish Socialist* (Westport, CT: Greenwood Press, 1979).

83 Salvatore, *Eugene V. Debs*, 162.

84 Bell, "The Background and Development of Marxian Socialism in the United States," 259.

85 Paul Krause, *The Battle for Homestead, 1890–1892: Politics, Culture, and Steel* (Pittsburgh: University of Pittsburgh Press, 1992). Philip S. Foner, *Jack London: American Rebel* (New York: Citadel Press, 1947), 15.

86 Richard Schneirov, Shelton Stromquist, and Nick Salvatore, eds., *The Pullman Strike and the Crisis of the 1890s: Essays on Labor and Politics* (Urbana: University of Illinois Press, 1999).

87 Eugene V. Debs, "How I Became a Socialist," *New York Comrade*, April 1902. Bell, "The Background and Development of Marxian Socialism in the United States," 261–62. Salvatore, *Eugene V. Debs*, 150.

88 Sally M. Miller, *Victor Berger and the Promise of Constructive Socialism, 1910–1920* (Westport, CT: Greenwood Press, 1973).

89 Salvatore, *Eugene V. Debs*, 164–67.

90 Jack Ross, *The Socialist Party of America: A Complete History* (Lincoln, NE: Potomac Books, 2015).

91 Buhle, *Marxism in the United States*, 68. Salvatore, *Eugene V. Debs*, 165.

92 Tim Davenport and David Walters, eds., *The Selected Works of Eugene V. Debs*, vol. 3, *The Path to a Socialist Party, 1897–1904* (New York: Haymarket Books, 2020), 303. Salvatore, *Eugene V. Debs*, 192.

93 Salvatore, *Eugene V. Debs*, 192–93. Dubofsky, *We Shall Be All*, 63.

94 Janine Giordano Drake, *War for the Soul of the Christian Nation: Christianity and American Socialism, 1880–1920* (London: Oxford University Press, 2022).

95 Franklin Monroe Sprague, *Socialism from Genesis to Revelation* (Boston: Lee and Shepard Publishers, 1893). Cort, *Christian Socialism*, 265–75.

96 Bell, "The Background and Development of Marxian Socialism in the United States," 215, 267. Ross, *The Socialist Party of America*.

97 Dubofsky, *We Shall Be All*, 27. Peter Carlson, *Roughneck: The Life and Times of Big Bill Haywood* (New York: W. W. Norton, 1983). Bruce Watson, *Bread and Roses: Mills, Migrants, and The Struggle for the American Dream* (New York: Viking-Penguin, 2005).

98 William Philpott, *The Lessons of Leadville; or, Why the Western Federation of Miners Turned Left* (Denver: Colorado Historical Society, 1995). Dubofsky, *We Shall Be All*, 68.

99 Elizabeth Jameson, *All That Glitters: Class, Conflict, and Community in Cripple Creek* (Urbana: University of Illinois Press, 1998). Dubofsky, *We Shall Be All*, 55.

100 Anthony J. Lukas, *Big Trouble: A Murder in a Small Western Town Sets off a Struggle for the Soul of America* (New York: Simon & Schuster, 1997).

101 Transcript, Convention, Industrial Workers of the World (June 27, 1905), Marxists Internet Archive, accessed July 8, 2024, https://www.marxists.org/history/usa/unions/iww/1905/convention/.

102 Dubofsky, *We Shall Be All*, 96.

103 Fred Thompson, *The I.W.W.: Its First Fifty Years* (Chicago: IWW Publishing Bureau, 1955).

104 Salvatore, *Eugene V. Debs*, 198. William M. Adler, *The Man Who Never Died: The Life, Times, and Legacy of Joe Hill, American Labor Icon* (New York: Bloomsbury, 2011), 5.

105 Buhle, *Marxism in the United States*, 101. Salvatore, *Eugene V. Debs*, 198.

106 Paul Frederick Brissenden, *The IWW: A Study of American Syndicalism* (New York: Columbia University Press, 1919), 221–31.

107 Watson, *Bread and Roses*. 2006. Salvatore, *Eugene V. Debs*, 250–51.

108 "Preamble to the IWW Constitution," Industrial Workers of the World (1905).

109 John Duda, ed., *Wanted! Men to Fill the Jails of Spokane: Fighting for Free Speech with the Hobo Agitators of the Industrial Workers of the World* (Chicago: Charles H. Kerr, 2009).

110 *IWW Songs—to Fan the Flames of Discontent: A Reprint of the Nineteenth Edition (1923) of the Famous Little Red Song Book* (Chicago: Charles H. Kerr, 2003). Adler, *The Man Who Never Died*.

111 William A. Glaser, "Algie Martin Simons and Marxism in America," *Mississippi Valley Historical Review* 41, no. 3 (December 1954): 419–34. Salvatore, *Eugene V. Debs*, 193.

112 Allen Ruff, *"We Called Each Other Comrade": Charles H. Kerr & Company, Radical Publishers* (Urbana: University of Illinois Press, 1997), xiv. Charles H. Kerr Publishing Company Archives, Special Collections, Newberry Library, Chicago, IL. Series 3: Author Files, Box 7.

113 Jason D. Martinek, *Socialism and Print Culture in America, 1897–1920* (New York: Routledge, 2016). A. M. Simons, "How to Read *Capital*," *International Socialist Review* (January 1907).

114 Pittinger, *American Socialists and Evolutionary Thought*, 123.

115 Karl Marx, *The German Ideology* (1845), Marxists Internet Archive, accessed July 9, 2024, https://www.marxists.org/archive/marx/works/1845/german -ideology/. Ruff, *"We Called Each Other Comrade,"* 90.

116 Ernest Untermann, *Marxian Economics: A Popular Introduction to the Three Volumes of Marx's "Capital"* (Chicago: Charles H. Kerr, 1907).

117 Pittinger, *American Socialists and Evolutionary Thought*, 133–37.

118 Sven-Eric Liedman, *A World to Win: The Life and Works of Karl Marx*, trans. Jeffrey N. Skinner (London: Verso, 2018), 509–10. Untermann, *Marxian Economics*, 57–59.

119 Untermann, *Marxian Economics*, 12.

120 Untermann, *Marxian Economics*, 19.

121 Marx, *Capital*, vol. 1, 714–15, 875. Untermann, *Marxian Economics*, 147–48.

122 Foner, *Jack London*, 24.

123 James L. Haley, *Wolf: The Lives of Jack London* (New York: Basic Books, 2010). Foner, *Jack London*, 25–44.

124 Foner, *Jack London*, 44–55.

125 Foner, *Jack London*, 55–78.

126 Jack London, *The Iron Heel* (1907; New York: Hill and Wang, 1957). Foner, *Jack London*, 87.

127 London, *The Iron Heel*, 24, 128.

128 London, *The Iron Heel*, 75, 84.

129 London, *The Iron Heel*, 114–15.

130   London, *The Iron Heel*, 186–87, 192.

131   Bell, "The Background and Development of Marxian Socialism in the United States," 215, 217.

CHAPTER THREE

1   John Reed, *Ten Days That Shook the World* (New York: Boni & Liveright, 1919). George Kennan, *Russia Leaves the War: Soviet-American Relations, 1917–1920* (1956; Princeton, NJ: Princeton University Press, 1989), 68–69. "Condoleezza Rice on the 10 Days Still Shaking the World," *New York Times*, October 17, 2017.

2   John Stuart, *The Education of John Reed* (New York: International Publishers, 1955).

3   Theodore Roosevelt, "Bolshevism and Applied Anti-Bolshevism," *The Outlook*, September 18, 1918.

4   Eric Rauchway, *Murdering McKinley: The Making of Theodore Roosevelt's America* (New York: Hill and Wang, 2004). Theodore Roosevelt, "Sixth Annual Message," National Archives, December 3, 1906, accessed at millercenter.org.

5   Maurice Hamington, "Jane Addams," *The Stanford Encyclopedia of Philosophy*, ed. Edward N. Zalta and Uri Nodelman, last modified July 7, 2022, https://plato .stanford.edu/cgi-bin/encyclopedia/archinfo.cgi?entry=addams-jane.

6   A. F. Kantor, "Upton Sinclair and the Pure Food and Drugs Act of 1906: 'I Aimed at the Public's Heart and By Accident I Hit It in the Stomach,'" *American Journal of Public Health* 66, no. 12 (December 1976): 1202–5. Roosevelt quoted in Max Eastman, *Love and Revolution: My Journey through an Epoch* (New York: Random House, 1964), 144. Upton Sinclair, *The Jungle* (New York: Doubleday, Page and Co., 1906).

7   Gabriel Kolko, *The Triumph of Conservatism: A Reinterpretation of American History, 1900–1916* (New York: Free Press, 1963). Alana Toulin, "'Old Methods Not Up to New Ways': The Strategic Use of Advertising in the Fight for Pure Food After 1906," *The Journal of the Gilded Age and Progressive Era* 18, no. 4 (October 2019): 461–79.

8   James Chace, *1912: Wilson, Roosevelt, Taft, and Debs—The Election That Changed the Country* (New York: Simon and Schuster, 2004).

9   The Socialist Party of America, *Platform of 1912*. H. Wayne Morgan, "'Red Special': Eugene V. Debs and the Campaign of 1908," *Indiana Magazine of History* 54, no. 3 (September 1958): 211–36.

10   H. Wayne Morgan, *Eugene V. Debs: Socialist for President* (Syracuse: Syracuse University Press, 1962), 134.

11   Morgan, *Eugene V. Debs*, 131.

12   Carl E. Schorske, *German Social Democracy, 1905–1917: The Development of the Great Schism* (Cambridge, MA: Harvard University Press, 1955).

13   Leszek Kolakowski, *Main Currents of Marxism: It's Rise, Growth, and Dissolution*, trans. P. S. Falla (Oxford: Clarendon Press, 1978), 379–402. Jack London, *The Iron Heel* (1907; New York: Hill and Wang, 1957), 114–15.

14   Kolakowski, *Main Currents of Marxism*, 433–46.

15   Jukka Gronow, *On the Formation of Marxism: Karl Kautsky's Theory of Capitalism,*

the Marxism of the Second International and Karl Marx's Critique of Political Economy (Chicago: Haymarket Books, 2016).

16   Paul Heideman, "The Rise and Fall of the Socialist Party of America," *Jacobin*, February 20, 2017. Mark Pittinger, *American Socialists and Evolutionary Thought, 1870–1920* (Madison: University of Wisconsin Press, 1993), 23. Sally M. Miller, *Victor Berger and the Promise of Constructive Socialism, 1910–1920* (Westport, CT: Greenwood Press, 1973).

17   Elmer A. Beck, *The Sewer Socialists: A History of the Socialist Party of Wisconsin, 1897–1940* (Fennimore, WI: Westburg Associates, 1982). John Nichols, *The "S" Word: A Short History of an American Tradition* (London: Verso, 2011), 101–40.

18   Will Stratford, "Rediscovering Revolutionary Socialism in America: The Marxism of Victor Berger at the Height of the Second International," *Moving the Social: Journal of Social History and the History of Social Movements* 68 (2022).

19   Victor Berger, "Socialism and Liberty," *Social Democratic Herald* 14, no. 22 (September 30, 1911): 1. Stratford, "Rediscovering Revolutionary Socialism in America."

20   Worth Robert Miller, *Oklahoma Populism: A History of the People's Party in the Oklahoma Territory* (Norman: University of Oklahoma Press, 1987).

21   Jim Bissett, *Agrarian Socialism in America: Marx, Jefferson, and Jesus in the Oklahoma Countryside, 1904–1920* (Norman: University of Oklahoma Press, 1999). Richard L. Harris, "Marxism and the Agrarian Question in Latin America," *Latin American Perspectives* 5, no. 4 (Autumn, 1978): 2–26.

22   Michael Levien, Michael Watts, and Yan Hairong, "Agrarian Marxism," *The Journal of Peasant Studies* 45 (2018): 853–83.

23   Chris Maisano, "When America's Red States Were Red," *Jacobin*, July 8, 2021.

24   Bissett, *Agrarian Socialism in America*, 66.

25   Bissett, *Agrarian Socialism in America*, 183.

26   Bissett, *Agrarian Socialism in America*, 96, 104, 90–91.

27   Philip S. Foner, *American Socialism and Black Americans: From the Age of Jackson to World War II* (Westport, CT: Greenwood Press, 1977), 259–60.

28   Jeffrey B. Perry, *Hubert Harrison: The Voice of Harlem Radicalism, 1883–1918* (New York: Columbia University Press, 2009), 7. Foner, *American Socialism and Black Americans*, 209–10.

29   Foner, *American Socialism and Black Americans*, 214–15.

30   Perry, *Hubert Harrison*, 200–215.

31   Mari Jo Buhle, *Women and American Socialism, 1870–1920* (Urbana: University of Illinois Press, 1981), 223–38. Meredith Tax, *The Rising of Women: Feminist Solidarity and Class Conflict, 1880–1917* (New York: Monthly Review Press, 1980).

32   Buhle, *Women and American Socialism*, 226. Philip S. Foner, ed., *Helen Keller: Her Socialist Years, Writings and Speeches* (New York: International Publishers, 1967), 33.

33   Lara Vapnek, *Elizabeth Gurley Flynn: Modern American Revolutionary, 1890–1964* (Boulder, CO: Westview Press, 2015), 7–9.

34   Vapnek, *Elizabeth Gurley Flynn*, 13.

35   Vapnek, *Elizabeth Gurley Flynn*, 20.

36   Tax, *The Rising of Women*, 12.

37   Vapnek, *Elizabeth Gurley Flynn*, 39.

38   Vapnek, *Elizabeth Gurley Flynn*, 37, 55.

39   Cook, "The Bohemian Bolsheviks" (master's thesis, James Madison University, 2020).

40   Thomas A. Maik, *The Masses Magazine (1911–1917): Odyssey of an Era* (New York: Garland Publishing, 1994), xii.

41   Eastman, *Love and Revolution*, 4, 15. Karl Marx, *The German Ideology* (1845), Marxists Internet Archive, accessed July 9, 2024, https://www.marxists.org/archive/marx/works/1845/german-ideology/.

42   The historian Allen Churchill is quoted in Maik, *The Masses Magazine*, 21.

43   Eastman, *Love and Revolution*, 12. Max Eastman, "Knowledge and Revolution," *The Masses*, December 1912, 6.

44   Eastman, *Love and Revolution*, 13–14.

45   Eastman, *Love and Revolution*, 15. Christoph Irmscher, *Max Eastman: A Life* (New Haven, CT: Yale University Press, 2017). John P. Diggins, *Up from Communism: Conservative Odysseys in American Intellectual History* (New York: Harper and Row, 1975).

46   Karl Marx, *Capital*, vol. 1, trans. Ben Fowkes (1867; New York: Vintage, 1977), 899. Fowkes translates it as "silent compulsion." Søren Mau translates it as "mute compulsion" in *Mute Compulsion: A Marxist Theory of the Economic Power of Capital* (London: Verso, 2023). The more commonly known translation is "dull compulsion." Eastman, *Love and Revolution*, 15.

47   Stuart, *The Education of John Reed*, 17–18.

48   Stuart, *The Education of John Reed*, 19.

49   Stuart, *The Education of John Reed*, 21.

50   Walter Lippman, "Legendary John Reed," *The New Republic*, December 26, 1914, 15–16.

51   Michael Kazin, *War against War: The American Fight for Peace, 1914–1918* (New York: Simon & Schuster, 2017).

52   John Maxwell Hamilton, *Manipulating the Masses: Woodrow Wilson and the Birth of American Propaganda* (Baton Rouge: LSU Press, 2020). Nick Fischer, *Spider Web: The Birth of American Anticommunism* (Urbana: University of Illinois Press, 2016).

53   John Reed, "The Traders' War," *The Masses* (September 1914). John Reed, "Whose War?" *The Masses* (April 1917). Eastman, *Love and Revolution*, 22, 30.

54   Cook, "The Bohemian Bolsheviks," 21.

55   Eastman, *Love and Revolution*, 63–64.

56   Sheila Fitzpatrick, *The Russian Revolution*, 4th ed. (London: Oxford University Press, 2017). China Miéville, *October: The Story of the Russian Revolution* (London: Verso, 2017). Alan Wald, "Imagined Solidarities: The Bolshevik Revolution and the U. S. Literary Left," *Science and Society* 81, no. 4 (2017): 570–79.

57   Isaac Deutscher, *The Prophet: The Life of Leon Trotsky* (1954, 1959, 1963; London: Verso Books, 2015).

58   Leon Trotsky, *My Life: An Attempt at an Autobiography* (New York: Charles Scribner's Sons, 1930), 268, 270.

59   Tony Michels, "The Russian Revolution in New York, 1917–19," *Journal of Contemporary History* 52, no. 4 (October 2017): 961.

60 Trotsky, *My Life*, 274–75.
61 Michels, "The Russian Revolution in New York," 959–60.
62 Michels, "The Russian Revolution in New York," 966.
63 Michels, "The Russian Revolution in New York," 967. Floyd Dell, "Trotsky," *Liberator*, March 1918, 33.
64 Reed, *Ten Days that Shook the World*, preface. Stuart, *The Education of John Reed*, 31.
65 Eastman, *Love and Revolution*, 78.
66 Eastman, *Love and Revolution*, 160, 77–78. Michels, "The Russian Revolution in New York," 969.
67 Eastman, *Love and Revolution*, 77, 162.
68 Reed, *Ten Days that Shook the World*, preface.
69 Reed, *Ten Days that Shook the World*, preface.
70 Reed, *Ten Days that Shook the World*, 63.
71 Reed, *Ten Days that Shook the World*, 66.
72 Reed, *Ten Days that Shook the World*, preface.
73 Eastman, *Love and Revolution*, 47.
74 Reed, *Ten Days that Shook the World*, 39. Eastman, *Love and Revolution*, 46–47.
75 Eastman, *Love and Revolution*, 127–44.
76 Stuart, *The Education of John Reed*, 213.
77 Foner, *American Socialism and Black Americans*, 276.
78 Theodore Kornweibel Jr., *No Crystal Stair: Black Life and the "Messenger", 1917–1928* (Westport, CT: Greenwood Press, 1975), 29.
79 Kornweibel, *No Crystal Stair*, 30. Foner, *American Socialism and Black Americans*, 267.
80 Kornweibel, *No Crystal Stair*, 26–27.
81 Foner, *American Socialism and Black Americans*, 272. Manning Marable, "A Philip Randolph and the Foundations of Black American Socialism," *Radical America* 14, no. 3 (May–June 1980): 6–29. "Who Shall Pay for the War?" *The Messenger* (November 1917): 7.
82 "The Rioting of Negro Soldiers," *The Messenger* (November 1917): 7.
83 "Who Should Be Mayor," *The Messenger* (November 1917): 19; "The Deportation of Agitators, *The Messenger* (March 2019): 3.
84 Foner, *American Socialism and Black Americans*, 278.
85 Joint Legislative Committee Investigating Seditious Activities, *Revolutionary Radicalism: Its History, Purpose and Tactics with an Exposition and Discussion of the Steps being Taken and Required to Curb It*, April 24, 1920, Senate of the State of New York.
86 A. Philip Randolph, "An Open Letter to the Union League Club of New York" (1921), found at the Samuel Gompers Papers website.
87 Peter G. Filene, *Americans and the Soviet Experiment, 1917–1933* (Cambridge, MA: Harvard University Press, 1967).
88 Ann Hagedorn, *Savage Peace: Hope and Fear in America, 1919* (New York: Simon & Schuster, 2007).
89 Vapnek, *Elizabeth Gurley Flynn*, 54. Jane Little Botkin, *Frank Little and the IWW: The Blood That Stained an American Family* (Norman: University of Oklahoma Press, 2017).
90 Bissett, *Agrarian Socialism in America*, 150–53.

91   Bissett, *Agrarian Socialism in America*, 146–47, 169. Christopher Phelps, "Lenin and American Radicalism," *Science & Society* 60, no. 1 (Spring 1996): 80–86.

92   Nick Salvatore, *Eugene V. Debs: Citizen and Socialist*, 2nd ed. (1982; Urbana: University of Illinois Press, 2007), 291–94. Eugene V. Debs, *Canton Speech*, reprinted in *Writings and Speeches of Eugene V. Debs* (Ewing Township, NJ: Hermitage Press, 1948), 417–33.

93   Salvatore, *Eugene V. Debs*, 294–96.

94   Eastman, *Love and Revolution*, 87–89.

95   Eastman, *Love and Revolution*, 120.

96   Hagedorn, *Savage Peace*, 80–90.

97   Fischer, *Spider Web*, 59–60.

98   David Brody, *Labor in Crisis: The Steel Strike of 1919* (Champaign: University of Illinois Press, 1987).

99   Hagedorn, *Savage Peace*, 171–78.

100   Hagedorn, *Savage Peace*, 53–60.

101   Hagedorn, *Savage Peace*, 152–54. Joint Legislative Committee Investigating Seditious Activities, *Revolutionary Radicalism*.

102   Hagedorn, *Savage Peace*, 223–25.

103   Hagedorn, *Savage Peace*, 229. Beverly Gage, *G-Man: J. Edgar Hoover and the Making of the American Century* (New York: Viking, 2022).

104   Robert K. Murray, *Red Scare: A Study in National Hysteria, 1919–1920* (Minneapolis: University of Minnesota Press, 1955).

105   Emma Goldman, "Deportation to Russia," *My Disillusionment in Russia* (New York: Doubleday, Page & Company, 1923).

106   Cameron McWhirter, *Red Summer: The Summer of 1919 and the Awakening of Black America* (New York: Henry Holt and Company, 2011). Hagedorn, *Savage Peace*, 317, 402.

107   Hagedorn, *Savage Peace*, 301.

108   Foner, *American Socialism and Black Americans*, 294–96.

109   Philip S. Foner, *History of the Labor Movement in the United States*, vol. 8, *Postwar Struggles, 1918–1920* (New York: International Publishers, 1988). Melvyn Dubofsky and Foster Rhea Dulles, *Labor in America: A History*, 6th ed. (Wheeling, IL: Harlan Davidson, 1999).

110   Theodore Draper, *The Roots of American Communism* (1957; New York: Routledge, 2003).

111   Christopher Lasch, *The Agony of the American Left* (New York: Vintage, 1968), 42.

112   Paul Buhle, *Marxism in the United States: A History of the American Left*, 3rd ed (1987; London: Verso, 2013), 121.

113   Eric Hobsbawm, "Problems of Communist History," *New Left Review* (March/April 1969). Paul M. Buhle, *A Dreamer's Paradise: Louis C. Fraina/Lewis Corey (1892–1953) and the Decline of Radicalism in the United States* (Atlantic Highlands, NJ: Humanities Press, 1995), 62.

114   Buhle, *A Dreamer's Paradise*, 4–6.

115   Buhle, *A Dreamer's Paradise*, 32–33, 75.

116   Buhle, *A Dreamer's Paradise*, 76.

117   Buhle, *A Dreamer's Paradise*, 76, 52–53. Louis C. Fraina, *Revolutionary Socialism: A Study in Socialist Reconstruction* (New York: The Communist Press, 1918).

118   Vladimir Lenin, *Imperialism, the Highest Stage of Capitalism* (1917), in *Lenin's Selected Works*, vol. 1 (Moscow: Progress Publishers, 1963), 667–766; accessed at Marxists Internet Archive, accessed July 8, 2024, https://www.marxists.org /archive/lenin/works/1916/imp-hsc/.

119   Fraina, *Revolutionary Socialism*, 20.

120   Fraina, *Revolutionary Socialism*, i.

121   Fraina, *Revolutionary Socialism*, 5.

122   Fraina, *Revolutionary Socialism*, 23–24. Daniela Spenser, *The Impossible Triangle: Mexico, Soviet Russia, and the United States in the 1920s* (Durham, NC: Duke University Press, 1999).

123   Fraina, *Revolutionary Socialism*, 37. J. P. Nettl, *Rosa Luxemburg* (London: Oxford University Press, 1969).

124   Harry Haywood, *Black Bolshevik: Autobiography of an Afro-American Communist* (Chicago: Liberator Press, 1978), 117.

125   Haywood, *Black Bolshevik*, 157–61.

126   "Interview with Harry Ring," James Cannon Papers, Box 1, Folder 14, Wisconsin Historical Society, Madison, WI (hereafter Cannon Papers).

127   Minkah Makalani, *In the Cause of Freedom: Radical Black Internationalism from Harlem to London, 1917–1939* (Chapel Hill: University of North Carolina Press, 2011). Mark Solomon, *The Cry Was Unity: Communists and African Americans, 1917–1936* (Jackson: University of Mississippi Press, 1998).

128   Haywood, *Black Bolshevik*, 172–74. Melvyn Dubofsky, *"Big Bill" Haywood* (New York: St. Martin's Press, 1987).

129   Robin D. G. Kelley, *Hammer and Hoe: Alabama Communists During the Great Depression* (Chapel Hill: University of North Carolina Press, 1990).

130   "Interview with Harry Ring," Cannon Papers. Bryan D. Palmer, *James P. Cannon and the Origins of the American Revolutionary Left, 1890–1928* (Urbana: University of Illinois Press, 2007).

131   Palmer, *James P. Cannon and the Origins of the American Revolutionary Left*, 52. Box 1, Folder 10, Cannon Papers.

132   "Interview with Harry Ring," Cannon Papers.

133   "Interview with Harry Ring, Cannon Papers. Palmer, *James P. Cannon and the Origins of the American Revolutionary Left*, 91–93.

134   "Interview with Harry Ring," Cannon Papers.

135   Palmer, *James P. Cannon and the Origins of the American Revolutionary Left*, 98–110.

136   Henry Adams, *The Education of Henry Adams: An Autobiography* (1918; New York: Modern Library, 1999).

137   Buhle, *Marxism in the United States*, 123–26.

138   Isaac Deutscher, *Trotsky: The Prophet Outcast* (1963; London: Verso, 2003). Leon Trotsky, *The Revolution Betrayed* (1937; trans. Max Eastman), Marxists Internet Archive, accessed July 9, 2024, https://www.marxists.org/archive/trotsky /1936/revbet/. Alex Callinicos, *Trotskyism* (Minneapolis: University of Minnesota Press, 1990).

139   Martin Abern, "International Labor Defense Activities," *James P. Cannon and the Early Years of American Communism: Selected Writings and Speeches, 1920–1928* (New York: Spartacist Publishing Company, 1992).

140   "Introduction," Cannon Papers. Leon Trotsky, "Declaration to the Sixth Com-

intern Congress" (July 12, 1928), Leon Trotsky, *The Challenge of the Left Opposition (1928–1929)* (New York: Pathfinder Press, 1981), 132–50.

141   Leon Trotsky, "Tasks of the American Opposition," *The Militant* (June 1, 1929). "Trotsky Correspondence—1929–1936," Box 12, Folder 8, Cannon Papers.

142   James P. Cannon, *The History of American Trotskyism*, Second Edition (New York: Pathfinder Press, 1974).

143   "Interview with Harry Ring," Cannon Papers.

144   "Interview with Harry Ring," Cannon Papers.

CHAPTER FOUR

1   Anthony Badger, *The New Deal: The Depression Years, 1933–1940* (New York: Hill and Wang, 1989).

2   Studs Terkel, *Hard Times: An Oral History of the Great Depression* (New York: Pantheon Books, 1970), 54.

3   Edmund Wilson, "Progress and Poverty," *New Republic* 67, no. 859 (May 20, 1931): 13–16, in Howard Brick, Paul LeBlanc, and Brian Whitener, eds., *"Leftward Ho!" Revolutionary Intellectuals, 1928–1948* (unpublished manuscript).

4   Mary Gabriel, *Love and Capital: Karl and Jenny Marx and the Birth of a Revolution* (Boston: Back Bay, 2012), 176–77.

5   Katherine A. S. Sibley, ed., *A Companion to Warren G. Harding, Calvin Coolidge, and Herbert Hoover*, Blackwell Companion to American History (Hoboken, NJ: Wiley & Sons, 2014).

6   John Kenneth Galbraith, *The Great Crash 1929* (1954; New York: Mariner Books, 2009).

7   Eric Rauchway, *The Money Makers: How Roosevelt and Keynes Ended the Depression, Defeated Fascism, and Secured a Prosperous Peace* (New York: Basic Books, 2015).

8   James Livingston, "Their Great Depression and Ours," *Challenge* 52, no. 3 (2009): 34–51.

9   Donald Worster, *Dust Bowl: The Southern Plains in the 1930s* (1979; Oxford: Oxford University Press, 2004).

10   James Noble Gregory, *American Exodus: The Dust Bowl Migration and Okie Culture in California* (Oxford: Oxford University Press, 1989). John Steinbeck, *The Grapes of Wrath* (New York: Viking Press, 1939). Marci Lingo, "Forbidden Fruit: The Banning of *The Grapes of Wrath* in the Kern County Free Library," *Libraries & Culture* 38, no. 4 (Fall 2003): 351–77.

11   Joan Hoff Wilson, *Herbert Hoover: Forgotten Progressive* (Long Grove, IL: Waveland Press, 1992); William E. Leuchtenberg, *Herbert Hoover: The American Presidents Series: The 31st President, 1929–1933* (New York: Times Books, 2009).

12   Henryk Grossman, *Capitalism's Contradictions: Studies in Economic Theory Before and After Marx* (Chicago: Haymarket Books, 2017).

13   Karl Marx, *Capital: A Critique of Political Economy*, vol. 3, trans. David Fernbach (New York: Penguin Books, 1981).

14   Sven-Eric Liedman, *A World to Win: The Life and Works of Karl Marx*, trans. Jeffrey N. Skinner (London: Verso, 2018), 326.

15   Karl Marx, *Grundrisse: Foundations of the Critique of Political Economy (Rough*

Draft), trans. Martin Nicolaus (New York: Penguin Books, 1973), 20. Letter of Marx to Engels (July 11, 1868), in *Marx Engels Selected Correspondence* (Moscow: Progress Publishers, 1975), 194.

16   Marx, *Capital*, vol. 3, 318.

17   Marx, *Capital*, vol. 3, 318.

18   Will Wilkinson, "Capitalism and Human Nature," *Cato Policy Report* 27, no. 1 (Jan-Feb 2005).

19   Michael Henrich, "Crisis Theory, the Law of the Tendency of the Profit Rate to Fall, and Marx's Studies in the 1870s," *Monthly Review* (April 1, 2013).

20   Louis Corey, "The NRA is Doomed," *Modern Monthly* 7, no. 10 (1932): 605–19, in Brick, LeBlanc, and Whitener, *"Leftward Ho!"* Lewis Corey, *The Decline of American Capitalism* (New York: Covici Friede Publishers, 1934). Paul Buhle, *A Dreamer's Paradise Lost: Louis C. Fraina/Lewis Corey (1892–1953) and the Decline of Radicalism in the United States* (Atlantic Highlands, New Jersey: Humanities Press International, 1995), 119, 121. John Maynard Keynes, *A Treatise on Money* (London: Macmillan & Co., 1930). John Maynard Keynes, *The General Theory of Employment, Interest, and Money* (London: Palgrave Macmillan, 1936).

21   Karl Marx, *Capital*, vol. 2, trans. David Fernbach (New York: Penguin Books, 1978). Robert Skidelsky, *John Maynard Keynes: 1883–1946: Economist, Philosopher, Statesman* (New York: Penguin Books, 2005), 329.

22   Paul Mattick, "Marx and Keynes," *Western Socialist* (November–December 1955).

23   James Livingston, *Pragmatism and the Political Economy of Cultural Revolution, 1850–1940* (Chapel Hill: University of North Carolina Press, 1994), 106–7. Corey, *The Decline of American Capitalism*, 232.

24   Corey, *The Decline of American Capitalism*, 246.

25   Fraser M. Ottanelli, *The Communist Party of the United States: From the Depression to World War II* (New Brunswick: Rutgers University Press, 1991).

26   Victor G. Devinatz, "The CPUSA's Trade Unionism during Third Period Communism, 1929–1934," *American Communist History* 18 (2019): 251–68.

27   Mike Davis, *Prisoners of the American Dream: Politics and Economy in the History of the U.S. Working Class* (London: Verso, 1986), 54. Leilah Danielson, *American Gandhi: A. J. Muste and the History of Radicalism in the Twentieth Century* (Philadelphia: University of Pennsylvania Press, 2014), 185. John A. Salmond, *The General Textile Strike of 1934: From Maine to Alabama* (Columbia: University of Missouri Press, 2002).

28   Robert H. Zieger, *The CIO, 1935–1955* (Chapel Hill: University of North Carolina Press, 1995). Lizbeth Cohen, *Making a New Deal: Industrial Workers in Chicago, 1919–1939* (London: Cambridge University Press, 2008).

29   Sidney Fine, *Sit-Down: The General Motors Strike of 1936–1937* (Ann Arbor: University of Michigan Press, 1969).

30   J. Peters, "The Communist Party: A Manual on Organization," (New York: Worker's Library Publishers, 1935).

31   Maurice Isserman, *Which Side Were You On?: The American Communist Party During the Second World War* (Middletown, CT: Wesleyan University Press, 1982). Leo P. Ribuffo, *Left Center Right: Essays in American History* (New Brunswick, NJ: Rutgers University Press, 1992).

32 Harvey Klehr, John Earl Haynes, Fridrikh Igorevich Firsov, *The Secret World of American Communism* (New Haven, CT: Yale University Press, 1996).

33 Marx, *Capital*, vol. 1, 414. Oscar Berland, "The Emergence of the Communist Perspective on the 'Negro Question' in America: 1919–1931: Part Two," *Science & Society* 64, no. 2 (Summer 2000): 194–217.

34 Randolph is quoted in Touré F. Reed, *Toward Freedom: The Case against Race Reductionism* (London: Verso, 2020), 39.

35 Dan T. Carter, *Scottsboro: A Tragedy of the American South* (Louisiana State University Press, Baton Rouge, 1979). Robin D. G. Kelley, *Hammer and Hoe: Alabama Communists During the Great Depression* (Chapel Hill: University of North Carolina Press, 1990). Mark Naison, *Communists in Harlem during the Depression* (Champaign: University of Illinois Press, 1983). Erik S. McDuffie, *Sojourning for Freedom: Black Women, American Communism, and the Making of Black Left Feminism* (Durham: Duke University Press, 2011).

36 Vivian Gornick, *The Romance of American Communism* (New York: Basic Books, 1977), 7–8, 29. Howard Sachar, *A History of the Jews in America* (New York: Vintage, 1993), 428–36.

37 Gornick, *The Romance of American Communism*, 29.

38 Gornick, *The Romance of American Communism*, 65.

39 William Z. Foster, *Toward Soviet America* (New York: Coward-McCann, Inc., 1932). Matthew Worley, ed., *In Search of Revolution: International Communist Parties in the Third Period* (New York: I. B. Tauris, 2004).

40 Shachtman is quoted in Terkel, *Hard Times*, 299.

41 Robert Weiner, "Karl Marx's Vision of America: A Biographical and Bibliographical Sketch," *The Review of Politics* 42, no. 4 (Oct 1980): 486.

42 Paul Sweezy, "Marx on the Significance of the Corporation," *Science and Society* 3, no. 2 (Spring 1939): 238–41.

43 "Hugo Gellert," *Spartacus Educational Online Encyclopedia*, accessed July 8, 2024, https://spartacus-educational.com/ARTgellert.htm. Hugo Gellert, *Karl Marx's Capital in Lithographs* (New York: Ray Long & Richard R. Smith, 1934).

44 Babak Amini, "A Brief History of the Dissemination and Reception of Karl Marx's *Capital* in the United States and Britain," *World Review of Political Economy* 7, no. 3 (Fall 2016): 334–49. Gellert, *Karl Marx's Capital in Lithographs*, 1.

45 Gellert, *Karl Marx's Capital in Lithographs*, 7.

46 Gellert, *Karl Marx's Capital in Lithographs*, 28.

47 Gellert, *Karl Marx's Capital in Lithographs*, 33.

48 Gellert, *Karl Marx's Capital in Lithographs*, 1.

49 Sidney Hook, *Towards the Understanding of Karl Marx: A Revolutionary Interpretation* (New York: John Day, 1933). Christopher Phelps, *Young Sidney Hook: Marxist and Pragmatist* (1997; Ann Arbor: University of Michigan Press, 2005). Max Eastman, "An Interpretation of Marx," *New York Herald Tribune* (April 16, 1933), 6.

50 Phelps, *Young Sidney Hook*, 67.

51 Phelps, *Young Sidney Hook*, 51.

52 Phelps, *Young Sidney Hook*, 71.

53 Sidney Hook, *From Hegel to Marx: Studies in the Intellectual Development of Karl Marx* (London: Victor Gollancz, 1936), 272. Hook, *Towards the Understanding of Karl Marx*, 9.

54   James T. Kloppenberg, "Pragmatism: An Old Name for Some New Ways of
     Thinking?" *The Journal of American History* 83, no. 1 (June 1996): 101. David A.
     Hollinger, "The Problem of Pragmatism in American History," *The Journal of
     American History* 67, no. 1 (June 1980): 88–107. See also James Kloppenberg,
     *Uncertain Victory: Social Democracy and Progressivism in European and American
     Thought, 1870–1920* (New York: Oxford University Press, 1986).

55   Robert Westbrook, *John Dewey and American Democracy* (Ithaca: Cornell Univer-
     sity Press, 1991); Alan Ryan, *John Dewey and the High Tide of American Liberalism*
     (New York: W. W. Norton, 1995).

56   Phelps, *Young Sidney Hook*, 58. Richard H. Pells, *Radical Visions and American
     Dreams: Culture and Social Thought in the Depression Years* (New York: Harper &
     Row, 1973). Randolph Bourne, "Twilight of Idols," *The Seven Arts* 11 (October
     1917): 688–702.

57   Richard Wightman Fox, *Niebuhr: A Biography* (Ithaca, NY: Cornell University
     Press, 1997).

58   Reinhold Niebuhr, *Moral Man and Immoral Society: A Study in Ethics and Politics*
     (New York: Charles Scribner's Sons, 1932).

59   Niebuhr, *Moral Man and Immoral Society*, 147.

60   Niebuhr, *Moral Man and Immoral Society*, 153–55, 160.

61   Hook, *Towards the Understanding of Karl Marx*, 9.

62   Max Eastman, *Marxism: Is it Science?* (London: George Allen & Unwin, 1941), 9.

63   Karl Korsch, *Marxism and Philosophy* (1923; New York: Monthly Review Press,
     1970). György Lukács, *History and Class Consciousness: Studies in Marxist Dialectics*
     (1923; London: Merlin Press, 1967). Karl Marx, "Theses on Feuerbach" (1845),
     Marxists Internet Archive, accessed July 9, 2024, https://www.marxists.org
     /archive/marx/works/1845/theses/theses.htm. Marx, *Capital*, vol. 1, 198.
     Hook, *Towards the Understanding of Karl Marx*, 79.

64   Hook, *Towards the Understanding of Karl Marx*, 86.

65   Hook, *Towards the Understanding of Karl Marx*, 33.

66   Hook, *Towards the Understanding of Karl Marx*, 33–36.

67   Marx, *A Contribution to the Critique of Political Economy*, preface, Marxists Inter-
     net Archive, accessed July 8, 2024, https://www.marxists.org/archive/marx
     /works/1859/critique-pol-economy/index.htm.

68   Daniel Aaron, *Writers on the Left: Episodes in American Literary Communism* (1961;
     New York: Columbia University Press, 1992). V. F. Calverton, "What Social-
     ism Means to Me," *Socialist Call* (1940); "Nemesis" (n.p., n.d.). V. F. Calverton
     Papers, Manuscripts and Archives Division, New York Public Library (Hereon:
     Calverton Papers), Box 21.

69   Philip Abbott, *Leftward Ho! V. F. Calverton and American Radicalism* (Westport,
     CT: Greenwood Press, 1993).

70   V. F. Calverton, "What Socialism Means to Me." Eric Homberger, "Proletarian
     Literature and the John Reed Clubs, 1929–1935," *Journal of American Studies* 13,
     no. 2 (August 1979): 228. Aaron, *Writers on the Left*, 331.

71   Calverton, "Marx: Idealist or Materialist," (n.p., n.d.), Calverton Papers, Box
     21. V. F. Calverton, *For Revolution* (New York: John Day, 1932).

72   Sheila Fitzpatrick, *The Cultural Front: Power and Culture in Revolutionary Russia*
     (Ithaca, NY: Cornell University Press, 1992).

73   Williams Phelps and Philip Rahv, "Problems and Perspectives in Revolutionary Literature," *Partisan Review* 1, no. 3 (June–July 1934): 3–11. V. F. Calverton, "Can We Have a Proletarian Literature?" *Modern Quarterly* 6 (Autumn 1932): 38–50. James D. Bloom, *Left Letters: The Culture Wars of Mike Gold and Joseph Freeman* (New York: Columbia University Press, 1992), 9, 56. Mike Gold, "Towards Proletarian Culture," *The Liberator* (February 1921).

74   Alan Wald, *Exiles from a Future Time: The Forging of the Mid-Twentieth-Century Literary Left* (Chapel Hill: University of North Carolina Press, 2002), 39, 57.

75   Mike Gold, *Jews Without Money* (New York: Horace Liveright, 1930).

76   V. F. Calverton, *The Newer Spirit: A Sociological Criticism of Literature* (1925; London: Octagon Books, 1974). Aaron, *Writers on the Left*, 326, 331.

77   Abbott, *Leftward Ho!*, 77.

78   V. F. Calverton, *The Liberation of American Literature* (New York: Charles Scribner's Sons, 1932). Calverton, *For Revolution.*

79   Abbott, *Leftward Ho!*, 80.

80   Letter from Calverton to Harry Elmer Barnes (undated), Calverton Papers, Box 1.

81   Calverton, *For Revolution.* Werner Sombart, *Why Is There No Socialism in the United States* (1905; New York: Sharpe, 1976).

82   Robert Genter, *Late Modernism: Art, Culture and Politics in Cold War America* (Philadelphia: University of Pennsylvania Press, 2010).

83   Michael Denning, *The Cultural Front: The Laboring of American Culture* (London: Verso, 1997), 102. Kenneth Burke, *Permanence and Change: An Anatomy of Purpose* (New York: New Republic, 1935), 55, 65.

84   Kenneth Burke, "Revolutionary Symbolism in America," (1935), in *The Legacy of Kenneth Burke*, ed. Herbert W. Simons and Trevor Melia (Madison: University of Wisconsin Press, 1989). Kenneth Burke, *Attitudes Toward History*, 3rd ed. (1937; Berkeley: University of California Press, 1987).

85   Burke, *Attitudes Toward History*, 56; *Permanence and Change*, 93.

86   V. F. Calverton, ed., *Anthology of American Negro Literature* (New York: Modern Library, 1929). Calverton, *The Liberation of American Literature*, 438.

87   W. E. B. Du Bois, *Black Reconstruction in America: An Essay Toward a History of the Part Which Black Folk Played in the Attempt to Reconstruct Democracy in America, 1860–1880* (1935; Cleveland, OH: Meridian Books, 1964). C. L. R. James, *Black Jacobins: Toussaint L'Ouverture and the San Domingo Revolution*, 2nd ed. (1962; New York: Vintage Books, 1989).

88   David Levering Lewis, *W. E. B. Du Bois: The Fight for Equality and the American Century, 1919–1963* (New York: Henry Holt, 2000), 352–73. W. E. B. Du Bois, *The Souls of Black Folks* (1903). Paul Buhle, *C. L. R. James: The Artist as Revolutionary*, new and expanded edition (1988; London: Verso, 2017).

89   Cedric Robinson, *Black Marxism: The Making of the Black Radical Tradition* (Chapel Hill: University of North Carolina Press, 1983).

90   Marx, *Capital*, vol. 1, 915. Lucia Pradella, "Crisis, Revolution and Hegemonic Transition: The American Civil War and Emancipation in Marx's *Capital*," *Science & Society* 80, no. 4 (October 2016). Kevin B. Anderson, *Marx at the Margins: on Nationalism, Ethnicity, and Non-Western Societies*, expanded edition (2010; Chicago: University of Chicago Press, 2016).

91   Marx and Engels, *The Civil War in the United States*.

92   John David Smith and J. Vincent Lowery, eds. *The Dunning School: Historians, Race, and the Meaning of Reconstruction* (Lexington: University Press of Kentucky, 2013).

93   Letter from Du Bois to Abram Harris (January 6, 1933), W. E. B. Du Bois Papers, digitized and online, University of Massachusetts, Amherst (hereafter Du Bois Papers). Lewis, *W. E. B. Du Bois*, 360–76. Du Bois, *Black Reconstruction*, 358.

94   W. E. B. Du Bois, "Marxism and the Negro Problem," *Crisis* 40, no. 5 (May 1933): 103–4, 118, in Brick, LeBlanc, and Whitener, eds., *"Leftward Ho!"*

95   Du Bois, *Black Reconstruction*, 5. Karl Marx, *The Poverty of Philosophy* (1847), Marxists Internet Archive, accessed July 8, 2024, https://www.marxists.org /archive/marx/works/1847/poverty-philosophy/.

96   Du Bois, *Black Reconstruction*, 29.

97   Andrew Zimmerman, "From the Rhine to the Mississippi," *Journal of the Civil War Era* 5, no. 1 (March 2015): 3–37. Du Bois, *Black Reconstruction*, 55–67.

98   Claire Parfait, "Rewriting History: The Publication of W. E. B. Du Bois's *Black Reconstruction in America*," *Book History* 12 (2009): 266–94. Abram Harris, "Reconstruction and the Negro," *The New Republic*, August 7 1935, 367–68, in Brick, LeBlanc, and Whitener, eds., *"Leftward Ho!"*

99   Ira Berlin, Barbara J. Fields, Steven F. Miller, Joseph P. Reidy, and Leslie S. Rowland, *Slaves No More: Three Essays on Emancipation and the Civil War* (New York: Cambridge University Press, 1992).

100 "Letter from W. E. B. Du Bois to Ben Stolberg" and "Letter from Benjamin Stolberg to W. E. B. Du Bois," Du Bois Papers. Du Bois, *Black Reconstruction*, 345.

101 "Letter from Benjamin Stolberg to W. E. B. Du Bois," Du Bois Papers.

102 Keeanga-Yamahtta Taylor, "Review of *Black Reconstruction in America*," *International Socialist Review* 57 (January–February 2008). Marx, *Capital*, vol. 1, 329.

103 Du Bois, *Black Reconstruction*, 329.

104 Du Bois, *Black Reconstruction*, 700. David Roediger, *Wages of Whiteness: Race and the Making of the American Working Class* (1991; London: Verso, 2007).

105 Du Bois, "Marxism and the Negro Problem."

106 Harris, "Reconstruction and the Negro." Du Bois, *Black Reconstruction*, 591–92.

107 C. L. R. James, *Toussaint Louverture: The Story of the Only Successful Slave Revolt in History; A Play in Three Acts* (1934; Durham, NC: Duke University Press, 2012).

108 Gornick, *The Romance of American Communism*, 23. James, *Black Jacobins*, 365.

109 James, *Black Jacobins*, x. For more on the differences between Marxism and the black radical tradition, see Robinson, *Black Marxism*.

110 James, *Black Jacobins*, x.

111 James, *Black Jacobins*, 85.

112 James, *Black Jacobins*, 109.

113 James, *Black Jacobins*, 47.

114 Du Bois, *Black Reconstruction*, 122.

CHAPTER FIVE

1   Roger Daniels, *Franklin D. Roosevelt: Road to the New Deal, 1882–1939* (Champaign: University of Illinois Press, 2015).

2   Roy Jenkins, completed with the assistance of Ricard E. Neustadt, *Franklin Delano Roosevelt*, ed., Arthur Schlesinger Jr. (New York: Times Books, 2003).

3   Harvey J. Kaye, *FDR on Democracy: The Greatest Speeches and Writings of President Franklin Delano Roosevelt* (New York: Skyhorse Publishing, 2020). Maurine H. Beasley, *Eleanor Roosevelt: Transformative First Lady* (Lawrence: University Press of Kansas, 2010).

4   Franklin Roosevelt, "Speech to the People's Forum, Troy, New York" (March 3, 1912), in Kaye, *FDR on Democracy*.

5   John Dewey, *Democracy and Education: An Introduction to the Philosophy of Education* (New York: Macmillan, 1916), 52.

6   A. S. Goldman, E. J. Schmalstieg, C. F. Dreyer, F. C. Schmalstieg Jr, D. A. Goldman, "Franklin Delano Roosevelt's 1921 Neurological Disease Revisited: The Most Likely Diagnosis Remains Guillain-Barré Syndrome," *Journal of Medical Biography* (November 2016): 452–59.

7   Franklin D. Roosevelt, "The First Inaugural Address as Governor" (January 1, 1929), *Public Papers of the Presidents of the United States, Franklin D. Roosevelt* (Washington, DC: Federal Register Division, National Archives and Records Service, General Services Administration, 1937), 75.

8   Franklin D. Roosevelt, "The First Inaugural Address as Governor."

9   Franklin D. Roosevelt, "The Forgotten Man" (April 7, 1932), in Kaye, *FDR on Democracy*.

10   Franklin D. Roosevelt, "The Forgotten Man."

11   Roosevelt, "A New Deal for the American People."

12   Franklin D. Roosevelt, "Re-Nomination Acceptance Speech at Democratic National Convention," Philadelphia, Pennsylvania, June 27, 1936, in Kaye, *FDR on Democracy*.

13   Robert S. McElvaine, ed., *Down and Out in the Great Depression: Letters from the Forgotten Man* (Chapel Hill: University of North Carolina Press, 1983), 218–27.

14   Alonzo Hamby, *For the Survival of Democracy: Franklin Roosevelt and the World Crisis of the 1930s* (New York: Free Press, 2004).

15   John Maynard Keynes, "An Open Letter to President Roosevelt," *New York Times*, December 16, 1933. Studs Terkel, *Hard Times: An Oral History of the Great Depression* (New York: Pantheon Books, 1970), 247–48. Kaye, *FDR on Democracy*.

16   Jewel Bellush, "Old and New Left Reappraisals of the New Deal and Roosevelt's Presidency," *Presidential Studies Quarterly* 9, no. 3 (Summer 1979): 243–66. Karl Marx and Frederick Engels, *The Manifesto of the Communist Party* (1848), Marxists Internet Archive, accessed July 8, 2024, https://www.marxists.org/archive/marx/works/download/pdf/Manifesto.pdf.

17   William E. Leuchtenburg, *Franklin D. Roosevelt and the New Deal, 1932–1940* (New York: Harper and Row, 1963).

18   Susan Estabrook Kennedy, *The Banking Crisis of 1933* (Lexington: University of Kentucky Press, 1973).

19   David M. Kennedy, *Freedom from Fear: The American People in Depression and War, 1929–1945* (Oxford: Oxford University Press, 1999).

20   Alan Brinkley, *The End of Reform: New Deal Liberalism in Recession and War* (New York: Alfred A. Knopf, 1995).

21   Mike O'Connor, *A Commercial Republic: America's Enduring Debate over Demo-
     cratic Capitalism* (Lawrence: University Press of Kansas, 2014), 117–44.

22   Ira Katznelson, *Fear Itself: The New Deal and the Origins of Our Time* (New York:
     Liveright, 2013), 230–34.

23   O'Connor, *A Commercial Republic*, 141. Katznelson, *Fear Itself*, 230–34.

24   Katznelson, *Fear Itself*, 230–34.

25   Rhonda F. Levine, *Class Struggle and the New Deal: Industrial Labor, Industrial
     Capital, and the State* (Lawrence: University Press of Kansas, 1988).

26   Kim Phillips-Fein, *Invisible Hands: The Businessmen's Crusade against the New Deal*
     (New York: W. W. Norton, 2010). Gabriel Kolko, *Railroads and Regulation 1877–
     1916* (Princeton, NJ: Princeton University Press, 1965). *A.L.A. Schechter Poultry
     Corp. v. United States*, 295 U.S. 495 (1935).

27   Alan Brinkley, *Voices of Protest: Huey Long, Father Coughlin, and the Great Depres-
     sion* (New York: Alfred A, Knopf, 1982).

28   Jim Pope, "Worker Lawmaking, Sit-Down Strikes, and the Shaping of Amer-
     ican Industrial Relations, 1935–1958," *Law & History Review* 24, no. 1 (2006):
     45–113.

29   Eric Hobsbawm, *Interesting Times: A Twentieth-Century Life* (London: Allen
     Lane, 2002), 388. Oliver Cromwell Cox, *Caste, Class and Race: A Study in Social
     Dynamics* (Garden City: Doubleday and Company, 1948), 262.

30   Studs Terkel, *Hard Times*, 309. James Burnham, "Attacks on NLRB Reflect
     Blows Suffered by Labor," *Socialist Appeal* 2, no. 36 (September 1938): 4.

31   Studs Terkel, *Hard Times*, 129. Sidney Fine, *Sit-Down: The General Motors Strike of
     1936–1937* (Ann Arbor: University of Michigan Press, 1969).

32   Irving Bernstein, *The Turbulent Years: A History of the American Worker, 1933–1941*
     (Boston: Houghton-Mifflin, 1969).

33   Charlie Post, "The Popular Front Didn't Work," *Jacobin*, October 17, 2017.

34   Maurice Isserman, *Which Side Were You On?: The American Communist Party
     During the Second World War* (Middletown, CT: Wesleyan University Press,
     1982), 4.

35   James Gilbert Ryan, *Earl Browder: The Failure of American Communism* (Tusca-
     loosa: University of Alabama Press, 2005).

36   Michael Denning, *The Cultural Front: The Laboring of American Culture* (London:
     Verso, 1997), 437, 156. Robert Genter, *Late Modernism: Art, Culture, and Politics in
     Cold War America* (Philadelphia: University of Pennsylvania Press, 2010).

37   Michael Denning, "'The Special American Conditions': Marxism and
     American Studies," *American Quarterly* 38, no. 3 (1986): 356–80. Lucy Maddox,
     ed., *Locating American Studies: The Evolution of a Discipline* (Baltimore: Johns
     Hopkins University Press, 1999). Daniel Boorstin, *The Americans: The Democratic
     Experience* (New York: Vintage, 1974). Henry Steele Commager, ed., *America
     in Perspective: The United States through Foreign Eyes* (New York: Random House,
     1947), xii.

38   F. O. Matthiessen, *American Renaissance: Art and Expression in the Age of Emerson
     and Whitman* (London: Oxford University Press, 1941), ix, xv.

39   Alan Wald, *New York Intellectuals: The Rise and Decline of the Anti-Stalinist Left
     from the 1930s to the 1980s* (Chapel Hill: University of North Carolina Press,
     1987).

40   Terry A. Cooney, *The Rise of the New York Intellectuals: "Partisan Review" and Its Circle, 1934–1945* (Madison: University of Wisconsin Press, 1986).

41   Irving Howe, "The *Brilliant Masquerade*: A Note on Browderism," in *Socialism and America* (New York: Harcourt Brace Jovanovich, 1985), 87–104.

42   Norman Podhoretz, *Ex-Friends: Falling Out With Allen Ginsberg, Lionel and Diana Trilling, Lillian Hellman, Hannah Arendt, and Norman Mailer* (New York: The Free Press 1999). Joseph Dorman, *Arguing the World* (First Run Features, 1998).

43   Daniel Kelly, *James Burnham and the Struggle for the World* (Wilmington, DE: ISI Books, 2002). Leon Trotsky, *The History of the Russian Revolution*, 3 vols., trans. Max Eastman (Ann Arbor: University of Michigan Press, 1932).

44   Helmut Fleischer, *Marxism and History* (New York: Harper & Row, 1973). Lucio Colletti, *Marxism and Hegel* (London: Verso, 2011). Karl Marx, *Critique of Hegel's Philosophy of Right* (1843; London: Oxford University Press, 1970).

45   Irving Howe, ed., *The Basic Writings of Leon Trotsky* (New York: Schocken Books, 1976).

46   Trotsky, *The Revolution Betrayed*; "The Workers' State, Thermidor, and Bonapartism," *New International* 2, no. 4 (July 1935): 116–22.

47   Isaac Deutscher, *Trotsky: The Prophet Outcast* (1963; London: Verso, 2003).

48   Daniel Oppenheimer, *Exit Right: The People Who Left the Left and Reshaped the American Century* (New York: Simon & Schuster, 2016), 141. Trotsky, "Petty-Bourgeois Opposition in the Socialist Workers Party," "An Open Letter to Comrade Burnham," James Burnham, "Science and Style: A Reply to Comrade Trotsky," all in Trotsky, *In Defense of Marxism* (New York: Pioneer, 1942).

49   Edmund Wilson, *To the Finland Station: A Study in the Writing and Acting of History* (1940; New York: Farrar, Straus and Giroux, 1972), 197.

50   Bernard D'Mello, "Karl Marx: 'Ruthless Criticism of All That Exists,'" *Monthly Review*, May 7, 2018.

51   Joseph Dorman, *Arguing the World: The New York Intellectuals in their Own Words* (New York: Free Press, 2000).

52   Benjamin L. Alpers, *Dictators, Democracy, and American Public Culture: Envisioning the Totalitarian Enemy, 1920s–1950s* (Chapel Hill: University of North Carolina Press, 2003).

53   David McCullough, *Truman* (New York: Simon & Schuster, 1992), 262.

54   James Burnham, *The Managerial Revolution* (New York: Penguin Books, 1941).

55   John P. Diggins, *Up from Communism: Conservative Odysseys in American Intellectual History* (New York: Harper & Row, 1975), 189. C. Wright Mills and Hans Gerth, "A Marx for the Managers," (1942), in *Power, Politics, and People: The Collected Essays of C. Wright Mills*, ed. Irving Horowitz (Oxford: Oxford University Press, 1967).

56   Isaiah Berlin, *Karl Marx: His Life and Environment* (London: Thornton Butterworth, 1939).

57   John Gray, *Isaiah Berlin*, (Princeton: Princeton University Press, 1996).

58   Berlin, *Karl Marx*, 9, 27.

59   Berlin, *Karl Marx*, 13.

60   Berlin, *Karl Marx*, 26.

61   Lewis M. Dabney, *Edmund Wilson: A Life in Literature* (New York: Farrar, Straus and Giroux, 2005).

62 Marshall Berman, *Adventures in Marxism* (London: Verso, 1999), 59.
63 Wilson, *To the Finland Station*, 161.
64 Richard Greenleaf, "The Social Thinking of F. Scott Fitzgerald," *Science & Society* 16, no. 2 (Spring 1952): 97–114.
65 Wilson, *To the Finland Station*, 231.
66 Louis Menand, "The Historical Romance: Edmund Wilson's Adventure with Communism," *New Yorker*, March 16, 2003. Walter Kauffman, *Hegel: A Reinterpretation* (New York: Anchor Books, 2003).
67 Max Eastman, *Marxism: Is it Science?* (London: George Allen & Unwin, 1941), 49, 24.
68 Eastman, *Marxism: Is it Science?*, 19.
69 Eastman, *Marxism: Is it Science?*, 22.
70 Reinhold Niebuhr, *The Children of Light and the Children of Darkness: A Vindication of Democracy and a Critique of Its Traditional Defenders* (1944; London: Nisbet, 1945), 29.
71 Niebuhr, *The Children of Light and the Children of Darkness*, 46.
72 Stephen J. Whitfield, *A Critical American: The Politics of Dwight Macdonald* (Hamden: Archon, 1984). Dwight Macdonald, *The Root Is Man* (1946; New York: Autonomedia, 1994), 39.
73 Macdonald, *The Root Is Man*, 54.
74 Kevin Coogan, introduction to the 1994 edition of *The Root Is Man*, by Dwight Macdonald, 9.
75 Israel Getzler, *Kronstadt, 1917–1921: The Fate of a Soviet Democracy* (Cambridge: Cambridge University Press 2002). Coogan, introduction to *The Root Is Man*, 9.
76 Coogan, introduction to *The Root Is Man*, 9.
77 David Riesman, *The Lonely Crowd: A Study of the Changing American Character* (1950; New Haven, CT: Yale University Press, 1961). William H. Whyte, *The Organization Man* (New York: Simon and Schuster, 1956).
78 Macdonald, *The Root Is Man*, 58–59.
79 Macdonald, *The Root Is Man*, 64.
80 Alonzo Hamby, *Beyond the New Deal: Harry S. Truman and American Liberalism* (New York: Columbia University Press, 1976).
81 Arthur Schlesinger Jr., *The Vital Center: The Politics of Freedom* (1949; London: Andre Deutsch, 1970), xxii, 46–47.
82 K. A. Cuordileone, *Manhood and American Political Culture in the Cold War: Masculinity, the Vital Center and American Political Culture in the Cold War, 1949–1963* (New York: Routledge, 2005). Schlesinger, *The Vital Center*, 86–87.
83 Schlesinger, *The Vital Center*, 86–87. George Fitzhugh, *Sociology for the South, or, the Failure of Free Society* (A. Morris, 1854).
84 Sidney Hook, *Marx and the Marxists: The Ambiguous Legacy* (Princeton: D. Van Nostrand Company, 1955), 18.
85 David Sidorsky, "Charting the Intellectual Career of Sidney Hook: Five Major Steps," *Partisan Review* 70, no. 2 (2003): 324–42. Frances Stonor Saunders, *The Cultural Cold War: The CIA and the World of Arts and Letters* (New York: The New Press, 1999).
86 Sidney Hook, *Heresy, Yes—Conspiracy, No!* (New York: The John Day Company, 1953).

87   Christopher Phelps, *Young Sidney Hook: Marxist and Pragmatist* (1997; Ann
      Arbor: University of Michigan Press, 2005), 4.

88   Hook, *Marx and the Marxists*, 41.

89   Eric Hobsbawm, *Age of Extremes: The Short Twentieth Century, 1914–1991* (Lon-
      don: Michael Joseph, 1994).

90   Hook, *Marx and the Marxists*, 42.

91   Hook, *Marx and the Marxists*, 38.

92   Louis Hartz, *The Liberal Tradition in America: An Interpretation of American Politi-
      cal Thought Since the Revolution* (New York: Harcourt, Brace & World, 1955), 3.

93   Hartz, *The Liberal Tradition in America*, 10.

94   James Livingston, "On Richard Hofstadter and the Politics of 'Consensus His-
      tory,'" *boundary 2* 34, no. 3 (2007): 33–46. Richard Hofstadter, *The Progressive
      Historians: Turner, Beard, Parrington* (1968; New York: Vintage, 1970), 452. John
      Higham, *Beyond Consensus: The Historian as Moral Critic*, *The American Historical
      Review* 67, no. 3 (April 1962): 609–25. Ian Tyrrell, "What, Exactly, Is 'American
      Exceptionalism,'" *Aeon*, October 21, 2016.

95   Heinz D. Kurz, "Transatlantic Conversations: Observations on Marx and
      Engels' Journalism and Beyond," *Social Research* (Fall 2014): 646–48. Robert
      Weiner, "Karl Marx's Vision of America: A Biographical and Bibliographical
      Sketch," *The Review of Politics* 42, no. 4 (Oct 1980): 486.

96   Hannah Arendt, *The Human Condition* (Chicago: University of Chicago Press,
      1958). Arendt, *The Origins of Totalitarianism* (New York: Schocken Books, 1951),
      463–64. Richard H. King, *Arendt and America* (Chicago: University of Chicago
      Press, 2015).

97   Hannah Arendt, "Karl Marx and the Tradition of Western Political Thought,"
      Social Research 69, no. 2 (Summer 2002): 273–319.

98   Arendt, *The Human Condition*, 86.

99   Arendt, *The Human Condition*, 105, 45, 121.

100   W. W. Rostow, *Stages of Economic Growth: A Non-Communist Manifesto* (Cam-
      bridge University Press, 1960).

101   David Milne, *America's Rasputin: Walt Rostow and the Vietnam War* (New York:
      Hill and Wang, 2008), 7, 25.

102   Milne, *America's Rasputin*, 60, 64.

103   Rostow, *Stages of Economic Growth*.

104   Milne, *America's Rasputin*, 64.

105   Nils Gilman, *Mandarins of the Future: Modernization Theory in Cold War America*
      (Baltimore: Johns Hopkins University Press, 2007).

106   Daniel Bell, *The End of Ideology: On the Exhaustion of Political Ideas in the Fifties*
      (1960; New York: The Free Press, 1962).

107   Daniel Bell, *Marxian Socialism in the United States* (1952; Ithaca, NY: Cornell
      University Press, 1996), x. Howard Brick, *Daniel Bell and the Decline of Intellec-
      tual Radicalism: Social Theory and Political Reconciliation in the 1940s* (Madison:
      University of Wisconsin Press, 1986). Bell, *The End of Ideology*, 275.

108   Bell, *The End of Ideology*, 275–78.

109   *Public Papers of the Presidents of the United States, Dwight D. Eisenhower* (Washing-
      ton, DC: Federal Register Division, National Archives and Records Service,
      General Services Administration, 1955), 852.

110   Bell, *The End of Ideology*, 297, 283.
111   Clinton Rossiter, *Marxism: The View from America* (New York: Harcourt, Brace and Company, 1960), 9.
112   Rossiter, *Marxism*, 5, 4.
113   Rossiter, *Marxism*, 14.
114   Rossiter, *Marxism*, 42, 75.
115   Rossiter, *Marxism*, 248.
116   Rossiter, *Marxism*, 8.
117   Richard H. Pells, *The Liberal Mind in a Conservative Age: American Intellectuals in the 1940s and 1950s* (New York: Harper & Row, 1985). Touré F. Reed, "Oscar Handlin and the Problem of Ethnic Pluralism and African American Civil Rights," *Journal of American Ethnic History* 32, no. 3 (Spring 2013): 37–45. Thomas Borstelmann, *The Cold War and the Color Line: American Race Relations in the Global Arena* (Cambridge, MA: Harvard University Press, 2001).
118   Paul Buhle, *C. L. R. James: the Artist as Revolutionary*, new and expanded edition (1988; London: Verso, 2017), 4. C. L. R. James, *American Civilization*, ed. Anna Grimshaw and Keith Hart (Cambridge, MA: Blackwell Publishers, 1993), 13.
119   Charles A. Beard and Mary R. Beard, *The American Spirit: A Study of the Idea of Civilization in the United States* (New York: Macmillan, 1942). James, *American Civilization*, 305.
120   James, *American Civilization*, 116–17.

CHAPTER SIX

1   Richard M. Freeland, *The Truman Doctrine and the Origins of McCarthyism: Foreign Policy, Domestic Politics, and Internal Security, 1946–1948* (New York: Knopf, 1972).
2   Ellen Schrecker, *Many Are the Crimes: McCarthyism in America* (Princeton: Princeton University Press, 1998). Corey Robin, *The Reactionary Mind: Conservatism from Edmund Burke to Donald Trump*, 2nd ed. (Oxford: Oxford University Press, 2018).
3   Elizabeth Dilling, *The Red Network: A 'Who's Who' and Handbook of Radicalism for Patriots* (Chicago: self published, 1934); *The Roosevelt Red Record and Its Background* (Chicago: self published, 1936), 25–26. Christine K. Erickson, "'I Have Not Had One Fact Disproven': Elizabeth Dilling's Crusade against Communism in the 1930s," *Journal of American Studies* 36, no. 3 (2002): 473–89.
4   Dilling, *The Roosevelt Red Record*, 13.
5   Kim Phillips-Fein, *Invisible Hands: The Making of the Conservative Movement from the New Deal to Reagan* (New York: W. W. Norton, 2009).
6   M. J. Heale, *American Anticommunism: Combating the Enemy Within, 1830–1970* (Baltimore: Johns Hopkins University Press, 1990), 111. Leo P. Ribuffo, *The Old Christian Right: The Protestant Far Right from the Great Depression to the Cold War* (Philadelphia: Temple University Press, 1983), 15.
7   Gerald L. K. Smith, Federal Bureau of Investigation, File number 62-43818, accessed July 8, 2024, https://archive.org/details/GeraldL.K.Smith/Smith%2C%20Gerald%20L.K.-HQ-11%20thru18/.

8   Ribuffo, *The Old Christian Right*, 178–224.

9   George H. Nash, *The Conservative Intellectual Movement in America, Since 1945* (1976; Wilmington, DE: Intercollegiate Studies Institute, 2006).

10   George Lipsitz, *Class and Culture in Cold War America: "A Rainbow at Midnight"* (South Hadley, MA: J. F. Bergin Publishers, 1981), 95.

11   Nelson Lichtenstein, *State of the Union: A Century of American Labor* (Princeton: Princeton University Press, 2002), 105.

12   Lipsitz, *Class and Culture in Cold War America*, 113.

13   Roger Biles, *The South and the New Deal* (Lexington: University of Kentucky Press, 1994).

14   Barbara S. Griffith, *The Crisis of American Labor: Operation Dixie and the Defeat of the CIO* (Philadelphia: Temple University Press, 1988).

15   Michael Bowen, *The Roots of Modern Conservatism: Dewey, Taft, and the Battle for the Soul of the Republican Party* (Chapel Hill: University of North Carolina Press, 2011).

16   Lipsitz, *Class and Culture in Cold War America*, 143.

17   C. Wright Mills, *The New Men of Power: America's Labor Leaders* (1948; Champaign: University of Illinois Press, 2001); Lichtenstein, *State of the Union*, 99.

18   Schrecker, *Many Are the Crimes*, 359–415.

19   John Lewis Gaddis, *George F. Kennan: An American Life* (New York: Penguin Press, 2011).

20   *The Charge in the Soviet Union (Kennan) to the Secretary of State* (Moscow, February 22, 1946), National Security Archive, www.nsarchive2.gwu.edu.

21   Joyce Kolko and Gabriel Kolko, *The Limits of Power: The World and United States Foreign Policy, 1945–1954* (New York: Harper and Row, 1972). Mr. X, "The Sources of Soviet Conduct," *Foreign Affairs*, July 1947.

22   Andrew Bacevich, "'Permanent War for Permanent Peace': American Grand Strategy since World War II," *Historically Speaking* 3, no. 2 (November 2001): 2–5. Denise M. Bostdorff, *Proclaiming the Truman Doctrine: The Cold War Call to Arms* (College Station: Texas A&M Press, 2008).

23   Thomas J. McCormick, *America's Half-Century: United States Foreign Policy in the Cold War* (Baltimore: John Hopkins University Press, 1989). Charles L. Mee, *The Marshall Plan: The Launching of the Pax Americana* (New York: Simon and Schuster, 1984).

24   William Appleman Williams, *The Tragedy of American Diplomacy* (1959; New York: W. W. Norton, 2009). Michael Cox and Caroline Kennedy-Pipe, "The Tragedy of American Diplomacy? Rethinking the Marshall Plan," *Journal of Cold War Studies* 7, no. 1 (2005): 97–134.

25   Melvyn P. Leffler, *A Preponderance of Power: National Security, the Truman Administration, and the Cold War* (Palo Alto, CA: Stanford University Press, 1992).

26   David Holloway, *Stalin and the Bomb: The Soviet Union and Atomic Energy 1939–1956* (New Haven, CT: Yale University Press, 1994).

27   E. J. Kahn, *The China Hands* (New York: Penguin Books, 1976). Schrecker, *Many Are the Crimes*, 372–73.

28   Bruce Cumings, *The Korean War: A History* (New York: Random House, 2010).

29   Lorraine Boissoneault, "The True Story of Brainwashing and How It Shaped

America," *Smithsonian Magazine*, May 22, 2017. Tim Weiner, "Remembering Brainwashing," *The New York Times*, July 6, 2008. Mark Fenster, *Conspiracy Theories: Secrecy and Power in American Culture* (Minneapolis: University of Minnesota Press, 1999).

30 Harvey Klehr, John Earl Haynes, Fridrikh Igorevich Firsov, *The Secret World of American Communism* (New Haven, CT: Yale University Press, 1996).

31 Walter Goodman, *The Committee: The Extraordinary Career of the House Committee on Un-American Activities* (New York: Farrar, Straus and Giroux, 1968). Larry Ceplair and Steven Englund, *The Inquisition in Hollywood: Politics in the Film Community, 1930–1960* (Champaign: University of Illinois Press, 2003). Victor Navasky, *Naming Names* (New York: Viking, 1980).

32 Eric Bentley, ed., *Thirty Years of Treason: Excerpts from Hearings before the House Committee on Un-American Activities, 1938–1968* (London: Thames and Hudson, 1971), 214. Robert E. Stripling, *The Red Plot against America* (Drexel Hill, PA: Bell Publishing Company, 1949).

33 Allen Weinstein, *Perjury: The Hiss-Chambers Case* (New York: Knopf, 1978). Victor Navasky, "Hiss in History," *The Nation*, April 12, 2007. Jason Roberts, "New Evidence in the Hiss Case: From the HUAC Files and the Hiss Grand Jury," *American Communist History* 1, no. 2 (2002): 143–62.

34 Michael Kimmage, *The Conservative Turn: Lionel Trilling, Whittaker Chambers, and the Lessons of Anti-Communism* (Cambridge, MA: Harvard University Press, 2009), 205.

35 Whittaker Chambers, *Witness* (London: Andre Deutsch, 1953), 7.

36 Chambers, *Witness*, 8, 9. Karl Marx, "Theses on Feuerbach" (1845), Marxists Internet Archive, accessed July 8, 2024, https://www.marxists.org/archive /marx/works/1845/theses/theses.htm.

37 Robert A. Nisbet, *The Quest for Community* (1970; London: Oxford University Press, 1953), 34. Gary Scott Smith, *Heaven in the American Imagination* (Oxford: Oxford University Press, 2011).

38 Karl Marx and Friedrich Engels, *The Communist Manifesto*, Marxists Internet Archive, accessed July 8, 2024, https://www.marxists.org/archive/marx /works/download/pdf/Manifesto.pdf. Michael R. Belknap, *Cold War Political Justice: The Smith Act, the Communist Party, and American Civil Liberties* (Westport, CT: Greenwood Press, 1977). *Yates v. United States* 354 U.S. 298 (1957).

39 "Speech of Joseph McCarthy," Wheeling, West Virginia (February 9, 1950), Senate, State Department Loyalty Investigation Committee on Foreign Relations, 81st Congress.

40 David M. Oshinsky, *A Conspiracy So Immense: The World of Joe McCarthy* (New York: Free Press, 1983).

41 Blanche Wiesen Cook, "The Impact of Anti-Communism in American Life," *Science & Society* 53, no. 4 (Winter 1989/1990): 470–75. "Speech of Joseph McCarthy."

42 "Speech of Joseph McCarthy."

43 Richard Gid Powers, *Secrecy and Power: The Life of J. Edgar Hoover* (London: Hutchinson, 1987). "Menace of Communism," Statement of J. Edgar Hoover Before the Committee on Un-American Activities, House of Representatives (March 26, 1947).

44   David Halberstam, review of *The Vantage Point Perspectives of the Presidency 1963–1969* by Lyndon Baines Johnson, *The New York Times*, October 31, 1971. Sam Roberts, *The Brother: The Untold Story of the Rosenberg Case* (New York: Random House, 2003). David J. Garrow, *The FBI and Martin Luther King, Jr.: From "Solo" to Memphis* (New York: W. W. Norton, 1981).

45   J. Edgard Hoover, *Masters of Deceit: The Story of Communism in America* (London: J. M. Dent & Sons, 1958), vi. Powers, *Secrecy and Power*, 344.

46   Hoover, *Masters of Deceit*, 13.

47   Hoover, *Masters of Deceit*, 13–18.

48   Hoover, *Masters of Deceit*, 18. Jonathan P. Herzog, *The Spiritual-Industrial Complex: America's Religious Battle against Communism in the Early Cold War* (Oxford: Oxford University Press, 2011).

49   Karl Marx, "Introduction to *A Contribution to the Critique of Hegel's Philosophy of Right*" (1843), Marxists Internet Archive, accessed July 8, 2024, https://www.marxists.org/archive/marx/works/1843/critique-hpr/intro.htm.

50   Marx, "Introduction to *A Contribution to the Critique of Hegel's Philosophy of Right*."

51   Marx, "Introduction to *A Contribution to the Critique of Hegel's Philosophy of Right*."

52   Nash, *The Conservative Intellectual Movement in America*, 52.

53   Patricia Cohen, "Leftist Scholars Look Right at Last, And Find A History," *The New York Times*, April 18, 1998. Russel Kirk, *The Conservative Mind* (London: Faber and Faber, 1953). Edmund Burke, *Reflections on the Revolution in France* (1790).

54   Kirk, *The Conservative Mind*, 17–18. Russell Kirk, *A Program for Conservatives* (Chicago: Henry Regnery Company, 1954). Ronald Lora, *Conservative Minds in America* (1971; Westport, CT: Praeger, 1980), 184.

55   Kirk, *The Conservative Mind*, 233. The sentence that Kirk attributed to Marx does not exist in any English version of *Capital*. It is entirely made up, perhaps by Kirk, perhaps by someone else whom he failed to cite.

56   Kirk, *The Conservative Mind*, 230.

57   Sven-Eric Liedman, *A World to Win: The Life and Works of Karl Marx*, trans. Jeffrey N. Skinner (London: Verso, 2018), 395–466.

58   Kirk, *The Conservative Mind*, 232–33.

59   Richard Weaver, *Ideas Have Consequences* (Chicago: University of Chicago Press, 1948), 122–24.

60   Kirk, *The Conservative Mind*, 235.

61   Kirk, *The Conservative Mind*, 233.

62   Kenneth L. Deutsch, John A. Murley, eds., *Leo Strauss, The Straussians, and the Study of the American Regime* (Lanham, MD: Rowman & Littlefield Publishers, 1999).

63   Leo Strauss and Joseph Cropsey, eds., *History of Political Philosophy*, 2nd ed. (1963; Chicago: Rand McNally College Publishing Company, 1972).

64   Joseph Cropsey, "Karl Marx," in Strauss and Cropsey, *History of Political Philosophy*, 755–81. Allan Bloom, *The Closing of the American Mind* (New York: Simon and Schuster, 1987), 79. Andrew Hartman, *A War for the Soul of Amer-*

ica: A History of the Culture Wars (Chicago: University of Chicago Press, 2015), 228–37.

65 Karl Marx, *The Poverty of Philosophy* (1847), Marxists Internet Archive, accessed July 8, 2024, https://www.marxists.org/archive/marx/works/1847/poverty-philosophy/. Cropsey, "Karl Marx," 758.

66 Cropsey, "Karl Marx," 760.

67 Cropsey, "Karl Marx," 778.

68 Catherine H. Zuckert and Michael P. Zuckert, *The Truth about Leo Strauss: Political Philosophy and American Democracy* (Chicago: University of Chicago Press, 2006).

69 Cropsey, "Karl Marx," 780.

70 Peter Viereck, *Conservatism Revisited: The Revolt against Ideology* (1949; New York: Transaction Publishers, 2005), 152.

71 Peter Viereck, "Will America Prove Marx Right?" *The Antioch Review* 12, no. 3 (Autumn, 1952): 335. Whittaker Chambers, "Big Sister is Watching You," *National Review*, December 28, 1957. Peter Viereck, *Shame and Glory of the Intellectuals: Babbitt Jr. vs. the Rediscovery of Values* (Boston: Beacon Press, 1953), 150.

72 Viereck, *Shame and Glory of the Intellectuals*, 11. Viereck, "Will America Prove Marx Right?", 332.

73 Quinn Slobodian, *Globalists: The End of Empire and the Birth of Neoliberalism* (Cambridge, MA: Harvard University Press, 2018).

74 Angus Burgin, *The Great Persuasion: Reinventing Free Markets since the Depression* (Cambridge, MA: Harvard University Press, 2012).

75 F. A. Hayek, *The Road to Serfdom* (London: Routledge, 1944), 113.

76 Nicholas Wapshott, *Keynes Hayek: The Clash that Defined Modern Economics* (New York: W. W. Norton and Company, 2012).

77 F. A. Hayek, "History and Politics," in *Capitalism and the Historians*, ed. F. A. Hayek (London: Routledge & Kegan Paul, 1954), 10.

78 Hayek, "History and Politics," 16.

79 Richard M. Ebeling, *Political Economy, Public Policy, and Monetary Economics: Ludwig von Mises and the Austrian Tradition* (New York: Routledge, 2010).

80 Ludwig von Mises, "Economic Calculation in the Socialist Commonwealth" (1920), in *Collective Economic Planning*, ed. Friedrich A. Hayek (Clifton, NJ: Kelley Publishing, 1975), 87–130.

81 Ludwig von Mises, *Marxism Unmasked: From Delusion to Destruction* (Irving-on-Hudson, NY: Foundation for Economic Education, 2006), 16.

82 Mises, *Marxism Unmasked*, 26.

83 Mises, *Marxism Unmasked*, 21.

84 Mises, *Marxism Unmasked*, 29.

85 Peter Clarke, *Keynes: The Twentieth Century's Most Influential Economist* (London: Bloomsbury, 2009).

86 Mises, *Marxism Unmasked*, 98, 102.

87 Frank Chodorov, *Out of Step: The Autobiography of an Individualist* (New York: Devin-Adair, 1962). Frank Chodorov, "About Socialism and Socialists," in *Fugitive Essays: Selected Writings of Frank Chodorov*, ed. Charles Hamilton (Indianapolis: Liberty Press, 1980), 131.

88   Chodorov, "About Socialism and Socialists," 133.

89   Chodorov, "About Socialism and Socialists," 133.

90   Chodorov, "The 'Crime' of the Capitalists," in *Fugitive Essays*, 143, 149, 188–89.

91   Hamilton, ed., *Fugitive Essays*, 91. Karl Marx, *Critique of the Gotha Programme*, Marxists Internet Archive, accessed July 8, 2024, https://www.marxists.org /archive/marx/works/1875/gotha/.

92   Joseph A. Schumpeter, *Capitalism, Socialism, and Democracy* (London: George Allen & Unwin, 1943), x.

93   John E. Elliott, "Marx and Schumpeter on Capitalism's Creative Destruction: A Comparative Restatement," *The Quarterly Journal of Economics* 95, no. 1 (August 1980): 45–68.

94   Schumpeter, *Capitalism, Socialism, and Democracy*, 47.

95   Thomas K. McCraw, *Prophet of Innovation: Joseph Schumpeter and Creative Destruction* (Cambridge, MA: Belknap Press of Harvard University Press, 2007).

96   Schumpeter, *Capitalism, Socialism, and Democracy*, 83.

97   Angus Burgin, "The Reinvention of Entrepreneurship," in *American Labyrinth: Intellectual History for Complicated Times*, ed. Raymond Haberski Jr. and Andrew Hartman (Ithaca, NY: Cornell University Press, 2018), 163–81.

98   Schumpeter, *Capitalism, Socialism, and Democracy*, 32.

99   Schumpeter, *Capitalism, Socialism, and Democracy*, 32.

100   C. Wright Mills, *White Collar: The American Middle Classes* (London: Oxford University Press, 1951); David Riesman, *The Lonely Crowd: A Study of the Changing American Character* (1950; New Haven, CT: Yale University Press, 1961).

101   James Buchanan, "Socialism is Dead" (1993), cited in S. M. Amadae, *Rationalizing Capitalist Democracy: The Cold War Origins of Rational Choice Liberalism* (Chicago: University of Chicago Press, 2003), 133.

102   Nancy MacLean, *Democracy in Chains: The Deep History of the Radical Right's Stealth Plan for America* (New York: Viking, 2017). Andrew Hartman, "The Master Class on the Make," *The Baffler*, December 2017, 105–11.

103   Nancy MacLean, *Democracy in Chains*, 12–19. Jill Ogline Titus, *Brown's Battleground: Students, Segregationists, and the Struggle for Justice in Prince Edward County, Virginia* (Chapel Hill: University of North Carolina Press, 2014). Milton Friedman, "The Role of Government in Education," in *Economics and the Public Interest*, ed. Robert A. Solo (New Brunswick, NJ: Rutgers University Press, 1955).

104   James Buchanan and Gordon Tullock, *The Calculus of Consent: Logical Foundations of Constitutional Democracy* (Ann Arbor: University of Michigan Press, 1962).

105   Buchanan and Tullock, *The Calculus of Consent*.

106   Gordon Tullock, *Rent Seeking* (Brookfield, VT: Edward Elgar, 1993).

107   Alexander Taborrok and Tyler Cowen, "The Public Choice Theory of John C. Calhoun," *Journal of Institutional and Theoretical Economics* 148, no. 4 (December 1992): 655–74.

108   Buchanan and Tullock, *The Calculus of Consent*, 12.

109   Buchanan and Tullock, *The Calculus of Consent*, 12.

110   Ralph Milliband, "Marx and the State," *The Socialist Register* (1965), 278–96.

111 William Clare Roberts, *Marx's Inferno: The Political Theory of* Capital (Princeton, NJ: Princeton University Press, 2017), 1, 19.

112 Buchanan and Tullock, *The Calculus of Consent*, 12–13.

113 Richard Hofstadter, *The American Political Tradition* (1948; New York: Vintage Books, 1989), 90, 112.

CHAPTER SEVEN

1   Stephen Resnick and Richard Wolff, *Rethinking Marxism: Essays for Harry Magdoff and Paul Sweezy* (Brooklyn, NY: Autonomedia, 1985). Cody Stephens, "In Search of an Agent: *Monthly Review* and the Precursors to New Left Third Worldism, 1950–1961" (unpublished paper).

2   John J. Simon, "Sweezy v. New Hampshire: the Radicalism of Principle," *Monthly Review*, April 1, 2000.

3   John Bellamy Foster, "Memorial Service for Paul Marlor Sweezy (1910–2004)," *Monthly Review*, February 27, 2004. Paul Sweezy, "*The Communist Manifesto* After 100 Years," *Monthly Review*, in Paul Sweezy, *The Present as History: Essays and Reviews on Capitalism and Socialism* (New York: Monthly Review Press, 1953), 5.

4   Simon, "Sweezy v. New Hampshire."

5   Sweezy, "Schumpeter's Theory of Innovation" (1943), in *The Present as History*, 282.

6   John Bellamy Foster and Paul Sweezy, "On the Laws of Capitalism: Insights from the Sweezy-Schumpeter Debate," *Monthly Review*, May 1, 2011.

7   J. W. Mason, "The Economy During Wartime," *Dissent* (Fall 2017).

8   Paul Sweezy, *The Theory of Capitalist Development: Principles of Marxian Political Economy* (1942; London: Dennis Dobson, 1949).

9   Sweezy, *The Theory of Capitalist Development*, 115.

10   Simon, "Sweezy v. New Hampshire." Ellen Schrecker, *No Ivory Tower: McCarthyism and the Universities* (Oxford: Oxford University Press, 1986).

11   Leo Huberman and Paul Sweezy, *Cuba: Anatomy of a Revolution* (New York: Monthly Review Press, 1960).

12   Max Elbaum, *Revolution in the Air: Sixties Radicals Turn to Lenin, Mao, and Che* (London: Verso, 2002).

13   Marx, *Capital*, vol. 1, chap. 31, "Genesis of the Industrial Capitalist."

14   Karl Marx, *Economic and Philosophical Manuscripts of 1844*, Marxist Internet Archive, accessed July 8, 2024, https://www.marxists.org/archive/marx/works/1844/manuscripts/preface.htm; Tom Hayden, *The Port Huron Statement: The Visionary Call of the 1960s Revolution* (New York: Thunder's Mouth Press, 2005), 45.

15   Sven-Eric Liedman, *A World to Win: The Life and Works of Karl Marx*, trans. Jeffrey N. Skinner (London: Verso, 2018), 59–68, 87–101. Gareth Stedman Jones, *Karl Marx: Greatness and Illusion* (Cambridge, MA: Belknap Press of Harvard University Press, 2016), 129–32.

16   Marx, *Economic and Philosophical Manuscripts of 1844*.

17   Jonathan Sperber, *Karl Marx: A Nineteenth-Century Life* (New York: Liveright, 2013), 145–47.

18   Liedman, *A World to Win*, 13–15. Sidney Hook, *Towards the Understanding of Karl Marx: A Revolutionary Interpretation* (New York: John Day, 1933), 9.

19   Raya Dunayevskaya Papers, "Retrospective" (1986), Archives of Labor and Urban Affairs, Wayne State University.

20   Dunayevskaya Papers, "Retrospective."

21   Kevin Anderson, "*Marxism and Freedom* After Sixty Years, For Yesterday and Today," *New Politics* 17, no. 1 (Summer 2018). Joel Kovel, Foreword to the 2000 edition of Raya Dunayevskaya, *Marxism and Freedom: From 1776 until Today* (1958; New York, Humanity Books, 2000).

22   Anderson, "*Marxism and Freedom* After Sixty Years." Stephen M. Ward, *In Love and Struggle: The Revolutionary Lives of James and Grace Lee Boggs* (Chapel Hill: University of North Carolina Press, 2016). Eugene Gogol, *Raya Dunayevskaya: Philosopher of Marxist-Humanism* (Eugene, OR: Resource Publications, 2004).

23   Paul Buhle, *C. L. R. James: The Artist as Revolutionary*, new and expanded edition (1988; London: Verso, 2017). C. L. R. James, Raya Dunayevskaya, and Grace Lee, *State Capitalism and World Revolution* (1950; Chicago: Charles H. Kerr Publishing Company, 1986).

24   Kent Worcester, *C. L. R. James: A Political Biography* (Albany: State University of New York Press, 1996), 55–65. Ward, *In Love and Struggle*, 101–14.

25   Dunayevskaya Papers, "Retrospective." Anderson, "*Marxism and Freedom* After Sixty Years." Khrushchev's Secret Speech, "On the Cult of Personality and Its Consequences," Delivered at the Twentieth Party Congress of the Communist Party of the Soviet Union, February 25, 1956, Wilson Center Digital Archive, digitalarchive.wilsoncenter.org.

26   Paul Lendvai, *One Day That Shook the Communist World: The 1956 Hungarian Uprising and Its Legacy* (Princeton, NJ: Princeton University Press, 2008). Dunayevskaya, *Marxism and Freedom*, 60, 21.

27   Dunayevskaya, *Marxism and Freedom*, 89.

28   Dunayevskaya, *Marxism and Freedom*, 81–91. Herbert Marcuse, preface to the 1957 edition of Dunayevskaya, *Marxism and Freedom*, xxiii.

29   C. L. R. James, *American Civilization*, ed. Anna Grimshaw and Keith Hart (Cambridge, MA: Blackwell Publishers, 1993), 314.

30   Dunayevskaya, *Marxism and Freedom*, 279–81.

31   Stephen G. Rabe, *The Most Dangerous Area in the World: John F. Kennedy Confronts Communist Revolution in Latin America* (Chapel Hill, NC: University of North Carolina Press, 1999).

32   Robert A. Caro, *The Passage of Power: The Years of Lyndon Johnson*, vol. 4 (New York: Vintage, 2013). Julian E. Zelizer, *The Fierce Urgency of Now: Lyndon Johnson, Congress, and the Battle for the Great Society* (New York: Penguin, 2015).

33   Richard Hofstadter, "The Paranoid Style in American Politics," *Harper's Magazine*, November 1964.

34   Maurice Isserman and Michael Kazin, *America Divided: The Civil War of the 1960s* (Oxford: Oxford University Press, 2004).

35   Jason Sokol, *There Goes My Everything: White Southerners in the Age of Civil Rights, 1945–1975* (Vintage: New York, 2007).

36   Jeff R. Woods, *Black Struggle, Red Scare: Segregation and Anti-Communism in the South, 1948–1968* (Baton Rouge: LSU Press, 2003).

37   Dunayevskaya, *Marxism and Freedom*, 281.

38   Britta Waldschmidt-Nelson, *Dreams and Nightmares: Martin Luther King Jr. Malcolm X, and the Struggle for Black Equality* (Gainesville: University Press of Florida, 2012). Van Gosse, *Rethinking the New Left: An Interpretive History* (New York: Palgrave Macmillan, 2005). Bruce Watson, *Freedom Summer: The Savage Season That Made Mississippi Burn and Made America a Democracy* (New York: Viking, 2010).

39   Gabriel Kolko, *Anatomy of a War: Vietnam, the United States, and the Modern Historical Experience* (New York: New Press, 1994). Michal R. Belknap, *The Vietnam War on Trial: The My Lai Massacre and the Court-Martial of Lieutenant Calley* (Lawrence: University Press of Kansas, 2002).

40   Mary Susannah Robbins, *Against the Vietnam War: Writings by Activists* (New York: Rowman & Littlefield, 2007).

41   Socialist Worker's Party Resolution, "The Fight against the Vietnam War," *SWP Discussion Bulletin* 27, no. 2 (June 1969).

42   Robert Cohen, *Freedom's Orator: Mario Savio and the Radical Legacy of the 1960s* (New York: Oxford University Press, 2009).

43   David Steigerwald, "Where Have You Gone, Holden Caulfield? Why We Aren't 'Alienated' Anymore," *Origins: Current Events in Historical Perspective* 4, no. 4 (January 2011).

44   Andrew Hartman, *A War for the Soul of America: A History of the Culture Wars* (Chicago: University of Chicago Press, 2015), 9–37.

45   Cletus E. Daniel, "Cesar Chavez and the Unionization of California Farm Workers," *Labor Leaders in America*, ed. Melvyn Dubofsky and Warren Van Tine (Champaign: University of Illinois Press, 1987).

46   Jacques E. Levy, *Cesar Chavez: Autobiography of La Causa* (New York: W. W. Norton, 1975), 188.

47   Martin Luther King Jr., *Stride Toward Freedom: The Montgomery Story* (New York: Harper & Brothers, 1958), 94. Thomas F. Jackson, *From Civil Rights to Human Rights: Martin Luther King, Jr., and the Struggle for Economic Justice* (Philadelphia: University of Pennsylvania Press, 2007).

48   Thomas Wheatland, *The Frankfurt School in Exile* (Minneapolis: University of Minnesota Press, 2009).

49   Martin Jay, *The Dialectical Imagination: A History of the Frankfurt School and the Institute of Social Research, 1923–1950* (1973; Berkeley: University of California Press, 1996), 294.

50   Russell Jacoby, *Dialectic of Defeat: Contours of Western Marxism* (Cambridge: Cambridge University Press, 2002). Theodore Adorno and Max Horkheimer, *The Dialectic of Enlightenment* (1944; New York: Herder and Herder, 1972).

51   Max Weber, *The Protestant Ethic and the Spirit of Capitalism*, trans. Talcott Parsons (New York: Scribner, 1958).

52   Michael Paul Rogin, *The Intellectuals and McCarthy: The Radical Specter* (Cambridge, MA: MIT Press, 1969).

53   T. W. Adorno, Else Frenkel-Brunswik, Daniel Levinson, R. Nevitt Sanford, eds., *The Authoritarian Personality* (New York: Harper & Row, 1950), ix. Hof-

stadter, "The Paranoid Style in American Politics." Leo P. Ribuffo, "Donald Trump and 'Paranoid' Style in American (Intellectual) Politics," *ISSF*, June 13, 2017.

54 Sigmund Freud, *Civilization and Its Discontents*, reprint edition (1930; New York: W. W. Norton, 2010).

55 Erich Fromm, *Marx's Concept of Man* (New York: Frederick Ungar, 1961). Lawrence J. Friedman, *The Lives of Erich Fromm: Love's Prophet* (New York: Columbia University Press, 2013).

56 Karl Marx, *Critique of the Gotha Programme*, (1875), Marxists Internet Archive, accessed July 8, 2024, https://www.marxists.org/archive/marx/works/1875/gotha/.

57 Fromm, *Marx's Concept of Man*, viii, 1.

58 Fromm, *Marx's Concept of Man*, 11–14.

59 Fromm, *Marx's Concept of Man*, 4.

60 Fromm, *Marx's Concept of Man*, 21.

61 C. Wright Mills, *White Collar: The American Middle Classes* (Oxford: Oxford University Press, 1951); C. Wright Mills, *The Power Elite* (1956; Oxford: Oxford University Press, 2000), 18.

62 Daniel Geary, *Radical Ambition: C. Wright Mills, the Left, and American Social Thought* (Berkeley: University of California Press, 2009).

63 C. Wright Mills, *Listen Yankee: the Revolution in Cuba* (New York: Ballantine Books, 1961). A. Javier Treviño, *C. Wright Mills and the Cuban Revolution: An Exercise in the Art of Sociological Imagination* (Chapel Hill: University of North Carolina Press, 2017).

64 C. Wright Mills, *The Marxists* (New York: Penguin Books, 1962), *The Marxists*, 28.

65 Mills, *The Marxists*, 36–37.

66 Mills, *The Marxists*, 39.

67 C. Wright Mills, *The Sociological Imagination* (Oxford: Oxford University Press, 1959), 7. Mills, *The Marxists*, 40. Marx, *Capital*, 668.

68 Mills, *The Marxists*, 103.

69 Marx, *Economic and Philosophical Manuscripts of 1844*.

70 Mills, *The Marxists*, 111.

71 Michael Harrington, *The Other America: Poverty in the United States* (New York: Macmillan Publishers, 1962). Maurice Isserman, *If I Had a Hammer: The Death of the Old Left and the Birth of the New* (Champaign: University of Illinois Press, 1993).

72 *Studies on the Left* Papers, Wisconsin Historical Society, Madison, WI (hereon *SotL* papers): Box 3: "Correspondence: Eugene Genovese."

73 Tim Barker, "Wars of Position: *Studies on the Left* and the New American Marxism, 1959–1976" (BA thesis, Columbia University, 2012).

74 *SotL* Papers: Box 1: "History" (1959–1967); Box 2: "Correspondence: Harold Cruse"; "Correspondence: W. E. B. DuBois."

75 Matthew Levin, *Cold War University: Madison and the New Left in the Sixties* (Madison: University of Wisconsin Press, 2013).

76 *SotL* Papers: Box 6: "Correspondence Herbert Marcuse."

77 Casey Nelson Blake, *Beloved Community: The Cultural Criticism of Randolph*

Bourne, Van Wyck Brooks, Waldo Frank, and Lewis Mumford (Chapel Hill: University of North Carolina Press, 2000).

78 *SotL* Papers: Box 6: "Correspondence: Staughton Lynd."

79 *SotL* Papers: Box 6: "Correspondence: Staughton Lynd."

80 Howard Zinn, *SNCC: The New Abolitionists*, 2nd ed. (1962; Chicago: Haymarket Books, 2013). Karl Marx, "Theses on Feuerbach" (1845), Marxists Internet Archive, accessed July 8, 2024, https://www.marxists.org/archive/marx/works/1845/theses/theses.htme. Howard Zinn, "Marxism and the New Left," in *Dissent: Explorations in the History of American Radicalism*, ed. Alfred F. Young, (Dekalb, IL: Northern Illinois University Press, 1968), 362.

81 Zinn, "Marxism and the New Left," 361. Martin Duberman, *Howard Zinn: A Life on the Left* (New York: The New Press, 2012).

82 Ronald Meek, review of *Marxism and Freedom* by Raya Dunayevskaya, *Studies on the Left* 2, no. 1 (Winter 1960).

83 Zinn, "Marxism and the New Left," 366.

84 Eleanor Hakim, "Brecht: A World Without Achilles," *Studies on the Left* 2, no. 2 (1961): 59–72.

85 Hakim, "Brecht," 67. Bertolt Brecht, *The Good Woman of Setzuan*, trans. Eric Bentley (1961; Minneapolis: University of Minnesota Press, 1999).

86 Martin Sklar, *The Corporate Reconstruction of American Capitalism, 1890–1916* (Cambridge: Cambridge University Press, 1988). John Judis, "Meet the Sarah Palin Enthusiast Who May Have Been the Best American Historian of His Generation," *The New Republic*, June 17, 2014.

87 Martin J. Sklar, "Woodrow Wilson and the Political Economy of Modern United States Liberalism," *Studies on the Left* 1, no. 3 (Fall 1960).

88 Murray Rothbard, "The Hoover Myth," *Studies on the Left* 6, no. 4 (Summer 1966), in James Weinstein and David Eakins, eds., *For a New America: Essays in History and Politics from* Studies on the Left, *1959–1967* (New York: Random House, 1970), 164.

89 Eugene Genovese, "On Antonio Gramsci," *Studies on the Left* 7, no. 2 (March–April 1967), Weinstein and Eakins, *For a New America*, 301. Antonio Gramsci, *Prison Notebooks*, vols. 1–3, trans. Antonio Callari and Joseph A. Buttigieg (New York: Columbia University Press, 2011). Alastair Davidson, *Antonio Gramsci: Towards an Intellectual Biography* (Chicago: Haymarket Books, 2016).

90 Martin Nicolaus, "Proletariat and Middle Class in Marx: Hegelian Choreography and the Capitalist Dialectic," *Studies on the Left* 7, no. 1 (January–February 1967); Weinstein and Eakins, *For a New America*. Karl Marx, *Grundrisse: Foundations of the Critique of Political Economy (Rough Draft)*, trans. Martin Nicolaus (1973; London: Penguin Books, 1993).

91 Nicolaus, "Proletariat and Middle Class in Marx," 254, 261.

92 Nicos Polantzas: *The Polantzas Reader: Marxism, Law, and the State*, ed. James Martin (London: Verso, 2008).

93 Zinn, "Marxism and the New Left," 365.

94 Vladimir Lenin, *Imperialism, the Highest Stage of Capitalism* (1917), Marxists Internet Archive, accessed July 8, 2024, https://www.marxists.org/archive/lenin/works/1916/imp-hsc/.

95 Harry Magdoff, *The Age of Imperialism: The Economics of U.S. Foreign Policy* (New York: Monthly Review Press, 1969). Douglas Martin, "Harry Magdoff, Economist, Dies at 92," *The New York Times*, January 9, 2006.

96 Susan Green, "The Sage of Imperialism," *Seven Days*, May 3, 2003. John Bellamy Foster, "The Optimism of the Heart: Harry Magdoff (1913–2006)," *Monthly Review*, January 2, 2006.

97 Magdoff, *The Age of Imperialism*.

98 Leo P. Ribuffo, "Moral Judgments and the Cold War: Reflections on Reinhold Niebuhr, William Appleman Williams, and John Lewis Gaddis," in *Cold War Triumphalism: The Misuse of History After the Fall of Communism*, ed. Ellen Schrecker (New York: New Press, 2004), 27–70. Paul Buhle and Edward Rice-Maximin, *William Appleman Williams: The Tragedy of Empire* (New York: Routledge, 1995). William Appleman Williams, *The Tragedy of American Diplomacy* revised and enlarged version (1959; New York: A Delta Book, 1962).

99 Gordon N. Levin Jr., "The Open Door Thesis Reconsidered," *Reviews In American History* 2, no. 4 (1974).

100 William Appleman Williams, "The Wisdom of an Open Door for Revolutions," *A William Appleman Williams Reader: Selections from His Major Historical Writings*, ed. Henry W. Berger (Chicago: Ivan R. Dee, 1992), 156–61. Jeffrey P. Kimball, "The Big Picture: William Appleman Williams, the Vietnam War, and the Economic Interpretation of U.S. Foreign Relations," *New England Journal of History* 66 (Fall 2009),:79–102.

101 Williams, "The Wisdom of an Open Door for Revolutions," 159. Kevin Mattson, *Intellectuals in Action: The Origins of the New Left and Radical Liberalism, 1945–1970* (State College: Penn State University Press, 2002).

102 William Appleman Williams, *The Great Evasion: An Essay on the Contemporary Relevance of Karl Marx and on the Wisdom of Admitting the Heretic into the Dialogue about America's Future* (Chicago: Quadrangle Paperbacks, 1964).

103 Williams, *The Great Evasion*, 18, 28.

104 Eugene D. Genovese, "William Appleman Williams on Marx and America," *Studies on the Left* 6, no. 1 (Jan–Feb 1966): 70–86.

105 William Appleman Williams, "The Central Utility of Marx," *A William Appleman Williams Reader*, 269. Williams, *The Great Evasion*, 14.

106 Williams, *The Great Evasion*, 69.

107 Williams, "The Central Utility of Marx," 268.

108 Williams, "The Central Utility of Marx," 268.

109 Sean L. Malloy, *Out of Oakland: Black Panther Party Internationalism During the Cold War* (Ithaca: Cornell University Press, 2017). Fred Hampton, "It's A Class Struggle Goddammit!" Speech delivered at Northern Illinois University, November 1969.

110 Peniel E. Joseph, *Waiting 'til the Midnight Hour: A Narrative History of Black Power in America* (New York: Henry Holt and Company, 2006). Scott McLemee, "Forty Years of the "Crisis of the Negro Intellectual," *Inside Higher Ed*, August 29, 2007. Jerry Gafio Watts, ed., *Harold Cruse's The Crisis of the Negro Intellectual Reconsidered* (New York: Routledge, 2004).

111 *SotL* Papers: Box 2: "Correspondence: Harold Cruse."

112   Harold Cruse, *The Crisis of the Negro Intellectual: A Historical Analysis of the Failure of Black Leadership* (1967; New York: New York Review Books, 2005), 7–8.

113   Cruse, *The Crisis of the Negro Intellectual*, 455.

114   Kwame Turé and Charles V. Hamilton, *Black Power: The Politics of Liberation* (1967; New York, Vintage, 1992), 44.

115   Cruse, *The Crisis of the Negro Intellectual*, 43, 158.

116   Christopher Lasch, "Black Power: Cultural Nationalism as Politics," *The Agony of the American Left* (New York: Vintage Books, 1969), 127. Andrew Hartman, "Christopher Lasch: Critic of Liberalism, Historian of Its Discontents," *Rethinking History* 13, no. 4 (2009): 499–519.

117   Lasch, "Black Power," 157.

118   Cruse, *The Crisis of the Negro Intellectual*, 139.

119   Douglas Kellner, *Herbert Marcuse and the Crisis of Marxism* (London: Macmillan, 1984). "Adorno-Marcuse Correspondence," *New Left Review* (January/February 1999). Andrew Hacker, "Philosopher of the New Left," *New York Times*, March 10, 1968, 1, 33–34.

120   Herbert Marcuse, *Eros and Civilization: A Philosophical Inquiry into Freud* (Boston: Beacon Press, 1955). Hacker, "Philosopher of the New Left." Kenneth A. Briggs, "Marcuse, Radical Philosopher, Dies," *New York Times*, July 31, 1979.

121   Herbert Marcuse, *One-Dimensional Man: Studies in the Ideology of Advanced Industrial Society* (Boston: Beacon Press, 1964), ix. Mark Greif *The Age of the Crisis of Man: Thought and Fiction in America, 1933–1973* (Princeton, NJ: Princeton University Press, 2015).

122   Marcuse, *One-Dimensional Man*, 1.

123   Marcuse, *One-Dimensional Man*, 21.

124   Marcuse, *One-Dimensional Man*, 32.

125   Marcuse, *One-Dimensional Man*, 256–57.

126   Frantz Fanon, *The Wretched of the Earth*, trans. Constance Farrington (New York: Grove Press, 1963).

127   Barbara Ehrenreich, "What is Socialist Feminism," *WIN Magazine* (1976), reprinted by *Jacobin Magazine*, July 30, 2018.

128   Robin Morgan, *The Word of a Woman: Feminist Dispatches*, 2nd ed. (New York: W. W. Norton, 1994), 29, 62, 70. Alice Echols, *Daring to Be Bad: Radical Feminism in America, 1967–1975* (Minneapolis: University of Minnesota Press, 1989).

129   Juliet Mitchell, *Women: The Longest Revolution* (New York: Pantheon Books, 1984), 18.

130   Friedrich Engels, *The Origins of the Family, Private Property and the State* (1884), Marxists Internet Archive, accessed July 8, 2024, https://www.marxists.org/archive/marx/works/1884/origin-family/.

131   Engels, *The Origins of the Family, Private Property and the State*.

132   Mitchell, *Women*, 26.

133   Shulamith Firestone, *The Dialectic of Sex: The Case for Feminist Revolution* (New York: William Morrow and Company, 1970).

134   Firestone, *The Dialectic of Sex*, 10.

135   Firestone, *The Dialectic of Sex*, 11.

136   *SotL* Papers: "Letter from George Rawick to Ellie Hakim" (January 23, 1961); "Letter from Ellie Hakim to George Rawick" (February 28, 1961).

137   Angela Davis, *Angela Davis: An Autobiography* (New York: Random House, 1974), 167.

138   Ibram X. Kendi, *Stamped from the Beginning: The Definitive History of Racist Ideas in America* (New York: Nation Books, 2016), 381–496.

139   Angela Davis, "Women and Capitalism: Dialectics of Oppression and Liberation," *The Angela Y. Davis Reader*, ed. Joy James (Malden, MA: Blackwell Publishers, 1998).

140   Davis, "Women and Capitalism," 161–63.

141   Davis, "Women and Capitalism," 163.

142   Davis, "Women and Capitalism," 164.

143   Davis, "Women and Capitalism," 165.

144   Davis, "Women and Capitalism," 166.

145   Davis, "Women and Capitalism," 175.

146   Robert Self, *All in the Family: The Realignment of American Democracy Since the 1960s* (New York: Hill and Wang, 2012).

147   Herbert Marcuse, "Marxism and Feminism," *The New Left and the 1960s: Collected Papers of Herbert Marcuse*, vol. 3 (London: Routledge, 2005), 166.

CHAPTER EIGHT

1   Branko Milanovic, Twitter, February 26, 2020, confirmed via email.

2   Alfred B. Evans, *Soviet Marxism-Leninism: The Decline of an Ideology* (Santa Barbara, CA: ABC-CLIO, 1993).

3   Michael Harrington, *Socialism* (New York: Saturday Review Press, 1972), 3.

4   Harrington, *Socialism*, 77.

5   Harrington, *Socialism*, 79, 108.

6   Harrington, *Socialism*, 5, 79.

7   Maurice Isserman, *The Other American: The Untold Life of Michael Harrington* (New York: HarperCollins/Public Affairs, 2000).

8   Ronald Reagan, Speech at Arlington National Cemetery, 1987, as quoted in Giles Scott-Smith, *Western Anti-Communism and the Interdoc Network: Cold War Internationale* (New York: Palgrave Macmillan, 2012), 1.

9   Harrington, *Socialism*, 37–40, 5–6.

10   Harrington, *Socialism*, 42, 54, 55.

11   Harrington, *Socialism*, 59–60.

12   E. H. Carr, *Michael Bakunin* (London: Macmillan And Co., 1937). Robert L. Bussard, "The 'Dangerous Class' of Marx and Engels: The Rise of the Idea of the Lumpenproletariat," *History of European Ideas* 8, no. 6 (1987): 675–92. Harrington, *Socialism*, 62.

13   Herbert Marcuse, *Counter-revolution and Revolt* (Boston: Beacon Press, 1972).

14   Harrington, *Socialism*, 63.

15   Jefferson Cowie, *Stayin' Alive: The 1970s and the Last Days of the Working Class* (New York: New Press, 2012).

16   Harrington, *Socialism*, 70.

17   Harrington, *Socialism*, 70.

18   Harrington, *Socialism*, 57.

19   Leszek Kolakowski, *Main Currents of Marxism: It's Rise, Growth, and Dissolution*, trans. P. S. Falla (Oxford: Clarendon Press, 1978).

20   Tony Judt, "Goodbye to All That?," *New York Review of Books*, September 21, 2006.

21   Kolakowski, *Main Currents of Marxism*, 5.

22   Kolakowski, *Main Currents of Marxism*, 412.

23   Kolakowski, *Main Currents of Marxism*, 6.

24   Kolakowski, *Main Currents of Marxism*, 128, 144.

25   Kolakowski, *Main Currents of Marxism*, 130–31, 411.

26   Kolakowski, *Main Currents of Marxism*, 417–20.

27   William Buckley Jr. and Charles R, Kessler, eds., *Keeping the Tablets: Modern American Conservative Thought* (New York: Harper & Row, 1988), 458. Michael Harrington, review of *Main Currents of Marxism*, *The New Republic*, February 3, 1979, 28–32.

28   Karl Marx, *Critique of the Gotha Programme*, Marxists Internet Archive, accessed July 8, 2024, https://www.marxists.org/archive/marx/works/1875/gotha/. Harrington, Review of *Main Currents*.

29   Harrington, Review of *Main Currents*.

30   Eric Hobsbawm, *The Age of Extremes: A History of the World, 1914–1991* (New York: Vintage, 1996). Quinn Slobodian, *Globalists: The End of Empire and the Birth of Neoliberalism* (Cambridge, MA: Harvard University Press, 2018). David Harvey, *A Brief History of Neoliberalism* (London: Oxford University Press, 2007).

31   Rick Perlstein, *Nixonland: The Rise of a President and the Fracturing of America* (New York: Scribner, 2008). Dan T. Carter, *The Politics of Rage: George Wallace, the Origins of the New Conservatism, and the Transformation of American Politics* (New York: Simon & Schuster, 1995). Sarah Mergel, *Conservative Intellectuals and Richard Nixon: Rethinking the Rise of the Right* (New York: Palgrave Macmillan, 2010).

32   William Glenn Gray, "Floating the System: Germany, the United States, and the Breakdown of Bretton Woods, 1969–1973," *Diplomatic History* 31, no. 2 (2007): 295–323.

33   Noam Chomsky has called Nixon "the last liberal president," "The Columbia Plan," *Z Magazine*, June 2000.

34   Ken Hughes, "Richard Nixon: Domestic Affairs," (Charlottesville, VA: Miller Center for Public Affairs, 2016).

35   Judith Stein, *Pivotal Decade: How the United States Traded Factories for Finance in the Seventies* (New Haven, CT: Yale University Press, 2011).

36   Yanek Mieczkowski, *Gerald Ford and the Challenges of the 1970s* (Lexington: University Press of Kentucky, 2005).

37   Michael H. Belzer, *Sweatshops on Wheels: Winners and Losers in Trucking Deregulation* (London: Oxford University Press, 2000).

38   Leo P. Ribuffo, *The Limits of Moderation: Jimmy Carter and the Ironies of American Liberalism* (Washington, DC: Westphalia Press, 2023).

39   Erik Loomis, *A History of America in Ten Strikes* (New York: The New Press, 2018), 157–78. Cowie, *Stayin' Alive*, 3.

40   Herbert Marcuse, *An Essay on Liberation* (Boston: Beacon Press, 1969). Howard

Brick and Christopher Phelps, *Radicals in America: The U.S. Left Since the Second World War* (New York: Cambridge University Press, 2015), 182.

41   Cowie, *Stayin' Alive*, 239.

42   William E. Pemberton, *Exit With Honor: The Life and Presidency of Ronald Reagan* (New York: Routledge, 1998).

43   Stephen F. Hayward, *The Age of Reagan: The Conservative Counterrevolution, 1980–1989* (New York: Crown Forum, 2009). Marable Manning, *Reaganism, Racism, and Reaction: Black Political Realignment in the 1980s* (New York: Taylor & Francis, 1981).

44   Matthew Dallek, *The Right Moment: Ronald Reagan's First Victory and the Decisive Turning Point in American Politics* (New York: Free Press, 2000).

45   Gil Troy, *Morning in America: How Ronald Reagan Invented the 1980s* (Princeton: Princeton University Press, 2005).

46   Loomis, *A History of America in Ten Strikes*, 179–200.

47   Ronald Reagan, "Address to the Nation on United States Policy in Central America," May 9, 1984, Ronald Reagan Presidential Library and Museum website.

48   Sidney Blumenthal, "Reaganism and the Neokitsch Aesthetic," in Sidney Blumenthal and Thomas Byrne Edsall, eds., *The Reagan Legacy* (New York: Pantheon Books, 1988). Cowie, *Stayin' Alive*, 310.

49   Robert A. Rosenstone, "*Reds* as History," *Reviews in American History* 10, no. 3 (September 1982): 297–310.

50   Kwame Turé and Charles V. Hamilton, *Black Power: The Politics of Liberation* (1967; New York, Vintage, 1992), 9. Robin Morgan, *The Word of a Woman: Feminist Dispatches*, 2nd ed. (New York: W. W. Norton, 1994), 69. Karla Jay and Allen Young, eds., *Out of the Closets: Voices of Gay Liberation* (New York: Jove/ HBJ Books, 1972), 34.

51   Arnold Beichman, "Marxism: The Communism of the 1980s," unpublished paper, Arnold Beichman Papers, Hoover Institution Archives, Palo Alto, CA., Box 87. Patrick Buchanan, "The Cultural War for the Soul of America," speech, September 14, 1992.

52   Allan Bloom, *The Closing of the American Mind* (New York: Simon and Schuster, 1987).

53   Turé and Hamilton, *Black Power*.

54   Touré F. Reed, *Toward Freedom: The Case against Race Reductionism* (London: Verso, 2020).

55   Davis Roediger, *The Red and the Black: Class, Race, and Marxism* (London: Verso, 2017).

56   Angela Davis, "Women and Capitalism: Dialectics of Oppression and Liberation," *The Angela Y. Davis Reader*, ed. Joy James (Malden, MA: Blackwell Publishers, 1998), 186.

57   Keeanga-Yamahtta Taylor, ed., *How We Get Free: Black Feminism and the Combahee River Collective* (Chicago: Haymarket Books, 2017). *Combahee River Collective Statement* (1974).

58   Marshall Berman, *Adventures in Marxism* (London: Verso, 1999), 79–90. Bertell Ollman, *Class Struggle is the Name of the Game: True Confessions of a Marxist Businessman* (New York: William Morrow and Company, 1983). Darío Fernández-

Morera, *American Academia and the Survival of Marxist Ideas* (Westport, CT: Praeger, 1996), 3.

59   Berman, *Adventures in Marxism*, 80.

60   E. P. Thompson, *The Making of the English Working Class* (1963; New York: Vintage Books, 1966). Harvey J. Kaye, *The British Marxist Historians* (1995; New York: Zero Books, 2022).

61   Daniel Rodgers, *Age of Fracture* (Cambridge, MA: Belknap Press of Harvard University Press, 2011), 15–40.

62   Gary B. Nash, *Red, White, and Black: The Peoples of Early America* (Englewood Cliffs, NJ: Prentice-Hall, 1974), 3.

63   Eugene D. Genovese, *Roll, Jordan, Roll: The World the Slaves Made* (New York: Pantheon Books, 1974). Richard H. King, "Marxism and the Slave South: a Review Essay," *American Quarterly* 29, no. 1 (1977): 117–31.

64   Peter Novick, *That Noble Dream: The 'Objectivity Question' and the American Historical Profession* (Cambridge: Cambridge University Press, 1988), 412. Timothy Barker, "Hegemony without Dominance? Eugene Genovese and the Gramscian Moment in American Intellectual Politics," (unpublished paper).

65   Barker, "Hegemony without Dominance?" Dorothy Ansart and Judith Grier, "Inventory to the Records of the Office of Public Information on the Vietnam War Teach-Ins, 1965–1966," Special Collections and University Archives, Rutgers University Libraries (1992).

66   Eugene Genovese, *In Red and Black: Marxian Explorations in Southern and Afro-American History* (New York: Vintage Books, 1968), 19.

67   Genovese, *Roll, Jordan, Roll*, xvii.

68   Perry Anderson, "The Antinomies of Antonio Gramsci," *New Left Review* (November–December 1976): 5–78. Antonio Gramsci, *Selections from the Prison Notebooks* (1971; New York: International Publishers, Co., 1989).

69   Eugene Genovese, "On Antonio Gramsci," *Studies on the Left* 7, no. 2 (March–April 1967). Genovese, *Roll, Jordan, Roll*, 5.

70   Manisha Sinha, "Eugene Genovese: The Mind of a Marxist Conservative," *Radical History Review* 88 (Winter 2004): 4–29.

71   Eugene D. Genovese, "Reflections on the 1960s," preface to the Italian edition of *In Red and Black*, *Socialist Review* 8, no. 2 (1978): 60.

72   Genovese, *In Red and Black*, 318.

73   Genovese, *In Red and Black*, 321–25.

74   Genovese, *In Red and Black*, 327.

75   Elizabeth Fox-Genovese and Eugene D. Genovese, "The Political Crisis of Social History: A Marxian Perspective," *Journal of Social History* 10, no. 22 (1976): 205–20. Edward E. Ericson Jr., *Radicals in the University* (Stanford: Hoover Institution Press, 1975), 26. Sinha, "Eugene Genovese."

76   Leo Ribuffo, "Eugene D. Genovese (1930–2012)," *Jacobin*, October 3, 2012.

77   Terry Eagleton, "Jameson and Form," *New Left Review* (September–October 2009): 123–37.

78   Fredric Jameson, *Marxism and Form: Twentieth-Century Dialectical Theories of Literature* (Princeton: Princeton University Press, 1971), x.

79   Fredric Jameson, *The Political Unconscious: Narrative as a Socially Symbolic Act* (Ithaca: Cornell University Press, 1981), 9–10.

80 Fredric Jameson, *The Cultural Turn: Selected Writings on the Postmodern, 1983–1998* (London: Verso, 1998). James Seaton, "Marxism Without Difficulty: Fredric Jameson's *The Political Unconscious*," *The Centennial Review* 28, no. 4; 29, no. 1 (Fall 1984–Winter 1985): 122–42.

81 Jameson, *The Political Unconscious*, 19–20.

82 Jameson, *Marxism and Form*, xii–xiii.

83 Fredric Jameson, *Postmodernism, or, The Cultural Logic of Late Capitalism* (Durham, NC: Duke University Press, 1992).

84 Marx, *Capital*, vol. 1, 163–77.

85 Marx, *Capital*, vol. 1, 165.

86 Jameson, *Marxism and Form*, 296. Marx, *Capital*, vol. 1, 166–67.

87 Jameson, *Marxism and Form*, 296, 336, 375.

88 Jameson, *Marxism and Form*, xiii.

89 Judith Butler, *Gender Trouble: Feminism and the Subversion of Identity* (New York: Routledge, 1990). Francois Cusset, *French Theory: How Foucault, Derrida, Deleuze & Co. Transformed the Intellectual Life of the United States* (Minneapolis: University of Minnesota Press, 2008).

90 Michel Foucault, *Power/Knowledge: Selected Interviews and Other Writings, 1972–1977* (New York: Vintage, 1980); *Discipline and Punish: The Birth of the Prison* (1977; New York: Vintage, 1995).

91 James Atlas, "On Campus: The Battle of the Books" *The New York Times Magazine* (June 5, 1988).

92 Cedric Robinson, *Black Marxism: The Making of the Black Radical Tradition* (Chapel Hill: University of North Carolina Press, 1983). Robin D. G. Kelley, "Introduction: Race, Capitalism, Justice," *Boston Review* (Winter 2017): 7.

93 Robinson, *Black Marxism*, 36–44.

94 Stephanie Smallwood, "What Slavery Tells Us About Marx," *Boston Review* (Winter 2017), 81.

95 Robinson, *Black Marxism*, 185–286.

96 Robinson, *Black Marxism*, 238.

97 Robinson, *Black Marxism*, 276.

98 Anderson, *Marx at the Margins*.

99 Karl Marx and Friedrich Engels, *Marx and Engels on Ireland*, Marxists Internet Archive, accessed July 8, 2024, https://www.marxists.org/archive/marx/works/subject/ireland/index.htm. Roediger, *The Red and the Black*.

100 Angela Davis quoted in Gaye Theresa Johnson and Alex Lubin, *Futures of Black Radicalism* (London: Verso, 2017), 247.

101 Ward Churchill, *Speaking Truth in the Teeth of Power: Lectures on Globalization, Colonialism, and Native North America* (Chico, CA: AK Press, 2004). Ward Churchill, ed., *Marxism and Native Americans* (Boston: South End Press, 1983), 4, 8.

102 Churchill, ed., *Marxism and Native Americans*, 20, 23.

103 Churchill, ed., *Marxism and Native Americans*, 24–26.

104 Churchill, ed., *Marxism and Native Americans*, 28.

105 Churchill, ed., *Marxism and Native Americans*, 36, 59. Mark Oppenheimer, "Free Bob Avakian," *Boston Globe*, January 27, 2008.

106 Churchill, ed., *Marxism and Native Americans*, 36–38. Karl Marx, *Grundrisse:*

Foundations of the Critique of Political Economy (Rough Draft), trans. Martin Nicolaus (New York: Penguin Books, 1973), 81.

107   Stephen Hymer, "Robinson Crusoe and the Secret of Primitive Accumulation," *Monthly Review*, September 1971. Churchill, ed., *Marxism and Native Americans*, 39.

108   Roxanne Dunbar-Ortiz, *An Indigenous Peoples' History of the United States* (Boston: Beacon Press, 2014).

109   Churchill, ed., *Marxism and Native Americans*, 76.

110   Leslie Marmon Silko, *Almanac of the Dead* (New York: Penguin Books, 1991). Amanda Walker Johnson, "Silko's *Almanac*: Engaging Marx and the Critique of Capitalism," *Howling for Justice: New Perspectives on Leslie Marmon Silko's* Almanac of the Dead, ed. Rebecca Tillet (Tucson: University of Arizona Press, 2014), 91–104.

111   Ellen Arnold and Leslie Marmon Silko, "Listening to the Spirits: An Interview with Leslie Marmon Silko," *Studies in American Indian Literatures* series 2, 10, no. 3 (Fall 1998): 1–33.

112   Silko, *Almanac of the Dead*, 311, 312, 316.

113   Walter Benjamin, "Theses on the Philosophy of History," *Illuminations* (1968; New York: Schocken Books, 2007), 255.

114   Cornel West, *Ethical Dimensions of Marxist Thought* (New York: Monthly Review Press, 1991), xxvii–xxviii.

115   West, *Ethical Dimensions of Marxist Thought*, xxviii.

116   West, *Ethical Dimensions of Marxist Thought*, xx, ix.

117   Cornel West, *The American Evasion of Philosophy: A Genealogy of Pragmatism* (Madison, WI: University of Wisconsin Press, 1989).

118   West, *Ethical Dimensions of Marxist Thought*, xxi.

119   West, *Ethical Dimensions of Marxist Thought*, 37, 170.

120   West, *Ethical Dimensions of Marxist Thought*, xxii.

121   David Lehman, *Sign of the Times: Deconstruction and the Fall of Paul de Man* (New York: Simon and Schuster, 1991).

122   Jacques Derrida, *Specters of Marx* (1994; New York: Routledge Classics, 2006). Bernd Magnus and Stephen Cullenberg, eds., *Whither Marxism? Global Crises in International Perspective* (New York: Routledge, 1994). Peggy Kamuf, "The Time of Marx: Derrida's Perestroika," *Los Angeles Review of Books*, April 23, 2013.

123   Derrida, *Specters of Marx*, 14.

124   Francis Fukuyama, *The End of History and the Last Man* (New York: The Free Press, 1992), xi–xii.

125   Fukuyama, *The End of History*, 65.

126   Kamuf, "The Time of Marx." Derrida, *Specters of Marx*, 45–46.

127   Russell Jacoby, "Wither Marxism?" *Transition* 69 (1996): 100–115. Terry Eagleton, *After Theory* (New York: Basic Books, 2004).

128   Jacoby, "Wither Marxism?"

129   Moishe Postone, *Time, Labor, and Social Domination: A Reinterpretation of Marx's Critical Theory* (Cambridge: Cambridge University Press, 1993).

130   Marx, *Grundrisse*, 712. Postone, *Time, Labor, and Social Domination*, 23, 27.

131   Postone, *Time, Labor, and Social Domination*, 37.

132 Postone, *Time, Labor, and Social Domination*, 12.
133 Marx, *Grundrisse*, 832–33. Postone, *Time, Labor, and Social Domination*, 23.
134 Postone, *Time, Labor, and Social Domination*, 32.

CHAPTER NINE

1 Ben Jacobs, "How Gen X Became the Trumpiest Generation," *Politico*, May 20, 2022.
2 Colin Devenish, *Rage against the Machine* (New York: St. Martin's Griffin, 2001).
3 Rage against the Machine, "Down Rodeo," *Evil Empire* (Los Angeles: Epic, 1996).
4 Howard Zinn, *A People's History of the United States, 1492–Present* (1980; New York: HarperPerennial, 1995). Sales figures quoted by HarperAcademic on its website.
5 Sam Wineburg, *Why Learn History (When It's Already on Your Phone)* (Chicago: University of Chicago Press, 2018), 51.
6 Scott Jaschik, "The Governor's Bad List," *Inside Higher Ed*, July 16, 2013.
7 Michael Kazin, "Howard Zinn's History Lessons," *Dissent* (Spring 2004). Howard Zinn, "Interpreting History," *Dissent* (Summer 2004). Nick Witham, "A People's History of Howard Zinn: Radical Popular History and Its Readers," *Marxism and America: New Appraisals*, ed. Christopher Phelps and Robin Vandome (Manchester: Manchester University Press, 2021), 195–216. Howard Zinn, "*Je ne suis pas un Marxiste*," *The Zinn Reader: Writings on Disobedience and Democracy* (Boston: Seven Stories Press, 1997), 574–78.
8 Witham, "A People's History of Howard Zinn," 195.
9 Zinn, *A People's History of the United States*, 209.
10 Zinn, *A People's History of the United States*, 252.
11 Howard Zinn Papers, Tamiment Library and Robert F. Wagner Labor Archive, New York University, Box 14, Folder 22: "Marx in Soho—Background (Capital)." Howard Zinn, *Marx in Soho: A Play on History* (New York: Haymarket Books, 2014), vii. Howard Zinn, *You Can't Be Neutral on a Moving Train: A Personal History of Our Times* (Boston: Beacon Press, 2002).
12 Howard Zinn, *Declarations of Independence: Cross-Examining American Ideology* (New York: HarperPerennial, 1990), 268.
13 Zinn, "*Je ne suis pas un Marxiste*."
14 Zinn, *Marx in Soho*, xvii–xviii.
15 Zinn, *Marx in Soho*, 8.
16 Zinn, *Marx in Soho*, 26.
17 Donald Cohen and Allen Mikaelian, *The Privatization of Everything: How the Plunder of Public Goods Transformed America and How We Can Fight Back* (New York: The New Press, 2023).
18 Tristram Hunt, "Eric Hobsbawm: A Conversation About Marx, Student Riots, the New Left, and the Milibands," *The Guardian*, January 15, 2011. Sebastian Edwards, *The Chile Project: The Story of the Chicago Boys and the Downfall of Neoliberalism* (Princeton, NJ: Princeton University Press, 2023).

19 Gary Gerstle, *The Rise and Fall of the Neoliberal Order: America and the World in the Free Market Era* (New York: Oxford University Press, 2022), 156.

20 Bruce Miroff, *The Liberals' Moment: The McGovern Insurgency and the Identity Crisis of the Democratic Party* (Lawrence: University Press of Kansas, 2007). Jon F. Hale, "The Making of the New Democrats," *Political Science Quarterly* 110, no. 2 (Summer 1995): 207–32.

21 Gerstle, *The Rise and Fall of the Neoliberal Order*, 151–57.

22 Dawn L. Rothe and Victoria E. Collins, "The Integrated Spectacle: Neoliberalism and the Socially Dead," *Social Justice* 43, no. 2 (2016): 1–20. Economic Research Service, "Food Security Status of US Households, 2022," (Washington, DC: U.S. Department of Agriculture, 2022). National Institute on Drug Abuse, "Drug Overdose Rates" (June 2023).

23 Mike Davis, *Planet of Slums* (London: Verso, 2006). Naomi Klein, *The Shock Doctrine: The Rise of Disaster Capitalism* (New York: Picador, 2008).

24 John Cassidy, "The Return of Karl Marx," *New Yorker*, October 12, 1997.

25 "The Prophet of Capitalism," *The Economist*, December 23, 1999.

26 Howard Brick and Christopher Phelps, *Radicals in America: The U.S. Left Since the Second World War* (New York: Cambridge University Press, 2015), 284. Howard Zinn, "A Man for All Seasons," *In These Times*, September 4, 2000.

27 Mark Engler, "The Seattle Protests Showed Another World Is Possible," *The Nation*, November 29, 2019.

28 Subcomandante Marcos, "The Slaves of Money—and Our Rebellion," *The Guardian*, September 10, 2003.

29 Brick and Phelps, *Radicals in America*, 275. Andrew Hartman, "Beyond the Whack-a-Mole Left," *Jacobin*, June 10, 2016.

30 Daniel Bensaïd, *Marx for Our Times: Adventures and Misadventures of a Critique*, trans. Gregory Elliott (London: Verso, 2002), 15.

31 Michael Hardt and Antonio Negri, *Empire* (Cambridge, MA: Harvard University Press, 2001).

32 Gilles Deleuze and Felix Guattari, *Capitalism and Schizophrenia* (1972; 1980; New York: Penguin Classics 2009). Michael Hardt and Antonio Negri, *Multitude: War and Democracy in the Age of Empire* (New York: Penguin Press, 2004).

33 Antonio Negri, *Marx Beyond Marx: Lessons on the Grundrisse* (New York: Pluto Press, 1984).

34 Hardt and Negri, *Empire*, 43, 57–59, 393.

35 Gopal Balakrishnan, "Hard and Negri's Empire," *New Left Review* (Sept/Oct 2000).

36 Balakrishnan, "Hard and Negri's Empire." Thomas Friedman, *The Lexus and the Olive Tree: Understanding Globalization* (New York: Farrar, Straus and Giroux, 1999).

37 Hardt and Negri, *Empire*, 413. Balakrishnan, "Hard and Negri's Empire."

38 Hardt and Negri, *Empire*, 168.

39 Hardt and Negri, *Empire*, 375.

40 Tom Lansford, *9/11 and the Wars in Afghanistan and Iraq: A Chronology and Reference Guide* (Santa Barbara, CA: ABC-CLIO, 2012).

41 Anthony R. Dimaggio, *Mass Media, Mass Propaganda: Understanding the News in the "War on Terror"* (Blue Ridge Summit, PA: Lexington Books, 2008).

42   Rahul Mahajan, "Iraq and the New Great Game," *Socialist Viewpoint* 2, no. 8 (September 2002). "Millions Join Global Anti-War Protests," *BBC News*, February 17, 2003.

43   Stephen Benedict Dyson, "'Stuff Happens': Donald Rumsfeld and the Iraq War" *Foreign Policy Analysis* 5, no. 4 (October 2009), 327–47. Daniel Finn, "The US Invasion Was a Catastrophe for the People of Iraq: An Interview with Dina Rizk Khoury," *Jacobin*, March 19, 2023.

44   Greg Muttitt, "The Bush Administration Turned the War on Terror Into a War for Oil," *Jacobin*, September 11, 2021.

45   Paul Blumenthal, "The Largest Protest Ever Was 15 Years Ago. The Iraq War Isn't Over. What Happened?" *Huff Post*, February 15, 2018.

46   Robin Blackburn, "The Subprime Crisis," *New Left Review* (March/April 2008). Renae Merle, "A Guide to the Financial Crisis—10 Years Later," *Washington Post*, September 10, 2018.

47   Andrew Clark and Jill Treanor, "Greenspan—I Was Wrong About the Economy, Sort Of," *The Guardian*, October 23, 2008.

48   Thomas Geoghegan, "Infinite Debt: How Unlimited Interest Rates Destroyed the Economy," *Harper's*, April 2009.

49   Gerstle, *The Rise and Fall of the Neoliberal Order*, 173–176.

50   Jacob S. Rugh and Douglas S. Massey, "Racial Segregation and the American Foreclosure Crisis," *American Sociological Review* 75, no. 5 (October 2010): 629–51.

51   Michael Lewis, *The Big Short: Inside the Doomsday Machine* (New York: W. W. Norton, 2011). Andrew Ross Sorkin, *Too Big to Fail: The Inside Story of How Wall Street and Washington Fought to Save the Financial System—and Themselves* (New York: Viking Press, 2010).

52   Oliver Burkeman, "Look Out for Number One—America Turns to Prophet of Self-Interest as Crash Hits," *The Guardian*, March 9, 2009. Rachel M. Blum, *How the Tea Party Captured the GOP: Insurgent Factions in American Politics* (Chicago: University of Chicago Press, 2020).

53   China Miéville, *A Spectre, Haunting: On the Communist Manifesto* (Chicago: Haymarket Books, 2022), 239. Timothy Shenk, "Thomas Piketty and Millennial Marxists on the Scourge of Inequality," *The Nation*, May 5, 2014. Leo Panitch, "Thoroughly Modern Marx," *Foreign Policy* 172 (May/June 2009): 140–45. Francis Wheen, *Marx's Das Kapital: A Biography* (New York: Atlantic Monthly Press, 2006), 121.

54   Janey Byrne, ed., *The Occupy Handbook* (Boston: Back Bay Books, 2012). Sanford Schram, *The Return of Ordinary Capitalism: Neoliberalism, Precarity, Occupy* (London: Oxford University Press, 2015).

55   Doug Henwood, "Occupy Wall Street at 10: It Was Annoying, But it Changed the World," *Jacobin*, September 17, 2021. John L. Hammond, "The Anarchism of Occupy Wall Street," *Science & Society* 79, no. 2 (April 2015): 288–313. Drake Bennett, "David Graeber: The Anti-Leader of Occupy Wall Street," *Bloomberg*, October 26, 2011.

56   David Graeber, *Debt: The First 5000 Years* (New York: Melville House, 2011).

57   David Harvey, "Reading Marx's *Capital* with David Harvey" (lecture series),

accessed July 8, 2024, https://davidharvey.org/reading-capital/. David Harvey, *A Companion to Marx's Capital* (London: Verso, 2010).

58 Harvey, "Reading Marx's *Capital Volume 1*," Class 1, Introduction.

59 Harvey, "Reading Marx's *Capital Volume 1*," Class 1, Introduction.

60 Mike Davis, *Old Gods, New Enigmas: Marx's Lost Theory* (London: Verso, 2018), 23. Harvey, "Reading Marx's *Capital Volume 1*," Class 1, Introduction.

61 David Harvey, *The Enigma of Capital and the Crises of Capitalism* (Oxford: Oxford University Press, 2010), 6, 71.

62 Benjamin Kunkel, *Utopia or Bust* (London: Verso, 2014), 26. Harvey, *The Enigma of Capital*, 46.

63 Harvey, *The Enigma of Capital*, 47.

64 Harvey, *The Enigma of Capital*, 30, 58.

65 Harvey, *The Enigma of Capital*, 66.

66 Harvey, *The Enigma of Capital*, 117, 66.

67 Harvey, *The Enigma of Capital*, 30, 117.

68 Kunkel, *Utopia or Bust*, 38. Harvey, *The Enigma of Capital*, 10.

69 Kim Moody, "Does the American Experience Refute Marxism?" *Marxism and America*, 266–20.

70 Tim Jelfs, "Will the Revolution Be Podcast? Marxism and the Culture of 'Millennial Socialism' in the United States," *Marxism and America*, 242–43.

71 Jelfs, "Will the Revolution Be Podcast?" 250. Adryan Corceone, "Who Is Karl Marx? Meet the Anti-Capitalist Scholar," *Teen Vogue*, May 10, 2018.

72 Kunkel, *Utopia or Bust*, 17. Jennifer Schuessler, "A Young Publisher Takes Marx into the Mainstream," *New York Times*, January 20, 2013.

73 "Dancing on Liberalism's Grave," *Jacobin*, July 14, 2011.

74 Jia Tolentino, "What Will Become of the Dirtbag Left?" *New Yorker*, November 18, 2016. Nellie Bowles, "The Pied Pipers of the Dirtbag Left Want to Lead Everyone to Bernie Sanders," *New York Times*, February 29, 2020.

75 Andrew Hartman, "The Millennial Left's War against Liberalism," *Washington Post*, July 20, 2017. Chapo Trap House, *The Chapo Guide to Revolution: A Manifesto against Logic, Facts, and Reason* (New York: Atria Books, 2018), 2.

76 Chapo Trap House, podcast, "Post Hoc, Ergo Propter Hoc," episode 101, April 19, 2017.

77 Max Foley-Keene, "You Can't be a Marxist and a Nihilist: Chapo Trap House Visits D.C. to Talk Politics," *The Diamondback*, September 7, 2018.

78 "*The Nation* names Bhaskar Sunkara Its New President," *The Nation* press release, February 23, 2022.

79 Robin Blackburn, "Lincoln and Marx," *Jacobin*, August 28, 2012.

80 Jelfs, "Will the Revolution Be Podcast?" 251.

81 Bhaskar Sunkara, *The Socialist Manifesto: The Case for Radical Politics in an Era of Extreme Inequality* (New York: Basic Books, 2019), 2, 41.

82 Sunkara, *The Socialist Manifesto*, 41–43.

83 Sunkara, *The Socialist Manifesto*, 2.

84 Sunkara, *The Socialist Manifesto*, 46–47, 185.

85 Steven Greenhouse, "Wage Strikes Planned at Fast-Food Outlets," *New York Times*, December 1, 2013.

86 Michael Rozworski, "Having the Hard Conversations: And Interview with Jane McAlevey," *Jacobin*, October 4, 2015. Liza Featherstone, "After Almost a Decade, Fight for $15 Has Made Progress—But It's Not Enough," *Jacobin*, May 20, 2021.

87 Bhaskar Sunkara, "Bernie for President," *Jacobin*, May 1, 2015. Bernie Sanders (@BernieSanders), "If there is going to be class warfare in this country, it's about time the working class won that war," X (formerly Twitter), August 21, 2019, https://x.com/BernieSanders/status/1164228993169723398.

88 Seth Ackerman, "Why Bernie Sanders Matters," *Jacobin*, September 27, 2019.

89 Matt Karp, "Bernie Sanders's Five Year War," *Jacobin*, August 28, 2020.

90 Gregory Krieg, "Inside the Rise of the Democratic Socialists of America," *CNN*, July 17, 2018.

91 Hadas Their, "Marxism in a Minute"; "What is Marxist Economics?"; "What is the Labor Theory of Value?" Haymarket Books YouTube channel, last updated July 29, 2021, https://www.youtube.com/playlist?list=PLcqXhvSDf0zIMa542dgTMpzLcfwfl7kwV. Bhaskar Sunkara, "Project Jacobin: Interview," *New Left Review* (Nov/Dec 2014).

92 Aaron Blake, "The Extraordinary Rise of Democratic Socialists in Nevada," *Washington Post*, March 10, 2021. Aliya Uteuova, "New York Takes Big Step Toward Renewable Energy in 'Historic' Climate Win," *The Guardian*, May 3, 2023. Lisa Friedman, "What is the Green New Deal? A Climate Proposal, Explained," *New York Times*, February 21, 2019.

93 John Bellamy Foster, *Marx's Ecology: Materialism and Nature* (New York: Monthly Review Press, 2000), 72.

94 Andreas Malm, *Fossil Capital: The Rise of Steam Power and the Roots of Global Warming* (London: Verso, 2016), 1, 3.

95 Malm, *Fossil Capital*, 2, 18.

96 Malm, *Fossil Capital*, 19, 307, 314.

97 Kohei Saito, *Karl Marx's Ecosocialism: Capital, Nature, and the Unfinished Critique of Political Economy* (New York: Monthly Review Press, 2017), 14, 9. Justin McCurry, "'A New Way of Life': The Marxist, Post-Capitalist, Green Manifesto Captivating Japan," *The Guardian*, September 9, 2022.

98 Saito, *Karl Marx's Ecosocialism*, 18, 20.

99 Saito, *Karl Marx's Ecosocialism*, 40–41.

100 Kohei Saito, *Marx in the Anthropocene: Towards the Idea of Degrowth Communism* (Cambridge: Cambridge University Press, 2023). Maya Goodfellow, "A Greener Marx? Kohei Saito on Connecting Communism with the Climate Crisis: An Interview," *The Guardian*, February 28, 2023.

101 Matt Huber (@Matthuber78), X (formerly Twitter), March 5, 2023, https://x.com/Matthuber78/status/1632505118334541824?lang=en. Matt Huber, *Climate Change as Class War: Building Socialism on a Warming Planet* (London: Verso Books, 2022).

102 Matt Huber, "Only a Mass Working-Class Climate Politics Can Free Us from the Climate Doom Cycle," *Jacobin*, March 3, 2023. Matt Huber, "The Problem with Degrowth," *Jacobin*, July 16, 2023.

103 Jonas Elvander, "Degrowth is Not the Answer to Climate Change: An Interview with Leigh Phillips," *Jacobin*, January 8, 2023.

104   Robin D. G. Kelley, "Why Black Marxism, Why Now?" *Boston Review*, February 1, 2021.

105   Deva Woody, *Reckoning: Black Lives Matter and the Democratic Necessity of Social Movements* (London: Oxford University Press, 2021).

106   Phil Helsel, "'Black Lives Matter' Activists Disrupt Bernie Sanders Speech," *NBC News*, August 9, 2015. Matt Taibbi, "The Line That May have Won Hillary Clinton the Nomination," *Rolling Stone*, April 28, 2016. Ta-Nehisi Coates, "The Case for Reparations," *The Atlantic*, June 15, 2014. Touré F. Reed, *Toward Freedom: The Case against Race Reductionism* (London: Verso, 2020), 158.

107   Robin D. G. Kelley, "What Did Cedric Robinson Mean by Racial Capitalism?" *Boston Review*, January 12, 2017.

108   Miéville, *A Spectre, Haunting*, 116–17.

109   Kevin Anderson, "No, Karl Marx Was Not Eurocentric," *Jacobin*, July 19, 2022.

110   Eric K. Arnold, "The Life of Riley," *East Bay Express*, April 26, 2006. The Coup, "5 Million Ways to Kill a C.E.O.," *Party Music* (75 Ark Records, 2001). Street Sweeper Social Club, "100 Little Curses," *Street Sweeper Social Club* (Warner Music Group, 2009).

111   Boots Riley, *Sorry to Bother You* (Focus Features, 2018). "Boots Riley on *Sorry to Bother You* and Communism," *The Dig Radio*, podcast, August 9, 2018, https://thedigradio.com/podcast/boots-riley-on-sorry-to-bother-you-and -communism/.

112   "Boots Riley on How His Hit Movie 'Sorry to Bother You' Slams Capitalism and Offers Solutions," *Democracy Now!*, July 17, 2018.

113   "The History of Political Correctness" (Free Congress Foundation), https:// www.youtube.com/watch?v=EjaBpVzOohs. Bill Berkowitz, "'Cultural Marxism' Catching On," *Intelligence Report* (Southern Poverty Law Center) (August 15, 2003). Martin Jay, "Dialectic of Counter-Enlightenment: The Frankfurt School as Scapegoat of the Lunatic Fringe," *Salmagundi Magazine*, 168/169 (Fall 2010–Winter 2011): 30–40.

114   "Political Correctness: The Frankfurt School."

115   Berkowitz, "'Cultural Marxism' Catching On."

116   "Andrew Breitbart on the Frankfurt School of Cultural Marxism," Hoover Institute Videos, June 14, 2011, https://www.youtube.com/watch?v =ftZfdrqpOk; accessed at YouTube. "Ben Shapiro on Frankfurt School Infiltration," Hillsdale College, Feb 22, 2016, https://www.youtube.com/watch?v =WxKwmy5AGKI .

117   Mark Levin, *American Marxism* (New York: Threshold Editions, 2021), 82. Miéville, *A Spectre, Haunting*, 2. "The Manifesto with China Miéville," *The Dig Radio*, podcast, July 9, 2023, https://thedigradio.com/podcast/the-manifesto -w-china-mieville/.

118   William Clare Roberts, *Marx's Inferno: The Political Theory of* Capital (Princeton, NJ: Princeton University Press, 2017), 1.

119   Roberts, *Marx's Inferno*, 19.

120   Martin Hägglund, *This Life: Secular Faith and Spiritual Freedom* (New York: Anchor Books, 2019), 8, 19.

121   Hägglund, *This Life*, 22, 23, 213.

122   Hägglund, *This Life*, 225.

123 Hägglund, *This Life*, 250.
124 Hägglund, *This Life*, 258, 251.
125 Jacob Rosenberg, "Workers Got Fed Up. Bosses Got Scared. This Is How the Big Quit Happened," *Mother Jones*, January–February 2022.
126 Terri Gerstein, "The Supreme Court Sided with Corporations Over Workers— Again," Economic Policy Institute, June 9, 2023. Margaret Poydock, Jennifer Sherer, and Celine McNicholas, "Major Strike Activity Increased Nearly 50% in 2022," Economic Policy Institute, February 22, 2023.
127 Miéville, *A Spectre, Haunting*, 98.

ILLUSTRATION CREDITS

0.1   Karl Marx portrait (1875), by John Jabez Edwin Mayal.

2.1   William Liebknecht, Eleanor Marx Aveling, and Edward Aveling portrait (1886), unknown source.

2.2   Big Bill Haywood mugshot (1918), Inmate Case Files, Leavenworth Prison, National Archives, Kansas City, Missouri.

3.1   John Reed portrait (1920), Widener Library, Harvard University, Cambridge, Massachusetts.

3.2   Elizabeth Gurley Flynn, (date unknown, 1910s), Library of Congress Prints and Photographs Division, Washington, DC.

3.3   *The Messenger* (1917), Schomburg Center for Research in Black Culture, Manuscripts, Archives and Rare Books Division, The New York Public Library, New York City, New York.

3.4   Eugene V. Debs mugshot (1919), Inmate Case Files, National Archives at Atlanta, RG 129, Atlanta, Georgia.

4.1   Hugo Gellert, "Frontispiece," *Capital in Pictures* (1934), permission granted by the Museum of Modern Art, New York City, New York.

4.2   Hugo Gellert, "Primary Accumulation: The Expropriation Whereby the Countryfolk Were Divorced from the Land," *Capital in Pictures* (1934), permission granted by the Museum of Modern Art, New York City, New York.

4.3   Dorothea Lange, "Migrant Mother" (1936), Library of Congress
       Prints and Photographs Division, Washington, DC.

4.4   Hugo Gellert, "Transformation of Money into Capital: Purchase and
       Sale of Labor Power," *Capital in Pictures* (1934), permission granted by
       the Museum of Modern Art, New York City, New York.

4.5   Hugo Gellert, "Degree of Exploitation of Labor Power," *Capital in
       Pictures*, (1934), permission granted by the Museum of Modern Art,
       New York City, New York.

4.6   W. E. B. Du Bois at the grave of Karl Marx, Highgate Cemetery, Lon-
       don, September 1958, W. E. B. Du Bois Papers (MS 312), Robert S.
       Cox Special Collections and University Archives Research Center,
       University of Massachusetts-Amherst Libraries, Amherst, Massa-
       chusetts, permission granted by the literary legacy of the estate of
       W. E. B. Du Bois.

4.7   C. L. R. James (1938), unknown source.

5.1   Walt W. Rostow et al. with President Lyndon B. Johnson, in the Oval
       Office (1967), photo by Yoichi Okamoto, Lyndon Baines Johnson
       Presidential Library, Austin, TX.

6.1   Elizabeth Dilling (1939), Library of Congress Prints and Photo-
       graphs Division, Washington, DC.

6.2   Whittaker Chambers (1948), Library of Congress Prints and Photo-
       graphs Division, Washington, DC.

7.1   *Monthly Review*'s trip to Cuba (1963), permission granted by the
       Monthly Review Foundation, New York City, New York.

7.2   Diego Rivera, Raya Dunayevskaya, Leon Trotsky, (1940), Princeton
       University Library Special Collections, Princeton, New Jersey.

7.3   The Tendency (late 1940s), permission granted by the James and
       Grace Lee Boggs Foundation, Detroit, Michigan.

7.4   William Appleman Williams (1960s), William Appleman Williams
       Papers (MSS Williams WA), Oregon State University Special Collec-
       tions and Archives Research Center, Corvallis, Oregon.

7.5   Harold Cruse (1970s), University of Michigan News and Informa-
       tion Services Photograph Series D (Faculty Portraits), Ann Arbor,
       Michigan.

7.6   Herbert Marcuse and Angela Davis (1970), photo by Nancy Chase,
       Newsweek.

8.1   Michael Harrington (1978), *Sacramento Bee*, Center for Sacramento
       History, Sacramento, California.

8.2   *Heterodoxy* (May 1992), permission granted by David Horowitz.

8.3   Cedric Robinson (2006), photo by Doc Searls.

9.1   Bob Weick and Howard Zinn (*Marx in Soho*), Boston, Massachusetts
       (2006), photo and permission granted by John Doyle.

INDEX

Page numbers in italics refer to figures.